SEX, CHRIST, AND EMBODIED COGNITION

EMORY STUDIES IN EARLY CHRISTIANITY

Editors
Vernon K. Robbins & David B. Gowler

Associate Editor
Robert H. von Thaden Jr.

Editorial Board
Richard S. Ascough
L. Gregory Bloomquist
Peder Borgen
J. J. Bernard Combrink
David A. deSilva
Anders Eriksson
Thomas H. Olbricht
Russell B. Sisson
Duane F. Watson

Number 16

SEX, CHRIST, AND EMBODIED COGNITION

Paul's Wisdom for Corinth

by
Robert H. von Thaden Jr.

SBL PRESS
Atlanta

Copyright © 2017 by SBL Press
Originally published by Deo Publishing, 2012

Publication of this volume was made possible by the generous support of the Pierce Program in Religion of Oxford College of Emory University.

All rights reserved. No part of this work may be reproduced or transmitted in any form or by any means, electronic or mechanical, including photocopying and recording, or by means of any information storage or retrieval system, except as may be expressly permitted by the 1976 Copyright Act or in writing from the publisher. Requests for permission should be addressed in writing to the Rights and Permissions Office, SBL Press, 825 Houston Mill Road, Atlanta, GA 30329 USA.

The Odyssea Greek font used in the publication of this work is available from Linguist's Software, Inc., www.linguisticsoftware.com, P.O. Box 580, Edmonds, WA 98020-0580 USA, tel. (425) 775-1130.

Library of Congress Control Number: 2017934922

Cover design is an adaptation by Bernard Madden of Rick A. Robbins, Mixed Media (19" x 24" pen and ink on paper, 1981). Online: http://home.comcast.net/~rick1216/Archive/1981penink.htm. Cover design used by permission of Deo Publishing.

Printed on acid-free paper.

In memory of Judy Von Thaden
(1947-2009)

μὴ ἀπώσῃ θεσμοὺς μητρός σου.
(Prov 1:8)

Contents

List of Figures x
Acknowledgments xi

Introduction 1
Conversation Partners 4
    Ferdinand Christian Baur: The Historical Paradigm 6
    Johannes Weiß: Partitions and Slogans 7
    John Coolidge Hurd: Getting Behind the Text 10
    O. Larry Yarbrough: Paul and Marriage 13
    Margaret Mitchell: Historical Rhetorical Analysis 15
    Renate Kirchhoff: Cultural and Social Analysis 18
    Brian S. Rosner: Scripture and Ethics 22
    Will Deming: Paul's Hellenistic Background 24
    Dale Martin: Ideology and the Body 26
    Kathy L. Gaca: Paul, Sex, and Metaphor 28
    Summary of Conversation Partners 31
The Roadmap 34

Chapter 1
A Cognitive Turn: Conceptual Blending within a Socio-Rhetorical Framework
Introduction 37
Cognitive Science of Religion: Embodied Cognition 38
    The Textual/Linguistic End of the Spectrum:
    Conceptual Integration Theory (Conceptual Blending) 43
        The Conceptual Integration Network (CIN) 46
        Framing Networks 50
        Different Types of Networks 53
        Governing Principles 57
A Socio-Rhetorical Framework: Embracing Embodied Cognition 61
Conclusion 74

Chapter 2
Wisdom

Introduction 76
What is "Wisdom"? 77
Jewish Wisdom Discourse 84
    Wisdom and Creation: Generative Righteousness 85
    Wisdom and Law: Right Action and Purity 94
    Wisdom's Self-Critique: The Limits of Human Wisdom 104
Conclusion 107

Chapter 3
Jewish Resource Zones

Introduction 109
Women 112
    Positive Views of Women 114
    Negative Views of Women 119
Sex and Marriage 129
Holiness 138
Freedom 147
Conclusion 158

Chapter 4
Setting the Wisdom Context: 1 Corinthians 1–4

Introduction 159
Community Behavior: The Context for Paul's Exposition on Wisdom 160
1 Corinthians 1:18–2:5: Apocalyptic Wisdom 163
1 Corinthians 2:6–3:4: Paul as Teacher of Eternal Wisdom 170
1 Corinthians 3:5–4:13: Blended Wisdom Analogies 176
1 Corinthians 4:14-21: "Be Imitators of Me"— Paul Asserts Authority 180
Conclusion 184

Chapter 5
The Wisdom of Fleeing Porneia: Introducing 1 Corinthians 6:12–7:7

Introduction 186
Establishing the Pericope 191
The Question of Slogans in 1 Corinthians 6:12–7:7 196
Constructing the Christian Σῶμα 202
Conclusion 205

Chapter 6
Why Porneia Should be Avoided: The Rhetography of 1 Corinthians 6:12–6:20

Introduction 206
Introduction to the Argument (6:12): Wisdom Rhetorolect 208
    Permitted and Beneficial: 6:12ab 213

Freedom and Self-Mastery: 6:12cd 220
Summary 224
Destruction of the Belly, Resurrection of the Body (6:13-14):
Wisdom-Apocalyptic Blended Rhetorolect 225
Member of Christ, Member of a Whore; Union with a Whore, Union
with Christ (6:15-17): Wisdom-Priestly-Apocalyptic Blended Rhetorolect ... 233
    Believers' Bodies as "Members" (6:15) 234
    "Clinging" Leads to Union (6:16-17) 240
Temples, Slaves, and Glorifying God (6:18-20): Wisdom-Priestly
Blended Rhetorolect 252
    Fleeing πορνεία (6:18) 253
    Temples and Slaves (6:19-20) 255
Conclusion 260

Chapter 7
How Porneia Should be Avoided: The Rhetology of 1 Corinthians 7:1–7:7

Introduction 263
The Basic Pauline Options (7:1-2): Wisdom-Priestly Blended Rhetorolect 264
Commanding Sex (7:3-4): Wisdom Rhetorolect 272
A Time to Pray (7:5-6): Wisdom-Priestly-Apocalyptic Blended Rhetorolect .. 281
Paul's Wish and Corinthian Reality (7:7): Wisdom-Priestly Rhetorolect 286
Conclusion 290
    A Holistic Argument 290

Conclusion 293

Bibliography 302
Index of Names 327
Index of Ancient References 333

Figures

Figure 1: Apocalyptic Binary Oppositions 165
Figure 2: Conceptual Network for 6:12ab 214
Figure 3: Conceptual Network for 6:12cd 221
Figure 4: Conceptual Network for 6:13-14 233
Figure 5: Conceptual Network for 6:15a 237
Figure 6: Conceptual Network for 6:15b 238
Figure 7: Conceptual Network for 6:16 241
Figure 8: Conceptual Network for 6:17 243
Figure 9: Conceptual Network for the Mega-Blend in 6:16-17 244
Figure 10: Conceptual Network for 6:18 254
Figure 11: Conceptual Network for 6:19a 256
Figure 12: Conceptual Network for the Mega-Blend of 6:19-20a 259
Figure 13: Conceptual Network for 7:1-2 271
Figure 14: Conceptual Network for 7:3-4 279
Figure 15: Conceptual Network for 7:5 284
Figure 16: Conceptual Network for 7:7 288

Acknowledgments

I feel a profound sense of gratitude to numerous people who had a hand in helping this project develop from conception, through various stages of growth, and finally to publication. While the creation of a book involves countless hours in solitary confinement translating ideas into words, it requires just as many hours of community support in order to reach completion. I have been the beneficiary of a tremendous amount of support from mentors, colleagues, friends, and family.

I would especially like to thank my tireless mentor, Vernon K. Robbins, for his encouragement, enthusiasm, and hard work as he patiently taught me modes of socio-rhetorical interpretation and as we explored the new ideas of conceptual integration theory. I can never repay him for over a decade's worth of continual support or for all of the opportunities he continues to provide. I would not be where I am, nor would this book exist in its current form, were it not for his seemly inexhaustible energy expended on my behalf. No one has worked harder in helping me produce this book than he has.

I would also like to thank David B. Gowler, Director of the Pierce Institute for Leadership and Community Engagement, for his help with the publication of this volume. I especially thank the Pierce Program in Religion of Oxford College of Emory University for its financial support. The production of scholarship requires financial investment and I am honored that the Pierce Program in Religion has deemed my work worthy of support.

My current institution, Mercyhurst University (Erie, PA), provided me with two research contracts (for academic years 2008-2009 and 2009-2010) that gave me the necessary time to complete the manuscript. Teaching is what we do at Mercyhurst and I appreciate the institution's recognition that great teaching requires the support of scholarship. I am grateful for the encouragement of my department chair, Thomas Forsthoefel, in the pursuit of those research contracts. And I especially thank my departmental colleague and friend, Verna M. Ehret, for all of her time spent reading (and re-reading) numerous drafts of various chapters. Her insightful comments and critiques enabled me to make more cogent arguments. Finally, I thank Ms. Renée Kiefer, my research assistant for two years, for all her patience and hard work.

I also owe a debt of gratitude to members of the Emory University community for help during earlier stages in the development of this project. I thank Gail R. O'Day (currently Dean of Wake Forest University School of Divinity), Walter T. Wilson, and Cynthia B. Patterson for their time, wisdom, and encouragement. I thank all of my former graduate student colleagues in the Graduate Division of Religion, especially those who were frequent denizens of the Student Lounge, for their camaraderie and friendship. I especially thank Susan Haddox, Brian Alderman, Juan Hernández, Jr., Bart Bruehler, James Strange, Erika Fitz, and Bryan Whitfield for reading innumerable early drafts and for doing the lion's share of the work in helping to save me from lack of clarity, logical fallacies, and crimes against the English language.

Finally, I thank my family for all of the love and care they have given me throughout my whole life. First and foremost I thank my amazing spouse, Hilary L. Copp, for her unfailing love and encouragement during this book's exceedingly long gestation period. She bore the brunt of my anxiety and frustration when writing was not going well and she shared in my joy when I managed to solve interpretive problems. There are no words to express my deep and abiding love and appreciation for her presence. If not for her, none of this would have any value. I thank my sister, Kim N. Veltri, for never letting me forget my essential humanity. Her grace under pressure and her love of family are qualities to which I can only aspire. And I offer my deepest thanks to my parents, Bob and Judy, for always loving and supporting me and for raising me to believe that I could accomplish anything I set my mind to. Sadly, my mother did not live to see the publication of this book and I dedicate it to her memory. I miss you, Mutti.

Introduction

When exegetes attempt to understand the meanings nurtured by the texts of the New Testament, they are, to borrow a quotation from Peter Brown, confronted "with a Christianity whose back is firmly turned toward us, untroubled by our own most urgent, and legitimate questions."[1] This is nowhere more the case than in the Pauline epistles. Not only are biblical scholars attempting to find meaning in texts written in a time and place remote from our own, but we must deal with the added obstacle of reading other people's mail, and only one side of the correspondence at that. More specifically, the difficulty of understanding 1 Cor 6:12–7:7 is well known. The number of divergent interpretations assigned to this passage has prompted Brian Rosner to claim that this pericope contains what "is widely acknowledged to be one of the most difficult passages of the Pauline corpus."[2]

It is also well known that much ink has been spilled in wrestling with Paul's language in 1 Cor 6:12–7:7. Given the sheer volume of material written on 1 Cor 6:12–7:7, especially since the beginning of the 1990s, anyone attempting yet another study of Paul's discussion of πορνεία in 1 Corinthians must first explain the need for such a project. The intellectual effort that has been expended on this pericope, from F.C. Baur in the nineteenth century to Kathy Gaca in the twenty-first, is extraordinary. Yet, as Vernon Robbins notes, "Interpretation is more like a ritual than a single act" because "[a] text is a thick matrix of interwoven networks of meanings and meaning effects."[3] Because of the complex nature of textual interpretation "[n]o complete interpreta-

---

[1] Peter Brown, *The Body and Society: Men, Women, and Sexual Renunciation in Early Christianity* (New York, Columbia University Press, 1988), xvii.

[2] Brian Rosner, "Temple Prostitution in 1 Corinthians 6:12-20," *NovT* 40 (1998): 336. See also Bruce N. Fisk, "ΠΟΡΝΕΥΕΙΝ as Body Violation: The Unique Nature of Sexual Sin in 1 Corinthians 6.18," *NTS* 42 (1996): 540.

[3] Vernon K. Robbins, *The Tapestry of Early Christian Discourse: Rhetoric, Society and Ideology* (New York: Routledge, 1996), 20.

tion of a text is humanly possible."[4] Thus, while many scholars have undertaken to investigate all or parts of 1 Cor 6:12–7:7, I believe that there are important questions that remain to be asked and solutions that have yet to be explored.

A full-fledged socio-rhetorical investigation of 1 Cor 6:12–7:7 that opens up new avenues of investigation has yet to be undertaken. The reigning interpretation, since at least the beginning of the twentieth century, has been to regard 6:12–7:7 as discourse rife with Corinthian slogans that Paul is forced to confront, modify, and overturn.[5] Such

---

[4] Vernon K. Robbins, *Exploring the Texture of Texts: A Guide to Socio-Rhetorical Interpretation* (Valley Forge, Pa.: Trinity Press International, 1996), 2.

[5] For examples of major authors who argue for the presence of slogans in 6:12-20, see especially Michael D. Goulder, *Paul and the Competing Mission in Corinth* (Library of Pauline Studies; Peabody, MA: Hendrickson, 2001), 118: "It is clear that Paul is citing catch phrases used by his opponents and then demolishing them, and there are some persuasive suggestions on how to see which is which." Ben Witherington, III, *Conflict and Community in Corinth: A Socio-Rhetorical Commentary on 1 and 2 Corinthians* (Grand Rapids: Eerdmans, 1994), 167: "Beginning with v. 12 Paul quotes some of the Corinthians' slogans and then qualifies or rejects them." For a chart of various slogan hypotheses see John Coolidge Hurd, *The Origin of First Corinthians* (New York: Seabury Press, 1965; repr., Macon, GA: Mercer University Press, 1983), 68. On the near ubiquity of regarding 1 Cor 6:12a and 12c as a slogan see, e.g., C.K. Barrett, *A Commentary on the First Epistle to the Corinthians* (HNTC; New York: Harper & Row, 1968), 144; Raymond F. Collins, *First Corinthians* (SP 7; Collegeville, MN: The Liturgical Press, 1999), 236; Hans Conzelmann, *A Commentary on the First Epistle to the Corinthians* (Hermeneia; trans. James W. Leitch; Philadelphia: Fortress Press, 1975), 108; Michael D. Goulder, "Libertines? (1 Cor 5-6)," *NovT* 41 (1999): 341; Gordon D. Fee, *The First Epistle to the Corinthians* (NICNT; Grand Rapids: Eerdmans, 1987), 251; Victor Paul Furnish, *The Theology of the First Letter to the Corinthians* (New York: Cambridge University Press, 1999), 56; Dale Martin, *The Corinthian Body* (New Haven: Yale University Press, 1995), 175; Margaret M. Mitchell, *Paul and the Rhetoric of Reconciliation: An Exegetical Investigation of the Language and Composition of 1 Corinthians* (HUT 28; Tübingen: J.C.B. Mohr (Paul Siebeck), 1991), 232; Wolfgang Schrage, *Der erste Brief an der Korinther* (4 vols; EKK 7; Düsseldorf/Neukirchen-Vluyn: Benzinger Verlag/Neukirchener Verlag, 1991-2001), 10; Anthony C. Thiselton, *The First Epistle to the Corinthians: A Commentary on the Greek Text* (NIGTC; Grand Rapids: Eerdmans, 2000), 460; Johannes Weiß, *Der erste Korintherbrief* (Göttingen: Vandenhoeck & Ruprecht, 1910), 157. But note that while "All NT scholars agree that much of 1 Cor 6,12-20 is Paul quoting from the Corinthians" they "unfortunately cannot agree where to put the quotation marks!" Timothy Radcliffe, "'Glorify God in your Bodies': 1 Corinthians 6,12-20 as Sexual Ethic," *NBf* 67 (1986), 306-314. For an attempt to address programmatically the issue of what, exactly, constitutes a slogan, see Paul Charles Siebenmann, "The Question of Slogans in 1 Corinthians" (Ph.D. diss., Baylor University, 1997) esp. 162, 172, 185, 195. Siebenmann also traces the origin of several slogan hypotheses (6-8). For those who argue that 1 Cor 7:1b is a quotation from the Corinthian Letter see, e.g., Barrett, *First Epistle to the Corinthians*, 154; R. Collins, *First Corinthians*, 252; Fee, *First Epistle to the Corinthians*, 270-271; Goulder, *Paul*, 125; Hurd, *Origin*, 68, 163-165; Thiselton, *First Epistle to the Corinthians*, 498-500; Schrage, *Der erste Brief an die Korinther*, 2:53-54; Witherington, *Conflict and Community*, 167; William E. Phipps, "Is Paul's Attitude toward Sexual Relations Contained in 1 Cor 7.1?" *NTS* 28 (1982): 125-131; O. Larry Yarbrough, *Not Like the Gentiles: Marriage Rules*

interpretations, I argue, serve a historical-reconstructionist project that attempts to divine the local situation in Corinth on the basis of the contents of Paul's letters. I argue that this type of reading obscures the unified nature of Paul's argument in 1 Cor 6:12–7:7 and thus inadequately treats Paul's overarching concern with the religious danger posed by πορνεία and the cultural relevance of his response to it. Rather than focus on local historical reconstruction, the interpretative principles of socio-rhetorical interpretation seek to discover, in the words of cognitive scientists Gilles Fauconnier and Mark Turner, "how language prompts for meaning" in a broader cultural environment.[6] The use of conceptual integration theory, a branch of cognitive science developed by Fauconnier and Turner, within a socio-rhetorical framework offers exegetes the ability to think about Paul's teaching against πορνεία in new ways. In their efforts to refine further the description of what meanings certain combinations of language can prompt, socio-rhetorical exegetes have identified types of discourse in the New Testament that they refer to as "rhetorical dialects," or rhetorolects for short.[7] As I will discuss in my following chapters, these rhetorolects help me, and other socio-rhetorical exegetes, to explain how Paul's language makes efficient use of background information while at the same time generating new meaning that has powerful rhetorical effects.

I argue that Paul's teaching against πορνεία in 1 Cor 6:12–7:7 is best understood as an example of early Christian wisdom discourse. Paul constructs his argument in two parts, the first which explains *why* the sin of πορνεία is to be avoided (6:12-20) and the other, which Paul ties into the concrete concerns that Corinthians have (7:1a), explains *how* this can be best achieved by members of the Corinthian community in their sexual bodies (7:1b-7). Thus, while I recognize that 1 Cor 6:12–7:7 represents different moments in Paul's argumentation, the essential exegetical unity of these 16 verses remains at the forefront of my interpretation. In order to demonstrate this, I situate Paul's teaching within

---

in the Letters of Paul (SBLDS 80; Atlanta: Scholars Press, 1985), 93-94, 121. For two scholars who critique the reigning slogan hypotheses regarding 6:12 and 7:1, respectively, see Brian J. Dodd, "Paul's Paradigmatic 'I' and 1 Corinthians 6.12," *JSNT* 59 (1995): 39-58; idem, *Paul's Paradigmatic 'I': Personal Example as Literary Strategy* (JSNTSup 177; Sheffield: Sheffield Academic Press, 1999), 78-90; Peter Nejsum, "The Apologetic Tendency in the Interpretation of Paul's Sexual Ethics," *ST* 48 (1994): 48-62.

[6] Gilles Fauconnier and Mark Turner, *The Way We Think: Conceptual Blending and the Mind's Hidden Complexities* (New York: Basic Books, 2002), 139 (also 277). I discuss cognitive science in general and conceptual integration theory in particular at greater length in ch. 1.

[7] See esp. Vernon K. Robbins, "The Dialectical Nature of Early Christian Discourse," *Scriptura* 59 (1996): 353-62.

the multi-faceted cultural matrix of Jewish wisdom literature, focusing especially on Jewish wisdom written in Greek and its permutations during the Hellenistic period. When placed within this web of significance, Paul's mode of teaching, as well as the specific content of his instruction, begins to lose some of the difficulties that enshroud it.

Conversation Partners

The work done on 1 Corinthians (1 Cor) over the centuries, from the early Church Fathers to the present day, is prodigious. An entire volume could be written that simply narrates the twists and turns of interpretation regarding Paul's teaching on sexual comportment found in this letter. Recognizing that every work on 1 Cor, or any biblical text for that matter, stands always already in dialogue with the work of many other scholars, I have opted not to cover some ground so well tread by others in this brief discussion of my immediate conversation partners.[8] Many of the works discussed below also contain excellent summaries of the literature available on 1 Cor 6:12–7:7 that need not be repeated here. What I have chosen to do, in selecting the ten scholars discussed below, is to interact with those thinkers whose ideas have left their stamp on much of subsequent scholarship, that is, those scholars with whom later interpreters feel compelled to interact – either explicitly or implicitly.

I have chosen to start with the seminal work of F.C. Baur because it is his framing of the historical investigation into the Corinthian correspondence that continues to be felt to this day. Johannes Weiß's thoughts as found in his commentary on 1 Cor are essential to understand, not only because of his influential partition theory and use of the idea of "slogans," but more importantly for the way in which he

---

[8] For an excellent work tracing the interpretation of Paul's teaching about proper sexual behavior in the early Church see Elizabeth A. Clark, *Reading Renunciation: Asceticism and Scripture in Early Christianity* (Princeton: Princeton University Press, 1999). In a similar, but more general, vein see Douglas Burton-Christie, *The Word in the Desert: Scripture and the Quest for Holiness in Early Christian Monasticism* (New York: Oxford University Press, 1993). More specifically, see as well J. Massingberd Ford, "St Paul the Philogamist (I Cor. VII in Early Patristic Exegesis," *NTS* 11 (1965): 326-48. As with many biblical texts, there is a lacuna in scholarship about the intricacies of medieval interpretation, but see the following works edited and written by Mark D. Jordan: *Ad Litteram: Authoritative Texts and their Medieval Readers* (ed. Mark D. Jordan and Kent Emery, Jr.; Notre Dame, Ind.: University of Notre Dame Press, 1992); Mark D. Jordan, *The Invention of Sodomy in Christian Theology* (Chicago: University of Chicago Press, 1997); idem, *The Ethics of Sex* (New Dimensions to Religious Ethics 3; Oxford: Blackwell, 2002). For the Reformation era see especially John L. Thompson, "Apostolic Doctrine and Apostolic Advice in 1 Corinthians 7: A Study in Sixteenth-Century Exegesis and Hermeneutics" (*American Society of Church History Papers*; Portland, Ore.: Theological Research Exchange Network, 1993).

roamed freely among Jewish and non-Jewish Hellenistic-Roman resources to help explicate Paul's argument in 1 Cor 6:12–7:7. And J.C. Hurd pushed the historical critical project of getting behind the text of 1 Cor farther than others before him, thereby showing in greater relief the promises and problems of such a methodology.

The amount of work done on 1 Cor 6:12–7:7 in the past quarter of a century is astonishing. O. Larry Yarbrough's work recalls the bicultural investigation of Weiß even as he asks questions about cultural formation rather than historical reconstruction. Margaret Mitchell's work, while still operating within the historical-critical paradigm, brings the importance of Paul's rhetoric to the fore. Four works clustered in the mid-1990s, those of Renate Kirchhoff, Brian Rosner, Will Deming, and Dale Martin, demonstrate the new, and somewhat fragmentary, ways in which thinking about Paul's teaching on sexual behavior has moved. Kathy Gaca's reading of Paul finishes this brief introduction because her scholarship demonstrates the interconnectedness of multiple academic disciplines at the beginning of the twenty-first century.

The thinkers with whom I engage here have been arranged in simple chronological order. This was done to avoid forcing the complex work many of these scholars have undertaken into some preconceived, arbitrary taxonomy. The works discussed below can be grouped in any number of combinations, but I feared that grouping these scholars according to methodology, framing, presuppositions, etc. would serve only to cover up other relations the reader might infer in the absence of such explicit categories. By discussing these works in chronological order I do not intend to create some evolutionary model of interpretation. What I do intend is to demonstrate that these important scholars, while making tremendous advances in our understanding of 1 Cor, depend on those who went before them, as does my own work.

Ferdinand Christian Baur: The Historical Paradigm
Almost any work that deals with the Corinthian Correspondence must take the seminal ideas of Ferdinand Christian Baur into account. Although the specifics of much of his work on the Corinthian letters have been much maligned,[9] he remains a crucial figure in the modern history of interpretation. His usefulness for the study of 1 Cor 6:12–7:7 is not self-evident, however, given that this pericope does not illuminate the main argument Baur makes regarding the differentiation between Petrine and Pauline Christianity. Yet his discussion of the characteristics of the Corinthian parties and his argument regarding the addressees

---
[9] See Goulder, *Paul*, 5-6.

of the various sections of 1 Cor make Baur's work pertinent to the present project. Baur launched a historical project that influenced many succeeding discussions of 1 Cor in general.[10]

In his important 1831 essay, "Die Christuspartei in der korinthischen Gemeinde," Baur lays the framework for understanding both of the Corinthian letters in a context of a struggle between two versions of early Christianity – one Petrine and the other Pauline.[11] The overall argument of this essay is well known and need not be rehearsed here. What is important for this study is that in this 1831 work and also in his *Paulus, der Apostel Jesu Christi*, which first appeared in 1845,[12] Baur contends that, by reading the Corinthian letters closely, one can reconstruct the nature of the opponents whom Paul was battling. In "Die Christuspartei," Baur argues that the key to unlocking the identity of the opponents lies in 1 Cor 1:12, where Paul mentions four "parties." However, these four parties are actually two, since the Paul and Apollos parties are similar and the Peter and Christ party are likewise aligned. In Baur's reading, the situation in Corinth is a battle between Jewish Christianity on the one hand (embodied by the Peter and Christ parties) and Pauline Christianity on the other (embodied by the Paul and Apollos parties).[13]

Baur's method of identifying the nature of Paul's opponents and reconstructing the historical situation in Corinth through a close reading of the Corinthian correspondence has proven exceedingly influential. After the opponents have been identified through the clues found in

---

[10] See Werner Georg Kümmel, *The New Testament: The History of the Investigation of Its Problems* (trans. S. McLean and Howard C. Kee; New York: Abingdon Press, 1972), 143; trans. of *Das Neue Testament: Geschichte der Erforschung seiner Probleme* (Freiburg/Munich: Verlag Karl Alber, 1958), 176: "Since Baur's time, scientific work on the NT has been possible only when the fundamental methodological principles he indicated have been followed and his overall historical view has been superseded or improved." And as recently as 2001, Michael Goulder (*Paul*) argues that Baur's interpretation of the situation in Corinth is essentially correct.

[11] Ferdinand Christian Baur, "Die Christuspartei in der korinthischen Gemeinde, der Gegensatz des petrinischen und paulinischen Christentums in der alten Kirche, der Apostel Petrus in Rom," in *Ausgewählte Werke in Einzelgaben* (ed. Klaus Scholder; 4 vols.; Stuttgart–Bad Cannstatt: Friedrich Frommann Verlag [Günther Holzboog], 1963-1970): 1:1-146; repr. from *Tübinger Zeitschrift für Theologie* 4 (1831): 61-206.

[12] The second edition of this work is used here. Ferdinand Christian Baur, *Paulus, der Apostel Jesu Christi. Sein Leben und Wirken, Seine Briefe und Seine Lehre: Ein Beitrag zu einer Kritischen Geschichte des Urchristentums* (2nd ed.; 2 vols.; Leipzig: Fues's Verlag, 1866-1867). ET, *Paul, The Apostle of Jesus Christ, His Life and Works, His Epistles and His Doctrine: A Contribution to a Critical History of Primitive Christianity* (2nd ed.; trans. Eduard Zeller; 2 vols.; London: Williams & Northgate, 1873-1875).

[13] See Baur, "Christuspartei," 74-76. Note also Baur's comment in *Paulus*, 1:289 (ET 1:259), where he argues that the Jewish-Christian opponents used a different mode of attack in Corinth than they did in Galatia.

the text, Baur then proceeds to interpret the letters in light of these reconstructed opponents. This way of interpreting 1 Cor has had a lasting influence, as have the problems associated with it. William Baird describes Baur's work as follows: "Indeed, his argument tends to be circular: NT documents are used to reconstruct early Christian history; the reconstruction of early Christian history provides the framework for the assessment of NT documents."[14] While Baur's research opened a new chapter in the interpretation of the New Testament, the problems inherent in his methodology continue to recur through many later interpreters.

Johannes Weiß: Partitions and Slogans

If Baur was one of the exemplars of a "consistently historical view of the New Testament" according to Werner Kümmel,[15] Johannes Weiß, although not adhering to the exact same ideological commitments as Baur, continued the tradition of historical investigation into 1 Cor.[16] As Weiß states at the end of the introduction to his commentary (1910), exegesis will always demonstrate "what an invaluable historical document we possess in 1 Corinthians."[17] By situating his exegesis within the historical paradigm, Weiß legitimates his interpretive strategy of partitioning the letter in order to make better sense of it. Citing the historical reality that no autographs of the Pauline letters survive, Weiß reminds his readers that the extant letters derive from the early collections of Pauline material, a "corpus Paulinum." On the basis of evidence found in 1 and 2 Corinthians, Weiß argues that Paul wrote, at minimum, four letters to the Corinthian community. How likely, he asks, is it that the archivist at Corinth would lose track of these "relics"? The solution, Weiß proposes, is that 1 Cor is not a unitary letter, but rather a synthesis of (at least) two letters.[18]

Weiß's importance for the legitimization of partition theories for 1 Cor in twentieth-century biblical scholarship can hardly be overesti-

---

[14] William Baird, *History of New Testament Research, Volume One: From Deism to Tübingen* (Minneapolis: Fortress, 1992), 262.

[15] See Kümmel, *Das Neue Testament*, ch. 4: "die konsequent geschichtliche Betrachtung des neuen Testament."

[16] See Kümmel, *Das Neue Testament*, 286-91, 294, 302-306, 337, 351-58, 367, 581 (ET 226-30, 238-40, 266, 276-81, 288).

[17] Weiß, *Der erste Korintherbrief*, xliii: "ein wie unschätzbares geschichtliches Dokument wir im 1 Kor. besitzen."

[18] Weiß, *Der erste Korintherbrief*, xl-xlii, although on p. xl Weiß notes Jülicher's objection that theories of partition are too "abenteuerlich" ["adventurous"].

mated.[19] Weiß did, it must be remembered, employ a rhetoric of humility about his proposed partition of the letter – "I can bring forward the following [ideas about partition] only with much timidity, since I myself know best how many difficulties still remain" – that is generally absent in the partition theories of later scholars.[20] In trying to make exegetical sense of the various arguments employed by Paul, Weiß suggests that two letters can be discerned in 1 Cor, although he admits, as noted, that his hypothesis is not without its difficulties.[21] The first letter (A) was composed in Ephesus and contains the following: 10:1-22 (or 23); 6:12-20; 9:24-27; 11:2-34; 16:7b-9, 15-20. The rest of 1 Cor he assigns, "although not without concerns" (*Bedenken*),[22] to *one* other letter (B) which seems to have been written in Macedonia and which Weiß suggests contained: 1:1-6:11; 7; 8; 13; 10:24-11:1; 9:1-23; 12; 14; 15; 16:1-7a, 10-14, 21-24.

The second letter (B), moreover, can be further broken down. Weiß notes that 1 Cor 1:1–6:11 appears to be an undivided unity, but the tone is different from that found in the "instructive chapters" (7 and following in Weiß's reconstruction). He argues that this can be explained if Paul wrote the "instructive chapters" first, answering the questions found in the letter the Corinthians sent to Paul (7:1a), but then heard about the conflict involving the "parties" orally before sending letter B. Paul, Weiß argues, penned 1:1–6:11 after receiving this oral information and placed this at the front of his already completed letter. Weiß thus argues for the composite nature of letter B (B_1 [the instructive chapters] and B_2 [1:1–6:11]). Weiß concludes "that form and content distinguish three different writings within the letter from one another" (A, B_1, B_2).[23]

Weiß's ideas about the partition of 1 Cor are important not only because of the power they exert over later NT interpretation, but for the rationale behind dividing up the letter. Hypothesizing about the existence of two letters in 1 Cor allows Weiß to argue that one can see the developmental history (*Entwicklungsgeschichte*) of the Corinthian community. The partition theory proposed by Weiß thus serves the histor-

---

[19] See e.g. Mitchell, *Paul and the Rhetoric of Reconciliation*, 2, esp. n. 5 in which she notes P. Vielhauer's claim that "later theories are mostly variations on Weiss's insights." Also see Hurd, *Origin of 1 Corinthians*, 44.

[20] Weiß, *Der erste Korintherbrief*, xl: "Ich kann das Folgende [ideas about partition] nur sehr schüchtern vortragen, da ich selbst am besten weiß, wieviel Schwierigkeiten noch übrig bleiben."

[21] Weiß notes (xlii) that there is a "geographic-chronological" difficulty inherent in his reconstruction of the two letters.

[22] Weiß, *Der erste Korintherbrief*, xli.

[23] Weiß, *Der erste Korintherbrief*, xlii:"daß formell und inhaltlich drei verschiedene Schriften innerhalb des Briefes sich von einander abheben."

ical agenda – not only can certain problems with the text of 1 Cor be explained away, but the two letters allow modern scholars a window into the historical evolution of an early Christian community. Additionally, Weiß's partition theory is important in that it solves the problem of the seemingly different audiences addressed by separating 6:12-7:7 into portions of two separate letters. While 6:12-20 was written to address opponents whom Weiß describes as "freethinking (*freigeistigen*) 'Gnostics,'" or "Libertines,"[24] in 7:1-7 Paul is writing against a "hyperascetic mood" (*Stimmung*)[25] that, Weiß suggests, could have derived from a certain understanding that extended Paul's arguments against πορνεία in the first letter to sex within the bounds of marriage.[26] In Weiß's reading, chapter 7 is readily understandable as explicating a possible confusion which arose from Paul's discussion of sexual immorality in letter A.[27]

In addition to his influential theory of partition, Weiß's commentary on 1 Cor is crucial for subsequent scholarship for the way in which he engages *both* Jewish and non-Jewish Hellenistic contexts. Ranging from the LXX to the Pseudepigrapha to Philo and Josephus to rabbinic material, Weiß situates Paul's thinking about sexual matters within a living Jewish interpretive tradition. Likewise, he discusses Cynic and Stoic popular philosophical ideas in general, but also refers, especially in the notes, to specific non-Jewish Hellenistic thinkers, most especially Epictetus and Musonius Rufus. In drawing from various cultural worlds in order to shed light on what Paul is doing in 6:12-20 and 7:1-7, Weiß provides an important model for reading Paul's argument within its broader cultural context to show how it draws from multiple symbolic worlds.[28] While his theory of partition has been discarded, Weiß's practice of situating Paul in both Jewish and non-Jewish Hellenistic-Roman symbolic worlds provides his work with a depth that continues to benefit contemporary scholarship.

John Coolidge Hurd: Getting Behind the Text

Moving into English language scholarship, one prominent work which has left an indelible mark on the history of interpretation of 1 Cor is John Coolidge Hurd's *The Origin of 1 Corinthians* (1965). In this book

---

[24] Weiß, *Der erste Korintherbrief*, 157, 159 respectively.

[25] Weiß, *Der erste Korintherbrief*, 169.

[26] Weiß, *Der erste Korintherbrief*, xlii. Weiß describes those who might take such a view to be "ernste, ängstliche, unfreie Gemüter" (169).

[27] Weiß, *Der erste Korintherbrief*, xlii, where Weiß also argues that 1 Cor 15 is an answer (in letter B) to objections which might have been raised against 6:14 (in letter A).

[28] See Luke Timothy Johnson, *The Writings of the New Testament: An Interpretation* (rev. ed.; Minneapolis: Fortress, 1999), 21-91.

Hurd argues that not only is understanding the specific situation that caused Paul to write 1 Cor essential to understanding the letter's meaning, but that it is in fact possible to reconstruct various exchanges which took place between Paul and the Corinthians before the writing of 1 Cor. In mapping out what took place "behind" 1 Cor, Hurd asserts that he can demonstrate not only *that* Paul changed his ideas over time, but he argues that he has discovered the reason *why* such changes took place.[29] According to Hurd, Paul alters his original message to the Corinthians due to the compromise articulated in the Apostolic Decree (Acts 15:20, 29; 21:25) and thus he argues that 1 Cor and Acts are both "independent witnesses to a single formula of agreement in the early Church."[30] Not only does Hurd's study attempt to tease out the meaning of 1 Cor on the basis of a historical reconstruction arrived at by scouring the letter itself (see Baur above), but it also notes the historical significance (see Weiß above) of the letter in reconstructing early Christian history, especially in relation to the Apostolic Decree.

Significantly, Hurd reads 1 Cor as a unity, thus arguing against the partition theories made by Weiß and scholars after him. He declares that the evidence for partition is simply not strong enough to support such "radical and somewhat arbitrary" theories.[31] Yet, in practice, Hurd's study divides 1 Cor in a way that achieves somewhat similar results to traditional partition theories. For Hurd, 1 Cor can be profitably analyzed by dividing the letter into those sections in which Paul reacts to events he has heard orally (either from Chloe's people [1 Cor 1:11] or from Stephanus, Fortunatus, and Achaius [1 Cor 16:17]) and those sections in which Paul is responding to a letter he has received from the Corinthians (7:1). It is possible to separate these two sections from one another, according to Hurd, primarily on the basis of the tone of Paul's response; Paul is more "emotionally involved than usual" in those parts of the letter which respond to oral information and this contrasts with the "calmer and more detached" manner evident in those sections of 1 Cor in which he is responding to information he has received in written form. Hurd claims that Paul's repeated use of the περὶ δέ formula is also critical in determining which portions of 1 Cor deal with the letter from the Corinthians.[32] Relying on the above

---

[29] Hurd, *Origin of 1 Corinthians*, xxiii–xxiv.

[30] Hurd, *Origin of 1 Corinthians*, ch. 7. The quotation is from p. 260.

[31] Hurd, *Origin of 1 Corinthians*, 46-47. But see p. 47 n. 1 where Hurd acknowledges that Weiß considered his partition theory "only a working hypothesis." See the section on Weiß above.

[32] Hurd, *Origin of 1 Corinthians*, 48-49, 62, 65. While these criteria are the primary ones Hurd refers to throughout the study they are not the only ones he articulates. See p. 82 for a full summary of what characterized Paul's response to oral communication

criteria, Hurd argues that 1 Cor 1:10-5:8; 5:13b-6:11; and 11:17-34 deal with information Paul has obtained through oral reports, while 5:9-13a; 7:1-11:16; 12:1-14:40; 15:1-58 (perhaps); and 16:1-9, 12 stem from a response to written communication from the Corinthians.[33] Interestingly, Hurd argues that 6:12-20 is the only portion of 1 Cor which seems to make use of both types of communication. This pericope, he concludes, "was intended by Paul as a transitional passage to conclude his treatment of the oral information and to introduce his answers to the Corinthians' questions."[34]

Hurd's analysis serves to partition the text of 1 Cor, albeit in a different manner than does Weiß, in order to develop a means to trace the historical events that lie behind the letter. Hurd's project focuses on those portions of 1 Cor that respond to the letter the Corinthians sent to Paul,[35] because he believes that from these responses he can argue backward[36] to reconstruct not only much of the content of the Corinthians' letter, but also much of the content of Paul's Previous Letter to the Corinthians (1 Cor 5:9) as well as some aspects of the founding message Paul preached to the Corinthian community. 1 Corinthians thus represents the fourth stage in an ongoing exchange between Paul and the Corinthian community, but Hurd believes it is possible to recover much of stages three (the Corinthians' letter to Paul), two (Paul's Previous Letter), and one (the founding of the community).[37] Hurd is cognizant of the fact that his conclusions become more and more tenuous the farther he moves from the text of 1 Cor, but he believes that reasonably certain claims can be made about the relationship among these various levels of communication.[38] Hurd argues that the slogans found in 1 Cor, which Paul neither accepts nor rejects, but which he modifies, shed light on the contents of the Corinthian letter to Paul. Moreover, Hurd contends that his reconstruction of the different portions of the Corinthians' letter "show a coherence and general point of view" which he argues validates his interpretation of this stage in the communication between Paul and the community. These por-

---

and see p. 74 for his summary of the characteristics of material which responds to the Corinthians' letter.

[33] Hurd, *Origin of 1 Corinthians*, 93.
[34] Hurd, *Origin of 1 Corinthians*, 89.
[35] In the new preface to the reprinted edition of his book (xx) Hurd acknowledges that those portions which he considers Paul's reaction to the oral reports he received from some Corinthians (1 Cor 1–4 and much of 5–6) do not receive significant attention in this study.
[36] Hurd, *Origin of 1 Corinthians*, 289.
[37] Hurd, *Origin of 1 Corinthians*, 57-58.
[38] Hurd, *Origin of 1 Corinthians*, 213.

tions of the letter from the Corinthians, he goes on to argue, "give the impression of being *counter*statements."[39] Not only was the Corinthian letter a counter-statement to something Paul had said, but "their letter was very probably a topic-by-topic *reply* to Paul's Previous Letter."[40] This conclusion allows Hurd to go back further and reconstruct the Previous Letter itself. By further arguing that 2 Cor 6:14–7:1 is a fragment of this Previous Letter, Hurd is certain that a reasonable reconstruction of this letter, or at least the portions of it to which the Corinthians objected in their letter to Paul, can be made.[41]

As seen with Weiß above, the presence of so-called slogans in 1 Cor allows the interpreter to argue that he or she can discern the historical situation that lies behind the letter and, based on this information, can more effectively interpret the letter. Hurd moves away from postulating the existence of several (sometimes rival) opponents Paul faced in Corinth to argue that the community as a whole has questions about what they see as a change in Paul's message.[42] By reconstructing three stages of communication that lie behind 1 Cor, Hurd argues that his exegesis is able to deal with the presence of apparent slogans in a coherent fashion that explains both their origins and the reason why Paul does not simply reject them out of hand.

Hurd's treatment of 1 Cor demonstrates his full commitment to the historical paradigm. He mines the letter not simply to recreate the situation on the ground in Corinth, though he does this as well, but for clues which can illuminate not just one moment in the relationship between Paul and the Corinthians, but a chain of correspondence. In doing so, Hurd enters the same cycle as did Baur – Hurd uses 1 Cor to reconstruct a history of interaction between the community and Paul, and then uses this history to interpret what Paul is arguing in 1 Cor. Although he does not engage in this activity as explicitly as does Baur, Hurd's aim at reconstructing the different stages in the Paul-Corinthian dialogue is to explain the letter of 1 Cor in light of what he sees as a change in the message Paul communicated to the Corinthians. While his project, I argue, is inherently problematic for this reason, this is not to discount the careful work Hurd has done in exegeting various portions of the letter.

O. Larry Yarbrough: Paul and Marriage

In 1985 O. Larry Yarbrough published *Not Like the Gentiles: Marriage Rules in the Letters of Paul*, which has become required reading for any

---

[39] Hurd, *Origin of 1 Corinthians*, 209. Emphasis in the original.
[40] Hurd, *Origin of 1 Corinthians*, 216. Emphasis in the original.
[41] See Hurd, *Origin of 1 Corinthians*, 237, 239.
[42] See Hurd, *Origin of 1 Corinthians*, 68, table 5.

study of Paul that deals with issues surrounding sexual conduct and marriage. The importance of Yarbrough's study lies in the fact that he examines *both* Jewish and Greco-Roman moral traditions in order to help illuminate Paul's teachings on marriage and sexual ethics. By opening up the boundaries of his study to both of these traditions, Yarbrough, like Weiß before him, recognizes the bi-cultural nature of Paul's discourse. Yarbrough intends

> to establish points of contact between the Pauline mission and the larger Greco-Roman society (of which Judaism was a part) and thereby determine more precisely how the nature of Pauline ethics as it relates to marriage and sexual morality may have affected his followers who, after all, continued to live in a world dominated by Greco-Roman culture.[43]

Yarbrough's study of the Jewish moral tradition focuses primarily on Jewish apocryphal and pseudepigraphal writings, as well as on Rabbinic material. In focusing on these materials Yarbrough explicitly notes that he is not simply looking for verbal parallels.[44] It is clear, in reading Yarbrough's work, that his focus on the function of Jewish moral arguments about sex and marriage demands that his comparative method move beyond seeking verbal antecedents. In fact, it is Yarbrough's interest in the *effects* of Jewish moral teaching – rather than simply regarding this body of literature as source material – that explains his interest in the Rabbinic literature, which is arguably later than Paul's writing.[45] While I do not explicitly interact with the Rabbinic writings, Yarbrough's practice of using comparative materials as more than just "source" material undergirds the practice I follow in chapters 2 and 3.

Yarbrough's treatment of 1 Cor 7 is illuminating. In an allusion to Hurd, Yarbrough explicitly states that any attempt to reconstruct the Corinthians' letter to which Paul refers in 7:1a before first analyzing Paul's argument in 1 Cor 7 "puts the methodological cart before the

---

[43] Yarbrough, *Not Like the Gentiles*, 5. See pp. 3-4 for Yarbrough's discussion of earlier studies from which he distinguishes his own work: Herbert Preisker, *Christentum und Ehe in den ersten drei Jahrhunderten: Eine Studie zur Kulturgeschichte der alten Welt* (Berlin: Trowitzsch, 1927); Gerhard Delling, *Paulus' Stellung zu Frau und Ehe* (Stuttgart: Kohlhammer, 1931); Heinrich Baltenweiler, *Die Ehe im Neuen Testament: Exegetische Untersuchungen über Ehe, Ehelosigkeit und Ehescheidung* (ATANT; Zürich: Zwingli, 1967).

[44] Yarbrough, *Not Like the Gentiles*, 8.

[45] Yarbrough, *Not Like the Gentiles*, 18 explains the inclusion of Rabbinic material as follows: "To be sure, some of the material ... is much later than Paul. Nevertheless these late traditions demonstrate that the issues addressed by sectarian Judaism were also important in what was to become the main body of Jewish thought." Although it should also be noted that Yarbrough does eventually focus on what he believes (relying on the work of Jacob Neusner) are five topics on which the "pre-70 sages" focused (idem, 24-27).

horse."[46] Yarbrough attempts first to exegete the chapter, and only then does he offer his reconstruction of the Corinthian situation. Yarbrough analyzes 1 Cor 7 in its entirety, but in order to ground the arguments accurately which follow from it, he spends a good deal of time examining 1 Cor 7:1-7 and he even draws 1 Cor 6:12-20 into this analysis.

In making a connection between the sexual immorality he warns against in 1 Cor 6:12-20 and the rules on having a spouse in 1 Cor 7, Paul, according to Yarbrough, is following the advice he gave the Thessalonians in 1 Thess 4. But, because some Corinthians argue that sexual activity is outside the bounds of acceptable behavior for believers, Paul has to adapt his earlier teaching to the new situation in Corinth.[47] This situation, which Yarbrough describes after his exegesis of 1 Cor 7, is not one of division between libertinistic and ascetic factions within the community, but rather a dispute between "ascetics and those who would continue normal sexual relations within marriage."[48] Although Yarbrough claims that 1 Cor 7:1b represents a Corinthian "slogan," he does recognize that, while it is unlikely that they are quoting Paul directly, in their use of such maxims "[i]n all probability ... the Corinthians derived their position from Paul."[49] In order to counter the Corinthian argument against sexual activity, Yarbrough notes that Paul's argument differs from that of either the Jewish or non-Jewish Hellenistic moralists in that he does not employ the usual arguments for favoring marriage (e.g., producing children). Rather, the only reason Paul gives for marriage is the avoidance of sexual immorality. While such a concern resonates within Jewish tradition, the Hellenistic-Roman moralists do not employ this rationale.[50] By deftly weaving Jewish and Hellenistic-Roman moral traditions, Yarbrough's study situates Paul's argument in a rich cultural landscape.

Margaret Mitchell: Historical Rhetorical Analysis

In 1991 a work appeared which, for the purposes of this project at the very least, must be considered groundbreaking: Margaret M. Mitchell's *Paul and the Rhetoric of Reconciliation: An Exegetical Investigation of the Language and Composition of 1 Corinthians*. Mitchell's work is so critical in the history of interpretation because, influenced by the work of

---

[46] Yarbrough, *Not Like the Gentiles*, 92.
[47] Yarbrough, *Not Like the Gentiles*, 97, 101.
[48] Yarbrough, *Not Like the Gentiles*, 119.
[49] Yarbrough, *Not Like the Gentiles*, 121.
[50] Yarbrough, *Not Like the Gentiles*, 109. Although Yarbrough quotes (p. 109) Antipater as the closest to this type of argument when he criticizes "his contemporaries who neglect marriage and its obligations because of their 'inclination to sexual pleasure and the easy life' [ἡ ἐπὶ καταφερὲς καὶ ῥάθυμον ἐπίκλισις]."

Hans Dieter Betz, she undertakes what she describes as an historical rhetorical analysis of 1 Cor.[51] Her study of 1 Cor moves beyond the historical paradigm as constructed by Baur and even beyond the traditional historical-literary studies of the early twentieth century. Although Mitchell still understands her work to fall under the rubric of the "historical-critical method," her focus on the rhetorical nature of Paul's argumentation allows her interpretation to ask new questions about the function of Paul's language throughout the letter. Indeed, there is, in my opinion, some tension between Mitchell's focus on language and the pull of the historical throughout her book. This tension is overcome by Mitchell's insistence that modern rhetorical studies "should not be put in the service of historical studies."[52] Mitchell retains the historical focus of her project by laying out "five mandates" of historical rhetorical criticism in her first chapter:

1. Rhetorical criticism as employed here is a historical undertaking.
2. Actual speeches and letters from antiquity must be consulted along with the rhetorical handbooks throughout the investigation.
3. The designation of the rhetorical species of a text ... cannot be begged in analysis.
4. The appropriateness of rhetorical form and content must be demonstrated.
5. The rhetorical unit to be examined should be a compositional unit, which can be further substantiated by successful rhetorical analysis.[53]

Mitchell self-consciously reads 1 Cor "in the light of the literary/rhetorical conventions operative in the first century."[54] Moreover,

---

[51] Mitchell, *Paul and the Rhetoric of Reconciliation*, 6 where Mitchell notes her indebtedness to Betz. For the importance of Betz's work in bringing a rhetorical focus to NT studies, see also Vernon K. Robbins, "Social-Rhetorical Criticism: Mary, Elizabeth and the Magnificat as a Text Case," in *The New Literary Criticism and the New Testament* (ed. Elizabeth Struthers Malbon and Edgar V. McKnight; Sheffield: Sheffield Academic Press, 1994), 169.

[52] Mitchell, *Paul and the Rhetoric of Reconciliation*, 7 where she cites Wilhelm Wuellner, "Where is Rhetorical Criticism Taking Us?" *CBQ* 49 (1987): 448 n. 1 for a list of such modern works.

[53] Mitchell, *Paul and the Rhetoric of Reconciliation*, 6.

[54] Mitchell, *Paul and the Rhetoric of Reconciliation*, 8; see n. 24 on the same page where Mitchell notes Wuellner's "vastly different" view of rhetorical criticism. See Lauri Thurén, "Is There a Biblical Argumentation?" in *Rhetorical Argumentation in Biblical Texts: Essays from the Lund 2000 Conference* (ed. Anders Eriksson et al.; Emory Studies in Early Christianity 8; Harrisburg, Penn.: Trinity Press International, 2002), 77-92 whose view is also vastly different from the one Mitchell puts forth and who specifically cites Mitchell as representative of those whose projects are primarily historical.

given her focus on factionalism as the issue governing 1 Cor, Mitchell reads not just the rhetorical handbooks, but actual political writings from the ancient world in order to demonstrate a link between the "terms and *topoi*" used in political speeches and those Paul employs in 1 Cor.[55] Although she herself does not employ the term, Mitchell's analysis of Paul's use of deliberative rhetoric is a study in intertextuality. Mitchell's project is firmly grounded in Paul's use of language and has thus moved Pauline scholarship forward. My work is indebted to Mitchell's study even as it asks different questions and employs a different interpretive analytic.[56]

Mitchell's importance for the present project lies in specific arguments she puts forth as well. She vociferously argues against two trends of modern NT research: (1) partition theories,[57] varieties of which have been proposed since at least the time of Johannes Weiß;[58] and (2) the predilection of NT scholars to attempt to characterize Paul's opponents (a project which, as noted above, Baur undertook in 1831), the results of which have proven to be maddeningly inconsistent and contradictory.[59] She contests both of these developments by arguing that 1 Cor is a unity that represents Paul's own response to *his* understanding of the situation at Corinth. In contrast to J.C. Hurd, Mitchell has what I refer to as a strong Pauline reading of the letter. That is, she maintains that most analyses, like Hurd's, "which have depended with too much certainty on presumed historical factors have tended to downplay Paul's own creative role in fashioning his letter of response."[60] She, on the other hand, proposes to interpret 1 Cor as Paul's own creation, in

---

[55] Mitchell, *Paul and the Rhetoric of Reconciliation*, 15; see also ch. 3.
[56] Robbins, *Tapestry*, 11-13.
[57] Mitchell, *Paul and the Rhetoric of Reconciliation*, 298.
[58] Weiß, *Der erste Korintherbrief*, xxxix-xliii. See Hurd, *Origin*, 45 for a chart laying out the partition theories of various scholars. Also see Thiselton, *The First Epistle to the Corinthians*, 36-41.
[59] Mitchell, *Paul and the Rhetoric of Reconciliation*, 302.
[60] Mitchell, *Paul and the Rhetoric of Reconciliation*, 189-90. The tension in Mitchell's work between a focus on language and a concern for the historical is seen in this quotation and in n. 19 which follows it: "One does not want to stray into antihistorical bias, however. Surely Paul's letter responds to a very specific set of historical circumstances. But here I challenge the absolute validity of such presuppositions by asking if we can understand the letter's composition as Paul's own creation, by seeing how its composition is appropriate to the genre of deliberative letter, and the subject matter, an appeal to seek concord. The assumption that an ancient letter writer would *as a matter of course* follow the sequence of the varied correspondence which she or he has received has never been documented, and must be questioned, both in itself and in its applicability to this particular letter." See pp. 190-92 for her critique of projects such as Hurd's. Since her critique relies heavily on the interpretation of the περὶ δέ formula, see also Margaret M. Mitchell, "Concerning the ΠΕΡΙ ΔΕ in 1 Corinthians," *NovT* 31 (1989): 229-56; also Nejsum, "The Apologetic Tendency," 50.

which he makes use of deliberative rhetoric that is characterized by four traits:

> 1) a focus on future time as the subject of deliberation; 2) employment of a determined set of appeals or ends, the most distinctive of which is the advantageous (τό συμφέρον); 3) proof by example (παράδειγμα); and 4) appropriate subjects of deliberation, of which factionalism and concord are especially common.[61]

Once 1 Cor is understood as Paul's deliberative response to factionalism, as opposed to specific opponents, Mitchell argues that "one cannot methodologically proceed by reconstructing a 'Corinthian' position from 1 Corinthians."[62] Mitchell's conclusion that the project of reconstructing specific "opponents" is untenable, I argue, also helps move the study of 1 Cor forward, although not all later scholars follow Mitchell's lead.[63]

Mitchell notes that many commentators tend to separate chs. 5–6 from 7–11 by arguing that in the latter chapters Paul is responding to questions the Corinthians have put to him in a letter (7:1), whereas chs. 5–6 treat issues Paul is aware of through oral transmission (5:1).[64] She argues against such a treatment of 1 Cor and thus interprets 5:1–11:1 as a distinct section of proof that revolves around two related issues: πορνεία and εἰδωλόθυτα. Paul, according to Mitchell, develops these issues "under the overarching theme *of his own choice*: ἐξουσία/ἐλευθερία."[65] Thus Mitchell interprets 1 Cor 7 along with chs. 5–6, and not as somehow disconnected from them.[66] In doing so she notes that Paul is, in fact, discussing marriage under the topic of πορνεία.[67] Additionally, Mitchell has no trouble accepting 7:1b as the general principle Paul is expounding in a chapter which provides positive exceptions to this general rule that allow for sexual activity within marriage.[68] The link between Paul's discussion in 1 Cor 7 with his

---

[61] Mitchell, *Paul and the Rhetoric of Reconciliation*, 23.
[62] Mitchell, *Paul and the Rhetoric of Reconciliation*, 302.
[63] See my discussion of Dale Martin below.
[64] See especially Hurd, *Origin of First Corinthians*.
[65] Mitchell, *Paul and the Rhetoric of Reconciliation*, 226. Emphasis in the original.
[66] As does, for example, Will Deming, *Paul on Marriage and Celibacy: The Hellenistic Background of 1 Corinthians 7* (SNTSMS 83; New York: Cambridge University Press, 1995), 118. See more on Deming below. See also Christian D. von Dehsen, "Sexual Relationships and the Church: An Exegetical Study of 1 Corinthians 5–7" (Ph.D. diss., Union Theological Seminary, 1987), 28.
[67] Mitchell, *Paul and the Rhetoric of Reconciliation*, 235.
[68] Mitchell, *Paul and the Rhetoric of Reconciliation*, 236. It is interesting to note, in light of the ideological critique leveled against much Protestant scholarship on 1 Cor 7 by Nejsum, "Apologetic Tendency," 48–62 (esp. 49: "The most widespread apologetic interpretation of 7:1b is to read it as a Corinthian slogan which Paul refutes."), that

argument in 6:12-20 is an important one and is an area in which my work is heavily indebted to Mitchell, especially her treatment of 7:1a: "The introductory formula Περὶ δὲ ὧν ἐγράψατε served more specifically to define the sphere of reference of the next topic for the Corinthians (who wrote that letter), than it does for us who stand apart from that extended conversation."[69] Although Mitchell's focus is different from mine, and thus some of her conclusions do not mesh with mine, without the rhetorical analysis that she performs on 1 Cor my project would not be possible in its present form.

Renate Kirchhoff: Cultural and Social Analysis

In her 1994 book, *Die Sünde gegen den eigenen Leib*, Renate Kirchhoff undertakes a socio-cultural investigation into the reasons some Corinthian Christian men were visiting πόρναι.[70] Heavily influenced by Gerd Theißen,[71] Kirchhoff attempts to examine the cultural factors which would have surrounded the practice of prostitution (as well as other forms of illicit sexual congress which did not involve the transfer of money or goods) and the type of censure, or lack thereof, Roman society leveled against men who availed themselves of such services. Having established these, she moves on to examine Paul's arguments in 1 Cor 6:12-20. Although she is interested in historical questions, Kirchhoff's main concern is the social and cultural location of those in Corinth to whom Paul was writing, which she ascertains by examining the understanding of the practice of prostitution in Roman Corinth in the first century. The historical picture she paints, then, is derived not from the text of 1 Cor itself, but from external evidence about the status of prostitution in the Roman socio-cultural world. In her three main chapters she: (1) undertakes a semantic investigation into the terms πόρνη and πορνεία and uses social history to analyze the "living environment (*Lebensraum*) of prostitutes" in Roman antiquity; (2) attempts to locate the addressees of 1 Cor socially; and (3) undertakes a "text-linguistic analysis" of 1 Cor 6:12-20 in which she identifies exegetical problems she proceeds to examine.

Before she begins her study, Kirchhoff usefully discusses the idea that the Greek terms beginning with the πορν- stem are completely understood. In order to better understand what the terms πόρνη and πορνεία might have meant for Paul and the Corinthians, Kirchhoff undertakes a

---

Mitchell, a Catholic scholar, has little difficulty dealing with Paul's lack of enthusiasm for marriage. See Yarbrough, *Not Like the Gentiles*, 107.

[69] Mitchell, *Paul and the Rhetoric of Reconciliation*, 235.

[70] Renate Kirchhoff, *Die Sünde gegen den einigen Leib: Studien zu πόρνη und πορνεία in 1 Kor 6,12-20 und dem socio-kulturellen Kontext der paulinischen Adressaten* (SUNT 18; Göttingen: Vandenhoeck & Ruprecht, 1994), 11.

[71] She specifically thanks his involvement in her project in the foreword.

semantic analysis of these word groups in the ancient world. In her study she examines the Hebrew Bible, the Dead Sea Scrolls, Greek Jewish and Christian writings, and Greek pagan writings. She concludes that the terms have different connotations in Jewish/Christian texts than they do in so-called pagan texts.[72] In the first place, non-Jewish/non-Christian Greek texts rarely use the terms πόρνη and πορνεία. Secondly, when these texts do make use of these terms, they possess a narrower meaning than that found in Jewish and Christian literature: for the Greeks a πόρνη was a prostitute, a πόρνος was a man who prostituted himself, and πορνεία was sexual intercourse between a man and a πόρνη or πόρνος. While some Jewish or Christian texts might restrict themselves to these narrow meanings, for the most part they use the term πορνεία/ זנות to denote various kinds of forbidden sexual activity; it can sometimes also stand for the specific sexual crime of μοιχεία/נאפים. According to Kirchhoff, Paul is standing firmly within the Jewish tradition when he uses πορν- words in 1 Cor 6:12-20. The πόρνη (זונה), for Paul, is a woman with whom Corinthian men should not be engaging in sexual activity; a prostitute is one such woman. And πορνεία is any such forbidden sexual activity.[73]

Kirchhoff's importance for the development of Pauline studies lies in the fact that, along with Mitchell (but for different reasons), she does not believe one can find "opponents" to Paul in 1 Cor 6:12-20. Those exegetes who find evidence of opponents in this pericope base their argument on what they see as three clues in the text:

> 1) πάντα μοι ἔξεστιν [all things are lawful for me] in v. 12 is understood as a quotation of the oppositional slogan, with which Paul's adversaries (and others) legitimate their behavior in sexual matters. 2) The promiscuity, to which 6:12-20 reacts, leads to the assumption that the addressees are enthusiasts who live libertinistically because they hold the body to be indifferent. 3) The argumentation about the transitoriness of stomach/food in contrast to σῶμα/Christ is considered a further piece of evidence that the addressees were of the opinion that the body was not affected by the Christ relationship or that the bodily matters, to which they reckoned food and also sexuality, did not affect the Christ relationship.[74]

Kirchhoff proceeds to show how each of these supposed clues turns out to be false. The main thesis that governs her investigation is that, given the fact that men in Roman society were not censured for going to prostitutes, the men who engaged in this form of πορνεία would

---

[72] Kirchhoff, Sünde, 18-37.
[73] Kirchhoff, Sünde, 34-35.
[74] Kirchhoff, Sünde, 73-74 (translation is my own).

not feel the need to justify their actions philosophically or theologically.[75] Thus, 6:12 does not represent a slogan of Paul's "opponents." Moreover, the phrase, πάντα μοι ἔξεστιν, is simply too broad a statement to align with any particular group with certainty.[76]

Kirchhoff, in renouncing the project of reconstructing Paul's "opponents," examines the wider socio-cultural conceptions of prostitution and other extra-marital sexual activity. Yet, she also pays a good deal of attention to how Paul constructs his argument in 6:12-20. Once one gives up the notion of reconstructing specific "opponents" behind 1 Cor, the need to interpret 1 Cor 6:12 (or other verses) as a slogan of these opponents becomes both less urgent and less compelling. Kirchhoff concludes that 6:12 is form-critically best described as a gnomic saying. "By beginning his text with a gnomic saying Paul claims the same authority for his argumentation that follows it as the gnomic saying itself has. He addresses his listeners as those who can learn from him and he arouses (in them) a readiness to listen as well as suspense."[77]

Once Kirchhoff has concluded that the search for Paul's so-called opponents hinders scholarly investigation into the meaning of 1 Cor 6:12-20, she is able to see the πάντα μοι ἔξεστιν in 6:12 not as an oppositional slogan, but as a gnomic maxim which Paul employs for the rhetorical purpose of lending his argument more authority.[78] For Kirchhoff, the first person pronoun in 6:12 is a "rhetorical I" (*rhetorische[s] Ich*) which Paul makes use of again in 6:15aβ (ἄρας ... ποιήσω) where he "provokes the identification with the addressee, in order to convict this person of his misconduct." By utilizing this "rhetorical I" (with whom the hearer is led to identify and to agree) Paul, according to Kirchhoff, scores rhetorical points with the authority he invokes and his *pathos* also sets up the command of 6:18a.[79]

Not only does Kirchhoff attend to rhetorical aspects of Paul's argumentation, as seen above, but her work deals with the figurative aspects of certain elements of Paul's language in 1 Cor 6:12-20.

---

[75] Kirchhoff, *Sünde*, 75, 197.

[76] Kirchhoff, *Sünde*, 76.

[77] Kirchhoff, *Sünde*, 109 (translation is my own).

[78] For more on Paul's use of maxims see Rollin A. Ramsaran: *Liberating Words: Paul's Use of Rhetorical Maxims in 1 Corinthians 1-10* (Valley Forge, Pa.: Trinity Press International, 1996); idem, "Living and Dying, Living is Dying (Philippians 1:21): Paul's Maxim and Exemplary Argumentation in Philippians," in *Rhetorical Argumentation in Biblical Texts: Essays from the Lund 2000 Conference* (eds. Anders Eriksson et al.; Emory Studies in Early Christianity 8; Harrisburg, Pa.: Trinity Press International, 2002), 325-38.

[79] Kirchhoff, *Sünde*, 113: "provoziert die Identifikation der Angesprochenen, um diese dann ihres Fehlverhaltens zu überführen." See Dodd, "Paul's Paradigmatic 'I'," 39-58.

Kirchhoff briefly analyzes several metaphorical elements in Paul's argumentation. For example, she investigates "where Paul's use of πορνεία falls on the scale between metaphorical and mythological manner of speech (*Redeweise*)."[80] She also devotes a section to the "Role of the πόρνη"[81] which is closely tied to her discussion of πορνεία and whether either represents a "power" which rules over the Christian. Into this discussion she injects a treatment of the figurative use of "body" and "members" based on a reading of how Paul uses the terms (in a somewhat different fashion) in 1 Cor 12. She also notes the metaphors of "fleeing" πορνεία,[82] "cleaving" to a sexual partner and thus becoming "one body" with her,[83] "indwelling" of the spirit,[84] the body as a "temple,"[85] and the use of slave motifs.[86] In noting and discussing the metaphors Paul makes use of in his argument, Kirchhoff demonstrates the fruitfulness of attending closely to the figurative language Paul employs in this pericope.

Brian S. Rosner: Scripture and Ethics

Brian Rosner's book (also published in 1994), *Paul, Scripture and Ethics: A Study of 1 Corinthians 5–7*, begins with an explicitly modest goal: to determine *whether* Paul used Scripture in the development of his ethic in these three chapters of 1 Cor.[87] Yet, as he argues for his thesis that the Scriptures are "a crucial and formative source for Paul's ethics,"[88] Rosner goes further and declares, in a section entitled "Paul's Jewishness," that "Paul's Scriptural inheritance may thus be regarded as having priority over other sources, such as pagan law, Stoicism, Iranian religion and Graeco-Roman mystery religions."[89] With this emphasis on Paul's relationship to Judaism throughout his work, Rosner is advocating, as he notes in his conclusion, "a 'paradigm shift' for many students of Paul."[90] In doing this Rosner notes that he is not alone, but in line with some recent work done on Paul.[91] In highlighting the degree

---

[80] Kirchhoff, *Sünde*, 147-48.
[81] Kirchhoff, *Sünde*, 152-58.
[82] Kirchhoff, *Sünde*, 148, 151, 182.
[83] Kirchhoff, *Sünde*, 168, 171.
[84] Kirchhoff, *Sünde*, 174.
[85] Kirchhoff, *Sünde*, 185.
[86] Kirchhoff, *Sünde*, 188.
[87] Brian S. Rosner, *Paul, Scripture, and Ethics: A Study of 1 Corinthians 5–7* (AGJU 22; Leiden: Brill, 1994; repr., Grand Rapids: Baker Books, 1999), 13.
[88] Rosner, *Paul, Scripture, and Ethics*, 177.
[89] Rosner, *Paul, Scripture, and Ethics*, 17. See the section on Kathy Gaca below.
[90] Rosner, *Paul, Scripture, and Ethics*, 180.
[91] Rosner, *Paul, Scripture, and Ethics*, 180 where he cites: Peter J. Tomson, *Paul and the Jewish Law: Halakha in the Letters of the Apostle to the Gentiles* (Assen/Maastricht: Van

to which Paul is dependent on Jewish Scripture (through the mediation of Jewish moral teaching[92]), Rosner thus provides NT scholarship with a picture of Paul to complement that found in writers such as Mitchell who, while not discounting Jewish elements, tend to highlight non-Jewish Hellenistic aspects in Paul's rhetoric.[93]

Rosner's treatment of 1 Cor 6:12-20 is illuminating in that he highlights multiple "contacts" between what Paul argues and the Jewish Scriptures and Jewish moral teaching influenced by these Scriptures. The "Hosea-like Paul"[94] Rosner describes uses the quotation from Gen 2:24 as the center around which he organizes this pericope.[95] But the influence of Scripture is not to be found only in this direct citation. Rosner links Paul's arguments in 6:12-20 with the story of Joseph fleeing Potiphar's wife in Gen 39. This influence could either be direct, or, since this chapter from Genesis exerted influence on biblical and post-biblical ideas of sexual immorality, through the mediation of some other writing such as the *Testament of Reuben* 5:5, for example.[96] The image of God dwelling within the believer and its relation to sexual chastity is also, Rosner argues, reminiscent of *Testament of Joseph* 10.[97]

In an interpretive move reminiscent of the work of J.C. Hurd, Rosner makes a distinction between what Paul heard as oral report (1 Cor 5–6) and what Paul learns via the letter the Corinthians sent him.[98] In 1 Cor 7, Rosner grapples with the problem that Paul's opinions here seem, to some interpreters' eyes, decidedly un-biblical and un-Jewish. After first arguing that 1 Cor 7:1b is a quotation from the Corinthian letter, Rosner argues that in ch. 7 not only is Paul not as strongly in favor of celibacy as has been thought, but that ascetic tendencies were widespread throughout varieties of first-century Judaisms and thus ascetic tendencies are not, in and of themselves, un-Jewish. As I will discuss below, Dale Martin focuses on non-Jewish Hellenistic ideals which valorized sexual abstinence, but Rosner fills out this picture by discussing the prevalence of such notions among Jewish groups. Rosner recognizes that, in the complex world of Jewish moral teaching

---

Gorcum, 1990); Martin Hengel, *The Pre-Christian Paul* (trans. John Bowden; London: SCM Press, 1991); Karl-Wilhelm Niebuhr, *Heidenapostel aus Israel: Die jüdische Identität des Paulus nach ihrer Darstellung in seinen Briefen* (WUNT 62; Tübingen: Mohr Siebeck, 1992); and Frank Thielman, *From Plight to Solution: A Jewish Framework for Understanding Paul's View of the Law in Galatians and Romans* (NovTSup 61; Leiden: Brill, 1989).

[92] Rosner, *Paul, Scripture, and Ethics*, ch. 2.
[93] But see Mitchell, *Paul*, 300.
[94] Rosner, *Paul, Scripture, and Ethics*, 137.
[95] Rosner, *Paul, Scripture, and Ethics*, 145.
[96] Rosner, *Paul, Scripture, and Ethics*, 140, 137.
[97] Rosner, *Paul, Scripture, and Ethics*, 141.
[98] Rosner, *Paul, Scripture, and Ethics*, 147. See Hurd, *Origin of First Corinthians* and my discussion of this work above.

during the Hellenistic period, different communities developed different ways of dealing with sexual practice. Moreover, while Paul's specific argument in 1 Cor 7:1-7 does not follow the biblical and Jewish preference for marriage, the way Paul conceives of marriage in these verses is, according to Rosner, quite biblical and Jewish.[99]

Within this section of his book, Rosner cites the work of O. Zöckler, who argues that the ascetic elements found in ancient Judaism were also found in the pagan world, especially among the Stoics, and these elements were inherited by the early Christians.[100] Thus, although Rosner's work clearly strives toward achieving a "Jewish Paul," he notes points of contact with the non-Jewish world of Late Antiquity in places. Even someone with Rosner's stated goal of arguing for the primacy of Jewish Scriptures in Paul's teaching on sexual behavior recognizes, in the act of interpretation, that Judaism cannot be taken out of the larger Hellenistic world in which it found itself. The careful work that Rosner has undertaken in demonstrating the relationship of 1 Cor 5–7 to Jewish Scripture and Jewish moral teaching challenges NT scholars to provide a fuller Jewish intertextual analysis of this pericope.

Will Deming: Paul's Hellenistic Background

Whereas Rosner makes a deliberate turn toward Jewish Scripture and moral teaching in order to interpret 1 Cor 5–7, Will Deming, in his 1995 book, *Paul on Marriage and Celibacy: The Hellenistic Background of 1 Corinthians 7*, takes an almost diametrically opposite approach. He argues that:

> Paul's discussion cannot be fitted into any presumed trajectory of ascetic thought. Rather his words draw on a reservoir of ideas about marriage and celibacy that is neither ascetic, nor Judeo-Christian in origin, nor confluent with much of the later church's thinking, but one in which the basic anxieties of Greek culture in the Hellenistic age lay restlessly submerged.[101]

Thus, the "conceptual framework" of Paul's argumentation in 1 Cor 7 lies not, as Rosner would have it, in Jewish tradition, but rather in the Stoic-Cynic debates on marriage.[102] Deming argues that Paul, like

---

[99] Rosner, *Paul, Scripture, and Ethics*, 150.

[100] Rosner, *Paul, Scripture, and Ethics*, 158.

[101] Deming, *Paul on Marriage and Celibacy* (1995), 49. In this Introduction I reference the first edition of Deming's work in order to keep the original content and context of his work that influenced scholars after him. In my exegesis chapter, however, I make use of the second edition of his book.

[102] Which Rosner does mention in his use of the work of Zöckler in *Paul*, 158.

the Stoics and the Cynics, discusses marriage in terms of duty[103] and responsibility, and not in terms of sex. Paul, he asserts, took a "Stoic hybrid view" in that he argues that "under certain circumstances the duties of married life interfere with one's allegiance to a higher cause."[104]

The value of Deming's study is that it takes seriously the effect non-Jewish Hellenistic-Roman philosophical debates about marriage had on Paul's argumentation, thereby complementing the picture painted by scholars such as Rosner. Deming's close reading of the Stoic and Cynic sources (ch. 2) and his identification of possible Stoic and Cynic elements in 1 Cor 7 (ch. 3) have proven to be of immense help in understanding this Pauline chapter by noting how influential these non-Jewish debates are for interpreting Paul. Deming's work moves beyond the discussion of similar elements in Yarbrough's work, which Deming critiques for being too "diffuse."[105] Methodologically, Deming aims "to locate in 1 Corinthians patterns of thought, argumentative structures, terminology, and phrasing that draw directly or indirectly on Stoic and Cynic traditions, and explain how they function in Paul's discussion with the Corinthians."[106]

Deming's work is important for the study of 1 Cor 7 not only because of his careful study of non-Jewish Hellenistic material, but in that he moves beyond the NT and attempts to map out an understanding of Christian asceticism and Paul's relation to these early Christian ascetic impulses. However, his negative assessment of later Christian teaching on sexuality[107] and his understanding of asceticism are no longer viable, given the amount of scholarly work done on ascetic theory and praxis since the mid-1990s.[108] Early on, Deming notes that there is a

---

[103] See Martin, *Body*, 209.

[104] Deming, *Paul on Marriage and Celibacy* (1995), 2-3. See my discussion of O. Larry Yarbrough above. See also Stanley K. Stowers, "A 'Debate' over Freedom: 1 Corinthians 6.12-20," in *Christian Teaching: Studies in Honor of Lemoine G. Lewis* (ed. Everett Ferguson; Abilene, Tex.: Abilene Christian University Press, 1981), 67-68.

[105] Deming, *Paul on Marriage and Celibacy* (1995), 8.

[106] Deming, *Paul on Marriage and Celibacy* (1995), 109.

[107] See also Phipps, "Is Paul's Sexual Attitude toward Sexual Relations Contained in 1 Cor 7.1?" 129-30, notably his statements, "Ironically, those who denounce Paul as one who denigrated sexual intercourse show that they are unable to liberate themselves from the warped patristic and monastic interpretations of his letters." And, "Tertullian, Jerome, Ambrose, Augustine and other prominent sexual ascetics have contaminated the Biblical outlook on sexuality."

[108] Deming, *Paul on Marriage and Celibacy* (1995), describes sexual asceticism as "the rejection of one's erotic nature in order to become more holy or closer to God" (2) and "a regime that fosters self-induced privation and hardship" (221). He also implies that sexual continence is, in ascetic theology, "an aspiration in itself" (220-221). For more recent studies on and discussion of ascetic practice see Vincent L. Wimbush and Richard Valantasis, eds., *Asceticism* (Oxford: Oxford University Press, 1998); Leif E.

major theological statement implicit in his work because, he argues, "the understanding of 1 Corinthians 7 held by most scholars and church leaders today derives from an early Christian reinterpretation of Paul, and that this text has been essentially misunderstood almost since its composition."[109] Although he uses the term "early Christian," I fear that the Protestant polemic against *Frühkatholizismus* hovers around Deming's book. While my project will not follow Deming's lead and trace the use of Paul through later Christian centuries, it is important to note Deming's discussion of this material because it affects his treatment of the Pauline chapter in question. By arguing that Paul has been misunderstood almost from the outset, Deming provides an ideological warrant for setting aside much work on Paul, from the early Fathers onward, which locates a "Judeo-Christian" element in Paul's discussion of marriage and celibacy.[110] While his work has greatly deepened our understanding of Paul's discussion in 1 Cor 7, his theoretical insistence on severing the link between this chapter and Judaism and later Christian interpretation must be re-evaluated.

Dale Martin: Ideology and the Body

Dale Martin, in his 1995 book *The Corinthian Body*, strives to undertake an ideological analysis of 1 Cor through the lens of the social construction of the body. Although Martin strives to step outside of the historical-critical paradigm by focusing his analysis on ideology of the body in Corinth, his work relies on a similar hermeneutic to that outlined in the work of Baur, Weiß, and Hurd above, namely that the text provides clues that allow scholars to reconstruct the historical situation in Corinth and this reconstruction is used to interpret Paul's arguments in the letter. Yet, it must be emphasized that Martin casts his interpretive net wide before turning his focus on the first letter to the Corinthians itself. Martin's analysis of "The Body in Greco-Roman Culture" in the first chapter of his book is exceedingly helpful in demonstrating his thesis that Hellenistic-Roman constructions of the body do not match our own. In this first chapter Martin successfully argues against reading Late Antique discussions of the body through the lens of a Cartesian ontological dualism. Rather, he contends that

---

Vaage and Vincent L. Wimbush, eds., *Asceticism and the New Testament* (New York: Routledge, 1999); Nejsum, "Apologetic Tendency." See also the important work of Clark, *Reading Renunciation*. Also Brown, *Body and Society*, 56: "Ascetic readers of Paul in Late Antiquity did not mis-hear the tone of his voice."

[109] Deming, *Paul on Marriage and Celibacy* (1995), 3.

[110] Deming by no means ignores this work. In fact, his chapter on the history of interpretation of 1 Cor 7 (ch. 1) is excellent and quite extensive and should be consulted for an intellectual history of the thesis Deming puts forth.

thinkers in this period thought more in terms of a "hierarchy of essence."[111] Moreover, he demonstrates that the ideas of the philosophers were not the only sources for the ideological construction of the body in the ancient world. Martin spends a good portion of his ideological analysis focusing on ancient medical theories as well as the theoretical musing of ancient physiognomy – "the art of interpreting a person's character and inner state on the basis of physiological characteristics."[112] By opening the boundaries of his investigation to medicine and physiognomy, Martin hopes to uncover ancient ideological constructions of the body which may have had wider currency than those found only in philosophical circles.[113] To be sure, Martin recognizes the interplay among all of these ancient writings, but by moving away from the standard philosophical tracts, Martin's work shows a desire to expand the intertextual boundaries commonly used when interpreting 1 Cor.

Building on the conclusions of his first chapter, Martin goes on to argue that 1 Cor can best be explained in light of a conflict of ideologies of the body held by the Strong on one hand and the Weak (and Paul) on the other.[114] Thus, although Martin presupposes the unity of 1 Cor that Margaret Mitchell has demonstrated, he argues that 1 Cor holds clues to the specific reason behind the disunity at Corinth, namely a conflict rooted in status issues.[115] One notes that, like Baur, Martin argues that there are two basic parties in conflict at Corinth, although for Martin it is not a conflict between Pauline and Petrine branches of Christianity, but rather between those of higher status (the Strong) and lower status (the Weak). Paul, according to Martin, argues against the ideology of the Hellenistic-Roman ruling class and often sides with the Weak, thus the views of the latter are not that difficult to map out. It is the position of the Strong that requires some digging in 1 Cor.[116]

Even though Martin recognizes the variety of hypotheses concerning the identity of Paul's "opponents"[117] and even though he is aware of Mitchell's work, he still believes that, in the conflict around issues relating to status, he has found the key to unlock the identity of the

---

[111] Martin, *The Corinthian Body*, 15. See Martin's statement on p. 12 referring to Plato ("the most dualistic of the ancient philosophers"): "We are still dealing with something more like a spectrum of essences than a dichotomy of realms."

[112] Martin, *Corinthian Body*, 18.

[113] Martin, *Corinthian Body*, 15.

[114] Martin, *Corinthian Body*, 163 where he notes that 1 Cor 5; 6:12-20; 8-10; and 11:17-24 "are particular instances of what is essentially a single conflict regarding the boundaries of the body." See also Mitchell, *Paul and the Rhetoric of Reconciliation*, 225-56 for her discussion of "The Integrity of the Corinthian Community against Outside Defilement."

[115] Martin, *Corinthian Body*, 56.

[116] Martin, *Corinthian Body*, 60, 86, 95-96, 101, 133, 168 (see also 178), 185, 208.

[117] Martin, *Corinthian Body*, 69.

group Paul was debating with. Moreover, unlike Mitchell, he believes it is possible to sketch out the "plausible social location of the Strong" using the so-called slogans found in 1 Cor (6:12 and 10:23; 6:13; 8:1; 8:4; and others embedded in the text such as 7:1), the existence of which he does not feel necessary to argue beyond stating that "commentators have long noted" their presence.[118] Using these slogans in 1 Cor, Martin has created a position for the Strong that he believes will help shed light on Paul's meaning in 1 Cor. This reconstruction of the position of the Strong is, in my view, the weakest part of Martin's analysis. As I hope to show, building on the work of Renate Kirchhoff, it is not at all certain that the so-called slogans can be used in the way that Martin has deployed them. The issue of the presence of slogans in 1 Cor has been part of the scholarly conversation at least since Johannes Weiß, and most fully exploited by John Hurd. The question of how these slogans can be used, indeed, the debate about what exactly constitutes a slogan, has dogged much scholarship on 1 Cor. In Chapter 5 I will suggest ways of reading 1 Cor 6:12–7:7 that relativize this contentious issue.

Kathy L. Gaca: Paul, Sex, and Metaphor

The work of the classicist Kathy L. Gaca in *The Making of Fornication* (2003) helps set my project within a broader conversation at the beginning of the twenty-first century. Gaca's work is important, on a general level, in that her study straddles three disciplines which are usually kept distinct within the academy: classics, biblical studies, and patristics. In attempting to "resolve an important philosophical and historical problem about the making of sexual morality in Western culture," Gaca traces teachings about proper and appropriate sexual behavior from Plato, the Stoics and the Pythagoreans; through Paul and Philo; and finally to the early Christian writers Tatian, Clement of Alexandria and Epiphanes.[119] More specifically for this project, Gaca's work is pivotal for a number of other reasons. First, her study undertakes an analysis of texts in which she examines how later authors "reconfigured" ideas from various philosophical/religious arenas.[120] Second, she notes

---

[118] Martin, *Corinthian Body*, 70. See also Mark Allen Plunkett, "Sexual Ethics and the Christian Life: A Study of 1 Corinthians 6:12–7:7" (Ph.D. diss., Princeton Theological Seminary, 1988), ch. 3, esp. 98; Stowers, "A 'Debate' over Freedom," 59.

[119] Kathy L. Gaca, *The Making of Fornication: Eros, Ethics, and Political Reform in Greek Philosophy and Early Christianity* (Hellenistic Culture and Society 40; Berkeley: University of California Press, 2003), 1.

[120] See Gaca, *Fornication* parts II and III. More specifically, see p. 12. For the concept of "reconfiguration," which Gaca expands somewhat, see Robbins, *Tapestry*, 107-108; idem, *Exploring*, 50.

the importance of the Septuagint over the Hebrew Masoretic text when exploring early Christian documents.[121] And third, she brings the discussion of figurative language to the fore when discussing Paul's argument against πορνεία in 1 Cor.[122]

The sheer scope of Gaca's work is extraordinary. Any future study which touches upon sexual morality in Greek-speaking antiquity (whether so-called pagan, Jewish, or Christian) will need to take Gaca's scholarship into account. Her primary aim is to understand the relation of post-apostolic Christian notions of sexual morality to those of the earlier Greek philosophers, or in her words: "My aim is to establish a clear understanding of the underlying principles that made many early Christian sexual restrictions take the radically ascetic forms they did."[123] In working out this goal, Gaca takes aim at the ideas of Michel Foucault. Gaca maintains that Foucault erred in his primary assessment of the basic continuity between Greek pagan and Christian sexual ethics. Instead, she argues that the later Christian encratite and ecclesiastical positions, stemming from ideas found in Paul and Philo, differ "radically" from those of the Greek philosophers.[124] Gaca intends to correct Foucault's inaccurate view of continuity, not through the usual method

---

[121] Gaca, *Fornication*, 16-18. As Gaca notes: "I use the Septuagint as a source in its own right to explore the Hellenistic ways of reading Greek scripture that helped generate the encratite and ecclesiastical sexual ethics of Tatian and Clement. The most formative players in this hermeneutic arena antedate the Christian idealizing of the Hebrew as the preferred vehicle of scriptural truth, *for the* hebraica veritas *movement takes hold only later with Origen and becomes more prominent with Jerome. For Paul, scripture is exclusively or predominantly Greek*. The Septuagint Pentateuch likewise provides the basis for Philo's conception of the biblical God's sexual rules" (p. 16-17; italics mine). Further, Gaca notes that "we must not regard the Greek and Hebrew exegetical traditions as though they were unanimous in the sexual norms they promote" (p. 122). While I agree with Gaca in this regard it is important to note the other side of the argument. For this see John J. Collins, *Between Athens and Jerusalem: Jewish Identity in the Hellenistic Diaspora* (2nd ed.; The Biblical Resource Series; Grand Rapids, Mich.: Eerdmans, 2000), 19-20.

[122] Gaca, *Fornication*, ch. 6; see also p. 20.

[123] Gaca, *Fornication*, 10.

[124] Gaca, *Fornication*, 6, 293. But see David M. Halperin, "Forgetting Foucault: Acts, Identities, and the History of Sexuality," in *The Sleep of Reason: Erotic Experience and Sexual Ethics in Ancient Greece and Rome* (ed. Martha C. Nussbaum and Juha Sihvola; Chicago: University of Chicago Press, 2002), 21-54, who cautions that many thinkers who rely on the English translation of Foucault's work have created a system of "Foucaultian" ideas that Foucault himself did not create. Although Gaca maintains Foucault favored a "thesis of continuity," she does note his "occasional hesitations." Whether Foucault himself truly espoused this idea is almost beside the point for Gaca. Her real concern is the growing consensus regarding the idea of continuity, resulting from the popularity of Foucault's work, that she believes "is settling in comfortably as the right way to think" (p. 5).

of social history, but rather through examining the "motivating philosophical and religious principles behind Christian sexual asceticism."[125]

In achieving her goal of unraveling the strands of thought that came together to form early Christian teachings on sexual morality, Gaca studies the ideas of Paul and Philo as key figures who began the transmutation of septuagintal teachings about proper sexual behavior. Although her analysis of these two Jewish thinkers produces immense returns, it must be noted that Gaca's primary use for them is to help explain how certain septuagintal ideas became combined, if only superficially, with ideas from the Greek philosophers in the writings of Tatian and Clement. Gaca's interaction with biblical studies, relying heavily on the ideas of Brian Rosner in part II of her book, demonstrates that she has a firm grasp of the exegetical issues surrounding the interpretation of Paul. Yet, as Gaca herself notes in her introduction, her "hermeneutical project is not bible studies for its own sake, but serves [an] interest in ethics and political philosophy."[126] Thus, far from having the final word on Paul's treatment of πορνεία, in light of her findings, Gaca's work invites a reassessment of Paul's argumentation from those of us who do undertake "bible studies for its own sake."

Gaca's study notes how Paul combines the Septuagint Pentateuch's metaphor of spiritual fornication with the prophetic metaphor of spiritual adultery. In her treatment of "the sexual poetics of the Pentateuch, Prophets, and Paul,"[127] Gaca argues that the biblical πόρνη is not necessarily, nor even primarily, a prostitute. Rather, "[a] harlot in the biblical sense is any woman whose sexual conduct is out of line with the regulations that biblically grounded communities construct and value as the word of God."[128] Hence, in the study of early Christian literature, "we must not simply assume that ... *pornai* are prostitutes, even though a few of them may be. If we make such a quick assumption, we are likely to take a complex biblical metaphor literally."[129]

Gaca further argues that Paul combines these two "didactic metaphors," the Pentateuchal metaphor of spiritual fornication and the pro-

---

[125] Gaca, *Fornication*, 9.
[126] Gaca, *Fornication*, 11.
[127] Gaca, *Fornication*, 159.
[128] Kathy L. Gaca, "The Sexual and Social Dangers of *Pornai* in the Septuagint Greek Stratum of Patristic Christian Greek Thought," in *Desire and Denial in Byzantium: Papers from the Thirty-first Spring Symposium of Byzantine Studies, University of Sussex, Brighton, March 1997* (ed. Liz James; Society for the Promotion of Byzantine Studies Publications 6; Brookfield, Vt.: Ashgate/Variorum, 1999), 36. See also Gail Corrington Streete, *The Strange Woman: Power and Sex in the Bible* (Louisville, Ky.: Westminster John Knox, 1997), 51, 98-100.
[129] Gaca, "Sexual and Social Dangers," 40.

phetic metaphor of spiritual adultery, wherein the community itself (both male and female members) is symbolized as God's sexually deviant wife.[130] However, she argues that in Paul's "marital theology the sexual force of the Prophets' metaphor takes on a more literal sexual significance."[131] In a bit of metaphoric gender bending, the men of the community are urged not to engage in fornication because they are members of a community which is, collectively, the bride of Christ.[132] Gaca argues that this means the community symbolically shares female sexual anatomy, which explains Paul's stress on fleeing literal fornication: "Christians need to uphold the bride's chastity through their own sexual bodies; they must internalize the requirement through keeping their own genitals untouched by sexual fornication."[133] This explains, Gaca contends, why Paul's ideal moves toward sexual renunciation even though he realizes this cannot be required for all Christians: "Insofar as the collective bride is vaginal, it is best to remain virginal."[134] Gaca's exploration of the use of biblical metaphor in these verses, like the work of Kirchhoff before her, opens up new questions about Paul's use of language that I hope to explore. I believe that these questions can serve as a means to move beyond a type of historical reconstructionist approach that does not necessarily recognize how Paul deploys language in this passage.

Summary of Conversation Partners

The works of F.C. Baur and Johannes Weiß began this section because in their ideas one can find the beginnings, or at least an early influential moment, of paradigms for viewing the text that have continued down to the present day. Baur's work, for all the disparagement it has received, was such a powerful expression of the historical project that its influence has transcended issues of disagreement over content. That someone such as Dale Martin, who describes his work as ideological criticism rather than historical-critical interpretation, reinscribes a func-

---

[130] Gaca, *Fornication*, 160. See also J. Duncan M. Derrett, "Right and Wrong Sticking (1 Cor 6,18)?" *EBib* 55 (1997): 99.

[131] Gaca, *Fornication*, 182.

[132] See also John Calvin, *Commentary on the Epistles of Paul the Apostle to the Corinthians* (trans. John Pringle; 2 vols.; Grand Rapids: Eerdmans, 1948), 1:218. However, Calvin quickly notes that many may not find his interpretation of a spiritual marriage between the believer and Christ persuasive so he proceeds to offer another interpretation which "is more simple, and agrees better with the context" (219). Also, Brian S. Rosner, "The Function of Scripture in 1 Cor 5,13b and 6,16," in *The Corinthian Correspondence* (BETL 125; ed. R. Bieringer; Leuven: University Press, 1996), 515-517 and idem, *Paul, Scripture and Ethics*, 131-34.

[133] Gaca, *Fornication*, 180; esp. n. 47, where she notes that synecdoche is helpful in understanding Paul's position here.

[134] Gaca, *Fornication*, 183.

tionally similar reading of 1 Cor to Baur's – one that reads the text and distills two opposing factions behind Paul's words – demonstrates how powerful Baur's ghost can be. The historical reconstructionist approach held sway over much of twentieth-century scholarship and continues to do so into the twenty-first century.

Weiß's commentary on 1 Cor is so important not only because of the historical rationale given for his hypothetical partition of the letter, or its location at the initial stages of what later would become various theories about the presence of slogans in the letter, but also to describe how, at the beginning of the twentieth century, this German scholar recognized the bicultural aspects of Paul's symbolic worlds as well as his use of figurative language. These insights remain a powerful model for reading the letters of Paul, but one that is not always followed, as the arguments of Brian Rosner and Will Deming demonstrate. Whereas Weiß opened the intertextual boundaries when reading Paul, Rosner and Deming practice a much more restrained mode of reading by categorically ruling out the usefulness of Hellenistic-Roman and Jewish resources respectively. Reading Paul through the lens of either Jewish or non-Jewish Hellenistic-Roman resources is not inherently problematic. My project focuses primarily on understanding Paul through Jewish wisdom discourse, for example. It is when ideological positions turn a heuristic focus into a programmatic assertion about *the* way to read Paul that certain studies lose their dialogical potential. Indeed, as was shown above, even though Rosner and Deming's theoretical statements, with which they begin their monographs, are fairly extreme examples of this hardening of scholarly focus into a "position," when they actually engage the Pauline text directly they soften the edges of their theses and engage texts that fall outside their stated purview. It is as if the Pauline texts demand that scholars keep boundaries open.

The works of Mitchell and Martin focus primarily on Hellenistic-Roman resources in their exegesis of 1 Cor, but neither argues that this is the only way to go about this task. Mitchell, referencing her own work, warns readers against "too quickly claim[ing] another point for the 'Hellenistic' side of Paul." She argues that, "we must remember also the extent to which we have seen Hellenistic Judaism ... at home with many" Hellenistic-Roman topics and conventions.[135] Kathy Gaca, while situating her interpretation within a broad continuum of ancient and Late Antique philosophical and religious history, surprisingly falls into a rather hard ideological position when reading Paul. Her reliance on the work of Brian Rosner may explain this, along with the fact that she does not examine Jewish wisdom traditions in her analysis of Paul.

---

[135] Mitchell, *Paul and the Rhetoric of Reconciliation*, 300.

This leads her to create a Paul who is influenced only by the LXX Pentateuch and Prophets in his thinking on sexual behavior and not the larger Hellenistic-Roman world in which he lived and founded communities. It is in the works of O. Larry Yarbrough and Renate Kirchhoff where the spirit of Weiß regarding the use of Jewish and non-Jewish Hellenistic-Roman resources is most fruitfully at work.

John C. Hurd's attempt to "get behind" the text of 1 Cor in order to trace the development of Paul's interaction with the Corinthian community (indeed, to *explain* the reasons behind this development) is a prime example of the historical reconstructionist paradigm of the mid-twentieth century. Hurd's careful exposition of the four stages of communication between Paul and the Corinthian community pushes the limits of the historical-critical method. To be sure, as noted above, Hurd recognizes the diminishing certainty of his reconstruction the farther away from 1 Cor he journeys. Nevertheless, his analysis relies on mining 1 Cor (and other NT books) to recreate the specific history of the Corinthian church, much as Baur did in his historical projects. While this mode of analysis has yielded certain insights, its insistence on using NT documents themselves to recreate the background by which these same documents are interpreted is problematic. A more fruitful method of investigating NT texts, seen in the work of Weiß and more fully exploited in the latter half of the twentieth century, steps away from the NT texts and seeks evidence in the wider social and cultural worlds in which the texts were written and read.

A continuing issue for interpreters of 1 Cor revolves around the issue of the presence of so-called slogans. I argue that slogan hypotheses exist to serve various historical reconstructionist projects. Weiß was among the first to hypothesize the existence of slogans within the text of 1 Cor.[136] Hurd uses these slogans as part of his method for determining which parts of 1 Cor are Paul's reaction to information he received in writing. Dale Martin relies heavily on these catch phrases to reconstruct the ideological stance of the "Strong" within the Corinthian community. To be sure, Martin does an excellent job in locating 1 Cor in the larger debates in Late Antiquity about the role of the body in social discourse. However, Martin's reliance on the so-called slogans for the purposes of historical reconstruction is called into question by the work of Renate Kirchhoff, whose work actually precedes Martin's *The Corinthian Body* by one year. Kirchhoff, in my opinion, persuasively demonstrates the difficulty in treating πάντα μοι ἔξεστιν as a slogan used by some faction within the Corinthian community to

---

[136] It should be noted that Origen claimed that 1 Cor 7:1b reflected the opinion of the Corinthians rather than Paul. Thus, the issue of so-called slogans is not confined to the modern period. See Thiselton, *First Epistle to the Corinthians*, 494.

justify their behavior.[137] It is Kirchhoff's investigation into the wider Jewish and non-Jewish Hellenistic-Roman world that allows such an argument.

Like Weiß before him and Kirchhoff after him, O. Larry Yarbrough's work focusing on the creation of Christian culture demonstrates the fruitfulness of locating Paul's teachings on marriage within the wider cultural worlds of Late Antiquity. By moving away from studying either Jewish or non-Jewish Hellenistic-Roman materials simply as sources, Yarbrough demonstrates how exploring cultural formation in these materials is helpful to understand what kind of culture Paul's teachings on marriage create. By exploring a wide range of cultural resources before engaging in a reconstruction of the specific situation in Corinth, Yarbrough's work is an important step in late twentieth-century scholarship on 1 Cor.

It is the work of Margaret M. Mitchell on Paul's use of rhetorical conventions in 1 Cor that opens up a closer investigation into Paul's use of persuasive language. Although still tied to the historical project, Mitchell abandons its reconstructionist aspect, indeed she declares certain tendencies of the reconstructionist project to be methodologically untenable. Her reading of 1 Cor as a carefully argued unity lays the groundwork for much of the scholarship on 1 Cor in the last decade of the twentieth century. The focused work of Kirchhoff and Gaca on the specifics of Paul's teaching on sexual comportment in 1 Cor owes a debt to Mitchell's overarching work on the rhetorical aspects of the letter.

My project stands within the complex web of intellectual discourse on 1 Cor outlined above. I have chosen to revisit Paul's teaching on sexual behavior in 1 Cor 6:12–7:7 because, productive as scholarship on these verses has been in the modern period, certain elements remain to be adequately explained. I aim to investigate Paul's teaching on sexual behavior through the lens of Jewish didactic wisdom, and I strive to do this through careful attention to Paul's language. I hope to show how Paul's unitary argument in these sixteen verses stands within a living stream of Jewish wisdom that, in the Hellenistic period, engages categories both outside of traditional wisdom and from the wider Hellenistic-Roman world. By employing the tools of conceptual integration theory within the framework of socio-rhetorical interpretation, I believe this exegetical investigation can make new contributions to the understanding of how Paul's language makes meaning in this complicated passage. Yet it is important to keep in mind the dialogical nature of scholarship. The

---

[137] See also the work of Brian Dodd, "Paul's Paradigmatic 'I' and 1 Corinthians 6.12," and his book *Paul's Paradigmatic "I": Personal Example as Literary Strategy*.

work I undertake in the following chapters is possible only because of the hard work of scholars who have come before me.

The Roadmap

Before engaging the data of my investigation it is essential to explain the relatively new way of reading I employ to make sense of Paul's rhetoric in 1 Cor 6:12–7:7. In my first chapter, "A Cognitive Turn: Conceptual Blending within a Socio-Rhetorical Framework," I place my project within the ongoing development of the cognitive science of religion. Specifically, I engage the linguistic end of the cognitive science spectrum with my use of conceptual integration theory, also-called blending theory. I deploy the resources of conceptual blending within a socio-rhetorical interpretive framework, which itself is making use of the insights of blending theory. Through this interpretive analytic I hope not only to shed new light on the meaning Paul's language makes in 1 Cor 6:12–7:7, but also to demonstrate that this practice of reading is an exegetically fruitful one, and one that can be applied to other Pauline and early Christian texts.

In order to undertake any interpretive project that makes use of conceptual integration theory and socio-rhetorical interpretation, it is first necessary to examine the cultural contexts from which a text can draw meaning. Since πορνεία is primarily a religious problem for Paul, in the next two chapters I interact with Jewish resources. In my second chapter, "Wisdom," I narrate the scholarly difficulty inherent in the use of the term "wisdom" while offering my own functional definition of how I understand this analytical category. I then look at how various Jewish resources describe wisdom. I focus on Jewish wisdom literature because the problem at hand in 1 Cor 6:12–7:7 is πορνεία – a problem with which the sages were acutely concerned. The third chapter, "Jewish Resource Zones," moves away from a discussion *about* wisdom to a description of four prominent wisdom themes: women, sex and marriage, holiness, and freedom. This chapter engages Jewish wisdom concerns that serve as the religious background for understanding Paul's language in 1 Cor 6:12–7:7. In this chapter I primarily engage Proverbs, Sirach, Wisdom of Solomon, and Philo. While I engage other material where it is warranted, I have chosen these examples as my primary conversation partners. Proverbs is an obvious choice since it is perhaps the epitome of what Jewish wisdom looks like. Any discussion of Jewish wisdom inevitably can be traced, in some way or another, back to Proverbs. Sirach and Wisdom of Solomon are examples of Jewish wisdom texts written in a Hellenistic cultural milieu, although each differs as to its engagement with and resistance to the larger Hellenistic world. Finally, Philo is useful because he represents a Hellenistic Jew who participates in wisdom modes of thinking even as he interprets this tradition and his sacred texts through Hellenistic philosophical categories. It should also be noted that in my study I follow Kathy Gaca's program (see above) of relying primarily on the Septuagint (LXX), and not the Masoretic Text (MT), when examining Jewish scriptural resources for Christianity. As Gaca notes, "For Paul, scripture is exclusively or predominantly Greek."[138]

The final four chapters bring my discussion of Jewish wisdom and wisdom themes to bear on 1 Cor. Chapter 4, "Setting the Wisdom Context: 1 Corinthians 1–4," describes how Paul understands his Jewish wisdom heritage through the eschatological event of the cross. The paradox of God's wisdom demonstrated through the crucifixion of God's Christ reveals, according to Paul, the very structure of the universe as God had planned it before creation. Understanding this wisdom of God, Paul believes, is a necessary precondition for the development of the proper eschatological discernment that will enable the Corinthians to govern their behavior in this world. In this chapter I analyze how Paul's use of wisdom blends with other rhetorolects. In Chapters 5–7 – "The Wisdom of Fleeing *Porneia*: Introducing 1 Corinthians 6:12-7:7," "Why *Porneia* Should Be Avoided: The Rhetography of 1 Corinthians 6:12-20," and "How *Porneia* Should be Avoided: The Rhetology of 1 Corinthians 7:1-7" – I reiterate the interpretive analytical underpinnings of my exegetical work and bring the material from the previous chapters to bear on Paul's teaching on πορνεία. Using the insights of conceptual integration theory within a socio-rhetorical framework, I analyze the conceptual networks Paul's language creates through the cultural organizing frames of wisdom, apocalyptic, and priestly rhetorolects. Moreover, as can be seen in the chapter titles, in this pericope Paul makes use of two kinds of reasoning. In 6:12-20 he relies mainly on rhetography, which evokes images to show the Corinthians why they ought to avoid πορνεία, while in 7:1-7 he relies more on rhetology, which evokes logical reasoning to explain to the Corinthians the various ways they can achieve this goal.[139]

---

[138] Gaca, *Fornication*, 16 and her discussion of this in n. 43 on the same page. See also Martin Hengel, *The Septuagint as Christian Scripture: Its Prehistory and the Problem of Its Canon* (trans. Mark E. Biddle; OTS; Edinburgh: T & T Clark, 2002; repr., Grand Rapids: Baker Books, 2004). It should also be noted that when I refer to a portion of an LXX verse I use lower case Greek letters (e.g. 13:4α). This is to avoid confusion with LXX additions, which are designated by lower case Latin characters (e.g. 13:4a).

[139] For more on rhetography and rhetology, see Chapter 1 below; Vernon K. Robbins, "Rhetography: A New Way of Seeing the Familiar Text," in *Words Well Spoken: George Kennedy's Rhetoric of the New Testament* (ed. C.C. Black and D.F. Wat-

Although I do interact with non-Jewish material in the exegetical chapters of this book, my primary goal is to demonstrate that the robust Jewish wisdom traditions of the Hellenistic period create useful cultural tapestries that allow us to understand some of the meaning that Paul's language evokes in 1 Cor 6:12–7:7. In focusing my investigation in this way, I am not discounting the importance of the larger non-Jewish cultural matrix in which Paul's language is set. Rather, given Paul's religious characterization of the Corinthian problem and his method of dealing with it, Jewish wisdom traditions have emerged as a fruitful exegetical lens through which to view this particular pericope. It is my hope that this project contributes not only to our understanding of the conceptual logic that drives Paul's teaching about proper sexual comportment, but that it also demonstrates the usefulness of conceptual integration theory for exegeting biblical texts when used within a socio-rhetorical framework.

son; Studies in Rhetoric and Religion 8; Waco, Tex.: Baylor University Press, 2008), 81-106; idem, *The Invention of Christian Discourse, Volume I* (Rhetoric of Religious Antiquity 1; Blandford Forum, UK: Deo, 2009), xxvii, 16-17; idem, "Enthymeme and Picture in the *Gospel of Thomas*," in *Thomasine Traditions in Antiquity* (ed. J.M. Asgeirsson, A.D. DeConick, and R. Uro; Leiden: Brill, 2006), 175.

1

A Cognitive Turn: Conceptual Blending within a Socio-Rhetorical Framework

Language is invocation, a meditative translation of our contact with the world.[1]

– Christopher Tilley

Introduction

This is an exciting time to be engaged in religious studies in general and biblical studies in particular. Developments in the cross-disciplinary endeavor known as cognitive science, a "blanket term for a set of disciplines ... concerned with the empirical investigation of the human mind," have opened up new avenues of inquiry in the study of religion.[2] The development of the cognitive science of religion promises to reorient the way some scholars of religion study and analyze this particular human phenomenon.[3] Cognitive science brings to the table an interdisciplinary array of tools that can, in principle, allow us to rethink our work and our conversation partners.[4] By taking advantage

---

[1] Christopher Tilley, *The Materiality of Stone: Explorations in Landscape Phenomenology* (New York: Berg, 2004), 29.

[2] Edward Slingerland, *What Science Offers the Humanities: Integrating Body and Culture* (New York: Cambridge University Press, 2008), 10. See also Raymond W. Gibbs, Jr., *Embodiment and Cognitive Science* (New York: Cambridge University Press, 2005), 276; Petri Luomanen, Ilkka Pyysiäinen, and Risto Uro, "Introduction: Social and Cognitive Perspectives in the Study of Christian Origins and Early Judaism," in *Explaining Christian Origins and Early Judaism* (ed. Petri Luomanen, Ilkka Pyysiäinen, and Risto Uro; Biblical Interpretation Series 89; Leiden: Brill, 2007), 1-33.

[3] Harvey Whitehouse, "Theorizing Religions Past," in *Theorizing Religions Past: Archeology, History, and Cognition* (ed. Harvey Whitehouse and Luther H. Martin; Cognitive Science of Religion Series; Walnut Creek, Calif.: Alta Mira, 2004), 230.

[4] E. Thomas Lawson, "The Wedding of Psychology, Ethnography, and History: Methodological Bigamy or Tripartite Free Love?" in *Theorizing Religions Past: Archeology,*

of some of these newer modes of analyzing religion and religious discourse, I hope to shed light on a particularly intractable Pauline problem in biblical studies. Before engaging Paul's discourse, however, it is necessary to lay out the relatively new interpretive analytics that will guide my investigation.[5] I engage an aspect of the cognitive science of religion, described in more detail below, referred to as conceptual integration theory, also known as blending theory.[6] I will be using the insights of conceptual integration theory within the overall interpretive framework of socio-rhetorical interpretation (SRI) in order to produce a richly textured interpretation of 1 Cor 6:12–7:7.[7]

Cognitive Science of Religion: Embodied Cognition

Petri Luomanen, Ilkka Pyysiäinen, and Risto Uro have recently written an excellent primer on the promise of the cognitive science of religion for the study of formative Christianity and Judaism in which they note that "a basic presupposition [of the cognitive science of religion] is that there are no specifically religious cognitive mechanisms or processes; what is known as 'religion' is based on ordinary cognitive

---

History, and Cognition (ed. Harvey Whitehouse and Luther H. Martin; Cognitive Science of Religion Series; Walnut Creek, Calif.: Alta Mira, 2004), 5.

[5] For works that engage the same area of cognitive science of religion in biblical studies that I do, see esp. Bonnie Howe, *Because You Bear This Name: Conceptual Metaphor and the Moral Meaning of 1 Peter* (Biblical Interpretation Series 61; Leiden: Brill, 2006); Hugo Lundhaug, "Conceptual Blending in the *Exegesis of the Soul*," in *Explaining Christian Origins and Early Judaism* (ed. Petri Luomanen, Ilkka Pyysiäinen, and Risto Uro), 141-60; Vernon K. Robbins, "Conceptual Blending and Early Christian Imagination," in *Explaining Christian Origins and Early Judaism* (ed. Petri Luomanen, Ilkka Pyysiäinen, and Risto Uro), 161-95. For the epistemological ramifications of this area of cognitive science see Slingerland, *What Science Offers the Humanities*. The relative newness of this approach to religious studies for the guild at large can be seen in the fact that the Cognitive Science of Religion Consultation began in the American Academy of Religion only at its 2008 meeting. The 2009 meeting of the Society of Biblical Literature saw the first meeting of the Cognitive Linguistics in Biblical Interpretation group as a section, after three years as a consultation. On the philosophical difference between a method and an interpretive analytic, see Robbins, *Invention*, 5; idem, "Socio-Rhetorical Interpretation," in *Blackwell Companion to the New Testament* (ed. David E. Aune; Malden, Mass.: Wiley-Blackwell, 2010), 192-219.

[6] See esp. Fauconnier and Turner, *The Way We Think*. Also Seana Coulson and Todd Oakley, "Blending Basics," *Cognitive Linguistics* 11 (2000): 175-96.

[7] Although used in 1984 in Robbins's *Jesus the Teacher: A Socio-Rhetorical Interpretation of Mark* (Philadelphia: Fortress, 1984; repr. with new introduction Minneapolis: Fortress, 1992) and described in various essays, the full program of classical socio-rhetorical interpretation was most fully explicated in two books by Robbins published in 1996, *The Tapestry of Early Christian Discourse* and *Exploring the Texture of Texts*. For the newer developments in this interpretive analytic see Robbins, *Invention*. For a brief history of the development of SRI, see Robbins, "Socio-Rhetorical Interpretation."

processes that also support non-religious behavior."[8] Whatever one might say about religion, in order for it to have phenomenological meaning for human beings it must be processed through the same brains that apprehend and make sense of the rest of the physical/cultural world.[9] Moreover, human brains are located within, not apart from, human bodies. Human bodies are critical in this understanding of human cognition, since, as Raymond Gibbs argues, "embodiment provides the foundation for how people interpret their lives and the world around them."[10] Any means to investigate the production and understanding of meaning by humanity must simply take into account the fact that humans are embodied, social agents. This is a point upon which cognitive scientists and socio-rhetorical interpreters agree and which demonstrates the usefulness of cognitive science approaches to religion within a socio-rhetorical framework. Vernon Robbins conceives of SRI as an interpretive analytic that strives "to nurture a 'full-body' mode of interpretation, rather than to continue a tradition of mind-body dualism in interpretation."[11] Along similar lines, Edward Slingerland argues that cognitive science fosters "an intellectual environment where bracketing our human disposition toward dualism may finally be a *real*, rather than merely notional, possibility for us."[12]

Cognitive science, deployed to analyze religion or any other aspect of human meaning making, is quite obviously based on scientific principles that rely on empirical data. This, of course, means that the claims made in the cognitive science of religion are provisional. Should further empirical data emerge to challenge previous assumptions, interpretive analytics will need to be overhauled accordingly, but this is the nature of scientific, critical thinking in any field, *Bibelwissenschaft* included.[13] Currently, Gibbs argues, "the mass of empirical evidence [is]

---

[8] Luomanen, Pyysiäinen, and Uro, "Introduction," 1.

[9] Gibbs, *Embodiment and Cognitive Science*, 10 and 13. See also Edward Slingerland, "Who's Afraid of Reductionism? The Study of Religion in the Age of Cognitive Science," *Journal of the American Academy of Religion* 76 (2008): 398: "Moral space is as much a reality as physical space for us."

[10] Gibbs, *Embodiment and Cognitive Science*, 2. For Gibbs's "embodiment premise," see idem, 9 and 276. See also Jerome A. Feldman, *From Molecule to Metaphor: A Neural Theory of Language* (Cambridge, Mass.: MIT Press, 2008); Shaun Gallagher, *How the Body Shapes the Mind* (New York: Clarendon Press, 2005); Mark Johnson, *The Meaning of the Body: Aesthetics of Human Understanding* (Chicago: University of Chicago Press, 2007); George Lakoff and Mark Johnson, *Philosophy in the Flesh: The Embodied Mind and Its Challenge to Western Thought* (New York: Basic Books, 1999).

[11] Robbins, *Invention*, 1:8. See Gibbs, *Embodiment and Cognitive Science*, 3.

[12] Slingerland, *What Science Offers the Humanities*, 10, emphasis in the original.

[13] See Slingerland, *What Science Offers the Humanities*, 297. See also Pascal Boyer, *Religion Explained: The Evolutionary Origins of Religious Thought* (New York: Basic Books, 2001), 78-89.

in favor of an embodied view of thought and language."[14] The human body, in the work of many theorists of language and meaning, provides the foundation for meaning construction and thus provides the possibility for cross-cultural understanding.[15] Edward Slingerland contends that "the basic stability of the human body and the environment with which it interacts across cultures and time would lead us to expect a high degree of universality" in basic cognitive structures of thought.[16] For all the differences in human culture across the globe and throughout history, members of the species *homo sapiens* share the same basic physiology with which to engage the world.

Despite humanity's common embodied nature, human cultures across space and time have demonstrated a remarkable creative diversity. Any credible theory of thought, language, and meaning needs to be able to explain how the universal nature of human embodiment fits with the obvious data of human diversity. Simply put, the human body does not exist in a vacuum, rather it is always already located within this or that human culture. While human bodies are generally the same, the *experience* of these bodies is always a cultural experience. Raymond Gibbs explains that, "Bodies are not culture-free objects, because all aspects of embodied experience are shaped by cultural processes. Theories of human conceptual systems should be inherently cultural in that the cognition that occurs when the body meets the world is inextricably culturally based."[17] The cultural nature of human embodiment requires scholars of religion (as well as scholars in any

---

[14] Gibbs, *Embodiment and Cognitive Science*, 275. See also Zoltán Kövecses, *Metaphor in Culture: Universality and Variation* (Cambridge: Cambridge University Press, 2005), 8, 285.

[15] See esp. the work of Raymond Gibbs, Edward Slingerland, and Zoltán Kövecses in the bibliography.

[16] Edward Slingerland, "Conceptions of the Self in the *Zhuangzi*: Conceptual Metaphor Analysis and Comparative Thought," *Philosophy East and West* 54 (2004): 328. On the stability of the structures of the brain in particular, see Coleen Shantz, *Paul in Ecstasy: The Neurobiology of the Apostle's Life and Thought* (Cambridge: Cambridge University Press, 2009), 71. Shantsz draws upon the work of Antonio Damasio, *The Feeling of What Happens: Body and Emotion in the Making of Consciousness* (New York: Harcourt Brace, 1999).

[17] Gibbs, *Embodiment and Cognitive Science*, 13. Gibbs further argues that "A body is not just something we own, it is something we are," idem, 14. Pauline scholars, no doubt, will recognize Bultmann's famous description of σῶμα in that quotation (see Rudolf Bultmann, *Theology of the New Testament* [trans. Kendrick Grobel; 2 vols.; New York: Charles Scribners' Sons, 1951-55], 1:194-195). The common phenomenological underpinnings of both Bultmann's and Gibbs's thought can explain this commonality, esp. the ideas of Husserl and Heidegger (see Gibbs, *Embodiment and Cognitive Science*, 25). Gibbs's work, of course, draws on more recent phenomenological thinking. See Shantz, *Paul in Ecstasy*, 10 for the influence of the phenomenology of Maurice Merleau-Ponty on embodied theories of meaning.

field) to be able to deal with the particularities of culture when analyzing meaning production and interpretation. This is especially necessary for a project such as this one that aims to make sense of an ancient argument set down in writing. Dealing with embodiment within physical and cultural space demands that human thought, indeed consciousness, be conceived of "in terms of dynamical interactions of brain, body, and world."[18]

Theories about the embodied and dynamic realities of human cognition give scholars of religion the ability to analyze persuasive arguments from an angle other than that of cold, propositional logic. This is crucial because, as Antonio Damasio argues, "Emotion, feeling, and biological regulation all play a role in human reason. The lowly orders of our organism are in the loop of high reason."[19] To be sure, the importance of emotion in human reasoning has been recognized in Western intellectual history since at least Aristotle, but cognitive theorists are providing new tools to help scholars of religion describe and explain how arguments can tap into biological and cultural resources to achieve their rhetorical ends. Damasio's research has led to the development of what he refers to as the "somatic marker hypothesis," which has become influential in the field of the cognitive science of religion. A somatic marker can work consciously or unconsciously as a "gut feeling" that pushes people toward or away from certain actions.[20] What is important for the current discussion is Damasio's contention that while somatic markers have their roots in biology, they have been "tuned to cultural prescriptions designed to ensure survival in a particular society."[21] Humans are embodied agents who always already exist embedded in particular cultures. A dynamic systems understanding of human cognition, in which human consciousness is conceived of as an emergent property of the interactions within and among various systems, can help biblical scholars flesh out the emotional texture of the rhetoric of biblical texts in order to make sense of them. The added bonus of using this approach is that it provides a base from

---

[18] Gibbs, *Embodiment and Cognitive Science*, 272. See also Slingerland, "Who's Afraid of Reductionism?" 378.

[19] Antonio R. Damasio, *Descartes' Error: Emotion, Reason, and the Human Brain* (New York: Grosset/Putnam, 1994), xiii. See George Lakoff and Mark Turner, *More Than Cool Reason: A Field Guide to Poetic Metaphor* (Chicago: University of Chicago Press, 1989).

[20] Joel B. Green, *Body, Soul, and Human Life: The Nature of Humanity in the Bible* (Studies in Theological Interpretation; Grand Rapids, Mich.: Baker Books, 2008), 86.

[21] Damasio, *Descartes' Error*, 200; see idem, 179.

which to engage other scholars who work in other areas of religious studies and in the humanities in general.[22]

While the embodied nature of human thought within a cultural world informs all work in the cognitive science of religion, it is important to pause for a moment to recognize that scholars of religion engage cognitive science in different ways. Among the various models of performing the cognitive science of religion, one might heuristically hold up two: that which emerges out of an ethnographic background, and that which emerges out of a textual or linguistic background. The former mode of thinking about the cognitive science of religion can be seen in the influential work of Harvey Whitehouse, while the latter has received its most robust explication in the recent work of Edward Slingerland.[23] To be sure, neither of these models exists as an ideal, each walled off from the other, but these are helpful categories for making sense of the burgeoning literature on the topic. Luomanen, Pyysiäinen, and Uro tend to focus on the ethnographic model in their essay and regard the more linguistic based approach found in conceptual blending theory to be a subset of the larger cognitive science of religion project, describing it as "a helpful cognitive tool for analyzing religion as crystallized in textual traditions" and "a mediating approach between the standard model of the cognitive science of religion and more content oriented approaches."[24] With all due respect to these scholars, I think such a description does not fully reflect the diverse ways to approach religion from a cognitive perspective, but rather tries to rank the ethnographic and the linguistic models in such a way that the ethnographic takes precedence. While it is true that the ethnographic and linguistic models engage religion at different interpretive levels, so to speak, I believe Slingerland's epistemological work using

---

[22] See Slingerland, "Who's Afraid of Reductionism?" 378.

[23] Harvey Whitehouse, *Inside the Cult: Religious Innovation and Transmission in Papua New Guinea* (Oxford: Oxford University Press, 1995); idem, *Arguments and Icons: Divergent Modes of Religiosity* (Oxford: Oxford University Press, 2000); idem, *Modes of Religiosity: A Cognitive Theory of Religious Transmission* (Cognitive Science of Religion Series; Walnut Creek, Calif.: Alta Mira, 2004); Edward Slingerland, "Conceptual Metaphor Theory as Methodology for Comparative Religion," *JAAR* 72 (2004): 1-31; idem, "Conceptions of the Self in the *Zhuangzi*" (2004); idem, "Who's Afraid of Reductionism? (2008): 275-411; idem, *What Science Offers the Humanities* (2008).

[24] Luomanen, Pyysiäinen, and Uro, "Introduction," 2, 15. These authors (idem, 12) discuss the work of Thomas E. Lawson and Robert N. McCauley as part of the "standard model" of the cognitive science of religion where they also place Whitehouse's work (Lawson and McCauley, *Rethinking Religion: Connecting Cognition and Culture* [Cambridge: Cambridge University Press, 1990]; and McCauley and Lawson, *Bringing Ritual to Mind* [Cambridge: Cambridge University Press, 2002]). Whitehouse, however, argues that his work is theoretically distinct from that of Lawson and McCauley, esp. their theory of ritual explicated in *Bringing Ritual to Mind*: Whitehouse, *Modes of Religiosity*, 139-55.

conceptual blending demonstrates that these are sibling approaches in the cognitive science of religion rather than related as ethnographic parent to linguistic child.[25] Moreover, as important as Whitehouse's work is in the field of the cognitive science of religion, my project does not directly engage his theoretical apparatus. As a biblical scholar, I find the tools from the textual/linguistic end of the cognitive science spectrum to be more helpful for the task at hand.

The Textual/Linguistic End of the Spectrum: Conceptual Integration Theory (Conceptual Blending)

The so-called rediscovery of the power of metaphor in the twentieth century by theorists of language has been nothing short of revolutionary for the way many of us who work in textual fields go about our work. To be sure, an understanding of the importance or power (positively or negatively assessed) of metaphor is nothing new. But, as Lynn Huber points out, the "[reintroduction] of metaphor into philosophical discussion" can be traced back to the mid-twentieth century in Max Black's concisely titled essay: "Metaphor."[26] Although metaphor theory has progressed by leaps and bounds since Black's essay was published, Huber nevertheless notes that it was Black who "made space for the question of how metaphorical language can create meaning."[27] It was the answers provided by George Lakoff and Mark Johnson in their influential book, *Metaphors We Live By*, however, that allowed for the cognitive turn in metaphor theory. In that work, Lakoff and Johnson argue that metaphor is not simply a matter of language, but rather is something that grounds human cognition. According to Bonnie Howe, "research data support the claim that metaphor is essentially conceptual, not linguistic, in nature and that metaphorical expressions in language are 'surface manifestations' of conceptual metaphor."[28] Lakoff, Johnson, and other theorists such as Mark Turner, see themselves, in the words of Huber, returning to and advancing an older view of metaphor, "in the tradition of Aristotle and Cicero, who assumed a vital connection between thought and language."[29]

---

[25] In this description I am following a self-consciously socio-rhetorical approach to interpretive analytics. See Robbins, *Invention*, 1:4-5.

[26] Lynn R. Huber, *Like a Bride Adorned: Reading Metaphor in John's Apocalypse* (Emory Studies in Early Christianity 12; New York: T & T Clark, 2007), 70.

[27] Huber, *Like a Bride Adorned*, 73.

[28] Howe, *Because You Bear This Name*, 60. See Slingerland, *What Science Offers the Humanities*, 19.

[29] Huber, *Like a Bride Adorned*, 76.

The exegetical benefits of using conceptual metaphor theory, as articulated by Lakoff, Johnson, Turner, and others, in the field of biblical studies has, to all intents and purposes, been established at this point in time. Detailed descriptions of the development of metaphor theory in the Western intellectual tradition in the recent works of Huber and Howe not only demonstrate this point, but provide important resources for biblical scholars.[30] In this project, however, I am not directly engaging conceptual metaphor theory, but a related theory of meaning construction that I believe will prove just as helpful, if not more so, to biblical scholars as well as other scholars of religion and the humanities: conceptual integration (blending) theory. Edward Slingerland, whose own theoretical work progresses from using conceptual metaphor theory to conceptual blending, describes blending theory as "what we might call 'second generation' cognitive linguistics, which portrays conceptual metaphor as merely one form of mapping involving a multiplicity of mental spaces."[31]

According to Lakoff and Johnson, "The essence of metaphor is understanding and experiencing one kind of thing in terms of another."[32] Thus, there are two domains in this model, a source and a target, where the "structure-rich source transfers information to the relatively structure-poor target,"[33] In view of some theorists, such a model, while highlighting the way thought can draw from multiple domains of understanding, is too limiting on at least three related fronts. First, conceptual metaphor theory, quite naturally, tends to limit analysis to conceptual structures behind figurative language such as metaphor and analogy. However, as Gilles Fauconnier and Mark Turner, the "fathers" of conceptual blending theory, argue, "metaphor and analogy phenomena are only a subset of the range of conceptual integration phenomena."[34] Conceptual blending, by contrast, provides an account of meaning not *only* for metaphor and analogy, but *also* for language, encountered repeatedly in Fauconnier and Turner's data, that does not

---

[30] For a brief discussion of the usefulness of metaphor in thinking about Israelite wisdom traditions see Leo G. Perdue, *Wisdom Literature: A Theological History* (Louisville, Ky.: Westminster John Knox, 2007), 8-14.

[31] Slingerland, *What Science Offers the Humanities*, 176. Compare this view with Slingerland's 2004 essay, "Conceptual Metaphor Theory as Methodology for Comparative Religion." Slingerland's work clearly demonstrates an intellectual progression from conceptual metaphor theory to conceptual blending.

[32] George Lakoff and Mark Johnson, *Metaphors We Live By* (Chicago: University of Chicago Press, 2003 [1980]), 5.

[33] Todd V. Oakley, "Conceptual Blending, Narrative Discourse, and Rhetoric," *Cognitive Linguistics* 9 (1998): 325.

[34] Gilles Fauconnier and Mark Turner, "Conceptual Integration Networks," *Cognitive Science* 22 (1998): 183. See also Tony Veale and Diarmand O'Donoghue, "Computation and Blending," *Cognitive Linguistics* 11 (2000): 253.

fit into these categories.[35] Thus conceptual blending theory is related to metaphor theory – Slingerland refers to it as an "amendment to conceptual metaphor theory" – but moves beyond it to show that similar conceptual mapping processes unite metaphors with a host of other aspects of human cognition.[36]

The second limitation stems from the fact that, as Seana Coulson notes, the data on how certain metaphors are meaningful often does not correlate to a straightforward correspondence between source and target. She notes how in the metaphor MY JOB IS A JAIL the source undergoes "accommodation so as to be more compatible with [the] target." Also, certain metaphors seem to have emergent structure that comes from neither the source nor the target. In the phrase THE SURGEON IS A BUTCHER the central insight yielded is that a surgeon so described is incompetent. Yet the idea of incompetence does not exist in either of the inputs – both a surgeon and a butcher are skilled in what each does. Conceptual blending, however, can explain how such emergent properties form.[37] Todd Oakley notes that the two domain model typically used to describe metaphor and analogy "[t]hough parsimonious … oversimplifies the projection process." On the other hand, "Fauconnier and Turner's conceptual blending model offers a more suitable, though less parsimonious, account."[38]

Third, while conceptual metaphor theory has provided scholars with a number of important tools for analyzing thought and language, one

---

[35] Fauconnier and Turner, "Conceptual Integration Networks," 135. See also idem, *The Way We Think*, 141.

[36] Slingerland, *What Science Offers the Humanities*, 176. While scholars such as Slingerland, Howe, Philip Eubanks ("Globalization, '*Corporate Rule*,' and Blended Worlds: A Conceptual-Rhetorical Analysis of Metaphor, Metonymy, and Conceptual Blending," *Metaphor and Symbol* 20 [2005]: 173-97), and Joseph E. Grady, Todd Oakley, and Seana Coulson ("Blending and Metaphor," in *Metaphor in Linguistics: Selected Papers from the Fifth International Cognitive Linguistics Conference* [ed. Raymond W. Gibbs, Jr. and Gerard J. Steen; Amsterdam: John Benjamins, 1997], 101-124) describe blending theory as related to, and thus inherently compatible with, conceptual metaphor theory, see the new 2003 afterword of Lakoff and Johnson's *Metaphors We Live By*, esp. 261-64, where the authors argue that "The Neural Theory of Language and Blending Theory are very different enterprises, which happen to overlap in subject matter in certain cases" (264).

[37] Seana Coulson, *Semantic Leaps: Frame Shifting and Conceptual Blending in Meaning Construction* (New York: Cambridge University Press, 2001), 166; Oakley, "Conceptual Blending," 326. For a discussion of the same phrase see Slingerland, *What Science Offers the Humanities*, 180; Kövecses, *Metaphor in Culture*, 268-69. Mark Turner notes that the input spaces of a Conceptual Integration Network need not be related to each other as source and target in *The Literary Mind* (New York: Oxford University Press, 1996), 68. See Gilles Fauconnier, "Compression and Emergent Structure," *Language and Linguistics* 6 (2005): 523-38.

[38] Oakley, "Conceptual Blending," 326.

drawback tends to be its limited focus on a specific source-target expression. Conceptual blending theory, much more than standard theories of metaphor, gives the interpreters the tools to trace the accumulation and creative development of complex conceptual blends throughout an extended piece of discourse and to analyze how they organize and serve the rhetoric of the text.[39] The ability to explain various kinds of conceptual blends that are produced "on the fly" in a progressive piece of discourse also, according to Slingerland, helps explain the dynamics of human creativity, or "cognitive nimbleness" to use the language of Philip Eubanks, in a way that the source-target model of metaphor theory cannot: "Seeing A as B certainly provides us with a degree of conceptual flexibility, but what seems really unusual about human beings is their ability to go beyond A and B and create an entirely new structure, C."[40] This new thing (C) that human cognition produces is referred to as the "emergent structure" of a conceptual network. These emergent properties can explain human conceptual creativity as well as the power of rhetoric to persuade people to think and *act* in new ways.

What makes conceptual integration theory more flexible than standard theories of metaphorical and analogical meaning construction lies in its ability to explain different kinds of conceptual integration networks that allow for the creation of novel emergent structures. Indeed, Eubanks argues that "[b]ecause blends take so many forms and so readily build on one another, the pervasiveness and recursiveness of conceptual blends would be difficult to overestimate."[41] Despite the radical creativity that blends prompt, however, Fauconnier and Turner argue that all blends are grounded in the same basic cognitive processes that can be described through the conceptual integration network model.

The Conceptual Integration Network (CIN)

Conceptual integration theory is a "theoretical framework for exploring human information integration" that makes use of mental space theory.[42] Gilles Fauconnier and Mark Turner describe mental spaces as

---

[39] Coulson, *Semantic Leaps,* 267; Slingerland, *What Science Offers the Humanities,* 22, 188, 196; Eubanks, "Globalization,"174.

[40] Slingerland, *What Science Offers the Humanities,* 175; Eubanks, "Globalization," 189. See Kövecses, *Metaphor in Culture,* ch. 11: "Creativity: Metaphor and Blending," 269-82.

[41] Eubanks, "Globalization," 189.

[42] Coulson and Oakley, "Blending Basics," 176. The standard work cited for the explication of mental space theory is Gilles Fauconnier, *Mental Spaces: Aspects of Meaning Construction in Natural Language* (Cambridge, UK: Cambridge University Press, 1994). For other summaries of specific aspects of conceptual blending theory, see: Slingerland,

"small conceptual packets constructed as we think and talk for the purposes of local understanding and action" that "can be used generally to model dynamic mappings in thought and language."[43] This model is referred to as a conceptual integration network (CIN). It is this network which allows Fauconnier and Turner to explain how the processes of conceptual blending operate.[44]

At its most basic, a CIN contains four elements: two input spaces, a generic space, and a blended space. The input spaces contain elements and structures from different cognitive arenas. Through a process known as cross-space mapping, "[t]here is *partial* mapping of counterparts between input spaces" which means that some elements and structures of the inputs carry over into the blend, while others are left out. The generic space "reflects some common, usually more abstract, structure and organization shared by the inputs and defines the core cross-space mapping between them."[45] The generic space is the most abstract of the four and, while having an important theoretical role, tends not to have a major functional role in actual analyses of extended pieces of discourse. For example, in order to ensure that an analysis of blending is illustrative, rather than confusing, Slingerland does not focus on generic space in his analysis of the *Mencius*. Coulson and Oakley, likewise, do not employ the generic space in their 2005 article, "Blended and Coded Meaning."[46] Following this practice, I generally omit specific reference to the generic space from my analysis of Paul's discourse in later chapters.

What Science Offers the Humanities, 176-88; Kövecses, *Metaphor in Culture*, 259-82; Howe, *Because You Bear This Name*, 84-95.

[43] Fauconnier and Turner, *The Way We Think*, 40. See also Gilles Fauconnier, *Mappings in Thought and Language* (New York: Cambridge University Press, 1997), 11: "Mental spaces are partial structures that proliferate when we think and talk, allowing fine grained partitioning of our discourse and knowledge structures." Also Fauconnier and Turner, "Conceptual Integration Networks," 137; Coulson and Oakley, "Blending Basics," 177; idem, "Metonymy and Conceptual Blending," in *Metonymy and Pragmatic Inferencing* (ed. Klaus-Uwe Panther and Linda L. Thornburg; Pragmatics & Beyond New Series 113; Amsterdam: John Benjamins, 2003), 52-54; Slingerland, *What Science Offers the Humanities*, 188.

[44] Fauconnier and Turner, *The Way We Think*, 40-50; Coulson and Oakley, "Metonymy," 54.

[45] Fauconnier, *Mappings*, 149. See Todd V. Oakley, "Conceptual Blending," 337, n. 1: "The generic space is a distinct mental space operating at a low level of description which can provide the category, frame, role, identity, or image-schematic rationale for cross-domain mapping."

[46] Slingerland, *What Science Offers the Humanities*, 188-206; Couslon and Oakley, "Blending and Coded meaning: Literal and Figurative Meaning in Cognitive Linguistics," *Journal of Pragmatics* 37 (2005): 1510-1537.

The blended space, or simply "the blend," contains only selected elements from each input space. Because of this *selective projection*, the blend prompts a new *emergent structure* throughout the network. This emergent structure is located neither in either of the two input spaces, nor in the blended space, but in the dynamic system of the network taken as a whole.[47] It is through this emergent structure that creative cognitive and rhetorical work gets accomplished in the blend – work that often helps to sustain reasoning as any given discourse unfolds.[48] This emergent structure is achieved in three ways – composition, completion, and elaboration. Composition occurs when the elements brought together in the blend make new relations possible. That is, when elements that come from separate input spaces are brought together in the blend, these elements taken together prompt for new meanings not found in either input space. Completion involves the use of background knowledge to fill in the gaps created by the pattern of the elements selectively projected from the input spaces. Elaboration is a process that "consists in cognitive work performed within the blend, according to its own emergent logic." These three ways of "running the blend" to produce emergent structure do not operate in isolation, but rather work together in dynamic relationships to produce meaning in a network that can invite new understanding.[49]

It is worth noting that the idea of emergent structure in a blend is related to Gibbs's dynamic systems model of consciousness described above. In each, "the whole is not the mere sum of its parts."[50] Rather, something new and different from its constituent elements, although related to them to be sure, emerges out of the dynamic interplay of various inputs. "How," Fauconnier asks, "can we start out with input mental spaces and end up with more than we started out with?" He answers this question by noting that "The paradox of simple, and yet conceptually creative, emergent structure is resolved when we understand that emergent structure is not confined to the blended mental spaces, but instead resides in the entire integration network and the compressions that operate within that network."[51] I will discuss the nature of compression in more detail below, but for the moment it is enough to note that compression allows various elements in the input spaces to be linked in the blend. For any blend to function well, of

---

[47] Fauconnier emphasizes this point in "Compression and Emergent Structure," (2005) more so than he and Turner did in *The Way We Think* (2002).

[48] Coulson and Oakley, "Blending Basics," 180; Eubanks, "Globalization," 174.

[49] Fauconnier, *Mappings*, 150-51. Also Fauconnier and Turner, *The Way We Think*, 48-49; Coulson, *Semantic Leaps*, 122-23.

[50] Howe, *Because You Bear This Name*, 84; Fauconnier, "Compression and Emergent Structure," 524. See Slingerland, "Who's Afraid of Reductionism?" 378.

[51] Fauconnier, "Compression and Emergent Structure," 524, see idem, 527-28.

necessity it needs to be rather simple and to recruit structure that already exists in the input spaces in order to be quickly grasped and understood. The "simple" nature of blends is important since they are produced, as noted above, "on the fly," thus in order for them to work (and be rhetorically persuasive) they must be simple enough to apprehend in a moment. The "power of integration" lies in the "linking of such simple structure to the array of mental spaces in the entire network."[52] It is the dynamism of the entire network that allows for creative emergent structure.

To illustrate their CIN model, I take an example directly from Fauconnier and Turner,[53] who imagine a contemporary philosophy professor leading a class discussion who states:

> I claim that reason is a self-developing capacity. Kant disagrees with me on this point. He says it's innate, but I answer that that's begging the question, to which he counters, in *Critique of Pure Reason*, that only innate ideas have power. But I say to that, What about neuronal group selection? And he gives no answer.

This is a fairly complicated example, but I will only touch on certain points for illustrative purposes. In this example there are two input spaces, one that contains Kant and his attendant elements (input-1) and one that contains the philosophy professor and her attendant elements (input-2). In each input space there is a thinker who is expressing philosophical ruminations – Kant through his writing, the professor through speaking. Thus the generic space, which facilitates cross-space mapping in the network, contains abstract elements such as "thinker," "philosophical ideas," and "expression of ideas." In the blend, Kant and the professor occupy the same space and time and express their ideas to one another. In the blend, each is aware of the other's ideas and they are engaged in a conversation. Clearly this scenario is patently absurd as far as realistic representation is concerned, but it nonetheless has discursive power. The power lies in the fact that none of the students thinks the professor has lost her sanity because she really believes she is conversing with a dead German thinker. Rather, "the blended space is valuable only because it is conceptually linked to the inputs."[54] The emergent structure arises from the dynamic interaction of the different spaces of the network. Through the imaginary conversation that takes place in the blend the professor can instruct students about the strengths and weakness of Kantian ideas and arguments. What is

---

[52] Fauconnier, "Compression and Emergent Structure," 532.
[53] This example is found in Fauconnier and Turner, *The Way We Think*, 59-62.
[54] Fauconnier and Turner, *The Way We Think*, 61. See Fauconnier, "Compression and Emergent Structure."

important to note in this example is that there is only a *partial* mapping of elements from the input spaces to the blend. Kant, his ideas, and the fact that he expressed his ideas are projected from input-1 into the blend. However, "Kant's time, language, mode of expression, the fact that he's dead, and the fact the he was never aware of the future existence of our professor are not projected."[55] This selective projection ensures that the blend runs smoothly and is not compromised by non-relevant elements.

Framing Networks

The mental spaces in a CIN do not exist in a conceptual vacuum, but are usually *framed*. A frame is typically understood as the requisite background knowledge that is required to make sense of the elements within and among mental spaces.[56] Fauconnier and Turner refer to a frame as "long-term schematic knowledge" and it is this knowledge that helps emergent logic to develop in the blend.[57] It is the use of frames that makes conceptual blending a particularly useful way to investigate biblical texts. "The appeal of frames," Seana Coulson writes, "lies chiefly in their ability to account for all the 'extra' information readers infer in the course of meaning construction."[58] I am following Coulson's practice by including a variety of different concepts under the umbrella term "frame." Noting that she herself is following the lead of Charles J. Fillmore, Coulson uses "the term *frame* as a cover term for a whole set of related concepts, including script, schema, scenario, idealized cognitive models, and folk theory. Although differences exist in the scope of these constructs, they are all used to represent structured background knowledge, have important experiential character, and so forth."[59] By making theoretical space for explicating that which struc-

---

[55] Fauconnier and Turner, *The Way We Think*.
[56] See Coulson, *Semantic Leaps*, 20.
[57] Fauconnier and Turner, *The Way We Think*, 40. Note that Fauconnier and Turner (*The Way We Think*, 103) also describe frames as "entrenched mental spaces that we can activate all at once." One notes, in this quotation, that Fauconnier and Turner are not as exact with their descriptive language as one might hope. In this quotation they seem to suggest a frame *is* a mental space. A better description, for the sake of clarity, would be that a frame *structures* elements and relations in and among mental spaces in a way that is easily retrievable. See Fauconnier and Turner, "Conceptual Integration Networks," 134.
[58] Coulson, *Semantic Leaps*, 83.
[59] Coulson, *Semantic Leaps*, 20 note. See also Robbins, *Invention*, 1:100; Peter Stockwell, *Cognitive Poetics: An Introduction* (London: Routledge, 2002), 76-77. Here Stockwell notes that that the term "frame," which Fauconnier and Turner employ, tends to be reserved for visual fields whereas terms such as "script" and "schema" are used more in the linguistic field. Regardless of specific terminology employed, Stockwell notes that since "language exhibits conceptual dependency" in any given discourse "[o]ften, both

tures the elements within and among mental spaces, conceptual blending analysis allows interpreters to move from a general theory about human cognition to a usable interpretive analytic for unraveling the specific meanings prompted by a discourse written in a particular social and cultural milieu for local, rhetorical purposes. In order to implement an analysis of conceptual blending properly, understanding the social and cultural worlds out of which the discourse arose is crucial.

Frames, while lending conceptual blending greater utility for the biblical scholar, also have the potential to muddy the exegetical waters because of their complexity. A frame can have a greater or lesser degree of specificity, therefore for just about every frame described, there exists also super- and sub-frames.[60] Determining what level of frame specificity yields the greatest exegetical returns is the job of the interpreter. In other words, the analyst may map out several levels of framing, but opt to focus the interpretation on that level which yields the most plausible and productive explanation for the meaning production of the rhetoric within the discourse being examined.[61] Typically, the most useful level of framing is referred to as an "organizing frame." In the section on socio-rhetorical interpretation below and in the exegetical chapters in this book, I will make use of what I refer to as cultural organizing frames. These cultural frames organize the logic and background information of a particular piece of discourse and structure the ways in which the elements of the discourse are rhetorically employed. Close exegetical analysis, however, can also identify what I refer to as local frames. These local frames, called "sub-frames" by Fauconnier and Turner, function below the level of the cultural organizing frame and allow exegetes a more precise tool to explicate the meaning of a certain segment of discourse. By using cultural and local frames together, a rich analysis of biblical texts is possible.

To return to the Kant example from above, one notes that the input spaces each contain thinkers who are expressing their philosophical ideas. The frame that governs each input space is the same and can be described as "philosophical reflection and expression." This frame recruits cultural ideas of a thinker engaged in deep reflection in order to arrive at some truth about the world, humanity, or both. In the blend, however, a different frame emerges. In the blend, two philosophers are

---

speaker and hearer are familiar with the situation that is being discussed, and therefore every single facet will not need to be enumerated for the situation to be understood."

[60] Fauconnier and Turner, *The Way We Think*, 102. When examining discourse one can also speak of frames that operate in the background and those that are at work in the foreground.

[61] See Coulson, *Semantic Leaps*, 120 for a discussion of "the hierarchal organization of frames."

having a conversation that involves pitting their ideas against each other. "The *debate* frame comes up easily in the blend through pattern completion, since so much of its structure is already in place in the composition of the two inputs."[62] The fact that the blend contains two indi-individuals who disagree means that the frame of *argument* could just as easily have been recruited for the blend. However, the fact that it is two *philosophers* who are engaged in this disagreement suggests, to someone with the appropriate cultural background knowledge of the Western academic setting, a reasoned discussion with rationales given for each position, thus more clearly a debate than an argument. Had the individuals in the blended space not been philosophers, but, say, patrons in a bar disagreeing about the merits of different sports teams, the frame of argument would be more readily recruited in the blend. Thus cultural background knowledge plays a key role in determining which frames are valuable for understanding the blend under evaluation. However, it is conceivable that two interpreters will disagree about what frame provides the most help in explaining a given piece of discourse.

Most of the research and writing involving conceptual integration theory takes its examples, like the Kant debate above, from contemporary language and cultural settings. This is done so that readers will readily "know" what types of frames the authors are interpreting, that is, so that readers will already possess the requisite cultural background information. For example, Seana Coulson, in a section analyzing framing in her published dissertation, chooses to examine the topic of abortion "chiefly because it is familiar to most Americans."[63] The challenge for the biblical scholar lies in excavating the culturally shared frames, also called "cultural models" by Coulson, that a given piece of biblical discourse might activate. This type of activity, while less certain than that in which most cognitive scientists engage, is not new to biblical studies.[64] Before any study that uses conceptual blending analysis can begin, the exegete must fully investigate these cultural models, what Luke Timothy Johnson calls the "symbolic worlds," out of which the NT writings emerged.[65] By striving to uncover the plausible "taken-for-granted models shared by members of a given social group," in this case Paul and the Corinthian Christians, my project systematically ex-

---

[62] Fauconnier and Turner, *The Way We Think*, 60.
[63] Coulson, *Semantic Leaps*, 224.
[64] See Luther H. Martin, "Toward a Scientific History of Religions," in *Theorizing Religions Past: Archeology, History, and Cognition* (ed. Harvey Whitehouse and Luther H. Martin; Cognitive Science of Religion Series; Walnut Creek, Calif.: Alta Mira, 2004), 7-14 for a discussion about using the ethnographic model developed by Whitehouse from his study of Papua New Guinea to explain ancient religious traditions.
[65] Johnson, *Writings of the New Testament*, 21-91.

amines how "[f]raming prompts speakers to integrate shared cultural models with conceived scenarios."[66] For the biblical scholar this will always carry with it a degree of uncertainty. The goal of my project is to demonstrate which cultural organizing frames are most beneficial for understanding what Paul's rhetoric in 1 Cor 6:12–7:7 is doing. As Coulson notes, "By employing diverse rhetorical strategies, speakers adapt cultural models to suit a variety of ideological outlooks and argumentative needs. ... Cultural models, pragmatic scales, and rhetorical strategies are all tools we use to construct and reconstruct a cultural understanding of the world we both inhabit and create."[67] Analyzing the text in this way does not try to arrive at some kind of positivist knowledge of the cultural frames Paul thought he was employing, but rather attempts to understand how Paul's argument makes sense in its cultural context.[68]

Framing is of interest to me because of its role in rhetorical persuasion. As Coulson notes in her study of American views on abortion, the contested issues are not over "mere semantics," but over how the debate is framed.[69] The frames that structure cognitive elements in mental spaces are often contested because they are "so central to social experience. Another reason people argue about framing is that framing is *arguable*."[70] Skilled rhetoricians will employ all manner of cognitive tools, sometimes unconsciously, as a means to move people to think and act in ways that conform to the rhetorical world being created – a world that has roots in, but moves beyond that which is already available in a culture. Frames provide a powerful resource to help us explain how arguments employ background information as they go about trying to persuade people to think and act in certain ways.

Different Types of Networks
The basic network model of conceptual blending, then, is comprised of four mental spaces (two input spaces, a generic space, and a blended space) with accompanying frames and the links between and among

---

[66] Coulson, *Semantic Leaps*, 223, 245. A similar stress on cultural background knowledge is found in the study of metaphor by cultural anthropologist James W. Fernandez. See esp. his *Persuasions and Performances: The Play of Tropes in Culture* (Bloomington, Ind.: Indiana University Press, 1986); idem, ed., *Beyond Metaphor: The Theory of Tropes in Anthropology* (Stanford: Stanford University Press, 1991). See below for how metaphor fits into conceptual integration theory.

[67] Coulson, *Semantic Leaps*, 266. See Eubanks, "Globalization," 195-96.

[68] For this distinction between understanding and knowledge I am indebted to L. Gregory Bloomquist, personal communication.

[69] Coulson, *Semantic Leaps*, 227-45.

[70] Coulson, *Semantic Leaps*, 245, emphasis in the original.

various elements in the mental spaces. Human thought, Fauconnier and Turner recognize, requires that an interpreter have the ability to model far more complicated arrangements. "In the unfolding of a full discourse, a rich array of mental spaces is typically set up with mutual connections and shifts of viewpoint and focus from one space to another."[71] Mapping the mental space relations of a full discourse is more like creating a web of interconnected meaning than the simple four space network model suggests. Fauconnier and Turner use the simple network model only as a stepping off point for more complicated mappings of multiple blends. These multiple blends are, they would argue, more in keeping with what is encountered in full discourses.

There are basically two ways to create a multiple blend. In the first, several input spaces, not merely two, are blended "in parallel." That is, elements and framing structures of multiple inputs are all selectively projected into the blend, which receives its emergent properties from those selective elements and frames. The second way to form a complex blend is when the inputs are "projected successively." That is, a blend might be formed by only two inputs, but then this blend is itself one of the inputs for a more complex blend, which itself serves as an input in another network, and so on. And, of course, both of these complex blending processes might occur in the same discourse.[72] For example, Paul uses the term σῶμα in multiple, complex ways in 1 Cor.[73] The exegete may find that this term is so slippery in Paul's written discourse because it always already exists as a blended space, or, to be more precise, different blended spaces. Yet Paul can take this blended space and use it in an input space in his argument in 1 Cor 6:12–7:7. Fauconnier and Turner's idea of multiple blends provides categories to tackle such difficult issues.

In addition to the recognition that blends multiply throughout extended discourse, what makes conceptual integration theory more flexible than standard theories of metaphorical and analogical meaning construction lies in its ability to explain different *kinds* of conceptual integration networks. Fauconnier and Turner describe four common types of networks that they claim "the network model predicts ... from theoretical principles, and, indeed, when we look at the laboratory of Nature, we find very strong evidence that they exist." These four net-

---

[71] Fauconnier and Turner, *The Way We Think*, 103. See Coulson, *Semantic Leaps*, 267; Eubanks, "Globalization,"174; Slingerland, *What Science Offers the Humanities*, 22, 188, 196.

[72] Fauconnier and Turner, *The Way We Think*, 279-298; see also 334-36.

[73] See B.J. Oropeza, *Paul and Apostasy: Eschatology, Perseverance, and Falling Away in the Corinthian Congregation* (WUNT 2nd series 115; Tübingen: Mohr Siebeck, 2000), 98.

works are: simplex networks, mirror networks, single-scope networks, and double-scope networks.[74]

A simplex network, on the surface, does not even appear to be a blend at all. It is characterized as being compositional and truth-functional. In this network a frame with its roles is projected from one input, while the second input space projects elements that become values to those roles in the blend. An example is the phrase "Paul is the father of Sally." In this network, one input space is organized by the frame of *family* and contains the roles father and daughter. The second input space contains two individuals, Paul and Sally, with no organizing frame. The blended space inherits the family frame and the roles, in this case *father* and *daughter*, from input-1 and the elements in input-2, Paul and Sally, become the values of these roles in the blended space.

A mirror network is one in which all the spaces of the CIN share an organizing frame. An example of this type of network is when an athlete, a runner for example, "competes" against the world record holder in an event – a person who ran sometime in the past and who might even be dead. Input-1 contains the world record holder and the race he or she ran. Input-2 contains the present runner and the race he or she is running. The frame of "competitive foot race" organizes both input spaces and the blended space. In the blend the runners from each input are projected as themselves, but the race that each runs, instead of being historically distinct, is fused into one and the same event. Hence the present runner and the world record holder are competing against each other in the blend. In the simplex and mirror networks, there are no clashes at the level of the organizing frame. This is because in the former only one input space is structured by an organizing frame, while in the latter the organizing frame for all spaces is the same. There can be clashes below the level of organizing frame in the mirror network, however. In the example of the two runners, there is, at the simplest level, a clash of time – two racers from different times cannot actually compete. However, the time relation is not projected and thus does not interfere with the blended space.

Simplex and mirror networks are relatively simple CINs. Single- and double-scope networks are considerably more complex. As Fauconnier and Turner note, "Single-scope networks are the prototype of highly conventional source-target metaphors."[75] It is in this type of network that conceptual blending and metaphor theory have the most in com-

---

[74] Fauconnier and Turner, *The Way We Think*, 119. Unless otherwise noted, the discussion of the four kinds of networks and their illustrative examples discussed in this and the following paragraphs all derive from idem, 119-35.

[75] Fauconnier and Turner, *The Way We Think*, 127.

mon. In a single-scope network the two input spaces have different organizing frames. However, only the organizing frame from one input is projected into the blend. The blended space does not disrupt the frame of the framing input (called the source in metaphor theory) even as it blends in the elements of the focus input (called the target in metaphor theory). For example, when two CEOs (input-1) are portrayed in a picture or a story as boxers in a ring (input-2) a single-scope network is at work. The organizing frame of boxing and many of its elements (gloves, a ring, etc.) carries over directly from the framing input to the blended space, while the values of CEO X and CEO Y, but not the business frame, are projected from the focus input.

The most complex network discussed by Fauconnier and Turner is the double-scope network which "has inputs with different (and often clashing) organizing frames as well as an organizing frame for the blend that includes parts of each of those frames and has emergent structure of its own."[76] The favorite example in the literature for a double-scope network is the idiom YOU ARE DIGGING YOUR OWN GRAVE, which, when used in discourse, implies that not only is the agent doing something that will have detrimental consequences, but that he or she is unaware that this is happening.[77] Thus a fiscally conservative father may say this to a child who continues to invest money in the stock market. In this scenario, the two input spaces are "grave digging" (input-1) and something like "unwitting failure" (input-2), since the father believes investing in the stock is throwing money away, an action that will result in financial ruin.

> In the blend (as opposed to the "digging the grave" input), digging one's grave is a serious mistake that makes dying more likely. In the blend, it becomes possible to be unaware of one's concrete actions – a situation that is projected from the "unwitting failure" input, where it is indeed fully possible, and common, to be unaware of the nature and significance of one's actions. But in the blend, it remains highly foolish to be unaware of such concrete actions – a judgment that is projected from the "digging the grave" input and will project back to the "unwitting failure" input to produce suitable inferences (i.e., to highlight foolishness and misperception of an individual's behavior).[78]

The double-scope network, then, provides the clearest platform for the strengths of conceptual integration theory. However, it is im-

---

[76] Fauconnier and Turner, *The Way We Think*, 131. Fauconnier and Turner go so far as to hypothesize that "the capacity for double-scope integration could well be the crucial distinctive feature of cognitively modern humans" (Fauconnier, "Compression and Emergent Structure," 528, citing Fauconnier and Turner, *The Way We Think*, ch. 9.).

[77] See Slingerland, *What Science Offers the Humanities*, 178-79.

[78] Fauconnier and Turner, *The Way We Think*, 133. For further discussion of this idiom, see Coulson, *Semantic Leaps*, 168-72.

portant to note that Fauconnier and Turner are adamant that the same processes of cognition are at work in all four of these prominent types of networks. Their conceptual integration network model aims to explain how human brains process a complex world in order to create meaning and communicate.

Governing Principles

The network model of human cognition outlined above provides the basis for conceptual integration theory. This model allows interpreters to explain how elements and frames associated with two or more input spaces are selectively projected into a blended space. This blended space is cognitively important because of the novel structure created in it by means of composition, completion, and elaboration which generates emergent properties throughout the network. Although it is suitably complex to tackle the difficulties of meaning making in human discourse, one danger is that "blending theory runs the risk of being too powerful, accounting for everything, and, hence, explaining nothing."[79] In response to this critique, Fauconnier and Turner have developed "governing principles" that "characterize strategies for optimizing emergent structure"[80] within a network. These governing principles (also called "optimality" principles) constrain how effective blends can be created and strive to make the analysis of conceptual blending a more principled endeavor.[81]

The governing principles developed by Fauconnier and Turner are useful in that they more accurately describe how the processes of composition, completion, and elaboration take place in a blend. Since these principles are based on the data analyzed by Fauconnier, Turner and others, they are subject to development as more research and analysis lead to a more nuanced understanding of how meaning is constructed in conceptual networks.[82] Based upon their continuing research, Fauconnier and Turner explicate a number of governing principles, in-

---

[79] Coulson and Oakley, "Blending Basics," 186; idem, "Metonymy," 58. See also Raymond W. Gibbs, Jr., "Making Good Psychology out of Blending Theory," *Cognitive Linguistics* 11 (2000): 347-58 for critiques of and recommendations for Fauconnier and Turner's theory. This critique has also been leveled against the category of "wisdom" in biblical studies.
[80] Fauconnier and Turner, *The Way We Think*, 311.
[81] Coulson and Oakley, "Metonymy," 59.
[82] See, for example, Fauconnier and Turner's discussion of the optimality principles in "Conceptual Integration Networks," 162: "Here we discuss the principles we have been able to substantiate..." Much of the literature that presently exists on conceptual integration theory interacts with the six optimality principles articulated by Fauconnier and Turner in their 1998 article "Conceptual Integration Networks," 162-63, 170. This list is itself a development from the one found in Fauconnier's 1997 work, *Mappings*, 186.

cluding Compression, Typology, Integration, Web, Unpacking, among others.[83] Of these, the most important, for this project and the ongoing development of blending theory, is Compression.[84]

Fauconnier argues that "a central feature of integration networks is their ability to compress diffuse conceptual structure into intelligible and manipulable human-scale situations in a blended space."[85] The notion of Compression has evolved in the development of blending theory and now has perhaps the most explanatory power when analyzing how the links among mental spaces become conceptually and rhetorically powerful in the creation of novel emergent structure.[86] Compression describes how the elements located in various mental spaces within a conceptual integration network can have numerous inner- and outer-space relations, that is, relations within and among spaces. There are about twenty or so of these "vital relations" that play an important role in understanding how Compression happens, including Analogy and Disanalogy, Part-Whole, Representation, Identity, Similarity, and Uniqueness.[87] "It is vital relations," Coulson and Oakley write, "that tend to be subject to compression in the blended space."[88] Thus, to use an example that comes up repeatedly in the literature, when pointing to a picture hanging on the wall, a person might state: "That's Jane." This statement involves compressing the vital relation of Representation, between a two-dimensional photograph and a human being, to that of Identity and Uniqueness where the photograph and the human it represents become fused in one element. "Uniqueness," according to Fauconnier, "is fusion, the strongest possible form of compression."[89] Compression helps explain how links between elements are formed and strengthened and will play a pivotal role in my exegesis of 1 Cor 6:12-20.

The goal of conceptual integration is to achieve *human scale* so that conceptually difficult situations can be more easily grasped in a blend than in its diffuse input spaces. According to Fauconnier and Turner, "The most obvious human-scale situations have direct perception and action in familiar frames that are easily apprehended by human be-

---

[83] See Fauconnier and Turner, *The Way We Think*, 309-36 for a complete discussion of all governing principles.

[84] See Fauconnier, "Compression and Emergent Structure"; Fauconnier and Turner, *The Way We Think*, 312-25.

[85] Fauconnier, "Compression and Emergent Structure," 523.

[86] See Fauconnier, "Compression and Emergent Structure," 527-28.

[87] Fauconnier and Turner, *The Way We Think*, 92-101; Fauconnier, "Compression and Emergent Structure," 523-24.

[88] Coulson and Oakley, "Metonymy," 60.

[89] Fauconnier and Turner, "Compression and Emergent Structure," 527.

ings."⁹⁰ Blended spaces often appear simple because they have achieved this human scale and it is this simplicity that allows the blend to work rhetorically by giving power to the entire network. Compressing vital relations to achieve human scale simplifies conceptually complex situations so that "[t]he logical, emotional, and social inferences within the blended space are inescapable; their validity is not in question."⁹¹ Thus, to use a biblical example, the book of Sirach describes wisdom as something that is like a man's mother *and* his virginal wife (Sir 15:2). While this is a complicated double-scope network, it does manage to explain an abstract principle such as wisdom in human, in this case familial, terms. Achieving human scale often requires a great deal of mental work as elements and structures are selectively projected to the blended space (notice that wisdom is not a man's mother *and* wife simultaneously in this network). In this example notions of different kinds of nurturing and love are being activated in rapid succession. This is rhetorically persuasive because the hearer/reader possesses easily accessible cultural knowledge about the love, comfort, and support mothers and wives are supposed to offer men. This imaginative mental work reconfigures these elements and relations and in so doing provides meaning for rhetorical persuasion which is necessary for argumentative discourse to be effective. As I will demonstrate, Paul's argument against πορνεία in 1 Cor 6:12–7:7 efficiently achieves human scale and this, I argue, gives it its rhetorical power.

Achieving human scale in the blend often has rhetorical power because of its ability to activate human emotions in the reasoning process. Slingerland concludes that "the primary purpose of employing a metaphoric blend to achieve human scale is not to help us intellectually *apprehend* a situation, but rather to help us to know how to *feel* about it." Slingerland connects the importance of emotion prompted by blends to Damasio's somatic marker hypothesis, introduced above.⁹² In full, Damasio argues that a somatic marker:

> forces attention on the negative outcome to which an action may lead, and functions as an automated alarm signal which says: Beware of danger ahead if you choose the option which leads to this outcome. The signal may lead you to reject, *immediately*, the negative course of action and thus make you choose among other alternatives. The automated signal protects you against future losses, without further ado, and then allows you *to*

---

⁹⁰ Fauconnier and Turner, *The Way We Think*, 312.
⁹¹ Fauconnier, "Compression and Emergent Structure," 529.
⁹² Slingerland, *What Science Offers the Humanities*, 185. For the importance of emotion in blends, see Coulson, *Semantic Leaps*, 200-210. For the importance of embodiment in understanding emotion, see Gibbs, *Embodiment and Cognitive Science*, 243.

choose from fewer alternatives. There is still room for using a cost/benefit analysis and proper deductive competence, but only *after* the automated step drastically reduces the number of options.[93]

The immediacy of the visceral reaction prompted by a somatic marker fits well with blending theory's notion that CINs allow for rapid, online reasoning. Moreover, notice that the somatic marker hypothesis does not discount deductive reasoning and other logic mechanisms. Somatic markers do not explain the entirety of human decision making, but they do stack the deck as it were, and skilled rhetoricians can exploit the persuasive potential of these markers to the fullest.[94] Slingerland returns to the DIGGING YOUR OWN GRAVE blend to demonstrate how the visceral response prompted by the blend turns a clumsy expression into a powerful persuasive tool by invoking somatic markers such as graves, corpses, and death.[95] Thus the reasoning prompted by blends often relies on the power of emotions and achieving human scale is an important element in provoking such emotional reactions. Slingerland highlights this when he writes that "human scale inputs are recruited polemically to inspire somatic-normative reactions in the listeners."[96] As I will demonstrate in my exegesis, this is precisely Paul's rhetorical strategy in 1 Cor 6:12–7:7.

Fauconnier argues that an optimal blend has the following properties: "human scale, only two objects, simple concrete action, clear-cut outcome."[97] The governing principles outlined above, most significantly Compression, serve to constrain how optimal blends can be formed. Yet not every blend satisfies these principles in the same fashion. Indeed, satisfaction of certain principles often comes at the expense of others. For example, Coulson and Oakley argue that metonymic expressions often violate the Topology principle in order to satisfy the Integration principle.[98] Fauconnier and Turner note that Compression also competes with the Topology principle, and that Integration also stands in tension with the Unpacking principle.[99] Such clashes, rather than demonstrating a problem with the governing principles, are where

---

[93] Damasio, *Descartes' Error*, 173, emphases in the original. See Martha C. Nussbaum's discussion of "The Cognitive Content of Disgust" in *Hiding from Humanity: Disgust, Shame, and the Law* (Princeton: Princeton University Press, 2004), 87-98.

[94] Slingerland, *What Science Offers the Humanities*, 196.

[95] Slingerland, *What Science Offers the Humanities*, 185.

[96] Slingerland, *What Science Offers the Humanities*, 188. See idem, 307: "A growing number of cognitive scientists and philosophers have come to agree with Hume and the Greek Stoics that ... normative judgments are ultimately derived from human emotional reactions."

[97] Fauconnier, "Compression and Emergent Structure," 531.

[98] Coulson and Oakley, "Metonymy," 61, 65.

[99] Fauconnier and Turner, *The Way We Think*, 336.

the messy work of creating a meaningful blend take place. Moreover, as the complexity of discourse increases, such "trade-offs between optimality principles become inevitable."[100] Coulson and Oakley contend that conceptual analyses "suggest that meaningful acts are not always supported by orderly structures with neat analogical mappings between domains, but, rather, unruly, ad hoc, conglomerations that, nonetheless, adhere to a few basic principles."[101] These governing principles allow the exegete to explain how complex, often messy, biblical discourse works as meaningful rhetorical argumentation.

A Socio-Rhetorical Framework: Embracing Embodied Cognition

Socio-Rhetorical interpretation (SRI) is an interpretive analytic that enables exegetes to examine how persuasive language works from multiple angles. Vernon Robbins argues that there is a philosophical difference between an interpretive analytic, such as SRI, and a method. "The philosophy of a method," Robbins writes, "is grounded in a belief that the true nature of something is 'in something itself.' In contrast, the philosophy of an interpretive analytic is grounded in a belief that the true nature of something is exhibited in the way it relates to all other things. This is a difference between a philosophy of essence or substance and a philosophy of relations."[102] Because SRI provides theoretic space for putting multiple analytical tools into conversation with one another when examining relations that allow interpreters to make sense of texts, it is possible to adopt a late twentieth/early twenty-first century theory of meaning construction (conceptual integration theory) to help explain a first century document. Part of the reason this is possible, as I have argued above, is because cognitive science focuses on the "capacity for meaning shared by all human beings" based on common physiology, yet it also "successfully takes into account cultural and situational data."[103] Based on common human anatomy, including neural anatomy, cognitive science understands itself to possess the tools necessary to begin to understand human meaning making in general while maintaining that human subjects are embodied in specific cultural environments. Thus, the full tapestry of human meaning pro-

---

[100] Coulson and Oakley, " Metonymy," 76.
[101] Coulson and Oakley, " Metonymy," 77.
[102] Robbins, *Invention*, 1:5.
[103] Todd V. Oakley, "The Human Rhetorical Potential," *Written Communication* 16 (1999): 94; Fauconnier, *Mappings*, 7.

duction is only understandable in relation to specific social and cultural worlds.

Conceptual integration theory, the linguistic end of the cognitive science spectrum that I engage, seems a natural fit to Robbins's SRI approach, which is why new socio-rhetorical works are making use of it.[104] Gilles Fauconnier argues that "discourse configurations are highly organized and complex within wider social and cultural contexts, and the raison d'être of grammatical constructions and words within them is to provide us with (imperfect) clues as to what discourse configurations to set up."[105] Although developed independently, the ideas about relational meaning construction found in conceptual blending theory fit well into SRI's concern to look at multiple aspects of textual discourse. Conceptual integration theory's concern with "how language prompts for meaning" makes it a powerful exegetical tool when combined with a programmatic interpretive analytic such as SRI.[106]

A full-fledged socio-rhetorical interpretation of Paul's argument in 1 Cor 6:12–7:7 has yet to be undertaken.[107] I argue that conceptual blending theory within a socio-rhetorical framework provides the tools necessary to ask newer questions of Paul's teaching against πορνεία than have been investigated in the past and thus promises to shed exegetical light on how the rhetoric of the argument functions. SRI is particularly suited to the task at hand because of the promise it holds, in the words of L. Gregory Bloomquist, to move "New Testament criticism from the limited examination of historical questions to an exploration of the fascinating web of reality spun by each of the New Testament writers and their worlds."[108] The tools of conceptual blend-

---

[104] I am referring specifically to the Rhetoric of Religious Antiquity series published by Deo, Blandford Forum, UK.

[105] Fauconnier, *Mappings*, 5. For more on the importance of culture in conceptual integration theory, see Fauconnier and Turner, *The Way We Think*, esp. 72-73, 102, 217, 259, 356, 369, 382-83, 393, 396; Slingerland, *What Science Offers the Humanities*, ch. 4.

[106] Fauconnier and Turner, *The Way We Think*, 139; see also 277.

[107] See Duane F. Watson's critique of the socio-rhetorical work done by Ben Witherington III (*Conflict and Community in Corinth: A Socio-Rhetorical Commentary on 1 and 2 Corinthians* [Grand Rapids: Eerdmans, 1995]; *The Acts of the Apostles: A Socio-Rhetorical Commentary* [Grand Rapids: Eerdmans, 1998]): "Two commentaries claiming to be socio-rhetorical, although excellent as commentaries, did not move beyond traditional historical-critical methods of interpretation with an emphasis on social history" ("Why We Need Socio-Rhetorical Commentary and What It Might Look Like," in *Rhetorical Criticism and the Bible* [ed. Stanley E. Porter and Dennis L. Stamps], 129).

[108] L. Gregory Bloomquist, "A Possible Direction for Providing Programmatic Correlation of Textures in Socio-Rhetorical Analysis," in *Rhetorical Criticism and the Bible* (ed. Stanley E. Porter and Dennis L. Stamps), 61. See also Bloomquist's comment on p. 93: "… I believe that the strength of SR[I] is precisely in its potential for leading us out of the modernist focus on history."

ing can help socio-rhetorical interpreters explain how these webs of rhetorical reality hang together.

There is some tension in the guild between scholars who focus on history, or "getting behind the text," and those who focus on the nature and use of language in Paul's discourse. This tension can be seen in the continuing discussion about how best to use rhetoric to interpret biblical texts. Margaret Mitchell, for example, regards the use of rhetoric as part of the historical-critical project and therefore restricts herself to a discussion of rhetorical devices that would have been in use in the first century CE.[109] Lauri Thurén critiques this exegetical restriction to ancient rhetoric when interpreting biblical texts.[110] In this he is joined by other scholars such as Elisabeth Schüssler Fiorenza and Thomas H. Olbricht.[111] For Thurén, such a restriction only makes sense "[i]f rhetorical conventions in the New Testament are seen mainly as historical phenomena" and then only "if we can reasonably assume that the authors had learnt those techniques by name at school." Thurén argues, rather, that NT writings "should be analyzed with the best means available, whether ancient or modern. When the goal is to understand the text, not only to identify historical features in it, this perspective is feasible."[112]

---

[109] Which she calls "historical rhetorical criticism," Mitchell, *Paul and the Rhetoric of Reconciliation*, 6. But note Stanley E. Porter's observation: "Even though rhetorical features are found in other ancient writings besides speeches ..., so far as I know letters – primarily because of their sub-literary status (literary letters are excluded from this) – were never analysed or examined in this way by the ancients or considered part of rhetoric or of the body of rhetorically influenced literature" ("Ancient Rhetorical Analysis and Discourse Analysis of the Pauline Corpus," in *The Rhetorical Analysis of Scripture: Essays form the 1995 London Conference* [ed. Stanley E. Porter and Thomas H. Olbricht; JSNTSup 146; Sheffield: Sheffield Academic Press, 1997], 251-52). Referring specifically to Mitchell's work Porter goes on to note that "the idea of a hybrid letter combining epistolary form and deliberative oration is simply a *non sequitur*, so far as established categories from the ancient world are concerned" (272).

[110] Thurén, "Is There Biblical Argumentation?" 77-92.

[111] Elisabeth Schüssler Fiorenza, "Challenging the Rhetorical Half-Turn: Feminist and Rhetorical Biblical Criticism," in *Rhetoric, Scripture and Theology: Essays from the 1994 Pretoria Conference* (ed. Stanley E. Porter and Thomas H. Olbricht; JSNTSup 131; Sheffield: Sheffield Academic Press, 1996), 32. Thomas H. Olbricht, "Introduction," in *Rhetorical Argumentation in Biblical Texts: Essays from the Lund 2000 Conference* (ed. Anders Eriksson et al.; Emory Studies in Early Christianity 8; Harrisburg, Pa.: Trinity Press International, 2002), 3, 6. See also Porter, "Ancent Rhetorical Analysis," 268.

[112] Lauri Thurén, "On Studying Ethical Argumentation and Persuasion in the New Testament," in *Rhetoric and the New Testament: Essays from the 1992 Heidelberg Conference* (ed. Stanley E. Porter and Thomas H. Olbricht; JSNTSup 90; Sheffield Academic Press, 1993), 470-71. This view is echoed, though in a slightly different fashion, by Hebrew Bible scholar Karl Möller when he uses Greco-Roman rhetorical categories, especially the insights of Aristotle, to interpret the book of Amos. He defends the use of these

Thurén's remarks touch on a point elucidated by Anders Eriksson. Eriksson notes that since H.D. Betz's reintroduction of rhetorical analysis to NT studies there has been some confusion "whether rhetoric is the tool used for analysis or the object of study." Historical critics, he notes, often have difficulty differentiating between these two aspects.[113] SRI, as conceived by Robbins, offers biblical scholars a way out of this difficulty.[114] "Socio-rhetorical critics," according to Robbins, "are interested in the nature of texts as social, cultural, historical, theological and ideological discourse." He goes on to state that "Within this approach, historical, social and cultural data stand in an intertextual relation to signs in texts."[115] With its multi-texture approach, discussed below, I take Robbins and SRI to be offering NT exegesis a "both/and" opportunity. The historical investigation of ancient rhetorical forms and praxis *always* has a place within SRI on at least the level of intertexture, that is, the NT's relationship to other texts that aim to persuade.[116] It may also have a place within the examination of the inner workings of a text as it goes about persuading, provided, as Thurén suggests, that it is the best means of explicating what the text is doing.[117] However, if other theories of meaning and language serve the interpreter better, then these other theories are used instead of ancient categories. SRI, with its programmatic analysis of different "textures"

---

categories against charges of anachronism and argues that "Aristotle and his successors, after all, did not *invent* rhetorical discourse. ... Aristotle and others merely investigated rhetorical utterances and then developed a concept of rhetoric that was based partly on their observations and partly on philosophical ideas and concepts" (Karl Möller, *A Prophet in Debate: The Rhetoric of Persuasion in the Book of Amos* [JSOTSup 372; Sheffield: Sheffield Academic Press, 2003], 43). For Möller, Greco-Roman rhetorical categories provide a useful means of interpreting the book of Amos, regardless of the fact that such categories were not indigenous to Amos' cultural context.

[113] Anders Eriksson, "Enthymemes in Pauline Argumentation: Reading between the Lines in 1 Corinthians," in *Rhetorical Argumentation in Biblical Texts: Essays from the Lund 2000 Conference* (ed. Anders Eriksson et al.; Emory Studies in Early Christianity 8; Harrisburg, Pa.: Trinity Press International, 2002), 246.

[114] But note Wuellner's critique of SRI as expounded by Robbins in his 1984 book, *Jesus the Teacher*. "... the sociorhetorical method proposed by V. Robbins ... ends up in the service of the historian's interest in social description" ("Where is Rhetorical Criticism Taking Us?" 454).

[115] Robbins, "Socio-Rhetorical Criticism," 164-65.

[116] In this view, Mitchell's work can be seen primarily as an intertextual investigation.

[117] The inner workings of a text is called "inner texture" in SRI (see below). See e.g. Robbins, *Exploring*, 21-29 where, in Robbins's discussion of the argumentative texture and pattern in an inner textual analysis, his examples derive mainly from ancient rhetoric. But also note that he ends the first paragraph of this subsection with this statement: "Rhetorical theory, both ancient and modern, presents extensive analytical tools for analyzing the argumentative texture of texts" (p. 21). Something similar is found in *Tapestry*, 58-64; see pp. 59 and 61 for Robbins's treatment of modern rhetorical theory.

of texts thus allows the interpreter consciously to treat rhetoric as *both* a tool for analysis *and* an object of historical study as well.

The classic texts of SRI remain Robbins's dual works published in 1996, *The Tapestry of Early Christian Discourse* and *Exploring the Texture of Texts*.[118] These twin volumes programmatically lay out an interpretive analytic that explores multiple textures found in texts. Using the image of examining a thick tapestry, Robbins argues that "when we explore a text from different angles, we see multiple textures of meanings, convictions, beliefs, values, emotions and actions. These textures within texts are a result of webs or networks of meanings and meaning effects that humans create."[119] The textures analyzed within SRI are: inner texture, intertexture, social and cultural texture, ideological texture, and in *Exploring the Texture of Texts*, sacred texture. Although not often recognized by its critics, SRI does *not* require an exegete to "run through the paces," as it were, of all the different textures. Rather it offers a means whereby an "interactive analysis" of texts can take place "within multiple arenas of texture."[120] Depending upon the exegetical project, different textures will be of greater or lesser importance.

According to Robbins, "Inner textual analysis focuses on words as tools for communication."[121] In this texture the exegete stays within the boundaries of the text under consideration and examines what the language of the text is doing. Intertexture moves beyond the boundaries of the language and structure of the text itself and recognizes that "texts stand in dynamic relation to phenomena outside of them."[122] Intertexture describes the various ways in which any given text utilizes, changes, or amplifies other texts (oral or written), cultural/social knowledge, and/or historical events. Social and cultural texture explores, among other things, the "social and cultural systems presupposed in the text" and "reveal[s] the potential of the text to encourage its readers to adopt certain social and cultural locations and orientations rather than others."[123] Ideological texture concerns both how the message of the text is evoked and received. The main issues an interpreter sees through this texture include "the social, cultural, and individual location and perspective of writers and readers."[124] Sacred texture is

---

[118] *Tapestry* provides the reader with a more detailed exposition of the theoretical underpinnings of SRI whereas *Exploring* is more of a "how-to" volume, which is evident in the latter's subtitle: *A Guide to Socio-Rhetorical Interpretation*.
[119] Robbins, *Tapestry*, 18; *Exploring*, 2-3.
[120] Robbins, *Tapestry*, 237; *Exploring*, 5-6.
[121] Robbins, *Exploring*, 7; *Tapestry*, 46.
[122] Robbins, *Tapestry*, 32, 96; *Exploring*, 40.
[123] Robbins, *Exploring*, 71, 72.
[124] Robbins, *Exploring*, 95; *Tapestry*, 36-40.

"embedded deeply" within the other four textures and enables the interpreter to analyze "the nature of the relation between human life and the divine."¹²⁵ When exploring each of these textures, the exegete strives to uncover various modes of meaning embedded in texts. Ideally, the results of analyzing several textures are put into dialogue and a thick narrative of interpretation is produced, or, to use the language of conceptual integration theory, various textural inputs are blended in the final exegesis so that interpretive emergent structure is produced that creates new insight into the text.

As a dynamic interpretive analytic, SRI grows and develops over time. As noted above, currently Robbins is moving the classical socio-rhetorical textured approach forward by incorporating the insights of the cognitive science of religion into his theoretical explication of SRI.¹²⁶ This newer stage in the development of SRI is described in Robbins's monumental two-volume work, *The Invention of Christian Discourse,* and will guide the forthcoming volumes of the Rhetoric of Religious Antiquity Series. Because socio-rhetorical interpreters are interested in exegetical practices that take human embodiment seriously, the tools of the cognitive science of religion, especially those of conceptual blending, are extremely productive when used within a socio-rhetorical framework. Taking human embodiment in geophysical space seriously demands, according to Robbins, a mode of analysis wherein "it is necessary not only to interpret reasoning in argumentation but also to interpret picturing of people and the environments in which they are interacting." Robbins creates two new terms to differentiate the analysis of rhetorical reasoning from the analysis of the graphic images rhetorical descriptions evoke. All too often, according to Robbins, exegesis re-inscribes a mind-body dualism that focuses predominantly on a text's rhetorical reasoning, that is, on its *rhetology*. Using the insights of the cognitive science of religion, Robbins pushes interpreters to take the rhetorical power of graphic picturing just as seriously. Robbins refers to this "graphic picturing in rhetorical description" as a text's *rhetography*.¹²⁷ As Robbins reminds exegetes, "the picture an argument evokes (its rhetography) is regularly as important as the reasoning it presents (its rhetology)."¹²⁸ The importance of rhetography for this newer stage of SRI's

---

¹²⁵ Robbins, *Exploring*, 130, 120.

¹²⁶ He is also incorporating insights from critical spatiality theory, but I do not engage this is my own work. See Bart B. Bruehler, *A Public and Political Christ: The Social-Spatial Characteristics of Luke 18:35–19:43 and the Gospel as a Whole in Its Ancient Context* (Princeton Theological Monographs 157; Eugene, Or.: Pickwick, 2011) for developments of critical spatiality within biblical studies.

¹²⁷ Robbins, "Rhetography"; idem, *Invention*, 1:16, xxvii.

¹²⁸ Robbins, *Invention*, 1:17. See Damasio, *Descartes' Error*, 96, 197-98; idem, *The Feeling of What Happens*, 318-19.

development cannot be overestimated and it is in analyses of the images evoked by the rhetoric of texts that the indebtedness to and usefulness of cognitive science in a socio-rhetorical framework is most prominently demonstrated.[129] Attending to the rhetography of a text provides exegetical space in which to analyze images evoked by texts that frequently function as somatic markers, as will be demonstrated in the analysis of 1 Cor 6:12–7:7 below.

Far from supplanting the classical textured approach, the newer emphasis on rhetography in SRI demonstrates how the use of cognitive science moves socio-rhetorical analysis forward. The concern about the images evoked by a text is already apparent in Robbins's description of sensory-aesthetic texture, a sub-category of inner texture. Images in texts, according to Robbins, will involve people's imaginations as the rhetoric of the text unfolds.[130] The images attended to via an analysis of a text's sensory-aesthetic textures may evoke any of the senses, as Damasio reminds scholars, "The word image does not refer to 'visual' images alone, and there is nothing static about images either."[131] While rhetography is certainly not a static element in texts, it does tend to focus on the visual in its analysis of mental picturing. According to Robbins, "Rhetography refers to the graphic images people create in their minds as a result of the visual texture of the text."[132] For SRI, accurately analyzing the rhetography of a text provides the interpreter with "the primary cultural clue to the logic of the discourse."[133] Rather than simply "mere" aesthetics, attending to the mental images a text creates helps the exegete understand what kinds of background information its rhetoric could evoke in meaning aware hearers/readers. SRI provides a critical space in which to take *both* the rhetography and rhetology of texts seriously and since arguments in NT documents rely more or less on some combination of these, such a critical space allows for newer exegetical insight.[134] For example, as I will discuss in my exegesis of 1 Cor 6:12–7:7, in the first half of Paul's argument (6:12-20) he relies heavily on rhetography to *show* the Corinthians *why* πορ-νεία is the worst of all bodily sins. Paul then moves, in the second half of his argument (7:1-7), to rely more on rhetology in order to *explain* to the Corinthians *how* πορνεία can be best avoided. To be sure, there

---

[129] See Robbins, "Rhetography," 81-106; idem, *Invention*, 1:85-88 for a discussion of the lack of vocabulary for analyzing visual texture outside of SRI.
[130] Robbins, *Tapestry*, 65.
[131] Damasio, *The Feeling of What Happens*, 318.
[132] Robbins, "Rhetography," 81.
[133] Robbins, "Rhetography," 100.
[134] For a discussion of the power effective blending of rhetology and rhetography provides early Christian discourse, see Robbins, *Invention*, 1:88.

are rhetological elements in 6:12-20 as well as rhetographical elements in 7:1-7, but SRI provides the tools that allow for an analytical discussion of both elements of textual discourse.

The study of the specific ways in which NT texts blend rhetography with rhetology has led Robbins to develop further a socio-rhetorical analytical category that emerged in 1996 known as a *rhetorolect*, short for "rhetorical dialect," which is defined as a "form of language variety or discourse identifiable on the basis of a distinctive configuration of themes, topics, reasonings, and argumentations."[135] In a later essay (2008) Robbins notes how this definition presupposes that early Christians created discourse that was "understandable" to the larger Greek and Roman culture of the eastern Mediterranean. Yet this early Christian discourse, while understandable, was also "highly unusual, in the manner in which a dialect is unusual."[136] This newer focus on rhetorolects demonstrates how SRI has developed into an interpretive analytic that analyzes discourse through frames and prototypes, rather than the more traditional biblical studies categories of form and genre. As discussed above, frames provide a way for meaning aware hearers/readers to contextualize the verbal cues language provides and thus allows for the production of meaning by human subjects. Rhetorolects function broadly as cultural frames that provide the necessary background information for hearers/readers to understand the picturing and reasoning evoked by discourse. Relying on the work of Seana Coulson and Charles Fillmore, Robbins understands frames to be "'any system of concepts related in such a way that to understand any one concept it is necessary to understand the entire system; introducing any one concept results in all of them becoming available.'"[137]

Rhetorolects, according to Robbins, are "cultural-religious frames that introduce multiple networks of thinking, reasoning, and acting that were alive and dynamic in early Christian thought, language, and practice."[138] While Coulson, following Fillmore, uses the term "frame" to denote a wide array of phenomena, Robbins correlates rhetorolects most closely with Idealized Cognitive Models (ICM) as described by

---

[135] Robbins, "Dialectical Nature," 356. Note that Robbins developed the term "rhetorolect" in the same year that *Tapestry* and *Exploring* were published. See Robbins, *Invention*, 1:xxvii-xxviii.

[136] Robbins, "Rhetography," 85; see idem, *Invention*, 1:78-81.

[137] Robbins, *Invention*, 1:100 citing Miriam R.L. Petruck, "Frame Semantics," in *Handbook of Pragmatics: Manual* (ed. J. Verschueren, J.-O. Östman, J. Bloomaert, and C. Bulcan; Philadelphia: J. Benjamins, 1997), 1.

[138] Robbins, "Rhetography," 99-100.

George Lakoff.[139] More specifically, Robbins suggests that rhetorolects, with their "distinctive configuration," most resemble what Lakoff refers to as "cluster ICMs." Cluster ICMs act as Gestalts in which the whole is conceptually easier to grasp than the parts. Like cluster ICMs, rhetorolects

> appear to contain clusters of topoi related to networks of meanings that configure first century Christian discourse in ways that are, at one and the same time, linked to multiple meaning networks in Mediterranean culture and distinctive of people with particular experiences in particular places and spaces in the Mediterranean world.[140]

For Robbins, cultural frames, ICMs, and rhetorolects are different ways of labeling similar conceptual phenomena.[141] To be sure, Coulson, Lakoff, and Robbins all have their own, somewhat idiosyncratic, intellectual enterprises, but it is important to note that these different cognitive projects can fruitfully be put in conversation with, and thus help support, one another.

Research among socio-rhetorical interpreters since the mid-1990s has led to the conclusion that, in the first century, "six rhetorolects functioned as prototypical modes of discourse that assisted early Christians in their energetic work of creating dynamic, adaptable, and persuasive modes of discourse within Mediterranean society and culture."[142] To be sure, these six modes of discourse do not exhaust early Christian discursive creativity, but rather reflect those that Robbins and other socio-rhetorical interpreters have documented, based on available data, in the first century of Christian rhetorical development.[143] Although the terminology for these six cultural frames has developed since their first exposition in 1996, socio-rhetorical interpreters now use the following terms for the six rhetorolects documented in the NT: wisdom, prophetic, apocalyptic, precreation, priestly, and miracle.[144] While each of these rhetorolects specifically moves Christian storylines forward, they are, as noted above, dialect variations

---

[139] Coulson includes ICMs in her understanding of "frame" (*Semantic Leaps*, 20 note); Robbins, *Invention*, 1:104. See George Lakoff, *Women, Fire, and Dangerous Things: What Categories Reveal about the Mind* (Chicago: University of Chicago Press, 1987), 68-76.

[140] Robbins, *Invention*, 1:119; see Lakoff, *Women, Fire, and Dangerous Things*, 74-76, 203.

[141] Robbins, *Invention*, 1:107.

[142] Robbins, *Invention*, 1:7, 115.

[143] See Robbins, *Invention*, 1:77 where he notes that "the NT writings are a small sample of the earliest ways the earliest Christians used language to communicate their picturing of God's world and to persuade others that their picturing was reasonable and truthful."

[144] Robbins, *Invention*, 1:114.

of larger ancient Mediterranean discourses. Robbins has made a provisional conclusion that there are three main discourses operative in the ancient Mediterranean world of which early Christians rhetorolects are local dialects: mantic discourses (divine communications), philosophical discourses (mental searching), ritual discourses (religious action). Robbins describes prophetic and apocalyptic rhetorlects as localizations of mantic discourses. Wisdom and precreation rhetorolects are Christian expressions of philosophical discourses, while priestly and miracle rhetorolects are Christian dialects for ritual discourses.[145] This typology helps interpreters understand how early Christian discourse was understandable to larger Mediterranean cultures while at the same time representing idiosyncratic expressions of specific belief systems and story-storylines of emerging Christian sub-cultures.

It is important to note, however, that while NT texts, and portions of them, may operate predominantly within one rhetorolect, Robbins explains that each of these modes of discourse regularly pushes outward and into the other modes.[146] The description of rhetorolects in SRI is not a static model since each mode of discourse stands in dynamic relation to the others. Such an understanding of these different types of discourse prevents exegetical myopia. While one rhetorolect tends to dominate a pericope or extended passage, this should not blind the interpreter to other modes of discourse that are being invited into the complex rhetoric of early Christian texts.[147] While these six modes of discourse all have the potential to interpenetrate one another, only three rhetorolects have emerged as generative for an analysis of Paul's argument in 1 Cor 6:12–7:7. Paul's arguments in this pericope are framed predominantly by wisdom rhetorolect that invites apocalyptic and priestly modes of discourse into its rhetoric.

---

[145] Robbins, *Invention*, 1:493-94.

[146] Vernon K. Robbins, "Argumentative Textures in Socio-Rhetorical Interpretation," in *Rhetorical Argumentation in Biblical Texts: Essays from the Lund 2000 Conference* (ed. Anders Eriksson, Thomas H. Olbricht, and Walter Übelacker), 27. For a similar discussion of different modes of discourse interpenetrating one another, see also Roland E. Murphy, *The Tree of Life: An Exploration of Biblical Wisdom Literature* (3rd ed.; Grand Rapids: Eerdmans, 2002), 101: "The sages were concerned in a broad way with (right) living, but they were not ethicists or framers of law. Because human conduct is the common denominator between wisdom and law, it is sometimes difficult to separate the two and to determine influence. ... These difficulties also occur with respect to the social concerns of the prophets."

[147] See Matthew J. Goff, *The Worldly and Heavenly Wisdom of 4QInstruction* (STDJ 50; Leiden: Brill, 2003), 65, where he states concerning wisdom and apocalypticism in 4QInstruction: "It is more important to understand how these traditions are combined than to argue that one should be emphasized at the expense of the other." Although he does not use the language of SRI, Goff's argument here rests on a similar interpretive principle.

Wisdom rhetorolect is not only the predominant frame for 1 Cor 6:12–7:7, but, Robbins argues, for emerging Christian rhetorical culture as well. According to Robbins, "Wisdom rhetorolect provided basic cognitive frames during the first century with which people could negotiate the meanings of other rhetorolects in Mediterranean culture and society." The foundational cognitive nature of wisdom rhetorolect stems from the fact that "people learn basic cognitive frames of wisdom discourse during childhood in the family household."[148] The emphasis in this rhetorolect is on instruction and it typically makes use of household and family imagery.[149] This rhetography is mapped onto God and the world God created. Thus God is the father of the household and the created world, esp. human beings, are members of that household.[150] "Wisdom rhetorolect," Robbins writes, "emphasizes 'fruitfulness' (productivity and reproductivity). The goal of wisdom rhetorolect is to create people who produce good, righteous action, thought, will, and speech with the aid of God's wisdom."[151] Wisdom rhetorolect is didactic in nature. As will become evident in the exegetical chapters below, this rhetorolect evokes cultural expectations of thinking and learning that should ideally lead to action. Wisdom attempts to prompt active fruitfulness through active thinking. Pauline wisdom rhetorolect, in particular, employs paradox to prompt active and critical thinking that should lead to righteous action. In so doing wisdom rhetorolect engages and evokes larger cultural expectations about the role and value of paradoxes within instructional discourse.[152] Moreover, just as every member of an actual household has different abilities and responsibilities, so too does the didactic nature of wisdom rhetorolect recognize that "righteous action" will look different for different people at different stages of life.[153]

Wisdom rhetorolect tends to blend organically with apocalyptic and priestly rhetorolects and this is evident in 1 Cor 6:12–7:7 as well.[154] As John Collins has noted, while both wisdom and apocalyptic texts focus on correct knowledge, a main difference lies in whence true knowledge comes.[155] This can be seen in the typology of Mediterranean dis-

---

[148] Robbins, *Invention*, 1:486-87; see 127.
[149] Thus the father's instruction to his son in Proverbs provides a powerful resource for this rhetorolect. See Goff, *Worldly and Heavenly Wisdom*, 45.
[150] Robbins, *Invention*, 1:129.
[151] Robbins, *Invention*, 1:110.
[152] Robbins, *Invention*, 1:158, 204, 508.
[153] Robbins, *Invention*, 1:129.
[154] Robbins, *Invention*, 1:191.
[155] John J. Collins, "The Sage in the Apocalyptic and Pseudepigraphic Literature," in *Seers, Sibyls and Sages in Hellenistic-Roman Judaism* (Supplements to the Journal for the

course discussed above. Wisdom rhetorolect is a dialect of ancient philosophical discourse in which true knowledge can be uncovered through observation of God's created world and through the teachings of elders. Apocalyptic rhetorolect, on the other hand, is a dialect of ancient mantic discourse in which true knowledge must come from a revelation from God. Much like wisdom, the goal of apocalyptic rhetorolect is to create righteous action among God's people. However, the manner in which it achieves this goal is different from wisdom. Whereas wisdom rhetorolect employs rhetography from households, apocalyptic rhetography tends to evoke imperial might and martial force. However, in apocalyptic rhetorolect the emperor (God) uses his army to eradicate evil and create perfect holiness across space and time. According to Robbins, the "special power of apocalyptic discourse lies in its reconfiguration of all time (past, present, and future) and all space (cosmic, earthly, and of personal bodies) in terms of holy and profane, good and evil." In the binary logic of this rhetorolect God and his angelic army will act to eradicate evil and (re)create a world of goodness.[156]

Like apocalyptic modes of discourse, priestly rhetorolect also evokes holiness and goodness, but again, the focus is different. Priestly rhetorolect is a dialect of broader ancient Mediterranean discourse involving religious ritual and the benefits that accrue to the practitioner (or beneficiary) of such ritual action. Priestly rhetorolect has as its primary focus beneficial exchange between human beings and God. This beneficial exchange often involves language of temple, sacrifice, and purity. Although a focus of this rhetorolect can be sacrificial action on the part of humans that, according to Robbins, "create[s] an environment in which God acts redemptively among humans in the world," oftentimes it is the sacrifice of Jesus the Christ through his death that plays a major role in this mode of discourse, especially in the Pauline literature. The sacrifice of Jesus the Christ forms the specifically Christian rationale for sacrificial action on the part of God's human children.[157]

In 1 Cor 6:12–7:7, Paul employs wisdom rhetorolect as the overarching cultural organizing frame in his discussion of πορνεία, teaching

---

Study of Judaism 54; Leiden: Brill, 1997), 339-50; repr. from *The Sage in Israel and the Ancient Near East* (ed. John G. Gammie and Leo Perdue; Winona Lake, Ind.: Eisenbrauns, 1990), 343-54; idem, "Cosmos and Salvation: Jewish Wisdom and Apocalypticism in the Hellenistic Age," in *Seers, Sybils and Sages in Hellenistic-Roman Judaism* (Supplements to the Journal for the Study of Judaism 54; Leiden: Brill, 1997), 334-36; repr. from *HR*17 (1977). See also Goff, *Worldly and Heavenly Wisdom*, 30-42, 47-51.

[156] Robbins, "Argumentative Texture," 54; idem, "Dialectical Nature," 359; idem, *Invention*, 1:110.

[157] Robbins, *Invention*, 1:112.

his Corinthian "children" (1 Cor 4:15) why it is to be avoided and how to best accomplish this. Tapping the internal logic of wisdom rhetorolect, Paul employs the local frames of freedom and self-mastery in the inauguration of his instruction on sexual comportment (1 Cor 6:12). These *topoi*, and the mode of argumentation in which these are situated, evoke wisdom-cultural resources in meaning-aware hearers/readers. As Paul's argument develops, he invites apocalyptic rhetorolect into his wisdom instruction as a means to describe what the true dangers of πορνεία are. This rhetorolect energizes Paul's wisdom discourse and provides him with more rhetorical tools with which to argue that πορνεία is the worst of all bodily sins. Apocalyptic rhetorolect is evident in 6:13–14 with Paul's description of the destruction and resurrection of the body. Paul increases the rhetorical power of his teaching still further by inviting priestly rhetorolect into various sections of this pericope that discuss holiness, more specifically temples, beneficial exchange, glorification, and prayer (6:15-20; 7:5). By exploring the different cultural and local frames that organize the elements of Paul's teaching as well as blends that Paul's discourse creates with them, I contend that we arrive at a fuller understanding of his teaching on the appropriate sexual use of the Christian body.

While prophetic, precreation, and miracle rhetorolects (the other Christian species of mantic, philosophical, and ritual discourses) do not play a major role in 1 Cor 6:12–7:7, they will be engaged in my discussion of 1 Cor 1–4, chapters which ground Paul's argument in wisdom rhetorolect. In brief, Christian prophetic rhetorolect emphasizes that God calls or chooses certain people or groups for special righteousness. The rhetography of this mode of discourse describes God as a king who sends out his special emissaries to confront leaders acting in ways contrary to the king's demands. These emissaries, therefore, often encounter resistance from the very leaders whose behavior they are sent to correct. When the people listen to the emissaries and obey God they are especially blessed and when they disobey, there are negative consequences.[158] Precreation rhetorolect focuses on the primal activity of God before the founding of the present order. Especially important in this rhetorolect is Christ's relationship to God before creation and the redemptive implications this has for the universe.[159] This rhetorolect falls on the speculative end of the philosophical discourse spectrum with its ruminations about eternity and rhetoric regarding the "nontime" in which God, the eternal emperor, dwells. The rhetography of this rhetorolect is related to that found in both wisdom and apocalyp-

---

[158] Robbins, "Argumentative Texture," 44-45; idem, *Invention*, 1:110.
[159] Robbins, "Argumentative Texture," 59.

tic: the emperor in his eternal household. The special emphasis in precreation rhetorolect is on eternal non-time and its goal, according to Robbins, is "to guide people towards community that is formed through God's love, which reflects the eternal intimacy present in God's precreation household."[160] Miracle rhetorolect is the one that is least important for the exegesis chapters below, but this mode of ritual discourse emphasizes the power of God to do marvelous, extraordinary things for the human beings in need.[161] The locus of need for humans in this rhetorolect tends to be on bodily malfunction and the embodied agent through whom God's restorative powers come. As Robbins notes, "[a] major goal of miracle rhetorolect is to effect extraordinary renewal within people that moves them toward speech and action that produces communities that care for the well-being of one another."[162]

The emergence of six rhetorolects, as well as the emphasis on rhetography (and not solely rhetology), within SRI creates an interpretive environment in which the insights of the conceptual integration theory can produce new exegetical fruit. While the terms and language of both of these interpretive analytics may be new to biblical studies, I hope to demonstrate that they are powerful instruments through which biblical scholars can engage their craft. The tools of conceptual integration theory, when set within the programmatic analysis demanded by SRI, provide a model for unraveling the complex argument Paul makes in teaching the Corinthians to avoid the sexual sin of πορνεία. This model provides a means to analyze how Paul's language prompts for specific meanings which, in turn, prompts the Christian community in Corinth to act in concrete ways to embody Paul's instruction. Such an interpretive analytic avoids a positivist emphasis on authorial intent as well as an overemphasis on actual community reception. Rather, an investigation employing conceptual integration theory within a socio-rhetorical framework proposes possibilities for how Paul's language about πορνεία could make meaning in its cultural context. What Paul actually intended and how the individual members of the community actually received this teaching remain beyond this, and every other, approach.

Conclusion

The constitutive and governing principles of conceptual integration theory as articulated by Fauconnier and Turner provide the basic inter-

---

[160] Robbins, *Invention*, 1:111.
[161] Robbins, "Argumentative Texture," 37-38; see also idem, "Dialectical Nature," 358.
[162] Robbins, *Invention*, 1:111.

pretive architecture I employ when exegeting Paul's argumentative discourse in 1 Cor 6:12–7:7. The insights this analysis yields will be set within the interpretive framework of socio-rhetorical interpretation that includes multiple textures and rhetorolects. This allows me to have a principled means of examining how Paul's discourse in this pericope is meaningful as well as a programmatic exegetical analytic in which to construct a coherent narrative of the results of this examination. Setting conceptual integration theory within, or beside, other interpretive frameworks is not something unique to my project. For example, Todd Oakley, in an extended analysis of a passage from Art Spiegelman's *Maus II: And Here My Troubles Began*, integrates the results he obtains from a study of blending with narratology and argumentation theory. He argues that "Such a study produces a new kind of analysis that is much stronger than each separately."[163] Using conceptual integration theory within a socio-rhetorical framework promises to yield a new kind of analysis of Pauline discourse.

Conceptual integration theory, by examining how language prompts for meaning, holds great promise for biblical exegesis. But more specifically, the theory of conceptual blending has particular usefulness for this project because the Pauline pericope under analysis deals with the topic of sexual comportment. As noted above, cognitive scientists stress that any model of meaning formation must take human embodiment into consideration. Fauconnier and Turner note that, "[h]uman sexual practices are perhaps the epitome of meaningful behavior because they constitute a deeply felt intersection of mental, social, and biological life." They further argue that, "the role of meaning construction and imagination in the elaboration of human sexual practices is phenomenal and has direct, real-world social consequences."[164] I have suggested that conceptual integration theory is a useful tool in general for analyzing biblical discourse, but my focus on Paul's instruction regarding the proper sexual use of the Christian body also means that the subject this study engages reflects a specific topic for which the applicability of conceptual blending is asserted by cognitive scientists themselves.

---

[163] Oakley, "Conceptual Blending," 357.
[164] Fauconnier and Turner, *The Way We Think*, 28. Also of interest to my project is their assertion that "Sexual fantasy, whether or not enacted, is a vast and important area of systematic human cognition that is imaginative but not explained by metaphor or analogy" (35-36).

2

Wisdom

Introduction

The basic premise of my project is that examining Paul's teaching on proper sexual comportment in 6:12–7:7 primarily through the cognitive resources of Jewish wisdom yields exegetical insights regarding how that teaching is conceptually and rhetorically meaningful. Immediately, however, this argument runs up against the problem of definition. The question of what, exactly, is meant by the term "wisdom" has bedeviled scholars. Modern scholarship is not alone in grappling with this conundrum. For example, the first-century Jewish thinker Philo recognizes that wisdom is a slippery category to engage:

> This too we must not fail to know, that wisdom [σοφία] which is the art of arts [τέχνη τεχνῶν] seems to change with its different subject matters, yet shows its true form unchanged to those who have clearness of vision and are not misled by the dense and heavy wrappings which envelop its true substance [ἀληθὲς εἶδος], but descry the form impressed by the art itself (*Ebr.* 88 [Colson & Whitaker, LCL]).

For Philo, wisdom can most basically be described as "the power in the wise man" [ἡ ἐν τῷ σοφῷ δύναμις] (*Ebr.* 91). It is this power that allows one to live a righteous life.

In this chapter I engage the problematic nature of the category wisdom. First I briefly rehearse some major voices of scholarship on wisdom. Building on this foundation I explain my own understanding and use of wisdom rhetorolect and provide a broad, but functional, definition of what I understand wisdom to mean. After establishing this, I then examine Jewish texts that discuss wisdom. I conduct this examination under three rubrics: wisdom and creation, wisdom and law, and wisdom's self-critique. By performing a close reading of these texts I hope to provide a thick description of Jewish resources that will help situate the conceptual categories employed by Paul within a wider cultural web of significance.

What is "Wisdom"?

The use of wisdom as a category for elucidating Pauline texts is not a new idea. Walter T. Wilson undertakes such an investigation in *Love without Pretense*. In this work Wilson analyzes gnomic wisdom in the ancient world and demonstrates how this can profitably be used to examine Rom 12:9-21. "It appears that the sapiential traditions conditioned the thought of the early Christians in numerous and diverse ways, and that these traditions have some bearing on our understanding not only of the theological and ethical aspects of the New Testament writings but of their literary and rhetorical characteristics as well."[1] It is difficult to overestimate the importance of Wilson's study. In his explication of the use of maxims in ancient gnomic wisdom traditions, Jewish and non-Jewish, Wilson provides a means to examine particularly intractable issues surrounding the interpretation of 1 Cor 6:12–7:7. By establishing that "sapiential themes or conventions" may be present in texts not, in themselves, regarded as sapiential,[2] noting that explanations attached to maxims may "limit the maxim's application,"[3] and concluding that "Paul views himself both as a bearer of traditional Jewish moral values and as an ethical role model for the audience,"[4] Wilson's study suggests ways to use wisdom as a category through which exegetes can interpret other examples of Pauline discourse. His findings have an added bonus for the present study as well in that they allow me to relativize the notorious issues surrounding the presence of so-called slogans in 1 Cor 6:12–7:7. Renate Kirchhoff enacts this kind of interpretation for 1 Cor 6:12, although she seems not to be aware of Wilson's work.[5]

---

[1] Walter T. Wilson, *Love without Pretense: Romans 12:9-21 and Hellenistic-Jewish Wisdom Literature* (WUNT 2nd series 46; Tübingen: Mohr Siebeck, 1991), 1. See also Robbins, *Invention*, 1:486.

[2] Wilson, *Love*, 2, 201. See also Giorgio Buccellati, "Wisdom and Not: The Case of Mesopotamia," *JAOS* 101 (1981): 40. See Lindsay Wilson, *Joseph, Wise and Otherwise: The Intersection of Wisdom and Covenant in Genesis 37-50* (Paternoster Biblical Monographs; Carlisle, U.K.: Paternoster, 2004), 30-35 for an overview of methodologies "to argue for the presence (or absence) of 'wisdom-like elements' in non-wisdom texts." He lists four broad categories for accomplishing this: 1. the formal approach (Wilson's study falls under this category); 2. the linguistic approach; 3. the social setting approach; 4. the content approach.

[3] Wilson, *Love without Pretense*, 43.

[4] Wilson, *Love without Pretense*, 207.

[5] See my discussion of Kirchhoff's work in the Introduction. See also Ramsaran, *Liberating Words*, who relies heavily on Wilson's study. In his analysis he maintains that 6:12 and 7:1b contain Corinthian maxims which Paul must refute. The evidence he gives for this is, in my mind, not entirely convincing.

Although his study readily demonstrates the exegetical usefulness of the category of wisdom, Wilson recognizes that its precise definition is more difficult to describe with accuracy, or at least in a way that satisfies everybody. In the first sentence of *Love without Pretense* Wilson follows his introduction of the term wisdom with the following caveat: "however it is to be defined."[6] John J. Collins notes that among the difficulties in defining what scholars mean by "wisdom" is the fact that, in the Hellenistic period at least, "[i]t is clear that wisdom literature is not held together by a single literary genre."[7] In an effort to delineate the term more accurately, James Crenshaw appeals to a literary corpus of Jewish texts that can be identified as wisdom literature: Proverbs, Job, Ecclesiastes, Sirach, and the Wisdom of Solomon.[8] Wilson also uses examples of specific texts as a beginning point for arriving at a functional definition, although his initial list of especially important texts includes the so-called wisdom psalms but not Job.[9] From this beginning point, Wilson suggests that certain "theological, ethical, or literary qualities comparable to these sources" found in other texts allow interpreters to posit sapiential influence.[10] Crenshaw has reservations about projects that he believes cast too wide a net in describing the influence of wisdom on non-sapiential texts, fearing that it will stretch the term into meaninglessness.[11] Yet whatever differences Cren-

---

[6] Wilson, *Love without Pretense*, 1, and on p. 2: "... the terms 'wisdom,' 'sapiential,' and so forth are notoriously difficult to define with precision." See also Gerald T. Sheppard, *Wisdom as a Hermeneutical Construct: A Study in the Sapientializing of the Old Testamant* (BZAW 151; Berlin: De Gruyter; 1980), 3-5. Whereas Wilson's study examines how wisdom traditions are used in a non-wisdom text, Sheppard comes at the question from the opposite end of the spectrum and examines how Jewish wisdom texts, especially Sirach and Baruch, "interpret non-wisdom traditions in terms of wisdom" (159; see also 12-18). For an overview of recent literature on wisdom, see James L. Crenshaw, *Old Testament Wisdom: An Introduction* (rev. ed.; Louisville, Ky.: Westminster John Knox, 1998), 1-3 and the supplements in Murphy, *The Tree of Life*, 191-281.

[7] John J. Collins, *Jewish Wisdom in the Hellenistic Age* (OTL; Louisville, Ky.: Westminster John Knox, 1997), 222. See Rosner, *Paul, Scripture and Ethics*, 40-45. But note a divergent view given by Richard Bauckham, *James: Wisdom of James, Disciple of Jesus* (New Testament Readings; New York: Routledge, 1999), 33: "It is essential to realize that in the later Second Temple period, the types of Jewish literature – such as wisdom paraenesis, law, apocalypse – are distinguished by literary genre and religious function, not by world-view."

[8] Crenshaw, *Wisdom*, 4.

[9] Wilson, *Love without Pretense*, 2. Wilson's list seems geared towards his specific project. Note Fox's assertion in *Proverbs*, 17: "No definition of Wisdom literature will identify precisely which works belong and which do not."

[10] Wilson, *Love without Pretense*, 2.

[11] Crenshaw, *Wisdom*, 30. See Coulson and Oakley, "Blending Basics," 186, and my discussion of conceptual blending in ch. 1, for a similar worry about the power of conceptual blending "accounting for everything, and, hence, explaining nothing."

shaw and Wilson have on this issue, both are agreed that wisdom is a universal phenomenon in human culture.[12]

The universality of wisdom described by Crenshaw and Wilson provides the warrant for looking beyond a bounded corpus of Jewish texts. These Jewish texts function more as a control group that determines what Near Eastern and Hellenistic material should be included, to a greater or lesser extent, within the wisdom constellation.[13] This constellation is characterized, according to Crenshaw, by the "reasoned search for specific ways to ensure personal well-being in everyday life, to make sense of extreme adversity and vexing anomalies, and to transmit this hard-earned knowledge so that successive generations will embody it."[14] While Crenshaw's understanding of wisdom reflects a reliance on Jewish biblical models without, perhaps, taking full account of later Hellenistic permutations,[15] the idea that wisdom deals with practical issues of behavior and that it gives rationales for its instruction in this area is generally agreed upon.[16]

In order to refine a functioning definition of the term "wisdom," it is also necessary to understand that the concern for instruction coupled with rationales for inculcating beneficial behavior is tied primarily to only one aspect of this category. In the literature on the subject, two classes of wisdom emerge: didactic and speculative[17] – although it is

---

[12] Crenshaw, *Wisdom*, 3; Wilson, *Love without Pretense*, 3.
[13] See, e.g., Wilson, *Love without Pretense*, 3, 6, 51-56.
[14] Crenshaw, *Wisdom*, 3.
[15] J.J. Collins, *Jewish Wisdom*, 224.
[16] See, e.g., Bauckham, *James*, 29, 31; J.J. Collins, *Jewish Wisdom*, 222-223; Michael V. Fox, *Proverbs 1-9: A New Translation with Introduction and Commentary* (AB 18A;. New York: Doubleday, 2000), 18; Wilson, *Love without Pretense*, 19, 21, 24, 209-210; Roland E. Murphy, "Wisdom in the OT," *ABD* 6:925-26; Vernon K. Robbins, "A Comparison of Mishnah Gittin 1:1-2:2 and James 2:1-13 from a Perspective of Greco-Roman Rhetorical Elaboration," appendix to *Mishnah and the Social Formation of the Early Rabbinic Guild: A Socio-Rhetorical Approach*, by Jack N. Lightstone (Studies in Christianity and Judaism 11; Waterloo, Ontario: Wilfrid Laurier University Press, 2002), 213-14; idem, "The Present and Future of Rhetorical Analysis," in *The Rhetorical Analysis of Scripture: Essays from the 1995 London Conference* (ed. Stanley E. Porter and Thomas H. Olbricht; JSNTSup 146; Sheffield: Sheffield Academic Press, 1997), 36; idem, "Argumentative Textures," 32; Eckhard J. Schnabel, *Law and Wisdom from Ben Sira to Paul: A Tradition Historical Enquiry into the Relation of Law, Wisdom, and Ethics* (WUNT 2nd series 16; Tübingen: Mohr Siebeck, 1985), 336. Note Roland Murphy's remark: "In a narrow sense, then, one might speak of wisdom only where there is a didactic purpose, where teaching is going on" (*Tree of Life*, 101-102).
[17] See Crenshaw, *Wisdom*, 5; Fox, *Proverbs*, 17-18; Goff, *Worldly and Heavenly Wisdom*, 42; Johann Cook, *The Septuagint of Proverbs – Jewish and/or Hellenistic Proverbs? Concerning the Hellenistic Colouring of LXX Proverbs* (VTSup 69; New York: Brill, 1997), 48 argues that in pre-Socratic Greek thought σοφία tended to have more practical connotations (along with τέχνη and ἔργον) whereas one finds "speculative wisdom" more pre-

perhaps more descriptive to view these classes as two ends of a continuum. It is didactic wisdom that is the focus of my investigation because it is the class of wisdom most related to moral formation,[18] and one of the main themes of this moral formation is the danger of sexual immorality.[19] Instruction with an eye towards ethical behavior is the key for my use of didactic wisdom.[20] In fact, Burton Mack goes so far as to argue that the nearest analog for Hebrew wisdom in the Hellenic world is παιδεία.[21] Speculative, otherwise described as critical or theoretical, wisdom is, as noted by Fox, an "amorphous"[22] class that appears to stem from reflection on the instructions proffered by didactic wisdom and not to provide guidance on practical matters itself.[23] Although these two types of wisdom are often used to distinguish the various wisdom *books*, this distinction is critical for understanding wisdom as a broader hermeneutical category. Casting this distinction in terms of rhetorolects, it is didactic wisdom that provides resources for Christian wisdom rhetorolect. Wisdom rhetorolect is typically concerned with teaching hearers/readers how to live a productive and righteous life. Speculative wisdom, on the other hand, provides resources that generate pre-creation rhetorolect in early Christian discourse. It is didactic wisdom with which I am concerned in this investigation. Speculative wisdom, and Paul's critique of it, does not, for the most part, help interpret the argumentative discourse in 1 Cor 6:12–7:7.[24] Keeping the

---

dominant in Socrates, Plato and Aristotle. See Philo, who notes numerous manifestations of wisdom. Among them he discusses two important avatars of wisdom: its relationship with piety (εὐσέβεια) and holiness (ὁσιότης) and with ethics (ἠθική). When wisdom is concerned with piety and holiness it deals with "the things concerning the one who is" (speculative wisdom) and with ethics, it deals with the moral improvement of humanity (didactic wisdom) (*Ebr.* 91).

[18] On wisdom as moral formation see Crenshaw, *Wisdom*, 3; Murphy, "Wisdom in the OT," 6:925; J.J. Collins, *Between Athens and Jerusalem*, 182; Corrington Streete, *Strange Woman*, 106, 116; Goulder, *Paul* 49; Walter T. Wilson, *The Mysteries of Righteousness: The Literary Composition and Genre of the Sentences of Pseudo-Phocylides* (TSAJ 40; Tübingen: Mohr Siebeck, 1994), 181; also note Robbins, "Argumentative Textures," 31.

[19] See J.J. Collins, *Jewish Wisdom*, 67–71, 114–118, 170, 191; idem, *Athens and Jerusalem*, 157–160; Corrington Streete, *Strange Woman*, ch. 4; Crenshaw, *Wisdom*, 12–15.

[20] Robbins, *Invention*, 1:186; Leo G. Perdue, *Wisdom Literature: A Theological History* (Louisville, Ky.: Westminster John Knox, 2007), 8.

[21] Burton Mack, *Wisdom and the Hebrew Epic: Ben Sira's Hymn of Praise of the Fathers* (CSHJ; Chicago: University of Chicago Press, 1985), 156–59. See Robbins, *Invention*, 1:15.

[22] Fox, *Proverbs*, 17.

[23] Note Johannes Thomas, *Der jüdische Phokylides: Formsgeschichtliche Zugänge zu Pseudo-Phokylides und Vergleich mit der neutestamentlichen Paränese* (NTOA 23; Freiburg, Switzerland/Göttingen: Universitätsverlag/Vandenhoeck & Ruprecht, 1992), 25–28.

[24] However, as I will show in ch. 4, speculative wisdom as expressed in pre-creation rhetorolect is important for Paul's initial discourse on wisdom in 1 Cor 1–4.

distinction of these two classes in mind allows for greater clarity in the exegesis of 1 Cor vis-à-vis Paul and wisdom.

The discussion of wisdom so far has been based on the functional definitions given by Crenshaw and Wilson. This definition tends to rely on analogies to certain Jewish texts and thus, especially for Crenshaw but less so for Wilson, wisdom as a concept is bound up in the idea of wisdom literature. Yet Giorgio Buccellati cautions that "it is clear that we must separate wisdom from literature. The correlation between the two is important, but not exclusive."[25] To be sure, neither Crenshaw nor Wilson maintains that wisdom is to be understood *solely* as a literary category.[26] Crenshaw argues that wisdom "constitutes an attitude toward life, a living tradition, and a literary corpus,"[27] while Wilson prefers to discuss "sapiential qualities" that reside in certain texts and then seek how these qualities might influence other texts, even non-sapiential ones. In line with my discussion of resource zones in the next chapter, Wilson notes that, since direct borrowing is rare, exegetes must examine "more subtle matters of shared theological perspectives and themes as well as common literary and rhetorical practices."[28] Wilson's concern with literary forms and conventions makes sense given his examination of the form and function of gnomic sayings in Rom 12:9-21. While a discussion of literary forms will play a role in interpreting 1 Cor 6:12–7:7, it does not have as central a role in this socio-rhetorical study as it does in Wilson's.[29] I am therefore following Buccellati and will move my use of wisdom a step further away from its identification with literature. As Buccellati notes, "Thus it can be said that wisdom has an internal coherence of its own, but as a dimension or attitude, not as an institution; it is not amorphous, but it

---

[25] Buccellati, "Wisdom and Not," 44. See also Katherine Dell, *"Get Wisdom, Get Insight": An Introduction to Israel's Wisdom Literature* (Macon, Ga.: Smyth & Helwys, 2000), 1: "An important distinction needs to be made between 'wisdom' as an attribute that is God-given and that we should all strive to 'Get'; and wisdom as denoting a genre of material contained in the Bible and other books which have the nature of specialist wisdom writings from the past."

[26] See esp. Crenshaw, *Wisdom*, 9-15, where he notes seven elements: a literary corpus, similar texts in Egypt and Mesopotamia, a special attitude, thematic coherence, a search for propriety, the fear of the Lord, and authority; Wilson, *Love without Pretense*, 2-3, where after giving his functional description he notes: "In practice, of course, such descriptions can be problematic; as we will see below, not the least difficulty is posed by the fact that the Jewish wisdom texts themselves exhibit considerable diversity."

[27] Crenshaw, *Wisdom*, 15.

[28] Wilson, *Love without Pretense*, 3.

[29] See Robbins, *Invention*, 1:98-103.

also is not organized along systematic lines. It is, we might say, a cultural tradition."[30]

Burton Mack also brings in the notion of culture when he notes that "as a mode of discourse" wisdom was much more pervasive in Israelite culture than some might suppose.[31] The understanding of Buccellati and Mack of wisdom as available within a wide cultural tradition allows me to tie the broader scholarly discussion of wisdom into the more recent developments in socio-rhetorical interpretation (SRI) discussed in ch. 1. Robbins, along with Buccellati and Mack, refers to wisdom as a mode of discourse emerging out of and propagating culture. Thus socio-rhetorical interpreters describe wisdom as a cultural frame or rhetorolect. Robbins posits three foci of wisdom in the Hellenistic era: "(1) the relation of the created world to God; (2) the relation of humans to God; and (3) the relation of humans to one another as a result of the relation of God to the created world and to humans."[32] Wisdom rhetorolect functions by arguing about these foci "by means of analogy from human relationships to God" and focuses on how humans behave in relationships in the context of a created order established by God.[33] The connection between wisdom and creation, seen especially in Prov 3:18-20 (cf. Gen 2:9; 3:23) and 8:22-31, has long been noted, although the exact nature of this relationship is a matter of much debate.[34] Wisdom's concern for community and for

---

[30] Buccellati, "Wisdom and Not," 44. See also J.J. Collins, *Jewish Wisdom*, 1; Schnabel, *Law and Wisdom*, 6; Robbins, *Invention*, 1:131: "When early Christianity emerged during the first century CE, it participated vigorously in a cultural environment in which wisdom discourse was pervasively present and highly valued."

[31] Mack, *Wisdom and the Hebrew Epic*, 141, where he also notes: "To speak of a mode of wisdom discourse is, however, already to delimit the range of reference to the term itself."

[32] Robbins, "Argumentative Textures," 31; see also idem, "Dialectical Nature," 357. These foci are also present in biblical wisdom texts, as Roland Murphy notes in *Tree of Life*: wisdom "deals with daily human experience in the good world created by God" (1). "Wisdom recognizes a dynamic relationship between humans and their environment. ... The sages analyzed the environment – the created world and its inhabitants – for signs and conclusions. ... The autonomy of creation is recognized for what it can teach humans about themselves, about God's creation, and even about God's own self" (113). Leo G. Perdue, *Wisdom and Creation: The Theology of Wisdom Literature* (Nashville: Abingdon, 1994), 35, suggests that "creation is truly the 'center' of wisdom theology, meaning that creation integrates all other dimensions of God-talk as well as anthropology, community, ethics, epistemology (both reason and revelation), and society."

[33] Robbins, "Argumentative Textures," 31.

[34] See esp. Peter Doll, *Menschenschöpfung und Weltschöpfung in der alttestamentlichen Weisheit* (SBS 177; Stuttgart: Katholisches Bibelwerk, 1985); Roland E. Murphy, "Wisdom and Creation," *JBL* 104 (1985): 3-11; idem, "Wisdom in the OT," 6:924-25; J.J. Collins, *Jewish Wisdom*, 3; Kirchhoff, *Sünde*, 79-80; Perdue, *Wisdom and Creation*; Schnabel, *Law and Wisdom*, 16-20, 103-106, 130-31, 256-57, 318-21. But note Crenshaw's qualified dissent, *Wisdom*, 12, 198-200.

individuals' relationship to God has also been discussed in scholarship. Leo Perdue argues that the stereotypical view of wisdom as secular and individualistic simply does not hold up under scrutiny. Rather, wisdom traditions represent an integral dimension of Israel's religious understanding[35] while they also provide guidance in social interactions with an eye toward what would be most beneficial for individual and community alike.[36] The world, created good and productive, sets the stage for the human struggle to lead lives of right relationships informed by "the fear of the Lord."[37] While wisdom rhetorolect found in Christian texts is not necessarily tied to specific literary models, it does actively incorporate Jewish as well as non-Jewish Hellenistic moral traditions into its elaboration of these three themes or foci and their implications for ethical behavior. Recent developments in SRI, then, provide a means to examine how Paul's argument in 1 Cor 6:12–7:7 is meaningful given cross-cultural wisdom traditions.[38]

The problem of definition still is not yet solved, but some general parameters have been established which guide this investigation.[39] Robbins's description of wisdom rhetorolect as sketched in ch. 1 establishes the general characteristics for how I will use the term "wisdom" in my exegesis of 1 Cor 6:12–7:7. Since my focus is on didactic wisdom, in this book I understand the term to mean a mode of discourse that can be described as reasoned instruction, delivered to discerning and active autonomous subjects, that deals with "the concrete, how and when and why certain actions are to be performed and certain insights appropriated"[40] in the context of the lived interrelationship among creation, God, and human community. Wisdom as rhetorolect, then, focuses on how discourse prompts the retrieval of cultural cognitive resources to create meaning that leads to productive action.

As noted, in this project I understand wisdom as a rhetorolect, which is a "form of language variety or discourse identifiable on the

---

[35] See also Murphy, *Tree of Life*; idem, "Wisdom and Creation."

[36] Perdue, *Wisdom and Creation*, 46. See also Crenshaw, *Wisdom*, 14: "A union of religion and ethics characterized ancient wisdom."

[37] Robbins, *Invention*, 1:121.

[38] Note Leo G. Perdue, "The Social Character of Paraenesis and Paraenetic Literature," *Semeia* 50 (1980): 5: "The paraenetic literature of Judaism and early Christianity drew heavily from two major cultural spheres: the ancient Near East (especially Israelite and Jewish wisdom influenced by the sages of Egypt and Mesopotamia) and Graeco-Roman civilization (notably the moral philosophers)." While in this chapter and next I focus on Jewish resources, in my exegesis chapter (ch. 6) I bring in Hellenistic-Roman resources where they provide a means to understand Paul's teaching.

[39] This is a problem that most every treatment of wisdom wrestles with and recognizes. See esp. J.J. Collins, *Jewish Wisdom*, 1.

[40] Murphy, *Tree of Life*, 113; Robbins, *Invention*, 1:186.

basis of a distinctive configuration of themes, topics, reasonings, and argumentations."[41] Although wisdom is understood as a mode of discourse, this is not to deny that the ways of being envisioned by and enacted via this discourse can be fruitfully described in multiple ways. Following a tradition found among the Greeks as well as Jews, wisdom can be personified, which is most clearly seen in the figure of woman wisdom in Proverbs 1–9.[42] Likewise traditions that produce and nurture this type of discourse can be referred to as "wisdom traditions" and the specific books, especially within Judaism, that grow out of this tradition can be grouped together as belonging to a "wisdom genre." However wisdom is described – as a mode of thinking, as personified as a woman, as a tradition, as a genre – it is important to remember that all these different permutations relate back to the primary referent: wisdom as an identifiable mode of discourse.

Jewish Wisdom Discourse

Wisdom in the Jewish resources is a complex discourse that deals with multiple issues.[43] I do not intend to tease out the totality of wisdom's concern in this section, but rather I engage Jewish wisdom discourse in order to illustrate three main themes. The first grows out of the theoretical discussion of wisdom above and has to do with wisdom's relationship to the created order and, by extension, to God. While it is speculative wisdom that concerns itself with this matter in and of itself,[44] since my focus is on didactic wisdom, I concentrate on the generative nature of wisdom's instruction that allows one to live a productive life (materially as well as morally) in God's creation. The second theme concerns wisdom's relationship to the law and to the commandments of God and of the father, who in many ways functions as God's proxy in the wisdom literature.[45] The third and final theme

---

[41] Robbins, "The Dialectical Nature of Early Christian Discourse," 356.

[42] In much scholarship, when the abstract notion of wisdom is personified it is signified by capitalizing the initial letter as in a proper name: Wisdom. Because I believe this practice has the effect of losing sight of the poetic (as opposed to hypostatic) nature of much of this personification and because I want to remind the reader that the personification is related to a mode of discourse, I do not follow this practice. See J.J. Collins, "Cosmos and Salvation," 326: "In Hebrew tradition, personified wisdom represents an intermediary stage between mythology and logic."

[43] Citing von Rad, J.J. Collins, "Cosmos and Salvation," 317, notes "the encyclopedic interests of wisdom."

[44] See e.g. 4 Macc 1:16.

[45] See Murphy, *Tree of Life*, 101: "The sages were concerned in a broad way with (right) living, but they were not ethicists or framers of law. Because human conduct is the common denominator between wisdom and law, it is sometimes difficult to separate the

revolves around the ability, and necessity, of wisdom discourse to critique itself and those who believe they are wise. A close reading of the Jewish texts reveals a concerted effort to determine how wisdom can be achieved and enacted. These texts also take pains to differentiate between those who are actually wise and those who only believe they possess this trait. These issues will help provide a framework for Chapters 4–7, in which Paul's arguments in 1 Cor will be read as participating in a mode of Jewish wisdom discourse in a Hellenistic setting.

Wisdom and Creation: Generative Righteousness

In the creation account of Genesis 2–4, the relationship of humans to knowledge is not a positive one. In 2:16 God tells the first human that he may eat of any tree in the garden,[46] but he is prohibited from eating from the tree of the knowledge of good and evil [ξύλον τοῦ γινώσκειν καλὸν καὶ πονηρόν] in 2:17 (cf. 2:9). The penalty for violating this command is death. Despite this prohibitive command, the serpent, first introduced into the narrative in ch. 3, claims that, should the first human couple eat the fruit of the tree, they will be as gods knowing good and evil [γινώσκοντες καλὸν καὶ πονηρόν] (3:5). They eat, their eyes are opened, and the first thing the couple "knows" is that they are nude and so they make clothes for themselves (3:7). The first element of knowledge that the protoplasts receive thus has to do with shame and given that this shame revolves around nudity, the narrative suggests that this is sexual shame.

The dialogue scene between the serpent and the woman leading up to the eating of the forbidden fruit is redolent with images and phrases symbolizing wisdom, at least in ancient Near Eastern cultures. The serpent, the tree, and even the woman offering the fruit of knowledge to the man are all evocative of the gaining of wisdom.[47] The repetition of words related to knowing in Genesis 2–3 also serves to demonstrate that, in the word David Carr, "the forbidden fruit is not sex, but wisdom."[48] This claim is bolstered by the fact that the first act the human couple undertake after recognizing their nudity is not to engage in sexual activity, but to cover up their naked bodies, thus preventing

two and to determine influence… These difficulties also occur with respect to the social concerns of the prophets."

[46] John William Wevers, *Notes on the Greek Text of Genesis* (SBLSCS 35; Atlanta: Scholars Press, 1993), 30: "As in MT the verb (future) is permissive in meaning."

[47] See Phyllis A. Bird, *Missing Persons and Mistaken Identities: Women and Gender in Ancient Israel* (OBT; Minneapolis: Fortress, 1997), 183-85; David M. Carr, *The Erotic Word: Sexuality, Spirituality, and the Bible* (Oxford: Oxford University Press, 2003), 45-46.

[48] Carr, *Erotic Word*, 45.

sexual relations and perhaps also desire. The wisdom gained from the tree complicates the relationship between the sexes, a topic discussed in more length in the next chapter, however the most dire result of this illicit gain in knowledge is the couple's banishment from the garden due to God's fear that the couple, who now possess knowledge such as God has, will eat from the tree of life [ξύλον τῆς ζωῆς] and live forever (3:22).

In this account of creation several elements are worthy of note. First, God does not desire that human beings gain the knowledge of good and evil. The wisdom of human beings seems antithetical to God's intended plan for the created couple.[49] Second, though related to the first point, the first command God gives in this narrative is the prohibition of eating from the tree of knowledge of good and evil (2:16-17; 3:1-3, 11). Again, the human acquisition of wisdom is antithetical to the commandment of God. Third, the acquisition of knowledge results in the human couple being denied the fruit of the tree of life and banished from the garden. David Carr suggests that this creation story, although featuring "legal genres like law, disobedience, interrogation, and pronouncement of punishment," is, additionally, a narrative of human maturation. Although the story appears etiological, it is actually describing the complicated situation in which human beings always already find themselves.[50]

There is no going back to the garden, thus humans have to learn to make their way in the world. This helps explain why a wisdom tradition was able to flourish in Jewish thinking. The wisdom tradition offers human beings a means to live in the world outside of the garden by employing a wisdom that is in line with the commands of God. Acquiring wisdom in the first place violated the command of God, but now wisdom is to be used as a means of navigating the complexities of life while trying to follow what God intends for humanity. Since human beings do possess the knowledge of good and evil, it is incumbent upon them to choose right action. However, this Genesis story also reminds Jewish tradition that human wisdom itself is problematic.[51] This reminder is crucial in understanding how Paul creates his own Christian wisdom discourse.

Despite the initial problem human wisdom and knowledge caused in the garden, early on in Israel's remembered past possession of these

---

[49] Carr, *Erotic Word*, 45 notes: "'Knowledge of good and evil' is a phrase often used to describe wisdom." See Goff, *Worldly and Heavenly Wisdom*, 62-63.

[50] Carr, *Erotic Word*, 46.

[51] Robbins, *Invention*, 1:146-47.

traits was recognized as essential for the leaders of God's people.[52] Moses, noting that the number of God's people was increasing beyond what he himself could directly regulate, had the tribes choose leaders from among themselves who were "wise and knowledgeable and understanding" [σοφοὺς καὶ ἐπιστήμονας καὶ συνετούς] (Deut 1:13). But it is in the person of Israel's second king that these gifts, according to tradition, are most fully expressed.[53] Solomon's gifts of wisdom and understanding are described in 3 Kingdoms:

> And the Lord gave to Solomon understanding [φρόνησιν] and exceedingly much wisdom [σοφίαν] and largeness of heart as sand along the sea, and Solomon increased greatly beyond the understanding of all the ancient people and beyond the wise men [φρονίμους] of Egypt and became wise [ἐσοφίσατο] beyond all other people ... And all peoples were arriving to hear the wisdom [σοφίας] of Solomon, and he received gifts from all the kings of the earth, as many as heard his wisdom [σοφίας] (3 Kgdms 5:9-11α, 14; cf. 10:23-25).[54]

Solomon's great wisdom is a gift from God, but one for which he had the good sense to ask. Solomon asks God for help in ruling God's people in order to be able "to perceive between good and evil" [τοῦ συνίειν ἀνὰ μέσον ἀγαθοῦ καὶ κακοῦ] (3 Kgdms 3:9). It is thus no surprise that it is to this wise king that God gives permission to build God's house (2 Kgdms 7:1-13; 3 Kgdms 5:15-19).[55] Yet, as will be explored in the next chapter, Solomon's reign will be marred by a stunning lack of obedience to God. Although Solomon's wisdom is praised worldwide, his failure to follow the commands of God regarding marriage and worship will have painful political consequences for the kingdom of Israel. Although his name is attached to three books of the wisdom corpus (Proverbs, Ecclesiastes, and Wisdom of Solomon), his wisdom does not prevent him from disobeying God's commandments.[56] It is Solomon's famed wisdom coupled with his equally famous sexual/religious sins (3 Kgdms 11:1-4) that reverberate throughout the wisdom tradition and, I would argue, serve as a tem-

---

[52] For an introduction to "cultural memory," see Philip R. Davies, *Memories of Ancient Israel: An Introduction to Biblical History – Ancient and Modern* (Louisville, Ky.: Westminster John Knox, 2008), 105-23, 175-78.

[53] For a discussion of "Solomon as Sage Par Excellence," see Crenshaw, *Wisdom*, 35-54; see also Gale A. Yee, *Poor Banished Children of Eve: Woman as Evil in the Hebrew Bible* (Minneapolis: Fortress, 2003), 147.

[54] See Rahlf's LXX additions 2:35a-o; 2:46a-l.

[55] Note the intersection of wisdom and priestly concerns.

[56] Solomon's name is, of course, also connected to the Song of Songs. The Song's relation to wisdom is contested. See Carey Ellen Walsh, *Exquisite Desire: Religion, the Erotic, and the Song of Songs* (Minneapolis: Fortress, 2000).

plate for a story line that warns against the dangers of sexual misconduct – dangers to which even the wisest king in the world succumbed.

The Proverbs attributed to Solomon (Prov 1:1) connect wisdom to creation in two ways. First, Proverbs places wisdom at the beginning of the world as the agent through which God creates (8:22-31). God sets up the earth "by wisdom" [τῇ σοφίᾳ], the heavens "by understanding" [ἐν φρονήσει], and the abyss is broken up "by knowledge" [ἐν αἰσθήσει] (3:19-20). Wisdom, and those elements within its semantic range, has a crucial, generative role to play in the foundation of the world. It is this function of wisdom that will produce much speculation in later Jewish thought about the possible hypostatic qualities of the figure "wisdom" and that will, as noted, provide resources for Christian pre-creation rhetorolect.

Second, in addition to being an agent of creation at the beginning, wisdom continues to generate life. Although the first human couple were thrown out of the garden in an attempt to prevent them from eating from the tree of life in the creation account of Genesis, Prov 3:18 declares that this tree is no longer located in some mythical garden to which humans do not have access. Rather wisdom herself is a tree of life [ξύλον ζωῆς].[57] Although, in Proverbs, this tree does not allow one to live forever (Gen 3:22), it does give the one who possesses her "length of life" [μῆκος βίου] and "years of life" [ἔτη ζωῆς] (Prov 3:16). While the life-giving power of wisdom can be seen in cognitive activity (15:24; 16:22), it is also displayed through wise speech. That this is a popular *topos* of the sages is demonstrated by the wealth of metaphors used to laud this gift, which even go as far as identifying wise speech with the tree of life itself [δένδρον ζωῆς] (15:4).[58] Additionally, the image of the tree of life, as well as other descriptors of generative power, is used throughout Proverbs to describe right action. Using a seed metaphor, Prov 11:30 teaches that the tree of life [δένδρον ζωῆς] grows out of the "fruit of righteousness." This idea is also found in the couplet of 10:16, where the works of the righteous create life, whereas "the fruit" of the impious creates sin. Wisdom, according to the teaching found in Proverbs, helped to create the liv-

---

[57] See Robbins, *Invention*, 1:145.

[58] For a detailed study of the use of metaphor in MT Proverbs relating to wise speech, see William P. Brown, "The Didactic Power of Metaphor in the Aphoristic Sayings of Proverbs," *JSOT* 29 (2004): 133-54. See esp. p. 153: "In the Solomonic collection, the 'fruit of the mouth' finds its place on 'the tree of life' within an Edenic world of gushing streams and honeycombs that populate the landscape of appropriate discourse." In contrast, notice that "destruction will cover the mouth of the impious" (Prov 10:11).

ing world and continues to teach individuals how to lead a generative, fruitful life of righteousness.[59]

The book of Sirach also stresses the importance of the lessons one can learn from creation. Wisdom's role in creation, while acknowledged (24:1-9), is not paramount for Ben Sira. Rather, creation is used to stress the power of God (17:10; 18:1-6; 42:15-43:33). These are not mutually exclusive, however, since in Sirach part of God's glory is that God alone possesses wisdom, who herself was created before all things (1:1-2).[60] In his retelling of the story of the immortal God (18:1) of creation, Ben Sira reconfigures the role of God in acquisition of human knowledge.[61] Whereas the creation story of Gen 2–4 suggests that God impeded this acquisition through God's prohibitive command (Gen 2:17), Ben Sira teaches that it was God who filled the human beings whom he created (17:1) with "knowledge of understanding" [ἐπιστήμην συνέσεως] and who showed them "good and evil" [ἀγαθὰ καὶ κακά] (17:7). For Ben Sira, the human ability to think [διανοεῖσθαι] (17:6) was part of God's plan from the beginning. By retelling the creation story so that human wisdom and the ability to discern good from evil are part of the divine plan, Ben Sira is able to declare without contradiction: "For the Lord made all things and to the pious he has given wisdom" [σοφίαν] (43:33). Human wisdom in Sirach is thus part of the original created order of things.

Although not as extensive as in Proverbs, Sirach also uses language that brings together wisdom and tree imagery. Recalling the understanding found in Proverbs, Sirach teaches that "The beginning of wisdom is to fear the Lord" (1:14).[62] Although not explicitly naming wisdom as the tree of life, Ben Sira does make use of various elements of this metaphor. "The root of wisdom is to fear the Lord, and her branches [are] length of days" (1:20).[63] Leaving the tree imagery behind, the sage continues the theme of wisdom as life giving by noting that "The one who loves her, loves life" (4:12). More directly refer-

---

[59] See Perdue, *Wisdom Literature*, 37.

[60] Cf. Sir 15:18: "For great [πολλή] [is the] wisdom of the Lord." For more on the connection between wisdom and creation in Sirach, see Perdue, *Wisdom Literature*, 236-56.

[61] On reconfiguration, see Robbins, *Tapestry*, 107.

[62] See Prov 1:7, 9:10; 15:33; 22:4; Sir 1:11-30; 19:20; 21:11; 40:27. See also Alexander A. Di Lella, "Fear of the Lord as Wisdom: Ben Sira 1,11-30," in *The Book of Ben Sira in Modern Research: Proceedings of the First International Ben Sira Conference 28-31 July 1996 Soesterberg, Netherlands* (ed. Pancratius C. Beentjes; BZAW 255; Berlin: de Gruyter, 1997), 113-33. Di Lella notes: "Fear of the Lord forms the basis of biblical faith; see, e.g., Exod 14:31; Deut 6:2; 10:12, 17:19; 31:12, 13; Josh 24:14; 1 Sam 12:14; Prov 14:2; Ps 66:11; 112:1; 128:1" (p. 120).

[63] See also Sir 1:12.

encing the creation story, Ben Sira likens the fear of the Lord to a "garden of blessing" [παράδεισος εὐλογίας] which is held above other kinds of glory [δόξαν] (40:27).[64] The wisdom that Ben Sira argues is so generative can be learned from the instruction [παιδείαν] of those who are wise (8:8-9). The counsel [βουλή] of the wise man is itself a "fountain of life" (21:13).[65] The role of wisdom in the actual process of creation is more muted in Sirach than it is in Proverbs, yet in his retelling of the creation of humanity Ben Sira locates human wisdom and discernment as one of God's original gifts to his creation. For this reason, perhaps, Ben Sira is able to stress the creative power of wisdom to give life to those who possess her.

The reader notes that the Wisdom of Solomon, to return to a work that tradition has linked to Solomon, is written in a different style and presents a different focus than either Proverbs or Sirach.[66] As Crenshaw writes:

> Here one encounters exquisite rhetoric in a philosophical vein rather than gnomic sayings. In addition, one comes up against reflective poems about personified Wisdom and historical retrospect akin to that in some psalms. The boldness of the author is astonishing, particularly the understanding of wisdom as a reflection of the divine being and the manner in which history becomes intrinsic to his thought, not just a supplement, as in Sirach.[67]

Because of its philosophical focus, the Wisdom of Solomon often pushes its wisdom discourse toward the speculative end of the spectrum thereby providing a resource for early Christian pre-creation discourse.[68] Yet the didactic element of wisdom is not lost. Wisdom is discussed as both life-giving and as something that is related to the way one lives and acts in the world.

While the Wisdom of Solomon is clear that it is God who is the creator, wisdom does have an important relation to the process of crea-

---

[64] See Gen 2:8-10, 15-16; 3:2-3, 8, 23-24.
[65] See Gen 2:6 and Prov 13:14; 14:27 above.
[66] On the similarities between Proverbs and Sirach, see J.J. Collins, *Jewish Wisdom*, 44: "Sirach's model was undoubtedly the book of Proverbs." See also Crenshaw, *Wisdom*, 150; Murphy, *Tree of Life*, 70.
[67] Crenshaw, *Wisdom*, 165.
[68] Wisdom of Solomon is divided by many scholars into three sections: "the 'book of eschatology' in 1:1-6:21, the 'book of wisdom' in 6:22-10:21, and the 'book of history' in 11-19" (J.J. Collins, *Jewish Wisdom*, 179, see esp. n. 9 for a survey of literature on this question). See also Crenshaw, *Wisdom*, 166; Murphy, *Tree of Life*, 86-94; Perdue, *Wisdom Literature*, 294-95. Note that "the book of eschatology" provides a resource for blending wisdom with apocalyptic discourse, whereas "the book of history" provides a resource for blending wisdom with miracle discourse.

tion.⁶⁹ Wisdom is described as the "breath [ἀτμίς] of God's power and a pure emanation [ἀπόρροια] of the glory of the almighty... For she is a reflection of everlasting light and a spotless mirror of the working [ἐνεργείας] of God and an image [εἰκών] of his goodness" (7:25-26).⁷⁰ The description of wisdom as the "breath," "reflection," and "image" echo the creation of the world and humanity presented in Genesis 1 (esp. 1:2-3, 26).⁷¹ Her role in the creation of the world is more explicit in 7:21, where she is described as the "craftswoman [τεχνῖτις] of everything."⁷² In verses such as this the functions of God and wisdom are beginning to blur. While God is described as "a guide even of wisdom" in 7:15 and is the one who is teaching Solomon the secrets of the structure of creation in 7:17-21, in 7:21 Solomon relates that he knows these things because he was taught them by wisdom. Although it is always God who is in control of the process of creation, wisdom is always close at hand – by God's throne (9:4), present when God creates the world (9:9), and the means by which humanity was created (9:2). Furthermore, as she was involved in creation in the past so wisdom is also generative in the present. It is she who teaches humans to produce that which is most profitable: self-control, discernment, righteousness, and courage (8:6).⁷³ Wisdom enables human beings to create offspring of virtue, which is more important in the eyes of the narrator than actual flesh-and-blood children (3:13; 4:1).

In addition to her role in creation and the production of virtue, the instruction in the Wisdom of Solomon takes a radically different turn from the wisdom literature which came before it in that it teaches that "The righteous will live forever" (5:15). In obtaining wisdom one thereby receives immortality (8:13, 17).⁷⁴ This fits with the overall logic of the book in which God is not the originator of death (1:13),

---

[69] Although it is wisdom's relationship to creation that concerns us here, it should be noted that the narrator is more interested in wisdom's role in human history, especially the history of Israel (Wis 10-11, 16-19). See Perdue, *Wisdom Literature*, 319-22.

[70] See J.J. Collins, *Jewish Wisdom*, 199-200 for a discussion of these verses.

[71] J.J. Collins, *Jewish Wisdom*, 199, notes that in Wis 9:1-2 "Word and Wisdom are parallel to each other as God's means of creation." Wis 9:2 reconfigures Gen 1:28.

[72] See 8:1, 6; Crenshaw, *Wisdom*, 168.

[73] See Crenshaw, *Wisdom*, 168.

[74] J.J. Collins, *Jewish Wisdom*, 186, notes that the noun ἀθανασία occurs in Wis 3:4; 4:1; 8:13, 17; 15:3 and that the adjective ἀθάνατος occurs in 1:15. Note that Solomon calls himself mortal [θνητός] in 7:1 referring to his birth as a descendant of the γηγενοῦς πρωτοπλάστου, but in 8:13 he declares that "on account of [wisdom] I will have immortality."

but one who created "in order for all things to be" (1:14).⁷⁵ Reconfiguring Gen 1:26-27, 2:17, and 3:1-24, the narrator in Wis 2:23-24 argues "that God created the human being for incorruptibility [ἐπ' ἀφθαρσίᾳ] and he made him an image of his own eternity, but on account of the devil's jealousy death entered into the world [κόσμον]."⁷⁶ By granting immortality, wisdom allows those who possess her to regain the incorruptibility which God intended for the created order.⁷⁷

Philo echoes the understanding of wisdom's role in creation found in Proverbs when he describes her as older [πρεσβυτέραν] than the created order (*Virt.* 62),⁷⁸ "through which everything came into being" (*Fug.* 109). Elsewhere he describes wisdom as God's "archetypal light" [ἀρχέτυπον φέγγος] of which the created sun is copy (*Migr.* 40). Not only does wisdom serve as an archetype for God's creation of the most glorious element of the created world, but the very fact that God fashioned the universe [κόσμον] is clear proof of God's wisdom (*Migr.* 41). The closeness of wisdom to God in his treatment of creation places Philo's exposition of wisdom within the continuum of Jewish discourse on this topic discussed above.⁷⁹ However, when Philo turns to describing the actual process of creation, he speaks not so much of God's wisdom, but of God's λόγος.

The relation of divine σοφία and λόγος can be seen, and possibly summarized, in Philo's allegorical treatment of the Garden of Eden. The garden itself Philo interprets as "the wisdom of God" (*Leg.* 1.64, 65). The main river that flows out of the garden (Gen 2:10) Philo calls ὁ θεοῦ λόγος as well as "generic virtue" [γενικὴ ἀρετή] (*Leg.* 1.65). Granted, this interpretation is an allegorical one in which Philo is discussing virtue, but it demonstrates Philo's understanding that divine σοφία and λόγος stand in relationship to one another in his thought. This relationship is explained elsewhere with a parental metaphor in which God (*Leg.* 2.49; 3.219) or God's λόγος (*Ebr.* 81) serves as the father and God's σοφία as the mother of all (*Leg.* 2.49; *Det.* 116).⁸⁰ Within this formulation it is typically God's λόγος that serves as the

---

[75] J.J. Collins, *Jewish Wisdom*, 187-88, notes, regarding the assertion that God did not create death, that the "contrast with Ben Sira could not be more stark" citing Sir 17:1 and 41:4.

[76] Cf. Wis 1:16. See J.J. Collins, *Jewish Wisdom*, 185-90.

[77] Again, note how wisdom is discussed in terms more at home in a priestly environment.

[78] Colson, LCL points the reader to Prov 8:22-30. See also *Leg.* 1.43.

[79] See *Sobr.* 55.

[80] See *Ebr.* 81, where God's λόγος is the father and παιδεία, rather than σοφία, is the mother. And see *Fug.* 109, where the divine λόγος has God for its father and Wisdom for its mother.

active creating agent and σοφία that nurtures the offspring these two forces have created.[81]

It is within divine λόγος that creation begins (*Opif.* 20, 24, 36; *Leg.* 1.21).[82] Yet it is important to remember that, for Philo, this beginning of creation is on the level of idea. The first human created in Gen 1:26 is called the image of God not in a bodily sense, but rather in reference to his mind [νοῦς] (*Opif.* 69), which exists in this world of ideas. Philo stresses that this intelligible world is used as a pattern from which to create the material, or perceptible, world (*Opif.* 16, 130).[83] The λόγος of God, which created the "original of mind ... and the original of sense-perception" (*Leg.* 1.21 [Colson & Whitaker, LCL]) in the intelligible world, moves on to create the material world in the second chapter of Genesis.

The relationship of λόγος and σοφία to the human being created within the material world is illustrative for this investigation. Philo notes that the human created in Gen 2:7 is different from the being described as the image of God in Gen 1:26. The human of Gen 2:7 is formed out of two elements, earth and divine breath [πνεῦμα], and is thus made up of mortal and immortal elements (*Opif.* 134-45; *Leg.* 1.31-32). The divine breath that God breathed into the material man's face imbues his soul or mind with divine λόγος (*Opif.* 139, 146). Because this second man lives embodied in the perceptible material world he needs to learn "earthly wisdom" [ἐπίγειον σοφίαν] and "earthly virtue" [ἐπίγειον ἀρετήν], which are, as all things in the perceptible realm, copies of the intelligible archetype (*Leg.* 1.43-45). While the being created in the image of God in Gen 1:26 "possesses virtue instinctively," the human created in the material world stands in need of instruction [διδασκαλίας] or else he "could have no part in wisdom" [φρονήσεως] (*Leg.* 1.92). It is because he lives in the perceptible world within a body that the first material man must be taught in order to possess wisdom and virtue.

As wisdom is the mother of creation, so does she care for and nourish her children (*Det.* 115-17; *Opif.* 158; *Leg.* 3.152). The first material man is placed in the Garden of Eden, which Philo allegorically interprets as virtue (*Leg.* 1.45). I have noted above that Philo also interprets Eden as God's wisdom (*Leg.* 1.64-65). By placing the mind within

---

[81] See J.J. Collins, *Jewish Wisdom*, 199 where he notes that in Wis 9:1-2 "Word and Wisdom are parallel to each other as God's means of creation."

[82] See *Leg.* 1.19, where, playing on the meanings of λόγος, Philo argues that the "book" spoken of in Gen 2:4 refers to God's τέλειος λόγος.

[83] This holds for even the smallest elements of the created world. As Philo teaches, "before grass sprang up in the field, there was in existence invisible grass" (*Opif.* 129 [Colson & Whitaker, LCL]).

wisdom, Adam, whom Philo refers to as the mind, is being trained in the ways of virtue (*Leg.* 1.47).[84] Adam, however, rejected heavenly wisdom [τὴν οὐράνιον σοφίαν] and this rejection severs the bond linking the divine element in human beings (mind) with God and thus humans now wallow with the other "earthly things" [τοῖς γεώδεσι] (*Leg.* 3.252). Humanity thus becomes trapped in the prison of the body, from which one needs to be rescued by God (*Leg.* 3.42). The way that human beings are now able to access this escape from the mortal element of their constitution and access God is by wisdom alone (*Deus.* 160). Even before the first man rebelled, however, he needed instruction in order to know what was wise. Given the general decline in the quality of the human species in Philo's thought the farther each generation is removed from the original (*Opif.* 141) it is a wonder that humans have any understanding of God at all.[85] This sad state of affairs is only remedied through the care of wisdom, through whom humans are able to know that which is wise (*Migr.* 39), and thus wisdom is rightly called the wise man's mother and nurse [μητέρα καὶ τιθήνην] (*Conf.* 49).

Wisdom and Law: Right Action and Purity

Using a seed metaphor, Prov 11:30 teaches that the tree of life [δένδρον ζωῆς] grows out of the "fruit of righteousness." This idea is also found in the couplet of 10:16 where the works of the righteous create life, whereas "the fruit" of the impious creates sin. Shifting metaphors somewhat, the text explains where one can learn how to act with righteousness. This instruction is found in the "law of the wise" and the "commands [πρόσταγματα] of the Lord," both of which are referred to as a "fountain of life" (13:14; 14:27).[86] Already in the book of Proverbs, one notes that wisdom and law are not entirely separate categories.[87]

The idea that the law is communal in nature whereas wisdom discourse focuses on the individual has been challenged by Leo Perdue.[88] Prov 9:12 itself should be enough to overturn this simple dichotomy:

> Son, if you are wise for yourself, you will be wise for your neighbors also; but if you prove to be evil, you will draw up evil alone.

---

[84] Recall that in *Leg.* 1.65 Philo refers to the river flowing out of Eden as "generic virtue." The relationship among λόγος, wisdom, and virtue (ἀρετή) in Philo's thought is complex. See my discussion on law and wisdom in Philo below.

[85] Cf. *4 Ezra* 5:51-55.

[86] See Gen 2:6.

[87] See Schnabel, *Law and Wisdom*, 1-7.

[88] Perdue, *Wisdom and Creation*, 46.

Nor is wisdom as singularly humanistic as some have argued.[89] The foundation of wisdom, according to Proverbs, is the fear of the Lord [φόβος θεοῦ].[90] In Prov 7:1-3, between the father's exhortation to his son to keep his "words" and "commandments," a septuagintal addition appears in which the son is told to honor the Lord and fear none but him (7:1a). This addition suggests that following the commands of the father is how one properly enacts fearing the Lord.[91] This is made even more explicit in Prov 9:10-10a, another addition, which demonstrates the theistic orientation of Jewish wisdom in a Greek medium, as well as its communal aspect and its relationship to the law:

> [The] beginning of wisdom [is the] fear of the Lord,
> and [the] counsel [βουλή] of the holy ones [is] understanding;
> for knowing [the] law is [to be] of a good mind [διανοίας].

As noted above, the commands the son receives in Prov 1–9 come from the father. It is he who transmits the law to his son in the hopes that his son will emulate him[92] by following the law and also teaching his own son in turn (2:1-2).[93] These commands not only will enable the son to live rightly and enjoy a long life, they also have bodily benefit. As the father tells his son, his counsel is "a healing to your flesh" [ἴασις ταῖς σαρξί σου] (3:22a).[94] It is thus not surprising to find throughout the aphoristic sections of Proverbs the repeated claim that a son who has found wisdom causes his father to rejoice (10:1; 15:20; 17:21; 29:3).

Although the father repeatedly refers to the instruction, words, commandments, customs, counsel, understanding, wisdom, and law that he gives his son as "his,"[95] it seems likely that these elements, including law, stand in relationship to God since they all are designed to help the son enact wisdom, which begins with the fear of the Lord. Moreover, in the list of instructions the father gives his son in Prov 1–9

---

[89] See Crenshaw, *Wisdom*, 15, 42, 44; Goff, *Worldly and Heavenly Wisdom*, 44; Perdue, *Wisdom Literature*, 49.

[90] Prov 1:7; 9:10; see also 15:33; 22:4.

[91] For more on MT Proverbs 1–9, which obviously does not include the addition discussed above, as instruction from father to son, see Carol A. Newsom, "Woman and the Discourse of Patriarchal Wisdom," in *Reading Bibles, Writing Bodies: Identity and the Book* (ed. Timothy K. Beal and David M. Gunn; Biblical Limits; London: Routledge, 1997), 116-31.

[92] See also 4 Macc 9:23.

[93] See also Prov 4:1-9.

[94] Prov 4:22 contains a similar notion. Here the father's word "is life to the ones who find them and healing (ἴασις) to all flesh."

[95] E.g. Prov 1:8; 2:1; 3:1, 21; 4:1-2, 10, 20; 5:1; 6:20; 7:1. The mother's teaching is also included in 1:8 and 6:20.

stands the command that the son should "not take lightly [the] instructions [παιδείας] of the Lord" because "whom the Lord loves he instructs" [παιδεύει] (3:11-12). Although this is just one example, I believe that it situates the father as transmitter of God's wisdom and law to the son. This can also be seen in Prov 10:8, which teaches that it is the wise man who will receive the commandments. Further, the son who possesses understanding [υἱὸς συνετός] is the one who keeps the law (28:7). That this law is related to God even though it is transmitted through the father is seen by the fact that Proverbs describes the one who turns [ἐκκλίνων][96] from the law as one whose very prayers "have become abominable" [ἐβδέλυκται] (28:9). Here the wise and understanding son is one who keeps the law of God as transmitted by the father. The one who does not keep the law is both a disappointment to his father (28:7) and the consequences of this failure to keep the law are described using cultic language of prayer and purity.

Wisdom, according to Proverbs, is important for knowing how to act correctly and thus for maintaining physical and social well-being. "[The] offspring of wisdom [are the] fear of the Lord[97] and wealth and glory and life" (Prov 22:4).[98] Wisdom is so desired because it allows one to lead a productive life. Whereas the concern in the Genesis 1 creation account is to fill the world with physical offspring (Gen 1:22, 28), the concern in Proverbs is the "offspring" produced by the one who lives by wisdom.[99] The fruits of living life according to wisdom are right relationship with God, material benefit, social acclaim, and, at the root of everything, life itself. It is no wonder that wisdom is widely sought.

The relationship of wisdom to law in Sirach does not diverge from that expressed in Proverbs. It offers, rather, an intensification of this relationship as well as a fuller explanation of it.[100] In the prologue to the Greek translation of the work, Ben Sira's grandson notes that his grandfather had written this book after immersing himself "in the reading of the law and of the prophets and of the other books of [the] fathers" (lines 7-10). The book of Sirach is, according the translator, "instruction and wisdom" [παιδείαν καὶ σοφίαν] (line 12) that will help the one who reads it live according to the law [διὰ τῆς ἐννόμου

---

[96] For more on the importance of the verb ἐκκλίνω, see the "Women" and "Sex and Marriage" sections in ch. 4.

[97] Note here a reversal of the dictum that "The beginning of wisdom is the fear of the Lord." While the fear of the Lord initiates one on the path of wisdom, apparently growing wise reinforces this initial condition.

[98] Cf. Eccl 2:26: "For to the good person before his face he has given wisdom (σοφίαν) and knowledge (γνῶσιν) and cheerfulness (εὐφροσύνην)."

[99] See Robbins, *Invention*, 1:121.

[100] See Schnabel, *Law and Wisdom*, ch. 1; J.J. Collins, *Jewish Wisdom*, ch. 3.

βιώσεως] (line 14). This understanding of his grandfather's intent seems to be borne out in the first chapter, where Ben Sira teaches "You who desire wisdom keep the commandments [ἐντολάς] and the Lord will supply her to you" (1:26).[101] Returning to the theme of fearing the Lord, one notes how this state of being is enacted according to Ben Sira:

> All wisdom [is the] fear of the Lord,
> and in all wisdom [is the] doing of the law [ποίησις νόμου] (19:20).

The cognitive state of fearing of the Lord is established, as in Proverbs, as the basis for wisdom, which in turn is achieved in practice by living a life in accordance with the law.[102]

This notion of right cognition translated into right action is further demonstrated in Sir 14:20-27, where the sage declares blessed the man who will study with wisdom [ἐν σοφίᾳ μελετήσει],[103] "who will reason [διαλεχθήσεται] with his understanding" (14:20), and "who thinks over [διανοούμενος] her ways in his heart and ponders [ἐννοηθήσεται] her secrets." While Ben Sira goes on to use metaphors of active seeking to finish this chapter (14:22-27), the concentration of verbs relating to cognition is remarkable. Ben Sira then teaches that "The one fearing the Lord will do this *and* the one who masters [ἐγκρατής] the law will take possession of [wisdom]" (15:1, emphasis added). For Ben Sira, the cognitive aspect of apprehending wisdom is insufficient. It is only when this understanding is translated into right action through a mastery of the law that one can be said to have obtained wisdom. When both of these conditions are met, Ben Sira uses two female metaphors to promise that wisdom "will meet him as a mother and will receive him as a virginal wife" [γυνὴ παρθενίας] (15:2). These complex conceptual blends paint wisdom as one who gave the wise man life and who cared for him as well as the one who provides him with legitimate offspring. Here again the generative power of wisdom is displayed – she is like one who gives birth to the wise man by providing

---

[101] Ben Sira also promises those who meditate on the commands (προστάγμασιν) and commandments (ἐντολαῖς) of the Lord that "the desire of wisdom will be given to you" (6:37). Codex Vaticanus reads "your desire of wisdom will be given to you."

[102] See Di Lella, "Fear of the Lord as Wisdom," 114: "Practical wisdom (the discipline and perfection of the will that enables one to make right moral choices), which Ben Sira identifies with the Law in chap. 24 ...become[s] possible only when one fears the Lord by keeping the commandments ..."

[103] Sir 14:20 contains a textual issue. I follow Rahlf's reading of μελετήσει although this comes from the corrector of Codex Sinaiticus. The original reading of Sinaiticus, Vaticanus and Alexandrinus read τελευτήσει.

him with right thought, but she also provides him with offspring in the form of the blessings that flow from his right actions.

Sirach 24 contains wisdom's hymn in which Ben Sira comes the closest to speculative wisdom in that the personification of wisdom here could be interpreted hypostatically.[104] In the hymn wisdom sings of her presence in the heavenly assembly (24:2) and alludes to her activity before and within creation (24:3-7; 9). However, this hymn strives to place wisdom within the history of Israel (24:8) and extols her activity "in the midst of her people" (24:1). Her throne is said to be in a pillar of cloud (24:4; cf. Exod 13:21-22) and she declares that "in the holy tent" she ministered before God and thus was "firmly fixed in Zion" (24:10; cf. Exod 33:9-10). In this hymn to wisdom, Ben Sira provides a resource for multiple modes of discourse. He provides fodder for pre-creation discourse when he praises wisdom's creation from "before the ages, in the beginning" (24:9), but then he placplaces wisdom in two cultic settings – the tent of meeting and the Temple (24:10)[105] – where she is serving God, thus providing material for priestly discourse. Wisdom's hymn praising herself ends with the note that those who work with her will not sin (24:22). From there Ben Sira moves to interpret his personification of wisdom by stating that "All these things [are the] book of [the] covenant of [the] most high God, [the] law which Moses commanded us" (24:23).[106] For Ben Sira, one finds wisdom most fully expressed in the textual tradition of Israel, most especially in the law of Moses (24:25-27).

John Collins argues that "[u]nlike Ben Sira and Pseudo-Phocylides, Pseudo-Solomon provides no instruction on social relations." According to Collins, the goal of immortality has "transformed" the traditional teaching of wisdom literature and created an "ethics of immortality."[107] The relationship of wisdom to law in Wisdom of Solomon, not surprisingly, is thus considerably more complex than what is found in Sirach, where wisdom and law are functional equivalents. Wis 6:17-20 is a useful pericope to examine in light of this in that it combines elements seen in the discussion of other Jewish texts above with the newer concerns of this Hellenistic Jewish text.

> For the beginning of [wisdom is] the most true desire for instruction [παιδείας ἐπιθυμία],

---

[104] But see Sir 3:20-24.
[105] See Sir 51:13-14.
[106] See Bar 3:9–4:4 and Mark E. Biddle's notes to these verses in "Baruch," in *The New Oxford Annotated Bible* (ed. Michael D. Coogan; 3rd ed.; Oxford: Oxford University Press, 2001), 180 Apocrypha. See also Schnabel, *Law and Wisdom*, 23: "Closely related to the theme of wisdom in Israel is the relationship between Ben Sira's concept of wisdom and Israel's cult. This is not surprising since Ben Sira was a priest."
[107] J.J. Collins, *Jewish Wisdom*, 190-91.

and thought [φροντίς] of instruction [is] love,
and love [is] observance of her laws,
and attention to laws [is the] establishing of incorruptibility [ἀφθαρσίας],[108]
and incorruptibility makes [one] to be near to God;
therefore [the] desire for wisdom leads to a kingdom.

This pericope begins with a familiar reference to the "beginning of wisdom," but in place of the familiar "fear of the Lord" we find in Proverbs, here wisdom stems from the desire to be instructed. That this desire is a cognitive activity is evident by its replacement by φροντίς in the second strophe of v. 17. The thought of instruction is described as ἀγάπη, which can be viewed as a border category between an internal cognitive state and the concrete activity that flows from it. The argument then moves to show that wisdom is enacted, in a manner similar to that seen in Proverbs and Sirach, by observing "her laws." The nature of these "laws" is a matter for debate. Eckhard Schnabel notes that the author of Wisdom of Solomon seems to avoid reference to particularistic Jewish laws in favor of emphasizing the universalistic ethical aspects of "the law."[109] However, Wis 18:4 clearly demonstrates that the concept of "law" in Wisdom of Solomon is tied to the Mosaic law. In this verse, located within a retelling of the Exodus narrative, it is God's children "through whom the incorruptible [ἄφθαρτον] light of [the] law was to be given to the world [τῷ αἰῶνι]." That wisdom's law is a circumlocution for this Mosaic law is further illustrated in Wis 9:9 where wisdom is described as being with God and knowing "what is right according to [God's] commandments."

Up to this point the teaching in Wis 6:17-18a is similar to the teachings located in Proverbs and Sirach. However, the reward for keeping wisdom's law is where the Hellenistic text of Wisdom of Solomon innovates. In 6:18β the one who follows the law is not given wealth and honor in this lifetime. Rather, the one who attends to the law, which is described as possessing "incorruptible light," will lay the groundwork for his own "incorruptibility," that is immortality.[110] This incorruptibility brings one closer to God in that it returns the wise man to his created state: "for God created the human being for incorruptibility" (2:23).[111] It is only by wisdom, enacted through the law, leading to incorruptibility/immortality, and thus being near God, that one can

---

[108] Note that this can also be translated, as does NRSV, as "immortality."

[109] Schnabel, *Law and Wisdom*, 131-32. Schnabel notes that references to the Jewish law probably appear at 2:12; 6:4; 9:9; 18:4.

[110] See Collins, *Jewish Wisdom*, 187: "There is no practical difference between immortality and incorruptibility in Wis. Sol."

[111] See Wis 1:15: "for righteousness is immortal."

receive a true kingdom. Given that the narrator is supposedly Solomon, this kingdom language is not surprising. In 6:9 and 21 he makes clear that his teaching is especially applicable to his fellow rulers and he urges them to "honor wisdom, in order that you might rule forever." Unlike the fatalistic Solomon of Ecclesiastes, the Solomon of this Hellenistic text argues that wise kings can continue to reign after death.[112]

Since the purpose of the law in the Pentateuch is to create a holy and priestly nation for God (Exod 19:5-6; Lev 20:22-26; Deut 26:18-19), analyzing the concerns for holiness and purity found in the Wisdom of Solomon will help toward understanding how attending to wisdom's laws leads to incorruptibility. In describing the spirit of wisdom with multiple epithets, Solomon begins the list with "intelligent, holy" [ἅγιον] and sums up her attributes by claiming that she is "one who comes through intelligent, pure [καθαρῶν], subtle spirits" (7:22-23). Because of her purity [καθαρότητα] wisdom is able to pervade all things (7:24), but because of her closeness to God, "nothing having been polluted gains entrance into her" (7:25).

It is due to the holiness and purity of wisdom that she enters only those souls that can be described as holy [ὁσία] (7:27). This discussion helps explain why those with "crooked thoughts" are separated from God (1:3). Because of her holiness and purity "wisdom will not enter into a deceitful soul and she will not settle in a body involved in sin. For a holy spirit of instruction will flee trickery" [ἅγιον πνεῦμα παιδείας φεύξεται δόλον] (1:4-5α).[113] Wisdom helps Israel, in part, because it is a holy [ὅσιος] nation (10:15, 17). It is for this reason that Solomon instructs the monarchs [τύραννοι] to learn wisdom so that they do not err, "for the ones keeping holy things [ὅσια] with holiness [ὁσίως] will be made holy" [ὁσιωθήσονται] (6:9-10). Becoming holy opens one up to the salutatory effects of wisdom and allows one, like Solomon, to take wisdom for a bride [νύμφη] (8:2), which in turn leads to the ultimate goal of the text: immortality (8:17).[114] According to what we have seen above, this holiness is achieved by enacting "the incorruptible light of the law" (18:4).

As with the other Jewish texts analyzed above, in the Philonic corpus there is an interplay between what is considered wise and those things which are considered "law." Although wisdom takes care to show humans that which is wise, this statement in itself has no actionable content. How the wise man should behave is once again found in

---

[112] See Eccl 2:16; 3:18-22; 9:7-10.
[113] See Wis 8:20: "being good I entered into an undefiled (ἀμίαντον) body."
[114] Looking ahead to the "Women, Sex, and Marriage" section in the next chapter, note that in Wis 8:2 Solomon states that from his youth (ἐκ νεότητος) he sought wisdom for his bride.

understanding and doing God's law, which is itself explained though its relationship to God's λόγος. Philo argues that the law is the same as the divine word [λόγος]. Doing the law thus means doing what the divine λόγος articulates and the wise man thereby enacts the words [λόγους] of God (Migr. 129-30). Law, λόγος, and enacting wisdom are all interrelated in Philo's thinking and produce right conduct in the wise man.[115] These three elements are bound together in Philo's teaching because all stand in fundamental relationship with the creation. As the world is created through divine λόγος and nurtured through divine wisdom, so Moses teaches that

> the world [κόσμου] is in harmony with the Law, and the Law with the world, and that the man who observes the Law is constituted thereby a loyal citizen of the world, regulating his doing by the purpose and will of Nature, in accordance with which the entire world itself also is administered (Opif. 3 [Colson & Whitaker, LCL]).[116]

Enacting what the law requires puts one in harmony with the natural created world (Mos. 2.52)[117] and allows one to live a "true life" [ἀλήθειαν ζωήν] (Congr. 87). This naturalness of the law also makes it the legitimate purview of wisdom in that "the task of wisdom is to investigate all that nature [φύσει] has to show" (Prov. 1 [Colson, LCL]).[118] Philo also demonstrates the connection between the naturalness of the law and wisdom by narrating the life of Abraham, who lived before God formally gave the law to Moses. According to Philo, the wise man Abraham performed the law that he was taught "by unwritten nature" [ἀγράφῳ τῇ φύσει] so that he himself was a law [νόμος αὐτός] (Abr. 275-76).[119] Since the law is in harmony with nature, the wise man, who investigates nature, will conform his actions to it.

The relationship between wisdom and law is also displayed in Philo's treatment of his multifaceted hero Moses.[120] According to Philo, Moses was "king, lawgiver, high priest, and prophet" (Mos. 2.292).[121] What is missing from this list is Philo's overarching category for which Moses, like Abraham before him, serves as an exemplum: the wise man. Moses

---

[115] See Ebr. 84.

[116] See also Mos. 2.48.

[117] See also Mos. 2.14; Abr. 3-6.

[118] On the relation of biblical wisdom and nature see Goff, *Worldly and Heavenly Wisdom*, 43.

[119] For Abraham as a wise man see: Abr. 77, 78, 83, 118, 132, 142, 168, 202, 213, 229, 255, 275; Migr. 122, 149; Congr. 48.

[120] See Mos. 2.211 where Philo describes Moses as "great in everything" (ὁ πάντα μέγας Μωυσῆς).

[121] See also Mos. 2.2.

is best considered *the* exemplum of this class of human being in that he is repeatedly and consistently described by Philo as "all wise" [πάνσοφος].[122] Like all mortals, however, Moses needed to be instructed in order to learn wisdom. Unlike other mortals, Philo claims that Moses was instructed by God (*Mos.* 1.80). Important for this investigation is that the all-wise Moses is also a lawgiver [νομοθέτης]. This "wise lawgiver" (*Congr.* 44) is described as one whose wisdom is "entirely most original" (*Deus.* 125) and whose "sacred [ἱερός] books" are "wondrous memorials of his wisdom" (*Mos.* 1.4). Moses' wisdom is not found only in his books, but also in his person. Much like Abraham before him, Philo describes Moses as a "living law" [νόμος ἔμψυχός] (*Mos.* 1.162) through whom the entire nation of Israel learned "the first things [προτέλεια] of wisdom" (*Deus.* 148).

The blend of wisdom and legal descriptors in the person of Moses is furthered in Philo's discussion of the properties of the law. As noted above, this law is first of all in harmony with nature (*Opif.* 1-3). The law must also be understood in light of the multiple kinds of directives available to the lawgiver for its explication. Philo distinguishes three ways whereby human behavior can be regulated: 1. command [πρόσταξις], 2. prohibition [ἀπαγόρευσις], and 3. commandment and exhortation [ἐντολή καὶ παραίνεσις].[123] A command concerns behavior one is supposed to produce while prohibition concerns behavior not to be produced. Exhortation, according to Philo, involves a neutral subject who is neither sinning nor behaving correctly. A person like this, such as a child, needs to be taught [διδάσκω] to keep away from evil and persuaded [προτρέπω] to do what is right (*Leg.* 1.93). Philo is at pains to show that the law of Moses, unlike other laws which are given to tyranny and despotism, is modeled on exhortation rather than command and prohibition.[124] Moses "suggests and admonishes rather than commands [κελεύει]." Moreover, his instructions are explained "by forewords and after-words, in order to persuade [τοῦ προτρέψασ-θαι] rather than to enforce" (*Mos.* 2.49-50 [based on Colson, LCL]). Moses' law, as Philo describes it, looks almost exactly like the model of instruction found in the older Jewish wisdom texts. When Philo describes Moses as a "wise lawgiver" (*Congr.* 44) he is not simply heaping

---

[122] *Det.* 126; *Post.* 28, 169; *Gig.* 24, 56; *Agr.* 20, 43; *Plant.* 27; *Migr.* 45, 76; *Fug.* 58; *Abr.* 13; *Mos.* 2.204; *Spec.* 2.194, 4.69, 157, 175. Others described as "all wise" include Abraham, *Cher.* 18; Isaac, *Cher.* 47; Sacr. 43; Jacob, *Sacr.* 48; God, *Plant.* 28; *Somm* 1.207; nature, *Spec.* 2.100; Joshua, *Virt.* 60; ἡγεμόνος, *Virt.* 61; a hypothetical artisan (to explain the actions of God), *Prov.* 1.

[123] Although he combines ἐντολή with παραίνεσις in this list, Philo only mentions the latter in his exposition. Hence Colson and Whitaker's translation of "command accompanied by exhortation" (LCL).

[124] But see *Migr.* 130.

multiple encomia upon his hero's memory, rather he is explicating how Moses is first and foremost a wise man with lawgiving being but one manifestation of his wisdom. Indeed, Moses "exhorts [προτρέπει] everyone everywhere to pursue piety and justice" [δικαιοσύνης] (*Virt.* 175 [Colson, LCL]). In Philo's corpus, the specific nature of Moses as lawgiver is almost entirely subsumed under his generic nature as "all-wise."

Although Moses writes his law from the perspective of the wise man with the broad goals of inculcating piety and righteousness, this is not to say that the law is devoid of particular content. Indeed, Philo notes that only hearing the law does not make it effective, one must translate what the law teaches into practice (*Praem.* 82). Although he strenuously argues that the law of Moses exhorts one to actions that are in accord with the universe, there are, nevertheless, particularistic aspects of Jewish law that do not fit well in Philo's naturalistic program that employs allegory as a hermeneutical category. Philo recognizes this tension and moves to resolve it. He notes that some may think it acceptable to neglect enacting the specific teachings of the actual words of the law in favor of "symbols of intelligible things" [σύμβολα νοητῶν] (*Migr.* 89). According to Philo this would be a mistake. However valuable the intelligible (i.e., allegorical) interpretation of the law may be, the fact that human beings occupy physical bodies in the material world demands that the "literal" injunctions of the law be kept. Those who would abandon the particular aspects of the law act as if they are "living alone by themselves in a desert" or as if they are "bodiless souls" [ἀσώματοι ψυχαί]. Corporeal existence in human community necessitates enacting those things enjoined by the law (*Migr.* 90). The law consists of something that resembles body (the literal sense) and soul (the intelligible sense). Just as humans must care for their bodies because it is the dwelling place of the soul, so must the "body" of the law be attended to. If this argument from analogy is not enough for his readers, Philo ends by stating that enacting the literal sense of the laws allows one to achieve a deeper understanding of their σύμβολα (*Migr.* 93).

Philo uses embodied human existence, which is lived out within a community, as a warrant for following the letter of the law. This helps to explain why his presentation of both Moses and the Mosaic law echoes the themes of Jewish wisdom. Although the law is always related to God and God's λόγος in Philonic thought (e.g. *Migr.* 130, 143), Philo's rationale for following the particular demands of the law is an anthropocentric one that is related to ethics, which, as noted above, is one of the manifestations of wisdom (*Ebr.* 91). This interpretation of the law through the lens of wisdom makes sense in light of Philo's contention that the commands of Moses allow one "to philosophize genuinely" [φιλοσοφεῖν ἀνόθως] (*Decal.* 58) and his further claim that legitimate philosophy "is woven from three strands – thoughts [βουλευμάτων], words [λόγων] and deeds [πράξεων]" (*Mos.* 2.212 [Colson, LCL]).[125] The law provides specific content for "the one who practices wisdom" [ὁ σοφίας ἀσκητής] (*Ebr.* 48).

In addition to wisdom being related to law in Philonic thought, both of these elements are related to holiness. Philo speaks of the wonder that "the sanctity of the legislation" [τὸ τῆς νομοθεσίας ἱεροπρεπές] inspires not only in Jews, but among the gentiles as well (*Mos.* 2.25 [Colson, LCL]).[126] The wise man, who will enact the law, acts as both priest and that which is offered. This man devotes [καθαγιάζει] his whole soul as a pure offering to God (*Leg.* 3.141). The model for priestly activity among the wise is, of course, Moses whom Philo calls a high priest (*Mos.* 2.2, 292).[127] Although Moses is the model, Philo contends that "An honour well-becoming the wise is to serve the Being Who truly is, and the service of God is ever the business of the priesthood" [ἱερωσύνη] (*Mos.* 2.67 [Colson, LCL]). This wise man must be, as Moses was, pure in both body and soul, which for Philo means disdaining those things of mortal nature, "food and drink and intercourse with women" [τῆς πρὸς γυναῖκας ὁμιλίας] (*Mos.* 2.68 [Colson, LCL]). In Philo's thought there exists the intersection of wisdom, law, and holiness with each presupposing and supporting the others.

Wisdom's Self-Critique: The Limits of Human Wisdom

Along with its exhortation to achieve wisdom, the book of Proverbs contains an indigenous critique of those who would too readily claim this mantle for themselves. Wisdom, apparently, is a designation ideally supplied by others to the sage, not something applied to oneself. Humility before God marks those who are truly wise. The father in Proverbs teaches his son to trust God with his whole heart, and then continues with an antithetical parallelism, "but do not be exalted in your wisdom" [σῇ σοφίᾳ] (3:5). Again he urges his son, this time reversing the parallelism, "Be not wise [φρόνιμος] according to yourself, but fear God and turn [ἔκκλινε] from every evil" (3:7). The indictment against those who seem wise to themselves rises to such a pitch

---

[125] See also *Virt.* 184.

[126] See *Mos.* 1.4 where the books of Moses are called sacred; *Opif.* 128 where the tablets upon which the law is inscribed are also designated with this term.

[127] Philo's full discussion of Moses as high priest occurs in *Mos.* 2.66-186. Philo also refers to the divine λόγος as a high priest (*Fug.* 108ff.; *Migr.* 102).

that the fool, the negative foil to the wise in Proverbs, is declared to have more hope than such a person (26:12). According to the teaching found in the book of Proverbs, attaining wisdom is the highest goal, and this is accomplished by fearing God and keeping the law and the commandments. Yet exalting one's own wisdom reveals one for what one truly is, a fool rather than a sage.[128] Those who are truly wise have no need to exalt their wisdom.

Although Ben Sira believes that one is able to keep God's commandments (15:15) and argues that "every understanding man knows wisdom" (18:28), it would be a serious misunderstanding of Sirach to assume that wisdom is thereby presented as easy to obtain. Due to the strenuous cognitive and ethical activity required to grasp wisdom, men of understanding "will give praise to the one who finds her" (18:28). Because the wise man receives praise, Ben Sira also warns, as does Proverbs, against thinking too much of oneself: "The greater you are, so much more humble yourself, and you will find grace before the Lord" (3:18). In contrasting human beings with God, Ben Sira reminds his readers that "all things are not able to be in human beings because a son of man [υἱὸς ἀνθρώπου] [is] not immortal" (17:30). Moreover, although Ben Sira teaches that God filled human beings with knowledge and the ability to think (17:6-7), he stresses the difference between humans and God when he notes that "the first man did not know [wisdom] completely and so the last man did not trace her out" [ἐξιχνίασεν] (24:28). The passing on of knowledge and wisdom throughout all of the generations of humanity will not be enough to comprehend all of God's wisdom. Because of this reality, it is not surprising that Ben Sira teaches: "Do not exalt [ἐξύψου] yourself, lest you fall" (1:30). The truly wise do not exalt themselves; rather it is wisdom who exalts [ἀνύψωσεν] her children (4:11).

The warnings against being wise "according to yourself" (Prov 3:7), are not as explicitly stated in Wisdom of Solomon as they are in Proverbs or Sirach. The narrator-as-Solomon even promises to provide information on "what wisdom is and how she came to be," by tracing her out "from the beginning of [her] origin" (6:22; cf. Eccl 1:13). This

---

[128] The narrator-as-Solomon in Ecclesiastes also participates in a critique of those who would be wise, but with a different valence. The teacher declares that although he has set his heart "to know wisdom" (8:16), and even though he has seen all the works of God, he has come to the conclusion that "no person will be able to discover [εὑρεῖν] the work that has been done under the sun; however much a person might toil to seek he will also not find [εὑρήσει]; and, moreover, however much the wise man might speak of knowing, he will not be able to discover" [εὑρεῖν] (2:17). This fits in well with the overall pessimism of the book about the inability of anyone, even the wise, to truly know anything.

contrasts with the declaration found in Sir 24:28, discussed above, that no one will be able to trace out wisdom.[129] Yet in the recitation of his own search for wisdom in chs. 7–9, Solomon, the wisest of kings, presents himself as the model for appropriate humility.[130] Although Wis 6:12-14 suggests that it is a rather easy task to obtain wisdom, the narrator-as-Solomon overturns the notion that this can be accomplished by humans on their own. In Wis 7:1-6 Solomon, reminiscent of the tone struck by the Solomonic teaching found in Ecclesiastes, stresses the equality of all human beings before God from the king down to the commoner: "Even I am a mortal human being, the same as everyone" (7:1). Moreover, "[There is] for all one entry into life and equally [one] exit" (7:6). The only reason Solomon has the reputation for wisdom is because he prayed and the spirit of wisdom [πνεῦμα σοφίας] came to him (7:7). He recognizes that whatever honor he receives comes to him solely on account of this relationship with wisdom (8:9-15).

As his discourse unfolds, Solomon further enacts the proper humility of the wise man when he restates that he would never be able to possess wisdom unless it was granted to him by God. Not only that, but he teaches that being able to achieve that insight is itself a sign of true understanding (8:21). In petitioning God for wisdom, the great king Solomon declares "that I am your slave and a son of your slave girl,[131] a weak human being and short-lived and inferior in understanding of judgment and laws" (9:5). In his estimation of his standing before God, Solomon models the appropriate humility of the sage. Solomon is driven to God because of the little value he accords the power of human reasoning (9:13-17), again echoing the pessimism of Ecclesiastes.[132] For Solomon, wisdom is not in the realm of unaided human discovery, nor is the ability to discern what God wants from humanity. Only God can give wisdom and thereby show people how to live correctly (9:17). Thus at the end of his speech Solomon declares "We were saved by wisdom" [τῇ σοφίᾳ ἐσώθησαν] (9:18).[133]

As with the other examples of Jewish literature examined above, Philo urges his readers to embody and enact the instruction of divine wisdom while at the same time reminding them that since they inhabit the perceptible world they always already fall far short of perfection (*Gig.* 29-31). Though humans know the difference between good and evil, they often knowingly choose the latter (*Migr.* 40). Ever mindful of

---

[129] See also Sir 3:21-24.
[130] See Murphy, *Tree of Life*, 88-90.
[131] Although see LSJ s.v. παιδίσκη II.2, which notes that this word can also mean prostitute. Note that a παιδισκεῖον is a brothel.
[132] Cf. Wis 1:16–2:1.
[133] Cf. Wis 6:24.

the imperfect nature of human beings Philo argues that not only does Moses urge his people to avoid the sin of pride [ὑπεροψία] (*Virt.* 163), but God himself demands that individuals free themselves of self-conceit [οἴησις], which is by nature unclean [ἀκάθαρτον] (*Leg.* 1.52).

Since part of the nature of wisdom, according to Philo, is to investigate "the things concerning the one who is" (*Ebr.* 91) there is a particular danger that human beings may think they know more about God than they do. According to Philo, no mortal is capable of seeing God (*Praem.* 86; *Leg.* 3.206; *Migr.* 135), and it is God alone who knows his own nature exactly as it is (*Leg.* 3.206). Philo argues that the human soul should fear trying to ascend to God on its own power rather than at the direction of God. Moreover, "it is better to stay where we are, roaming, with the bulk of mankind, through this mortal life, rather than lift ourselves heavenward and incur shipwreck as impostors" (*Migr.* 171 [Colson & Whitaker, LCL]).[134] God is the "fountain of wisdom" [ἡ πηγὴ τῆς σοφίας] and Philo argues that it is God alone who possesses wisdom (*Sacr.* 64).[135] In light of this Philo teaches that for human beings "the end of knowledge is knowing [that] we know nothing" (*Migr.* 134). After this gnomic saying he launches into an attack on those who would claim the mantle of wisdom that is similar to Paul's attack on the Corinthians in 1 Cor 3:18-23 (*Migr.* 136-38).[136] Philo and Paul, both Hellenistic Jews, urge their communities to seek the wisdom of God and enact it through concrete behavior, and both have little patience for the arrogance of mere human wisdom.

Conclusion

By performing a close reading of how some Jewish resources describe wisdom in this chapter, I hope to have laid the foundation for my examination of wisdom in 1 Cor 1–4 in ch. 4. The multiple ways Jewish traditions discuss and understand wisdom, noted by Philo in my introduction to this chapter, are the main reasons why wisdom as a hermeneutical category is so difficult to define precisely. Yet, wisdom can be fruitfully employed as a heuristic category through which certain modes of discourse can be analyzed and related to other texts exhibiting similar conceptual qualities.[137] Such a mode of interpretation requires an investigation of inner texture, intertexture, and cultural

---

[134] See Sir 1:30.
[135] See also *Conf.* 39; *Congr.* 114; *Migr.* 40, 134.
[136] See also *Conf.* 110-25 where Philo uses the story of the tower of Babel to critique the dangers of presumptuous human wisdom.
[137] On "sapiential qualities" see Wilson, *Love without Pretense*, 3.

texture as it explores how certain conceptual categories and blends are exploited for rhetorical effect.[138] My investigation above has also highlighted the great plasticity of wisdom as it operates in different cognitive arenas. This supports Matthew J. Goff's conclusion that "Israel's sapiential tradition was both conservative and flexible. Great value was placed on wisdom that was handed down from generation to generation. Yet wisdom tradition was able to merge with other ideas and newer developments."[139] Although Goff does not use SRI or categories from conceptual integration theory, his description of Jewish wisdom explains how it is such fertile ground for the kinds of conceptual blending Paul's rhetoric creates in 1 Cor.

The didactic aspects of wisdom are bound up with its role in the creation of the world and its continued ability to lead people to fruitful and productive lives. This grounding in the natural created order provides the rationale for why people ought to perform right action that generates purity and holiness in imitation of the creator. However, wisdom discourse also warns people against thinking they can achieve perfect wisdom, and its concomitant righteousness and purity, on their own, or even at all. For many voices of Jewish wisdom, the fact that humanity is imperfect, unlike their creator, means that the search for wisdom is necessarily a life-long pursuit. This pursuit requires attention to specific behavior and necessitates appropriate arguments and rationales for specific actions. In my next chapter I explore how Jewish resources deal with issues that will bear on my interpretation of 1 Cor 6:12–7:7. The way different texts, written at different times, engage the categories of women, sex and marriage, and holiness under the general conceptual category of freedom demonstrates the multiplicity of voices and conceptual categories available to a Hellenistic Jew such as Paul as he struggles to warn his Corinthian community of the dangers of πορνεία.

---

[138] As noted in the methodology chapter, these textures will be engaged implicitly, rather than explicitly, in my exegesis of 1 Cor 6:12–7:7.

[139] Goff, *Worldly and Heavenly Wisdom*, 41. See Robbins, *Invention*, 1:486.

3

Jewish Resource Zones

Introduction

In the previous chapter I wrestled with the problem of definition that is encountered by any project hoping to make use of the category of wisdom. I also performed a close reading and thick description of multiple ways wisdom itself is discussed by some Jewish texts. In this chapter I move beyond a focus on wisdom *per se* and analyze a small segment of wisdom's "encyclopedic interests."[1] The primary aim of this chapter is to provide some necessary conceptual context for Paul's teaching in 1 Cor 6:12–7:7. As such, I interact with four main themes from a selection of Jewish resources: women, sex and marriage, holiness, and freedom. The related themes of women and sex/marriage are rather self explanatory when engaging Paul's argument against πορνεία in 1 Cor 6:12–7:7. Paul's rhetography in 6:12-20 hinges on the malevolent figure of the πόρνη (whore) while his rhetology in 7:1-7 will rely heavily on monogamous heterosexual coupling as he explains how to avoid sexual sin.[2] Paul's argument, as will be demonstrated in ch. 6, also evokes priestly concerns about holiness and thus a full-bodied exegesis requires a thick description of this theme as well. Finally, it is necessary to explore a broad conceptual field that I am naming freedom since Paul's gnomic sayings in 6:12 activate cultural debates surrounding the proper use of freedom and personal authority. Indeed, recall Mitchell's argument that Paul develops his arguments in this section of 1 Cor (5:1–11:1) "under the overarching theme *of his own choice*: ἐξουσία/ἐλευθερία."[3] While freedom is a much broader category than the first three, especially in light of Hellenistic Jewish thought of the first century, understanding how freedom, authority, and virtue

---

[1] J.J. Collins, "Cosmos and Salvation," 317.
[2] I discuss my translation of πόρνη as "whore" in ch. 6.
[3] Mitchell, *Paul and the Rhetoric of Reconciliation*, 226. Emphasis in the original. See idem, 118: "Discussion of what is true freedom was especially common in political discourses and appears throughout 1 Corinthians." See my discussion of Mitchell in the Introduction.

were discussed among Jewish voices in a Greek idiom is crucial for correctly reading the opening texture of 1 Cor 6:12–7:7 that so firmly roots Paul's teaching in wisdom rhetorolect by evoking a fairly typical moral debate. I confine myself to Jewish resource zones in this chapter because the problem of πορνεία is for Paul primarily a *religious* problem.[4] This presentation does not pretend to be exhaustive, but rather illustrative in a way that provides a solid foundation for my exegetical analysis of 1 Cor 6:12–7:7.

In order to be able to use the insights available from conceptual integration theory it is necessary to have as full a picture as possible about the cultural worlds out of which Paul's admonition in 1 Cor to avoid πορνεία emerged. As Gilles Fauconnier and Mark Turner note, "Human culture and thought are fundamentally conservative. They work from the mental constructs and material objects that are already available... Indeed, for conceptual blending to happen at all, continuity is essential."[5] New insight is achieved not by abandoning all previous frames and blends, but in combining them in new ways.[6] In this way new emergent properties are understandable because they are tied to the familiar, but they move thought forward through the creative framing and blending of resources available from the symbolic worlds at hand.[7] This stress on continuity, coupled with Seana Coulson's insight that "meaning is never fully context-independent," compels the biblical interpreter to situate the text under investigation in its environment as she or he is best able in order to employ properly the principles of conceptual integration.[8]

The importance placed on continuity and context in conceptual integration theory finds a similar expression in the foundational underpinnings of socio-rhetorical interpretation (SRI). Vernon Robbins notes that "There is no way ... for a text to be what it is and to be outside the world."[9] In order to make sense of the meaning found in biblical texts, the interpreter must elucidate how these texts relate to other texts as well as to social and cultural environments.[10] In the pro-

---

[4] To be sure, non-Jewish material will be engaged in chs. 6 and 7 as I perform the exegetical analysis of the pericope.
[5] Fauconnier and Turner, *The Way We Think*, 382-83. See also Oakley, "Human Rhetorical Potential," 94, 96, 109, and 124.
[6] See Goff, *Worldly and Heavenly Wisdom*, 41 for this in Jewish sapiential traditions.
[7] See Johnson, *Writings of the New Testament*, 21-91, esp. 21: "A symbolic world is made up of the social structures in which people live, and the symbols attached to and supporting those structures. In the case of the NT, it might be better to speak of the symbolic *worlds*, so complex and pluralistic was its setting" (emphasis in the original). See also Perdue, *Wisdom Literature*, 8.
[8] Coulson, *Semantic Leaps*, 8; see also 25.
[9] Robbins, *Tapestry*, 19.
[10] See Robbins, *Tapestry*, 14, 30-36, 96-191. See also idem, *Exploring*, 3, 40-94.

grammatic explication of SRI by Robbins in *The Tapestry of Early Christian Discourse* and *Exploring the Texture of Texts* these relationships are explored primarily under the rubrics of "intertexture" and "social and cultural texture." Intertexture describes the various ways in which any given text utilizes, changes, or amplifies other texts (oral or written) and social/cultural knowledge. Social and cultural texture explores, among other things, the "social and cultural systems presupposed in the text" and "reveal[s] the potential of the text to encourage its readers to adopt certain social and cultural locations and orientations rather than others."[11] This mutual concern for situating the biblical text within its various symbolic worlds is another demonstration of how a systematic exegetical investigation is able to employ conceptual integration theory within a socio-rhetorical framework. Conceptual blending is a tool that requires setting the discourse under investigation into its social and cultural contexts and this is precisely what SRI demands from exegetes.

Given that the focus of my interpretive project is discourse, it seems appropriate that written discourse provide the basis upon which to build a description of the social and cultural landscape surrounding 1 Cor.[12] However, I do not utilize these contextual materials merely as "sources" from which Paul directly drew, although some texts examined below certainly perform this function. As David Gowler notes, placing a text in its social and cultural contexts within a socio-rhetorical project is not done in order to find "'parallels' that function as proof texts." Rather, the data gathered about the symbolic worlds out of which the text emerges function "as *comparative* texts that show a range of possibilities for interpreters."[13] Socio-rhetorical exegetes use the descriptive expression "resource zones" as a short hand for designating this use of contextual material. This comparative use of resources does not simply rely on lexical parallels, but also explores conceptual fields that can help explain how certain language constructions can prompt different meanings. It is important to note here that many interpreters utilize background material in a similar way even though they are not undertaking a socio-rhetorical analysis and therefore do not make use of this terminology. For example, Michael Fox, in his commentary on Proverbs 1–9, notes that he explores what he

---

[11] Robbins, *Exploring*, 71, 72.

[12] Note Carol A. Newsom's contention that "discourse embodies and generates a symbolic world," in "Woman and the Discourse," 116.

[13] David B. Gowler, "Introduction: The Development of Socio-Rhetorical Criticism," in *New Boundaries in Old Territory: Form and Social Rhetoric in Mark*, by Vernon K. Robbins (ed. David B. Gowler; Emory Studies in Early Christianity 3; New York: Peter Lang, 1994), 28, emphasis in the original.

calls "parallels" to Proverbs not because these represent similarities "due to genetic influence or borrowing," but rather because they function as analogies that "give insight into how a certain theme, form, or idea was treated in ancient Wisdom literature."[14] Similarly, Dale Martin notes that he spends so much time discussing ancient medical theories "not because I think Paul ever read these medical texts ... or because there is any direct relation between what they say and what he says." Rather, Martin argues, he uses medical texts because he is "comparing the unspoken assumptions about the body underlying the two kinds of texts, Paul's and the doctors'."[15] Thus whether or not the term "resource zone" is used elsewhere, the understanding that lies behind this convenient expression is at work in much responsible biblical scholarship that makes use of comparative material.

Women

Given that Paul uses both "good" and "bad" women, the wife and the whore respectively, in his rhetography and rhetology of 1 Cor 6:12–7:7, it is essential to map the conceptual contours of the *topos* of women within Jewish resources. Perhaps the most logical place to begin a description of women in the Jewish resources is with creation.[16] The portrait of the woman in the accounts of creation is a complicated one and one that illustrates the ambivalent manner in which other Jewish resources describe the female sex. On the positive side the female, as much as the male, portion of humanity is described as the image of God (Gen 1:27). Neither gender alone, according to Genesis 1, is closer to the divine εἰκών, but only as a pair do men and women reflect their creator and, as a pair, they are commanded to increase and multiply (Gen 1:28). However, as I discuss below, an allegorical interpretation of Genesis 1 will do much to cast these positive images in a negative light. Further, in the garden story of Genesis 2, the creation of woman is celebrated by the first man. Though she is taken "from her husband" [ἐκ τοῦ ἀνδρὸς αὐτῆς], it is the man who will leave his

---

[14] Fox, *Proverb*, 18-19.

[15] Martin, *Corinthian Body*, xiii.

[16] The various source and redaction critical theories about authorship of various elements in the Hebrew creation accounts do not concern me in this project. The accounts of creation in Greek translations of Genesis known to Hellenistic Jews such as Paul form a narrative unity as "Scripture." See Wevers, *Notes on the Greek Text of Genesis*, xii-xiii. Also note Loader's argument, *Septuagint, Sexuality, and the New Testament*, 120: "It is almost to be expected that the translator would treat Genesis 1–2 as a whole. We see minor indications of this in the smoothing of the transition between the two accounts of creation. Genesis 2 is now an account of how God formed the creation which he 'began' to create in Genesis 1." See his further discussion of this theme on pp. 30-42.

familial household and cling "to his wife" [πρὸς τὴν γυναῖκα αὐτοῦ] (Gen 2:23-24). If not entirely reciprocal, there is a certain mutuality in the description of the relationship between men and women. Yet in narrating the disobedience of the first human couple in Genesis 3, the text turns from a positive evaluation of the woman to a decidedly negative one. Although the man is clearly with her, it is the woman who engages in dialogue with the serpent.[17] She is the one who sees the beauty of the fruit and she is the one who first eats of it. The man places the majority of the blame for his disobedience on the woman.[18] While God punishes the man for *his* decision to eat the fruit, the pronouncement of punishment also appears to locate blame, at least in part, on the woman. God tells the man he is being punished because, instead of doing what God commanded, "you listened to the voice of your wife" [ἤκουσας τῆς φωνῆς τῆς γυναικός σου] (Gen 3:17). This paradigmatic story sets up an apparent dichotomy between the words of the woman and the commandments of God that will be exploited by later Jewish texts, especially in the Hellenistic era.[19] For example, Philo opines that it was woman who was "the beginning of blameworthy life" [ἀρχὴ τῆς ὑπαίτιου ζωῆς] for the first man (*Opif.* 151 [Colson & Whitaker, LCL]) and the book of Sirach goes so far as to claim: "From woman is the beginning of sin [ἀρχὴ ἁμαρτίας], and because of her we all die" (Sir 25:24).

The dual evaluation of women in the creation accounts briefly sketched above provides a heuristic lens through which to examine the portrayal of women in other Jewish resources. Mapping a thick description of the multiple ways women are described will help in exegeting the conceptual blends Paul's discourse creates in his discussion about and to women in 1 Cor 6:12–7:7. I will first examine the positive evaluations of women in the resources, typically as the good wife [γυνή],[20] but in the Hellenistic-Roman era also as virgin [παρθένος]. I will then move into a description of the negative ways in which wom-

---

[17] Loader, *Septuagint, Sexuality, and the New Testament*, 45 notes the LXX translates הִשִּׁיאַנִי, which has the meaning of "tricked me," with ἠπάτησεν, which has a meaning ranging from "deceive" to "seduce" and may have sexual connotations (he sites LXX Susanna 56 as an example of this). In using this word, Loader argues that the LXX thus makes possible later interpretations that the serpent seduced Eve sexually.

[18] Although the man also blames God since it was God who gave the woman to the man (Gen 3:12).

[19] See Yee, *Poor Banished Children of Eve*, 76.

[20] For a discussion of γυνή as a female married to, or having had sexual relations with, a man, as opposed to the more generic English word "woman," see Guilia Sissa, *Greek Virginity* (trans. Arthur Goldhammer: Cambridge, Mass.: Harvard University Press, 1990), 78; Ken Dowden, *Death and the Maiden: Girls' Initiation Rites in Greek Mythology* (New York: Routledge, 1989), 2.

en are depicted, typically as a strange or "other" woman [ἀλλοτρία], an adulteress [μοιχαλίς], and/or whore [πόρνη].²¹ The book of Proverbs encapsulates this distinction when it teaches:

> He who has found a good wife, has found grace,
>   and he has received happiness from God.
> He who gets rid of a good wife, gets rid of good things;
>   and the one who keeps an adulteress is foolish and impious.

> ὅς εὗρεν γυναῖκα ἀγαθήν, εὗρεν χάριτας,
>   ἔλαβεν δὲ παρὰ θεοῦ ἱλαρότητα.
> ὅς ἐκβάλλει γυναῖκα ἀγαθήν, ἐκβάλλει τὰ ἀγαθά·
>   ὁ δὲ κατέχων μοιχαλίδα ἄφρων καὶ ἀσεβής.
>   (Prov 18:22-22a; cf. Sir 7:19, 26; 26:1, 3)

Positive Views of Women

The good wife is generally depicted as a great asset to her husband (e.g. Prov 11:16)²² in Jewish wisdom literature, and one of the more extended treatments of this *topos*, and certainly the most well known, is Prov 31:10-31.²³ The "courageous wife" [γυναῖκα ἀνδρείαν] (Prov 31:10; cf. 12:4) is a blessing to her husband and he praises her as the best of all women (Prov 31:28-29). This type of wife looks to the economic stability of the household under her care and because of her unflagging work the house not only survives, it thrives (Prov 31:13-19, 21-22, 24, 27; cf. 14:1), thereby earning her husband praise in public spaces and affording him a role in public life (Prov 31:23, 31).²⁴ This wife is a blessing not only to her own family but she is also mindful of

---

²¹ Kirchhoff, *Sünde*, 18-21, has rejected the translation of "whore" for πόρνη not only because she feels it carries too much judgmental baggage, but also because she is unsure that the valance of the modern term "whore" is found in this ancient Greek lexical item. I agree with Kirchhoff that a πόρνη is best described as "eine Frau, die regelwidrigen Sexualverkehr hat" ["a woman whose sexual behavior is against the rules"] (36), however I do employ the shorthand "whore" as a translation and not Kirchhoff's "prostitute," since the latter term denotes an economic position, whereas the former stresses social status. I discuss this translation choice at greater length in ch. 6. See Kathy Gaca's discussion in *Fornication*, 165-70. For a fuller and graphic depiction of positive and negative roles of women in wisdom literature in particular, see Carole R. Fontaine, "The Social Roles of Women in the World of Wisdom," in *A Feminist Companion to Wisdom Literature* (ed. Athalya Brenner; FCB 9; Sheffield: Sheffield Academic Press, 1995), 48-49.

²² Note that the LXX of Prov 11:16 states specifically that the glory is the husband's [γυνὴ εὐχάριστος ἐγείρει ἀνδρὶ δόξαν], which the MT does not [אֵשֶׁת־חֵן תִּתְמֹךְ כָּבוֹד].

²³ Note that here I am referring to the *depiction* of the woman in Prov 31:10-31. In doing so, however, one should not forget the point made by Fontaine, "Social Roles of Women," 25: "... the elevated female figures such as Woman Wisdom (Prov. 1–9) or the Woman of Worth (Prov. 31.10-31) may be inversely proportional to the truth of real women's lives."

²⁴ Note that the LXX again inserts the husband in 31:31 where he is not present in the MT.

the less fortunate and gives to them (Prov 31:20). She is the wise woman who is extolled for her wisdom (Prov 31:30; see 14:1) – she opens her mouth only according to the ways of wisdom and the law (Prov 31:28), since she knows how to control her tongue (Prov 31:25).[25]

Though the woman described in Proverbs 31 is more subservient than probably most 21st-century North American tastes, mine included, are comfortable with, she can be seen as the embodiment of the "helper" described in Gen 2:18 and 20.[26] The necessity of such a helper by one's side is seen throughout much wisdom literature. The gloomy teacher of Ecclesiastes counsels a man to look out on life with a wife whom he loves, since that is his portion in this life of vanity (Eccl 9:9). The book of Sirach, which has in general a negative view of women,[27] even counsels a man: "Do not deprive yourself of a good and wise wife" (Sir 7:19).[28] Such a wife is, as in Ecclesiastes, a "good portion" [μερὶς ἀγαθή] to a wise man and brings him joy (Sir 26:3-4). To be sure, such a positive description of an ideal woman does not make Ben Sira a proto-feminist by any stretch of the imagination. As Warren Trenchard notes, Sirach's "view of women's status is such that she can be adjudged positive only in the context of her benefit to a man."[29] This ideal wife has several qualities: she is silent [σιγηρά], self-disciplined [πεπαιδευμένη ψυχῆς], modest [αἰσχυντηρά], self-controlled [ἐγκρατὴς ψυχῆς], and beautiful [κάλλος] (Sir 26:14-16).[30] Directly echoing the description of the woman at creation, Sirach notes that the lucky husband of such a wife has a "helper corresponding to him" [βοηθὸν κατ' αὐτόν] (Sir 36:24; cf. Gen 2:20).[31]

The image of the good wife, in addition to describing some ideal actual woman, is also used as a symbol or metaphor in the Jewish resources. In addition to the courageous woman mentioned above, the other well-known positive female figure in the book of Proverbs is woman wisdom in Prov 1–9. As Claudia Camp notes, "Female Wisdom is associated with the wife whom one is to love faithfully" (Prov

---

[25] Note that Sir 26:14 lists a silent wife as a gift from the Lord. Holding one's tongue and keeping quiet are important virtues in wisdom texts. See e.g. Prov 10:19; 11:12; 13:3; 17:25; 27:20a; 29:20; Eccl 5:5; 10:13-14α; Sir 20:5-8.

[26] LSJ notes the military connotations of βοηθός in Greek literature.

[27] J.J. Collins, *Jewish Wisdom*, 66-72.

[28] NRSV for LXX: μὴ ἀστόχει γυναικὸς σοφῆς καὶ ἀγαθῆς.

[29] Warren C. Trenchard, *Ben Sira's View of Women: A Literary Analysis* (BJS 38; Chico, Calif.: Scholars Press, 1982), 14.

[30] But see Prov 31:30.

[31] For a more extensive discussion of the good wife *topos* in Sirach, see Trenchard, *Ben Sira's View of Women*, 9-38.

4:6; 5:15-19; 7:4; 8:17).[32] Wisdom personified as a woman is, like the γυναῖκα ἀνδρείαν of Prov 31:10, "more valuable than costly stones" (Prov 3:15; cf. 8:11).[33] The LXX extends this description of her, noting that nothing evil will be able to oppose her, nor is anything valuable worth as much as she is. That something as valuable as wisdom, described as that which is *most* valuable, can be described in terms of a feminine symbol denotes the positive valance, albeit as wife, that the images of women can evoke in the Jewish resources.

In Prov 5:15-19, noted by Camp above, the son is counseled by his father (see Prov 4:1) to drink water from his own reservoir [πῖνε ὕδατα ἀπὸ σῶν ἀγγείων] rather than go to another [ἀλλοτρίαν] (Prov 5:20). Michael Fox notes that LXX Prov 5:19 expands the text found in the MT and he translates the Greek as:

> A doe of affection and a filly of your grace –
> let her be together [ὁμιλείτω] with you.
> And may your own one lead [ἡγείσθω] you
> and associate [συνέστω] with you at all times,
> for, consorting [συμπεριφερόμενος] in her affection,
> you will become very great.[34]

Fox notes that while an actual woman is being spoken of in this verse, the use of the phrase "let her lead you" suggests a symbolic valence to the son's own wife. The verb ἡγεῖσθαι can mean something more forceful than leading through guidance. When used with the genitive it can mean to rule or control somebody and Fox states that in the LXX "it commonly renders words for various types of ruler and chief" and in Wis 7:12 it is wisdom who controls [ἡγεῖται] everything good.[35] The woman being described here is *both* a real wife *and* a symbol of wisdom. There is, as Carol Newsom notes, "slippage" between the literal and the figurative. Newsom further argues that the protection offered by the wife and the good marriage in Prov 5:15-19 recalls "the themes of protection associated with Wisdom in 4:6-9."[36] Wis-

---

[32] Claudia V. Camp, *Wise, Strange and Holy: The Strange Woman and the Making of the Bible* (JSOTSup 320; Gender, Culture, Theory 9; Sheffield: Sheffield Academic Press, 2000), 75. In the second chapter of this work, from which the quotation comes, Camp discusses the "subtle unity of personified Wisdom and the Strange Woman ... as a representation of the necessary complementarity of human experience" (77). For an in-depth analysis of the personification of wisdom as female in the Hebrew text of Proverbs, see Camp's *Wisdom and the Feminine in the Book of Proverbs* (Bible and Literature Series 11; Decatur, Ga.: Almond: 1985).

[33] But see Wis 7:9.

[34] Michael V. Fox, "The Strange Woman in Septuagint Proverbs," *JNSL* 22 (1996): 35.

[35] Fox, "Strange Woman," 35.

[36] See Newsom, "Woman and the Discourse of Patriarchal Wisdom," 127.

dom portrayed as a wife who will protect the young man from the strange and evil woman is also found in Prov 7:4-5. This slippage between a real woman and a metaphorical statement will be seen below in my discussion of this "strange woman" in Proverbs and will factor into my exegesis of the conceptual blends found 1 Cor 6:12–7:7.

It is important to note, with Claudia Camp, that it is the portrait of the good wife sketched above, and *not* the image of the virgin, which typically serves as the foil for the sexually promiscuous woman in earlier Jewish texts.[37] This wife was, in accordance with the command of God in Genesis, expected to produce children, preferably sons, for her husband.[38] In the Hellenistic period, there is a shift towards valorizing a wise woman who does not fit the standard model of wifely fecundity and industry described in the book of Proverbs.[39] However, there are multiple voices in the Jewish resources of this period as well. For instance, the gnomic poem known as the *Sentences* of Pseudo-Phocylides recalls older wisdom teaching when it counsels a man:

> Remain not unmarried [ἄγαμος], lest you perish nameless.
> And give something to nature [φύσει] yourself: beget [τέκε] in turn as you were begotten [ἐλοχεύθης] (175-76).[40]

Here, although couched in the Greek idiom of nature rather than that of creation, the author of this Hellenistic text appeals to men to get married and reproduce. Not only does this prevent a man's name from dying out, but it inserts him into the natural cycle of life – marrying and having children are the way things should be.

Other Jewish-Hellenistic texts do not seem to value the production of children as highly as Pseudo-Phocylides. The Wisdom of Solomon goes so far as to bless "the sterile woman who is undefiled" [μακαρία στεῖρα ἡ ἀμίαντος] (Wis 3:13) because, in its calculation of goodness, being without children is no matter compared to the life lived with virtue. It is the memory of one's virtue which grants one immortality,

---

[37] Claudia V. Camp, "Woman Wisdom and the Strange Woman: Where is Power to be Found?" in *Reading Bibles, Writing Bodies: Identities and The Book* (ed. Timothy K. Beal and David M. Gunn; Biblical Limits; London: Routledge, 1997), 99. Camp makes this assertion regarding Prov 1–9 specifically, but I believe its appropriateness for the rest of Jewish scripture holds.

[38] See Fontaine, "Social Roles of Women," 30.

[39] J.J. Collins, *Jewish Wisdom*, 70 argues that the shift from the active, industrious wife running the household in Proverbs 31 to the passive wife typically portrayed in Sirach "reflects the transition from a rural to an urban culture."

[40] Text and translation from Walter T. Wilson, *The Sentences of Pseudo-Phocylides* (CEJL; Berlin: de Gruyter, 2005), 187, 221. See also P.W. van der Horst, *The Sentences of Pseudo-Phocylides: With Introduction and Commentary* (SVTP 4; Leiden: Brill, 1978), 98-99.

not simply the production of heirs (Wis 4:1). In fact, the "prolific brood of the ungodly" (Wis 4:3 [NRSV]; cf. 3:12) is said to be useless.[41] The blessed sterile woman also, according to the text, has "not known a bed with sin [ἐν παραπτώματι]" (3:13). Here the issue seems to be the transvaluation of the usual signifiers of sterility versus having many children.[42] It is the very women who are sterile and face social shame who are validated by their virtue. However, it is important to note that this text from Wisdom of Solomon discusses women who are involuntarily childless. To catch a glimpse of voluntary childlessness seen in a positive light it is necessary to turn to Philo who, in his description of the feast of the Therapeutae, notes the presence of virgin women approvingly. These women, he argues, have "spurned the pleasures of the body [τῶν περὶ σῶμα ἡδονῶν]" voluntarily, unlike the Greek priestesses, because of their desire for wisdom. The children these women desire are not those of flesh and blood, but "those immortal children" that come from the divine gift of discerning wisdom (*Contempl.* 68 [Colson, LCL]). In Wisdom of Solomon, but more so in Philo, one sees Hellenistic Jewish thinkers praising the productivity of virtue through wisdom over the sexual productivity commanded by God in Genesis 1.

Philo also uses the figure of the virgin allegorically in a positive fashion. As will be discussed below, Philo has decidedly negative views of sensual pleasure derived from sexual activity.[43] The virgin, one free from such activity, is thus a natural positive character in Philo's thought. Dorothy Sly notes that virginity in Philo's writings has three valences: it represents "freedom from lust and the other passions"; it can be "restored when human sexual relations are abandoned in favor of union with God"; and, finally, it is an escape from the body.[44] Although Philo admires the purported virgins among the Therapeutae, Richard Baer notes that his use of the virgin as an allegorical expression of the purity of a man's soul is more frequent.[45] In Philo, then, one arrives at the virgin as the foil for the dangerous sexually immoral woman – the pure soul over and against the defiled one.

---

[41] See also Sir 16:1-3.

[42] See J.J. Collins, *Jewish Wisdom*, 190-91.

[43] Note Dorothy Sly, *Philo's Perception of Women* (BJS 209; Atlanta: Scholars Press, 1990), 72-73: "As the object of physical intercourse, [woman] represents defilement. And as the instrument of generation, she also represents the beginning of corruption."

[44] Sly, *Philo's Perception of Women*, 71-72; see pp. 80-81 for examples from Philo's works contrasting virginity with defilement. See also Richard A. Baer, Jr., *Philo's Use of the Categories Male and Female* (ALGHJ 3; Leiden: Brill, 1970), 51-53 and Walter T. Wilson, "Sin as Sex and Sex with Sin: The Anthropology of James 1:12-15," *HTR* 95 (2002): 156, note that on this same page Wilson discusses the symbol of the childbearer in Philo.

[45] Baer, *Philo's Use of the Categories Male and Female*, 75.

Negative Views of Women

Although the good wife and, later, the virgin make strong showings in the Jewish resources, more striking in these texts is how often individual women, or the generic category "woman," are portrayed negatively. Gale Yee, in her book *Poor Banished Children of Eve*, investigates "the problem of the symbolization of woman as the incarnation of moral evil, sin, devastation, and death in the Hebrew Bible."[46] It is the symbolization of "woman," or a certain type of woman, that is important for contextualizing Paul's argument against πορνεία as well as for understanding his teaching on how to avoid this sexual sin. As noted above, despite the positive descriptions of women in Genesis, the activity of the first woman in Genesis 3 and God's speech afterward are usually seen as "the beginning" of using woman as the representation of evil in Jewish, and later Christian, tradition.[47] The good wife *topos* in the Jewish resources emphasizes the benefits women bring to their husbands, while it is Eve's less respectable daughters who highlight the dangers, seen in the story of creation, that women pose to men, as well as to other women, families, and communities.

The *topos* of woman as temptress, found in a certain way of reading Genesis 3, reappears throughout the narrative memory of the Jewish Scriptures. The story of Joseph and Potiphar's wife found in Genesis 39 is a good example of this.[48] Interestingly, the narrative seems to imply that it was Joseph's physical beauty that prompted the adulterous desire in Potiphar's wife – a reversal of the usual wisdom concern with men gazing upon beautiful (and tempting) women. Only after she "cast her eyes upon Joseph" does she command sex from him (Gen 39:6β-7). Joseph refuses to do this even though Potiphar's wife speaks to him every day (Gen 39:9-10). Once again, it is the woman's speech that tempts Joseph to sin against God by having a sexual relationship with

---

[46] Yee, *Poor Banished Children of Eve*, 1. In her study, which is more comprehensive than my descriptions in this chapter can be, Yee looks at four examples: Eve in Genesis (59-79), faithless Israel in Hosea (81-109), the two sisters in Ezekiel (111-134), and the other woman in Proverbs (135-165). Note also Crenshaw's statement that "loose women" were "a favorite topic of Israelite sages" in *Wisdom*, 12.

[47] Yee, *Poor Banished Children of Eve*, 59; see also Walsh, *Exquisite Desire*, 152, who notes: "That this story came to associate woman and sexuality with sin is a notorious postbiblical development."

[48] For the Joseph story in Genesis as wisdom literature, see esp. Gerhard von Rad, "The Joseph Narrative and Ancient Wisdom," in *Studies in Ancient Israelite Wisdom* (ed. James L. Crenshaw; The Library of Biblical Studies; New York: Ktav, 1976), 439-47, who concludes that "we may say that the Joseph narrative is a didactic wisdom-story..." (447). See also L. Wilson, *Joseph, Wise and Otherwise*; Crenshaw, *Wisdom*, 87 n. 52.

his master's wife. And it is the woman's lies that land the innocent Joseph in prison (Gen 39:11-20).

In retelling the Joseph story in a Hellenistic milieu, Philo intensifies both the woman's depravity and Joseph's self-control. Reading *Ios.* 40 confirms that it is Joseph's beauty that prompts Potiphar's wife's erotic desire for him. Philo narrates that the overly passionate woman was driven to grasp hold of Joseph's garment because she was "kindling and inflaming lawless desire" (*Ios.* 41). As Philo tells it, Joseph does not simply run away, but launches into a speech about the sexual chastity practiced by the Hebrews. Other nations, Joseph claims, allow their boys, after the age of fourteen, to have sex with "whores and prostitutes" [πόρναις καὶ χαμαιτύπαις] and any others who hire out their bodies. Among the Hebrews, however, a courtesan [ἑταίρα] is not even allowed to live (*Ios.* 43).[49] Moreover, Joseph continues, even when Hebrews do marry and engage in sexual intercourse, they do so not for the sake of pleasure [ἡδονή] but in order to sire children of known paternal lineage (*Ios.* 43). That he should put such words in Joseph's mouth is understandable given Philo's understanding that "no two things can be more hostile to each other than virtue is to pleasure" (*Ios.* 153 [Colson, LCL]). Joseph, the epitome of virtuous endurance [καρτερικός] and self-control [ἐγκράτεια] (*Ios.* 54-55), eloquently defends his chastity in the face of the sexual passion of a foreign woman.

The dangers of women, especially foreign women/wives [γυναῖκες ἀλλότριαι], are frequently depicted as so insidious that even the wisest of kings can succumb to their, usually sexual, charms.[50] Despite all of Solomon's gifts of wisdom and understanding (3 Kgdms 5:9-14; cf. 10:23-25), the narrative of the beginning of his reign presages the difficulties he will have later on. Immediately after the paean to Solomon's wisdom the LXX narrates that Solomon "took the daughter of Pharaoh to himself for a wife" (3 Kgdms 5:14a; 2:35c).

It is Solomon's foreign wives that cause the downfall of his house (3 Kgdms 11:9-13). The problem of these wives is twofold. First, like the daughter of Pharaoh, the other foreign women that Solomon brings into his household are from the nations which God commanded the sons of Israel not to "go into." Second, the rationale behind this prohibition was the ever present danger that these foreign women would "turn [ἐκκλίνωσιν] your (i.e. the sons of Israel) hearts after their

---

[49] In a note on this section Colson, LCL states that Philo's interpretation of Deut 23:17 here (and in *Spec.* 3.51) is more "extreme" than what the biblical text states.

[50] For a discussion of "Solomon as Sage Par Excellence," see Crenshaw, *Wisdom*, 35-54; see also Yee, *Poor Banished Children of Eve*, 147. *1 Enoch* 6-9 imagines that even angels can succumb to the sexual temptations they feel when looking at beautiful women (also 12:4; 15:3-7; 19:1).

idols" (3 Kgdms 11:2) and, in fact, this is what happens to Solomon when he becomes old (3 Kgdms 11:4). This turn of events is ironic since old age typically confers wisdom.[51] In his younger years Solomon had no difficulty judging the motives of two γυναῖκες πόρναι (3 Kgdms 3:16-28) or impressing the queen of Sheba [Σαβα] with his understanding (3 Kgdms 10:1-13). However, in his old age Solomon's foreign wives [αἱ γυναῖκες αἱ ἀλλότριαι] are able to exert their influence over his wise heart and he goes after their gods. The text narrates that these wives are able to do this because Solomon clung to them in order to love them [εἰς αὐτοὺς ἐκολλήθη Σαλωμων τοῦ ἀγαπῆσαι] (3 Kgdms 11:2; cf. 1 Cor 6:16).[52] The coupling of the verbs for clinging and loving seem to suggest that although it is Solomon's heart which is turned, the cause for this is physical desire for his wives.[53] Being a lover of women [φιλογύναιος] (3 Kgdms 11:1) and clinging to his foreign wives, Solomon's heart "was not perfect with the Lord his God" (3 Kgdms 11:4).[54] Once again, women have come between a man and the commands of God.

The Proverbs attributed to Solomon (Prov 1:1), although lauding the benefits the courageous woman brings to her husband and extolling the virtues of woman wisdom, also recognizes the "problematic" nature of women, at least as far as men are concerned. The man who loves wisdom, and brings joy to his father, is contrasted with the man who keeps πόρναι and thereby loses his wealth (Prov 29:3).[55] This could be read as simple economic reality – one who spends his money on women for sex, whether in the form of gifts or direct payment, will become impoverished, whereas the lover of wisdom maintains the economic stability of his household, which is a great virtue in the wisdom literature (e.g. Prov 8:18; 31:11-27).[56] This statement could have another level of meaning, however. The man "loving" [φιλοῦντος] wisdom is the opposite of the one who "cherishes" [ποιμαίνει][57] whores. The opposite of wisdom, which in the LXX tends to be impie-

---

[51] See Lev 19:32.
[52] See Herbert Weir Smyth, *Greek Grammar* (Cambridge, Mass.: Harvard University Press, 1984), 451, §2032 a and e.
[53] This is how Sir 47:19 interprets this situation.
[54] Cf. Exod 34:15-16.
[55] See also Prov 23:20-21.
[56] For a "broader economic reading of Proverbs 1-9" see Yee, *Poor Banished Children of Eve*, 135-58.
[57] Note that the literal meaning of this word is to herd, feed, or graze animals or to act as a shepherd. LSJ also notes that when used metaphorically, it means "cherish." Given the context, however, I do not think the idea of feeding animals should be kept too far away from the meaning of this verse.

ty and foolishness (e.g. Prov 1:7; 2:32; 3:35; 4:10-19; 26:1-12), seems to be personified by the πόρναι here.

The reading of Prov 29:3 offered above is bolstered by returning to Prov 1–9 to examine the foil for woman wisdom, namely the strange or "other" woman. Much ink has been spilled debating who the strange woman actually is, that is, determining what actual women she might be representing. Turning once again for guidance to Claudia Camp, it is perhaps more helpful to consider that this "figure operates at a less directly historically referential level of symbolism," rather she consolidates "a variety of images of female-identified evil into an archetype of disorder at all levels of existence."[58] Michael Fox concurs with this view, arguing that the strange woman is a "multivalent symbol with the potential for application to a variety of inimical realities."[59] Using the language of conceptual integration theory operative in this study, one can state that the strange woman of Prov 1-9 is already a blended space serving multiple rhetorical purposes.[60]

The strange woman[61] makes an appearance in chs. 5, 6, 7, and 9 of LXX Proverbs and is described in many ways: she is worthless (5:3), a whore [πόρνη] (5:3; 6:26), folly (5:5),[62] a stranger/foreigner/other [ἀλλοτρία] (5:20), not one's own (5:20), beautiful (6:25; 9:18a), an animal of prey (6:26), a married woman (6:29), strange and wicked [ἀλλοτρία καὶ πονηρία] (7:5), excited and profligate (7:11), having a shameless face (7:13), an adulteress (7:19-20), possessing a home that leads to Hades and death (7:27; cf. 5:5), foolish and bold [ἄφρων καὶ θρασεῖα] (9:13), immodest (9:13), a spring trap of Hades (9:18), and strange water [ὕδωρ ἀλλότριον] (9:18b-c). Given the multiple images used for this dangerous female figure Carol Newsom's contention that "with the Strange Woman ... the text discovers its primary image of otherness" is easily defended.[63]

The descriptions of the strange woman in Proverbs 5-9 tend to emphasize her erotic attractiveness. Her lips drip with honey (Prov 5:3), her beauty inflames powerful desire [ἐπιθυμία], and one must therefore guard against gazing at her (Prov 6:25; cf. 9:18a). Her outward appearance as a sexually immoral, and therefore available, woman

---

[58] Camp, *Wise, Strange and Holy*, 43, also 63-64; idem, "Woman Wisdom," 93. See also Yee, *Poor Banished Children of Eve*, 150.

[59] Fox, "Strange Woman," 31.

[60] For Camp's discussion of the inputs and frames constructing the blend of the strange woman, a discussion beyond the scope of my investigation, see *Wise, Strange and Holy*, 48-58.

[61] For the sake of convenience I will refer to this figure as the "strange woman" even though, as will be noted, she has many other descriptors.

[62] See Fox, "Strange Woman," 35.

[63] Newsom, "Woman and the Discourse of Patriarchal Wisdom," 121.

[πορνικός] causes young men's hearts to flutter (Prov 7:10). Her sexual brazenness leads her to play the aggressor and kiss the young man after catching him (Prov 7:13), tempting him with her sensuous bed (Prov 7:16-17) and with her explicit invitation: "Come and let us enjoy love [φιλίας] until morning, come here and let us be involved in love [ἔρωτι]" (Prov 7:18).[64] This bold sexual nature appears again in Proverbs 9 where this foolish woman sits in the doorways and urges senseless men to turn to her to enjoy secret and stolen pleasures (Prov 9:13-17). It is worth noting that here, in the Proverbs attributed to Solomon, the verb used by the foolish woman to turn men into her house is ἐκκλίνω. This same verb describes how Solomon turned after the gods of his foreign [ἀλλότριαι] wives (3 Kgdms 11:4) because of his desire for these women. The strange/foreign woman is so dangerous precisely because she is so attractive. Camp notes that "Woman Stranger of Proverbs is a full-blown force of evil, an evil that manifests itself in sexual form."[65]

Despite her erotic attractiveness, the imagery related to the strange woman suggests her proximity to death and Hades (Prov 5:5; 7:26-27; 9:18). As Carol Newsom writes, describing this figure in MT Proverbs, "her vagina is the gate of Sheol. Her womb, death itself."[66] The strange woman does not walk upon "the paths of life" (Prov 5:6) and following her is like being a dumb animal led to slaughter or confinement (Prov 7:22-23). This contrasts both with woman wisdom, who walks in the paths of righteousness (Prov 8:20), and the results of obtaining wisdom and understanding the law (Prov 9:10-10a). The one who walks with woman wisdom rather than the strange woman, is told: "you will live for a long time and years of your life will be added to you" (Prov 9:11). Claudia Camp speaks to the fact that it is through the image of woman that "the ideal conceptualization of good and evil" is represented. Camp argues that, "In their embodiment, Woman Wisdom and the Strange Woman are one, a fact that their speeches only partially mitigate. *As woman, her dual path runs from heaven to Sheol and back, never failing to pass through human territory.*"[67] It is this potential for "woman" to function in a multiplicity of conceptual blends that

---

[64] The description of the sexually attractive strange woman in Proverbs should be compared with the images found in the erotic poem of the Song of Songs, also attributed to Solomon (1:2, 13-14; 2:5; 3:6-7; 4:3, 10-15; 5:1, 5; 6:1; 8:1-2, 14).

[65] See Camp, *Wise, Strange and Holy*, 87, quotation from 62.

[66] Newsom, "Woman and the Discourse of Patriarchal Wisdom," 128. Cf. 4QWiles of the Wicked Woman (4Q184): 9-11.

[67] Camp, *Wise, Strange and Holy*, 87, emphasis mine. Note that Camp's analysis is of MT Proverbs, but I believe her insights, like Newsom's, hold for LXX Proverbs as well.

will be important for my exploration of Paul's arguments against πορ-νεία.

Turning to the later wisdom text of Sirach, it is worth noting with Claudia Camp that "nowhere in the canon (except perhaps in Ezekiel) is there the virulent attack on women that occurs here: not only against traditionally 'evil' women (harlots), but also against one's wife and daughters."[68] This estimation is difficult to argue against given the sweeping generalization of Sir 42:14: "Better the evil of a man than a woman doing good" [κρείσσων πονηρία ἀνδρὸς ἢ ἀγαθοποιὸς γυνή]. Despite the generally high praise for the good wife sketched above, even the best woman is problematic in the book of Sirach.

The traditional women one must guard against are listed in Sir 9:3-9.[69] One is to avoid every kind of dangerous and sexually marginal woman such as the courtesan [γυνὴ ἑταιριζομένη] (Sir 9:3), the singer [ψαλλούσῃ] (Sir 9:4), and the ever sinister πόρνη (Sir 9:6-7). This wisdom book also instructs men even not to look at a "shapely woman" [γυνὴ εὔμορφος] (Sir 9:8 [NRSV]). These types of women seem to be dangerous in and of themselves, even though, or perhaps because, they do not seem to be the sexual "property" of any socially respectable individual or group. Sirach also warns against intently gazing at a virgin, lest one lose self-control and suffer financial loss for violating her (Sir 9:5). Thus even a virgin, a sexually "good" woman, can be the downfall of a man who is not careful. The wife of another man can also effect this same outcome, especially if one spends too much time contemplating her beauty or dines and drinks with her, presumably at a banquet. In doing this the sage warns men that "your soul [ψυχή] might turn [ἐκκλίνῃ] to her" and cause your spirit to slide into destruction (Sir 9:8β-9). A wife, who again should be characterized as a "good" woman as seen above, can be a cause of sexual transgression if she happens to be the wife of another. As with Solomon in 3 Kingdoms and the senseless man in Proverbs 9, the danger is that a woman who is sexually off limits will "turn" one away from proper sexual comportment – with dire consequences.

As if the dangers lurking in just about every woman a man might meet outside of his family were not bad enough, Sirach begins ch. 9 discussing the dangers inherent in sexual expression with the only

---

[68] Claudia V. Camp, "Understanding Patriarchy: Women in Second Century Jerusalem through the Eyes of Ben Sira," in *"Women Like This": New Perspectives on Jewish Women in the Greco-Roman World* (ed. Amy-Jill Levine; SBLEJL 1; Atlanta: Scholars Press, 1991), 5 and also n. 17 on the same page. For an analysis of the *topoi* of woman as bad wife, as adulteress and prostitute, and as daughter see Trenchard, *Ben Sira's View of Women*, 57-94, 95-128, and 129-165 respectively.

[69] The chapter actually begins with a discussion about one's wife, but that will be taken up in a discussion below. See Camp, "Understanding Patriarchy," 20-21.

woman shown any courtesy in this text, namely one's own wife. A wife can be "bad" in any number of ways. Trenchard analyzes "a wide variety of negative domestic scenarios ranging from drunken wives to wives who are overly talkative, from wives hard to control to those who support their husbands financially, from suppression to divorce."[70] Claudia Camp has shown how Sir 9:1 demonstrates that even sexual relations with one's wife, supposedly the "correct" outlet for a man's carnal urges, is fraught with danger. In this verse Sirach teaches:

Μὴ ζήλου γυναῖκα τοῦ κόλπου σου
μηδὲ διδάξῃς ἐπὶ σεαυτὸν παιδείαν πονηράν.

An interpretive crux has traditionally been how to interpret the negative imperative μὴ ζήλου. Trenchard translates it as "do not be jealous" and argues that by being "groundlessly jealous" of one's wife a husband teaches her to be overly aware of any sexual indiscretions on his part, thus exposing him to public shame.[71] Camp rightly notes the problematic nature of this interpretation and suggests translating the verb as one does elsewhere, as "zealous, or passionate, for." If the verb is translated this way, the verse is rendered: "Do not be passionate for [the] wife of your bosom / lest you teach an evil lesson against yourself." In this understanding, a husband who shows unreserved sexual passion is teaching his wife the same.[72] The danger comes if one's wife takes this sexual passion learned from her husband and expresses it with other men. This is a real danger given Sirach's understanding of the sexual depravity of women. This is on display with "virtually pornographic lewdness"[73] in the argument Ben Sira makes from the following simile:

> Like a thirsty foot-traveler will open [his] mouth
> and will drink from every [source of] water close at hand,

---

[70] Trenchard, *Ben Sira's View of Women*, 57. Trenchard examines mainly Sir 26:5-9; 25:13-26, but also 9:2; 33:20 (= Heb 33:19 and 30:28 in some Gk); 47:19; 7:26; 37:11; 42:6. See also Claudia V. Camp, "Honor and Shame in Ben Sira: Anthropological and Theological Reflections," in *The Book of Ben Sira in Modern Research: Proceedings of the First International Ben Sira Conference 28-31 July 1996 Soesterberg, Netherlands* (ed. Pancratius C. Beentjes; BZAW 255; Berlin: de Gruyter, 1997), 182: "... the possibility of having an *evil wife* is not just raised, but given rather extensive treatment. The real possibility of women's evil, defined repeatedly as sexually transmitted shame, has moved from the streets of Proverbs into the heart of the man's home."

[71] Trenchard, *Ben Sira's View of Women*, 31.

[72] See also the *Sentences* of Pseudo-Phocylides 193-94 for a similar idea. As van der Horst notes in his commentary on line 193: "Self-restraint in marriage is a common theme in antiquity" (p. 240). Cf. 4Q416 (4QSap.Work A^b) Frag. 2 col. IV.

[73] Camp, "Understanding Patriarchy," 22.

>   she[74] will sit down opposite every peg
>   and will open [her] quiver before an arrow (Sir 26:12).

In addition to worrying about the sexual impropriety that women, even one's own wife, might tempt a man to, Sirach also worries about controlling the sexual activity of one's daughters (Sir 7:24).[75] Having a female child to begin with is a loss (Sir 22:3) and worrying about her keeps a man up at night (Sir 42:9). The main part of a man's fear about his daughter is that she will bring public shame upon him (Sir 42:11), usually in the form of sexual irregularities. The biggest fear is that a daughter will lose her virginity and become pregnant in her father's house, or that, once married off, she may be unfaithful to her husband (Sir 42:10). As Camp notes, a daughter is an everlasting source of anxiety regarding sexual improprieties. "An adulterous wife can be divorced, but a sexually deviant daughter has no place to go but home."[76]

Not only does Sirach describe worrying about female children through the lens of sexual misconduct, but also from the curious notion that daughters are not really safe anywhere. The beauty of one's daughter is not to be viewed by other men, but she is also not supposed to sit and listen to groups of, presumably married, women either (Sir 42:12).[77] The reason that even other women endanger virgin daughters is found in the gnomic saying of 42:13: "for from garments emerges the moth, and from a woman, woman's evil." Camp and Trenchard argue that the "woman's evil" that the daughter will learn from other women is the knowledge of her sexuality.[78] Women themselves thus participate, according to the androcentric text of Sirach, in their own corruption.

The negative portrayal of woman in the writings of Philo provides a rich and complex study of how Hellenistic Jews could use their texts in new conceptual environments to think creatively about the dangers

---

[74] There is some question about who lies behind the implied pronoun "she" in this passage. As it stands in the text as we have it, this verse is included in a unit that warns a man to control his "headstrong daughter" (26:10). Camp, citing Patrick W. Skehan and Alexander A. DiLella, *The Wisdom of Ben Sira* (AB 39; Garden City, NY: Doubleday, 1987), argues, however, that "the context describes wives" ("Understanding Patriarchy," 22 n. 45). In terms of my use of Sir 26:12 as a resource zone here, who the actual referent is (wife or daughter) matters less than the fact that, whoever she is, she is a *woman*.

[75] Literally this verse warns a man to be alert concerning his daughters' bodies: θυγατέρες σοί εἰσιν; πρόσεχε τῷ σώματι αὐτῶν.

[76] Camp, "Understanding Patriarchy," 37.

[77] The Greek of Sirach simply reads ἐν μέσῳ γυναικῶν, which could be rendered "in the midst of wives" or "in the midst of women." Camp, "Understanding Patriarchy," 35; Trenchard, *Ben Sira's View of Women*, 154-58; and the NRSV translation, relying on the Hebrew, argue that these women are married.

[78] Camp, "Understanding Patriarchy," 35; Trenchard, *Ben Sira's View of Women*, 158.

posed by women. As in some of the wisdom literature above, there is a certain amount of "slippage" in Philo between actual women and allegorical women. As Richard Baer notes:

> His deprecation of actual woman and of female sense-perception are frequently so closely intertwined that no clear separation of the two can be made. Philo's usual practice is to speak disparagingly of actual woman on the basis of the literal meaning of a text and then allegorize the passage in terms of sense-perception. In some instances, however, his pejorative references to the female are confined to actual woman, and in other cases refer only to sense-perception. But nowhere are these two foci really far apart, for it is precisely Philo's deprecation of woman that permits him to use her as a symbol of sense-perception, and, on the other hand, his castigation of female sense-perception and the material world leads in turn to a further devaluation of woman.[79]

What matters most for this discussion, however, is that, regardless of where on the continuum between actual and allegorical a female figure falls in Philo's writings, it is the image of *woman* that is used to convey Philo's understanding about certain negative elements of the world in which he finds himself.

In a discussion of that most dangerous figure in Greek-speaking Judaism, the πόρνη, Philo describes her not as some simple sex worker, but one who threatens the very fabric of society. This is perhaps counter intuitive at first glance, especially when considered in light of Gail Corrington Streete's argument that πόρναι are viewed in Jewish scriptural resources as less destructive than adulteresses because the former's sexuality is owned by no one.[80] Yet, she does note that, overall, "[f]emale sexual desire is portrayed as disturbing and destructive to the community when it is perceived to aim at no benefit to husband or household."[81] Philo's πόρνη is so dangerous because she actively hunts the young men [νέων] of the community for her *own* sexual and economic benefit, recalling the strange woman of Proverbs. Philo refers to the πόρνη as an outrage [λύμη], damaged goods [ζημία], and a polluted thing [μίασμα] (cf. 1 Cor 6:15-17) who not only endangers naïve men with sensual pleasures, but also threatens "the souls of men and women alike with licentiousness [ἀκολασίας]." The fact that the πόρνη sells her "blossoming" in the ἀγορά is bad enough, but her presence

---

[79] Baer, *Philo's Use of the Categories Male and Female*, 40. See also Judith Romney Wegner, "Philo's Portrayal of Women – Hebraic or Hellenic?" in *"Women Like This": New Perspectives on Jewish Women in the Greco-Roman World* (ed. Amy-Jill Levine; SBLEJL 1; Atlanta: Scholars Press, 1991), 41-66.

[80] Corrington Streete, *Strange Woman*, 43; see also Crenshaw, *Wisdom*, 13.

[81] Corrington Streete, *Strange Woman*, 17.

within the community is also likened to an infection that destroys the virtues of the citizens of the πολιτεία (*Spec.* 3.51).

The dangers of the πόρνη, or those women who are allowed to play the part, are further expanded in Philo's exposition on Num 31:16 found in Book One of the *Life of Moses*. In this retelling, Balaam counsels King Barak to use the attractive women of his region as weapons against the Israelites who are favored by God. Balaam argues that if the sons of Israel can be made to disobey God, they will lose God's favor and, thereby, their ability to win in battle. Balaam counsels the king that these women should hire and prostitute themselves out [μισθαρνεῖν καὶ δημοσιεύειν] that they might trap the young men [νεότητα] (296). The king agrees and allows any woman to have sexual relations with anyone she pleased, thereby throwing all laws governing sexual behavior to the wind (300). Balaam gives the rationale behind this: "when their desires [ἐπιθυμίαις] have them in their grip, there is nothing which they will shrink from doing or suffering" (297 [based on Colson, LCL]). With promises of sexual pleasure, the women get the young Israelites to leave the ways of their fathers and worship idols (298). These women, playing the role of prostitutes, were able to mislead the mind [τὴν διάνοιαν] of the young men through the pleasures of their bodies (301). These men suffered the ruin "of their bodies through lust [λαγνείαις], of their souls through impiety [ἀσεβείᾳ]" (305 [Colson, LCL]). For Philo, women have the potential to use their bodies for sensual pleasure to effect the destruction of what should be the more rational parts of men (*Virt.* 34ff.).[82] What is interesting to note in this section of Philo's corpus is that the women do not seem to need persuading.[83] All that the king needs to do is nullify the laws regulating female sexual behavior. Through this retelling of the biblical story, Philo lays bare his contention that the sexual power of women threatens to break out of control if not kept in check by the laws and customs of a society.[84]

From his concern with the sensual dangers posed by women's bodies, Philo, as noted by Baer above, easily moves into rhetoric wherein he refers to sense-perception, or anything material, as female. From the Genesis account of creation Philo makes an allegorical leap in which the mind refers to the male aspect and the senses the female aspect in individuals (*Opif.* 165).[85] As he states elsewhere, "the most proper and

---

[82] See Wilson, "Pious Soldiers," for an analysis of this scene in Philo's *De virtutibus* (*De fortitudine* = *De virtutibus* 1-50).

[83] But see *Virt.* 39 and Wilson, "Pious Soldiers."

[84] Cf. *Ebr.* 55.

[85] For a more complete analysis of Philo's discussion of the rational and irrational parts of the human soul see Baer, *Philo's Use of the Categories Male and Female*, 14-41; Wilson, "Sin as Sex and Sex with Sin," 149-57.

exact name for sense-perception [ὄνομα αἰσθήσεως] is woman" (*Leg.* 2.38 [Colson & Whitaker, LCL]).[86] This involves some creative interpretation of the Genesis account of creation. Eve, whom Philo allegorizes as sense-perception [αἴσθησις], is called ζωή by Adam, the earthly mind, even though she is his own death. Eve/Sense is only the mother to "those who are in truth dead to the life of the soul. But those who are really living have Wisdom [σοφίαν] for their mother, but Sense they take for a bond-woman, the handiwork of nature made to minister to knowledge" (*Her.* 52-53 [Colson & Whitaker, LCL]).[87] In this passage the feminine sense-perception can only be combated, or rather properly subordinated, by recourse to wisdom, which interestingly is also personified as feminine. Yet Philo relates that being the children of wisdom refers to those who live by the divine spirit of reason [θείῳ πνεύματι λογισμῷ], which is a "male" force, as opposed to those who are deceived by the pleasures of the flesh [σαρκὸς ἡδονῇ].[88] As Walter Wilson states, "in Philo's psychic hierarchy 'male' and 'manly' refer to what is rational, complete, superior, and active, while 'female' and 'effeminate' designate their opposites."[89]

Sex and Marriage

Having produced a fairly thick description of the *topos* of women in some Jewish resources, it is now necessary to turn to the related *topoi* of sex and marriage. To be sure, these themes do not exist sharply demarcated in the texts under investigation – concerns about sex and marriage are almost always close at hand when the ancients think about women. However, in this section I will explore the issues of sex and marriage more specifically, since these *topoi* form the backbone of the second half of Paul's argument in 7:1-7. It is best, once again, to begin this discussion with the creation account. David Carr notes that at the end of the garden story in Genesis 3, "[a]s a result of human wisdom, creation has been broken open to the new possibilities and compromises of human moral reasoning."[90] The seemingly uncomplicated command of the creator God to couple sexually and reproduce in Genesis 1 and the innocent, shameless nakedness of the protoplasts in the garden story of Genesis are no longer recognized as actual possibilities of lived human community in the Jewish resources. The

---

[86] Sly, *Philo's Perception of Women*, 61 also cites *Leg.* 49-50 for this idea.
[87] Wilson, "Sin as Sex and Sex with Sin," 154 also notes this curious passage.
[88] *Her.* 57; cited by Sly, *Philo's Perception of Women*, 63.
[89] Wilson, "Sin as Sex and Sex with Sin," 151.
[90] Carr, *Erotic Word*, 55.

knowledge that the first humans received from disobeying God in Genesis 3 seems to have thrust upon them the responsibility of negotiating the now complicated sexual relationships between men and women. The celebratory paean to the commensurate relationship between men and women of Gen 2:23-24 is overshadowed by the results of disobeying God pronounced in Gen 3:16-17. The goodness of sexual productivity along with the intrinsic desire of a man and woman to become one flesh now is burdened by pain, inexplicable dependence, misuse of power, and seeming opposition between the words of women and the word of God (Gen 3:17α). Denied the fruit from the tree of life (3:22), the only way for humanity to continue to live is through sexual knowledge.

Many of the resources for thinking about sex and marriage in Jewish texts have been implicitly touched upon in the discussion of women above. In discussing the treatment of sexual activity in the wisdom literature, Claudia Camp makes two important points. First she notes that "[s]exuality is celebrated, but only if it is properly controlled" and, second, she recognizes that by "sexuality" the Jewish resources really mean "heterosexuality."[91] Thus, in the Jewish resource zones, especially those counted among the wisdom books, permissible sexual expression is bound up with marriage. The regulations regarding whom a man is allowed to marry and have sexual relations with are dealt with at length in the legal codes, especially Leviticus 18 and 20.[92] Although the primary social-sexual role for free men is the continuation of their family line by producing legitimate male heirs with their legal wives, Gail Corrington Streete notes that there are very few biblical codes regarding male extra-marital sexual relations with women whose sexuality was not the property of other men – namely one's own female slaves[93] and πόρναι.[94] The rules that do exist regarding πόρναι typically involve prohibitions against turning one's daughter into this type of woman, or bringing a prostitute's fee as an offering to the Temple (Deut 23:19-19).[95] To be sure, although no legal prohibition from Torah explicitly bars men from having sex with women outside of the

---

[91] Camp, "Woman Wisdom," 99. For more on celebrating sexuality, see Walsh, *Exquisite Desire*, 26. For more on controlling sexual outlets, see Crenshaw, *Wisdom*, 14: "The wise never tired of discussing the dangers of sexual license."

[92] See also the *Sentences* of Pseudo-Phocylides 179-83. See Deborah L. Ellens, *Women in the Sex Texts of Leviticus and Deuteronomy: A Comparative Conceptual Analysis* (Library of Hebrew Bible/Old Testament Studies 458; New York: T. & T. Clark, 2008).

[93] But note Deut 21:10-14 where rules are given regulating sexual activity between a man and a newly acquired female captive.

[94] Corrington Streete, *Strange Woman*, 43 where she also notes that Lev 21:14 prohibits priests from marrying πόρναι (along with other non-virginal women), "but it is not said that other men may not marry or enjoy the services of prostitutes."

[95] See my section on "Holiness" below.

ownership sphere of other men, the wisdom literature, as noted above, discourages such activity. The books of Proverbs and Ecclesiastes counsel a man to be satisfied with the company of his own wife. Doing otherwise not only leads to financial ruin and the possibility of public shame, but it involves walking in the ways of death. Such unwise extra-marital sexual activity does not exhibit the ultimate virtue of fearing the Lord.

Before moving on to discuss the controls placed on sexuality (and sexual passion) found in Jewish resources from the Hellenistic era, it is worth pausing to reflect on its celebration in another book in the Septuagint with Solomon's name attached to it, namely Ἆισμα ᾀσμάτων, ὅ ἐστιν τῷ Σαλωμων, the Song.[96] Although she notes that it is unclear that any specifically wisdom traditions are found in it and that there is likewise a lack of clear moral teaching, Carey Ellen Walsh names the Song as a wisdom book along with the other two texts related to Solomon in the Hebrew textual tradition, Proverbs and Ecclesiastes.[97] Not everyone agrees that the Song should be considered wisdom literature. Roland Murphy declares that it is not, but rather a "collection of love poems." However even he notes that it is "the link between eros and wisdom that opens the Song of Songs to another level of understanding. While it is not wisdom literature, its echoes reach beyond human sexual love to remind one of the love of Lady Wisdom."[98] Regardless of how one categorizes the text, the power of the Song has endured and famously made Rabbi Aqiba declare that this text is "the Holy of Holies."[99]

The metaphor of Israel as the lover and wife of God has a long pedigree in the biblical texts, especially among the prophets.[100] Traditionally the sexual yearning expressed in the Song has been taken as a metaphor of Israel's yearning for God. Murphy, Walsh, and David Carr, however, make note of the "slippage" found in this text between sensual desire of two lovers for one another and the desire for the divine.[101] Whatever spiritual or allegorical plane the metaphors of the text may or may not point to, the fact remains that in the Song there is a celebration of erotic desire that verges on the edge of uncontrolled.

---

[96] For other references to Solomon see Song 1:5; 3:7, 9, 11; 8:11-12.

[97] Walsh, *Exquisite Desire*, 3, 5.

[98] R. Murphy, *Tree of Life*, 106-107, see n. 28 for reference to others who claim the Song is, or is at least related to, wisdom literature.

[99] See Walsh, *Exquisite Desire*, 30.

[100] Walsh, *Exquisite Desire*, 154, cites Hosea 1-3, Jeremiah 2:24, and Ezekiel 16; 23.

[101] R. Murphy, *Tree of Life*, 106-107; Walsh, *Exquisite Desire*, 31-36; Carr, *Erotic Word*, 9-11, 139-51, see p. 145 nn. 33-37 for other references to those who hold this view.

This yearning described in the Song is viewed in a positive, although not always unproblematic light. Like the strange woman of Proverbs, the beautiful young woman of the Song wants "kisses and plenty of them."[102] Unlike the strange woman, however, the woman of the Song is not described as a threat to the young man of the poem although her lips, too, drip with honey (Song 4:11) and she desires to lie with her lover in a perfumed bed (Song 1:5-6). This is perhaps because the woman of the Song is no stranger, but is described by her lover as his sister (Song 4:9, 10, 12; 5:1, 2) and young bride [νύμφη] (Song 4:8-12; 5:1; cf. Wis 8:2).[103]

Sirach's fear of sexual ardor even within marriage is far removed from the eroticism of the Song. In one of the Song's more explicit scenes, the man knocks on the woman's door and begs her to "open to me" [ἄνοιξόν μοι] (Song 5:2). In response to this, the woman describes how her belly [κοιλία] is stirred by his yearning (Song 5:4; cf. 1 Cor 6:13). When the young woman rises to open the door for her lover, he is gone (Song 5:6) and the searching and desiring begin again. This rising tension that almost, but never quite, reaches consummation sustains the energy of the poem. The desires felt by the young lovers are elaborated and celebrated throughout the poem, yet even in this bold, sensual text there is a warning about the power of these desires. For the third time in the poem (see Song 2:7, 3:5), the woman warns the daughters of Jerusalem not to arouse love until it is ready (Song 8:4) because, as she later tells her lover:

love [ἀγάπη] [is] as strong as death,
passion [ζῆλος] as harsh as Hades;
its (fem.) sparks [are] sparks of fire, its flames (Song 8:6).

Even in this erotic love poem, where the desire of the young woman and man is celebrated, the dangers of this desire are acknowledged, even if only to emphasize love's power. The link of sexual love and passion with death and Hades brings us full circle back to the paths of the strange woman in Proverbs. Though the overwhelming power of desire is celebrated in the Song, it is treated with much more caution and fear in the Jewish resources of the Hellenistic era, as summed up in the teaching of Pseudo-Phocylides: "For *Eros* is no god, but a passion [πάθος] destructive to all" (194).[104]

As noted already, sexual activity, even sex within marriage, is a problem for the author of Sirach. In his desire to withstand the yearning of the belly [κοιλία] and for intercourse [συνουσιασμός] he prays

---

[102] Song 1:2; Walsh, *Exquisite Desire*, 1.
[103] See Carr, *Erotic Word*, 95 for family epithets in ancient Mesopotamian love poetry.
[104] Text and translation from Wilson, *Sentences of Pseudo-Phocylides*, 187, 221.

to the Lord to "turn desire [ἐπιθυμίαν] away from me" (Sir. 23:5-6; cf. Song 5:4; 1 Cor 6:13). The fear appears to be that desire will lead a man into all manner of sexual sins. Sirach 23 lists three main types of sexual sins: the sexually immoral person who commits incest, described in the Greek as ἄνθρωπος πόρνος ἐν σώματι σαρκὸς αὐτοῦ (v. 17α); the general sexually immoral person to whom "all bread is sweet" and who will not weary of it until dead (v. 17β); and the man who sins against his marriage bed thinking that the darkness hides his actions from God (v. 18). Although couched in the generic ἄνθρωπος (cf. 1 Cor 7:1), the subject of these sexual transgressions is clearly male. The chief sin of a woman in this chapter is adultery, which is counted, keeping literary symmetry, as three wrongs: disobeying the law of God; committing an offense against her husband; and committing adultery through sexual immorality [ἐν πορνείᾳ ἐμοιχεύθη] (Sir 23:23) and bearing another man's children thereby. Additionally, and of great import to Sirach, sexual sins stain the honor of a man's family, hence the blanket admonition to "be ashamed about πορνεία before your father and mother" (Sir 41:17).

While it would be reductionistic to assign a single cause to Sirach's sexual anxieties, lurking in the background is the collective memory of what the sexual sins of a king did to God's chosen nation. Uncharacteristically for a wisdom text, Sirach 44–50 contains what the Greek text titles πατέρων ὕμνος, the hymn of the fathers, which focuses on certain great men in Israelite cultural memory.[105] When Ben Sira sings to king Solomon, he lauds how wise he was in his youth [ὡς ἐσοφίσθης ἐν νεότητί σου] (Sir 47:14) – an anomaly, since it is young men who are usually foolish. Paradoxically, as discussed above, it is when Solomon grows old that his heart is led astray.[106] As Sirach sings in obvious disappointment:

> You turned aside your loins to women (or: wives)
> and were mastered through your body.
> παρανέκλινας τὰς λαγόνας σου γυναιξὶν
> καὶ ἐνεξουσιάσθης ἐν τῷ σώματί σου (Sir 47:19; cf. 1 Cor 6:12; 7:1).

The national experience, at least in the literary symbolic world of the Septuagint, of the divided kingdom following Solomon's sexual and then religious misconduct is an object lesson in what the extreme effects of sexual sins can be.

Sexual activity is inherently dangerous according to the author of Sirach and therefore must be undertaken only within the prescribed

---

[105] For an analysis of the hymn, see Mack, *Wisdom and the Hebrew Epic*.
[106] Cf. Lev 19:32.

bounds of marriage and, even there, with self-control and moderation. It is important to note, however, that the lack of a socially acceptable sexual outlet is also considered a problem in this wisdom text. Already noted above is the concern evinced by Sirach for the bodily integrity of a man's virgin daughters. The fear of communal shame brought upon a man if his daughters become pregnant in his house before they are married is extreme.[107] Getting one's daughter married off to a good husband, while not alleviating all anxiety, is still considered completing a great task [ἔσῃ τετελεκὼς ἔργον μέγα] (Sir 7:25) by the sage. At least then one's daughter's sexual body legally belongs to another man. But it is not only unmarried daughters that are a concern. The community as a whole needs to be wary, according to Sir 36:25-27, of an unmarried man. Not only does this man wander around sighing, but who, the text asks, would trust a man without a legal domicile, with an implied wife to keep it, of his own? As the gnomic saying of 36:25α teaches: "where there is no fence, a piece of property is plundered" (cf. 1 Cor 7:2). The wandering man without a wife is not only unhappy, but a threat to the integrity of the community. Although sexual activity is, by definition, fraught with problems, avoiding it is also perilous. It is only marriage, accompanied by the virtue of self-control, that channels the dangerous sexual inclinations of both men and women into acceptable patterns that do not threaten society.

In the Wisdom of Solomon one finds a discussion of how sexual disorders began. In this text, especially, Crenshaw's assertion that "the sages concentrated on sexual deviancy" is well justified.[108] There are no words to the wise on how to conduct their own sexual lives within their marriages. What a marriage actually constitutes is taken for granted. Thus the author, under the guise of Solomon, can state that he sought [ἐζήτησα] wisdom for his bride [νύμφην] and this conceptual blend is apparently understood by the community (Wis 8:2; cf. Song 4:8-12; 5:1). What the author instructs concerning sexual immorality is its cause and its destructive effects. In its famous pronouncement, summing up the connection seen in many biblical texts, the Wisdom of Solomon states that "the beginning of sexual immorality [πορνείας] [is the] thought of idols" (Wis 14:12).[109] For the author of this text, the real perversion lies in not knowing God (Wis 13:1) and thus creating images to worship that did not exist "at the beginning" (Wis 14:13). Improper sexual comportment comes through ignorance of the God of creation. Because of this "confusion of good things" [θόρυβος ἀγαθῶν] the ignorant do not keep their marriages pure (Wis 14:24),

---

[107] See Sir 7:24-25; 23:3-5; 42:9-14.
[108] Crenshaw, *Wisdom*, 14.
[109] Cf. Philo, *Decal.* 8; *Spec.* 1.332.

but fall prey to "defiling of souls, sexual perversion, disorder in marriages [γάμων ἀταξία], adultery and debauchery" (Wis 14:26 [NRSV]). For Wisdom of Solomon, idolatry leads necessarily to sexual problems because the ignorant people ensnared in its grasp have forgotten the creator and thus also the proper function of sexual activity within the created order.[110]

Although Philo of Alexandria, as noted above, was quick to associate woman with the debased world of sense-perception and to laud the virgins of the Therapeutae, marriage was understood by him to be the normal state of affairs, with its attendant sexual practices. However, unlike Wisdom of Solomon, Philo spends a great deal of energy attempting to regulate the sexual practices of married couples; simply being married is not good enough to protect the spouses from the dangers of sexual activity. Philo, in an allegorical analysis of Gen 12:10-20, argues that there are two kinds of marriages.

> Now in a marriage where the union is brought about by pleasure [ἡδονή], the partnership is between body and body [σωμάτων κοινωνίαν], but in a marriage made by wisdom [σοφία] it is between thoughts [λογισμῶν] which seek purification and perfect virtues [ἀρετῶν]. Now the two kinds of marriage are directly opposed to each other (Abr. 100 [Colson, LCL]; cf. 1 Cor 7:32-35).

Although Philo's understanding of marriage here is on the level of allegory – he will continue the discussion by noting that in a marriage made by wisdom it is the "wife" (virtue [ἀρετή]) who sows and the "husband" (thought [λογισμός]) who receives (Abr. 101 [Colson, LCL])[111] – this passage does highlight his unease with embodied sexuality.

Even within marriage, as seen above in the discussion of Philo's retelling of the Joseph story, sexual expression has as its sole purpose the production of legitimate male heirs (Ios. 43).[112] Thus Philo argues that the law of nature [νόμον φύσεως] teaches that a man should refrain from sexual intercourse with his wife during her menstrual period, lest he waste his seed [γονάς] for the sake of pleasure (Spec. 3.32).[113] Even more so, men should not marry women who are known to be sterile [στείραις γυναιξί] because the only reason for such a marriage would be "the quest of mere licentious pleasure [ἡδονῆς ἀκράτορος]," which

---

[110] Cf. 1 Enoch 19:1-3.

[111] See Wilson, "Sin as Sex and Sex with Sin," esp. 155-56.

[112] See Gaca, Fornication, 204-16. She discusses the "procreationism" of the Pythagoreans, which she argues had an influence on Philo, in her fourth chapter (pp. 94-116).

[113] Colson, LCL cites Lev 18:19 as Philo's scriptural referent. Philo also employs an agricultural metaphor to support his argument in this section. See Wilson, "Sin as Sex and Sex with Sin," 151.

is a symptom of an incurable lack of self-control [ἀκρασίαν ἀνίατον] (*Spec.* 3.34 [Colson, LCL]). However, those men who marry young women ignorant of their future wives' sterility, but who refuse to divorce them once their inability to bear children is demonstrated over the course of many years, deserve sympathy according to Philo; it is only those who knowingly marry sterile women who deserve censure (*Spec.* 3.35-36). Even if one's wife is fertile, however, there still lurks the danger that "natural pleasure [ἡ κατὰ φύσιν ἡδονή]"[114] may prompt a yearning for sexual coupling beyond moderation. When this happens, these "lovers of women [φιλογύναιοι]"[115] (cf. 3 Kgdms 11:1) "behave unchastely, not with the wives of others, but with their own [γυναιξὶν οὐκ ἀλλοτρίαις ἀλλὰ ταῖς ἑαυτῶν]" (*Spec.* 3.9 [Colson, LCL]). Why does sexual expression among married couples stoke Philo's anxiety? I suggest that an answer can be found in two areas: his treatment of Gen 2:24 and his blanket condemnation based on the LXX Decalogue, of desire and with it, pleasure.

In his *Allegorical Interpretation of Genesis*, Philo directly engages the encomium the first man utters in Gen 2:24 to his wife immediately after her creation. But far from celebrating the fact that a man will leave his father and mother to cling to his wife to create an independent household, Philo reads this verse allegorically to show what has gone wrong with the original creation of the mind in Genesis 1 (*Leg.* 1.21). For Philo, the man is the mind [νοῦς] and woman is sense-perception [αἴσθησις].[116] What is important to note about Gen 2:24, according to Philo, is that it is the superior element, man/mind, that clings to the inferior element, woman/sense-perception, thereby becoming her slave [αὐτῇ δουλωθῇ]. Philo reads the man's leaving of his father and mother as the mind leaving behind God, the father of everything, and God's virtue and wisdom [τὴν ἀρετὴν καὶ σοφίαν τοῦ θεοῦ], the mother of all. By leaving its father and mother, the mind becomes one flesh [μία σάρξ] with sense-perception, the two becoming one passion [ἓν πάθος]. Thus, when the man clings to his wife, the

---

[114] Note *Contempl.* 59 where Philo describes the "love-sickness" of a man for a woman and vice versa as "passions paying tribute to the laws of nature [ὑποτελοῦσι γὰρ αἱ ἐπιθυμίαι αὗται νόμοις φύσεως]," which differs from the love of "men for other males differing from them only in age" described by Plato (Colson, LCL). Cf. *Leg.* 2.8, 17.

[115] Note that in *Opif.* 81 God is called: a lover of virtue [θιλάρετον], a lover of that which is beautiful/good [φιλόκαλον], and a lover of generic (see *Opif.* 76) humanity [φιλάνθρωπον]. On whether women were included by Philo in the generic category ἄνθρωπος see Sly, *Philo's Perception of Women*, 59-70, where she concludes that this is not the case.

[116] See Baer, *Philo's Use of the Categories Male and Female*, 38-39. Note also my treatment of Philo in the sub-section on women above.

Scripture is allegorically teaching that the mind has become a lover of passions [φιλοπαθές] instead of a lover of God [φιλοθέος] (*Leg.* 2.49-50). When this happens, Philo teaches elsewhere, the sons of the earth have turned the mind "into the lifeless and inert nature of the flesh" [εἰς τὴν ἄψυχον καὶ ἀκίνητον σαρκῶν φύσιν] (*Gig.* 65 [Colson & Whitaker, LCL). Although this is Philo's allegorical interpretation of this passage, I would argue that the frame of enslavement, of the heavenly mind to the earthly flesh, attaches to this verse and is present even when Gen 2:24 is invoked to describe the literal marriage of men to women.

Both Kathy Gaca and William Loader, apparently independently of one another, have noted the impact the last commandment of the LXX Decalogue has on Philo's understanding of sexual yearning and expression.[117] In Hellenistic Judaism in general, and in Philo in particular, the tenth commandment found in Exod 20:17 and Deut 5:21 is often condensed into the two-word imperative that repeats twice in both verses: οὐκ ἐπιθυμήσεις (*Spec.* 78).[118] Although direct objects follow each of these commands, distilling the meaning of the command down to a prohibition against desire in Hellenistic Jewish thought fit into Stoic and other Greek philosophical notions.[119] Gaca contrasts Philo's views with that of Wis 14:12, discussed above, which relegates sexual immorality to a symptom of a disordered relationship with the Creator.

> For Philo ... the "origin of wrongdoing" and "of violation of the Law" (*Spec.* 4.84; *Opif.* 151-2) is innate sexual desire and its tendency to excessive pleasure, as Plato argues, not the worship of competing gods in the vicinity. Eros is what needs dismantling. Religiously alien worship is simply one venue invented to accommodate the nefarious ways of eros.[120]

Reducing the force of the final element in the Decalogue to outlawing desire in general has the effect of privileging of sexual desire as the source of all that plagues humanity. Returning to *Opif.* 152, cited by Gaca, one sees the chain of destruction in Philo's treatment of creation. Love [ἔρως] creates desire for the other sex in the man and the woman. This desire [πόθος], in turn, produces bodily pleasure [τὴν τῶν

---

[117] Gaca, *Fornication*, 153, 194-201; Loader, *Septuagint, Sexuality, and the New Testament*, 10-14.

[118] See also *Decal.* 142. In the LXX see Num 11:4, 34; Prov 12:12; 13:4. But see Prov 13:12, where good desire is called a tree of life [δένδρον γὰρ ζωῆς ἐπιθυμία ἀγαθή]; also Prov 10:24; 13:19.

[119] Gaca, *Fornication*, 153; Loader, *Septuagint, Sexuality, and the New Testament*, 13-14. Both Gaca and Loader cite Paul in Rom 7:7 and 13:9 and 4 Macc 2:6 as other examples of this trend. See *Decal.* 142f. and *Spec.* 4.78f. for Philo's treatment of this issue.

[120] Gaca, *Fornication*, 200. Cf. *1 Enoch* 19:1-3.

σωμάτων ἡδονήν] "for the sake of which [they] bring upon themselves the life of mortality and wretchedness in lieu of that of immortality and bliss" (Colson & Whitaker, LCL).[121]

Although, as noted, Philo recognizes the difference between pleasure which is according to nature and that which is contrary to it (cf. *Opif.* 161), as a general category he defines pleasure negatively as "a courtesan and a wanton" [ἑταιρὶς καὶ μαλχάς] (*Opif.* 166 (Colson & Whitaker, LCL]).[122] The good man [σπουδῖος] only uses pleasure out of necessity [μόνον ἀναγκαίῳ], but those who take pleasure as a perfect good [ἀγαθῷ τελείῳ] (*Leg.* 2.17) make themselves "slaves of passion" [δοῦλοι … πάθους] (*Opif.* 167; cf. 1 Cor 6:12). Given that Philo states elsewhere that "every passion [πάθος] is blameworthy" (*Spec.* 4.79 [Colson, LCL]), it is clear how detrimental becoming enslaved to such a force is in his thought. The ignominy of being under pleasure's power is also explored in *Deus* 111, where Philo describes the mind that falls into pleasure's grasp as one that is a lover of the body [φιλοσώματος] and a lover of passion [φιλοπαθής].[123] Such an emasculated soul is "unable to receive divine messages [and is] debarred from the holy congregation [ἐκκλησίας τῆς ἱερᾶς]" ([Colson & Whitaker, LCL]; cf. 1 Cor 6:18-20). Thus while Philo recognizes that marriage, raising children, a host of other banal tasks "wither the flower of wisdom before it blooms," it is not marriage, or the other tasks of daily living per se, that are problematic (cf. 1 Cor 7:32-35).[124] The true culprit is humanity's "fleshy nature" [ἡ σαρκῶν φύσις] (*Gig.* 29-30 [Colson & Whitaker, LCL]) that, prompted by desire, pursues pleasure.[125] The natural pleasure found in the marriage bed is dangerous, but the σπουδῖος knows how to use this powerful force properly rather than be used by it.

Holiness

In addition to the important and obvious categories of women, sex, and marriage as resource zones for Paul's argument in 1 Cor 6:12–7:7, the theme of holiness also requires exploration along with its attendant elements such as purity, priestly activity, and sacred temple space. Investigating a topic such as holiness of necessity involves interacting with cultic regulations found in the Pentateuch. Since I have touched on the relations of wisdom and holiness in Chapter 2, my exploration of wisdom resources here will be somewhat briefer than in the previ-

---

[121] Cf. *Leg.* 2.72; 3.113.
[122] Cf. *Deus.* 115.
[123] In contrast to being, as noted above, a lover of God [φιλοθέος] (*Leg.* 2.49-50).
[124] See Sir 38:24-25.
[125] See 4 Macc 1:22.

ous sections of this chapter. It is in the Hellenistic era, especially in the book of Sirach and the works of Philo, that the blurring of the lines between cult, law, and wisdom – never sharp to begin with – is especially evident and represents, to use the words of James Crenshaw, an intrusion "on wisdom's self-sufficiency, until at last a wedding of Yahwism and wisdom took place."[126] Crenshaw clearly gives a negative valence to this union, but it is this complex blending of multiple frameworks in creative ways during the Hellenistic era that allows interpreters to catch a glimpse of the complex interaction among the cognitive resources available to Jewish thinkers of this time, of whom Paul is surely a good example.

The regulations delineating holiness and purity in the presence of sacred space found in the Jewish resources are extensive. In this section I attempt to map out a description of holy and priestly resources especially as they have to do with the sexual body and the relation of that body to sacred space. A paradigmatic example of the incompatibility of sexual activity and sacred space is found in Exodus 19. Here the people of Israel agree to uphold the commands that God has given them. In response to this assent, the Lord tells Moses that he will appear to the people in a dense cloud on Mount Sinai, thus making the mountain sacred space – so sacred that any who touch it, whether human or animal, are to be killed (19:12). God tells Moses that the people must be consecrated, wash their clothes, and "be ready for the third day" (19:10-11). However, when Moses relates this command to his (male) audience he adds another level of purity: "Be ready for three days, do not approach [προσέλθητε] a woman" (19:15).[127] The incompatibility of "approaching" women, a likely euphemism for sexual intercourse,[128] and standing in the presence of the Lord is something that echos throughout the, typically androcentric,[129] Jewish resources.

---

[126] Crenshaw, *Wisdom*, 15.

[127] John William Wevers, *Notes on the Greek Text of Exodus* (SBLSCS 30; Atlanta: Scholars Press, 1990), 301 notes that, in contrast to 19:11, "[t]he reference [in 19:15] to 'three days' is in the accusative, thus denoting extent of time."

[128] See LSJ, προσέρχομαι III; see Hippocrates *Epid.* 6.3.14 where προσέρχομαι is used in a sexual sense as well. Note that the BDB entry for נגשׁ, used in MT Exod 19:15, also suggests that this Hebrew verb is used as a sexual euphemism here.

[129] See Camp, "Woman Wisdom and the Strange Woman, 85-112; Corrington Streete, *Strange Woman*, esp. 1-19; Newsom, "Woman"; Walsh, *Exquisite Desire*, 39, 135-37; Athalya Brenner and Fokkelein van Dijk-Hemmes, *On Gendering Texts: Female and Male Voices in the Hebrew Bible* (Biblical Interpretation Series 1; Leiden: Brill, 1993), 57-62; Ilona N. Rashkow, *Taboo or not Taboo: Sexuality, Family and the Hebrew Bible* (Minneapolis: Fortress, 2000).

In the legal codes, there are numerous regulations ensuring the separation of sexual activity and sacred space.[130] For example, in the book of Leviticus, God repeatedly warns Moses that the people must be holy because their Lord God is holy (Lev 11:44; 19:2 20:7, 26; cf. Num 15:40-41) and this holiness is part of what is expected by a God who separated the people of Israel from "all the nations" [πάντων τῶν ἐθνῶν] (Lev 20:24, 26).[131] This holiness of the nation of Israel is assured if they keep and enact all of God's commands [προστάγματα] (Lev 20:8). It is their status as a holy nation which makes cultic cleanness and purity, especially regarding sexual matters, so important for Israel. This is made evident in Leviticus 15, although the topic discussed here is not restricted to sexual activity. This chapter has to do primarily with the emission of fluids, both pathological and natural, from the genitals of men and women. Any "flowing" from the penis (literally, σῶμα) renders a man unclean (Lev 15:2), even the natural emission of semen (Lev 15:16, 18).[132] So, too, any flowing of blood from a woman's vagina, either due to menstruation or disease, renders her unclean.[133] It is also important to note that Lev 15:18 specifically states that, in the act of coitus, if a man ejaculates, *both* he and the woman are unclean. Even though it is not the woman whose genitals are visibly emitting fluid (see Lev 15:33 and 18:19 for this), by receiving the discharge from her partner she too is unclean.[134] Knowing how one's genitals affect one's purity status is important in that if the people do not properly deal with bodily impurity they will die on account of it, because they will have polluted God's tabernacle that is among them [τὴν σκηνὴν ... τὴν ἐν αὐτοῖς] (Lev 15:31). Genital emissions, including those that occur during sexual activity, are problematic for the text of Leviticus due to the

---

[130] On the importance of legal codes for wisdom, see Goff, *Worldly and Heavenly Wisdom*, 46: "An important feature of the sapiential tradition in the late Second Temple period is the incorporation of Torah piety." See also Robbins, *Invention*, 1:150-71 for a discussion of what he refers to as "Torah Wisdom."

[131] See also Exod 19:6.

[132] See John William Wevers, *Notes on the Greek Text of Leviticus* (SBLSCS 44; Atlanta: Scholars Press, 1997), 224, where he notes that σῶμα is not a euphemism for the penis in Greek. However, Weavers argues that "it is here an obvious calque for בשר." See also Deut 23:11 for a man who becomes ritually unclean because of a nocturnal emission having to leave the camp.

[133] For an analysis of the structure of MT Leviticus 15, see esp. Deborah Ellens, "Menstrual Impurity and Innovation in Leviticus 15," in *Wholly Woman, Holy Blood: A Feminist Critique of Purity and Impurity* (ed. Kristin de Troyer, Judith A. Herbert, Judith Ann Johnson, and Anne-Marie Korte; SAC; Harrisburg, Penn.: Trinity Press International), 33-34. See also Leviticus 12, which discusses purity issues after childbirth. Note esp. Lev 12:4 where the woman impure from childbirth is prohibited from touching (οὐχ ἄψεται) anything holy and from entering the sanctuary [ἁγιαστήριον].

[134] Although note the ancient medical idea that both men and women release semen during sexual intercourse discussed in, e.g., Martin, *Corinthian Body*, 223-24.

fact that God's tabernacle is in the people's midst, which means they are always living in close proximity to sacred space (cf. 1 Cor 6:18-20).

Living with the tabernacle in their midst means that the sexual relations in which, and with whom, the Israelites engage must be controlled. More importantly, in terms of sexual behavior, the Israelites, as God's holy nation, are not to follow the practices [ἐπιτηδεύματα] or the customs [νομίμοι] of either the Egyptians or the Canaanites (Lev 18:2-3). Following this command in Leviticus 18 is a list of prohibited sexual activities.[135] The vast majority of these rules (Lev 18:6-18) deal with incest, while the remainder (Lev 18:19-23) cover a wide range of sexual "abominations" and activities by which one is "polluted," including sex during menstruation, adultery, treating males as female sexual partners, and bestiality.[136] The chapter ends (18:24-30) with the rationale for these sexual regulations – the people who occupied the land before the Israelites engaged in all these sex acts and through these activities the land became polluted, which, in turn, caused the land to become vexed [προσοχθίζω] with these inhabitants.[137] God charges the Israelites to keep his commandments and not to pollute themselves with any of the sexual activities enumerated in this chapter since "the souls [ψυχαί] who do [these abominations] will be destroyed out of their people" (Lev 18:29). Because of their relationship, and the relationship of the land, with the holy one whose self-designation is "the Lord your God," the people of Israel must live different sexual lives than those of their neighbors or predecessors.

Although all of Israel is a holy nation living in a holy land in close proximity to the sacred space of God's tabernacle, lay people were generally not, according to the scriptural resources, under the same purity strictures as the priesthood. As noted in the previous section, there is no regulation in the Pentateuch which states that sexual activity with a πόρνη makes a man any more impure than having intercourse with any other category of woman.[138] For example, in Genesis 38 Judah is not censured for sleeping with Tamar when he thought she was but a πόρνη and, as noted, Leviticus 18 deals only with incest and adultery. What the children of Israel *are* prohibited from doing, however, is turning their own daughters into πόρναι. The rationale behind this and

---

[135] See also Lev 20:10-21; Deut 27:20-23.

[136] Note that Lev 18:21 is not about sexual activity per se, but rather giving one's offspring, the result of sexual activity, over to the service of "a ruler" [ἄρχων] (מלך in MT Leviticus).

[137] Instead of becoming angry with the inhabitants, the MT uses more colorful imagery and has the land "vomit out" (קיא) its inhabitants. The translation of προσοχθίζω as "to be vexed with" comes from Wevers, *Notes on the Greek Text of Leviticus*, 285.

[138] See Lev 20:10-21.

for the regulations in Leviticus 18 seems to be concern for the land. If the daughters of Israel become πόρναι, "the land will be given to sexual immorality and the land will be full of lawlessness [ἀνομίας]" (Lev 19:29). The priests of Israel, however, are also commanded not to marry πόρναι or any other non-virginal women because of the priests' holy status and the position they have of offering gifts to God (Lev 21:7-8, 13-15). Furthermore, the daughters of priests are under stricter sexual controls than the daughters of ordinary Israelites. If a daughter of a priest is given to sexual immorality she is to be burned to death because she has profaned [βεβηλόω] her father's name. She has, that is, attached pollution to the name of a man holy to God (Lev 21:7-13).[139]

In addition to the censure Jewish wisdom texts give to sexually immoral women and the men who are intimate with them, especially those who pay for the privilege,[140] one also finds in the book of Proverbs a concern with purity issues regarding women who sell carnal favors. In a series of pithy gnomic sentences, Proverbs 19:13β states that the vows that are paid out of the earnings of an ἑταίρα are not pure.[141] The money earned from selling sex, according to this gnomic saying, is impure and should not, it is implied, be used to pay religious vows.[142] The linking of sexually immoral behavior with improprieties of worship, or other cultic expressions, is also seen in Prov 7:14. In this verse the strange woman says to the young man she has in her grasp: "I have a peace sacrifice, today I pay my vows." Claudia Camp notes that many interpreters see the sacrifice and vows discussed here to be from religiously alien cults. However, Camp makes a good case that the woman here represented is talking about the sacrificial system of the cult of YHWH.[143] That is, the woman is so threatening because she is a member of the community who has made herself "other" by flaunting the religious and purity codes of the community by treating the sacrificial system as one in which she can proleptically obviate the sexual sin she is about to commit.[144] In other words, the strange woman seems to treat sacrifice and the payment of vows as mere "ritual motions" that, having been dispensed with, allow her to engage in immoral sexual

---

[139] See also Lev 22:12-13 where the main concern seems not to be about with whom the priest's daughter has sex, but with the existence of offspring.

[140] See Prov 23:20.

[141] Although the term used here is ἑταίρα rather than πόρνη, the actual differences between the two are not that great in actual usage. Here, linking the ἑταίρα with wages [μισθώματα] (also "rent") puts this figure on the level of a sex worker. See Laura K. McClure, *Courtesans at Table: Gender and Greek Literary Culture in Athenaeus* (New York: Routledge, 2003), 11-18, for a discussion of these terms.

[142] See Sir 43:18.

[143] Camp, *Wise, Strange and Holy*, 44-46. See Prov 15:8; 21:27.

[144] Note the ἕνεκα clause in 7:15. See also Prov 30:20.

behavior without consequence. Moreover, the strange woman's desire for adulterous sex during what should be a time of religious ritual purity gives this section its heightened charge of religious horror.[145]

If the book of Proverbs brings together cultic ritual and sexual transgression to intensify the depravity of the strange woman, it is worth noting that there is evidence in the Jewish resources that shows that temple imagery can also be used in a vaguely erotic sense. This occurs, of all places, in the book of Sirach. In his description of the beauty of the good wife, Ben Sira uses similes that seem to echo the holy implements and structure of the temple. Her beautiful face is described as light upon a "holy lampstand" (Sir 26:17)[146] and her beautiful feet and steadfast heart are likened to "golden pillars upon a silver pedestal" (Sir 26:18).[147] Using temple imagery to laud the beauty of a woman may seem out of place, but since the woman is a "good wife" the positive valence of the temple is selectively projected on to the woman, thus building her up. In the example of the strange woman in Proverbs, she is an adulteress and her negative connotations are selectively projected onto the cultic rituals to their demerit.

The placement of wisdom within sacred space, both the tabernacle and the temple, is an important concept for Ben Sira. As personified wisdom teaches in Sir 24:10-12α:

> I served before him in [the] holy tabernacle [σκηνῇ]
> and thus I was established in Zion;
> likewise he gave me to rest in the beloved city,
> and in Jerusalem [is] my power [ἐξουσία];
> and I took root among a glorified [δεδοξασμένῳ] people...

In the famous "Hymn to the Fathers" (Sir 44–50), however, much descriptive ink is spilled discussing the activities of Israelite priests (Aaron, Phineas, Samuel, and Simon)[148] – their holiness (esp. Sir 25:12), zealousness (Sir 45:23), and their activities in and relation to sacred space (Sir 45:14, 16, 21, 23-24; 46:16; 50:1-21). Wisdom, on the other hand, appears at the beginning of the hymn (Sir 44:12-15) in Ben Sira's affirmation "that the best of men will produce *both* seed faithful to the covenant and lasting wisdom,"[149] but is not discussed

---

[145] Camp, "Woman Wisdom," 93, notes that Lev 7:11-21 prohibits sexual activity during the days of the peace offering. See also idem, *Wise, Strange and Holy*, 45-46.

[146] Cf. Ex 25:31; 37:17-24; Num 8:11-4; 3 Kgdms 7:35; 2 Chron 4:7, 20.

[147] Cf. Ex 26:15-30; 38:34-27; 3 Kgdms 7:26-29, 34-36; 2 Chron 3:15-4:10, 19-22.

[148] See Mack, *Wisdom and the Hebrew Epic*, 27.

[149] Claudia V. Camp, "Storied Space, or, Ben Sira 'Tells' a Temple," in *"Imagining" Biblical Worlds: Studies in Spatial, Social and Historical Constructs in Honor of James W. Flana-*

again until the postscript by the author, who describes himself as one "who pours forth wisdom from his heart" (Sir 50:27). Nonetheless, Burton Mack argues that the hymn is "one of the finer achievements of Ben Sira's intellectual efforts in a wisdom mode, even though the figure of wisdom no longer appears there."[150] Mack asserts that the repetition of the term "glory" in the hymn, primarily referring to the temple, alludes to wisdom, since this term "belongs as well to the linguistic field of wisdom discourse."[151] In Mack's analysis wisdom and temple cultic space are not antithetical, but both work together, or rather, wisdom works in the sacred space of the temple and both produce glory.

Claudia Camp has a different reading of the hymn and its relationship to wisdom. She argues that the similarities between woman wisdom in Sirach 24 and Simon the high priest in Sirach 50 do not serve complementary purposes, but rather the purpose of displacement. She notes that "[o]nce Simeon appears, Woman Wisdom disappears" and thus the displacement in the hymn is "of the female by the male."[152] Camp notices that women are missing from Sirach's hymn. The great men exist without mothers, sisters, or wives. The one exception, discussed in the section above, is with Solomon, the actual builder of the temple in Jerusalem. Solomon had wives, and plenty of them, which led to his religious sins. "But women do not depart from [Ben Sira's] space from their own accord, as the reference to Phinehas, both at the end of the Aaron pericope and at the end of Simeon's shows."[153] Camp notes that Ben Sira was not crass enough to explicate the exact nature of Phinehas's "zeal," but argues that the implied reader of the book of Sirach would readily be able to supply the background information from Num 25:6-18. Indeed, as Mack notes, Sir 45:23-24 makes intertextual allusions to this pericope in Numbers. Phinehas is portrayed as a priest in the hymn of Ben Sira, but the sacrifice by which he made expiation for Israel [ἐξιλάσατο περὶ τοῦ Ισραηλ][154] was not an animal sacrifice, but the killing of the Midianite woman engaged in copulation with one of the sons of Israel.[155] Reading Camp together with Mack one notes that they disagree not so much on the presence of wisdom in the temple – Camp agrees that Simon has taken on wisdom's attributes – but rather the representation of wisdom as woman. Perhaps it is best

---

gan (ed. David M. Gunn and Paula M. NcNutt; JSOTSup 359; London: Sheffield Academic Press, 2002), 74.

[150] Mack, *Wisdom and the Hebrew Epic*, 151; see also 159.
[151] Mack, *Wisdom and the Hebrew Epic*, 169.
[152] Camp, "Storied Space," 76.
[153] Camp, "Storied Space," 78.
[154] See Num 25:13: ἐξιλάσατο περὶ τῶν υἱῶν Ισραηλ.
[155] Mack, *Wisdom and the Hebrew Epic*, 28.

to say that, for Ben Sira, wisdom and temple holiness go hand in hand in glory, but precisely for this reason it is necessary for him to banish all images of (necessarily impure) female embodiment as they relate to wisdom in this sacred space.

Given the utter mistrust of the body and all things material, Philo can be expected to have concerns about humans coming into contact with the divinity – either in sacred spaces or via holy oracles. In *The Unchangeableness of God*, Philo makes an argument that assumes bodily purity is necessary to enter holy spaces. However, he uses this datum in an argument from the lesser to the greater. Both temples and bodies, being made of material things, are according to Philo "soulless" [ἄψυχον]. Thus "it is absurd to think that a man should be forbidden to enter temples save after bathing and cleansing his body, and yet should attempt to pray and sacrifice with a mind [διάνοια] still soiled and spotted" (8 [based on Colson & Whitaker, LCL]). If it is necessary to cleanse the physical body when entering a temple made of stones and timber, then how much more ought one's higher faculties be pure when encountering the purity of God. Although he verges on deprecating physical purity and sacred physical spaces, Philo does so to make the point that simply undertaking physical ablutions is no substitute for purifying one's intellect. His critique is effective only insofar as his implied audience accepts as common sense the necessity of bodily purity in sacred spaces. The thrust of his argument here is to combat the notion that while this might be a necessary element in approaching the sacred, it is not a sufficient one.

The fact of the matter is that Philo is intensely concerned with correct use of the body in the presence of the divine. In his retelling of Exod 9:14-19, Philo approvingly notes that the people, in preparation for Moses' reception of a divine oracle, only indulged in pleasures necessary to stay alive and, therefore, "had kept pure from intercourse with women" [ἀγνεύσας ὁμιλιῶν τῶν πρὸς γυναῖκας]. He also notes that the people cleansed their bodies with ablutions, washed their clothes and wore "the whitest of raiment" (*Decal.* 45). This description of the people fits with Philo's description of Moses himself. In Book Two of *The Life of Moses* Philo notes that his intention of writing such a work is to highlight several aspects of Moses' career. He states that he has covered the kingly and philosophical [βασιλικὴν καὶ φιλόσοφον] abilities of Moses' life in Book One. Book Two is reserved for a treatment of three others, those concerned with law-giving, the office of the high priest, and prophecy [περὶ νομοθεσίαν, ἡ δὲ περὶ ἀρχιερωσύνην, ἡ δὲ ... περὶ προφητείαν] (*Mos.* 2.2-3 [Colson, LCL]). In discussing Moses as priest, Philo declares, "An honor well-becoming the wise [σοφῷ] is to serve the Being Who truly IS [ὄν] and the service of God is ever the business of the priesthood [ἱερωσύνη]" (*Mos.* 2.67 [Colson, LCL]) thereby blending the conceptual realms of wisdom and priestly discourse. In order to enter the priesthood, however, Moses had to be cleansed in both body and soul [ὥσπερ τὴν ψυχὴν καὶ τὸ σῶμα] by purifying himself of those things "mortal nature" calls the body to partake in, namely "food and drink and intercourse with women [τῆς πρὸς γυναῖκας ὁμιλίας]" (*Mos.* 2.68 [Colson, LCL]). Regarding sexual intercourse, Philo makes the point that Moses had "disdained" such activity for a long time [ἐκ πολλῶν χρόνων], ever since he became a prophet and was possessed by God [θεοφορεῖσθαι].[156] The rationale behind this sexual abstinence on the part of Moses was so he could always be ready to receive an oracle of God (*Mos.* 2.69 [Colson, LCL]). Since Moses had such intimate contact with the deity by receiving God's revelation, Philo views it as a matter of course that sexual activity is out of the question.[157]

The purity of Moses, who regularly received divine revelations, is one thing, the actual lived existence of God's chosen people is quite another for Philo. In his retelling of Gen 12:10-20, where Pharaoh takes Sara into his house, thereby incurring God's wrath because she is Abram's wife, Philo notes that Sara's purity/chastity [ἁγνεία] is protected by God (*Abr.* 98). While in the biblical account, Pharaoh does not know he is violating a marriage due to Abram's ruse (Gen 12:13), Philo alters this part of the story and turns the Pharaoh into a lecherous monarch with no control [ἀκρασία], who desires to bring sexual shame upon Sara (*Abr.* 94).[158] By protecting Sara's ἁγνεία God honored Abram's piety and, furthermore, allowed his marriage to produce a nation most loved by God [θεοφιλέστατον] that "received the gift of priesthood and prophecy on behalf of all mankind" (*Abr.* 98 [Colson, LCL]). What is important to note here is that Philo argues that God saves Sara from improper sexual relations so that the proper arena for legitimate sexual intercourse, her marriage with Abram, is preserved from violation, thereby allowing the birth of a nation that receives divine gifts. While Moses stays away from women altogether to fulfill his divine role, Sara does not have the option of staying away from all men. However, she is protected from "unauthorized" men for the sake of her marriage. Her purity/chastity is not protected *from* marital relations, but preserved *for* them.

---

[156] But see Num 12:1.

[157] See John C. Poirier and Joseph Frankovic, "Celibacy and Charism in 1 Cor 7:5-7," *HTR* 89 (1996): 10-18, where they link this portrait of Moses in Philo to Paul's situation.

[158] In a similar fashion, Philo intensifies the depravity of Potiphar's wife in *Ios.* 40-53.

In reading Philo one gets the sense that, while the purity of the body matters to him, his concern is more on the way the intellect controls the passions. Thus the body matters insofar as it is the tool by which the mind controls or is enslaved by the passions. This distinction is summed up in a passage from *On Drunkenness* in which he compares the wise man, once again, to the priest who prays both at the outer altar of the body and the inner altar of reason, both of which are necessary due to the fact that "life is many-sided" (*Ebr.* 86 [Colson & Whitaker, LCL]):

Again, that master as he stands at the outer, the open and visible altar, the

> altar of common life, will seem to pay much regard to skin and flesh [σαρκῶν] and blood and all the bodily parts [πάντων ὅσα περὶ σῶμα] lest he should offend the thousands who, though they assign to the things of the body a value secondary to the things of the soul, yet do hold them to be good. But when he stands at the inner altar, he will deal only with what is bloodless, fleshless [ἀσάρκοις], bodiless [ἀσωμάτοις] and is born of reason [λογισμοῦ], which things are likened to the incense and the burnt spices. For as incense fills the nostrils, so do these pervade the whole region of the soul with fragrance (*Ebr.* 87 [Colson & Whitaker, LCL]).

Freedom

Paul explicitly discusses women, sex and marriage, and holiness in 1 Cor 6:12–7:7. With the dual gnomic sayings of 6:12, however, he firmly situates his argument in this pericope within wisdom rhetorolect with the following words: "Everything is permissible for me, but not everything is beneficial; everything is permissible for me, but I will not be enslaved by anything."[159] These sayings, I will argue in ch. 6, evoke an ongoing debate within many Hellenistic cultures regarding the tension between absolute freedom of action and activities that produce benefits or demonstrate self-mastery. Although the lexical item "freedom" does not exist in many of the resources discussed below, especially the earlier Jewish wisdom texts, I am arguing that the broad conceptual categories of self-determined action and its contrary, the inability to act as one wishes, are readily apparently through a host of images related to liberation and enslavement. Indeed, as will be seen, especially by the first century CE in the thought of Philo of Alexandria, life and death can serve as images for the possibility of freedom and its total absence, respectively. Life is the necessary pre-condition

---

[159] See Chapter 5 for why I read this verse "without quotation marks" (Dodd, "Paul's Paradigmatic 'I'," 54).

for engaging in purposeful behavior and death represents the ultimate enslavement, a state completely devoid of possibility. The resources discussed below often spend more time mapping out images and themes that address the *lack* of freedom (death, snares, imprisonment, passions, slavery, etc.) in order to paint in sharper relief that which actually constitutes true freedom of action. The debate surrounding freedom and lack of freedom was an important one in ancient Mediterranean cultures. Because of this, it is necessary to map out the conceptual constellations in Jewish resources relating to freedom and slavery in order to contextualize Paul's conceptual blends in 1 Cor 6:12–7:7.

Before discussing the broad conceptual category of freedom in Jewish wisdom texts, it is perhaps best to begin this discussion with that paradigmatic event in Jewish scriptural memory that relates to freedom from slavery – the Exodus from Egypt.[160] It is this narrative of liberation from enslavement that sets the stage for thinking about what freedom means for the Jewish resources.[161] When Jewish writings wrestle with what it means for individuals to be free, this discussion always occurs within a worldview that understands freedom through the lens of obedience to God. As will become evident in my analysis below, some Jewish texts simply assume this worldview, while other texts, typically those written in the Hellenistic period, will explicitly argue why obedience to God is the hallmark of true freedom.

Exodus 5–14 narrates the story of the miracles Moses worked in God's name that allowed the children of Israel to flee Egypt, culminating in the crossing though the sea (11:22). This section of the narrative ends with a description of Israel after the crossing that governs their future relationship with the God of Abraham, Isaac, and Jacob:

> And the Lord freed [ἐρρύσατο] Israel on that day from the hand of the Egyptians, and Israel saw the Egyptians dead along the edge of the sea. And Israel saw the great hand, [the things] which the Lord did to the Egyptians; and the people feared [ἐφοβήθη] the Lord and believed God and Moses his servant (Exod 14:30-31).

Although later texts will wrestle with how the emotion of φόβος impinges upon freedom, in the Jewish resources, especially the wisdom texts, it is only the fear of God that keeps God's people from slavery. It is within this Jewish idiom that the ideas of freedom from slavery must be evaluated.

---

[160] See Davies, *Memories of Ancient Israel*, 105-23.

[161] For a more in depth study on the recontextualization and reconfiguration of the Exodus story in Jewish and early Christian materials (esp. the Gospel of John), see Susan E. Hylen, *Allusion and Meaning in John 6* (BZNW 137; Berlin: de Gruyter, 2005).

In Exodus 19 God gives the people of Israel a choice. Noting that the people witnessed his power over the Egyptians and how he carried the people "on eagles' wings," a proposal is made. If the people obey his voice and keep his covenant they will be God's "peculiar people" [λαὸς περιούσιος]. Out of the entire earth that is God's, Israel is chosen to be God's "priestly kingdom and holy nation" (Exod 19:4-6). To this offer "all the people answered as one and said, 'Everything, as much as God said, we will do and obey'" (Exod 19:8). In Exodus 20-23 God relays various rules and regulations that will govern the lives of God's special people. After hearing these statutes, the people once again respond, "All the words, which the Lord spoke, we will do and obey'" (Exod 24:3). According to the text, the people positively affirm their acceptance of God's rules for being his special people, once after being reminded of the miracle of passing through the sea and a second time after actually hearing what it is that God expects of them.

The issue of obedience to God is raised once again in the law books of Leviticus and Deuteronomy, most especially in the lists of blessings and curses. Near the end of both of these texts, after the statutes and ordinances of God are exhaustively explained, God enumerates what blessings will come to the Israelites when they obey, and the curses that God will visit upon them should they disobey. In Lev 26:3-13 (cf. Deut 28:1-14) God lists the blessings of obedience, which include things such as good conditions for agriculture and herding, peace and security, protection from enemies, and having God's dwelling place in their midst. God gives the ultimate reason for these blessings, "I am the Lord your God who led you out of the land of Egypt, [where] you were slaves and I crushed the bonds of your yoke and led you with boldness [παρρησίας]" (Lev 26:13).[162] The results of not obeying God are listed in Lev 26:14-39 (cf. Deut 28:15-68) and consist of God sowing fear and want among the people by giving victory to their enemies. The land also rebels against the people for their disobedience and one of the reasons given for spreading a disobedient Israel among the nations (Lev 26:33) is so that the land can enjoy the Sabbaths denied it by Israel's failure to obey God (Lev 26:34).

It appears that freedom, in the book of Leviticus, is freedom from foreign domination, hunger, and fear. All of this is achieved because, in their own land, the people of Israel are free to obey their God. This idea is reiterated twice in Deuteronomy's extensive list of the results of disobedience. If the people do not serve God "with cheerfulness and a good heart" [ἐν εὐφροσύνῃ καὶ ἀγαθῇ καρδίᾳ][163] they will be forced

---

[162] LSJ translates μετὰ παρρησίας as "openly."
[163] Note that Codex Vaticanus reads "with ... a good mind" [ἀγαθῇ διανοίᾳ].

by their enemies, whom they must serve, to wear an iron collar [κλοιὸν σιδηροῦν] (Deut 28:47).[164] If the people persist in their disobedience, God even threatens to put them on boats and send them back to Egypt (Deut 28:68), thus reversing the narrative of liberation from slavery chronicled in Exodus. The Pentateuch thus has near its ending the warning that disobedience to God is functionally equivalent to a return to the very slavery from which God rescued the children of Israel. As God tells Israel in Deut 30:15, "Behold, I have presented before your face today life and death, good and evil."

When focus moves from the Pentateuch to the wisdom texts, one finds expressed a similar dichotomy to that described in the parallelism of Deut 30:15.[165] Prov 13:14 and 14:27 describe both the law of the wise and commandment of the Lord as a "fountain of life" [πηγὴ ζωῆς],[166] which is contrasted with the "snare" [παγίς] of death. Further, the command [πρόσταγμα] of the Lord is described as something that turns one [ποιεῖ δὲ ἐκκλίνειν] away from death and toward life (Prov 14:27).[167] When the enemy of Prov 1-9, the strange woman, is described, the text accuses her of causing the ruin of the young man "with the snares from [her] lips" [βρόχοις ... τοῖς ἀπὸ χειλέων] (Prov 7:21). The young man in her grasp is compared to an animal about to die. He is described as follows:

> just as an ox is led to [the] slaughter,
> and just as a dog to halters
> or as a deer having been struck with an arrow in the liver,
> he hastens as a bird into a snare [ὥσπερ ὄρνεον εἰς παγίδα],[168]
> not seeing that he runs for [his] life [περὶ ψυχῆς τρέχει] (Prov 7:22-23).

While the strange woman turns men into beasts being led on to death, God's law and commandments lead Israel to life.

The image of the snare [παγίς, θήρα, βρόχος] figures prominently in the wisdom resources of Judaism.[169] This is a favorite metaphor in wisdom texts for sexually marginal women (Prov 7:21-23; Eccl 7:27; Sir 9:3), but on a larger scale the image graphically portrays the predic-

---

[164] LSJ for κλοιός notes that while it does mean a (usually wooden) collar for prisoners, it also is used for collars worn by dogs.

[165] For the relationship between Deuteronomy and wisdom, see Ryan O'Dowd, *The Wisdom of Torah: Epistemology in Deuteronomy and Wisdom Literature* (FRLANT 225; Göttingen: Vandenhoeck & Ruprecht, 2009); Robbins, *Invention*, 1:150-64.

[166] See also Prov 16:22 where "understanding" [ἔννοια] is also described as a fountain of life.

[167] See Prov 9:16; cf. 3 Kgdms 11:4; Sir 47:19.

[168] See Eccl 9:12.

[169] See Prov 6:2, 5; 7:21, 23; 11:8, 9; 12:13, 27; 13:14; 14:27; 18:7; 20:25; 21:6; 22:5, 25; 29:6; Eccl 9:12; Wis 14:11; Sir 9:3, 13; 27:20, 26, 29; 51:2.

ament of the one who does not fear the Lord.[170] The image of being ensnared – by women, one's mouth (or tongue),[171] alcohol,[172] "crooked paths,"[173] anger,[174] dishonesty towards friends,[175] or idolatry[176] – functions in Proverbs (and the other wisdom texts) as a means to demonstrate that unwise actions not only restrict a person's life, but that such behavior takes life away. As wisdom herself teaches in Prov 8:36, "the one who hates me loves death."[177]

The image of the servant or slave is also employed in the book of Proverbs to persuade one to lead a righteous life. Prov 29:21 teaches that the one "who lives wantonly [κατασπαταλᾷ] from childhood, will be a slave [οἰκέτης]." Immoral, undisciplined living is not an expression of power or freedom, rather it is such behavior that enslaves. According to a Septuagintal addition, being properly instructed from childhood results in wisdom, and the one who grows to be wise "will use the fool [ἄφρονι] as a servant [διακόνῳ]" (Prov 10:4a). This addition is in agreement, not only with Prov 29:21, but also with what is taught elsewhere in Proverbs, namely that "a fool will be a slave [δουλεύσει] to a wise man [φρονίμῳ]" (Prov 11:29β). For Proverbs, the only way to live an unfettered life is to become wise – those who remain fools exist in a state of enslavement serving those who possess wisdom. It is important to note, however, that Proverbs argues that objective social status does not necessarily correlate with who is foolish or wise (cf. 1 Cor 1:26; 4:8-13). Prov 17:2 teaches that in a situation where the master is foolish and the house slave is wise, it is really the slave who "will rule [κρατήσει]," rather that the one whom society recognizes as the free man.[178] Wisdom confers immense power upon individuals that possess it. No matter what one's station in life, loving wisdom and living accordingly is what frees from slavery and grants mastery over others. Interestingly, it is only in another septuagintal addition, 25:10a, where the term "free" is actually used in the Prov-

---

[170] Using terminology from SRI, this type of rhetoric is based on rhetography, persuading via images.

[171] Prov 6:2; 11:9; 20:3 (using a slightly different image – συμπλέκω); Sir 51:2.

[172] Prov 20:1 also using the related image of συμπλέκω.

[173] Prov 22:5; cf. Sir 27:26, 29.

[174] Prov 22:24-25.

[175] Prov 29:5 using the related image of περιβάλλω.

[176] Wis 14:11.

[177] See also Prov 15:32: "Who[ever] disdains instruction [παιδείαν], hates himself"; Prov 24:9: "A fool [ἄφρων] dies in [his] sins." Also note the description of the father's words in Prov 4:22: "For they are life to those who find them and a healing [ἴασις] to all flesh [σαρκί]."

[178] Cf. Prov 22:11. See also Eccl 10:5-7, where this reversal of status is used negatively.

erbs. This addition teaches that "grace and love [φιλία] set [one] free [ἐλευθεροῖ]." However, although an ἐλευθερ- stem word is only used in this one addition, the concept of freedom is present in the book of Proverbs as a whole and is described as the opposite of those forces which ensnare or enslave humanity – forces that can only be combated through wisdom.

In the wisdom texts of the Hellenistic period, Sirach and Wisdom of Solomon, the teachings about freedom and slavery stand in continuity with the older wisdom text of Proverbs. However, one can also see the texts thinking through the particular Jewish idiom of freedom as obedience to God and God's commandments in a new environment. The text of Sirach displays sensitivity to this question and exegetes the apparent paradox of freedom through obedience. In general terms, the argument runs along the following lines: wisdom/instruction/the law is only oppressive to the wicked; to the righteous these elements are liberatory. In 4:17-19, Ben Sira argues using an educational model. When someone walks "crookedly," wisdom accompanies him causing him fear and cowardice [φόβον καὶ δειλία]. While still unwise, wisdom will torment [βασανίσει] that one with her instruction [παιδεία]. Once one has earned the trust of wisdom, usually achieved in the literature by learning her lessons, and is on the straight path, wisdom changes from tormentor to comforter. However, should the one now wise deviate from wisdom's straight path, she will leave him and "will deliver him into the hands of his fall [πτώσεως]." Following wisdom's instructions and avoiding evil are the avenues to prosperity.[179] Straying from the straight path is what makes one vulnerable to iniquity and calamity.[180]

Sirach 6:24-25 uses rhetography of imprisonment to describe the proper relation one should have with wisdom:

> and bring your feet into her fetters
> and your neck into her collar [κλοιόν] (cf. Deut 28:47);
> lay down your shoulder and bear her
> and do not be angry with her bonds [δεσμοῖς] (cf. Prov 7:22γ).[181]

Here Ben Sira uses the very images of enslavement that were employed to describe a life lived contrary to the dictates of the law and wisdom in Deuteronomy and Proverbs. However, the one who is wise knows that, when living in deference to wisdom, these implements of slavery are transformed. When one lives according to wisdom her fetters become a "strong protection (or: shelter)," her collar becomes a

---

[179] E.g. Sir 2:1-9; 7:1-2; 11:14; 24:22.
[180] E.g. Sir 3:26-28; 7:3; 27:7-30.
[181] See also Sir 51:26.

"robe of glory,"[182] and her bonds become a "hyacinth spray." Moreover, far from having to bear her demands with the brute strength of one's shoulders, she becomes for the wise person a "crown of rejoicing"[183] (Sir 6:29-31). Although the conditions for living according to wisdom in the proper fear of the Lord may seem to enslave, to the wise one who has been properly instructed these are actually the very things that offer one a safe life of honor and success.

The frames of education, enslavement, and glory are again blended in Sir 21:19 and 21. Here Ben Sira teaches that for the fool, παιδεία is like fetters on the feet "and as handcuffs upon [the] right hand," whereas for the wise this instruction is a "golden ornament"[184] and, instead of handcuffs, is "as a bracelet upon [the] right arm." Here again one notes the transformational effects of wisdom. The fetters-to-ornament and handcuffs-to-bracelet transformation does not result in a change in what wisdom demands from one's life. Rather it is the result of a cognitive change, recognizing the demands of wisdom stem from a concern for one's honor and prosperity, as well as a practical change, bringing one's actions in line with what the fear of the Lord and the law demand.[185] Paradoxically, for Ben Sira one can only be truly free when one is the willing slave to wisdom.[186]

The notion of beneficial slavery also appears in the Wisdom of Solomon. The narrator-as-Solomon who, in a prayer to God, declares "You chose me [as the] king of your people" (Wis 9:7) also tells God "I am your slave [δοῦλος]" (Wis 9:5). Here one sees in bold relief an example of the striking juxtaposition of roles – the king, the one with all power, is also a slave, the one with no power. The text notes, however, that God has given power to the people of Israel by teaching them what pleases him and by saving them through this wisdom (Wis 9:15). The saving power of wisdom is read back into the scriptural memory of Israel. Thus Cain killed his brother after he "withdrew from her [wisdom]," but the departure from wisdom caused this unrighteous man to perish because of the fratricide he committed (Wis 10:3). Although he killed his brother, his departure from wisdom also caused his own destruction. The Exodus story is also retold through

---

[182] LSJ s.v. κλοιός points one towards Gen 41:42 for the use of a *"collar of gold, as an ornament."* This passage in Genesis describes the various gifts Pharaoh gives to Joseph to honor him for his visions, which include a "linen robe" and the aforementioned "golden collar (or: necklace)." This suggests an interesting intertextual relationship between Sirach and the Joseph story in Genesis.

[183] See Sir 1:11.

[184] Sir 6:30 describes wisdom as having a "golden ornament" upon her.

[185] Sir 33:2: "A wise man will not hate the law."

[186] See my discussion of Paul's paradoxical teaching in 1 Cor 1–4 in Chapter 4.

the lens of wisdom in this Hellenistic text. According to Wisdom of Solomon, it was wisdom herself who saved Israel from a "nation of oppressors" (Wis 10:15) and it was she who allowed them to cross through the sea and who killed their enemies (Wis 10:18-19; cf. Exod 11:22; 14:3-31). Because of wisdom's actions the righteous slaves were able to plunder the army of Pharaoh (Wis 10:20).

Being a slave to God, and to God's wisdom, is what allows Israel to triumph over her enemies. The author of the Wisdom of Solomon, like the author of Sirach, seems to understand that this notion needs explication. For the author of Wisdom, the incorrect reasoning of the impious (Wis 2:1, 21), and its concomitant wickedness, blinds its perpetrators (Wis 2:21) and disqualifies them for the incorruptibility that comes from being made in the image of God (Wis 2:23; cf. Gen 1:27). Not only will the impious be punished for their faulty reasoning, but the narrator argues that their disregard for "wisdom and instruction" [σοφίαν ... καὶ παιδείαν] makes them miserable in their lives and renders everything they do pointless and useless (Wis 3:10-11). This misery stems from the very abominations [βδελύματα] the unrighteous undertake in their foolishness (Wis 12:23). This theme is continued in the retelling of the Exodus story. The lawless Egyptians supposed that they were the ones who wielded power over God's holy nation. However, when God sent the plague of darkness upon the land, the people of Egypt became "captives of darkness and prisoners of [the] long night" (Wis 17:2) – a fitting image for the lack of understanding evinced by Pharaoh regarding who possessed true power.

For the Wisdom of Solomon, things are not always as they appear (cf. 1 Cor 1–4). In the retelling of the scriptural stories of Cain and Abel and the Exodus, the author of Wisdom marshals evidence for this claim. While it is true that Cain killed Abel, it is also true that this very act of fratricide destroyed the murderer himself because it demonstrated his abandonment of God's wisdom. Likewise the Egyptians appeared to have power over their Hebrew slaves, but that was an illusion. It was the God of Israel, or rather God's wisdom, that demonstrated that a holy nation of slaves could overcome its oppressors. Although the foolish believe that they have the upper hand, their very ignorance enslaves them. It is the righteous one who recognizes that living with wisdom entails neither bitterness nor pain, but rather is a life marked by "cheerfulness and joy" [εὐφροσύνην καὶ χαράν] (Wis 8:16). Thus when the wicked see the righteous apparently punished, they do not realize that the righteous are disciplined only for a time as a matter of testing and that this discipline makes them acceptable to God "as a sacrificial whole burnt offering" [ὡς ὁλοκάρπωμα θυσίας]

(Wis 3:6; cf. 4 Ezra 7:14; 1 Enoch 96:1-3).[187] What the foolish do not know, according to Wisdom of Solomon, is that, though the righteous may seem to die, they are actually freed from death and destined for immortality (Wis 3:2-4).[188] Moreover the Wisdom of Solomon teaches that after the righteous achieve immortality, "They will judge [κρινοῦσιν] nations and rule [κρατήσουσιν] peoples and the lord will reign [βασιλεύσει] over them forever" (Wis 3:8; cf. 1 Cor 6:3). While the righteous may appear to be oppressed in this life, they happily bear up under this pressure because they have hope in a future immortality in which the actual state of affairs will be revealed – the righteous will rule. However, this rule of the righteous is subsumed under that larger reign of God (cf. 1 Cor 3:22-23). Thus even when the wise are finally able to judge and rule, they themselves are still under the rule of God, which is the ultimate joy for the Wisdom of Solomon.

Before moving on to a discussion of freedom in the works of Philo, it is instructive to interact with another philosophical Jewish treatise, namely the one known as 4 Maccabees. This text is a proof of and meditation upon the possibility of self-mastery, even in the face of enormous adversity. The author seeks to demonstrate that reasoning, or more accurately "pious reasoning" [ὁ εὐσεβὴς λογισμός] (4 Macc 1:1), is the master [αὐτοκράτωρ] of the passions [παθῶν] (4 Macc 1:7, 13).[189] For the Jewish author of this text, this pious reasoning is master over three general types of passions: those that interfere with self-control, such as gluttony [γαστριμαργία] and desire [ἐπιθυμία]; those that interfere with justice, such as maliciousness [κακοήθεια]; and those that interfere with courage, such as anger [θυμός], fear [φόβος], and pain/suffering [πόνος] (4 Macc 1:3-4). The main demonstrations given by 4 Maccabees to prove this point are the martyrdom stories of Eleazar (4 Macc 5–7) and the seven brothers (4 Macc 8–14), along with narration of the suicide and testament of the mother of the seven brothers (4 Macc 15–17:6). The mother, exhorting her children to be faithful to the religion of their fathers, explains why they should not avoid torture and death. According to the mother, "it is unreasonable for those having known piety not to withstand sufferings [πόνοις]" (4 Macc 16:23).[190]

---

[187] Note the priestly language used here.

[188] J.J. Collins, Jewish Wisdom, 184-87. See Sir 19:19, which is widely considered a late addition.

[189] See also 1:30 (where reason is also called the "leader of virtues" [τῶν ἀρετῶν ἡγεμών]); 6:31; 13:1; 18:1-2.

[190] See Philo, Prob. 113.

Though the treatise is mainly devoted to inductive reasoning via the martyrdom stories about the ability of pious reason to overcome the passions, the author also argues, early in the text, from the law and the narrative history of the Pentateuch. Part of this scriptural proof of the power of pious reasoning occurs in a discussion about the example of Joseph, described as self-controlled [σώφρων], who overcame "luxury" [ἡδυπάθεια] by being fully in command of his mind [διανοίᾳ περιεκράτησεν] (4 Macc 2:2).[191] He was able to do this because of his adherence to the law, which teaches not to desire the wife of one's neighbor (4 Macc 2:5).[192] From this commandment, which legislates against desiring, and from Jacob's testament in Genesis 49 where he curses the anger of Simeon and Levi (Gen 49:7) for slaughtering the men of Shechem to avenge the rape of their sister (Gen 34), the author of 4 Maccabees concludes that reason can overcome the passions. If it were not so, no commandment could or would be given to that effect, nor could Jacob justly curse the passion of his sons if it were not possible to master anger (4 Macc 2:6, 19-20). Thus not only does the law teach that the passions are to be controlled, but the very fact that it legislates this demonstrates *ipso facto* that pious reasoning is *able* to control the passions. The author of 4 Maccabees is realistic, however. He recognizes that although it cannot be entirely eradicated, reason makes it possible not to be enslaved by desire [μὴ δουλωθῆναι τῇ ἐπιθυμίᾳ] (4 Macc 3:2).[193] Proper use of pious reasoning, available through enacting the teaching of the law, thus represents for the author of this Hellenistic Jewish text the means to free oneself from the shackles of desire and passion.

In discussing Philo's understanding of freedom and slavery, this project benefits from the recent work of Lincoln Galloway, whose monograph, *Freedom in the Gospel*, puts Paul's discussion of freedom into conversation with not only Epictetus, but also Philo.[194] Echoing what has been discussed explicitly in the Hellenistic wisdom texts above, Galloway concludes, "Freedom may be portrayed on a master/slave template as a divine transaction in which the free find slavery to God to be their goal and highest boast." Moving beyond this master/slave relationship, "Philo can also use friendship and shared sovereignty with God who grants παρρησία as a mark of freedom."[195] In either case,

---

[191] Codex Alexandrinus and some other MSS read: τω λογισμω διανοια.

[192] See Exod 20:17; Deut 5:21; also Gaca, *Fornication*, 153; William Loader, *The Septuagint, Sexuality, and the New Testament: Case Studies on the Impact of the LXX in Philo and the New Testament* (Grand Rapids: Eerdmans, 2004), 13-14.

[193] See my discussion of self-mastery in my exegesis of 6:12 and 13 in ch. 6.

[194] Lincoln E. Galloway, *Freedom in the Gospel: Paul's Exemplum in 1 Cor 9 in Conversation with the Discourses of Epictetus and Philo* (CBET 38; Leuven: Peeters, 2004), ch. 3 for his discussion of Freedom in Philo's thought.

[195] Galloway, *Freedom in the Gospel*, 147, see also 123-24, where Galloway cites *Cher.* 107.

Galloway demonstrates that, for Philo, the only way to true freedom is via one's relationship with God.

Philo is of the opinion that "Slavery is to the free [τοῖς ἐλευθέροις] most unbearable" (*Praem.* 137). Yet Philo argues that slavery and freedom exist in two senses, those applied to the body and those applied to the soul. Bodily slavery involves being subject to human masters and bodily freedom entails "security ... from men of superior strength." Slavery of the soul or mind consists of being mastered by vices and passions while freedom of the soul or mind is described as "liberty from the domination of the passions."[196] Philo describes this latter kind of slavery in terms of four main passions: pleasure [ἡδονή], desire [ἐπιθυμία], grief [λύπης], and fear [φόβος].[197] Of these passions, pleasure is typically seen as the primary enemy while self-control [σωφροσύνη] is the wise man's primary weapon (*Leg.* 2.79).[198] As Galloway notes, "Freedom requires the mind to turn away from pleasure and cleave to virtue" (cf. 1 Cor 6:12).[199]

Philo ties pleasure, and the bodily senses through which it enters the mind, closely to his conception of the female. Thus he can argue that Gen 2:24 represents the mind becoming a slave to sense perception (*Leg.* 2.49; cf. 1 Cor 6:16). When this happens, the mind is reduced to a state of slavery [ἠνδραπόδισται][200] and does not function properly. Only when the mind is ruling can bodily sense perception be rendered powerless (*Leg.* 2.70). Evidence such as this from the Philonic corpus fits with Galloway's insightful observation that "any understanding of freedom in his work must take into account his own agenda for excising the female. Freedom will have to be defined in terms of the absence or obliteration of the female."[201]

While the whore and prostitute known as pleasure may promise indulgence [ἄνεσις] and freedom from fear [ἄδεια] (*Sacr.* 23), the wise, and therefore free, man recognizes that not only is his hope in following the law [*Abr.* 16], but that only those living a life under the law are

---

[196] *Prob.* 17 (Colson, LCL); Galloway, *Freedom in the Gospel*, 146. See also *Mos.* 1.299 (discussed in my "Women" section above) where Balaam counsels king Barak on how to make each Israelite man "a slave of passion [τοῦ πάθους δοῦλος]".

[197] Galloway, *Freedom in the Gospel*, 120 where he cites *Her.* 269-7 and *Prob.* 18.

[198] For the dangers of pleasure, see also Galloway, *Freedom in the Gospel*, 119, where he cites *Ebr.* 212. See also idem, 120 n. 98, in which Galloway cites *Sacr.* 21, where Philo describes pleasure as in "the guise of a whore and a prostitute [πόρνης καὶ χαμαιτύπης]." For more on self-control see also *Ios.* 54; *Mos.* 1.25; 2.185; *Contempl.* 34; *Opif.* 164.

[199] Galloway, *Freedom in the Gospel*, 120, where he points the reader to *Sacr.* 45.

[200] LSJ s.v. ἀνδραποδίζω "... *sell the free men* of a conquered place *into slavery.*"

[201] Galloway, *Freedom in the Gospel*, 127. See *Mos.* 1.299 (also cited above) for how women can be used to enslave male warriors. See also *Virt.* 34-39; Walter T. Wilson, "Pious Soldiers, Gender Deviants, and the Ideology of Actium: Courage and Warfare in Philo's *De Fortitudine,* " *StudPhilAnn* 2005 (17): 1-32.

truly free [ὅσοι δὲ μετὰ νόμου ζῶσιν, ἐλεύθεροι] (*Prob.* 45).[202] Philo argues that this is the case because the law teaches that which is virtuous and good. The good man will only want to act sensibly and virtuously, therefore the good man will not be prevented from doing what he wishes, therefore the good man is free (*Prob.* 59). It is through such reasoning that Philo tackles the notorious philosophical problem that while the "notion of ἐλευθερία allowed one to be self-determined, autonomous, independent and at liberty to do as one wishes," this idea "had to be reconciled with the life of virtue."[203] The wise and free person will not succumb to the false promises of pleasure, but using reason will recognize them for the snares they are. While Philo argues that "no two things are so closely related as independence of action [αὐτοπραγία] and freedom" (*Prob.* 21 [Colson, LCL]), he also argues that the wise man will only desire to do that which stems from virtue (*Prob.* 60) and is thus lawful.

Conclusion

The Jewish resource zones examined in this chapter provide a solid foundation on which to build an exegetical analysis of 1 Cor 6:12–7:7 that uses the tools of conceptual integration theory within a sociorhetorical framework. The themes of women, sex and marriage, holiness, and freedom will recur in Paul's argument against πορνεία. As I hope to have demonstrated, the wisdom resources of Judaism provide ample conceptual material to help biblical interpreters begin to make sense of Paul's teaching. I also hope that my presentation of the Hellenistic permutations of Jewish wisdom demonstrates the great creativity that Greek-speaking Jews displayed in reconfiguring traditional wisdom in a new environment. Hellenistic Jewish thought serves as an illustrative example of how texts that operate within a wisdom framework are not content to be bounded by the limits of traditional wisdom. Rather, other modes of discourse – priestly, legal, apocalyptic – are invited into these Jewish resources. The ability of Jewish wisdom discourse to open itself up to different modes of expression in the face of new realities makes Paul's blending of wisdom rhetorolect with other modes of discourse anything but novel. The fact that Paul invites apocalyptic and priestly rhetorolects into his wisdom discourse of 1 Cor 6:12–7:7 shows that his teaching is firmly in line with the tradition out of which it emerged – in practice if not always in content.[204]

---

[202] See *Sacr.* 127, where the ones who worship God have eternal freedom.
[203] Galloway, *Freedom in the Gospel*, 17.
[204] See Robbins, *Invention*, 1:191.

4

Setting the Wisdom Context:
1 Corinthians 1-4

Introduction

When discussing wisdom in 1 Corinthians, the majority of scholarship focuses on the first four chapters of this letter or on pericopae found within these chapters.[1] It is an oft cited fact that Paul engages wisdom and foolishness in these four chapters to a degree unrivaled in the other Pauline letters.[2] Yet determining Paul's relationship to wisdom in these chapters has befuddled exegetes and has created a wide divergence of opinion about how wisdom functions in 1 Cor. The crux of the confusion stems from Paul's apparent negative view of wisdom in 1:18–2:5 and the noted change of tone in 2:6–3:4, where Paul seems to discuss wisdom in a positive light and to portray himself as a wisdom teacher. This interpretive problem is bound up with this question – is wisdom an indigenous concept to Paul, or does he employ it only as a reaction to the situation in Corinth?[3] Since I argue that Paul's treatment of πορ-νεία is best understood as didactic Christian wisdom, answering the

---

[1] For a comprehensive modern *Forschungsbericht* on the investigation of wisdom in 1 Cor 1–4, see Joachim Theis, *Paulus als Weisheitslehrer: Der Gerkreuzigte und die Weisheit Gottes in 1 Kor 1–4* (Biblische Untersuchungen 22; Regensburg: Friedrich Pustet, 1991), ch. 1 (pp. 10-114). See also the references in Wilson, *Love without Pretense*, 4 n. 5; Ben Witherington, III, *Jesus the Sage: The Pilgrimage of Wisdom* (Minneapolis: Fortress, 1994), 299 n. 12; as well as the extensive notes in Sigurd Grindheim, "Wisdom for the Perfect: Paul's Challenge to the Corinthian Church (1 Corinthians 2:6-16)," *JBL* 121 (2002): 689-709.

[2] Noted, e.g., by E. Elizabeth Johnson, "The Wisdom of God as Apocalyptic Power," in *Faith and History: Essays in Honor of Paul W. Meyer* (ed. John T. Carroll, Charles H. Cosgrove, and E. Elizabeth Johnson; Atlanta: Scholars Press, 1990), 137. See also Richard B. Hays, "Wisdom According to Paul," in *Where Shall Wisdom be Found? Wisdom in the Bible, the Church and the Contemporary World* (ed. Stephen C. Barton; Edinburgh: T. & T. Clark, 1999), 111-12; L.L. Welborn, *Paul, the Fool of Christ: A Study of 1 Corinthians 1–4 in the Comic-Philosophic Tradition* (Library of New Testament Studies 293; New York: T. & T. Clark, 2005).

[3] See E. Johnson, "Wisdom of God," 138-39.

question of Paul's relationship to wisdom and exploring how wisdom functions in these opening chapters is necessary before moving on to an exegesis of 6:12–7:7.[4]

In this chapter I explore what Paul says *about* wisdom in 1 Cor 1–4. In so doing, I am here dealing with modes of discourse that operate near the speculative end of the wisdom spectrum, as I discussed in Chapter 2.[5] In these chapters, Paul strives to show the Corinthians what true wisdom looks like. God's true wisdom, Paul teaches, comes through the paradox of God's crucified Christ.[6] The cross, in Paul's thinking, lays bare the true structure of the universe as God had intended it in the non-temporal realm of eternity before creation (2:7). Paul apparently believes that understanding God's paradoxical wisdom as revealed through the eschatological event of the cross will provide the Corinthians with the eschatological discernment necessary to help them live lives worthy of the message Paul proclaims to them.[7] Moreover, although God had defined it before time, the wisdom that Paul teaches is not available to unaided human perception, but is rather a mystery (1 Cor 2:7).[8] This mystery is only available to the community through God's spirit and Paul's instruction. In this way, Paul's teaching regarding God's eternal wisdom is always already energized by apocalyptic and as such Paul's instruction participates in a broad cultural stream of Hellenistic Jewish teaching on wisdom.

Community Behavior: The Context for Paul's Exposition on Wisdom

The problems discussed by Paul in 1 Cor 1:10-17, reported to him by Chloe's people (1:11), revolve around the existence of divisions [σχίσματα] (v. 10) and quarrels [ἔριδες] (v. 11) within the community.[9] Unfortunately, what actually transpired in the community at Corinth will never be known. However, it is immediately after the description of the divisions in Corinth that Paul asserts that he did not preach ἐν σοφίᾳ λόγου (with eloquent wisdom [NRSV]: 1:17; cf.

---

[4] See Schnabel, *Law and Wisdom*, 300: "The issue of the place of wisdom in Paul's ethic seems never to have been dealt with systematically even though scholars are aware of the formal and material links between Paul's paraenesis and the Jewish wisdom tradition."

[5] See also Goff, *Worldly and Heavenly Wisdom*, 42; Robbins, *Invention*, 1:124-25.

[6] See Robbins, *Invention*, 1:158, 204, 508-509.

[7] I am indebted to Carl R. Holladay for suggesting the phrase "eschatological discernment" to me, personal communication.

[8] Cf. Dan 2:28; *4 Ezra* 4:2; *1 Enoch* 63:2-3; 108:15.

[9] See Baur's classic study on this issue: "Die Christuspartei." Although most biblical scholars no longer subscribe to Baur's conclusions, see Goulder, *Paul and the Competing Mission in Corinth*.

1:5).¹⁰ This juxtaposition supports Joachim Theis's idea of a link between ideas about wisdom and community behavior.¹¹ Whatever is causing the divisions in Corinth, Paul believes an explanation of wisdom viewed through the lens of the Christ event will help resolve the difficulty.

Paul's speculative wisdom discourse in 1 Cor 1:18–3:4 does not exist apart from his concern with community behavior. 1 Cor 1:17 signals the shift from a treatment of the concrete problems in the community to Paul's general discourse on the *topos* of wisdom, and 3:4-5 reintroduces issues of community behavior. "The principle of composition is therefore circular" (*ringförmig*), according to Theis, because the discussion of community behavior in 1:10-17 and 3:5–4:21 bracket Paul's "homily" in 1:18–3:4.¹² Theis further argues that Paul's placement of his exposition of wisdom within the discussion of the community's problematic behavior demonstrates "that a causal, situational, and thematic connection (*Abhängigkeit*) exists between the two problem areas."¹³ Thus while 1:18–3:4 presents the main data about wisdom in these introductory chapters, it is important to keep this exposition in its context – Paul's discussion of the problems in Corinth.

As noted, in 3:5–4:13 Paul shifts from his exposition on wisdom and returns to the problems of behavior in the Corinthian community. Recalling his concern with the divisions in the community, Paul moves to overturn their faulty understanding of the proper prophetic role of those who proclaim the gospel, as I will analyze in more detail below.¹⁴ Here Paul works to diminish the influence that human teachers should have among members of the Corinthian community, an influence that is either the cause or the symptom of the divisions among

---

[10] For the difficulties in translating this phrase see esp. Stephen M. Pogoloff, *Logos and Sophia: The Rhetorical Situation of 1 Corinthians* (SBLDS 134; Atlanta: Scholars Press, 1992), ch. 4 (pp. 99-127); also the review of treatments of this verse in Thiselton, *First Epistle to the Corinthians*, 143-44. Weiß, *Der erste Korintherbrief*, 22-23 already raised the difficulties this phrase poses.

[11] Note that Theis, *Paulus als Weisheitslehrer*, 126 describes 1:17 as "den Kern der Auseinandersetzung" [the core of the debate]. See also Schrage, *Der erste Brief an die Korinther*, 1:158; Witherington, *Conflict and Community*, 103-4; Hermann von Lips, *Weisheitliche Traditionen im Neuen Testament* (WMANT 64; Neukirchen-Vluyn: Neukirchener Verlag, 1990), 343-47; Johan S. Vos, "Die Argumentation des Paulus in 1 Kor 1,10–3,4," in *The Corinthian Correspondence* (BETL 125; Leuven: University Press, 1996), 91-97; Bruce W. Winter, *Philo and Paul among the Sophists: Alexandrian and Corinthian Responses to a Julio-Claudian Movement* (2nd ed.; Cambridge: Cambridge University Press, 1997; repr., Grand Rapids: Eerdmans, 2002), 187-95.

[12] Theis, *Paulus als Weisheitslehrer*, 125. See idem, 119 for his outline of 1 Cor 1–4.

[13] Theis, *Paulus als Weisheitslehrer*, 130: "daß ein ursächliche, situative und inhaltliche Abhängigkeit zwischen den beiden Problemkreisen besteht."

[14] Theis, *Paulus als Weisheitslehrer*, 119.

them (1:11-12; 3:5, 22).[15] Paul notes that he and Apollos were called to preach to the Corinthians,[16] but since Paul is at pains to reduce the cult of personality in Corinth, he uses language of slaves and servants to diminish the status of individuals who proclaim the gospel (cf. 9:16).[17] In 3:21-22 Paul argues that those who preach the gospel are not only slaves of Christ: his language of ownership implies that they are slaves of the Corinthians as well, "for everything is yours, whether Paul or Apollos or Cephas ... everything is yours."[18] Lest Paul's de-emphasis of the power of those who proclaim the gospel serve to increase the Corinthians' boasting (3:6-7), Paul concludes his argument with the definitive declaration: "but we [are] Christ's and Christ [is] God's" (3:23). The Corinthians are not their own masters, just as Christ is not his own.

Paul shifts into an ironic mode in 4:8-13 in which he reverses the Corinthians' "human" expectations, which he explained in 1:18–3:4.[19] Those called by God to proclaim the gospel do not live like those with wealth, status, and power. They are, rather, "the rubbish of the world, the dregs of all things" (4:13 [NRSV]; cf. 1:26; 2:3). As will be seen below, Paul sustains the same logic throughout most of 1 Cor 1–4. Namely, things in this world are not indicative of the true order of the cosmos as revealed through the eschatological Christ event. Paul reminds the Corinthians in 3:18-20 that if they wish to become truly wise, they must become fools in this age,[20] therefore how the Corinthians understand wisdom affects their behavior, and Paul in 1 Cor 1–4 is trying to change both.

---

[15] See Winter, *Philo and Paul*, 172-79 where he attributes this problem to the Corinthians acting like sophistic μαθηταί/ζηλωταί. Thus for Winter the divisions noted in 1:12 are a symptom of a larger issue. But see Mitchell, *Paul and the Rhetoric of Reconciliation*, 82-86.

[16] 1 Cor 3:5, 9, 10; 4:1, 9. Thus Paul employs a prophetic rhetorolect here. I will use rhetorolects below to analyze how Paul organizes his discussion of wisdom in 1:18–3:4.

[17] Note, however, θεοῦ γάρ ἐσμεν συνεργοί in 3:9. BDAG s.v. συνεργός notes the two possible ways this can be translated. I am opting for an understanding that "fellow workers" refers to Paul and Apollos working together serving God, rather than Paul and Apollos being fellow workers *with* God. Note that Dale Martin, *Slavery as Salvation: The Metaphor of Slavery in Pauline Christianity* (New Haven: Yale University Press, 1990) argues that Paul's slave metaphors do not necessarily denote lower status. However, as I argue here, I think Paul is employing the slave metaphor in this instance to reduce the status of the teachers in the estimation of the Corinthians.

[18] Fee, *First Epistle to the Corinthians*, 154; Thiselton, *First Epistle to the Corinthians*, 326; Witherington, *Conflict and Community*, 135. Schrage, *Der Erste Brief an die Korinther*, 1:314-15 and Theis, *Paulus als Weisheitslehrer*, 20, 138, 331-32, 505 emphasize Corinthian freedom in their analysis of this passage rather than the apostles being "owned."

[19] See my discussion of 4:8-13 below.

[20] See Sir 3:18-24; Philo, *Migr.* 134-38.

It is instructive to point to the work of Matthew Goff on 4QInstruction, from the Dead Sea Scrolls. This text, Goff argues, merges a sapiential pedagogical ethos with an apocalyptic worldview.[21] This, I will argue below, is similar to the dynamic Paul creates in 1 Cor. In each text the discussion of the mystery of God's wisdom "affects the addressee's ethical conduct and the way he handles his daily affairs."[22] Paul's exposition in 1 Cor 1-4 creates a rhetorical situation in which his specific wisdom instructions in 1 Cor 5:1-11:1 are always related to the revelation of God's eternal wisdom through the cross (1:24, 30; 2:7). This is also similar to the rhetoric of 4QInstruction, although the latter teaches not about the mystery of the cross, but rather the hyhn zr, which Goff translates as "the mystery that is to be."[23] Yet, as Paul does with the cross in 1 Cor, Goff argues that "4QInstruction combines the mystery that is to be with specific teachings that are similar to traditional wisdom."[24]

1 Corinthians 1:18–2:5: Apocalyptic Wisdom

The juxtaposition of "wisdom of the word" [σοφία λόγου] in 1:17 and "the word of the cross" [ὁ λόγος ὁ τοῦ σταυροῦ] in 1:18 introduces a decidedly negative view of wisdom at the outset of Paul's exposition. Richard Hays argues that if an "exploration of 'wisdom according to Paul' seeks to focus on what Paul actually says *about* wisdom, then we cannot avoid his relentless critique of it in 1 Corinthians."[25] This certainly seems to hold true of 1:18–2:5, but attention to 1 Cor 1–4 as a whole and to the various rhetorolects at work in these chapters suggests Hays's argument is incomplete, especially in light of the positive remarks Paul makes regarding wisdom in 2:6–3:4.[26] Paul is critical of wisdom in 1:18–2:5 to be sure, but as I observed in Chapter 2, wisdom discourse has a propensity for self-critique. This tendency is further accentuated when this discourse is blended with resources from apoca-

---

[21] Goff, "Wisdom, Apocalypticism and the Pedagogical Ethos of 4QInstruction," in *Conflicted Boundaries in Wisdom and Apocalypticism* (ed. Benjamin G. Wright, III and Lawrence M. Wills; SBLSymS 35; Atlanta: Society of Biblical Literature, 2005), 67; idem, *Worldly and Heavenly Wisdom*, 39.

[22] Goff, *Worldly and Heavenly Wisdom*, 73.

[23] Goff, "Wisdom, Apocalypticism and the Pedagogical Ethos of 4QInstruction," 61; idem, *Worldly and Heavenly Wisdom*, 33-34.

[24] Goff, *Worldly and Heavenly Wisdom*, 73.

[25] Hays, "Wisdom According to Paul," 112, although he does note on the same page that "Paul's relation to wisdom *traditions* is not unreservedly negative" (emphases in the original).

[26] See Theis, *Paulus als Weisheitslehrer*, 150-218 for a detailed analysis of 1 Cor 1:18–2:5.

lyptic rhetorolect through which Paul proclaims the saving act of God through the cross as an event that overturns the expectations of the present age by revealing the true structure of the universe. Proper eschatological discernment, achievable by attending to Paul's instruction, will allow the Corinthians to see this as well.

In 1:18 Paul organizes his discourse on wisdom with apocalyptic rhetorolect that focuses on the cross. The evidence for this rhetorolect is found immediately in the juxtaposition of the two dative participles – ἀπολλυμένοις and σῳζομένοις – that serve to create a binary world consisting of two opposing sides as this age nears its end (1:8). The cross is foolishness to those who are perishing, but it represents the power of God to those who are being saved. Building upon the verb ἀπόλλυμι, Paul recites from LXX Isa 29:14, where God promises that he will destroy [ἀπολῶ] "the wisdom of the wise" and nullify "the intelligence of the intelligent" (1:19; cf. 1 Cor 3:19-20).[27] Paul intensifies the apocalyptic nature of Isaiah's prophetic discourse by substituting the verb ἀθετήσω for Isaiah's κρύψω.[28] In Paul's recitation, God nullifies the intelligence of those who believe they possess it rather than simply hiding it.[29] Paul's discourse continues in this apocalyptic vein through a series of rhetorical questions that describes a divine reversal of the present order – God has "made foolish the wisdom of the world" [ἐμώρασεν ὁ θεὸς σοφία τοῦ κόσμου (1:20; cf. 3:19)]. Moreover, because the world was unable to know God via its wisdom, God, in God's own wisdom, decided that salvation will instead come to those who believe the foolishness of the kerygma (1:21). To those who believe the message proclaimed by Paul, Christ becomes "the power of God and the wisdom of God" (1:24; cf. 1:30).[30] Although the world deems the proclamation of God's crucified Christ foolish, Paul argues that the foolishness and weakness of God are wiser and stronger than mere human wisdom and power (1:25). Thus Paul argues that his message relies not on "persuasive words of wisdom" [πειθοῖς σοφίας λό-

---

[27] See Robbins, *Tapestry*, 104 and idem, *Exploring*, 41. See also Michael Fishbane, *Biblical Interpretation in Ancient Israel* (rev. ed.; New York: Oxford University Press, 1988), esp. Part Two: Legal Exegesis (pp. 91-277); Sheppard, *Wisdom as a Hermeneutical Construct*, ch. 5 (pp. 100-119). But see Dan 2:21.

[28] NA[27] and BDAG (s.v. ἀθετέω) suggest an allusion to Ps 32:10 (MT 33:10).

[29] See my discussion of "hidden wisdom" below in the section dealing with 1 Cor 2:6-3:4.

[30] Cf. *1 Enoch* 5:8: "And then wisdom shall be given to the elect. And they shall all live and not return again to sin, either by being wicked or through pride; but those who have wisdom shall be humble and not return again to sin." Translation from E. Isaac, "1 (Ethiopic Apocalypse of) Enoch," in *The Old Testament Pseudepigrapha* (ed. James H. Charlesworth; 2 vols.; Anchor Bible Reference Library; New York: Doubleday, 1983-1985), 1:5-89. See also *1 Enoch* 99:10.

4. Setting the Wisdom Context: 1 Cor 1–4

γοις],[31] but rather on the power of God in order that the belief of the Corinthians might rest on something more powerful (and efficacious) than human wisdom [ἐν σοφίᾳ ἀνθρώπων (2:5)].

Paul's thoroughgoing apocalyptic rhetoric in 1:18–2:5 proclaims that in light of the revelatory power of the cross every human thing in this age can be critiqued.[32] Apocalyptic rhetorolect governs his discourse about wisdom. This cultural organizing frame routinely creates two antithetical realms of good and evil into which Paul can place various elements. Surveying the specific elements Paul assigns each realm yields the following results:

Figure 1: Apocalyptic Binary Oppositions

Evil		Good	
the ones being destroyed	1:18	the ones being saved	1:18
Wisdom of the wise	1:19a		
intelligence of the intelligent	1:19b		
the wise, the scribe, the debater of this age	1:20a		
Wisdom of the world	1:20b	wisdom of God	1:21
Stumbling block	1:23	Christ crucified	1:23
		Christ the power of God	1:24
		Christ the wisdom of God	1:24
human wisdom	1:25a	foolishness of God	1:25a
human strength	1:25b	weakness of God	1:25b
Wisdom according to the flesh, power, noble birth	1:26		
Wise	1:27a	God chose the foolish of the world	1:27a
Strong	1:27b	God chose the weak of the world	1:27b
things that are [τὰ ὄντα]	1:28	God chose the things that are not [τὰ μὴ ὄντα]	1:28
		Jesus Christ – wisdom of God	1:30a
		righteousness, and holiness, and redemption	1:30b
Sublime words or wisdom	2:1	Jesus Christ crucified	2:2
		weakness, fear, much trembling	2:3
persuasive words of wisdom	2:4	proof of spirit and power[33]	2:4
human wisdom	2:5	power of God	2:5

These binary oppositional categories not only demonstrate that

---

[31] But note the textual difficulty of this phrase in NA[27]. Cf. Philo, *Prob.* 88, 96; *Contempl.* 31, 75; *1 Enoch* 49:4.

[32] Note especially the language of destruction and nullification: 1:18, 19a [ἀπόλλυμι]; 1:19b [ἀθετέω]; 1:28 [καταργέω].

[33] BDAG s.v. ἀπόδειξις.

Paul's rhetoric is drawing from the argumentative logic of apocalyptic rhetorolect, but they also denote a divine reversal of the current order of things – God bypasses the things that are [τὰ ὄντα] for the things that are not [τὰ μὴ ὄντα] (1:28).[34] Because of the lack of value he accords the wisdom of this world, Paul appears like the sage-heroes of Jewish apocalypses. As John Collins notes, "One finds, then, in the sages of the apocalypses a denial of earthly wisdom, but also a claim to a higher, superior wisdom."[35] Thus *4 Ezra* 4:21 teaches that "those who dwell on the earth can understand only what is on the earth, and he who is above the heavens can understand what is above the height of the heavens."[36] Wisdom *per se* is not devalued; rather, the wisdom that is available from this world is dismissed. Such a reliance on divine revelation rather than teaching based on observation and instruction from the natural created order, found in older Jewish wisdom, is evident in Wisdom of Solomon as well as in Daniel, *4 Ezra*, and *1 Enoch*.[37] As *1 Enoch* 99:12 teaches: "Woe to you ... who acquire worldly knowledge, for you shall be consumed by it."[38] For Paul, true wisdom cannot be found in the world, but only in Christ Jesus and him crucified (1:24, 30). And this wisdom is only available to those who are being saved (1:18).[39]

Although Paul leans heavily on the resources of apocalyptic rhetorolect to organize his teaching about wisdom, this is not the only rhetorolect at work in this passage. As Robbins's work has shown, early Christian use of rhetorolects is not a zero sum game; the use of one does not preclude the use of others. In fact, Robbins argues that Christian texts routinely invite multiple rhetorolects into their complex discourse.[40] In 1 Cor 1:18–2:6 Paul's instruction on wisdom and foolishness proceeds according to the logic of apocalyptic rhetorolect. However, the *topoi* of wisdom and foolishness are also, naturally, regular themes in wisdom rhetorolect as well, albeit at the speculative end

---

[34] Cf. Gen 1:2, especially in light of my discussion of pre-creation rhetorolect below.

[35] J.J. Collins, "Sage in Apocalyptic Literature," 350. But note the call to attend to the wisdom found in the natural world made in *1 Enoch* 2:1–5:3; 101:1-9. Yet nature is also full of mysteries that need revelation to comprehend them as noted in *1 Enoch* 41:3-9; 60:11-23 (cf. *4 Ezra* 4:5, 7; 5:36).

[36] Translation from B.M. Metzger, "The Fourth Book of Ezra," in *The Old Testament Pseudepigrapha* (ed. James H. Charlesworth) 1:516-59.

[37] See J.J. Collins, "Cosmos and Salvation," for an interpretation of Wisdom of Solomon in light of apocalypticism. Collins suggests that "the basis for such rapprochement as we find between apocalypticism and wisdom" should probably be sought "in the wider environment of the Hellenistic age" (idem, 319).

[38] Isaac (*OTP* 1:88) notes that there is a textual difficulty with this verse.

[39] Cf. Dan 2:21; *4 Ezra* 14:26; 46–47; *1 Enoch* 5:8.

[40] Robbins, "Argumentative Textures"; see idem, *Invention* 1:116-17.

of the spectrum. While Paul's critique, in light of the eschatological event of the cross, of the wisdom of this world in 1:18–2:5 resembles the arguments found in the apocalyptic sages, this should not completely obscure the fact that this critique is not antithetical to wisdom rhetorolect, but rather is an essential element of it.[41]

The main thrust of Paul's treatment of wisdom in this section of text can be seen in his recitation of Jer 9:23 in 1 Cor 1:31. Here Paul omits a number of words from the original context in order to create the following maxim: "Let the one who boasts, boast in the Lord."[42] Working from his admonition that "no flesh should boast before God" (1:29), Paul takes a prophetic text in which the Lord warns the wise and strong against boasting in their own abilities and creates a wise saying to instruct the Corinthian community. Although the elements derive from a prophetic text, Paul selects specific elements available in Jeremiah to form a maxim.[43] Such a saying is at home in the wisdom tradition of Judaism, in both form and content, and is reminiscent of Ben Sira's warning that "the greater you are, so much more humble yourself " (Sir 3:18).[44] Paul follows Ben Sira's lead in using Jewish scriptural traditions in his creation of wisdom teachings.[45] In following the Pauline maxim, the Corinthians will be able to embody a prime concern of Jewish wisdom, namely to avoid being exalted in *their own* wisdom (Prov 3:5, 7), which is a sure sign of one's foolishness (Prov 26:12). Such a wisdom concern carries over into Jewish apocalyptic literature as well. The narrator-as-Ezra of *4 Ezra* seems certain that he can know the judgment of God (*4 Ezra* 4:2-3; 5:34-35) until the angel Uriel questions him about his knowledge. These questions lay bare Ezra's ignorance and force him to declare: "I am without wisdom"

---

[41] As demonstrated in my discussion of wisdom in ch. 2. This is what Hays could be pointing towards with his statement that Paul's relationship with "wisdom *traditions*" is not entirely negative ("Wisdom According to Paul," 112).

[42] Robbins, *Tapestry*, 103-4; idem, *Exploring*, 41-42. See also Fishbane, *Biblical Interpretation*. Paul's recitation reads: ὁ καυχώμενος ἐν κυρίῳ καυχάσθω [Let the one who boasts, boast in the Lord], whereas Jer 9:23 in its original LXX context reads: ἀλλ' ἢ ἐν τούτῳ καυχάσθω ὁ καυχώμενος, συνίειν καὶ γινώσκειν ὅτι ἐγώ εἰμι κύριος ποιῶν ἔλεος καὶ κρίμα καὶ δικαιοσύνην ἐπὶ τῆς γῆς, ὅτι ἐν τούτοις τὸ θέλημά μου, λέγει κύριος ["but let the one who boasts boast in this, understanding and knowing that I am the Lord who performs mercy and judgment and righteousness upon the earth because in these things [is] my pleasure," says the Lord].

[43] For more on the form of the maxim, or gnomic saying and its use by Paul, see Wilson, *Love without Pretense*. See Sheppard, *Wisdom as a Hermeneutical Construct* for ways in which Hellenistic Jewish texts use wisdom as a lens through which other, non-wisdom, texts are read.

[44] See Fishbane, *Biblical Interpretation*, 541-42.

[45] Fishbane, *Biblical Interpretation*, 9.

(*4 Ezra* 5:39).[46] Paul's exhortation against the wisdom the Corinthians think they possess in 1:18–2:5 (cf. 1 Cor 3:18), while energized by apocalyptic rhetorolect, also draws its rhetorical power from specific Jewish wisdom resources.[47]

In addition to apocalyptic and wisdom rhetorolects, Paul's emphasis on the "calling" of the Corinthians and the things which God "chose" (1:26-29) is evidence that his discourse is organized by prophetic rhetorolect in this section. This rhetorolect is introduced at the beginning of the letter (1:1), when Paul notes that he was called to be an apostle by the will of God, and is applied to the Corinthians themselves by Paul in 1:9. Paul's use of this organizing frame in 1:26-29 in reference to the Corinthians thus recalls his earlier thanksgiving. As Robbins notes, "[t]he presupposition within most prophetic discourse is that people whom God previously selected to produce righteousness in the human realm have followed the path of unrighteousness. Therefore, God is choosing someone else ... to receive God's blessings."[48] The divine reversal Paul explains in 1:26-29, and which he applies directly to the Corinthians, is at home in prophetic Jewish discourse even as it mimics the larger apocalyptic argument in this section of 1 Cor. Taken as a whole, 1 Cor 1:18–2:5 thus represents a complex blend in which several inputs with different frames are projected in parallel.[49]

While I suggest 1 Cor 1:18–2:5 contains the intersection and blending of three rhetorolects – apocalyptic, wisdom, and prophetic – a complete analysis of 1 Cor 1:18–2:5 using the tools of socio-rhetorical interpretation (SRI) is beyond the scope of this chapter. However, a brief sketch of the dynamic of the conceptual integration in this pericope reveals that these rhetorolects act as organizing frames for Paul's treatment of the theme of wisdom. In this complicated multiple-scope network,[50] the three disparate frames do not clash but rather arrange themselves in a hierarchy so that the dominant apocalyptic frame highlights certain modes of thinking from the other two. In this instance apocalyptic rhetorolect elicits the binary oppositional features found in wisdom and prophetic rhetorolects and brings them to the fore-

---

[46] The humility of the sage is important in *4 Ezra*. See the Lord's response to Ezra in *4 Ezra* 8:47b-49: "But you have often compared yourself to the unrighteous. Never do so! But even in this respect you will be praiseworthy before the Most High, because you humble yourself, as is becoming for you, and have not deemed yourself to be among the righteous in order to receive the greatest glory." Cf. Dan 2:30; *1 Enoch* 5:8; 93:11-14.

[47] See Theis, *Paulus als Weisheitslehrer*, 192. Cf. *4 Ezra* 4:2.

[48] Robbins, "Argumentative Textures," 44-45.

[49] Fauconnier and Turner, *The Way We Think*, 279-98; see also idem 334-36. Please see ch. 1 for my full discussion of conceptual integration theory.

[50] See Fauconnier and Turner, *The Way We Think*, 131.

ground.⁵¹ Such oppositional features are not alien to wisdom or prophetic rhetorolects, but the apocalyptic frame pushes the entire discourse to the end of time and makes these oppositions ontological rather than instrumental.⁵² The oppositions are ontological in discourse organized by apocalyptic rhetorolect because, within the discourse, choices have already been made and judgment rendered; the time for change has past.⁵³ Oppositions that are instrumental, as in wisdom and prophetic rhetorolects, not only admit a change of status, but their *raison d'être* within these organizing frames is to encourage and facilitate such a change in the present *before* judgment is rendered. This blend draws upon the resources of wisdom rhetorolect to emphasize the contrast between the wise and foolish, the fate of those who fall into each camp, and the warning against falsely claiming wisdom. The resources of prophetic rhetorolect receive less stress and therefore run in the background, serving as a reminder that those in the "good" camp are only there because they have been called by God.⁵⁴ Thus the overarching conceptual blend created by this pericope is organized by apocalyptic-wisdom blended rhetorolect with prophetic undertones.⁵⁵

This brief analysis of 1 Cor 1:18–2:5 using the tools of SRI and conceptual integration theory argues against Hays's claim that Paul is critiquing wisdom *per se*. To be sure, Hays is correct to say that Paul has no use for human wisdom of this world. However, I believe that Hays's treatment is like that of most other interpreters who argue that Paul takes up wisdom only as a result of what his so-called opponents teach.⁵⁶ Such interpretations focus too exclusively on the primary apoc-

---

⁵¹ See Robbins, "Argumentative Texture," 54.

⁵² See J.J. Collins, "Cosmos and Salvation," 332.

⁵³ To be sure the *rhetorical* aim of such apocalyptic language can still be, and often is, deliberative.

⁵⁴ Something Paul reminds the Corinthians of in 4:7.

⁵⁵ For a surprisingly similar type of blending taking place in a different branch of Judaism during the Hellenistic period, see Goff, *Worldly and Heavenly Wisdom* in which he concludes that "4QInstruction is a sapiential text that attests a transformation of wisdom. ... 4QInstruction has an apocalyptic worldview." Furthermore, "The combination of sapiential and apocalyptic material in 4QInstruction demonstrates that the wisdom tradition, as it was passed on, could be combined with ideas and traditions that had no place in the ancient Israel in which it was originally developed" (pp. 216-17). Also, idem, "Wisdom, Apocalypticism and the Pedagogical Ethos of 4QInstruction."

⁵⁶ See e.g. Hays, "Wisdom According to Paul"; Witherington, *Jesus the Sage*, 299-314; Gail Paterson Corrington, "Paul and the Two Wisdoms: 1 Corinthians 1:18-31 and the Hellenistic Mission," in *Proceedings: Eastern Great Lakes and Midwest Biblical Societies* (ed. Paul Redditt; Eastern Great Lakes Biblical Society and the Midwest Region of the Society of Biblical Literature; Westerville, Ohio: 1986), 72-84; James A. Davis, *Wisdom and Spirit: An Investigation of 1 Corinthians 1:18-3:20 against the Background of Jewish Sapiential Traditions in the Greco-Roman Period* (Lanham, Md.: University Press of America,

alyptic frame governing Paul's teaching in 1:18–2:5 and, although they do not employ these SRI categories, they functionally argue that this rhetorolect supersedes all other rhetorolects rather than blending with them. Although organized primarily by apocalyptic rhetorolect where Paul argues that things are not as they seem in the present age, the discourse of 1:18–2:5 also draws from a Jewish wisdom tradition that is able to critique itself and sternly warn those who claim wisdom for themselves.[57] Paul negatively assesses the wisdom of the current age by drawing on an indigenous wisdom trait of self-critique which is only intensified in the overall apocalyptic frame in which he sets it. What matters for Paul is not those who are "wise according to the flesh" [σοφοὶ κατὰ σάρκα], but rather Christ Jesus "who became for us wisdom from God" [ὅς ἐγενήθη σοφία ἡμῖν ἀπὸ θεοῦ (1:30; cf. 1:24)]. It is to this wisdom that Paul turns in 2:6 as he begins to construct his positive account of the true wisdom of God.[58]

1 Corinthians 2:6–3:4: Paul as Teacher of Eternal Wisdom

After denouncing human wisdom by comparing it to the wisdom and power of God that was revealed in the event of the cross, Paul shifts the discussion in 2:6–3:4 arguing that, in fact, he *does* proclaim a message of wisdom [Σοφίαν δὲ λαλοῦμεν].[59] This wisdom, however, is one that can be made available only to "the mature" [ἐν τοῖς τελείοις]. Moreover, this wisdom about which Paul speaks is different from the wisdom of this age, a wisdom practiced by those who currently rule [ἀρχόντων].[60] Tying this section to the previous one, Paul begins this pericope within the argumentative logic of apocalyptic rhetorolect when he argues that these rulers of this age are "doomed to perish" [καταργουμένων (2:6)].[61] Those who rule in this age cannot understand the wisdom of God because Paul proclaims it "as a mystery having

---

1984); Michael D. Goulder, "ΣΟΦΙΑ in 1 Corinthians," *NTS* 37 (1991): 526-34; Richard A. Horsley, "Wisdom of Word and Words of Wisdom in Corinth," *CBQ* 39 (1977): 224-39.

[57] See Theis, *Paulus als Weisheitslehrer*, 504-5; also E. Johnson, "Wisdom of God," 141.

[58] Charles A. Wanamaker, "A Rhetoric of Power: Ideology and 1 Corinthians 1–4," in *Paul and the Corinthians: Studies on a Community in Conflict. Essays in Honour of Margaret Thrall* (ed. Trevor J. Burke and J. Keith Elliot; NovTSup 109; Leiden: Brill, 2003), 125. See Robbins, *Invention*, 1:147: "Wisdom, then, is a very puzzling, problematic thing."

[59] See Theis, *Paulus als Weisheitslehrer*, 218-76 for a detailed analysis of 2:6-3:4. See Thiselton, *First Epistle to the Corinthians*, 225.

[60] For a discussion of the ἄρχοντες in 1 Cor 2:6, 8 see the excursus in Theis, *Paulus als Weisheitslehrer*, 225-66; also Thiselton, *First Epistle to the Corinthians*, 233-39.

[61] BDAG s.v. καταργέω 3.

4. Setting the Wisdom Context: 1 Cor 1–4

been hidden away" [ἐν μυστηρίῳ τὴν ἀποκεκρυμμένην] (2:7),[62] an idea prevalent in Jewish apocalyptic literature.[63] Because they could not comprehend this mystery, the rulers of this age crucified "the Lord of glory" (2:8). The wisdom of God that Paul proclaims is not within the reach of unaided human ability, a claim substantiated by his recitation of some writing he considers authoritative (2:9),[64] rather this hidden wisdom must be revealed by the spirit of God (2:10-13; cf. 1:21, 24, 30; *4 Ezra* 4:10, 21).[65]

The idea of a "hidden wisdom" undetectable by human striving might seem to work against some strands of early biblical wisdom.[66] However, such a concept of hidden wisdom is found within segments of the Jewish sapiential tradition, especially later texts from the Hellenistic period that are influenced by apocalypticism.[67] Already in 3 Kingdoms one notes that Solomon has his great wisdom only as a gift from God (3 Kgdms 5:9; cf. Dan 1:17, 20-21), although admittedly the relationship between the asking for wisdom and receiving it is somewhat dialectical: only because Solomon had the wisdom to ask for wisdom

---

[62] See 1 Cor 2:1 and the textual difficulties surrounding μυστήριον there. Also recall that Paul substituted ἀθετέω for Isaiah's use of κρύψω in his recitation of Isa 29:14 (1 Cor 1:19). Although it cannot be demonstrated conclusively since it is not known exactly what text (if any) of Isaiah Paul had access to, this substitution of "nullify" for "hide" in 1:19 coupled with the use of ἀποκρύπτω in 1 Cor 2:7 suggests that Paul's treatment of wisdom here is a well conceived argument of his own making rather than simply a reaction to the situation in Corinth. The hidden wisdom, according to Paul, is the true wisdom.

[63] E.g. Dan 2:18-19, 22, 28-29, 47; *4 Ezra* 5:9-10; 10:38; 14:26, 46-47; *1 Enoch* 38:3; 41:3; 49:1-4; 51:3; 52:1, 5; 60:11; 63:2-3; 68:1; 71:4; 103:2; 104:10-12; 108:15. See Goff, *Worldy and Heavenly Wisdom*, ch. 2 and idem, "Wisdom, Apocalypticism, and the Pedagogical Ethos of 4QInstruction" for a discussion of the role of "the mystery that is to be" in 4QInstruction.

[64] Although Weiß, *Der erste Korintherbrief*, 57-58, notes "The content of that wisdom of God is displayed in the quotation," he concedes that "certainty has still not been attained concerning the origin of the quotation." Conzelmann, *1 Corinthians*, 63: "The quotation cannot be found in either the Old Testament or in extracanonical Jewish writings"; see nn. 70 and 71 on the same page. See also Thiselton, *First Epistle to the Corinthians*, 251-52 for his treatment of the possible sources of the quotation. See idem, 229 for a short bibliography of analyses of the quotation.

[65] An apocalyptic rationale, though not necessarily one Paul himself employs, for why wisdom cannot be found except through divine revelation is found in *1 Enoch* 42:1-2: "Wisdom could not find a place in which she could dwell; but a place was found (for her) in the heavens. Then Wisdom went out to dwell with the children of people, but she found no dwelling place. (So) Wisdom returned to her place and she settled permanently among the angels." For a similar idea, see *4 Ezra* 5:9-10.

[66] See Crenshaw, *Wisdom*, 3, 10-12, but see J.J. Collins, *Jewish Wisdom*, 224 for a critique of Crenshaw's position.

[67] J.J. Collins, "The Sage in the Apocalyptic and Pseudepigraphical Literature," 21-29.

from God – instead of a long life, wealth, or revenge – is it granted to him (3 Kgdms 3:9-12). This tradition is fleshed out in Solomon's discourse in the Wisdom of Solomon, a Hellenistic Jewish text where the necessity of asking for wisdom is crucial for obtaining it, as is the function of the "spirit" (cf. 1 Cor 2:10-13). In Wis 7:7 Solomon prays, evidently to God, and receives discernment [φρόνησις] (cf. Dan 2:23; *1 Enoch* 5:8; 37:3-5).[68] Furthermore, as the result of his invocation [ἐπεκαλεσάμην] "the spirit of wisdom" [πνεῦμα σοφία] comes to him. Solomon recognizes that the wisdom that derives from human sources is deficient and will never enable one to learn the "counsel of God" (Wis 9:13-16; cf. *4 Ezra* 4:2, 10). Discernment of the counsel of God is only possible, Solomon teaches, when God gives wisdom and sends his holy spirit (Wis 9:17). As in 3 Kingdoms, Solomon understands that he would not possess wisdom unless God had revealed it to him (Wis 8:21). This recognition on the part of the narrator-as-Solomon is echoed in the work of Philo who, recognizing that God alone possesses wisdom,[69] argues that for human beings "the end of knowledge is knowing [that] we know nothing" (*Migr.* 134; cf. 1 Cor 8:2). The notion that only God truly possesses knowledge and wisdom is found in Jewish apocalypses as well (*4 Ezra* 4:10-11; 5:34-35, 40; *1 Enoch* 93:11-14). It is within this stream of Jewish apocalyptic wisdom teaching that Paul stands. Having argued against the value of human wisdom (1 Cor 1:18–2:5) in light of God's wisdom that is Christ (1 Cor 1:21, 24, 30), Paul goes on to teach that true wisdom can only be revealed by the spirit of God (1 Cor 2:6-13).[70]

Since true wisdom is only available through the spirit (2:13), Paul teaches that only the one who is spiritual [πνευματικός] will be able to discern it (2:15; cf. *1 Enoch* 5:8). To the "natural" human being [ψυχικός ἄνθρωπος], who does not receive the things of the spirit of God, such gifts appear to be foolishness (2:14). Paul's use of μωρία in 2:14 recalls his teaching in 1:18–2:5: what appears foolish to this world is actually wisdom. It seems that there is a continuation of binary categories as well – πνευματικός vs. ψυχικός. However, the situation is

---

[68] In the Old Greek version Daniel praises the Lord for giving him σοφίαν καὶ φρόνησιν whereas Theodotion's translation reads σοφίαν καὶ δύναμιν.
[69] *Sacr.* 64; *Conf.* 39; *Congr.* 114; *Migr.* 40, 134.
[70] See Theis, *Paulus als Weisheitslehrer*, 221: "Die positive Darstellung der Weisheit in 2,6 kann als Modifikation und Differenzierung des zuvor in 1,18ff Gesagten verstanden werden." [The positive presentation of wisdom in 2:6 can be understood as a modification and differentiation of what was said before in 1:18.] See Goff, *Worldly and Heavenly Wisdom*, ch. 2 (pp. 30-79) where he notes: "4QInstruction is exceptional among sapiential texts because of its prominent appeals to revelation" (p. 30). Given my treatment of resources in the previous chapter and the discussion above, I would want to nuance Goff's statement about exactly how "exceptional" 4QInstruction is in this regard.

complicated by Paul's use of τέλειος in 2:6 and by his remarks in 3:1-4 which seem to juxtapose πνευματικός with σάρκινος/σαρκικός while also introducing the term νήπιος.[71]

In the confusing set of terms that Paul employs in 2:6–3:4, some see a blueprint for a division of different groups of Christians in Paul's thinking. The juxtaposition of τέλειος with νήπιος seems straightforward enough; the images of infants and mature adults echo the idea in Jewish wisdom tradition that one grows into wisdom. The main problem stems from Paul's use of *both* ψυχικός and σάρκινος/σαρκικός as foils for πνευματικός while giving no indication of the relationship between these two "unspiritual" groups. This complicates mapping spiritual, natural, and fleshly onto the categories of τέλειος and νήπιος. It seems that the "spiritual" maps easily onto those who are "mature," while, as Matthew Goff notes, "Paul's 'people of the flesh' are 'infants in Christ' who are not fully mature in terms of their development as ethical followers of Christ."[72] Goff's brief engagement with 1 Cor 1–4 does not wrestle directly with how the term ψυχικός fits into this schema. However, his reading of these chapters in light of 1 Cor 15 suggests a possible solution. Although ψυχικός is not the lexical item Paul usually contrasts with πνευματικός,[73] in 1 Cor 15 Paul uses these two terms in a developmental model that fits with his use of the terms "mature" and "infant" in 2:6 and 3:1. Paul contrasts the "natural body" [σῶμα ψυχικόν] with the "spiritual body" [σῶμα πνευματικόν] in 15:44 using the agricultural image of seed and plant. He then goes on in 15:46 to claim: "But the spiritual [πνευματικόν] [is] not first, but the natural [ψυχικόν], then the spiritual." Although the topic Paul is discussing in 1 Cor 15 is different from what he is arguing in 1 Cor 2–3, his use of the term ψυχικόν as the precursor to πνευματικόν sheds light on how these terms function in 2:6–3:4. It makes the most exegetical sense to regard ψυχικός as a synonym for σάρκινος/σαρκικός. While I will argue in my exegesis of 6:12–7:7 that Paul does recognize different degrees of "good" behavior, in this instance, regardless of the complications caused by Paul's many terms, 2:6–3:4 still manifests a mode of binary oppositional thinking that is endemic to apocalyptic

---

[71] Note that Hays, "Wisdom According to Paul," 119-20 suggests that Paul's ironic discourse begins at 2:6. In other words, Hays argues that Paul's treatment of wisdom is not at all positive in 2:6-3:4, but is, rather, a continuation of the critique begun in 1:18. For a discussion of "spiritual people" and the "fleshly spirit" in 4QInstruction, see Goff, *Worldly and Heavenly Wisdom*, ch. 3 (pp. 80-126), esp. pp. 123-26 where he has an excursus on "'Spiritual' and 'Fleshly' Types of Humankind in Paul."

[72] Goff, *Worldly and Heavenly Wisdom*, 124.

[73] See E. Johnson, "Wisdom of God, 142-43.

rhetorolect. However, the opposition here is between the wise (τέλειος and πνευματικός) and the foolish (νήπιος and ψυχικός/σαρκικος).

The use of rhetorolects has shifted in 2:6–3:4 from that of the previous pericope. The dominant cultural organizing frame of this part of Paul's teaching appears to have become that of wisdom. To be sure, Paul begins this cycle with apocalyptic language of destruction – "the rulers of this world [who are] doomed to perish" (2:6) – and he specifically uses the term ἀποκαλύπτω (2:10; cf. *4 Ezra* 5:32; 7:49; 10:38) while stressing the importance of revealed wisdom, but the emphasis has changed. Whereas in 1:18–2:5 Paul was intent on critiquing human wisdom based on the eschatological event of the cross, in 2:6–3:4 he is trying to convey his positive message of God's eternal wisdom (2:6-7) that is revealed to all believers by God's spirit (2:10-13). Paul insists that God's hidden wisdom must be revealed rather than discerned through human unaided ability and so his argument brings us to the porous border between apocalyptic and wisdom rhetorolects.[74] Here Paul uses revelation in a manner similar to the way it is employed in the apocalyptically influenced Wisdom of Solomon in that what the spirit reveals is not a destruction of evil at the end of time, which is assumed by Paul in 2:6, but rather the spiritual wisdom of God. The opposition between spiritual and "natural" or "fleshly" human beings is supposed to convince the Corinthians to change their behavior (3:3-4). "Paul presumes that one who is among the fleshly people can become a member of the spiritual people."[75] This exhortation is more closely aligned with the theme of opposition between the wise man and the fool that is central to argumentation in wisdom rhetorolect. The opposition presented in 2:6–3:4 is thus not descriptively ontological (as in apocalyptic rhetorolect), but rather is employed in an instrumental manner (as in wisdom rhetorolect) in order to effect a change in the Corinthians.[76] Paul's message in 3:1-4 shows a way for the Corinthians to move from one category into the other.

The equivalents of the wise man and the fool, the πνευματικός and the ψυχικός/σαρκικός, encounter the revelation of the spirit that takes place after the eschatological event of the crucifixion (2:8), and their status is defined by how they react to this revelation.[77] The focus, however, is not on how the ψυχικός/σαρκικός will be destroyed at the end of time, but on the wisdom of God revealed through the cross and

---

[74] See the essays in Benjamin G. Wright, III and Lawrence M. Wills, eds., *Conflicted Boundaries in Wisdom and Apocalypticism* (SBLSymS 35; Atlanta: Society of Biblical Literature, 2005).

[75] Goff, *Worldly and Heavenly Wisdom*, 124.

[76] Excepting, of course, Paul's discussion of "the rulers of this age" in 2:6 and 8 where the language is ontological – they are opposed to God in their being.

[77] See Wanamaker, "Rhetoric of Power," 129-30.

how that wisdom ought to change their behavior (3:1-4).[78] Despite Paul's recontextualization of a truncated and altered form of Isa 40:13 (2:16), there is no discernible use of a prophetic frame in this pericope.[79] However, resources from pre-creation rhetorolect are deployed at the beginning of this passage. The resources available in apocalyptic rhetorolect do not provide Paul the necessary tools he needs to teach the Corinthians that Christ crucified reveals the true architecture of the universe as God planned it from before time. In order to instruct the Corinthians on the eternity of the wisdom revealed through the cross, Paul must draw from pre-creation rhetorolect.

Not only is God's wisdom hidden, but Paul teaches that this wisdom is that "which God pre-defined before the ages for our glory" (2:7).[80] Here Paul moves his wisdom discourse to the far speculative end of the spectrum, which, as discussed in ch. 1, often provides resources for pre-creation rhetorolect.[81] The mysterious and hidden wisdom of God (2:6), which Paul defines as the proclamation of the Christ event (1:24, 30), was not a random act, but rather something that God had pre-defined, in God's wisdom (1:21), from before the beginning of time (cf. *4 Ezra* 6:1-6). Thus Paul moves from using an apocalyptic frame in 2:6 where he posits the fate of the rulers, to a pre-creation frame in 2:7. The focus shifts from the end of time to before time began. By shifting the frame at the outset of the pericope, Paul is able to argue that the wisdom he teaches, the gospel of Christ, is not a "new" wisdom, but the true wisdom that has operated from eternity.

The wisdom of God revealed through the cross, Paul teaches, has existed since before the creation of time. This is why apocalyptic rhetorolect is insufficient for Paul's argument in this pericope. Apocalyptic rhetorolect operates in the temporal realm, that is, after time began.[82] Paul wants to show the Corinthians that the cross does not *only* transform the value of the wisdom of this world, but rather that it lays bare the reality of the universe as conceived by God from eternity. For this, Paul must draw from the logic of pre-creation rhetorolect, which Robbins argues wrestles with "'non-time' before time began with the creation of the world."[83] Pre-creation rhetorolect also helps explain the function of the spirit in 1 Cor 2:10-16. It is only God's spirit, which hovered over the waters before creation (Gen 1:2), that

---

[78] See Goff, *Worldly and Heavenly Wisdom*, 27-28.
[79] Robbins, *Invention*, 1:162; idem, *Tapestry*, 107; idem, *Exploring*, 48.
[80] Robbins, *Invention*, 1:208. See Thiselton, *First Epistle to the Corinthians*, 242; BDAG s.v. ὁρίζω.
[81] See Robbins, *Invention*, 1:125.
[82] Robbins, "Argumentative Textures," 54.
[83] Robbins, *Invention*, 1:111.

can provide the discernment necessary to understand God's wisdom. Paul's use of pre-creation rhetorolect here is in the service of his wisdom teachings. What Collins argues concerning the logic of the Wisdom of Solomon fits for Paul's teaching here as well: "The wise man, who understands the structure of the world, also understands the principles of God's judgment and can live life in light of those principles."[84] Paul's innovation here is his understanding of the cross of Christ as that which reveals the structure of the universe as pre-defined in God's eternal wisdom.

Paul's innovative use of the resources and logic of pre-creation rhetorolect distinguishes his teaching from other examples of speculative Hellenistic Jewish wisdom. In this literature the eternal equivalent of wisdom is often the law.[85] Thus the true structure of the universe in many strands of Hellenistic Jewish thought is revealed through the teachings found in the law and therefore it is only natural that the law provides a sure blueprint for righteous action. Whereas those like Ben Sira understood wisdom by conceiving it in conjunction with Torah, Paul understands wisdom through its equivalence with the gospel he proclaims rather than through the law. Such a distinction affects how Paul will later argue against πορνεία in 6:12–7:7. Law, according to Paul, cannot teach the Corinthians why and how to live lives of righteousness. Only the eschatological discernment of God's eternal wisdom revealed by the cross can do that. 1 Cor 2:6–3:4 is thus organized by an overarching wisdom frame that invites the logic and resources available in apocalyptic and pre-creation rhetorolects into its exposition on God's hidden wisdom.[86]

1 Corinthians 3:5–4:13: Blended Wisdom Analogies

One of the characteristics of traditional Jewish wisdom is that it often, in the words of Goff, "encourages the pursuit of natural analogies."[87] The use of these analogies is typically based on wisdom's understanding of the world as "well-ordered, beneficent, and just."[88] As noted above, however, Paul's discourse paints a world that seems to be anything but

---

[84] Collins, "Cosmos and Salvation," 321; see also idem, 333.
[85] See my discussion of wisdom in ch. 2; also Robbins, "Argumentative Textures," 37; Goff, *Worldly and Heavenly Wisdom*, 46; Theis, *Paulus als Weisheitslehrer*, 281; E. Johnson, "Wisdom of God," 146: "Paul speaks of his gospel as the wisdom of God in much the same way his Jewish contemporaries speak of the Torah." Jewish apocalyptic writings also tie wisdom to the doing of the law as in *4 Ezra* 7:72, 81; 8:12, 29; 9:11; 13:38; *1 Enoch* 99:2; 108:1.
[86] Robbins, *Invention*, 1:208.
[87] Goff, *Worldly and Heavenly Wisdom*, 45; see Robbins, *Invention*, 1:144.
[88] Robbins, "Argumentative Textures," 31.

4. Setting the Wisdom Context: 1 Cor 1–4

this. The perceptible world cannot, according to Paul, teach the Corinthians the principles of God's eternal wisdom since this wisdom is hidden. Only the eschatological event of the cross can reveal God's wisdom. Once God's spirit gives an understanding of this wisdom to those who are being saved, everything in this world is no longer what it appears. Yet in 3:5–4:13 Paul has left his exposition on the nature of wisdom and has returned to specific issues relating to proper understanding and behavior within the community.[89] This, I argue, helps explain his return to a form of argumentation deeply rooted in wisdom rhetorolect. Although he will invite apocalyptic and prophetic rhetorolects into this pericope, Paul is concerned to help the community understand the roles of their apostolic teachers in order to change their behavior towards them and towards one another. To do this, he draws from the logic of analogical instruction as found in wisdom.

Throughout 3:5–4:13 Paul's rhetoric moves to diminish the cult of personality associated with human teachers in Corinth (cf. 1:12-13).[90] He begins this by portraying the spirit of God as the true teacher of God's mysterious wisdom (2:10-16). In 3:5–4:13 Paul tells the Corinthians that their human teachers are "assistants [ὑπηρέτας] of Christ and stewards [οἰκονόμους] of God's mysteries" (4:1; cf. 3:5). What is important, according to Paul, is not the human teacher, but whom the teacher serves and what mystery he or she has been charged with keeping and teaching. Yet, as Charles Wanamaker notes, while Paul moves to dismantle the teacher factionalism in this pericope he also positions himself as *the* authority figure to whom the Corinthians should listen by offering "a divine warrant for his dominant role within the Corinthian community" (3:10).[91] Although my focus is different from his, my analysis of 1 Cor 3:5–4:13 relies on Wanamaker's socio-rhetorical study of the ideology of power in 1 Cor 1-4.

In 3:5-9 and 3:10-15 Paul's rhetographical argumentation employs two metaphors in order to instruct the Corinthians about the proper role of teachers within their community through analogical reasoning about the community itself. As he tells the Corinthians in 3:9b: "You are God's field, God's building" [θεοῦ γεώργιον, θεοῦ οἰκοδομή ἐστε]. In the field analogy of 3:5-9, Paul describes himself and Apollos as mere servants [διάκονοι], who simply performed the tasks assigned to them by the Lord (3:5). Although Paul did the planting and Apollos did the watering, Paul stresses that it is only God who can make things grow. Thus, Paul argues, the Corinthians owe their allegiance only to

---

[89] See Theis, *Paulus als Weisheitslehrer*, 119, 125.
[90] See Wanamaker, "Rhetoric of Power," 130-33.
[91] Wanamaker, "Rhetoric of Power," 132.

the one who generates life. Paul claims that those who plant and tend are not anything (cf. 1:28) and are themselves working towards a common goal. Since it is only God who can actually make things grow, it is only God who matters (3:6-8). Although Paul teaches that he and Apollos are working toward the same goal, he does "[s]ubtly ... allow for differentiation between himself and Apollos when it comes to the rewards that they receive from God" (3:9).[92] Paul the planter seems to have precedence over Apollos the one who waters.

With the building metaphor of 3:10-15 Paul continues urging the community toward unity by stressing the same goals held by their various teachers, but he also further cements his role as the primary builder who controls, or should control, the entire operation. Paul stresses that the foundation of the building is Jesus Christ and that no one is able to lay another foundation than this one (3:11). Yet Paul positions himself as the "skilled master builder" [σοφὸς ἀρχιτέκτων] who laid that foundation (cf. 2:1-5) upon which all other builders must work (3:10). As Wanamaker argues:

> the master builder metaphor underscores [Paul's] role as the one taking responsibility for supervising the coordination and the overall project with respect to the other builders... Thus as the one who marked out and laid the foundation, which he identifies as Jesus Christ, and by implication in the context, Christ crucified, everyone else who exercises leadership in the community must build on the foundation which he laid. There is no other foundation according to Paul; there is no chance for anyone to supersede or replace his work. Ideologically the metaphor dissimulates his relation to the church and to the leaders of the community by subordinating both to him.[93]

Paul energizes his use of analogical reasoning so prevalent in wisdom rhetorolect by injecting an apocalyptic theme of judgment into this discourse. Not only is the work of other builders subordinate to Paul the skilled master builder, but the quality of the work that they build upon his foundation will be "revealed with fire" [ἐν πυρὶ ἀποκαλύπτεται]. With the apocalyptic image of fire (cf. *1 Enoch* 100:9; 102:1), Paul reminds the other teachers that their work will be judged based on its conformation to his foundation.

Paul extends his building metaphor in 3:16-17 by identifying the structure that he and the other teachers are actually constructing. The Corinthians are not just any building, but they are God's temple, which houses God's spirit. This image will play a key role in Paul's reasoning in 6:12–7:7. In 3:16-17 Paul's rhetoric, in an extremely efficient fashion, blends three rhetorolects: wisdom, priestly, and apoca-

---

[92] Wanamaker, "Rhetoric of Power," 131.
[93] Wanamaker, "Rhetoric of Power," 132.

lyptic. The use of metaphor and analogy is, as noted above, a hallmark of wisdom instruction. The fact that Paul uses the metaphor of God's holy temple draws from the background information available in priestly rhetorolect. Finally, Paul's threat of destruction [φθείρω][94] in 3:17 continues the logic of apocalyptic rhetorolect introduced in 3:12-15.

Following his rhetographical use of multiple metaphors in 3:5-17, Paul re-iterates his teaching in 1:18–3:4 with an exhortation for the members of the community to "become fools in order that you might become wise" [μωρὸς γενέσθω, ἵνα γένηται σοφός] (3:18). Although Paul has rhetorically positioned himself as the primary teacher with the Corinthian community through his analogical instruction, in the final verses of ch. 3 Paul makes a final push to delegitimize any cult of personality in Corinth by subordinating all the teachers to the Corinthians themselves. Yet he follows this by subordinating the Corinthians to Christ and subordinating Christ to God. In 3:5-23 Paul is performing a delicate dance. He must undercut the legitimacy of factionalism among the Corinthians by reducing the importance of individual teachers, yet he must also assert his credentials as one who has the primary authority to instruct the Corinthians. Moreover, he must constantly work to make sure that the Corinthians remember their proper role in relation to Christ and God.

Paul's description of Apollos and himself in 4:1-13 continues this delicate dance. In 4:1-5 Paul again works to diminish the influence of human teachers. Those who proclaim the gospel to the Corinthians are serving Christ and are mere "stewards" of God's mysteries (cf. 2:1, 7). Here Paul continues in the apocalyptic vein of 3:12-15 by stressing that stewards will be judged. However, his rhetoric here also serves to undercut any Corinthian judgment against him, since he declares that it is not human judgment that matters, but God's judgment. Not only is it God's place to judge, but it is also only God's place, after revealing hidden things, to offer commendation (4:5). The final judge who offers the only punishments and rewards that matter is God the giver of all gifts (4:7).

In 4:8-13 Paul drives home not only the paradoxical nature of leadership in this world, but he also firmly cements his authority as an authentic teacher sent by God. To do this, Paul relies heavily on the resources available in prophetic rhetorolect that, once again, overturn the expectations of this world. In 4:8 Paul sarcastically addresses the Corinthians with rhetoric that encompasses the exuberant possibilities

---

[94] Note that this lexical item has cultic and apocalyptic connotations. BDAG s.v. φθείρω.

found in traditional wisdom and prophetic traditions.[95] If worldly wisdom were a true picture of reality, the positive images Paul uses in 4:8 and 4:10 for the Corinthians would serve to bolster their status and honor. However, as Paul has demonstrated in 1:18-3:4, the wisdom of this world is not based on reality. The true structure of the universe is revealed through the cross of Christ. This reality is based on what appears to be weakness and foolishness to worldly eyes. Thus when Paul contrasts "us apostles" who are fools, weak, and held in disrepute with the Corinthians who are wise, strong, and held in honor his rhetoric is one that serves to shame the community. They are conformed to the reality of this world rather than the reality of God's eternal wisdom since they are apparently still too immature to know the difference (3:1-4).

The depiction of the abuse suffered by the true apostles in 4:8-13 serves to demonstrate to the Corinthians what living in conformity to God's wisdom actually looks like. And although he makes sarcastic use of the exuberant prophetic possibility of righteous kingship, Paul is able to selectively project other resources available in prophetic rhetorolect into his rhetoric. The fact that those specially called by God suffer abuse in this world is nothing new to Jewish prophetic tradition. This is amply demonstrated in 2 Chron 36:15-16 which describes a God who mercifully sends his messengers to his chosen people only to have his prophets mocked [ἐμπαίζοντες ἐν τοῖς προφήταις αὐτοῦ]. The experience of Elijah also serves as a graphic warning about the physical dangers faced by God's true prophets (3 Kgdms 19:10, 14).[96] The brutal treatment Paul has received at the hands of this world provides him with a prophetic warrant for the truth of the message he proclaims. Based on the order of the universe revealed through the cross, and the experience of Israel's prophets, Paul's persecution demonstrates that he lives his life in accordance with God's eternal wisdom and therefore is in a position to instruct the Corinthians.

1 Corinthians 4:14-21: "Be Imitators of Me" – Paul Asserts Authority

In 3:5–4:13 Paul tries to dismantle that cult of personality that the Corinthians have apparently created around certain teachers while subtly

---

[95] I am heavily indebted to Vernon K. Robbins for the reading of this section through the "exuberant possibilities" of wisdom and prophetic rhetorolects; personal communication. Gaining and maintaining wealth is a positive sign of wisdom (e.g. Prov 8:18; 31:11-27; Eccl 2:3-8; Goff, *Heavenly and Worldly Wisdom*, 43), whereas the production of a righteous kingdom is the goal of prophetic literature as any of the prophetic books amply demonstrate.

[96] The persecution of the prophets is a major *topos* of early Christian prophetic rhetorolect. See e.g. Matt 5:12; 23:37; Luke 11:47-48; 13:34; Acts 7:51-52.

insinuating the primacy of his own teaching authority into his analogical reasoning. In 4:14-15, after having recounted the trials he has suffered as an apostle (4:10-13), Paul abandons a subtle approach and appropriates the image of the primary teacher in the Jewish wisdom tradition for himself – the father who instructs his children.[97] As John Collins notes, "The classic form of [wisdom] instruction is cast as the advice of a father to his son, but variations are possible."[98] Paul refers to members of the Corinthian community as his beloved children [ὡς τέκνα μου ἀγαπητά] (4:14) of whom he states "I fathered you in Christ Jesus through the gospel" [ἐν γὰρ Χριστῷ Ἰησοῦ διὰ εὐαγγελίου ἐγὼ ἐγέννησα] (4:15).[99] Paul constructs the other teachers in Corinth as pedagogues – useful, but under the authority of the head of the household. Because of the father-child relationship between Paul and the Corinthians, Paul is able to urge them to "be imitators of me" [μιμηταί μου γίνεσθε] in 4:16.[100] As Wanamaker notes, "by virtue of the triad of interconnected metaphors which presents Paul as father, other leaders, including Apollos, as guardians and disciplinarians, and the Corinthians themselves as children, Paul reasserts his unique authority over the community in preparation for authoritatively addressing a range of divisive behavior."[101]

Paul not only activates the father-as-teacher model from Jewish wisdom tradition, but as Elizabeth Castelli observes, in his call to *mimesis* Paul also participates in the broader Hellenistic pedagogical ideal of

---

[97] Prov 1:8; 2:1; 3:1; 4:1-2, 10, 20; 5:1; 6:20; 7:1. See Crenshaw, *Wisdom*, 77-78 (also 45); Dell, "*Get Wisdom, Get Insight,*" 11, 23-24; Murphy, *Tree of Life*, 3-4. See esp. Newsom, "Woman and the Discourse of Patriarchal Wisdom," for more on MT Proverbs 1-9 as intergenerational instruction from father to son.

[98] J.J. Collins, *Jewish Wisdom*, 222.

[99] See Conzelmann, *1 Corinthians*, 91: "The phrasing shows that fatherhood is no mere metaphor; it is real, 'spiritual' fatherhood." Schrage, *Der erste Brief an die Korinther*, 1:354 notes that the "father" language Paul employs denotes an unbreakable relationship between Paul and the community: "Keiner von beiden kann sich davon emanzipieren." [Both are unable to emancipate themselves from it.] Wanamaker, "Rhetoric of Power," 135. See Trevor J. Burke, "Paul's Role as 'Father' to His Corinthian 'Children' in Sociohistorical Context (1 Corinthians 4:14-21)," in *Paul and the Corinthians: Studies on a Community in Conflict. Essays in Honour of Margaret Thrall* (ed. Trevor J. Burke and J. Keith Elliot; NovTSup 109; Leiden: Brill, 2003), 95-96, 107-108. Although Burke uses cognitive metaphor theory rather that conceptual integration theory, his analysis of 1 Cor 4:14-21 is similar in method to what I will employ to exegete 6:12-7:7 below.

[100] Fee, *First Epistle to the Corinthians*, 96 argues that 4:16 "now takes the father-child imagery a step further and in so doing enunciates the point of the entire paragraph." Burke, "Paul's Role as 'Father,'" 102: "Fathers in particular expected to model appropriate behaviour for their children, especially sons, to imitate." See also Witherington, *Conflict and Community*, 147; Crenshaw, *Wisdom*, 78.

[101] Wanamaker, "Rhetoric of Power," 136.

paideia – the imitation of a great teacher by the pupil. The blending of these two arenas, Castelli notes, is also found among other Hellenistic Jews, notably Philo and Josephus.[102] To be sure, the categories of father-child and teacher-pupil were not distinct in the ancient world, as Trevor Burke reminds exegetes when he notes that "[p]arents in antiquity, particularly fathers, were also expected to educate their offspring."[103]

Paul twice exhorts the Corinthians to imitate him in the letter and these exhortations in 4:16 and 1:11 form a rhetorical *inclusio*.[104] In 4:15-21 Paul looks back on his argument in 1:10–4:13 and concludes it with a call to the Corinthians to reform their behavior by using him, their father in Christ, as a model. These verses also show Paul looking forward because they set the context for his teachings in chapters 5-10, where he portrays himself as the παράδειγμα (esp. 1 Cor 9) of proper judgment and behavior in the Christian community.[105] This rhetorical unit ends in 11:1 with Paul's repeated exhortation that the Corinthians should imitate him.[106] Between 4:16 and 11:1, the repetitive texture of Paul's teaching emphasizes his role as the παράδειγμα to whom the Corinthians can look for guidance about proper judgment and conduct as he teaches them specific strategies for negotiating living in the world.[107]

Elizabeth Castelli recognizes that Paul's calls to imitation in 4:16 and 11:1 have to do with a reassertion of his authority over the Corinthians.[108] She notes the importance of the father figure in Greco-Roman

---

[102] Elizabeth A. Castelli, *Imitating Paul: A Discourse of Power* (Louisville, Ky.: Westminster John Knox, 1991), 81-85. Conzelmann, *1 Corinthians*, 92: "The summons to 'imitate' him is a paraenetic topos in Paul (11:1 etc.)... The word group μιμεῖσθαι, is used of the pupil's relation to his teacher." See n. 16 on the same page for references from Greek and Hellenistic Jewish resources. See also Winter, *Philo and Paul*, 172-79.

[103] Burke, "Paul's Role as 'Father'," 104. See Crenshaw, *Wisdom*, 24, 78; also J.J. Collins, *Jewish Wisdom*, 2.

[104] Dodd, Paradigmatic "I," 66-67.

[105] See Mitchell, *Paul and the Rhetoric of Reconciliation*, 49-60. "The purpose of this self-exemplification is manifestly to get the Corinthians to imitate his example in their behavior" (p. 60). Dodd, Paradigmatic "I," 67: "If we divide 4.14–15.58 into topics and set this list next to Paul's self-characterizations throughout these same chapters, we find that Paul's self-presentation is at the heart of each of these same chapters (except 11.17-34)."

[106] See Mitchell, *Paul and the Rhetoric of Reconciliation*, 206, 225 where she argues the rhetorical unit runs from 5:1-11:1. "5:1-11:1 is a distinct section of proof because it manifests rhetorical unity and coherence" (p. 225).

[107] 1 Cor 4:16; 5:3, 12; 6:7 (alluding to Paul's teaching in 4:8-13), 12, 15; 7:7, 8, 40; 8:13; 9:1-27; 10:33; 11:1. See Mitchell, *Paul and the Rhetoric of Reconciliation*, 53 where she notes that 4:16 and 11:1 "are not isolated incidents;" Burke, "Paul's Role as 'Father'," 105. See Robbins, *Tapestry*, 46-50; idem, *Exploring*, 8 for a discussion of repetitive texture.

[108] See Wanamaker, "Rhetoric of Power," 115-37. He notes on 116: "... in this paper I hope to move Castelli's work forward by looking at the ways in which Paul's rhetoric in 1 Cor. 1:10-4:21 functions ideologically to reassert power in the Corinthian community." But see Burke, "Paul's Role as 'Father'," 110.

society and the authority due him in Hellenistic culture,[109] but she argues that "one is hard pressed to produce a univocal, concrete expression of what exactly the Corinthians are being called to imitate."[110] However, Paul's teaching in 1 Cor 5-10 adduces specific points of imitation. Moreover, the context of 4:16-21 also calls into question this part of Castelli's analysis. Immediately after Paul urges the Corinthians to imitate him, he notes that he has sent his envoy Timothy, also described by Paul as his child, so that he can remind [ἀναμνήσει] them of Paul's "ways in Christ," which he teaches [διδάσκω] in every assembly (4:17).[111] Paul's call to imitation thus comes not only with concrete instructions found later in the letter, but coupled with the intent to send one who will be able to "remind" the Corinthians of Paul's teachings. Thus, contrary to Castelli's claim, Paul's call to imitation does possess content. However, since this content is organized by the logic of wisdom rhetorolect, it is not "univocal," but seeks rather to teach and persuade by means of rationales for different modes of behavior rather than simply to demand obedience through non-negotiable commands. Even when Paul does resort to commands that admit no deviation (e.g. 5:13; 6:18; 10:14), he provides rationales supporting them and offers various ways to adhere to these injunctions.[112] Paul does not attempt to cover every possibly exigency, rather he teaches the Corinthians to be able to recognize for themselves when to appropriate certain teachings and when to use others as their specific situation warrants. Such a mode of instruction is a fundamental characteristic of wisdom rhetorolect.[113]

Although I disagree with her specific analysis of how Paul's call to imitation functions in 1 Cor, Castelli does rightly emphasize Paul's overarching concern about power. Paul reminds the Corinthians not to become "puffed up," because when he returns, he will contrast their

---

[109] Castelli, *Imitating Paul*, 101. Reading Castelli and Newsom, "Woman and the Discourse of Patriarchal Wisdom," together provides excellent insight into the power dynamics of instruction based on a father-child model across biblical traditions. See Thiselton, *First Epistle to the Corinthians*, 371-73 for a critique of Castelli's thesis. See Burke, "Paul's Role as 'Father'," 100: "Undergirding every discussion of family in antiquity is the common assumption that parent-child relations were hierarchical in nature." And further, his conclusion on 105: "The evidence for the most part shows that as far as the typical expectations of father-child relations are concerned, Jewish families were little different to their non-Jewish counterparts at the turn of the eras." Burke cites various Jewish and Greco-Roman sources on pp. 100-105.

[110] Castelli, *Imitating Paul*, 109.

[111] See Burke, "Paul's Role as 'Father,'" 110-11. But note Witherington, *Conflict and Community*, 147.

[112] See Philo *Leg.* 1:93; *Mos.* 2:49-50.

[113] See Robbins, "Argumentative Texture," 31-37; Murphy, *Tree of Life*, 113; Goff, "Wisdom, Apocalypticism and the Pedagogical Ethos of 4QInstruction," 59.

power with that of the kingdom of God (4:18-20), which comes "by power" [ἐν δύναμει] and not "by a word" [ἐν λόγῳ] (4:20; cf. 1:17-18; 2:4-5). In his final warning before he turns to certain specific issues, Paul invokes the traditional power of the father in Jewish wisdom literature: "What do you wish? Should I come to you with a rod [ἐν ῥάβδῳ] or with a loving and gentle spirit?" (4:21). Certainly Castelli, and Wanamaker following her lead, is correct that, despite Paul's suggestion that he and the other teachers belong to the Corinthians (3:21-22), Paul here demands to have his specific authority recognized with his use of the image of a father disciplining his children.[114] Paul's description of himself as the father of the Corinthian congregation followed closely by his use of the term ῥάβδος in the context of reproving the Corinthians sets up the cultural organizing frame of wisdom for Paul's teaching that follows.

Conclusion

In the first four chapters of 1 Corinthians Paul attempts to resolve the problems he sees in the Corinthian community through a meditation upon wisdom. Throughout, he is at pains to make the Corinthians understand that appearances in this age are deceiving. According to Paul, "the wisdom of this world is foolishness in the sight of God" (3:19; cf. 1:21, 25). The wisdom of God is evident not through persuasive words of human wisdom, but through God's crucified Christ (1:24, 30).[115] Understanding this, Paul apparently believes, will help the Corinthians bring their behavior into conformity with the very structure of God's created order. Although the wisdom which Paul speaks in 1 Cor 1–4 is different from some aspects of traditional biblical wisdom, most notably in its aversion to eloquent speech,[116] "the conception of Old Testament wisdom teaching is still included in the Pauline argument. This applies especially to the concerns of Old Testament

---

[114] Wanamaker, "Rhetoric of Power," 136. See Prov 10:13; 13:24; 22:15; 23:13-14; 26:3; Sir 33:25 (for a donkey); for similar language of discipline without the specific term ῥάβδος, but often with a similar device, μάστιξ, see Sir 22:6; 23:2; 28:17; 30:1; 40:9. See also Philo *Leg.* 2:89-90: "... in truth the conduct of the virtuous man leans on discipline as a rod, settling and allaying the tumult and tossing of the soul ..." (2:90 [Colson & Whitaker, LCL]). Fee, *First Epistle to the Corinthians*, 192: "With one further use of the father-child metaphor, Paul ties the challenge of vv. 8-20 to the appeal of vv. 14-17." See also Dodd, *Paradigmatic "I,"* 74; Thiselton, *First Epistle to the Corinthians*, 378; Weiß, *Der erste Korintherbrief*, 122.

[115] See E. Johnson, "Wisdom of God," 145: "The conflict between human and divine wisdom is ... an eschatological power struggle between cosmic forces."

[116] Philo is also suspect of certain types of speech. See *Prob.* 88, 96; *Contempl.* 31, 75. See also Goff, *Worldly and Heavenly Wisdom*, 216-17 for the development of wisdom in 4QInstruction as distinct from that found in Israel of earlier periods.

4. Setting the Wisdom Context: 1 Cor 1–4

wisdom to proclaim the will of God with regard to the concrete, everyday management of life," as Theis rightly notes.[117] Having explicated the paradoxical nature of God's wisdom and secured his own position of pedagogical authority in 1 Cor 1–4, Paul goes on to discuss concrete methods for this "everyday coping" in 1 Cor 5:1–11:1.

Paul's discussion of wisdom in these opening chapters of 1 Cor, although undertaken in order to remedy problematic behavior within the Corinthian community, is of his own creation and not simply the adoption of some Corinthian *Stichwort*.[118] I am in agreement with Theis that "the formal link between community problems and wisdom themes in these thoroughly well thought out texts demonstrates that 1 Cor 1–4 first and foremost represents Pauline thinking."[119] From his discussion *about* wisdom, Paul turns to offer wisdom instruction to his community in subsequent chapters. However, Paul's wisdom instruction will invite resources from other rhetorolects in order to make his teaching as persuasive as possible. This demonstrates the opportunistic nature of early Christian discourse, which frustrates scholarly attempts at drawing neat boundaries. Yet it is by blending wisdom instruction with other modes of discourse that Paul is most like his Hellenistic Jewish contemporaries who also were combining their robust wisdom heritage with argumentation and themes from other arenas. It is within this messy Hellenistic wisdom context that Paul's treatment of πορνεία and the means to avoid it is set.[120]

---

[117] Theis, *Paulus als Weisheitslehrer*, 281: "Dennoch ist die Vorstellung der alttestamentlichen Weisheitslehre in die paulinische Argumentation aufgenommen. Dies trifft insbesondere auf das Anliegen der alttestamentlichen Weisheit zu, Gottes Willen im Hinblick auf die konkrete alltägliche Bewältigung des Lebens zu verkünden." See also ibid., 196.

[118] Theis, *Paulus als Weisheitslehrer*, 147: "Wisdom is a vitally important theme for Paul as well." E. Johnson, "Wisdom of God," 145; Witherington, *Jesus the Sage*, 307. Witherington notes that Paul uses sapiential material in 2 Cor 11, Phil 2:6-11ff.; Rom 10:6-8; 11:33-36 and that, according to NA[26], Paul makes twenty-six allusions to Sirach "and cites or alludes to the Wisdom of Solomon some forty times" (n. 47). In an interesting contrast of how similar data, end even similar conclusions, can be colored by the answer one gives this question, compare the work of James Davis (*Wisdom and Spirit*) with that of Joachim Theis (*Paulus als Weisheitslehrer*). Both agree that a Hellenistic Alexandrian Jewish wisdom model is at work in 1 Cor 1–4, but for Davis it is Paul's opponents who use this model as a resource, whereas for Theis it is Paul himself who draws from it. See Weiß, *Der erste Korintherbrief*, xxxii-xxxiii for a discussion of this in light of the "Apollos people."

[119] Theis, *Paulus als Weisheitslehrer*, 147: "die formale Verbindung von Gemeindeproblematik und Weisheitsthematik innerhalb dieser wohl durchdachten Texte bezeugt, daß 1 Kor 1–4 zuallererst das paulinische Denken darstellt."

[120] See Coulson and Oakley, "Metonymy," 77 where they discuss the construction of meaning as "unruly, ad hoc, conglomerations." See my discussion of the ways in which conceptual integration theory deals with the messiness of human meaning making in Chapter 1.

5

The Wisdom of Fleeing Porneia: Introducing 1 Corinthians 6:12-7:7

Introduction

Having established the proximate rhetorical wisdom context of 1 Corinthians 1–4 in the previous chapter, I now aim to use conceptual integration theory within a socio-rhetorical framework in order to elucidate Paul's discussion of πορνεία in 1 Cor 6:12–7:7. The primary goal of this exegesis is to shed light on how Paul constructs a meaningful wisdom argument, first by explaining *why* the Corinthians should avoid πορνεία (6:12-20) and then by providing various general options for *how* to go about doing this (7:1-7). A secondary goal will be to demonstrate that conceptual integration theory, when used in a broader interpretive analytic, provides biblical scholars useful exegetical tools for the undertaking of *Bibelwissenschaft*.

Given that the following exegetical chapters rely so heavily on the newer developments in socio-rhetorical interpretation (SRI) and the apparatus of conceptual integration theory, both of which have their own distinctive vocabulary, it is worth recalling the salient features of each from Chapter 1. Recent developments in socio-rhetorical interpretation (SRI) involve the exegetical use of rhetorical dialects, or *rhetorolects*, that socio-rhetorical interpreters have identified in early Christian discourse. Recall that a rhetorolect is a heuristic category that is defined as "form of language variety or discourse identifiable on the basis of a distinctive configuration of themes, topics, reasonings, and argumentations."[1] In addition to the term rhetorolect, SRI employs two other neologisms to discuss specific kinds of rhetoric in texts.[2] An

---

[1] Robbins, "The Dialectical Nature of Early Christian Discourse," 356; idem, *Invention*, 1:xxvii-xxviii; "Rhetography."

[2] On the usefulness of neologisms in rhetorical analyses see Willi Braun, "Rhetoric, Rhetoricality, and Discourse Performances," in *Rhetoric and Reality in Early Christianities* (ed. Willi Braun; Studies in Christianity and Judaism/Études sur le christianisme et le judaïsme 16; Waterloo, Ontario: Wilfrid Laurier University Press, 2005), 10.

argument can rely primarily either on images or on reasoned statements to make its case. The former type of argument is grounded in *rhetography* – rhetoric that evokes images – and the latter is built upon *rhetology* – rhetoric that evokes logical reasoning.[3] Certainly these two types of arguments rarely exist in any pure form, isolated from the other. Rather, they interact dynamically with one another. Some arguments, however, rely more heavily on one than the other. In the first part of Paul's argument (6:12-20), in which he explains why πορνεία is to be avoided, he relies heavily on rhetography in order to get the Corinthians to *see* that πορνεία is incompatible with the Christian body.[4] The images Paul employs drive his argument forward. In the second part of the argument (7:1-7), in which Paul teaches the Corinthians how to avoid this sexual sin, he relies more on rhetology. Reasoned explanations, rather than images, are the primary mode of argumentation in the part of the pericope in which Paul is *explaining* how the Corinthians can avoid πορνεία.

Although socio-rhetorical interpreters have so far identified six rhetorolects operative in the NT, Paul's didactic discourse in 6:12-7:7 only evokes three: *wisdom, apocalyptic,* and *priestly.* As I will demonstrate, the host rhetorolect, the one that evokes the cultural conceptual environment for the pericope as a whole, is wisdom. It is from within this host wisdom environment that Paul invites resources from the other two rhetorolects into the discussion. In 6:12 Paul introduces his teaching with gnomic reasoning about the topic of freedom, namely rhetology. Once this rhetology establishes the initial wisdom rhetorolect that hosts his discourse, Paul relies on rhetography that is more at home in apocalyptic and priestly rhetorical environments (6:13-20) to make his case for why the Corinthians should avoid πορνεία. In the second half of the pericope, where Paul moves to teach the Corinthians how to avoid sexual sin, he resumes the emphasis on rhetology and uses wisdom rhetorolect more explicitly to organize his teaching. However, Paul evokes other rhetorolects even here. In 7:1, Paul continues with a blend of wisdom and priestly rhetorolects when he relies on implicit purity rationales as the basis for the gnomic saying in 7:1b. Paul also evokes priestly rhetorolect in 7:5 to provide rationales, again based on purity, for allowing a couple to refrain from sexual relations. This rationale is important, especially given his teaching about the importance of regular sexual activity within marriage (7:3-4). However,

---

[3] See Robbins, "Enthymeme and Picture in the *Gospel of Thomas*," 175; idem, *Invention*, 1:xxvii.

[4] Cf. Aeschines' oration *Against Timarchus* in which he employs a similar strategy to *show* the Athenian jury that Timarchus lives in ways antithetical to the citizen's body.

in 7:5 Paul also uses apocalyptic rhetorolect to provide the rationale for why the couple should resume regular sexual activity as quickly as possible. The use of rhetorolects, as well as a focus on rhetography and rhetology, helps to explain the different modes of argumentation Paul's rhetoric embodies in each section of the pericope.

Conceptual integration theory is also rich with terminology that, while confusing for those not familiar with it, lends precision to my analysis. Recall that the *constitutive principles* of conceptual blending involve the *conceptual network* that has, at minimum, four mental *spaces*: two *input* spaces, a *generic* space, and the *blended* space (or, the *blend*).[5] A blend provides new meaning because of *selective projection*. In any blend only some elements, roles, values, and relations are projected while others are not. In the blend these selective projections allow for the creation of *emergent structure* in the network through which new insights are born. New emergent structure is created through three processes: *composition, completion,* and *elaboration*.[6] In order for new emergent structure to be effectively created, background information must be efficiently recruited in both the input spaces and the blended space. This recruitment is possible because input and blended spaces both often rely on entrenched meaning that allows the conceptual network function. The input and blended spaces are often organized by *frames*, which represent certain types and configurations of entrenched knowledge, or by entrenched *characters* with known attributes.

The process of blending additionally involves several *governing principles*. One main principle, and the one my exegesis relies heavily upon, involves the *compression* of *vital relations*.[7] Vital relations are what link various elements and structures between mental spaces.[8] Compression involves tightening these essential relationships. The vital relations of

---

[5] The exact nature and function, even the usefulness, of the generic space is debated by cognitive scientists themselves. See, e.g., Seana Coulson and Todd Oakley, "Blending and Coded Meaning ," 1516-17 where they do not employ a generic space in their analysis, but rather make use of what they refer to as a "grounding box." This shift is based on their reading of Ronald W. Langacker, *Concept, Image, and Symbol: The Cognitive Basis of Grammar* (2nd ed.; Berlin: de Gruyter, 2002).

[6] See Fauconnier and Turner, *The Way We Think*, 42-43 for a discussion of how these three work together in a single blend to create new insights. See also Seana Coulson and Todd Oakley, "Purple Persuasion: Deliberative Rhetoric and Conceptual Blending," § 1. Cited 13 May 2006. Online: http://cogsci.ucsd.edu/~coulson/purple.html. In *Cognitive Linguistics Investigations: Across Languages, Fields, and Philosophical Boundaries* (ed. J. Luchenbroers; Human Cognitive Processing 15; Amsterdam: H. Benjamins, 2006), 47-65.

[7] Fauconnier and Turner, *The Way We Think*, 114: "Blending is a compression tool *par excellence*." See also idem, 312; idem, "Compression and Global Insight," *Cognitive Linguistics* 11 (2000): 283-304.

[8] Fauconnier and Turner, "Compression and Global Insight," 290-91.

Analogy, Disanalogy, Part-Whole, and Identity will be important to my exegetical analysis below.[9] The vital relation of Identity, in which two elements from different inputs spaces are compressed into one element in the blend, will play a large role in exegeting the importance of the Christian body for Paul. In addition to Compression, there are other governing principles as well. Some of these remaining principles appear in my exegesis, but they happen not to play as central a role as the principle of Compression. The other principles are: Topology, Pattern Completion, Integration, Promoting Vital Relations, Web, Unpacking, and Relevance.[10] These governing principles, especially Compression, will help me understand how Paul's conceptual blends function and, thus, how they make rhetorical sense.

I combine the new insights of SRI with those of conceptual integration theory. Fauconnier and Turner argue that "Cultures work hard to develop integration resources that can be handed on with relative ease... The creative part comes in running the blend for a specific case."[11] Rhetorolects are these dynamic cultural "integration resources." They both provide cultural resources that help configure Paul's teaching and are themselves reconfigured by Paul's creative running of various blends. In other words, rhetorolects can help organize the background information necessary for a conceptual network to function in a meaningful way, but they are also enriched by the emergent structure produced by the conceptual blending that occurs within the conceptual networks Paul's rhetoric evokes. I therefore consider rhetorolects to be dynamic *organizing cultural frames* that account for the "distinctive configurations,"[12] and the logic that drives them, of Paul's conceptual networks. These distinctive configurations and *topoi* have led Vernon Robbins to suggest that rhetorolects are similar to George Lakoff's "cluster Idealized Cognitive Models (ICM)."[13] Thus one way wisdom rhetorolect traditionally argues against extra marital sexual behavior is economic – such sexual activity, either with sex workers or with women who expect gifts, leads to economic ruin for a man's household. Apocalyptic rhetorolect provides a different, special frame for this argument, viewing the πόρνη as a representative of the malevolent forces of this world working against the power of God. Priestly rhetorolect provides a frame of cultic impurity for the figure of the πόρνη and of the man who defiles himself by having sexual relations

---

[9] See Fauconnier and Turner, *The Way We Think*, 93-101 for a description of vital relations.
[10] See Fauconnier and Turner, *The Way We Think*, 325-34.
[11] Fauconnier and Turner, *The Way We Think*, 72.
[12] Robbins, "Dialectical Nature," 356.
[13] Robbins, *Invention*, 1:119; see Lakoff, *Women, Fire, and Dangerous Things*, 74-76, 203.

with her. These three cultural "integration resources" interact dynamically in Paul's argumentation. Since each rhetorolect, or organizing cultural frame, or cluster ICM relies on different background information to power its cognitive engine, their blending within Paul's teaching evokes highly complex processes of cognition. The "creative part" of Paul's teaching fosters emergent structure that enriches a single rhetorolect as well as creates new emergent structure that is achieved by the blending of multiple rhetorolects. This complex creativity not only nurtures a richness of reasoning, but it also creates the possibility of hearers/readers reasoning in different ways from one another.

In Chapter 1 I noted the great plasticity conceptual integration theory possesses in describing how the constitutive elements of conceptual networks are organized. The input spaces and the blend can be of varying levels of specificity.[14] Rhetorolects – cultural frames that organize mental spaces and facilitate new kinds of emergent structure – are sometimes as specific as biblical interpreters can get to explaining how a blending network functions. However, I argue that in detailed exegesis it is often possible to specify more closely how the discourse organizes input spaces and blends.[15] I refer to this level of specificity as a *local frame*. This more specific frame helps evoke more specific background information about "themes, topics, reasonings, and argumentations" available in a conceptual network.[16] Thus I argue that 1 Cor 6:12 is organized by the cultural frame of wisdom rhetorolect, but its rhetorical function is further specified by the local frame of freedom. By mixing the insights derived from an analysis of cultural and local frames, I argue that conceptual integration theory used in a socio-rhetorical framework gives biblical interpreters a powerful tool to use in exegesis. My discussion of the Jewish resources in Chapters 2 and 3 attempts to describe, in some detail, the cultural resources that help explain how a Hellenistic Jew like Paul could organize his teaching on the religious problem posed by πορνεία – or, more accurately, how an argument produced by a Hellensitic Jew such as Paul could prompt the activation of cultural resources in meaning aware hearers/readers. I will recall these Jewish resource zones in my analysis below while also bringing in relevant Hellenistic-Roman resources where I believe they

---

[14] Fauconnier and Turner, *The Way We Think*, 103-104.

[15] Note that in Chapter 4 I did not enter into a detailed exegesis of the rest of 1 Corinthians, but kept my analysis on the level of cultural frames. Bear in mind that an analysis of local frames is not always possible, or exegetically fruitful, even in the most careful exegesis.

[16] Fauconnier and Turner refer to these as sub-frames; see also idem, *The Way We Think*, 40 for a discussion of the difference between long-term schematic knowledge and long-term specific knowledge. See Oakley, "Human Rhetorical Potential," for a discussion of the importance of local purposes in rhetoric.

provide useful information to help fill out the meaning potential of the cultural and local frames Paul relies upon in 1 Cor 6:12–7:7.

In all of this, recall that the overarching goal of conceptual blending is to achieve *human scale*, that is, to make complex cognitive situations easily comprehensible. As Fauconnier and Turner explain it, "The most obvious human-scale situations have direct perception and action in familiar frames that are easily apprehended by human beings... They typically have very few participants, direct intentionality, and immediate bodily effect and are immediately apprehended as coherent."[17] An analysis of the conceptual networks that Paul's didactic discourse creates in 1 Cor 6:12–7:7, especially his rhetography, demonstrates that he fulfills this goal with amazing proficiency.

Establishing the Pericope

After reminding the Corinthians of their sanctification in the name of Christ and in the spirit of God (6:11), Paul begins his teaching regarding the sanctity of the Christian body and the consequent necessity of avoiding πορνεία in 1 Cor 6:12–7:7.[18] This span of text functions as a unified pericope in which Paul organizes his instruction in two parts. Paul first demonstrates why the Corinthians are to avoid sexual immorality and then he teaches the community how to achieve this goal.[19] The pericope is marked by a rhetorical *inclusio* in which Paul makes use of a "paradigmatic I" through which he attempts to get his hearers/readers to identify with the first person pronouns he uses. This recalls his exhortation in 4:16 (and later in 11:1) to "Be imitators of me."[20] Paul opens the argument in 6:12 with the double use of a gnomic saying that focuses on his freedom:

> All things are lawful for me, but not all things are beneficial;
> All things are lawful for me, but I will not be dominated by anything.

In each instance he curtails his freedom (cf. 1 Cor 9).[21] He ends the

---

[17] Fauconnier and Turner, *The Way We Think*, 312; see Robbins, *Invention*, 1:184.

[18] Note that Dodd, *Paul's Paradigmatic "I"*, 86-87 argues that 6:9-12 rhetorically belong together. However, see Goulder, *Paul and the Competing Mission*, 120: "The lack of a linking particle shows that 6.12 does not follow on from 6.11."

[19] This idea is suggested, although not demonstrated, by Nejsum, "Apologetic Tendency," 52. See also Plunkett, "Sexual Ethics and the Christian Life," 4, 15. But see Rosner, "Temple Prostitution," 338 who argues that the general argument against πορνεία begins at 7:2.

[20] Dodd, *Paul's Paradigmatic "I"*, 89-90: "The macro-strategy of personal example in the letter has suggested such an interpretation"; idem, "Paul's Paradigmatic 'I'," 39-58. See also Mitchell, *Paul and the Rhetoric of Reconciliation*, 49-60; Kirchhoff, *Sünde*, 105-20.

[21] Kirchhoff, *Sünde*, 109.

general argument in 7:7 with another reference to himself, summing up the second half of his argument: although it would be best if everyone could be as sexually controlled as he is (7:1b), pragmatically Paul recognizes that each person has differing gifts from God (7:2-6; cf. 12:27-31; 14). Paul thus begins and ends this pericope by re-inscribing the admonition of the rhetorical unit in which it is found – imitating Paul is the best means to embody correct behavior; he is an "I" who is worthy to be emulated. However, when direct *mimesis* is not possible, one should imitate Paul by making wise judgments (cf. 7:25, 40).

The division of the text that I have suggested requires further support in that Paul once again uses himself as an example in 7:8. Why is this verse not the end of the pericope? I maintain that in 7:1-7 Paul discusses general means for men and women in the community to avoid πορνεία, either by avoidance of sexual activity (7:1b), through monogamous marriage in which sexual activity between the marriage partners is not restricted (7:2-4), or a somewhat dangerous blend of the two (7:5).[22] In these instances Paul speaks in general terms: of a generic (male) "person," "each man," and "each woman." Beginning with 7:8, however, Paul turns from his general argument to specific groups, in this instance the unmarried and widows. Paul here employs a characteristic mode of argumentation found in wisdom rhetorolect where "on the basis of one or more generalized principles, it may offer any number of specific examples or analogies."[23] In 7:8-16 Paul offers specific advice to various groups: to the unmarried and widows (vv. 8-9), to the married (vv. 10-11), and to "the rest" (vv. 12-16).[24] Paul's use of himself as a παράδειγμα in 7:8 therefore serves to introduce the application of his general teaching in 7:1-7 to specific groups within the Corinthian community. In 7:17-24 Paul makes use of several analogies which serve to bolster his overall argument that the Corinthians are acceptable to God whether married or unmarried[25] and that changing one's current status is therefore unnecessary and unwarranted. In 7:25-30 Paul returns to giving advice to specific groups – this time to virgins (vv. 25-35), anyone fearing improper behavior with "his virgin" (vv. 36-40),[26] and women whose husbands have died (vv. 39-40). Paul ends

---

[22] See Conzelmann, *1 Corinthians*, 114; Witherington, *Conflict and Community*, 173.

[23] Robbins, "Argumentative Textures," 31.

[24] See R. Collins, *First Corinthians*, 262-73.

[25] But see Yarbrough, *Not Like the Gentiles*, 101: "Four times in vv. 8-40 Paul addresses the question of believers' marrying and in each instance he argues against it."

[26] The exact referent of παρθένος and the meaning of ὑπέρακμος have proven to be an interpretive crux for exegetes. See R. Collins, *First Corinthians*, 299-302; Conzelmann, *1 Corinthians*, 134-36 and esp. nn. 40, 41 (p. 135); Fee, *First Epistle to the Corinthians*, 350-52; Martin, *Corinthian Body*, 219-28; Schrage, *Der Erste Brief an die Korinther*, 2:197-210; Thiselton, *First Epistle to the Corinthians*, 594-98; William Loader, *Sexuality and the Jesus*

the chapter with a recapitulation of his teaching in vv. 8-9 and a reference to himself, not explicitly as a παράδειγμα as in v. 8, but as one who possesses the "spirit of God" and is therefore able to provide wise counsel (7:39-40; cf. 2:6-13, 15; 7:25).[27]

The presence of περὶ δέ in 7:1a has caused many commentators to treat what follows this formula as separate from that which came before.[28] Margaret Mitchell, however, has successfully demonstrated that "the περὶ δέ is nothing more or less than a way of introducing a topic the only requirement of which is that it be readily known to both writer and reader."[29] It does not provide a methodologically sound means to reconstruct specific, separate moments of Corinthian communication with Paul.[30] In the case of its use in 7:1a, the formula does not mark a completely new topic, but rather highlights the transition to a new sub-argument in Paul's treatment of πορνεία.[31] Paul shifts from showing why one should avoid sexual immorality, an argument couched in rhetography, to explaining general principles for enacting this avoidance, a way of arguing grounded in rhetology. Likewise, the use of περὶ δέ in 7:25 does not signal a complete change in topic but denotes a shift in emphasis from Paul's use of analogies in 7:17-24 back to his use of specific examples (7:8-16, 25-40). This is evident by the loose *inclusio* formed by 7:8-9 and 7:39-40.[32]

Tradition (Grand Rapids: Eerdmans, 2005), 180; Margaret Y. MacDonald, "Virgins, Widows, and Wives: The Women of 1 Corinthians 7," in *A Feminist Companion to Paul* (ed. Amy-Jill Levine; Cleveland: Pilgrim, 2004), 148-68. For the purposes of this project, these issues do not need to be settled here.

[27] See R. Collins, *First Corinthians*, 289-90.

[28] This formula is found in 7:1, 25; 8:1; 12:1; 16:1, 12. The break in NA[27] between 6:20 and 7:1, agreeing in this instance with the *kephalaia* of most MSS, suggests that these two sections of Paul's argument are distinct. R. Collins, *First Corinthians*, 251-58; Conzelmann, *1 Corinthians*, 114-15; Fee, *First Epistle to the Corinthians*, 266-67, 271; Thiselton, *First Epistle to the Corinthians*, 483, 498. On the question of whether this preposition and particle constitute a "formula," see Mitchell, "Concerning ΠΕΡΙ ΔΕ," 236 n. 30.

[29] Mitchell, "Concerning ΠΕΡΙ ΔΕ," 236.

[30] Mitchell, *Paul and the Rhetoric of Reconciliation*, 191. See idem, "Concerning ΠΕΡΙ ΔΕ," for a fuller treatment of this formula in which she provides comparative examples. See also Dodd, *Paul's Paradigmatic "I"*, 91. See Hurd, *Origin of 1 Corinthians* for the most extreme example of this type of reconstruction.

[31] See Mitchell, "Concerning ΠΕΡΙ ΔΕ," 256: "περὶ δέ ... is one of the ways in which Paul introduces the topic of the next argument or sub-argument." See also Martin, *Corinthian Body*, 212; Schrage, *Der Erste Brief an die Korinther*, 2:50.

[32] See Mitchell, "Concerning ΠΕΡΙ ΔΕ," 237 where she discusses the use of the formula in Diogenes Laertius's *Lives of Eminent Philosophers*. But see Stanley K. Stowers, "PERI MEN GAR and the Integrity of 2 Cor. 8 and 9," *NovT* 32 (1990): 345.

The use of the περὶ δέ plus the genitive to mark a shift to a different sub-argument within a larger discursive structure is not unique to Paul in 1 Cor 7, but can also be seen in other early Christian literature as well. Acts 21:18-26 contains a narrative in which Paul tells "all the elders" the things "God did among the Gentiles" [ἐποίησεν ὁ θεός ἐν τοῖς ἔθνεσιν (Acts 21:19)]. In 21:20-24 the elders discuss Jewish believers and then, in 21:25, shift back to the topic introduced in v.19: "And concerning the believing Gentiles ..." [περὶ δὲ τῶν πεπιστευκότων ἐθνῶν].[33] Here the περὶ δέ does not introduce a new topic, but returns the focus to the believing Gentiles who were already introduced earlier in the narrative.

A different function of the formula is found in *Did.* 6:1-3 where περὶ δέ is employed to mark a specific example within a broader category.[34] *Did.* 6:2 argues: "For if you can bear [δύνασαι βαστάσαι] the entire yoke of the Lord, you will be perfect; but if you cannot, do as much as you can" (Ehrman, LCL).[35] In 6:3a the author narrows the focus from "the entire yoke of the Lord" to food: "And concerning food, bear what you can" [περὶ δὲ τῆς βρώσεως, ὃ δύνασαι βάστασον (Ehrman, LCL)]. A similar case may be found in *Did.* 11:3, depending on how one relates the "teachers" in 11:1-2 with the "apostles and prophets" in 11:3-6. Since apostles and prophets seem an interchangeable title in 11:3-6, I see no reason for arguing that "teachers" somehow represent a distinct "office."[36] Rather, it seems that 11:1-2 discusses the broad category of "whoever comes and teaches you," with 11:3-6 discussing a narrower subsection of that group: περὶ δὲ τῶν ἀποστόλων καὶ προφητῶν.[37] The περὶ δέ formula alone, then, does not specify whether the shift is to a new topic, to a previously

---

[33] See Mitchell, "Concerning ΠΕΡΙ ΔΕ," 251 on Acts 21:25: "Because the subject of Gentile Christians is readily understood by the audience, it can be introduced with περὶ δέ." Mitchell fails to note that the περὶ δέ in this verse is not simply used to introduce a topic "readily understood," but serves to bring the discussion back to the main theme introduced in v. 19.

[34] And thus it appears to function here in much the same way that Stowers argues περὶ μὲν γάρ typically does (Stowers, "PERI MEN GAR," 342-45).

[35] This is surprisingly similar to what Paul argues in 1 Cor 7:1-7, 32-38.

[36] The hierarchy explicated by Paul in 1 Cor 12:28 does not appear operative in *Did.* 11.

[37] Both of these examples from the *Didache*, however, may fall under a rule, discussed by C. E. Faw, "On the Writing of First Thessalonians," *JBL* 71 (1952): 221, that περὶ δέ introduces the second point in a series of replies (quoted by Mitchell, "Concerning ΠΕΡΙ ΔΕ," 251). However, I argue that the best example of this rule is found in *Did.* 9:1-3. Here the Eucharist as a topic is introduced with the formula περὶ δέ and then the list of elements in the Eucharist is discussed. In 9:2 one reads "First, concerning the cup ..." [πρῶτον περὶ τοῦ ποτηρίου] followed by "And concerning the piece [of bread] ..." [περὶ δὲ τοῦ κλάσματος]. *Did.* 6:3 and 11:3, as I argue above, use the περὶ δέ formula to narrow the focus of a broader category.

mentioned topic, or to a sub-topic within a larger discussion; it is context alone that allows the exegete to make this determination. Given that Paul discusses monogamous heterosexual coupling only διὰ τὰς πορνείας (1 Cor 7:2) it seems reasonable to conclude that 1 Cor 7:1a, "and concerning the things which you wrote" [περὶ δὲ ὧν ἐγράψατε],[38] serves to link Paul's teaching in 7:1-7 to that which preceded it in 6:12-20.[39] Both sections discuss different moments in a coherent argument about avoiding πορνεία. The περὶ δέ in 7:1a simply serves to tie Paul's teaching into an ongoing discussion with the Corinthians about concrete concerns they already have (cf. 1 Cor 5:9) and about which they apparently wrote Paul, hence it refers to issues with which both are familiar.[40]

The opening (6:12) and closing (7:7) of the pericope contain Paul's reference to himself as a model who exemplifies correct behavior.[41] However, the imitation Paul expects from the Corinthians is not that they should do exactly that which he does, but rather that they should learn to judge as he judges. He teaches the skills needed to judge what mode of action is correct for the individual members of the heterogeneous Corinthian community, each of whom has different gifts (7:7; cf. 12:27-31; 14), based on the "facts on the ground" within certain non-negotiable parameters.[42] As Crenshaw notes, "If true wisdom consists of the appropriate deed for the moment, then different situations call for varied responses."[43] Thus Paul teaches that, while everything is permitted him, it is necessary to judge what is beneficial [συμφέρει] in order

---

[38] See Ehrman's new LCL translation of *Did.* 6:3 ("and concerning ... ") and compare this to his translation of *Did.* 11:3 ("but concerning ..."). The difference between the two is based on an interpretation of context, not inherent to the περὶ δέ formula itself. I discuss my translation for 1 Cor 7:1a below.

[39] So Martin, *Corinthian Body*, 212; Nejsum, "Apologetic Tendency," 49. See also Elaine H. Pagels, "Paul and Women: A Response to a Recent Discussion," *JAAR* 42 (1974): 542.

[40] See Mitchell, *Paul and the Rhetoric of Reconciliation*, 235: "It may be surprising to modern readers that Paul treats marriage under the topic of πορνεία, but that is the case." In n. 279 she further states that "Exegetes have been forced to admit that Paul does not provide a *positive* rationale for marriage in this chapter [i.e., 1 Cor 7]. It is acceptable διὰ τὰς πορνείας." See also Yarbrough, *Not Like the Gentiles*, 107. For περὶ δέ followed by verbs relating to writing, see Mitchell, "Concerning ΠΕΡΙ ΔΕ," 245.

[41] Outside of these verses, the only other place a first person singular pronoun is implied in this pericope is 6:15.

[42] See Robbins, *Invention*, 1:129; Murphy, *Tree of Life*, 113; Crenshaw, *Wisdom*, 3, 50, 56; Wilson, *Love without Pretense*, 22. Note also Faith Kirkham Hawkins, "1 Corinthians 8:1-11:1: The Making and Meaning of Difference" (Ph.D. diss., Emory University, 2001), chs. 4 and 5 (pp. 198-294) where she discusses Paul's "construction of difference."

[43] Crenshaw, *Wisdom*, 13. See idem, 200: "The goal was to know what to do or say on any given occasion."

not to be mastered [ἐξουσιασθήσομαι] by anything (6:12).[44] While he argues that avoiding πορνεία is an absolute that cannot be compromised (cf. 10:14), Paul recognizes that there will be different ways that different members of the community will be able to achieve this goal (7:7). The ἐξουσία of Paul and, by extension, the Corinthian community, demands the ability to make wise decisions.

The Question of Slogans in 1 Corinthians 6:12–7:7

A major issue that must be confronted when attempting an exegesis of 1 Cor 6:12–7:7 is the existence of various hypotheses regarding the presence of so-called Corinthian slogans in these verses. The twice repeated phrase "Everything is permissible for me" [πάντα μοι ἔξεστιν] (6:12a, c; cf. 10:23), as Wolfgang Schrage notes, enjoys almost universal recognition as a slogan that the Corinthians employed and against which Paul must argue.[45] With less unanimity, many scholars agree that a slogan is also located in 6:13, but there is some dispute over its exact length. The majority opinion holds that the slogan consists of 6:13ab: "Meats for the belly and the belly for meats, and God will destroy this and them" [τὰ βρώματα τῇ κοιλίᾳ καὶ ἡ κοιλία τοῖς βρώμασιν, ὁ δὲ θεὸς καὶ ταύτην καὶ ταῦτα καταργήσει].[46] Jerome Murphy-O'Connor has suggested that 6:18b, "Each sin which a person might commit is outside of the body" [πᾶν ἁμάρτημα ὃ ἐὰν

[44] See Philo, *Leg.* 3.194; *Sacr.* 23; cf. *Leg.* 3.149, 156; *Sacr.* 32. For why I read 6:12 "without quotation marks," see my discussion of the so-called slogans below (Dodd, "Paul's Paradigmatic 'I'," 54).

[45] Schrage, *Der erste Brief an die Korinther*, 2:10: "Daß Paulus mit V 12a und 12c die Losung freiheitsstolzer Korinther zitiert, ist heute fast allgemein anerkannt." [That Paul with verses 12a and 12c quotes the solution of the proudly free Corinthians is almost universally acknowledged today.] See also Conzelmann, *Commentary on the First Epistle to the Corinthians*, 108; Fee, *First Epistle to the Corinthians*, 251; Furnish, *Theology*, 56; Goulder, "Libertines?" 341; Martin, *Corinthian Body*, 175; Mitchell, *Paul and the Rhetoric of Reconciliation*, 232; Thiselton, *First Epistle to the Corinthians*, 460; Weiß, *Der erste Korintherbrief*, 157. See Dodd, *Paul's Paradigmatic "I"*, 79–81 for his discussion of various scholars who argue for the presence of slogans; Kirchhoff, *Sünde*, 73 n. 21 for her list of such scholars; Hurd, *Origin of 1 Corinthians*, 68 for a table of various authors' opinions on this issue.

[46] See R. Collins, *First Corinthians*, 244; Fee, *First Epistle to the Corinthians*, 254; Karl Olav Sandnes, *Belly and the Body in Pauline Epistles* (Cambridge: Cambridge University Press, 2002), 192–93; Schrage, *Der erste Brief an die Korinther*, 2:20; Thiselton, *First Epistle to the Corinthians*, 462; Jerome Murphy-O'Connor, "Corinthian Slogans in 1 Cor 6:12–20," *CBQ* 40 (1978): 394. But see the dissenting view of Furnish, *Theology of 1 Corinthians*, 58: "Paul's rhetoric here is not polemical but didactic." Although he does not use the terminology of SRI, Furnish's contention that these verses are didactic lends support to my reading them through a wisdom lens. Udo Schnelle argues that 1 Cor 6:14, while not a Corinthian slogan, is a post-Pauline addition, "1 Kor 6:14 – Eine Nachpaulinische Glosse," *NovT* 25 (1983): 217–19.

ποιήσῃ ἄνθρωπος ἐκτὸς τοῦ σώματος ἐστιν], is also a Corinthian slogan.⁴⁷ However, this hypothesis has met with little assent. Finally, as discussed above, 1 Cor 7:1b, "It is good for a person not to touch a woman" [καλὸν ἀνθρώπῳ γυναικὸς μὴ ἅπτεσθαι], is regarded by many scholars to be a quotation from the Corinthian letter to Paul.⁴⁸

Exegetes generally do not reflect on the process of distinguishing Corinthian slogans from Pauline discourse. An exception to this is Paul Charles Siebenmann's 1997 dissertation from Baylor University.⁴⁹ He undertakes his study "out of a growing concern in the community of NT scholars that the search for slogans is not being carried out in a fashion which is heuristically appropriate or beneficial."⁵⁰ Although his study re-inscribes the general consensus about the location of slogans in 1 Corinthians in general and in 6:12–7:7 in particular, he does voice a concern that their existence in some portions of the letter has tempted scholars to find slogans where they "would either resolve a dilemma or provide an opportunity to defend or promote a solution which corresponds to their favorite theory."⁵¹ I would go further and argue that the genesis of various slogan hypotheses, like that of partition theories from the last century,⁵² is the desire to resolve what scholars view as unsettling or intractable interpretive difficulties. Just as challenging and overcoming various theories of partition in the late twentieth century has helped moved our understanding of 1 Corinthians forward,⁵³ a reconsideration of the function of various slogan hypotheses allows for a more nuanced reading of Paul's didactic rhetoric in 1 Cor 6:12–7:7.

Brian Dodd has done the most work in contemporary scholarship in calling the ubiquity of various slogan hypotheses into question.⁵⁴ My

---

⁴⁷ Murphy-O'Connor, "Corinthian Slogans," 391-96. See Thiselton, *First Epistle to the Corinthians*, 471-72 for his discussion of this suggestion and others who hold it.

⁴⁸ See, e.g., Goulder, *Paul*, 125; Thiselton, *First Epistle*, 498-500; R. Collins, *First Corinthians*, 252; Schrage, *Der erste Brief an die Korinther*, 2:53-54; Witherington, *Conflict and Community*, 167; Fee, *First Epistle*, 270-71; Barrett, *First Epistle*, 154; Hurd, *Origin*, 68, 163-65; Yarbrough, *Not Like the Gentiles*, 93-94, 121; Phipps, "Is Paul's Attitude toward Sexual Relations Contained in 1 Cor 7.1?" 125-31.

⁴⁹ Siebenmann, "Question of Slogans," 162, 172.

⁵⁰ Siebenmann, "Question of Slogans," abstract, also 5.

⁵¹ Siebenmann, "Question of Slogans," 297. He identifies slogans in 1 Cor 6:12; 6:13; 6:18 (in agreement with Murphy-O'Connor); 7:1; 8:1; 8:4; 8:8; 10:23. See Nejsum, "Apologetic Tendency."

⁵² See Wieß, *Der erste Korintherbrief*, xl-xlii. Weiß is generally regarded as the foundational proponent of partition theories: see Mitchell, *Paul and the Rhetoric of Reconciliation*, 2 (esp. n. 5); Hurd, *Origin of 1 Corinthians*, 44.

⁵³ See esp. Mitchell, *Paul and the Rhetoric of Reconciliation*.

⁵⁴ See Dodd, *Paul's Paradigmatic "I"*; idem, "Paul's Paradigmatic 'I'." But see Thiselton, *First Epistle to the Corinthians*, 460: "There can be no question that the initial clause

purpose here is not to attempt to demonstrate that the Corinthians did not have a stock set of phrases which they bandied about. What I object to, and what my exegesis challenges, is the way various slogan hypotheses have been traditionally deployed in twentieth century biblical scholarship. They have generally been used in the service of historical reconstruction. My intent is to shift the exegetical focus from this kind of localized historical reconstruction to an analysis of Paul's rhetorical argumentation.[55] Biblical scholars can never know for certain what the Corinthians said. Even trying to falsify the slogan hypotheses requires the exegete to re-inscribe the very methodology that I find to be unhelpful for socio-rhetorical exegesis. Regardless of whether Paul incorporated Corinthian phrases into his teaching, I argue that the standard way of reading these so-called slogans obscures a holistic understanding of Paul's argument and does not take into account the paradoxes that are endemic to Paul's reasoning.[56]

In Paul's discussion of wisdom in 1 Cor 1–4, he speaks paradoxically of God choosing the foolish of the world to demonstrate God's wisdom (1:26), and he exhorts the Corinthians paradoxically to become fools so they may be wise in God's eyes (3:18-19). The ultimate source of this mode of Pauline argumentation is his understanding of the paradoxical nature of the cross that is foolishness to those who are perishing, but the power of God to those being saved (1:18). While a crucified messiah is "a stumbling block to the Judeans and foolishness to Gentiles," to those who are called from every people, this Christ is the power and wisdom of God (1:23-24).[57] The salvific event that undergirds Paul's proclamation is itself paradoxical, and Paul's argumentation draws upon and mimics this paradox for rhetorical effect. Thus I believe exegetes need to exercise extreme caution before concluding

---

of v. 12 represents a quotation used as a maxim by some or by many at Corinth, in spite of the recent argument to the contrary by B.J. Dodd."

[55] See Caroline Vander Stichele and Todd Penner, "Paul and the Rhetoric of Gender," in *Her Master's Tools? Feminist and Postcolonial Engagements of Historical-Critical Discourse* (ed. Caroline Vander Stichele and Todd Penner; SBL Global Perspectives on Biblical Scholarship 9; Atlanta: Society of Biblical Literature, 2005), 291, who have a similar exegetical goal for their interpretation of 1 Cor 11:2-16. Also Jennifer Wright Knust, *Abandoned to Lust: Sexual Slander and Ancient Christianity* (Gender, Theory, and Religion; New York: Columbia University Press, 2006), 75; Stanley K. Stowers, *A Rereading of Romans: Justice, Jews, and Gentiles* (New Haven: Yale University Press, 1994), 67. See also Daniel Boyarin, *Carnal Israel: Reading Sex in Talmudic Culture* (The New Historicism: Studies in Cultural Poetics 25; Berkeley: University of California Press, 1993), 12-13 for an analogous discussion about reconstructing the lives of the rabbis in studies of early rabbinic literature.

[56] See Robbins, *Invention*, 1:204.

[57] See my discussion in Chapter 4. Although generally regarded as pre-Pauline, this idea is found in the Christ hymn of Phil 2:5-11.

any part of 1 Corinthians does not have an organic place in Paul's rhetoric.

Rather than slogans, I suggest that a more helpful exegetical path is to be found in the phenomenon of rhetorical invention.[58] Employing invention, the rhetor makes use of various topics and ideas – from history, literature, culture, and local context – in crafting a persuasive argument.[59] This takes seriously the deliberative nature of Paul's teaching in 1 Corinthians, which Margaret Mitchell has demonstrated.[60] "Deliberative rhetoric," Duane Watson writes, "is advice giving, persuasion or dissuasion, and its end is the possible or impossible, advantageous or harmful, necessary or unnecessary, expedient or inexpedient."[61] The exact provenance of the rhetorical elements is, at best, ancillary to the goals of rhetorical invention. The important thing is that these elements work together to persuade the hearer/reader. This is not judicial rhetoric in which the speaker/writer proves his or her opponent wrong by countering with opposing claims.[62] Rather, reading 1 Cor 6:12–7:7 through the lens of deliberative rhetorical invention fits better, I argue, into Paul's didactic purposes of persuading the Corinthians to avoid πορνεία. Paul's rhetoric employs rhetorical invention and elaboration to persuade the Corinthians to take right action in the realm of sexual comportment.[63]

Rather than resort to so-called slogans that purport to tell biblical scholars what is taking place "behind" Paul's letter, it makes more exegetical and rhetorical sense to read Paul's teaching in 6:12–7:7 as a coherent example of didactic rhetoric that displays his paradoxical teaching, his binary apocalyptic view of the world, and his concern for the holiness of the Christian body as he attempts to persuade the Corinthians. Thus, as I will argue below, I believe that Paul in 6:12 is

---

[58] See Robbins, *Invention*, 1:12, 78-79.

[59] Duane Frederick Watson, *Invention, Arrangement, and Style: Rhetorical Criticism of Jude and 2 Peter* (SBLDS 104; Atlanta: Scholars Press, 1988), 14.

[60] Mitchell, *Paul and the Rhetoric of Reconciliation*, 1; see Martin, *Corinthian Body*, 38-39. But note Porter's objections in "Ancient Rhetorical Analysis," 272, as well as Thomas H. Olbricht's more general caution against using classical rhetorical categories when interpreting Paul in "The Foundations of Ethos in Paul and in the Classical Rhetoricians," in *Rhetoric, Ethic, and Moral Persuasion in Biblical Discourse: Essays from the 2002 Heidelberg Conference* (ed. Thomas H. Olbricht and Anders Ericksson; Emory Studies in Early Christianity 11; New York: T. & T. Clark, 2005), 138-59.

[61] Watson, *Invention, Arrangement, and Style*, 10; see also Coulson and Oakley, "Purple Persuasion," § 4.

[62] See Watson, *Invention, Arrangement, and Style*, 14.

[63] Note that "elaboration" is a *terminus technicus* in both rhetorical studies and conceptual integration theory. For the importance of the cognitive process of elaboration in deliberation, see Coulson and Oakley, "Purple Persuasion," § 1.

invoking a known cultural debate over how freedom ought to be enacted and that activating the competing voices of this debate serves his local rhetorical goals.[64] Toward this end, I presuppose that Paul employs the phrase πάντα μοι ἔξεστιν, along with its modifiers, in order to provide a rhetorically effective way to prompt critical reflection among the Corinthians as a means to lead them to change their behavior.[65] Suggesting that 6:12a and 12c are examples of a Corinthian slogan is unnecessary, since neither the phrase nor its modifications (6:12b, d) conflict with anything Paul writes elsewhere in the letter (see 1 Cor 9). Some scholars who support the slogan hypothesis for 6:12 recognize this fact and note that such a Corinthian slogan could have its ultimate origin in Paul himself.[66] About 6:12 as a whole, Conzelmann even states that "[w]hat Paul here presents is nothing else but the πάντα ὑμῶν – ὑμεῖς δὲ Χριστοῦ, 'all things are yours – but you are Christ's,' of 3:21ff."[67] However, in the end biblical scholars must admit ignorance as to the provenance of the phrase. No matter where it comes from, the surrounding culture, the Corinthians, or his own original thought, the saying "Everything is permissible for me" serves Paul's didactic rhetorical aims in the coherent argument he structures in 6:12–7:7 rather than functions as a position which he must modify or against which he must argue.

It is in the discussions of the supposed slogan in 6:13 that one begins to notice that which Siebenmann worried about: once scholars think they have found a slogan in one part of the letter, it becomes attractive to resort to a slogan hypothesis to explain away other sections that cause difficulty.[68] The phrase "Meats for the belly and the belly for meats and God will destroy this and them," whatever its ultimate source, is integral to Paul's argument in the pericope. Rather than viewing Paul's teaching in 6:13-14 as stemming from antithetical ideologies – that of Paul and his opponents – I suggest that a more exegetically fruitful reading considers both sayings to be Pauline wisdom instruction that teaches the Corinthians the apocalyptic reality of the world in which they live, including the final fate of different elements within the created order.

Finally, as noted in the section above and as will be explicated in the exegesis below, the phrase "It is good for a person not to touch a woman," fits seamlessly into Paul's teaching about how sexual immo-

---

[64] See Ramsaran, "Living and Dying, Living is Dying," 327.
[65] See Coulson and Oakley, "Purple Persuasion," § 4; Robbins, Invention, 1:186.
[66] See, e.g., Conzelmann, First Epistle to the Corinthians, 108; Furnish, Theology, 56; Mitchell, Paul and the Rhetoric of Reconciliation, 233 n. 261; Schrage, Der erste Brief an die Korinther, 2:18.
[67] Conzelmann, First Epistle to the Corinthians, 110.
[68] Siebenmann, "Question of Slogans," 297.

rality is best avoided. As Holger Tiedemann notes, "The verse fits perfectly with the rest of the chapter."[69] Paul's teaching in 7:2 is not a repudiation of this maxim, but rather yet another instance in which Paul offers his hearers/readers a complex view of the world in which they live in order to allow them to make wise decisions in it. Peter Nejsum argues that regarding 7:1b as a quotation from a Corinthian letter to Paul has more to do with apologetics than exegesis. I believe that Nejsum is correct.[70] To support his claim, Nejsum highlights "the welter of sexually ascetic undercurrents which manifested themselves in the age when Paul was active... We must accordingly acknowledge that Paul is not expressing any particularly divergent view when he says that he wishes that all could be abstinent, as he himself is."[71] Again, the ultimate origin of this saying is unknown to interpreters; however, in what follows I read it as an integral part of Paul's argument rather than yet another position he needs to overturn.

While my reading of these so-called slogans may be deeply unsatisfying on the level of local historical reconstruction, I believe that this interpretation restores a rhetorical integrity to the argument found in 6:12–7:7 that the search for Pauline opponents has obscured. The added bonus of this reading is that it obviates the need to explain the interpretive problem raised by viewing both 6:12 and 7:1 as verses that contain Corinthian sentiments.[72] An older solution to the problem raised by the slogan hypotheses, championed by Hans Jonas, declared that the Corinthians, unlike Paul, did not care about the body at all. This lack of care expressed itself *both* in libertinistic *and* ascetic excess. Mark Plunkett has demonstrated that this solution, while perhaps mak-

---

[69] Holger Tiedemann, *Paulus und das Begehren: Liebe, Lust und letzte Ziele. Oder: Das Gesetz in den Gliedern* (Stuttgart: Radius, 2002), 45-46: "Der Vers paßt vollkommen zum Rest das Kapitels." See idem, *Die Erfahrung des Fleisches: Paulus und die Last der Lust* (Stuttgart: Radius, 1998), 136-42.

[70] As does Tiedemann, *Erfahrung des Fleisches*, 140-42, where he reviews the argument in Nejsum's article, "Apologetic Tendency." See also idem, *Paulus und das Begehren*, 49-50, and also 45: "This information (in 1 Cor 7:1b) has given headaches mainly to Protestant theologians... hence Protestant theologians like to claim that the verse in question is probably only a quotation: In Corinth there was an ascetic faction and their slogan is quoted here by Paul and then in what follows the apostle corrects it."

[71] Nejsum, "Apologetic Tendency," 56-57; see also Brown, *Body and Society*, 51-56; Clark, *Reading Renunciation*, 264-69. But see Thiselton, *First Epistle to the Corinthians*, 498-500; also Phipps, "Paul's Attitude," 125-31.

[72] This problem is, in fact, created by "a methodological position which makes the historicity of the epistles, understood as the circumstances immediately surrounding them, into their axis of rotation." Found in Nejsum, "Apologetic Tendency," 60. See, e.g., MacDonald, "Virgins, Widows, and Wives," 153-54 and Martin, *Corinthian Body*, 207-208 for their respective solutions to this problem. Knust, *Abandoned to Lust*, 76 recognizes this problem, but answers it rhetorically rather than historically.

ing existential sense, does not mesh with the historical data. No such group can be found that was simultaneously libertine and ascetic based on the same underlying principle.[73] Moreover, work on asceticism since the 1990s makes this position untenable.[74] As this recent research shows, ascetic groups, far from despising the body or paying it no mind, actually had a great deal for respect for and concern about the body. I modestly suggest that handling the difficulties of 1 Cor 6:12–7:7 with slogan hypotheses, at least as they have traditionally been deployed in historical-critical studies, creates more problems than it solves. Paul certainly appropriated insights from all manner of resources, but given how paradoxical his thinking is I think it makes the best exegetical sense to put Paul back in control of his argument and to read 1 Cor 6:12–7:7 "without quotation marks."[75]

Constructing the Christian Σῶμα

Another major exegetical conundrum found in this pericope revolves around what Paul means by the term σῶμα.[76] As Rudolf Bultmann notes, "The most comprehensive term which Paul uses to characterize man's existence is *soma*, body; it is also the most complex and the understanding of it fraught with difficulty."[77] In the history of scholarship three main interpretations of the term σῶμα have dominated.[78] The first comes from Johannes Weiß who declares that although one might "feel" what Paul means by this term, actually describing it is a complicated task. While encompassing the idea of corporeality, Weiß argues that σῶμα has a broader meaning in Paul's thought. It is not *just* corporeality; rather the word denotes a "form" that can be filled by different contents, for example, with σάρξ or with πνεῦμα. The right understanding of the word is found, Weiß argues, in 1 Cor 6:14, where Paul writes ἡμᾶς exactly where one might expect the term σῶμα. Thus, Weiß concludes, the term σῶμα in Paul's argumentation carries with it

---

[73] Plunkett, "Sexual Ethics and the Christian Life," 295-97. See also Kirchhoff, *Sünde*, 76: "Neither such a mode of argumentation nor a corresponding practice has been proven among Gnostic, Stoic, and Jewish groups." See her further explanation in n. 36 of the same page. Also Tiedemann, *Paulus und das Begehren*, 45.

[74] See esp. the essays in Wimbush and Valantasis, *Asceticism* and, more recently, Gavin Flood, *The Ascetic Self: Subjectivity, Memory and Tradition* (Cambridge: Cambridge University Press, 2004).

[75] See Dodd, "Paul's Paradigmatic 'I'," 54.

[76] This term is used 46 times in 1 Corinthians and eight times in ch. 6, all which are found in vv. 12-20. The only chapters that have more occurrences of the word σῶμα are ch. 12 (18x) and ch. 15 (9x).

[77] Rudolf Bultmann, *TNT*, 1:192.

[78] Renate Kirchhoff, *Sünde*, 130-37 provides a detailed history of interpretation of Paul's use of σῶμα. She provides her own interpretation on pp. 138-45.

the idea of "personality."⁷⁹

Bultmann, in contrast to Weiß, argues that σῶμα does not mean form or shape. Bultmann suggests that a human being does not *have* a σῶμα – she or he *is* σῶμα.⁸⁰ Thus σῶμα describes the whole human being.⁸¹ It is from this idea that Bultmann makes his classic assertion:

> Man is called *soma* in respect to his being able to make himself the object of his own action or to experience himself as the subject of whom something happens. He can be called *soma*, that is, having a relationship to himself – as being able to distinguish himself from himself.⁸²

While Bultmann's interpretation allows for a more nuanced understanding of the existential importance that the term σῶμα has for Paul, his definition has difficulty dealing with the avowedly physical aspects the term sometimes has in Paul's letters. Hence he has great difficulty discerning how Paul uses the term, declaring that "[t]he nuances of meaning in the word *soma* melt into one another in a strange fashion in 1 Cor. 6:13-20."⁸³

A third option, and the one that is widely used in current scholarship, comes from Ernst Käsemann. He argues that σῶμα does not, as Bultmann contends, stand for the relationship a person has with him or herself. Rather it stands for "that piece of the world which we ourselves are and for which we ... also carry responsibility. It is for the Apostle the human being in his creatureliness [*Weltlichkeit*], hence in his ability for communication [*Kommunikationsfähigkeit*]."⁸⁴ With such a definition, Käsemann has less trouble than Bultmann in dealing with the corporeal aspects of the term σῶμα as found in Paul. For Käsemann, σῶμα thus denotes the human being as he or she is in the world and through which he or she is able to communicate with the world

---

⁷⁹ Weiß, *Der erste Korintherbrief*, 160-61.

⁸⁰ Bultmann, *TNT*, 1:194. See also John A.T. Robinson, *The Body: A Study in Pauline Anthropology* (Philadelphia: SCM Press, 1952; repr. Bristol, Ind.: Wyndham Hall, 1988), 14. For a similar view expressed by a cognitive scientist, see Gibbs, *Embodiment and Cognitive Science*, 14: "A body is not just something we own, it is something we are." As noted in Chapter 1, a common phenomenological philosophical foundation in the work of Bultmann and Gibbs helps to explain this similarity.

⁸¹ See Robert Gundry's critique of this position in *Sôma in Biblical Theology: With Emphasis on Pauline Anthropology*. New York: Cambridge University Press, 1976), 5: "So persuasive have Bultmann and Robinson been that it has become orthodoxy among New Testament theologians to say that in Pauline literature, and perhaps elsewhere as well, *soma* frequently and characteristically refers to the whole person rather than especially, or exclusively, the body." But note Robinson, *Body*, 9: "For no other writer of the New Testament has the word σῶμα any doctrinal significance."

⁸² Bultmann, *TNT*, 1:195.

⁸³ Bultmann, *TNT*, 1:194.

⁸⁴ Ernst Käsemann, *Zur Thema der urchristlichen Apokalyptik*," ZTK 59 (1962): 282.

and God. It is the *whole* person in his or her "creatureliness," that is, as a created being in the world created by God.[85] Wolfgang Schrage describes this use of σῶμα as expressing the whole person "so wie er leibt und lebt" [as he lives and breathes].[86]

A fourth option, beyond those suggested in German biblical scholarship earlier in the twentieth century, has been proposed by Renate Kirchhoff, who understands σῶμα in 1 Cor 6:12-20 as a *Verpflichtungsname*, a name describing one's reciprocal relationship to the Lord. In this pericope, Kirchhoff argues that "Σῶμα is here the Christian man, who stands in an obligatory relationship [*Verpflichtungsverhältnis*] to the Lord."[87] Thus the σῶμα, according to Kirchhoff, is still a physical body, but one that not everybody possesses. Rather, it refers only to the special bodies of those baptized into the Christian community, who have a relationship with the risen Lord. "This kind of body," Kirchhoff writes, "has, according to Paul, more capabilities [*Fähigkeiten*] than that of the unbaptized."[88] This Christian body, like all of creation, will die, but because of its relationship to the Christ, it will experience resurrection, unlike the bodies of the unbaptized.[89]

The problem confronting the exegete over how Paul employs the word σῶμα is lessened somewhat if interpreters accept B.J. Oropeza's insight that Paul uses the term in multiple ways throughout 1 Cor.[90] It may be exegetically impossible and even unwise to try to formulate some "essence" of theological meaning for the word σῶμα. I am thus theoretically closest to Kirchhoff's formulation in that hers arises from her exegesis of Paul's specific argument found in 1 Cor 6:12-20, although she does seem to suggest it has broader application in other Pauline letters.[91] I argue, gleaning from the insights of conceptual integration theory, that it makes more sense to regard the rhetorical meaning of σῶμα as context dependent. The conceptual networks that Paul's rhetography creates selectively project only certain meaning from the inputs that serve Paul's local rhetorical purposes in creating a local definition of σῶμα.[92] Recall that the great flexibility of human

---

[85] See Ernst Käsemann, *Perspectives on Paul* (trans. Margaret Kohl; Philadelphia: SCM Press, 1971; repr. Mifflintown, Pa.: Sigler Press, 1996), 22.

[86] Schrage, *Der erste Brief an die Korinther*, 2:22.

[87] Kirchhoff, *Sünde*, 140.

[88] Kirchhoff, *Sünde*, 144.

[89] Kirchhoff, *Sünde*, 145.

[90] Oropeza, *Paul and Apostasy*, 98. Oropeza, in other words, is arguing against trying to reconcile what Bultmann referred to as the "nuances of meaning" found in the term (Bultmann, *TNT*, 1:194).

[91] Kirchhoff, *Sünde*, 145.

[92] For more on selective projection, see Chapter 1. Also see Fauconnier and Turner, *The Way We Think*, 47-48; Coulson and Oakley, "Blending Basics," 180; idem, "Blending and Coded Meaning," 1510-11.

meaning production derives from the fact that, as Fauconnier and Turner note, "[n]ot all the elements and relations from the inputs are projected to the blend."[93] Certain elements *must* be projected for the term to make lexical sense to Paul's hearers/readers. However, as Paul argues against πορνεία he does so by constructing a local meaning for the Christian σῶμα – a meaning that cannot be predetermined, but only derived from exegetical work. It seems clear that the fact that the Christian σῶμα will be resurrected (6:14; 15:1-58) drives Paul's definition of the term in 6:12–7:7. It is thus possible to state at the outset that Paul's argument in 1 Cor 6:12–7:7 works to divorce his local definition of the Christian σῶμα from the appetites and the passions and to unite it with Christ and the holy spirit of God. This understanding of σῶμα, however, should not be understood as its "intrinsic" meaning, but simply the one that selectively activates certain elements and relations within Paul's wisdom teaching on the dangers of πορνεία.

Conclusion

Conceptual integration theory used within a socio-rhetorical framework provides the tools that allow me to ask newer exegetical questions of Paul's argument in 1 Cor 6:12–7:7 than have been investigated in the past. While the technical vocabulary of these interpretive analytics may prove daunting at the outset, the exegetical fruit they bear is well worth the effort. The socio-rhetorical analysis of 1 Cor 6:12–7:7 in the following two chapters depends on the insights of conceptual integration theory in order to demonstrate the holistic nature of Paul's argument against πορνεία in a way that does not require special appeals to unnecessary and unhelpful slogan hypotheses. Paul's general argument about the proper sexual use of the Christian body achieves rhetorical power by blending resources from wisdom, apocalyptic, and priestly rhetorolects in such a way that he achieves human scale. The conceptual networks Paul's rhetoric creates, and the emergent structures that arise from them, seem to fulfill Fauconnier's prediction that optimal blends contain the following properties: "human scale, only two objects, simple concrete action, clear-cut outcome."[94] The "simplicity" of Paul's blends, however, requires a great deal of cognitive work to achieve.

---

[93] Fauconnier and Turner, *The Way We Think*, 47.
[94] Fauconnier, "Compression and Emergent Structure," 531.

6

Why Porneia Should Be Avoided: The Rhetography of 1 Corinthians 6:12-20

Introduction

Unlike 1 Cor 5, which treats a specific expression of sexual immorality within the community, 1 Cor 6:12–7:7 examines the topic of πορνεία without any specific instance immediately in view. As Michael Goulder notes, "Surely if Paul heard that his converts were whoring he would hit the roof, as he does at 2 Cor 12:21, and the first reaction would be to specify the scandal."[1] Thus I argue that Paul in 1 Cor 6:12–7:7 is making a general argument against πορνεία rather than responding to any one instance of Corinthian misbehavior. I further maintain that Paul's argument against πορνεία begins with a demonstration of why the Corinthians ought to avoid this sin (6:12-20). Paul introduces this demonstration with gnomic reasoning in 6:12. After this rhetological introduction establishes wisdom rhetorolect as the host environment for his argument, however, apocalyptic and priestly rhetography dominates Paul's teaching in 6:13-20. In these verses Paul uses various *images* to *show* the Corinthians why the Christian body is incompatible with πορνεία.[2] In this local rhetorical context, Paul proceeds to argue that πορνεία is "a comprehensive and radical sexual sin," to quote Mark

---

[1] Goulder, "Libertines? 342-43; idem, *Paul,* 119. For others who argue that this section of 1 Corinthians constitutes a general argument rather that indicating specific behavior, see R. Collins, *First Corinthians,* 240; Hurd, *Origin of 1 Corinthians,* 86, 164; Mitchell, *Paul and the Rhetoric of Reconciliation,* 232; Furnish, *Theology,* 55-56; Archibald Robertson and Alfred Plummer, *A Critical Exegetical Commentary on the First Epistle of St. Paul to the Corinthians* (2nd ed.; New York: Charles Scribner's Sons, 1916), 121; Weiß, *Der erste Korintherbrief,* 157. See Brian Rosner, *Paul, Scripture and Ethics,* 125 and idem, "Temple Prostitution," 337-38 for the contrary view.

[2] See Coulson and Oakley, "Blending and Coded Meaning," 1514: "Conceptual blending processes proceed via the establishment and exploitation of mappings, the activation of background knowledge, and *frequently involve the use of mental imagery* and mental simulation" (emphasis mine). See my discussion of the importance of rhetography for socio-rhetorical interpretation in Chapters 1 and 5 and Robbins, *Invention,* 1:xxvii.

Jordan, that severs the relationship between the believer and Christ.[3] Brian Rosner, however, argues that Paul simply assumes the negative nature of πορνεία in 6:12-20 rather than actively argues the case. Following the work of Traugott Holtz, Rosner states that "Paul's arguments against fornication in this passage in effect *presuppose* that fornication is wrong. This point is borne out by the observation of several commentators that Paul's proofs are so strong that they could be used against all sexual activity."[4] Rosner's argument rests on a presupposition that assumes that Paul must view sexual expression positively.[5] This, however, is an ideological presupposition with which Rosner begins. Paul's understanding of the proper sexual use of the Christian body must be based on a thorough exegetical investigation of his statements about sexual activity. Paul's views on what, if anything, constitutes proper Christian sexual behavior can only be assessed at the conclusion of an exegetical analysis.

In 1 Cor 6:12 Paul evokes cultural resources consistent with wisdom rhetorolect. Paul's paradoxical wisdom teaching in this verse prompts the hearer/reader to prepare for reflection on proper behavior. However, the integration resources available in wisdom rhetorolect are insufficient for Paul's local rhetorical purposes. In order for Paul, *in this context*, to teach that πορνεία is the worst of all possible bodily sins he must draw from resources available in apocalyptic and priestly rhetorolects as well. Using rhetography drawn from these latter two rhetorolects within a wisdom host environment, Paul compresses the vital relations between the believer and Christ from Analogy to Identity (6:13-17).[6] He then elaborates this compression by activating the metaphor of the believer's body as a temple (6:18-20; cf. 3:16-17). Conceptual integration theory within a socio-rhetorical framework allows me to explain how the warrants Paul gives for avoiding πορνεία are meaningful and how Paul's use of apocalyptic and priestly rhetography enriches and energizes his use of wisdom rhetorolect. It is wisdom

---

[3] Jordan, *Ethics of Sex*, 27. Note that I am making this claim about Paul's argument *in this context* and not about that amorphous category called "Pauline theology."

[4] Rosner, *Paul, Scripture and Ethics*, 124 (emphasis in the original) where he cites Traugott Holtz, "Zur Frage der inhaltlichen Weisungen bei Paulus," *Theologische Literaturzeitung* 106 (1981): 387-88.

[5] See Nejsum, "Apologetic Tendency," 48-50.

[6] See Coulson and Oakley, "Blending and Coded Meaning," 1533 who note that "... compression of analogy to identity is a recurrent pattern." Fauconnier and Turner, "Compression and Global Insight," 299: "Identity is not only a vital relation, but perhaps the primary vital relation without which the others are meaningless. Human mental life is unthinkable without constant compression and decompression of identity."

rhetorolect that provides fertile ground for the emergent structures that arise from the conceptual networks Paul creates in his teaching.[7]

Paul's treatment of πορνεία in 1 Cor 6:12-20 consists of four main sections:

1. In the introduction to the argument Paul establishes the rhetology of wisdom rhetorolect as the argument's host environment (6:12) into which he will invite apocalyptic and priestly rhetography as his argument progresses.
2. In his next argumentative move Paul establishes a rhetographical Disanalogy between the destruction of the belly and meats with the resurrection of Christ and the body. Once he creates this difference between the belly and the Christian body, Paul compresses the vital relation between the believer's body and Christ's body to Analogy (6:13-14).
3. Paul then creates another rhetographical Disanalogy, between the characters of Christ and the πόρνη, which allows him to compress the relationship between the believer and Christ to Part-Whole and then, ultimately, to Identity (6:15-17).
4. After an argumentative progression that compresses the relationship between the believer and Christ from Analogy to Part-Whole to Identity, in the final portion of this section of his argument Paul elaborates his final compression with a metaphoric network that describes the body as a temple and crafts imperatives grounded in this image (6:18-20).[8] This conceptual creation of the body as sacred space will provide the foundation for the next section of Paul's argument where Paul explains *how* the Corinthians can best avoid πορνεία (7:1-7).

Introduction to the Argument (6:12): Wisdom Rhetorolect

Many acknowledge that exegesis of Paul's argument against πορνεία is a difficult undertaking for a host of reasons.[9] Among the more contentious issues is how to understand the twice repeated formula πάντα μοι ἔξεστιν in 6:12a and 12c. Since 6:12 introduces Paul's teaching in this pericope, it is essential to understand how it functions in his argument and I will thus take a fair amount of space to perform a close reading of this verse. As noted in the previous chapter, I call into question the exegetical usefulness of treating πάντα μοι ἔξεστιν as a Corinthian slogan. A more rhetorically sound interpretation, I argue, is

---

[7] For the foundational nature of Wisdom rhetorolect in the development of Christian rhetorical culture, see Robbins, *Invention*, 1:486.

[8] This breakdown of 6:12-20 is similar to that put forward by Kirchhoff, *Sünde*, 106.

[9] See Rosner, "Temple Prostitution," 336: "1 Cor 6:12-20 is widely acknowledged to be one of the most difficult passages of the Pauline corpus." See also Fisk, "ΠΟΡΝΕΥΕΙΝ as Body Violation," 540.

offered by Renate Kirchhoff, who reads this phrase not as a slogan of some specific group in Corinth, but as a general gnomic saying Paul employs in order both to claim authority as a wise teacher and as part of his overall strategy to have the Corinthians imitate him.[10] Her conclusion should not be surprising since, according to Walter Wilson, "the authors of various genres – among them letters, orations, diatribes, and different paraenetic genres – took advantage of gnomic forms and themes since they were of use in achieving their broader instructional or exhortatory objectives."[11] I argue that 6:12 contains two rhetological sayings through which Paul is able to activate a cultural debate surrounding the nature of freedom through the use of such pregnant words as ἔξεστιν, συμφέρει, and ἐξουσιασθήσομαι.[12] Paul employs these words in compact gnomic statements to introduce his didactic discourse and invite the resources of wisdom rhetorolect into the pericope.

Kirchhoff's assertion that πάντα μοι ἔξεστιν is a gnomic saying not only formally situates this verse firmly in wisdom rhetorolect, but it also points the way forward for this exegetical investigation in that it leaves the concern for reconstructing an oppositional Corinthian group behind. This allows me to proceed by examining both how the phrase functions in 6:12 and how this verse operates within Paul's argument.[13] Walter Wilson's work on gnomic sayings in the Greek speaking Hellenistic world supports Kirchhoff's thesis while offering concrete ways to advance her initial argument further. In his analysis of complex sayings that consist of multiple "topics and comments," Wilson provides a means to analyze the sayings in 6:12.[14] Each half of the verse contains a

---

[10] Kirchhoff, *Sünde*, 109, 113. See James G. Williams, *Those Who Ponder Proverbs: Aphoristic Thinking and Biblical Literature* (Bible and Literature Series 2; Sheffield: Almond, 1981), 26-32, his section entitled: "Authority: Tradition and the Fathers." For a discussion of the use of maxims in Paul's rhetoric see Ramsaran: *Liberating Words*; idem, "Living and Dying, Living is Dying (Philippians 1:21)," 325-38.

[11] Wilson, *Mysteries of Righteousness*, 15; see Robbins, *Invention*, 1:184.

[12] Such words are described by Wolfgang Fenske, *Die Argumentation des Paulus in ethischen Herausfoderung* (Göttingen: V & R unipress, 2004), 277 as follows: "Worte, die häufig verwendet, prägen sich fest ein, unterstreichen nicht nur die Argumentation, sondern sind quasi selbst Argument, allerdings nicht für die Ratio, sondern für die Emotion." [Words which are frequently used, firmly imprinted in memory, do not only underscore arguments, but rather are themselves arguments, certainly not rationally, rather emotionally.] See Damasio, *Descartes' Error*, 197-98.

[13] In socio-rhetorical terms, Kirchhoff moves the analysis of πάντα μοι ἔξεστιν out of historical intertexture, which she has found exegetically inconclusive, and into an exegesis firmly anchored in inner texture and cultural intertexture.

[14] Wilson makes use Alan Dundes' structural method for analyzing proverbs. See Wilson, *Love without Pretense*, 25-26. Note 45 on p. 25 gives the reference to the work of Dundes.

complex gnomic saying with two cola each. Making use of Wilson's categories, I note that 6:12a and 12c are the main topics (T) and 6:12b and 12d are the main comments (C). Yet within each cola there also exists a sub-topic (t) and a sub-comment (c):

> Πάντα μοι ἔξεστιν
> ἀλλ' οὐ πάντα συμφέρει·
> T: Everything (t_1) is permissible for me (c_1),
> C: but not everything (t_2) is beneficial (c_2); (6:12ab)
>
> πάντα μοι ἔξεστιν
> ἀλλ' οὐκ ἐγὼ ἐξουσιασθήσομαι ὑπό τινος.
> T: everything (t_1) is permissible for me (c_1),
> C: but I will not be enslaved (c_2) by anything (t_2). (6:12cd)[15]

Although the structural parallelism breaks down somewhat in the second cola of the latter half of the verse (6:12d),[16] note that the primary topic in each (T) contrasts with the comment (C), signaled by the "strongly adversative conjunction" ἀλλά followed by a lexical marker of negation [οὐ(κ)].[17] Each of these cola, however, likewise has its own topics (t_1, t_2) and comments (c_1, c_2).[18]

In the first half of the verse (6:12ab), the focus is on the contrasting sub-topics (πάντα, οὐ πάντα) while the comparative sub-comments (μοι ἔξεστιν, συμφέρει) serve to heighten the contrast.[19] Wilson isolates this type of complex gnomic saying and argues that "patterns of this sort may furnish authors with a striking means of expressing their ironic or paradoxical understanding of human behavior and experience."[20] The second half of the verse (6:12cd) functions similarly, although the focus shifts from the sub-topics (πάντα, τινος) to the first person pronouns of the comments, Paul's "rhetorical I" (μοι, ἐγώ).[21] While the structure is not as neat as that of 6:12ab, the passive verb (ἐξουσιασθήσομαι) still marks the first person pronoun as the recipient of the action. This time, however, the sub-topics are comparative rather than contrasting: τινός is a lesser group derived from the larger πάντα, which serves to highlight the contrast between the sub-comments (μοι ἔξεστιν, οὐκ ἐγὼ ἐξουσιασθήσομαι).

---

[15] Cf. Sir 47:19 regarding how Solomon was mastered through his body.
[16] The parallelism is structurally better maintained in 10:23.
[17] Smyth, *Greek Grammar*, §2775. Wilson, *Love without Pretense*, 34: "... contrast refers to delineating the differences or oppositional features." See Kirchhoff, *Sünde*, 108-9.
[18] Wilson, *Love without Pretense*, 35.
[19] See Wilson, *Love without Pretense*, 30-31 for his discussion of comparison.
[20] Wilson, *Love without Pretense*, 38; see Robbins, *Invention*, 1:204.
[21] See Dodd, "Paul's Paradigmatic 'I,'" 39-58, esp. 39, 45.

In 6:12 Paul functions as the wise father-teacher[22] dispensing gnomic sayings of a paradoxical nature so that the members of Corinthian community will think about the impact of their behavior.[23] As Wilson notes, "The gnomic style ... promotes a certain degree of intellectual reflection, ethical criticism, and personal creativity as individuals make sense of wisdom sayings for themselves in their daily moral judgments."[24] By means of these pithy statements, Paul begins his instruction about right judgment in matters concerning the Corinthians' sexual use of their bodies. Rather than treating 6:12a and 12c as a Corinthian idea against which Paul must argue, I maintain that they represent the main topics of Paul's dual gnomic sayings and that they activate culturally available debates surrounding notions of freedom of action. However, Paul's teaching is paradoxical in nature and, as Wilson suggests a teacher can do in such an instance, he expounds upon his topic (πάντα μοι ἔξεστιν) with comments that contrast with it.[25] By reading the elements of 6:12 as gnomic sayings integral to the logic of Paul's argument, my interpretation not only ties the verse formally to the larger wisdom rhetorolect operative in the letter, but it more firmly anchors Paul's argumentation and its linguistic markers in its indigenous religious and philosophical milieu.[26]

The synoptic Gospels frequently use the impersonal verb ἔξεστιν in debates about what is permitted vis-à-vis Torah.[27] Although 1 Corinthians provides no indications that specific Jewish legal restrictions are playing an explicit role, the question Paul grapples with in 6:12 touches on the notion of law (νόμος), but not necessarily only Jewish law.[28] Evoking a larger philosophical conversation concerning freedom of

---

[22] See 1 Cor 4:14-21 and my arguments in Chapter 4. See also Crenshaw, *Wisdom*, 78; Galloway, *Freedom in the Gospel*, 189; Williams, *Those Who Ponder Proverbs*, 26-32.

[23] See Chapter 4 for my discussion of Paul's paradoxical wisdom in 1 Cor 1–4. For gnomic sayings as a means of instruction see Abraham Malherbe, *Moral Exhortation: A Greco-Roman Sourcebook* (Philadelphia: Westminster, 1986), 109-11.

[24] Wilson, *The Mysteries of Righteousness*, 181.

[25] For paradox in wisdom instruction, see Williams, *Those Who Ponder Proverbs*, 33-34; 57-63, esp. 57: "Kohelet and Jesus both employ literary paradox to disorient their audience."

[26] See Coulson, *Semantic Leaps*, 12: "Whether or not a distinct *sense* is retrieved for lexical items, ultimately the language comprehension process involves the recruitment of knowledge about the likely nature of the particular referents of the utterances." See also idem, p. 17.

[27] See Mark 2:24; 3:4; 10:2; 12:14; Matt 12:2, 4, 12; 19:3; 22:17; Luke 6:2, 4, 9; 14:3; 20:22. See also John 5:10.

[28] That 6:12 represents some kind of "anti-judaizing" teaching was already discounted by Weiß in 1910 (*Der erste Korintherbrief*, 157). Although championed by Baur, the practice of reading the problem Paul deals with in the letter to the Galatians into 1 Corinthians is now generally avoided. An exception is Goulder, *Paul*.

action, the debate revolves around what produces right behavior in individuals. Paul's answer moves away from a solution that looks to law by focusing on the wisdom with which individuals make right judgments and enact them.[29] Law is not the answer for Paul; rather his moral teaching relies upon the sanctified community's eschatological discernment.[30] Prompting the community to make use of this discernment, Paul begins his treatment of πορνεία with two gnomic sayings that evoke the broader *topos* of freedom – more specifically, the concern with how freedom is to be virtuously enacted by an individual. The first saying (6:12ab) contrasts permission to do all things with the recognition that not every action is advantageous or beneficial (συμφέρει). Thus this first saying focuses on how freedom is to be used as a benefit, rather than a hindrance. In the second saying (6:12cd) Paul moves his point further forward by contrasting the idea of freedom of action with those things that exercise authority over a person. With this saying Paul argues, as Conzelmann notes, that "freedom cannot cancel itself by making me unfree."[31]

With the sayings in 6:12ab and 12cd Paul enters into an ongoing Hellenistic moral debate about freedom of action, that is, the permissibility to do anything. Given the international character of wise gnomic sayings, it makes logical sense for Paul to begin his teaching with a form and *topos* readily accessible to people across a wide swath of cultures.[32] My discussion of Judaic traditions concerning freedom (Chapter 3) sets the stage for cultural and local resources that Paul's dual gnomic sayings could evoke to make meaning. However, like other Hellenistic Jews, Paul also reconfigured ideas from the debate surrounding the proper use of freedom circulating in non-Jewish arenas as well. There are two main concerns in the conversation about freedom of action that these sayings in 6:12 evoke. The first, noted by Galloway, is that "[t]he notion that ἐλευθερία allowed one to be self-determined, autonomous, independent and at liberty to do as one wished, had to be reconciled with the life of virtue."[33] The second concern, analyzed in depth by Stanley Stowers in his re-reading of Romans, is with the

---

[29] But see Ryan O'Dowd, *The Wisdom of Torah: Epistemology in Deuteronomy and the Wisdom Literature* (FRLANT 225; Göttingen: Vandenhoeck & Ruprecht, 2009).

[30] Contra Philo, *Prob.* 45; see also *Mos.* 2.48, 52. See my discussion of eschatological discernment in Chapter 4.

[31] Conzelmann, *First Epistle to the Corinthians*, 108. See Mitchell, *Paul and the Rhetoric of Reconciliation*, 118: "Discussion of what is true freedom was especially common in political discourses and appears throughout 1 Corinthians."

[32] See my Chapter 3. Wilson, *Mystery of Righteousness*, 181: "gnomic paraenesis represents a truly international mode of communication, one that characterizes most every culture in antiquity." See also J.J. Collins, *Jewish Wisdom*, 2.

[33] Galloway, *Freedom in the Gospel*, 17.

"ethic of self-mastery," in which enslavement to the passions could mask itself with the guise of freedom.[34]

Permitted and Beneficial: 6:12ab

The cognitive blend created by the gnomic saying of 6:12ab is typical of paradoxical wisdom reasoning.[35] As Fauconnier and Turner predict, Paul does not need to come up with either the form or the content of his wisdom blend from scratch. The moral instruction of Jewish and non-Jewish Hellenistic teachers wrestled with the dual goods of freedom and beneficial action, as the quotation from Galloway above noted. I argue that Paul is able to evoke the background information of a widespread cultural debate in his pithy statement of 6:12ab because of framing.[36] Paul's gnomic saying in 6:12ab consists of a topic and a comment that stand in contrast to one another. The contrast is paradoxical and requires reflection to tease out its meanings. As Wolfgang Fenske notes, "Like the wisdom texts Paul can briefly and clearly address specific themes; with only a few words fundamental questions about human communal life are effectively set forth."[37] The content of the saying in 6:12ab deals with a known *topos* – freedom, specifically the freedom of action. The form and context prompt the hearer/reader to use the organizing cultural frame of wisdom rhetorolect to configure the elements in Paul's sayings. Given the prevalence of contrastive gnomic sayings in wisdom traditions, it seems likely that the Corinthians would be able to make sense of Paul's use of this form. More specifically, the rhetorical *topos* that Paul engages, freedom, functions as a local frame that further specifies the cultural resources available to the hearer/reader when encountering the saying.[38] These frames prompt the hearer/reader to place Paul's wise sayings in a larger cultural context and this background information helps "fill in the gaps" when the blend is run.

---

[34] Stowers, *Rereading of Romans*, 42-82; the quotation is from p. 42. See Wilson, *Sentences of Pseudo-Phocylides*, 34.

[35] See Wilson, *Love Without Pretense*, 35-39; see Robbins, *Invention*, 1:204.

[36] See Fenske, *Argumentation des Paulus*, 52-53 where he discusses "Frame Theory" in a section entitled "Argumentation aus der Perspektive der Kognitiven Linguistik: Abhängigkeit der Textentstehung und der Textrezeption vom Weltwissen" [Argumentation from the Perspective of Cognitive Linguistics: The Reliance of Text Development and Text Reception on Knowledge of the World], pp. 49-58.

[37] Fenske, *Argumentation des Paulus*, 271: "Wie die weisheitlichen Texte kann Paulus kurz und knapp ... bestimmte Thema ansprechen; wirkungsvoll werden mit wenigen Worten grundlegende Fragen menschlichen Zusammenlebens dargelegt." See Wilson, *Mysteries of Righteousness*, 15.

[38] What Fenske calls "Weltwissen" (*Argumentation des Paulus*, 49). See also Coulson, *Semantic Leaps*, 18.

The topic and comment of 6:12ab are blended together to form a more complex double-scope network that clashes on the level of the local frame. The clash created by the saying as a whole makes sense when viewed through the cultural frame of wisdom, since this clash, or contrast to use Wilson's term, of local frames is precisely one of the ways wisdom rhetorolect prompts hearers/readers to engage in active discernment. Conceptual integration theory helps explain how this clash functions in a rhetorically useful manner. The local frame of beneficial action is projected into the blend with "high asymmetry" compared to the freedom frame. That is, the frame of beneficial action determines how the frame of freedom of action will be viewed in the blend.[39] Graphically, the network looks like this:

Figure 2: Conceptual Network for 6:12ab

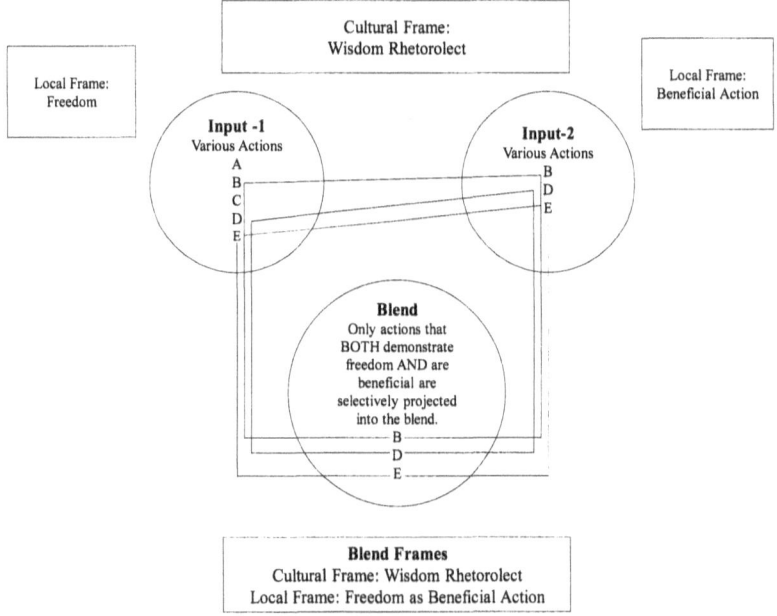

The emergent structure of the blend prompts for paradoxical thinking based on the contrast of the local frames in the topic (input-1) and comment (input-2), which is linguistically signaled by the conjunction followed by a negative: ἀλλ' οὐ. In the double-scope blend created by Paul's maxim in 6:12ab, only those elements that have cross-space mapping between the two input spaces (B, D, E – where these letters

---

[39] Fauconnier and Turner, *The Way We Think*, 134; Coulson and Oakley, "Blending and Coded Meaning," 1516.

represent certain categories of action) get selectively projected into the blend. That is, only those actions that exist in *both* input spaces – the one governed by freedom and the other by beneficial action – are projected into the blend. In the blend, the elements organized by the local frames of freedom and beneficial action compress to Identity and become functional equivalents – only those actions that are beneficial can now be described as a true expression of freedom. The topic and comment, though contrasting, are not antithetical in Paul's thought. Rather, the contrast prompts for a certain type of blend whose emergent structure allows for new insight into the nature of freedom of action – true freedom does not consist in doing all that is permitted, but rather in performing only those actions that are classified as beneficial. To be sure, the emergent structure that arises from this blending is neither particularly novel in the moral universe of the Hellenistic world, nor particularly Christian, as I will demonstrate below. Yet the emergent structure prompted by this conceptual network displays the richness of wisdom rhetorolect as both an integration resource for Paul and as an environment that creates conceptual space for paradoxical thinking about the nature of permissible action.

Understanding how this conceptual network is possible and rhetorically effective requires knowledge of the larger cultural web of significance in which Paul's wise saying is deployed. Recall my discussion of Jewish resources in Chapters 2 and 3. These resources provide useful cultural knowledge that can help exegetes understand the rhetorical impact of Paul's saying in 6:12ab. They provide a foundation for the paradox on which 6:12ab rests. As far as most of the Jewish writings discussed in Chapter 3 are concerned, God has declared that everything is *not* permissible. As noted in that chapter, even texts that function in the wisdom tradition recognize the importance of obedience to the law of God.[40] Also, in the paradigmatic Jewish story of liberation, the Exodus, freedom does not result in the newly liberated Israelites being able to do anything they wish. In fact, Exodus 32 narrates the catastrophic result of Israelites using their freedom to act in this myopic manner (cf. 1 Cor 10:6-13). The freedom of the children of Israel must be lived out through obedience to the God who carried the people out of slavery "on eagle's wings" (Ex 19:4). Freedom oriented toward obedience means life, whereas abusing this freedom through disobedience results in death (Deut 30:15).

The Hellenistic Jewish thinker Philo interprets his religious heritage by appropriating conventional philosophical categories and arguing that only those who live under the law of God are truly free [ὅσοι δὲ μετὰ

---

[40] Cf. Dio, *De lege* [*Or.* 75] 3.

νόμου ζῶσιν, ἐλεύθεροι] (*Prob.* 45).⁴¹ Philo is instructive for understanding Paul because, as Rosner has demonstrated, Paul does not simply appropriate and interpret Jewish Scripture in a vacuum. Rather he stands in a living stream of Jewish moral tradition.⁴² For Philo, unlike Paul, the law teaches that which is virtuous and good. Following the law, for Philo, allows one's mind to escape slavery and to live a life of "liberty from the domination of the passions" (*Prob.* 17 [Colson, LCL]). Echoing the Stoics who so influenced him, Philo argues that the good man only wants to act virtuously, therefore the good man will not be prevented from doing what he wishes, and therefore the good man is free (*Prob.* 59). Thus while Philo argues that "no two things are so closely related as independence of action and freedom" (*Prob.* 21 [Colson, LCL]), he also argues that the wise man will only desire to do that which stems from virtue (*Prob.* 60) and is thus lawful. Wisdom, law, freedom, and virtue do not, when understood correctly, conflict according to Philo's thought.

In addition to Jewish resources, Paul's rhetoric can be helpfully illuminated by reading surviving Stoic and Cynic writings alongside of it.⁴³ The conceptual network Paul creates in 6:12ab is able to prompt the hearer/reader to access a larger Hellenistic debate about freedom of action with a minimum number of linguistic cues. The writings of Dio Chrysostom provide a particularly illustrative resource when exploring the cultural knowledge that Paul's teaching on freedom could have evoked in order to make meaning.⁴⁴ Indeed, as noted, Paul's paradoxical formula in 6:12ab appears not to have been all that novel, but part of a well worn discussion.

Dio notes that freedom, which he argues all people desire, is not so readily understood as many would like to believe (1 *Serv. lib.* [*Or.* 14] 1). While some argue that freedom consists in being permitted [ἔξεστιν] to do everything one wishes, Dio argues that this is by no means the case (1 *Serv. lib.* [*Or.* 14] 13).⁴⁵ Despite his great respect for the ideal of law

---

⁴¹ See also *Sacr.* 127.

⁴² Rosner, *Paul, Scripture and Ethics*. See also Rosner's student, H.H. Drake Williams, III, *The Wisdom of the Wise: The Presence and Function of Scripture within 1 Cor. 1:18-3:2* (AGJU 49; Leiden: Brill, 2001).

⁴³ See esp. R. Collins, *First Corinthians*, 241, 243; Conzelmann, *First Epistle to the Corinthians*, 108; Schrage, *Der erste Brief an die Korinther*, 2:18-19; Weiß, *Der erste Korintherbrief*, 157-59; see also Mitchell, *Paul and the Rhetoric of Reconciliation*, 118-19 for her discussion of non-Jewish Hellenistic moral philosophers.

⁴⁴ For a treatment of freedom in the thought Cynics, Stoics, and in the writings of the Stoic Epictetus, see Galloway, *Freedom in the Gospel*, ch. 2 (pp. 57-102).

⁴⁵ Cf. 1 *Serv. lib.* [*Or.* 14] 3. Using a formula that Christian wisdom rhetorolect seems to have absorbed, Dio argues his case through the use of several analogies (1 *Serv. lib.* [*Or.* 14] 4-8). Unlike Paul, Dio has a high regard for the power of law to help people perform right action (*De lege* [*Or.* 75]). However, the functional usefulness of the law is

[νόμος], he knows that human laws fall far short in promoting ideal behavior.[46] Although their rationales are different, Paul's distrust in the law to produce right behavior is analogous to Dio's concerns. According to Dio, the truly free man, later equated with the wise man (1 *Serv. lib.* [*Or.* 14] 17), does *not* do all that is legally permitted to him, since this would include permissible but unseemly acts such as "collecting taxes, or keeping a brothel" [πορνοβοσκεῖν] (1 *Serv. lib.* [*Or.* 14] 14).[47] Dio thereby shifts the meaning of the word ἔξεστιν so that, in this context, it is the functional equivalent of συμφέρω.[48] Dio's rhetoric, like Paul's in 1 Cor 6:12ab, blends these two terms in such a way that permissibility becomes redefined through the process of compression. The properties of each word compress to Identity, that is, a single functional definition. Thus it is not permissible [οὐκ ἔξεστι], Dio contends later in his discourse, to do things that are "mean and unseemly and unprofitable" [φαῦλα καὶ ἄτομα καὶ ἀσύμφορα]. However, it is "both proper and permissible" [προσήκει τε καὶ ἔξεστιν] to undertake actions that are "just and profitable and good" [δίκαια καὶ συμφέροντα καὶ ἀγαθά] (1 *Serv. lib.* [*Or.* 14] 16 [Cohoon, LCL]). In the tension Dio highlights between what is permitted and what is beneficial/profitable, he comes down firmly on the side of what is beneficial via a blend that interprets freedom through the frame of beneficial action. And since the wise only wish for that which is beneficial, they alone can do whatever they wish, and therefore, they alone are free (1 *Serv. lib.* [*Or.* 14] 17).[49]

I want to highlight the juxtaposition of the terms ἔξεστιν and συμφέρω in Dio's treatment of freedom. As noted, through the cognitive process of compression Dio's discourse collapses the definition of these two terms into functional equivalents. Paul's paradoxical gnomic saying, in much more economical fashion, makes a similar cognitive

---

itself "a sign of the depravity of mankind" [Σημεῖον δὲ τῆς πονηρίας τῆς τῶν ἀνθρώπων] (*Virt.* [*Or.* 69] 9 [Crosby, LCL]). According to Dio, law is a necessary, but not sufficient, element of living a life of virtue. One must also obtain knowledge that allows one to distinguish what constitutes virtuous behavior (*Virt.* [*Or.* 69] 8).

[46] For Dio's encomium to law, see *De lege* [*Or.* 75] where the law functions almost like personified wisdom does in the Jewish sapiential materials. For his critique of laws made by human beings, see *Lib.* [*Or.* 80] 3.

[47] Note Cohoon's LCL introduction to 1 *Serv. lib.* [*Or.* 14] in which he notes that this discourse and the fifteenth are "our chief source for knowledge of the Stoic doctrine that the wise man alone is free" (LCL 2:123). See also *Gen.* [*Or.* 25] 1 for this idea as well.

[48] See Weiß, *Der erste Korintherbrief*, 158 for his argument that συμφέρει is a *terminus technicus* of popular Stoic philosophy.

[49] As noted above, Philo appropriates this Stoic line of reasoning in his treatise *Quod omnis probus liber sit* (That Every Good Person is Free). See esp. *Prob.* 59.

and rhetorical move. Indeed, it is worth pointing out that Dio uses the example of running a brothel to explain a case of something that is technically allowed but not beneficial. The constellation of words – ἔξεστιν, συμφέρω, and πορνοβοσκέω – that Dio employs in his discourse is striking when read alongside Paul's argument in 1 Cor 6:12-20. This, I would suggest, throws further doubt upon an interpretation of 6:12 based on the idea that Paul must counter the Corinthian slogan "Everything is permissible for me," which the Corinthians use as a philosophical warrant for visiting sex workers. While certainly not impossible, it seems curious that the historical reconstruction of the situation in the Corinthian assembly should so perfectly match what appears to be a philosophical trope. Moreover, Dio is not the only one to use sexual behavior in this way in a rhetorical argument concerning morality. Raymond Collins notes that Seneca, Musonius, and Epictetus also use this topic to probe the "relationship between law and morality."[50] Given the Hellenistic philosophical resources that use sex as a way to examine these principles, it should come as no surprise that Paul makes a similar rhetorical move. By opening his didactic discourse in this way, Paul shifts the focus from a debate about the permissibility of certain expressions of sexual behavior to a concern about discerning what actions are beneficial.

Paul's sarcastic reference to kingship in relation to the Corinthians in 1 Cor 4:8, coupled with his overarching concern about the wisdom of the members of the Corinthian community, makes another of Dio's discourses, namely one on kingship, a profitable comparative text when read in light of Paul's saying in 6:12ab and provides a bridge to the ideas found in 6:12cd. Walter Wilson notes that discourses on kingship were a "popular ... genre that was designed expressly to instruct persons of authority in their basic moral responsibilities." He goes on to note that "such treatises were in fact relevant for anyone who desired the moral status of those deemed worthy to govern."[51] When Dio is discussing the ideal king in *Discourse* 3, he writes:

> Such a king considers virtue [ἀρετήν] a fair possession for others but an absolute necessity for himself. Who, in fact must exercise greater wisdom [φρονήσεως] than he who is concerned with the weightiest matters; who a

---

[50] R. Collins, *First Corinthians*, 240 where he cites Seneca, *Epistles*, 1.69, 71; Musonious, "On Sexual Relations," frag. 12.84.32–86.1, 6–8, 10–15; 88.6; Epictetus, *Discourses*, 3.7.21; *Encheiridion* 33.8 (see also *Discourses*, 2.18.15–26; 3.22.13, 95 for Epictetus's argument that higher moral standards are expected from Stoics).

[51] Wilson, *Sentences of Pseudo-Phocylides*, 35; see Knust, *Abandoned to Lust*, 47, 85; Stowers, *Rereading Romans*, 55–56; Guilia Sissa, "Sexual Bodybuilding: Aeschines against Timarchus," in *Constructions of the Classical Body* (ed. James I. Porter; The Body, in Theories: Histories of Cultural Materialism; Ann Arbor: University of Michigan Press, 1999), 155.

keener sense of justice [δικαιοσύνης] than he who is above the law [τῷ μείζονι τῶν νόμων]; who, a more rigorous self-control [σωφροσύνης ἐγκρατεστέρας] than he to whom all things are permissible [ὅτῳ πάντα ἔξεστι]; who, a stouter courage [ἀνδρείας] than he upon whom the safety of everything depends? (3 *Regn*. [*Or.* 3] 9b-10 [Cohoon, LCL]).[52]

In this discourse, Dio notes that the king must possess the four cardinal virtues of wisdom, justice, self-control, and courage to a greater degree than all other men precisely *because* he is "above (lit., greater than) the law" and permitted to do all things.[53] According to Dio, the lack of external controls requires that the king know how to regulate his own actions, not only for his own benefit but also for that of his subjects. Although no radical message such as "for freedom Christ set us free" (Gal 5:1) is found in 1 Cor,[54] Paul's use of himself as the model of the free person who does not make use of all the ἐξουσία that his freedom entails (1 Cor 9), when read in light of Dio's concerns about the behavior of one above the law, suggests a conceptual cultural place for Paul's focus on the responsibility laid upon one for whom anything is permissible.[55] This situates Paul's saying of 6:12ab more firmly in the proximate rhetorical context of 4:16–11:1 where Paul is at pains to teach the Corinthians the principles of right judgment.

Although I am not suggesting that the thought found in the resources discussed in this section have some kind of essential similarity that trumps their distinctive characteristics, I am suggesting that the contrastive gnomic saying in 1 Cor 6:12ab, with which Paul begins his argument against πορνεία, would not be out of place among the variety of voices struggling to express the tension between individual freedom and self-controlled responsibility found in the various thought worlds of Hellenistic moral discourse – both Jewish and non-Jewish. The conceptual network Paul creates in 6:12ab, especially its blend and the emergent structure that arises from it, is not particular to Paul. The widely accessible nature of the topic and comment, as well as the emergent structure created by blending them, firmly situates this gnomic saying within the environment of wisdom rhetorolect. Paul begins his argument not with any specifically Christian teaching, but with a

---

[52] Cf. 1 Cor 16:13; Wis 9:1-18; Aeschines, *Tim.* 108. See also Dio's description of the wise man as "sensible and just and holy and brave" [τὸν φρόνιμον ... καὶ δίκαιον καὶ ὅσιον καὶ ἀνδρεῖον] in *Fel. Sap.* (*Or.* 23) 8 (Cohoon, LCL). For his description of virtue see *Virt*, (*Or.* 69) 2.

[53] For more on the cardinal virtues see Wilson, *Mysteries of Righteousness*, ch. 2, "The Canon of Cardinal Virtues in Antiquity" (pp. 42-59).

[54] But see 2 Cor 3:17.

[55] For a discussion of "The Mission of the Free" in Epictetus, see Galloway, *Freedom in the Gospel*, 82-83. See also Stowers, *Rereading Romans*, 56.

gnomic wisdom saying that has broad accessibility and that, because of this, has emergent structure that appears self-evident. This is the nature of wisdom rhetorolect.[56]

Freedom and Self-Mastery: 6:12cd
As with the first half of the verse, so the gnomic saying in 6:12cd represents an example of paradoxical wisdom. In the latter half of this verse Paul juxtaposes the idea that everything is permissible with the declaration that he will not allow anything to have authority over him. As noted above, 6:12cd contains comparative sub-topics (πάντα and τινος) and contrasting sub-comments (μοι ἔξεστιν and οὐκ ἐγὼ ἐξουσιασθήσομαι). If it were not for the adversative lexical marker followed by a negative (ἀλλ' οὐκ), however, the main topic (6:12c) and main comment (6:12d) would hardly seem contrastive at all. However, by placing this saying after 6:12ab and by repeating the contrasting conjunction "but," Paul sets up the expectation in this saying that his main comment will offer another paradoxical teaching about the nature of permissibility. The paradoxical wisdom is not found in the content of either the topic or the comment, however, but in the emergent structure of the network, which prompts the hearer/reader to consider how the danger of enslavement lurks behind the notion of absolute freedom.[57]

The work of Stanley Stowers on the importance of the concept of self-mastery in the Hellenistic world can help exegetes understand the moral concern Paul's blend activates in 6:12cd.[58] Although Stowers's focus is on the letter to the Romans, his contention that "[t]he theme of self-mastery would have loomed very large for ancient readers" holds for Paul's argument against πορνεία in 1 Cor as well. As Stowers notes, "Paul was fully implicated in the values and discourse of his society, time, and social group."[59] The dangers that one might use one's freedom to succumb to the dangerous enslavement of the passions weighed heavily on the minds of thinkers in the Hellenistic world.[60] As Jennifer Wright Knust argues, with an eye towards the cumulative effect of Paul's teaching in 6:12-14, "Allowing oneself to be mastered by either food or *porneia* was to fail in one's duties as a master of oneself and others."[61]

---

[56] See Wilson, *Love without Pretense*, 19; Crenshaw, *Wisdom*, 12; Robbins, *Invention*, 1:184.
[57] See Coulson, *Semantic Leaps*, 138; Philo, *Prob.* 6-7.
[58] Stowers, *Rereading Romans*, ch. 2 (pp. 42-82).
[59] Stowers, *Rereading Romans*, 42; also Wilson, *Pseudo-Phocylides*, 34.
[60] Especially, as Stowers notes, in the time of the moral politics initiated by Augustus (*Rereading Romans*, 52-56).
[61] Knust, *Abandoned to Lust*, 78.

The conceptual network in 6:12cd functions in much the same way as the one in 6:12ab. Here, as there, Paul's maxim is effective because of the emergent structure that arises out of his high-asymmetry double-scope blending of input spaces with different local frames. Here there are two input spaces governed by the local frames of freedom (input-1) and self-mastery (input-2). When the blend is run, by combining the simplex blends of each input space with the contrastive conjunction ἀλλά, the elements governed by the local frames are compressed into Identity and, once again, freedom is understood only through the frame of self-mastery. When the blend is elaborated, no action that threatens self-mastery can be viewed as a proper expression of freedom. The diagram for this high-asymmetry double-scope network in 6:12cd thus looks similar to the network mapped out for 6:12ab:

Figure 3: Conceptual Network for 6:12cd

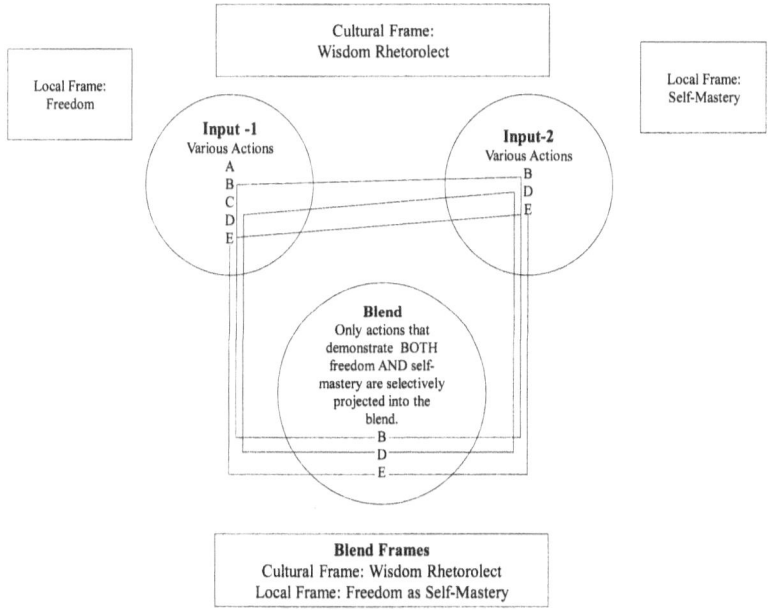

Lincoln Galloway notes that early Stoic thinkers conceived of ideas about slavery on at least three levels. These include "(i) the moral slavery of the bad, (ii) subordination, and (iii) slavery as property or chattel slavery."[62] It is the first view, that of moral slavery, that helps us under-

---

[62] Galloway, *Freedom in the Gospel*, 91 where he is dependent upon Andrew Erksine, *The Hellenistic Stoa: Political Thought and Action* (London: Duckworth, 1990), 43-63.

stand Paul's teaching in 6:12cd. Returning to Dio as an illustrative conversation partner, I note that he describes moral slaves as ignorant [ἀγνοοῦντες and ἀνοήτους] – they cannot make good decisions because they lack the knowledge to make, much less enact, them. Dio describes the wise, on the other hand, as those who know [ἐπιστάμενοι] how to make wise decisions and act upon them (1 Serv. lib. [Or. 14] 17).[63] Only through knowledge and wisdom can one avoid losing one's mastery over oneself, that is, mastery over one's passions. Moreover, as noted above, Dio teaches that it is the one for whom everything is permissible who needs to have "a more rigorous self-control" [σωφροσύνης ἐγκρατεστέρας] (3 Regn. [Or. 3] 10 [Cohoon, LCL]) than other people.

Dio also displays a concern that enslavement may come upon a person unawares. In his discourse On Freedom, Dio notes that moral slavery is an ever present danger to one who is not wise (Lib. [Or. 80] 10). This enslavement is so insidious,[64] according to Dio, because although it is "a mistress [δέσποινα] who is in other respects harsh and ill-disposed and treacherous," she looks happy and cheerful. The appearance of such cheerfulness is only an illusion (Lib. [Or. 80] 11). She comes to individuals promising to make them happy, but in reality she destroys [ἀπολλύῃ] them (Lib. [Or. 80] 12). Although they hardly seem that way to the ignorant, this mistress places fetters [δεσμά] upon them and around their necks she puts a collar [κλοιόν], although its appearance is that of silver or gold (Lib. [Or. 80] 11-12).[65]

Dio's description of the harsh mistress who traps the mass of ignorant people sounds surprisingly similar to the description of the "strange" woman in Jewish wisdom texts. That both use the image of a woman to represent the enticing nature of unwise actions is important for the analysis of Paul's teaching given his use of the figure of the πόρνη in 1 Cor 6:15-16. Turning to the Jewish material, recall the prevalence of the image of the snare.[66] This image, like that of Dio's fetters and collar, is used in Jewish sapiential literature for all manner of dangers that would morally enslave the unsuspecting fool. Also like Dio, Jewish wisdom texts use this image for women who are sexually

---

[63] Stowers, Rereading Romans, 57 notes that Dio, in multiple instances, argues that Egypt benefits from Roman control because of Roman self-mastery. See idem, 53 for a discussion of the creation of the degenerate East in Roman ideology; also McClure, Courtesans at Table, 28-29.

[64] Dio refers to it as "disgraceful, odious slavery" [τῆς αἰσχρᾶς καὶ δυσχεροῦς δουλείας] in Lib. (Or. 80) 9 (Crosby, LCL).

[65] For δεσμά see Prov 7:22; Sir 6:25; for κλοιόν see Deut 28:47; Sir 6:24. Cf. Sir 4:17-19; 21:19-21; 27:27; 51:26.

[66] See Prov 6:2, 5; 7:21, 23; 11:8, 9; 12:13, 27; 13:14; 14:27; 18:7; 20:25; 21:6; 22:5, 25; 29:6; Eccl 9:12; Wis 14:11; Sir 9:3, 13; 27:20, 26, 29; 51:2.

marginal (Prov 7:21-23; Eccl 7:27; Sir 9:3). In Proverbs the strange woman is depicted as erotically attractive, and this is why she is so dangerous.[67] Despite her beauty, consorting with the strange woman leads to death. As with those who fall under the spell of Dio's "harsh mistress," those whom the strange woman enslaves are led to their destruction as unaware of their predicament as are animals who are led to the slaughter (Prov 7:22-23).[68] The pleasure one encounters in the embodied figure of the strange woman in Jewish sapiential material must be avoided at all costs according to Philo of Alexandria.[69] While pleasure might be inviting and tempting, Philo, giving Jewish wisdom tradition a Hellenistic spin, argues that those who are wise will not become ensnared in its tendrils. Rather, they will live a life of virtue.[70] The fact that Greek and Jew alike use the figure of a sexually alluring woman to describe the danger of becoming enslaved to pleasurable things helps prepare the necessary cultural background information for Paul's teaching against πορνεία.[71]

The cultural resources discussed above suggest that the hearer/reader of Paul's wise saying would be able to make sense of the blend 6:12cd prompts and would be able to draw upon the insights created by the emergent structure of this network as Paul continues his teaching in the rest of the pericope. Not all of these cultural resources, to be sure, were necessarily available to all the recipients of Paul's teaching.[72] Yet the evidence from various cultural environments suggests that most hearers/readers would be able to run Paul's blend with a high probability of success. With a limited numbers of words, Paul's saying calls up a

---

[67] See Prov 5:3; 6:25; 7:10, 13, 16-18; 9:13-17.

[68] See Prov 5:5; 7:26-27; 9:18.

[69] See Philo, *Ios.* 153: "no two things can be more hostile to each other than virtue is to pleasure" (Colson, LCL). For more on the danger of pleasure in Philo, see, e.g., *Leg.* 3.149, 156, 194; *Sacr.* 23, 32.

[70] See Stowers, *Rereading Romans*, 58-74 for more on the presentation of Judaism as a school for self-mastery by Hellenistic Jewish writers, especially Philo.

[71] For the idea that women pose an inherent danger to society and thus can represent all manner of vices for the ancient authors, see Anne Carson, "Putting Her in Her Place: Woman, Dirt, and Desire," in *Before Sexuality: The Construction of Erotic Experience in the Ancient Greek World* (ed. David M. Halperin, John J. Winkler, and Froma I. Zeitlin; Princeton: Princeton University Press, 1990), 135-69. A different version of this essay appears as idem, "Dirt and Desire: The Phenomenology of Female Pollution in Antiquity," in *Constructions of the Classical Body* (ed. James I. Porter; The Body, in Theories: Histories of Cultural Materialism; Ann Arbor: University of Michigan Press, 1999), 77-100. See also, Judith M. Lieu, *Christian Identity in the Jewish and Greco-Roman World* (Oxford: Oxford University Press, 2004), 192-94.

[72] See Coulson and Oakley, "Blending and Coded Meaning," 1517: "... all sentences rely importantly on contextual assumptions that vary in their transparency to speakers and hearers."

debate that was playing out in both Jewish and non-Jewish cultural spheres. Those involved in this debate worried about individuals becoming enslaved to those things that they freely chose to do. Again, Paul compresses the definition of two phrases, μοι ἔξεστιν and οὐκ ἐγὼ ἐξουσιασθήσομαι, so that the former is always understood in terms of the latter. The one who is permitted to do all things, *will not* allow himself or herself to be mastered by any of those things, especially the pleasures associated with attractive women and sex.[73] Unlike other Hellenistic Jews such as Philo and the author of 4 Maccabees, however, Paul does not see Jewish law as a necessary or sufficient means to keep oneself free from enslavement. Rather, Paul hopes to develop the discernment of the Corinthians through his use of the gnomic saying of 6:12cd. As with his saying in 6:12ab, the gnomic saying in 6:12cd is configured within and conceptually productive for wisdom rhetorolect. The emergent structure produced by this saying is broadly applicable, as with many gnomic sayings, and, with 6:12ab, prepares the hearer/reader to accept Paul's teaching that follows.

Summary

1 Cor 6:12 represents the opening texture of Paul's didactic discourse on πορνεία.[74] This opening is made up of two gnomic sayings whose form, content, accessibility, and self-evident nature establish wisdom rhetorolect as the host environment for Paul's teaching that follows. Paul activates the tension between absolute freedom of action and activities that produce benefits or demonstrate self-mastery that is found in many Hellenistic cultures. He does this, not with an extended logical argument, as Dio undertakes, but with pithy apothegms. These short sayings blend together in such a way that the emergent structure that arises from them prompts the hearer/reader to "fill in the gaps" with the resources available from wisdom rhetorolect through the cognitive processes of completion and elaboration.[75] The emergent structure produced by these sayings enriches wisdom rhetorolect by creating the necessary space for paradoxical thinking as well as by creating the expectation that reflection and understanding will be necessary to embody Paul's teaching.

The local frame of freedom of action allows the blend to be more specific, and thus more rhetorically effective, within the larger cultural organizing frame of wisdom rhetorolect. Linking the problems of beneficial action and self-mastery vis-à-vis freedom with the topic of proper sexual comportment seems to be a fairly common occurrence in

---

[73] Cf. Dio, 3 *Regn.* [*Or.* 3] 10.
[74] For opening texture, see Robbins, *Exploring*, 19-21; idem, *Tapestry*, 50-53.
[75] See Fauconnier and Turner, *The Way We Think*, 42-44.

both Jewish and non-Jewish Hellenistic cultures. Such commonality not only demonstrates the predicted cultural conservatism of cognitive blends,[76] but also offers another reason to shy away from the typical deployment of a slogan hypothesis and its concomitant historical reconstruction of the Corinthian community when exegeting this verse. Moreover, not only is it suspicious that the historically reconstructed situation in Corinth seems to match popular strategies for wrestling with the problem of freedom, but an over emphasis on historical reconstruction by means of a slogan hypothesis threatens to overshadow the larger cultural relevance of the argumentative strategies Paul enacts in 6:12–7:7. By creating blends whose emergent structure is broadly accessible and apparently self-evident, Paul is rhetorically preparing his audience to accept the rest of his teaching in a similar manner.

Destruction of the Belly, Resurrection of the Body (6:13-14): Wisdom-Apocalyptic Blended Rhetorolect

With 6:13-14 Paul progresses from general wise sayings to sayings that move his audience towards the issue at hand: πορνεία. The progressive texture of Paul's argumentation in this pericope begins with a compression of the elements of freedom and beneficial action (6:12ab) into Identity – although free to do as he or she wishes, the wise have the discernment and self-control to do only that which is beneficial. This idea of control progresses in 6:12cd with the compression of the elements of freedom of action and self-mastery. 1 Cor 6:13ab continues this progression with a wise saying regarding the belly (κοιλία) and meats (βρώματα). How does this relate to 6:12? Although Fee argues that 6:13 is "an abrupt change of direction," I argue rather that the saying about meats and belly continues a discussion of self-mastery.[77] Both Stanley Stowers and Karl Olav Sandnes have demonstrated that self-mastery is typically discussed in terms of being stronger than one's belly in the moral discourse of the ancient Mediterranean world.[78] As Stowers notes, "In Greek thought, the stomach represents the bestial, wild, needy, and passionately desiring part of the human."[79] By employing the rhetography of meats and the belly (see Sir 36:18), Paul is progressing from a general idea about self-mastery (6:12d [οὐκ ἐγὼ

---

[76] See Fauconnier and Turner, *The Way We Think*, 382-83. See also Oakley, "Human Rhetorical Potential," 94, 96, 109, and 124.
[77] See Knust, *Abandoned to Lust*, 78.
[78] Fee, *First Epistle to the Corinthians*, 253; Stowers, *Rereading Romans*, 49 (where he is discussing Xenophon, *Mem* 1.5.1-6); Karl Olav Sandnes, *Belly and the Body in Pauline Epistles* (Cambridge: Cambridge University Press, 2002), esp. ch. 2 (pp. 24-34).
[79] Stowers, *Rereading Romans*, 49.

ἐξουσιασθήσομαι]) to a discussion of a specific part of the body that regularly is linked with lack of that mastery when sated on rich foods, such as meats (see Sir 37:30).[80] Paul uses the *topos* of the belly as a means to ease his audience into his main theme of πορνεία, which first appears in 6:14.[81]

The rhetorical link Paul's didactic discourse creates between a full belly and sexual licentiousness is not cognitively surprising in the context of medical and philosophical views current in late antiquity that "sexual appetite [Κύπρις] accompanies satiety" (Aristotle, *Probl.* 896a; cf. 1 Cor 10:7-8).[82] The link between the belly and sex is further concretized by cultural knowledge that likens women, the necessary "cause" of πορνεία (1 Cor 5; 6:15-17), to a stomach – each is a "power" that threatens male bodily integrity.[83] Stowers notes that, "According to Hesiod, woman is like an insatiable stomach who leads to a man's death."[84] An analogy between woman and stomach is also found in Sir 36:18-26 (cf. Sir 9:2).[85] Paul's conceptual move from the belly as a *topos* symbolizing the appetitive pleasures into an argument against sexual sin committed with a πόρνη thus seems not that unusual.

1 Cor 6:13-14 contain two sayings that are formally almost identical, as with the two sayings Paul uses in 6:12. Using Wilson's categories of topic (T) and comment (C) to analyze these sayings yields the following:

---

[80] See Sandnes, *Belly and the Body*, 61: "The belly was a catchword for a life controlled by pleasures." Cf. 1 Macc 1:63; 4 Macc 1:34.

[81] Sandnes, *Belly and Body*, ch. 3 (pp. 35-60) demonstrates that "belly" is a *topos* in ancient sources. Sandnes reviews the works of the following ancient writers: Euripides, Plato, Xenophon, Aristotle, Dio Chrysostom, Musonius Rufus, Epictetus, Plutarch, and Athenaeus.

[82] As quoted and translated by Sandnes, who explains that "Cypris was another name for Aphrodite" (*Belly and the Body*, 2). See also Bruce W. Winter, *After Paul Left Corinth: The Influence of Secular Ethics and Social Change* (Grand Rapids, Eerdmans, 2001), 84 n. 24: "Cypris was a name for Aphrodite from the island of Cypus and became an appellative for love or passion." Also Wilson, *Sentences of Pseudo-Phocylides*, 79; Knust, *Abandoned to Lust*, 78. See Gaca, *Fornication* for the correlation between a full belly and sexual desire in the thought of Plato (pp. 27, 34, 195), the Middle Platonists (p. 194), the Pythagoreans (pp. 94, 105), and Philo (pp. 196, 205); also James Davidson, *Courtesans and Fishcakes: The Consuming Passions of Classical Athens* (London: HarperCollins, 1997), 105. For more on this link as it relates to early Christian thought see esp. Teresa M. Shaw, *The Burden of the Flesh: Fasting and Sexuality in Early Christianity* (Minneapolis: Fortress, 1998), ch. 2 (pp. 27-78); also Martin, *Corinthian Body*, 207; Gillian Clark, "Women and Asceticism in Late Antiquity: The Refusal of Status and Gender," in *Asceticism* (eds. Vincent L. Wimbush and Richard Valantasis; Oxford: Oxford University Press, 1998), 39; Robert H. von Thaden, Jr., "Glorify God in Your Body: The Redemptive Role of the Body in Early Christian Ascetic Literature," *Cistercian Studies Quarterly* 38 (2003): 198-99.

[83] See Carson, "Putting Her in Her Place," 159: "Sexually the female is a pore."

[84] Stowers, *Rereading Romans*, 50.

[85] Note the use of βρῶμα with κοιλία in Sir 36:18.

Saying 1 (6:13ab):
τὰ βρώματα τῇ κοιλίᾳ καὶ ἡ κοιλία τοῖς βρώμασιν,
ὁ δὲ θεὸς καὶ ταύτην καὶ ταῦτα καταργήσει.
T: Meats for the belly and the belly for meats,
C: and God will destroy both this and them.

Saying 2 (6:13c, 14):
τό δὲ σῶμα οὐ τῇ πορνείᾳ ἀλλὰ τῷ κυρίῳ καὶ ὁ κύριος τῷ σώματι,
ὁ δὲ θεὸς καὶ τὸν κύριον ἤγειρεν καὶ ἡμᾶς ἐξεγερεῖ
διὰ τῆς δυνάμεως αὐτοῦ.
T: And the body not for sexual immorality but for the Lord and
the Lord for the body,
C: and God both raised the Lord and will raise us through his power.[86]

Although 6:13-14 have the form of wise sayings, the comments in each saying introduce images of destruction (6:13b) and resurrection (6:14), which are common images found in the rhetography of apocalyptic rhetorolect.[87] While Paul may be enacting the role of a wisdom teacher in trying to persuade the Corinthians to change their behavior, he undertakes this role within his apocalyptic worldview.[88] Here Paul uses binary oppositional categories typical of apocalyptic rhetorolect, as he did in 1 Cor 1-4, thus blending the resources of wisdom and apocalyptic rhetorolects. There are only two options in Paul's discussion of the belly and the body: destruction or resurrection.

In 6:13-14 Paul continues his teaching within the environment of wisdom rhetorolect, which he established in 6:12. This is demonstrated by the continuation of the theme of self-mastery and its concern with proper use of the body. Moreover, the link to wisdom rhetorolect also occurs on a formal level. In these two verses he creates a pair of gnomic sayings with "equational structure" that suggests "equivalence of topic and comment."[89] The structure of the topics and the comments in 6:13-14 is parallel.[90] When read together, however, these two gno-

---

[86] Note that I punctuate these sayings in a different way than what is found in NA[27]. On the translation of δέ see Smyth, *Greek Grammar*, §2834: "later it became a conjunction commonly represented by *but* or *and*, which are, however, mere makeshifts of translation."

[87] See Weiß, *Der erste Korintherbrief*, 162.

[88] See J.J. Collins, "Cosmos and Salvation," and "The Sage in the Apocalyptic Literature," 317-38 and 339-50 respectively. Also Goff, "Wisdom, Apocalypticism, and the Pedagogical Ethos of 4QInstruction," 57-67.

[89] Wilson, *Love without Pretense*, 27.

[90] Fee, *First Epistle to the Corinthians*, 254; see Fenske, *Argumentation des Paulus*, 101 although he states that the parallelism is not "theologically consistent, or rather the parallelism collapses" (translation mine). Fenske does not see the overall parallelism because he does not consider that Paul is discussing two sides of apocalyptic reality. He does, how-

mic sayings treat two pairs of elements in a way that serves, ultimately, to contrast their eschatological fate.[91] The contrast is found in the juxtaposition of God's action towards the elements in each saying.[92] Paul's instruction here proceeds in a manner similar to earlier chapters of the letter – the wisdom that God revealed through the crucified Christ allows one to discern the true nature of realty. His instruction to the Corinthians in these verses explains this embodied reality from two different vantage points, just as he explicated the proper use of freedom in 6:12 through two gnomic sayings that drew their rhetorical force from two different arenas. The reading of δέ as a strong adversative in 6:13c, for which Fee argues, assumes that Paul is trying to neutralize the saying of 6:13ab.[93] This, I argue, is not the case. The δέ of 6:13c moves Paul's overall argument forward by displaying an alternative apocalyptic reality. Thus this δέ marks "something new or different, but not opposed, to what precedes."[94] Although the maxims of 6:13ab and 6:13c-14 constitute an "anti-analogy" when read together, the vision of reality expressed in them is not antithetical, but rather forms two sides of the same apocalyptic coin.[95]

With the sayings of 6:13-14 Paul enters the middle texture of his argument that defines the Christian body in such a way that it is separated from the passions to which a person can fall prey.[96] By separating out "the passionately desiring part of the human," Paul is actually *decompressing* the relations between the body and its passionate appetites and thereby creating two different, and distinct, entities: belly *and* body [σῶμα].[97] Paul then invites the integration resources available in apocalyptic rhetorolect into his argument and declares the eschatological fate of "meats" [βρώματα] and the "belly" [κοιλία] – they are destined for destruction. In contrast to the desiring belly, Paul argues that the σῶμα exists not for the satisfaction of pleasurable appetites (in 6:13c he specifically singles out πορνεία) but for the Lord.[98] The rationale he gives

---

ever, note later that the *Motivespender* for 6:13-14 is judgment and the *Motivekomplex* is eschatology (p. 106).

[91] See Kirchhoff, *Sünde*, 109-11; see also Gundry, *Sôma in Biblical Theology*, 55-56.

[92] See Robertson and Plummer, *First Epistle to the Corinthians*, 124 where they note that it is the parallel ὁ δὲ θεός construction in 6:13b and 14 that "puts the contrast between the two cases in a very marked way."

[93] Fee, *First Epistle to the Corinthians*, 254.

[94] Smythe, *Greek Grammar*, § 2836.

[95] See Kirchhoff, *Sünde*, 111. For their discussion of "Disanalogy," see Fauconnier and Turner, *The Way We Think*, 99.

[96] For middle texture, see Robbins, *Exploring*, 19-21; idem, *Tapestry*, 50-53.

[97] Stowers, *Rereading Romans*, 49. Fauconnier and Turner, *The Way We Think*, 119; idem, "Compression and Global Insight," 299.

[98] Cf. Sir 18:30: "Do not go after your desires [τῶν ἐπιθυμῶν] and be hindered from your appetites [τῶν ὀρέξεων]." See Knust, *Abandoned to Lust*, 78.

for this also draws from apocalyptic rhetorolect – the σῶμα, like the Lord himself, is destined to be raised by God. Thus after Paul decompresses the relation of the body from its passions he begins to compress the relation of the Christian body and Christ. In 6:13c-14 he compresses the relationship between the two into the vital relation of Analogy. As Paul begins to demonstrate why πορνεία is to be avoided, it is important to note that he does not give rationales typically available in wisdom rhetorolect for avoiding this sexual sin,[99] but rather he uses apocalyptic rhetorolect to organize the comments (C) he gives to the wisdom topics (T) of his sayings. In so doing, Paul creates a conceptual network in which the resources of wisdom and apocalyptic rhetorolects are blended. The new emergent structure prompted by these networks is more powerful than the resources of any one rhetorolect on its own.

As noted, after Paul decompresses the relation between the body of the believer and the belly, he defines his local use of the term σῶμα in 6:13c where it is dependent upon its relationship to the Lord for meaning. The topic of Paul's second saying (6:13c-14) is rhetorically designed to mimic the relationship between meats and the belly. The first part of the topic – τὸ δὲ σῶμα οὐ πορνείᾳ ἀλλὰ τῷ κυρίῳ – introduces a Disanalogy between the body and sexual immorality. Πορνεία is a passionate appetite and thus, based on Paul's decompression of the body and belly in 6:13ac, this Disanalogy is conceptually logical within Paul's teaching. Moreover, this Disanalogy seems to blend Paul's teaching in 3:23 with his instruction in ch. 5. The final half of the topic – ὁ κύριος τῷ σώματι – has caused considerable exegetical and theological *Angst*.[100] However, the idea of a reciprocal relationship between the body and the Lord should not cause great concern based on the comment of this saying (6:14), which cements the vital relation between the Lord and the believer's body. It is precisely because the Lord was a *body* who both died on the cross (2:2; 15:2) and was resurrected and seen by many (15:3-9) that the relationship between the two is meaningful. Raymond Collins notes that "[b]odily existence (σῶμα) undergirds human solidarity with the risen and awaited one."[101] On a more specific level, this shared local frame of the human body in 6:13c-14 creates what Fauconnier and Turner refer

---

[99] Such as fear of economic ruin. See e.g. Prov 29:3; Sir 6:9; Davidson, *Courtesans and Fishcakes*, 95, 105, 255; McClure, *Courtesans at Table*, 10. Another wisdom concern is found in Prov 23:33: "Whenever your eyes behold a strange woman [ἀλλοτρίαν] then your mouth will speak crooked things [σκολιά]."

[100] See, e.g., Fee, *First Epistle to the Corinthians*, 256.

[101] Collins, *First Corinthians*, 246. See also Schrage, *Der erste Brief an die Korinther*, 2:23.

to as a mirror network. As Turner argues, "a mirror network is one in which all the inputs share a single organizing frame, which is also projected into the blend to organize it. The shared frame gives the inputs an analogical relation; each has the same set of roles."[102] This mirror network compresses the vital relation between the believer and Christ to Analogy. Both the believer and Jesus possess bodies on which God can act. Moreover, what God *has* done to the body of Jesus, God *will* do to the bodies of believers (6:14). What is being recruited into Paul's cognitive blend, then, is the notion that a believer's body should serve the Lord, because the Lord has shown *through his crucifixion and resurrection* the importance of the body in God's wisdom – Paul articulates an embodied theology here. The use of σῶμα elsewhere in Paul may have other conceptual trappings. However, as far as Paul's argument is concerned in 6:13c-14, its analogous relationship to the risen Lord is the one that matters for his local rhetorical purposes.

Taken as a whole, when each saying moves from the topic (6:13a; 6:13c) into the comment (6:13b; 6:14), apocalyptic rhetorolect energizes the host wisdom environment of the topic to create a rhetorically effective emergent structure in a complex double-scope network of topic plus comment. Fauconnier and Turner claim that "A double-scope network has inputs with different ... organizing frames as well as an organizing frame for the blend that includes parts of each of those frames and has emergent structure all its own."[103] Here we see that double-scope blends can emerge organically out of local mirror networks as Paul's rhetoric develops, but this is a dynamic, not linear, emergence and one that the hearer/reader can readily process "on the fly." Analyzing the specific mirror network Paul's discourse creates in 6:13c-14 allows interpreters to understand how Paul's Analogy between the believer and the Lord makes sense. However, understanding this network within the dynamics of the more complex double-scope networks of 6:13-14 taken together allows interpreters to see how Paul draws from a diversity of culturally available arguments. When he uses apocalyptic rhetorolect as the organizing frame for the comments of the sayings, Paul activates elements within Jewish religious culture that

---

[102] Mark Turner, "The Art of Compression," in *The Artful Mind: Cognitive Science and the Riddle of Human Creativity* (ed. Mark Turner; New York: Oxford University Press, 2006), 101. I am grateful to Bonnie Howe for pointing this reference out to me. See also Fauconnier and Turner, *The Way We Think*, 337-38.

[103] See Fauconnier and Turner, *The Way We Think*, 131. Technically, each saying is a non-clashing double-scope network. In such a network "both [organizing frames] contribute to a blend that incorporates both of them" (p. 135).

6. Why Porneia Should Be Avoided: 1 Cor 6:12-20

would be out of place in a non-Jewish Hellenistic environment.[104] In this way Paul is displaying what Fauconnier and Turner refer to as "multiple-scope creativity."[105] Here interpreters can begin to see the strength of conceptual blending theory that was discussed in Chapter 1 – the ability to trace the development and accumulation of complex conceptual networks within a piece of discourse while analyzing how different networks, dynamically working together, organize and serve the rhetoric of the text.[106] Paul's arguments in 1 Cor 6:13-14 bear exegetical fruit when analyzed on the level of local frames (the body) *as well as* on the level of cultural frames (apocalyptic and wisdom rhetorolects); the dynamic interaction of different levels of framing within the networks helps us understand how Paul's rhetoric is fertile ground for meaning production. It is through the cognitive creativity of blending wisdom and apocalyptic rhetorolects to form a wisdom-apocalyptic blended cultural organizing frame that Paul's reasoning is able to achieve such rhetorical force.[107] This new emergent structure, which blends the rhetorical power of wisdom and apocalyptic rhetorolects, drives Paul's argument forward in a way that wisdom rhetorolect alone would be unable to do.

In addition to beginning to create a local definition of the Christian σῶμα in this section of his argument, Paul also introduces of the term πορνεία for the first time in this pericope in 6:13. Renate Kirchhoff, after an extended analysis, points out that the lexical item πορνεία has different conceptual trappings in the non-Jewish and non-Christian Greek world than it does in the moral traditions of Judaism and Christianity.[108] In the non-Jewish and non-Christian Greek speaking world, the meaning of πορνεία is generally confined to an economic activity, and thus translated by the English word "prostitution."[109] Certainly in the LXX the word can and does have this same economic meaning, as, for example, in the well known story of Tamar and Judah (Gen 38:15-26). However, in the moral traditions of Judaism and nascent Christianity the word πορνεία has a broader (and more amorphous) meaning,

---

[104] Thus Brian Rosner, *Paul, Scripture and Ethics*, is correct to point to Paul's use of Jewish moral tradition. However, this only represents one of the cultural arenas upon which Paul draws when making his rhetorical blends.

[105] Fauconnier and Turner, *The Way We Think*, ch. 15 (pp. 299-308).

[106] Coulson, *Semantic Leaps*, 267; Slingerland, *What Science Offers the Humanities*, 22, 188, 196; Eubanks, "Globalization,"174.

[107] See Goff, *Worldly and Heavenly Wisdom*; idem, "Wisdom, Apocalypticism, and the Pedagogical Ethos of 4 QInstruction."

[108] Kirchhoff, *Sünde*, 18-37; see also Gaca, *Fornication*, 20.

[109] Kirchhoff, *Sünde*, 37; see McClure, *Courtesans at Table*, 10-11, 15-18; Davidson, *Courtesans and Fishcakes*, 73-74, 76, 95, 111-20, 124-25, 131-33, 194-200, 225.

as Kirchhoff has demonstrated, and covers any forbidden sexual activity, including prostitution, but also other specific acts such as μοιχεία.[110] Such a broad meaning of πορνεία can be seen in Sir 23:16-23 where the incestuous man and the man who lacks sexual self-control are both described as a πόρνος[111] (Sir 23:17) and where a woman who leaves her husband is described as "having committed adultery through sexual immorality" [ἐν πορνείᾳ ἐμοιχεύθη] (Sir 38:23). That Paul employs this broad definition of πορνεία is confirmed by how he first uses the term in 1 Cor 5:1. Here Paul is referring to the incestuous relationship between a man and his father's wife and refers to it as "such a kind [τοιαύτη] of πορνεία that is not even among the gentiles." When Paul recoils at the sexual transgressions of this sinful couple his rhetoric employs a general word for any kind of sexual irregularity: πορνεία. Thus I see no reason to restrict the translation of πορνεία in 6:13c to "prostitution." Rather, it functions in the broadest possible sense as a rather open-ended lexical item that covers every kind of sex act deemed immoral by Paul.[112]

In struggling with Paul's slippery use of the term σῶμα, with the help of B.J. Oropeza I suggest that striving to find a theological essence of the term misses the mark exegetically.[113] Part of Paul's rhetorical goal in 6:12-20 is to construct a local definition for the Christian σῶμα that is divorced from sexually irregular appetites and that stands in close relationship to Christ and God. What is important for Paul's argument in this context, what the new emergent structure his multiple-scope network in 6:13-14 projects, is the notion that the desiring belly along with its appetites is a distinct entity from the body. God will destroy the belly and its appetites. The body, on the other hand, is important in the life of the believer because the Lord was crucified and resurrect-

---

[110] Kirchhoff, *Sünde*. 37. See Mark D. Jordan, *Blessing Same-Sex Unions: The Perils of Queer Romance and the Confusions of Christian Marriage* (Chicago: University of Chicago Press, 2005), 189: "*Porneia* is a vaguer word than *moicheia*. Related to the word for 'prostitute,' it implies a range of sexual liberties outside marriage – or inside commerce." Also idem, *Ethics of Sex*, 26-27; William Loader, *Enoch, Levi, and Jubilees on Sexuality: Attitudes towards Sexuality in the Early Enoch Literature, the Aramaic Levi Document, and the Book of Jubilees* (Grand Rapids, Mich.: Eerdmans, 2007), 22, 169; Carolyn Osiek, "Female Slaves, Porneia, and the Limits of Obedience," in *Early Christian Families in Context: An Interdisciplinary Dialogue* (ed. David L. Balch and Carolyn Osiek; Religion, Marriage, and Family; Grand Rapids: Eerdmans, 2003), 268. Wilson, *Sentences of Pseudo-Phocylides*, 79 suggests a similar expansive use of "adultery" in early Judaism to refer to any sexual irregularity. For an analysis of the complexity of meaning inherent in μοιχεία/μοιχός, see Cynthia B. Patterson, *Family in Greek History* (Cambridge, Mass.: Harvard University Press, 1998), 114-25.

[111] Kirchhoff, *Sünde*, 35 notes that in non-Jewish and non-Christian Greek texts a πόρνος is typically a male prostitute. See also Knust, *Abandoned to Lust*, 33, 63, 75, 77.

[112] See BDAG s.v. πορνεία.

[113] Oropeza, *Paul and Apostasy*, 98.

ed precisely as a body. The crucifixion represents God's wisdom and the resurrection represents God's power. Both have to do with the embodied Lord. As the Lord's body is instrumental in God's wisdom and power, so too is the Christian's body crucial to the Lord and as God resurrected the Lord, so too will God resurrect the σῶμα of the believer. While the connection between the body of the believer and the Lord is established here through Analogy, this connection will receive fuller expression in Paul's next section of argumentation (6:15-17) where he compresses this vital relation of Analogy to Part-Whole and then, further, to Identity.

Figure 4: Conceptual Mega-Blend for 6:13-14

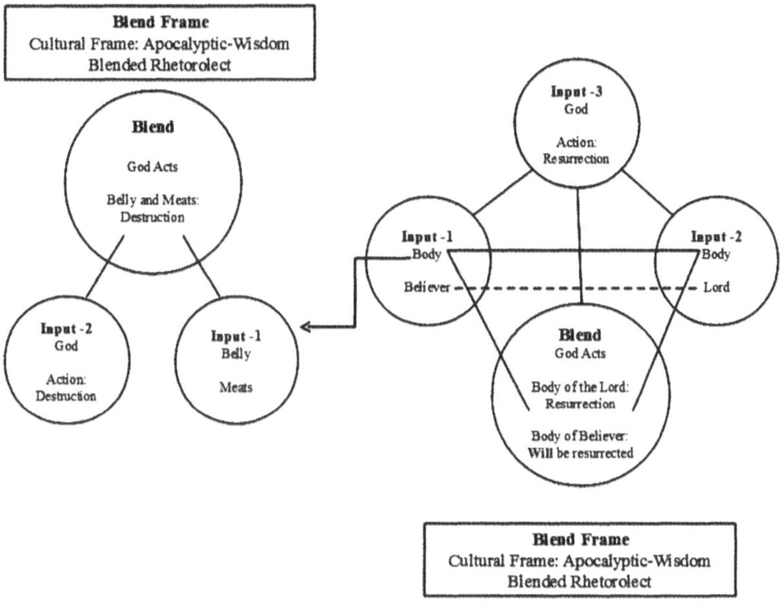

Member of Christ, Member of a Whore; Union with a Whore, Union with Christ (6:15-17): Wisdom-Priestly-Apocalyptic Blended Rhetorolect

In 6:15-17 Paul shows the Corinthians, using powerful rhetography, why the Christian body is incompatible with πορνεία. In these verses Paul continues to use the body as a shared frame in many of the mental spaces, but he also organizes his conceptual networks by deploying Characters who evoke meaningful background information— in this case the Characters of Christ/Lord (already introduced in 6:13) and the ever dangerous πόρνη.[114] By employing the Character of the πόρνη in vv.15-17 Paul creates a more rhetorically effective, even visceral, argument. The quick shift from the sin of πορνεία (6:13) to the agent of this sin, the πόρνη, serves Paul's rhetorical purposes by helping his argument achieve human scale. It does this by moving beyond the somewhat abstract idea of πορνεία to the concrete actor involved in this sexual sin.[115] According to Paul, the Corinthians must choose between Christ and the πόρνη. By simplifying the argument against πορνεία into a stark choice between two opposing and incompatible entities, Paul's teaching is conceptually easier to grasp and, thus, more rhetorically effective. In so doing, Paul's argument in these verses fulfills the properties of an optimal blend as articulated by Fauconnier: "human scale, only two objects, simple concrete action, clear-cut outcome."[116]

In the first part of this section (6:15), Paul discusses the bodies of the believers not as analogous to the body of Christ, but rather as members of the body of Christ. This rhetorical move is part of the overall progressive texture of the pericope in which Paul systematically compresses the conceptual relationship between the bodies of believers and Christ. Paul's argument in 6:15 compresses the vital relation of Analogy that he establishes in vv.13-14 into a Part-Whole relationship. Such rhetorical compression prepares for the second argument of this section (6:16-17) in which Paul further compresses the Part-Whole relationship achieved by the blend in v. 15 into the vital relation of Identity.[117] This final compression provides the major rationale for avoiding sex acts with a πόρνη.

Believers' Bodies as "Members" (6:15)

In 6:15 Paul asks, "Do you not know that [οὐκ οἴδατε ὅτι] your bodies are members of Christ?"[118] This question (the implied answer to which is yes) has the effect of stressing the connection of the believer's body to Christ, which Paul first raises in 6:13c[119] and which will be decisively confirmed in 6:17. The logic of Paul's argument in the first

---

[114] Recall the importance of characters in recruiting and organizing background information, see Fauconnier and Turner, *The Way We Think*, 251. See idem, 146 where they argue that "words and patterns into which words fit are triggers to the imagination. They are prompts we use to try to get one another to call up some of what we know and to work on it creatively to arrive at meaning." See also Martin, *Corinthian Body*, 176.

[115] See Kirchhoff, *Sünde*, 116; Fauconnier and Turner, *The Way We Think*, 312.

[116] Fauconnier, "Compression and Emergent Structure," 531.

[117] For the importance of Identity in human meaning construction see Fauconnier and Turner, *The Way We Think*, 6; idem, "Compression and Global Insight," 299.

[118] See 1 Cor 3:16; 5:6; 6:2, 3, 9, 15, 16, 19; 9:23, 24.

[119] See Weiß, *Der erste Korintherbrief*, 162.

rhetorical question of 6:15 stresses that the σῶμα of the believer is not for sexual immorality because it, not one's soul or spirit, is a member of Christ. Thus Paul compresses the relation of Analogy between the believer's body and Christ (vv. 13-14) into a Part-Whole relation.

In 6:15b, Paul poses a second rhetorical question: "Should I then take away[120] the members of Christ and make [them] members of a whore [πόρνη]?"[121] Paul supplies an immediate answer to this question: "By no means!" I translate the Greek term πόρνη as "whore" in 6:15-16 rather than as "prostitute" because I believe Paul is invoking the low social status of sexually marginal women rather than referring to a specific economic position certain women held.[122] I recognize the moralizing danger, so eloquently described by Renate Kirchhoff, that such a translation runs.[123] Kirchhoff herself concedes that the type of woman to which Paul refers is not necessarily a sex worker, but rather a woman whose sexual behavior is "against the rules" (regelwidrigen).[124] I choose the morally loaded English word "whore" because (pace Kirchhoff) I believe this translation lays bare for the English speaker the visceral power of Paul's graphic language in this pericope. To use Damasio's terminology, the whore functions as a "somatic marker" in Paul's argument.[125] Paul's rhetoric counts on a cultural revulsion in

---

[120] As Robertson and Plummer, *First Epistle to the Corinthians*, 125 and Fee, *First Epistle to the Corinthians*, 258 note, the participle means not simply "to take," but rather "to take away, remove." See BDAG s.v. αἴρω 3.

[121] See Robertson and Plummer, *First Epistle to the Corinthians*, 125: "It is impossible and unimportant to decide whether ποιήσω is deliberative subjunctive ('Am I to take away ... and make?') or future indicative ('Shall I take away' etc.). The two aorists would mark two aspects, simultaneous in effect, of one and the same act."

[122] See Tikva Frymer-Kensky, *Reading the Women of the Bible: A New Interpretation of Their Stories* (New York: Schocken Books, 2002), 270. For more on the economic position of prostitute see Thomas A.J. McGinn, *The Economy of Prostitution in the Roman World: A Study of Social History and the Brothel* (Ann Arbor: University of Michigan Press, 2004), ch. 2 (pp. 14-77); also Bettina Eva Stumpp, *Prostitution in der römische Antike* (2nd ed.; Antike in der Moderne; Berlin: Akademie Verlag, 1998), 230-47. Translating πόρνη as "prostitute" is the best option in the Apocalypse when it refers to the "great prostitute" (Rev 17:1) since Rev 17-18 provides an economic critique of empire. For a study of this economic critique as it relates to wisdom see Barbara R. Rossing, "City Visions, Feminine Figures and Economic Critique: A Sapiential *Topos* in the Apocalypse," in *Conflicted Boundaries in Wisdom and Apocalypticism* (ed. Bejamin G. Wright, III and Lawrence M. Mills; SBLSymS 35; Atlanta, Society of Biblical Literature, 2005), 181-96.

[123] See Kirchhoff, *Sünde*, 18-21. See Davidson, *Courtesans and Fishcakes*, 73 where he translates πόρνη as a "common whore."

[124] Kirchhoff, *Sünde*, 36: "eine Frau, die regelwidrigen Sexualverkehr hat." See also idem, 196 where Kirchhoff notes that while these women were not *necessarily* prostitutes, in practice non-slave owning men who had sex with women other than their wives most often engaged in this sexual behavior with sex workers. See Gaca, *Fornication*, 165-70.

[125] Damasio, *Descartes' Error*, 173.

bringing together Christ and a religiously "filthy" figure such as a whore.[126] As Dale Martin aptly notes, "The man who has sex with a prostitute is, in Paul's construction, Christ's 'member' entering the prostitute."[127] In the religious imagination of various sectors of Hellenistic Judaism the figure of the πόρνη is a malevolent sexual creature, but one who is not only or simply defined by the economic marker of "prostitute." Paul is drawing from a Jewish moral tradition in which the whore looms large as an appealing and dangerous temptation.[128] From non-Jewish Hellenistic culture Paul can also draw on the fairly standard practice of using the term πόρνη in invective.[129]

Conceptually, 6:15a is a network that contains two input spaces. Input-1 contains the elements "your bodies" and "Christ," while input-2 contains the element "members" and the implied element "body." The implied element of "body" is cognitively available to the hearer/reader of Paul's query due to what is known as a standard XYZ construction. This is more easily seen when the question is put into a statement format that the question prompts – "Your bodies are members of Christ."[130] As Fauconnier and Turner explain:

> In this construction – 'X be Y of Z' – X, Y, and Z are nouns or nounphrases. X and Z identify elements x and z in one input space, and Y identifies element y in a second input space. The copula *be* indicates that x and y are counterparts. And the understander must identify the two relevant domains and set up an implicit element w to be the counterpart of y.[131]

The correspondence of Paul's construction in 6:15a to this model is as follows: "Your bodies [x] are members [y] of Christ [z]." What is

---

[126] I am indebted to Mark D. Jordan for the connection between πορνεία/πόρνη and the conceptually powerful, yet ambiguous, term "filthy" as it is found in older English usage (personal communication). For more on disgust projected onto, and thus evoked by, the female whore, see Nussbaum, *Hiding from Humanity*, 137 (also 113).

[127] Martin, *Corinthian Body*, 176. Martin, like Kirchhoff, translates πόρνη as "prostitute."

[128] See J.J. Collins, *Jewish Wisdom*, 11.

[129] As McClure, *Courtesans at Table*, 10-11 notes is already the case in Greek writing of the archaic and classical periods, also idem, 53, 113. See also Leslie Kurke, *Coins, Bodies, Games, and Gold: The Politics of Meaning in Archaic Greece* (Princeton: Princeton University Press, 1999), 182: "The *pornē* had been a staple of blame poetry since Archilochos." The terms Archilochos uses to describe this type of woman, "even without their context, suggest the negative associations of the *pornē* – lewdness, pollution, the humiliating necessity of working for pay, and excessive commonality in the public sphere." See Knust, *Abandoned to Lust*, 48 where she notes "the importance of sexualized invective across genres, eras, and regions" in the rhetorical strategies of ancient Mediterranean cultures.

[130] See Fauconnier and Turner, *The Way We Think*, 139-59. Technically τὰ σώματα ὑμῶν is a blended space already, but in order to avoid infinite regress I will not discuss how this blend is formed.

[131] Fauconnier and Turner, *The Way We Think*, 144.

missing, and what the hearer/listener must supply, is the value for [w]. Arriving at the identity of [w] is fairly straightforward in this instance given the frame of the body that Paul began using in 6:13-14. The missing term to be supplied by the hearer/reader is thus "body."

Figure 5: Conceptual Network for 6:15a

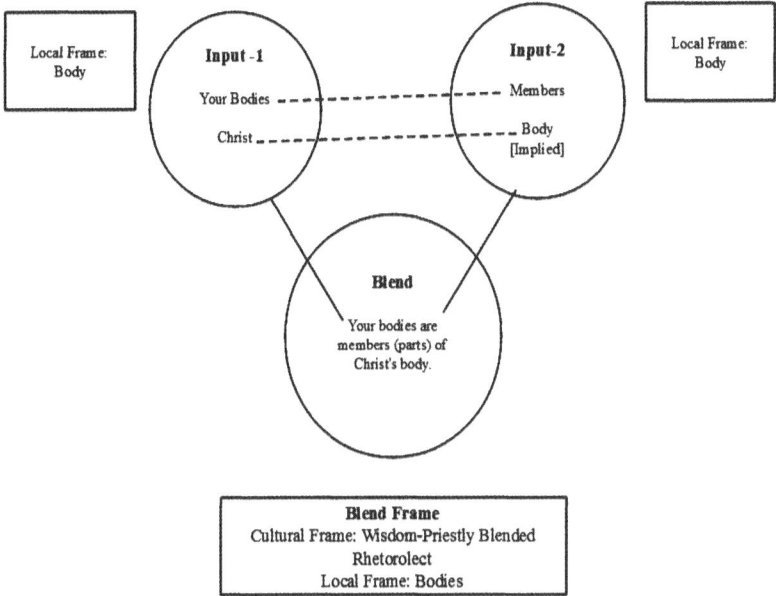

While the input spaces draw on the general local frame of the human body, Paul deploys Characters in this blend to further specify the meaning potential of the network. As Fauconnier and Turner note, "Frames give one basic way to organize a mental space. Character, Identity, and Ego give another."[132] The Character of Christ provides the organization and necessary background knowledge for input-1, while input-2 has no organizing Character. In the blend, the elements of input-1 (your bodies, Christ) get projected as values for the roles found in input-2 (members, body). The roles in input-2 have an inner-space Part-Whole relationship – bodies have parts. This vital relation is projected into the blend so the bodies of believers are now understood as a part of Christ.[133] Unlike either input space, the emergent structure created by this net-

---

[132] Fauconnier and Turner, *The Way We Think*, 255.
[133] Such a projection of a vital relationship from one input space into the blend is referred to as "borrowing for compression." Fauconnier and Turner, *The Way We Think*, 324. Paul will return to this blend in 1 Cor 12.

work is organized by a cultural frame. Paul's focus on knowledge [οὐκ οἴδατε] and the body in this blend ideally suits wisdom rhetorolect as described by Robbins.[134] However, the new emergent structure also draws upon resources found in priestly rhetorolect to make sense of believers as *members* of Christ's body. This Part-Whole relationship between the believer and Christ seems to be grounded in the cultic activity of baptism (1 Cor 1:1-16; 6:11; 15:29). In the blend, but not in either of the input spaces, wisdom rhetorolect hosts reasoning about the relationship between the believer and Christ that uses resources available in priestly rhetorolect. The emergent structure of this wisdom-priestly blend is crucial for Paul's argument in this pericope.

Figure 6: Conceptual Network for 6:15b

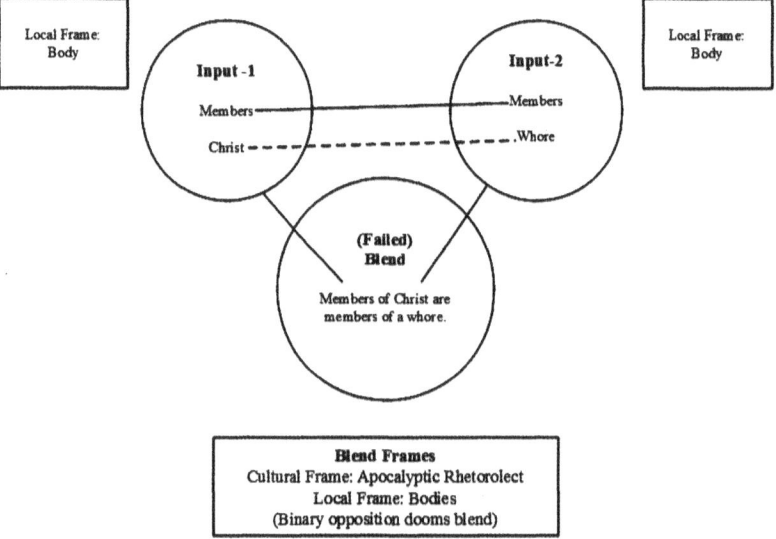

The emergent structure of the network created by 6:15a, where believers' bodies are conceptually identified as members of Christ's body, is used as an input in the next blend that Paul creates with the rhetorical question of 6:15b.[135] The emotional response required for this second question to be rhetorically effective means that the blend created in 6:15a needs to carry over. Paul does this lexically by referring to the "members of Christ" [τὰ μέλη τοῦ Χριστοῦ]. Although the verb Paul uses here [αἴρω] means "to take away, remove," the fact that he is still

---

[134] Robbins, *Invention*, 1:192.

[135] This re-use of an effective blend as an input space in another blending network is known as "recursion" in conceptual integration theory. Fauconnier and Turner, *The Way We Think*, 334-36.

referring to the blend of believers-as-members suggests that the mere act of taking away a member from Christ's body does not destroy Christ's ownership of that member. The connection between this severed member and Christ remains intact in the conceptual network created by 6:15b.

As with the previous network, the specific meaning potential of the input spaces in the conceptual network of 6:15b is organized by different Characters with known attributes. Within each input space of this conceptual network there is a Part-Whole relationship between the elements – an inner-space Part-Whole relation. In the blend the members of input-1 and the members of input-2 are the same. Thus a cross-space mapping between the two input spaces (each have "members") is compressed into the vital relation of Identity in the blend.[136] The blend pushes the hearer/reader to map this same compression to Identity onto the other elements of the input spaces based on the Topology and Integration principles. These other elements happen to be Characters with known attributes: Christ and the whore.[137]

The cultural knowledge available about the two Characters who organize the input spaces in this network resists their compression into a relationship of Identity in the blend.[138] The knowledge of the low status of whores in both Judaism and the non-Jewish Hellenistic world coupled with the high status awarded to the risen Christ in the nascent Christian culture in Corinth ensures that such a compression will fail and the blend along with it.[139] Martin notes that "The Christian man penetrating a prostitute constitutes coitus between two beings of such different ontological status that Paul can hardly contemplate the consequences."[140] It is this apocalyptic clash of two such ontologically different, and opposed, characters that dooms the blend. Yet it is precisely where the blend itself breaks down that *serves* Paul's argumentative goals.[141] Again, note that it is only out of the emergent structure prompted by the blend, and not in the input spaces themselves, where

---

[136] Fauconnier and Turner, *The Way We Think*, 95.

[137] Fauconnier and Turner, *The Way We Think*, 253 note how the term "prostitute" can be a frame or a character: "It can be construed as a frame that anybody can fall into, or as a frame with character implications: Someone who can fit into it aptly must have a certain character."

[138] See Fauconnier and Turner, *The Way We Think*, 330: "We often reject invitations to fuse two elements ..."

[139] See McClure, *Courtesans at Table*, 11: "Clearly, porne is what a speaker resorts to when he wants to insult a woman ..."

[140] Martin, *Corinthian Body*, 177.

[141] On the usefulness of failed blends in *reductio ad absurdum* arguments, see Fauconnier and Turner, *The Way We Think*, 233-36. The blend fails, in part, because the governing principle of Integration is resisted (idem, 328-29).

apocalyptic rhetorolect recruits background information about the incompatible nature of the characters of Christ and the whore. It is the integration resources available in this rhetorolect, most notably the idea of ontological binary oppositions, that ensure the blend will not function. As if to remove any doubt about the failure of the blend created by 6:15b, Paul answers his own rhetorical question with what Kirchhoff describes as "a cry of full pathos: μὴ γένοιτο."[142]

In 6:15 Paul's didactic discourse creates two conceptual networks. In these networks the specific meaning potential of the inputs spaces are organized by Characters whose attributes are well known. Out of the emergent structures created by these networks, however, the organizing cultural frames of wisdom, priestly, and apocalyptic rhetorolects provide integration resources necessary for the blends to serve Paul's rhetorical goals. In 6:15a wisdom provides the host environment for the use of priestly rhetorolect in the emergent structure that compresses the relation between the believer and Christ from Analogy to Part-Whole. In 6:15b Paul brings in the character of the πόρνη to create a blend in which she stands in binary opposition to Christ. The very apocalyptic rhetorolect that organizes such a binary worldview dooms the blend – one cannot be a member of both Christ and the whore. It is the failure of this blend, however, that moves Paul's argument forward.

"Clinging" Leads to Union (6:16-17)
In vv. 16-17 Paul once again relies on rhetography that produces an emotional response rather than on strict reasoned statements.[143] In these verses Paul asks another rhetorical question, for which he recites Gen 2:24 as a proof text for the implied affirmative answer. Building off of the failed blend in 6:15b, Paul asks, "Do you not know that the one who clings [ὁ κολλώμενος] to the whore is one body [with her]? For, [as] it says, 'The two will be [made] into one flesh.' But the one who clings [ὁ δὲ κολλώμενος] to the Lord is one spirit [with him]." Paul's argument compresses the vital relation between the believer and the whore from Part-Whole (6:15) into Identity. He uses a biblical quotation as a proof text for this compression. Paul likewise compresses the relation between the believer and Christ. Progressively, Paul's teaching has moved the believer and Christ closer together through the relations

---

[142] Kirchhoff, *Sünde*, 113. On this same page she refers to what I am calling a breakdown of blending as an oxymoron.

[143] Recall Slingerland from Chapter 1: "the primary purpose of employing a metaphoric blend to achieve human scale is not to help us intellectually *apprehend* a situation, but rather to help us to know how to *feel* about it" (*What Science Offers the Humanities*, 185). For the importance of emotion in blends, see Coulson, *Semantic Leaps*, 200-210. For the importance of embodiment in understanding emotion, see Gibbs, *Embodiment and Cognitive Science*, 243.

of Analogy (6:13-14), then Part-Whole (6:15), and now into Identity (6:17). However, Paul seems to shift focus when he makes the final compression of believer and Christ for, unlike the somatic union experienced with the whore, the believer and the Lord are "one spirit" [ἕν πνεῦμα (6:17)].[144] While this might seem to work against Paul's overall argumentative goal, namely that the body is important, the shift from body to spirit has a progressive argumentative function and can be explained on conceptual grounds based on Paul's lexical choices.[145] I will explain this lexical shift below.

Figure 7: Conceptual Network for 6:16

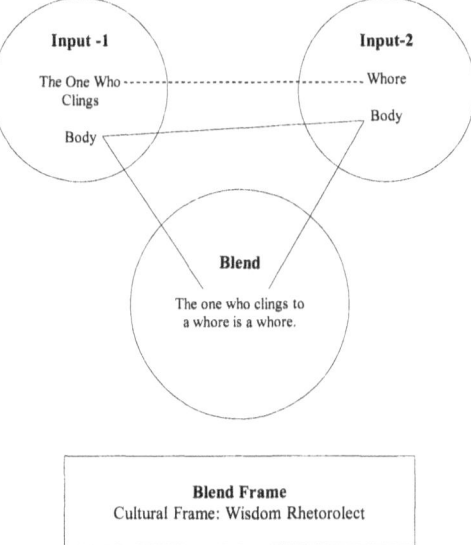

The elements in v. 16 and the elements in v. 17 each function as separate blends that combine into a more complex conceptual network. In v. 16, input-1 contains a person identified by his action, namely clinging, and his body. Input-2 contains the whore and her body. These input spaces are, once again, organized by the general local frame of the body. Here, as in 6:15, the whore functions as a Character who organizes her input space.

The rhetorical question of 6:16 compresses the cross-space mapping

---

[144] See Guy Williams, *The Spirit World in the Letters of Paul the Apostle: A Critical Examination of the Role of Spiritual Beings in The Authentic Pauline Epistles* (FRLANT 231; Göttingen: Vandenhoeck & Ruprecht, 2009), 286.

[145] The shift from body to spirit here may also have provided some scribes with the authorization for the addition to 6:20 that is found in many manuscripts: και εν πνευματι υμων, ατινα εστιν του θεου. See the apparatus in NA[27] for details.

of the element "body" found in each input space into Identity in the blend (hence, ἓν σῶμα). The Topology and Integration principles also push the other elements from each input space, "the one who clings" and the whore, into a relation of Identity. Unlike in 6:15, here the blend works: "the one who clings" and the whore, through the identity of their bodies, merge into the same Identity themselves. Since input-1 is not more specifically organized beyond the common local frame of the body, the Character from input-2, the whore, and all her attendant attributes organizes the blend. "The one who clings" thus inherits all of her attributes. This blend confirms Guilia Sissa's assertion that in the sexual ideology of the ancient Mediterranean, "your sexual body is yourself."[146] The recitation of Gen 2:24 simply reinforces this network by re-creating a similar blend while providing an authoritative source to give the conceptual network Paul has created scriptural legitimacy.[147] Based on the antithetical nature of the whore when compared to Christ in 6:15 and the cultural revulsion Hellenistic Jewish writings exhibits to such a character, this blend has a negative valence.

Paul is not alone in his negative assessment of men who "cling" to sexually marginal women. Using language similar to that used in 1 Cor 6:16, Sirach 19:2 teaches that "the one who clings to whores [ὁ κολλώμενος πόρναις] is reckless."[148] This negative valence, it is important to note, is created by the emergent structure created by the blend and is possible because the blend recruits the integration resources readily available in wisdom rhetorolect. As I noted in Chapter 3, concern over the dangers of consorting with a πόρνη is a recurring theme in wisdom texts and the negative assessment of such congress, like that found in Sirach, permeates the Jewish wisdom tradition.[149] Wisdom rhetorolect effectively recruits the background information necessary to fit the blend of 6:16 into its rhetorical context and provides it with the rhetorical power to move Paul's teaching forward.

Paul's discourse creates a similar network in v. 17. As in v. 16 there are two input spaces: input-1 contains "the one who clings" and his spirit and input-2 contains the Lord and his spirit.

---

[146] Sissa, "Sexual Bodybuilding," 164.

[147] Albeit one less specific – "the two," instead of naming specific characters.

[148] The context of Sir 19:2 makes the translation of πόρναις as "prostitutes" a viable option based on the economic concerns of 19:1. 19:3, however, signals that more than economic stability is in view, thus I have opted for the translation, as in 1 Cor 6:15-16, of "whores."

[149] See Crenshaw, *Wisdom*, 14: "The wise ever tired of discussing the dangers of sexual license."

Figure 8: Conceptual Network for 6:17

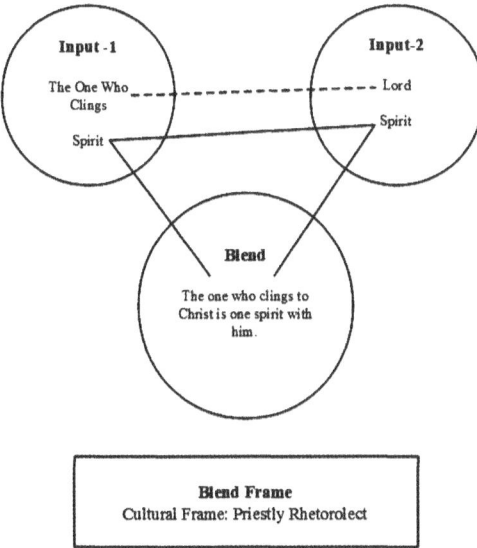

As in the previous verse, the text of 6:17 compresses the cross-space mapping of the element "spirit" in each input space into Identity in the blend (hence the ἕν πνεῦμα). Likewise, the undefined "one who clings" and the Character Christ mimic this compression to Identity through the same principles as above, namely Topology and Integration. As in v. 16, "the one who clings" is imbued with the attributes of the Character with whom he is blended, namely the Lord. While this sounds surprising, this is the very thing that serves Paul's didactic rhetorical goals and completes the argumentative progression, from Analogy to Identity, begun in 6:13.

Like the Part-Whole relation between the body of the believer and the body of Christ (6:15a), the relation of Identity in the blend between the spirit of the "one who clings" and Christ invites the resources of priestly rhetorolect into the blend. As seen above, this organizing cultural frame exists in the emergent structure of the blend. The union of πνεῦμα between the believer and the Lord that the blend creates draws from the resources available in priestly rhetorolect to make sense of this special relationship the believer has with the Lord. In the context of Paul's argument, 6:17 sets the believer off from the surrounding world (cf. 1 Cor 5:9-10) for a special relationship with the Lord. This reasoning activates the resources of priestly rhetorolect.

In 6:16, Paul keeps the focus trained on the whore and the results of having sexual intercourse with her.[150] This didactic treatment of the dire consequences of sex with a πόρνη is a characteristic of the resources found in wisdom rhetorolect. The conceptual network Paul creates in 6:17, where he teaches about the pneumatic unity of the believer and the Lord, relies on priestly rhetorolect. It is when the conceptual networks of 6:16-17 are read together that apocalyptic rhetorolect arises from Paul's teaching via the new emergent structure generated by the blending of these networks.

Figure 9: Conceptual Network for the Mega-Blend in 6:16-17

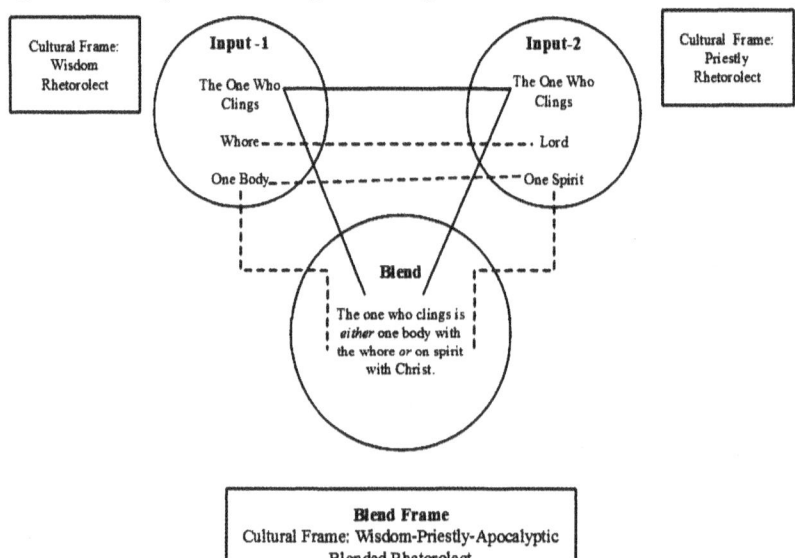

Note that apocalyptic rhetorolect does not exist in either input space. It only emerges from the mega-blend of 6:16-17 that contrasts the πόρνη with the Lord. In input-1 wisdom rhetorolect and the Character of the whore help organize the space, whereas priestly rhetorolect and the Character of Christ do the same for input-2. Paul has already established that these two Characters cannot occupy the same space (6:15) and thus the vital relations between them resist compression in this blend. This resistance reverberates throughout the network based on the Topology principle. Once again Paul has set up a blend that maintains the Topology of the inputs, but to the complete detriment of the Integration principle. The failure of the blend to achieve a complete Integration of all the elements from both input spaces serves

---

[150] The whore comprises the middle section of Paul's chiastic argument in 6:15-17: Christ, whore: whore, Christ. See Fee, *First Epistle to the Corinthians*, 257.

Paul's rhetoric. Thus while "the one who clings" from each input space is compressed to Identity in the blend via cross-space mapping, in order for the blend to function at all selective projection demands that *either* the whore and her body (input-1) *or* Christ and his spirit (input-2) get projected into the blend. As he does in 6:13-14, Paul is graphically describing two apocalyptic realities here in 6:16-17. One is either one body with a whore, or one is one spirit with Christ and the whorish body, as Paul teaches in 6:13b, will be destroyed.

In order to explore the meaning of the emergent structures Paul's discourse creates in 6:16-17 it is helpful to examine more fully the background information meaning aware hearers/readers could activate when presented with these conceptual networks. As noted, Paul uses the verb κολλάω to describe the interaction with the whore and with Christ.[151] In all likelihood this lexical choice is grounded in the LXX context of Gen 2:24. The Genesis text describes how a man will leave his mother and father "and will cling to his wife" [καὶ προσκολληθήσεται πρὸς τὴν γυναῖκα αὐτοῦ].[152] In the Greek speaking Jewish literary tradition, this verb has a wide semantic range. In Deut 6:13, 10:20; 4 Kgdms 18:6; and Sir 2:3, for example, it describes "clinging to God," a human-scale metaphor describing loyalty to God. In 2 Kgdms 20:2 the verb functions similarly in that it describes those of Judah who are loyal to David. Jeremiah also uses it in the graphic image of loincloths clinging to the loins. Although the verb is literal in this instance, the sign-act itself functions as a metaphor for Judah and Israel clinging to God (Jer 13:11). It can also, as in 1 Cor 6:16 and in Gen 2:24, have sexual connotations evoking the coupling of human bodies.

From out of the rich semantic tradition of κολλάω (metaphoric and literal) in Jewish texts, I maintain that Paul's wise teaching further evokes a story line from Jewish tradition regarding King Solomon. The character of Solomon provides crucial background information about "the one who clings" [ὁ κολλώμενος] to the whore in the mega-blend

---

[151] For an understanding of the verb κολλάω in economic terms, see S.E. Porter, "How Should ΚΟΛΛΩΜΕΝΟΣ in 1 Cor 6,16.17 be Translated?" *ETL* 67 (1991): 105-106.

[152] Note, however, that LXX Gen 2:24 uses a compound form of the verb, προσκολλάω, along with the preposition πρός. When Gen 2:24 is quoted in Matthew, the uncompounded form κολλάω plus the dative is used (as Paul does in 6:16), although many MSS, most notably Sinaiticus, read the LXX compound form in Matt 19:5. 1 Esdras 4:20 also uses the uncompounded form of the verb, but it does use πρός, in its paraphrase of Gen 2:24. Thus Paul's use of the uncompounded verb without the preposition could stem from a traditional recitation of Gen 2:24 as he and others know it. See Rosner, *Paul, Scripture and Ethics*, 131-32.

of vv. 16-17 (input-1). As noted in Chapter 3, although Solomon was the wisest king on the earth, he also had a weakness for women. In addition to being wise, he is described as being a φιλογύναιος (3 Kgdms 11:1) – a lover of women. Solomon took "strange women" [γυναῖκας ἀλλοτρίας], the daughters of foreign kings, for his brides (3 Kgdms 11:1; cf. Prov 5:20; 7:5; 9:18b-c). This resulted in Solomon's disastrously unwise decision to worship the gods of his foreign wives. The text explains that Solomon was led astray religiously because he "clung" [ἐκολλήθη] to these women (3 Kgdms 11:2). Solomon's sexual clinging to his foreign wives leads to actions that damage his relationship with God. Solomon clung to his wives instead of clinging to the God of his father (3 Kgdms 11:4).

In the Hellenistic period, Ben Sira teaches that because Solomon "bent [his] flanks for women" [παρανέκλινας τὰς λαγόνας σου γυναιξίν][153] he became enslaved to his body through the sexual allure of those women (Sir 47:19a). Solomon turned away from the worship of the God of his father and turned towards his foreign wives. Solomon's enslavement to these wives through his body (Sir 47:19b) leads to God's wrath [ὀργή] being visited upon Solomon's descendants (Sir 47:20). Thus, although Ben Sira does not employ the verb κολλάω in his epitome of the Solomon story, his argument focuses on the physical nature of Solomon's sins and thereby evokes a similar conceptual field. Josephus, another Hellenistic Jewish writer, also mourns Solomon's pursuit of pleasure through his sexual body. Though Solomon was "the most illustrious of all kings and most beloved by God," Josephus describes how he "became madly enamoured of women and indulged in excess of passion" [εἰς δὲ γυναῖκας ἐκμανεὶς καὶ τὴν τῶν ἀφροδισίων ἀκρασίαν] (A.J. 8.190-91 [Thackeray and Marcus, LCL]). In the pursuit of "irrational pleasure" [ἡδονὴν ἀλόγιστον] (A.J. 8.193), Solomon deserted the customs of his father in order to "gratify his wives and his passion for them" [ταῖς γυναιξὶ καὶ τῷ πρὸς αὐτὰς ἔρωτι χαριζόμενος] (A.J. 8.192 [Thackeray and Marcus, LCL]). In order to gratify himself sexually, Solomon indulges the religious desires of his foreign wives by participating in the worship of their gods. Although neither Ben Sira nor Josephus employ the lexical item κολλάω, their treatment of Solomon unpacks how the physical attachment Solomon experienced for his foreign wives caused him to turn away from the proper worship of the God of Israel. Clinging to his foreign wives, Solomon was unable to cling to his God.

The theme of enslavement to religiously dangerous women is also important for Paul's recitation of Gen 2:24 in its reconfigured envi-

---

[153] Following NETS. See LSJ s.v. παρεγκλίνω where "π.τὰς λαγόνας γυναιξί" is translated as "*lay beside* or *by*."

ronment of 1 Cor 6:16 (cf. Sir 47:19b).[154] Notably Paul does *not* recite this Genesis quotation when he teaches about the duties and obligations of the partners in a lifelong monogamous heterosexual union. Instead, he employs it when describing sexual intercourse with a πόρνη. For Paul, it is the union of bodies in the act of coitus that seems to stimulate the identification of man and woman as one body/flesh.[155] Paul does not see the quotation primarily describing a man and a woman about to marry, but rather as explaining the unifying nature intrinsic in the act of intercourse as it was constructed at creation. The negative valance Paul's argument gives to his reconfigured recitation of Gen 2:24 is not unique to Paul, but it may have had circulation in Jewish moral teaching of the first century.

An example of a negative interpretation of Gen 2:24 is found in Philo's *Allegorical Interpretation of Genesis*. Recall that Philo reads this verse allegorically to show what has gone wrong with the original creation of the mind in Genesis 1 (*Leg.* 1.21).[156] According to Philo, Gen 2:24 allegorically demonstrates that the superior element of creation, man/mind, clings to the inferior element, woman/sense-perception, and thereby becomes her slave [αὐτῇ δουλωθῇ]. Philo reads the action of the man leaving his father and mother as the mind leaving behind God, the father of everything, and God's virtue and wisdom [τὴν ἀρετὴν καὶ σοφίαν τοῦ θεοῦ], the mother of all. By leaving its father and mother, the mind becomes one flesh [μία σάρξ] with sense-perception, the two becoming ἕν πάθος. Thus, when the man clings to his wife, the Scripture is allegorically teaching that the mind has become a lover of passions [φιλοπαθές] instead of a lover of God [φιλόθεος] (*Leg.* 2.49-50).[157]

Although Philo's allegorical interpretation of this passage is not found in Paul, I would argue that the theme of enslavement that Philo employs is echoed in Paul's argument in 6:12-20, which begins with a reflection on the proper use of freedom and Paul's contention that he will not be mastered by anything (6:12cd) and ends with Paul reminding the Corinthians that they have been purchased by another (6:19b-20a). While Paul is concerned with the body, and not some asomatic νοῦς, he does contrast two types of bodies: the one ruled by the appe-

---

[154] See Robbins, *Tapestry*, 107; idem, *Exploring*, 50 for a discussion of reconfiguration. See Kirchhoff, *Sünde*, 158-76 for her exposition of the reconfiguration of Gen 2:24 in 1 Cor 6:16.

[155] In this instance it appears that Paul's ἕν σῶμα is equivalent to Genesis's μία σάρξ. See Schrage, *Der erste Brief an die Korinther* 2:27. But note Kirchhoff, *Sünde*, 172-76.

[156] See Loader, *Septuagint, Sexuality, and the New Testament*, 67-68. See Chapter 3 above.

[157] See also Philo, *Spec.* 3.9 especially in light of the tradition of Solomon.

tites united to the whore and the one destined for resurrection pneumatically united to Christ. Paul employs Gen 2:24 in 1 Cor 6:16 as a proof text for a situation that cuts one off from God's plan of salvation, which is analogous to Philo's use of it to describe the mind being cut off from God's original plan of creation.

Paul's audience would not necessarily need to know the Jewish scriptural traditions of Solomon or Jewish interpretive uses of these traditions to derive benefit from his teaching, however. Not only does a sex act between a believer and a sexually marginal woman join a member of Christ to such a low status and religiously impure figure, but the one who engages in this sex act *himself* becomes identified with the whore according to Paul's conceptual blend in 6:16, becoming, in effect, a whore himself. Such an argument would strike at the heart of Greek and Roman male self-conception. In ancient Athens a man who "whored" himself out lost his citizen status.[158] Laura McClure writes, about ancient Athens, that "[i]n addition to charges of citizen prostitution, the accusation of fraternizing with a porne or hetaera comprised a major portion of inflammatory abuse in fourth-century oratory."[159] She also notes that being a whore, more specifically a prostitute, was linguistically marked as an activity that males could engage in, but that it represented a *state of being* for women.[160] This can be seen in Aeschines' speech against Timarchus where he describes his opponent as one who has the body of man, but who is nevertheless guilty of the "sins of a woman" because he prostituted himself out to other men, (*Tim.* 185 [Adams, LCL]).[161] In the words of James Davidson, Aeschines paints his opponent as one who is "whorish as well as a whore."[162] Identification with a πόρνη would thus alter a man's status dramatically.

The fact that having sex with women considered πόρναι was not censured in non-Jewish Hellenistic culture to the degree that it was in Judaism and Christianity is beside the point given the way Paul's argu-

---

[158] Davidson, *Courtesans and Fishcakes*, 253; K.J. Dover, "Classical Greek Attitudes to Sexual Behavior," in *Sexuality and Gender in the Classical World: Readings and Sources* (ed. Laura K. McClure; Oxford, 2002), 27; Knust, *Abandoned to Lust*, 35; Sissa, "Sexual Bodybuilding," 153-54.

[159] McClure, *Courtesans at Table*, 16

[160] McClure, *Courtesans at Table*, 17. While the evidence McClure cites refers to classical Athens rather than a Roman colony in the Hellenistic period, I believe her insights are instructive for Paul's argument as I discuss below.

[161] τὸν ἄνδρα μὲν καὶ ἄρρενα τὸ σῶμα, γυναικεῖα δὲ ἁμαρτήματα ἡμαρτηκότα.

[162] Davidson, *Courtesans and Fishcakes*, 256. Earlier on the same page, Davidson notes: "In Aeschines' argument both prostitution and dissipation are merely side-effects of Timarchus' desperate attempts to satisfy other desires... Aeschinus emphasizes that Timarchus was simply careless with his body." See also Patterson, *Family in Greek History*, 161-62.

ment functions.[163] Paul's rhetography argues that the man who has sex with a whore *is* a whore. And in the ancient Mediterranean world, in Jennifer Wright Knust's words, "for a man to be called a 'prostitute' was a particularly sharp insult."[164] No matter how tacitly certain segments of Hellenistic and Roman cultures might have accepted the sex *acts* between free men and πόρναι, the πόρναι themselves were objects of derision. McClure notes that even when public brothels are being praised, the women themselves are denigrated for their public availability as a fragment from Philemon's *Adelphoi*, found in the compendium of Athenaeus, demonstrates:

> The women stand naked that you are not deceived.
> Look at everything.
> Maybe you are not feeling well. You have
> some sort of pain. Why? The door is open.
> One obol. Hop in. There is no coyness,
> no idle talk, nor does she snatch herself away.
> But straightaway, as you wish, in whatever way you wish.
> You come out. Tell her to go to hell [οἰμώζειν λέγ'].
> She is a stranger [ἀλλοτρία] to you.[165]

Such derision of women whose sexual activity exists in the public sphere is further seen in classical Greek vase painting. Leslie Kurke examines a sixth-century BCE kylix by the "Pedieus Painter" that depicts ribald sympotic sex scenes between men and women. In these scenes multiple men penetrate the women in multiple orifices. Kurke notes that on this kylix "all the women are portrayed in animal-like postures, squatting on all fours, their heads well below those of their male partners." Further, while the men are portrayed as elegantly slim, "the females have large, sagging bodies, in which the contours of

---

[163] See Knust, *Abandoned to Lust*, 33. But see, e.g., idem, 45 (where she discusses the moral teaching of Musonius Rufus); Plutarch, *Conj. praec.* 42, 44.

[164] Knust, *Abandoned to Lust*, 83.

[165] Athenaeus, *Deipn.* 13.569e-f (= Philemon, *Adelphoi*, F3 KA), as cited and translated by McClure, *Courtesans at Table*, 113; also idem, 117 on Athenaeus, *Deipn.* 13.570c-d. See Davidson, *Courtesans and Fishcakes*, 117 who notes the "comic descriptions of the brothel as a *kinētērion*, a 'fuck-factory' as if it were a workshop producing sexual commodities." On the use of κινῶ see David Bain, "Six Greek Verbs of Sexual Congress (βινῶ, κινῶ, πυγίζω, ληκῶ, οἴφω, λαικάζω)," *Classical Quarterly* 41 (1991): 63-67. Sarah B. Pomeroy, *Goddesses, Whores, Wives, and Slaves: Women in Classical Antiquity* (New York: Schocken Books, 1975), 139 claims that "the picture we have of the lives of prostitutes in the Hellenistic Age has been unduly embellished and enhanced by their presentation as characters in New Comedy." She notes the much grimmer reality.

breasts and buttocks are grotesquely exaggerated."[166] While this evidence cited by McClure and Kurke comes from material produced centuries before Paul is writing, I argue that it paints a sharp picture of the longevity of the culturally low status of sexually marginal women that continued into the Hellenistic period of the early Roman Empire.[167] This enduring and widely available cultural image of the "filthy" sexually marginal woman gives Paul's argument, based on the vital relation of Identity between a man and a whore, emotional traction in the wider Hellenistic world.[168]

In 6:17 Paul moves away from his negative teaching regarding the πόρνη and shifts his focus to the believer's identification with the Lord. Yet when Paul makes this rhetorical move he seems to shift abruptly from a concern with bodies to focus on a spiritual union with Christ. Margaret Mitchell writes that with a "nice *double entendre* Paul exhorts the Corinthians to cleave to the Lord ... instead of cleaving (sexually) with the prostitute."[169] Paul's play on the multiple meanings of the verb κολλάω, necessitating a parenthetical explanation by Mitchell, can partially explain his shift from σῶμα to πνεῦμα when moving from the union with the whore to union with Christ. Johannes Weiß was of the opinion that the picture (*Bild*) Paul's word play creates here is "very bold and, at any rate, not careful."[170] Using the insights from conceptual blending, I argue that Paul's language, while definitely bold, was more careful than Weiß gave him credit for.

As repeatedly noted, one of the central tenets of conceptual integration theory is that meaning is context dependent. Words are meaningful, not solely because of some intrinsic lexical essence, but rather by what conceptual blends they prompt in context.[171] In 6:16, Paul uses the verb κολλάω in a sexual sense, much like in the story of Solomon

---

[166] Kurke, *Coins, Bodies, Games, and Gold*, 209-11 describing Louvre, inv. no. G 13 (the quotations are from p. 211). See also Eva C. Keuls, *The Reign of the Phallus: Sexual Politics in Ancient Athens* (New York: Harper & Row, 1985), ch. 6 (pp. 153-86).

[167] Notably because the Philemon fragment McClure cites is found in the second century CE Hellenistic compendium of Athenaeus. See Knust, *Abandoned to Lust*, 48 for cultural conservatism when it comes to sexual invective. Also see Elaine Fantham et al., *Women in the Classical World: Image and Text* (New York: Oxford University Press, 1994), ch. 11 (pp. 294-329) on the moralizing legislation of Augustus. Also Huber, *Like a Bride Adorned*,116-20; Bruce W. Winter, *Roman Wives, Roman Widows: The Appearance of New Women in the Pauline Communities* (Grand Rapids: Eerdmans, 2003), ch. 3 (pp. 39-58).

[168] See Davidson, *Courtesans and Fishcakes*, 180: "Prostitutes and banquet-lovers are both called 'cisterns,' because they absorb what flows into them without distinction." See also idem, 85.

[169] Mitchell, *Paul and the Rhetoric of Reconciliation*, 234.

[170] Weiß, *Der erste Korintherbrief*, 164: "sehr kühn und jedenfalls nicht vorsichtig."

[171] See Fauconnier and Turner, *The Way We Think*, 142-43. "'Polysemy' – the fact that a single word seems to have 'many meanings' – is a very common phenomenon, a standard by-product of conceptual blending, but noticed in only a fraction of cases" (p. 143).

in 3 Kingdoms. In 6:17 Paul does make a *"double entendre,"* as Mitchell notes, in which the conceptual integration at work in that verse, while relying on the similarity of the verb κολλάω to shake the hearer/reader, does not project a sexual meaning into the blend, but rather a religious one. Paul's use of πνεῦμα to describe the type of union that exists between the believer and Christ increases the likelihood that the blend will function with the correct projections carefully selected. Priestly rhetorolect emerges from 6:17, prompted by Paul's blend of Identity between the believer and the Lord via the spirit, and allows the religious context to be projected rather than the sexual.[172] Far from being incautious, Paul's lexical choice of πνεῦμα in 6:17 puts pressure on the blend by prompting the hearer/reader to run Paul's daring use of images correctly instead of running the blend in such a way that founders on the shores of misunderstanding.

Paul's use of πνεῦμα when making his final compression to Identity between the believer and Christ does not, however, leave concern for body behind.[173] Dale Martin notes how Paul's assertion that the believer and Christ are "one spirit" actually intensifies the somatic relation between the believer and Christ: "The pneumatic union between the body of the Christian man and the body of Christ (6:17) is what identifies the Christian man. The man's body and Christ's body share the same pneuma; the man's body is therefore an appendage of Christ's body, totally dependent on the pneumatic life-force of the larger body for its existence."[174] Thus, though the union between the body of "the one who clings" and the Lord operates on a pneumatic level, whereas the union between "the one who clings" and the whore is somatic, both still deal with the body of the believer. As Schrage notes, "only with somatic embodiment does pneumatic unity with Christ also exist."[175] The somatic union with the whore prohibits the pneumatic union between "the one who clings" and Christ. The overall thrust of vv. 16-17, then, is that what one does with one's body affects one's relationship with the Lord.

---

[172] Moreover, note that the resurrected body (cf. 6:14) will be described by Paul as a "spiritual body" [σῶμα πνευματικόν] in 15:44.

[173] See esp. Martin, *Corinthian Body*, ch. 1 (pp. 3-37) where he cautions against the conceptual anachronism of reading ontological Cartesian dualism back into ancient discourse (esp. p. 15). Whatever one might think of Martin's treatment of 1 Corinthians in this book, his treatment of the conceptions of the body in antiquity is an important intellectual contribution.

[174] Martin, *Corinthian Body*, 176; also Kirchhoff, *Sünde*, 158.

[175] Schrage, *Der erste Brief an die Korinther*, 2:30: "nur bei somatischer Einverleibung auch eine pneumatische Einheit mit Christus vorliegt" [only with bodily incorporation is a pneumatic union with Christ also available].

Although Paul's discussion of pneumatic union with Christ has implications for somatic Christian behavior, the fact remains that in v. 17 Paul has shifted focus away from σῶμα, at least lexically. In the next, and final, section this part of his argument Paul connects his use of πνεῦμα with the body in a concrete fashion as his rhetography more explicitly evokes the resources of priestly rhetorolect, which arose from the emergent structure of the networks created in 6:15-17. The argument Paul makes about "the one who clings" being ἕν πνεῦμα with Christ *means*, according to his elaboration in vv.18-20, that the body is a temple in which God's holy spirit dwells.[176]

Temples, Slaves, and Glorifying God (6:18-20): Wisdom-Priestly Blended Rhetorolect

In 6:18-20 Paul's instruction reaches its goal for this section of his argument (cf. 10:14) when he writes: "Flee sexual immorality! Each sin that a person might commit is outside [ἐκτός] of the body, but the one who engages in sexual immorality sins against his own body [εἰς τὸ ἴδιον σῶμα ἁμαρτάνει]. Or do you not know that your body [τὸ σῶμα ὑμῶν] is a temple of the holy spirit within you, which you have from God, and that you are not your own? For you have been bought with a price; therefore glorify God in your body!"[177] Here Paul intensifies the use of elements from priestly rhetorolect within the host environment of his wisdom discourse. This is evidenced by his rhetographical use of temples, holiness, and cult to bring to a close his teaching that the believer must avoid using the sanctified body for πορνεία. Within this cultic rhetography, however, Paul also activates images of slavery to reinforce his argument that the Christian body is not for the Corinthians to do with as they please due to the fact that they have been purchased by God. According to Paul, πορνεία has particular significance because it is a special kind of sin that does something to destroy the integrity of the sanctified body. As Josephus, another Hellenistic Jew, writes in the context of explaining the prohibition of money made from sex work being used to pay for sacrifices in the house of the Lord (Deut 23:19): "no shame could be worse than the degradation of the body" [χείρων δ' οὐκ ἂν εἴη ἐπὶ τοῖς σώμασιν αἰσχύνης (*Ant.* 4.206; Thackeray, LCL)].[178]

---

[176] See Williams, *Spirit World*, 286.

[177] Cf. *T. Reu.* 5:5.

[178] Note that Josephus describes the πόρνη of Deut 23:19 as a γυναικὸς ἡταιρημένης. This demonstrates that McClure's claim that the same woman could be referred to both as a πόρνη and as an ἑταίρα in classical Athens (*Courtesans at Table*, 11) holds in Hellenistic Jewish writing as well.

Fleeing Πορνεία (6:18)

While Paul's command in 6:18a to flee πορνεία seems straightforward enough, it is important to note that this short command also represents a conceptual blend. This blend re-introduces the term πορνεία after Paul's focus on the πόρνη (6:15-17), yet it does so in a way that maintains human scale in Paul's didactic discourse. Instead of construing the sin of sexual immorality in some abstract way, in 6:18a Paul conceptualizes it as something or someone, most likely the πόρνη, that one can move away from spatially. Such a spatial metaphor seems as conceptually easy to grasp as personifying this sin by the Character of the πόρνη. The rhetography of fleeing that anchors Paul's command conserves the hard won human scale his previous blends have achieved.

Although Paul relies heavily on rhetography in 6:18, it is important to note that he uses images as a warrant to provide a rationale for the command to flee πορνεία.[179] This warrant, however, has been problematic for modern exegetes. The problem for interpreters has been explaining the difference between a sin[180] which is "outside of the body" [ἐκτὸς τοῦ σώματος] and sexual immorality which Paul argues is a sin "against one's own body" [εἰς τὸ ἴδιον σῶμα].[181] Bruce Fisk has created a helpful chart that maps out the history of interpretation of this verse and thus I will not rehearse this history here.[182] For our pur-

---

[179] For vv. 18b and 20a as rationales that support the premises of vv. 18a and 19 see Frederick J. Long, "From Epicheiremes to Exhortation: A Pauline Method for Moral Persuasion in 1 Thessalonians," in *Rhetoric, Ethic, and Moral Persuasion in Biblical Discourse: Essays from the 2002 Heidelberg Conference* (ed. Thomas H. Olbricht and Anders Eriksson; Emory Studies in Early Christianity 11; New York: T. & T. Clark, 2005), 180. See also Robbins, *Invention*, 1:17, 204.

[180] Here Paul uses ἁμάρτημα, which BDAG defines "as an individual act sin, transgression."

[181] See Robertson and Plummer, *First Epistle to the Corinthians*, 262. Martin, *Corinthian Body*, 178 argues that, although the preposition εἰς when coupled with the verb ἁμαρτάνω usually means "against," in this context it maintains a sense of "motion from the outside into something," the opposite of ἐκτός. This contention allows the following colorful interpretation: "... whereas in 6:16-17 Paul's rhetoric implied that sexual intercourse between the Christian man and the prostitute enacted sexual intercourse between Christ and the prostitute – in which case, Christ is sexually penetrating the evil cosmos – in 6:18 the roles are reversed: the man is fucked by sin, so Christ is fucked by the cosmos." Martin's analysis fails to take into account the entrenched nature of idioms in human understanding of language. See Fisk, "ΠΟΡΝΕΥΕΙΝ," 545: "Parallel uses of ἁμαρτάνειν εἰς elsewhere clarify the force of the preposition. The εἰς marks out the one *against whom* a sin is committed, the one violated by the sinner as it were." See n. 11 following this sentence where Fisk lays out the textual evidence. For the idea of sinning against one's own body see Aeschines, *Tim.* 22, 39, 94; cf. idem 31, 41, 87, 108, 116, 188.

[182] Fisk, "ΠΟΡΝΕΥΕΙΝ," 542-43. For the minority argument that 6:18b is yet another Corinthian slogan, see Murphy-O'Connor, "Corinthian Slogans," 391-96.

poses, we can use the tools of conceptual integration theory to map the difficult rhetography used in this verse:

Figure 10: Conceptual Network for 6:18

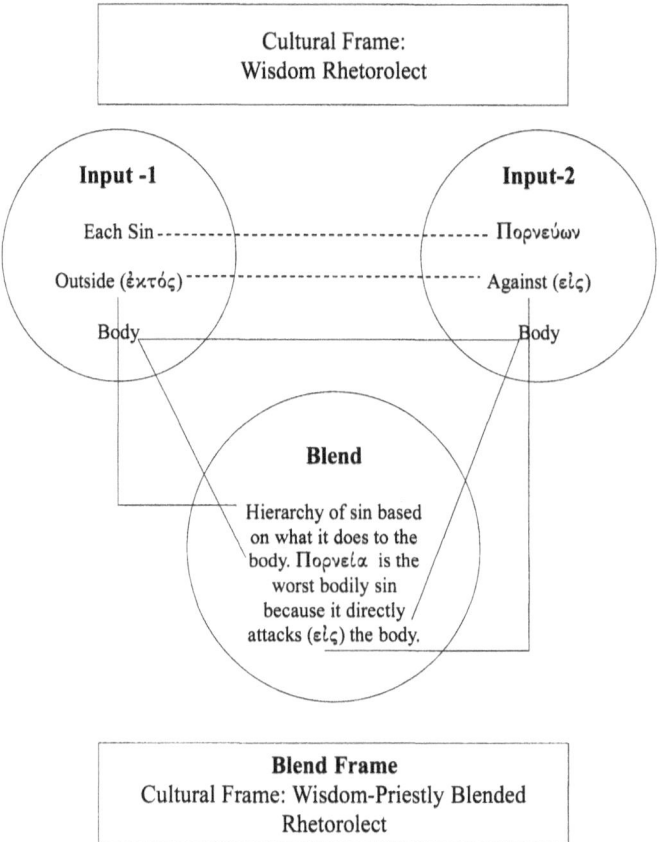

This conceptual network only has rhetorical traction because of the progressive texture of Paul's arguments in 6:13-17 that teach the importance of the sanctified Christian body. This progressive texture, as noted, compresses the relation between believer and Christ towards Identity, thus Fisk's contention that "for Paul, because sexual sin is uniquely body-joining, it is uniquely body-defiling" makes conceptual sense.[183] The input spaces seem to be loosely organized by wisdom

---

[183] Fisk, "ΠΟΡΝΕΥΕΙΝ," 558. See also Goulder, "Libertines?" 334-48. Cf. Prov 25:20: "As vinegar [is] not beneficial [ἀσύμφορον] [for] a sore, thus a passion [πάθος] attacking the body pains the heart."

rhetorolect. The focus on sinful deeds,[184] the sin of sexual immorality, and the concern for the body seem to be configured by traditional concerns of wisdom rhetorolect.[185] Due to cross-space mapping, the body found in each input-space is compressed in the blend to Identity. The other elements also get projected, but based on Paul's argument in 6:13-17 arrange themselves in a hierarchy with πορνεία being the worst of all the sins since it is committed against one's body.

The emergent structure that arises in the network formed in 6:18 can find the resources for configuring sexual immorality as an especially egregious sin against the body primarily in the Jewish wisdom literature of the LXX.[186] Fisk notes the various proverbs that warn against the danger of the "promiscuous woman," something I explored in Chapter 3.[187] The sin of sexual immorality unites the believer and the whore in one body (6:16). This somatic union with the malevolent figure of the πόρνη counts, in this wisdom context, as a unique threat against the integrity of the Christian body. Yet the emergent structure is also nurtured by priestly rhetorolect and its concern for protecting boundaries. The integration resources available in priestly rhetorolect are readily at hand because Paul's conceptual networks have relied on priestly rhetorolect to configure the emergent structures of some of the blends in 6:15-17 and this rhetorolect is crucial for understanding the next argument Paul makes in 6:19-20. In 6:18 Paul urges the Corinthians to flee πορνεία because it destroys the sanctified Christian body which Paul will describe as a temple (6:19). As Paul teaches in 3:16-17, where he first introduces the idea that the Corinthians are God's temple: "if someone destroys [φθείρει] the temple of God, God will destroy [φθερεῖ] that one." The corruption of the Christian body through the sin of πορνεία destroys the Christian body and its relationship with Christ.[188]

Temples and Slaves (6:19-20)

In the fourth and final rhetorical question of the pericope, Paul unites his concern about the believer's body and the spirit (6:19; cf. Wis

---

[184] See M. Miguens, "Christ's 'Members' and Sex (1 Cor 6,12-20)," *Thomist* 39 (1975): 38 where he notes that Paul only uses the noun ἁμάρτημα in 1 Cor 6:18 and Rom 3:25. He goes on to argue that "this term indicates a wrong deed or wrong doing, the sinful action rather than the sinful quality."

[185] Robbins, *Invention*, 1:186.

[186] Thiselton, *First Epistle to the Corinthians*, 473.

[187] Fisk, "ΠΟΡΝΕΥΕΙΝ," 546 n. 14 lists: Prov 2:16-19; 5:2-23; 6:23-35; 7:6-27; Sir 9:1-9; 23:16-27; 25:2; 26:22; 41:17-22; 47:19.

[188] Note the purity concerns contained in BDAG s.v. φθείρω 1. "to cause harm to in a physical manner or outward circumstances, *destroy, ruin, corrupt, spoil*." 2. "to cause deterioration of the inner life, *ruin, corrupt*." Cf. *T.Reu.* 4:6; 5:1-7. See Judith M. Lieu, *Christian Identity in the Jewish and Greco-Roman World* (Oxford: Oxford University Press, 2004), 194.

12:1). Like the first rhetorical question encountered in this argument (6:15), the statement Paul creates with his question, "your body is a temple of the holy spirit," is an XYZ formulation.

Figure 11: Conceptual Network for 6:19a

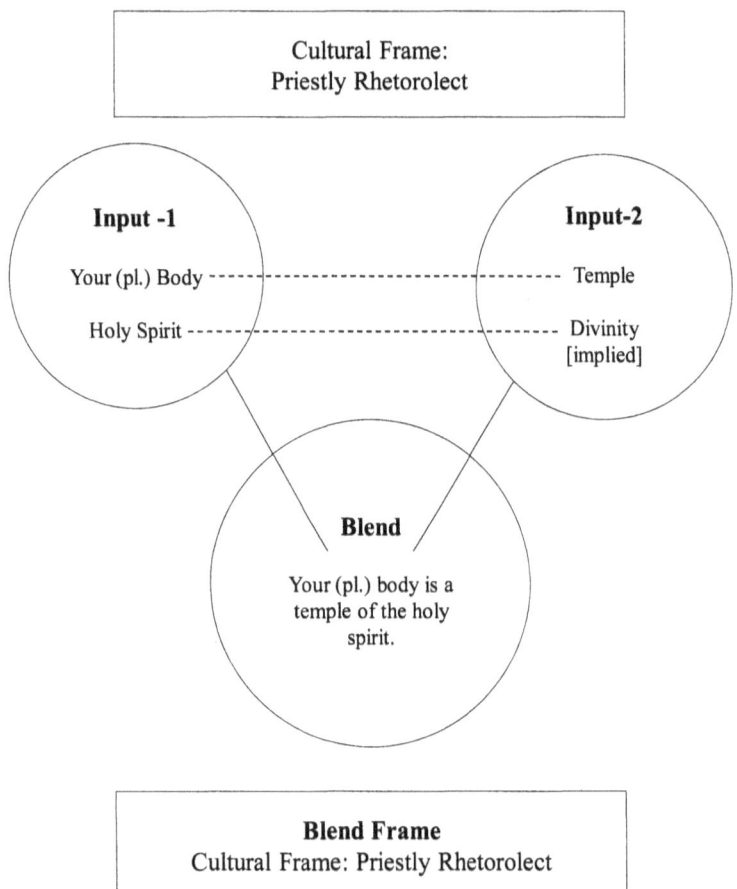

The missing element [w] that the blend prompts the hearer/reader to supply is a divinity that is worshipped in a temple. The holy spirit, which Paul describes as being "from God," corresponds to this divinity. Considering that Trinitarian categories are conceptually anachronistic in Paul's letters, there is no reason to conclude that God's holy spirit is anything other than the one spirit that unites the believer and Christ (6:17). This network is a typical single-scope metaphoric integration in which the body maps onto the temple and the holy spirit maps onto the divinity – body and holy spirit are values for the roles of temple and divinity.[189] Moreover, these roles (input-1) and values (input-2) are both organized by the cultural frame of priestly rhetorolect. Bodies, an element from input-1, are compressed to Identity with temples, the image from input-2. The blend is also culturally organized by priestly rhetorolect and locally organized by the image of the temple and, therefore, whatever the Corinthians do with their bodies reflects upon their estimation of the holy spirit whose temple their bodies are.[190] The emergent structure prompted by this network enriches priestly rhetorolect by nurturing a type of reasoning that regards the Christian body as worthy of the same respect accorded to a temple in which the holy spirit of God dwells.

The resources available from priestly rhetorolect recruit the cultural knowledge that cultic activity precludes impure sexual activity even as the emergent structure applies this knowledge to Christian bodies, thus serving Paul's rhetorical aims in this pericope.[191] Such a cultural understanding is not confined to Judaism, but would be available to the larger Hellenistic and Roman world in which the Corinthians lived. Laura McClure notes a comic fragment, cited by Plutarch in his recitation of the life of Demetrius (*Demtr.* 26.3), which notes the outrage of introducing courtesans into the temple of the virgin goddess Athena, thereby rendering it a brothel.[192] It was understood in the Greek speaking world that those guilty of sexual irregularities, usually adultery, are (or should be) barred from making sacrifices or offering public prayers to the gods.[193] And although some biblical scholars are unwilling to let go

---

[189] Fauconnier and Turner, *The Way We Think*, 154; idem, 127: "Single-scope networks are the prototype of highly conventional source-target metaphors."

[190] In 6:18 the Greek is τὸ σῶμα ὑμῶν. The plural possessive modifying a singular verb has caused some consternation in the MS tradition. A number of MSS read τὰ σώματα ὑμῶν. However, P[46], Sinaiticus, Vaticanus, and the corrector of Alexandrinus read σῶμα. Fee, *First Epistle to the Corinthians*, 263 n. 65 argues that τὸ σῶμα ὑμῶν "reflects semitic preference for a distributive singular." Coming at this grammatical construction from another cultural angle, Thiselton, *First Epistle to the Corinthians*, 474 notes that the reading of σώματα for σωμα is "an understandable secondary gloss. The singular with the genitive plural ὑμῶν may seem awkward, while classical Greek sources offer evidence to the distributive use of the singular where a plural meaning might be suggested." See Sandnes, *Belly and Body*, 79.

[191] See Martin, *Corinthian Body*, 178; Nejsum, "Apologetic Tendency," 57; also Loader, *Enoch, Levi, and Jubilees on Sexuality*, 288 on the sexual ideology of the book of *Jubilees*: "Sexual intercourse is not to take place in the temple nor should one be naked there…"

[192] McClure, *Courtesans at Table*, 138.

[193] Carson, "Phenomenology of Female Pollution," 86; Sissa, "Sexual Bodybuilding," 162; Mary R. Lefkowitz, "Wives and Husbands," in *Women in Antiquity* (ed. Ian McAuslan and Peter Walcott; Greece & Rome Studies; Oxford: Oxford University

of the idea, classicists have discounted the idea of sacred or temple prostitution for ancient Greece generally and for Corinth in particular.[194] To be sure, there are close associations between sex workers and Aphrodite because of the goddess's power of seduction, but McClure notes that a close relationship between courtesans and sacred places "transgress[es] religious norms" in the Greek speaking world.[195] Conceptually and discursively creating a body that functions as sacred temple space is an efficient way for Paul to argue against the sexual irregularities of πορνεία across cultural boundaries.

As Paul's teaching creates the emergent structure of the body-as-sacred-space blend, he is careful to note who the primary creator of this blended space is. Christian bodies are temples only because the holy spirit dwells within them and this holy spirit, Paul teaches, comes from God (ἀπὸ θεοῦ). The Corinthians "have" the spirit only because God gave it to them. This gift of the spirit that makes Christian bodies into temples means that the Corinthians no longer possess themselves, rather this gift signifies that they have been purchased, with something valuable (6:20a), by God.

Input-1 (*Fig. 12*) contains elements that are configured by priestly rhetorolect – the body-as-temple blend and the statement that this was a gift from God. Recall that the notion of beneficial exchange is among the resources available in priestly rhetorolect, wherein the devotee receives special blessing from God.[196] Input-2 is not well organized, although one could argue that the language of slavery draws from wisdom rhetorolect. While possible, I believe that wisdom rhetorolect only emerges in the blend. In the blend the idea of body-as-temple is linked to Paul's argument that the Corinthians are no longer their own masters. In fact, Paul's rhetography paints the Corinthians as slaves who have been purchased for a price.

Press, 1996), 75. See Demonsthenes, *Neaer.* [*Or.* 59] 73, 86, 111, 116; Aeschines, *Tim.* 19, 183, 188.

[194] Stephanie Lynn Budin, *The Myth of Sacred Prostitution in Antiquity* (Cambridge: Cambridge University Press, 2008). See also McClure, *Courtesans at Table*, 140. See Frymer-Kensky, *Reading Women of the Bible*, 271 for a critique of reading the *qedeshah* as a temple prostitute.

[195] McClure, *Courtesans at Table*, ch. 5 (pp. 137-63). The quotation is from p. 149.

[196] See Robbins, *Invention*, 1:112.

6. *Why* Porneia *Should Be Avoided: 1 Cor 6:12-20* 259

Figure 12: Conceptual Network for the Mega-Blend in 6:19-20a

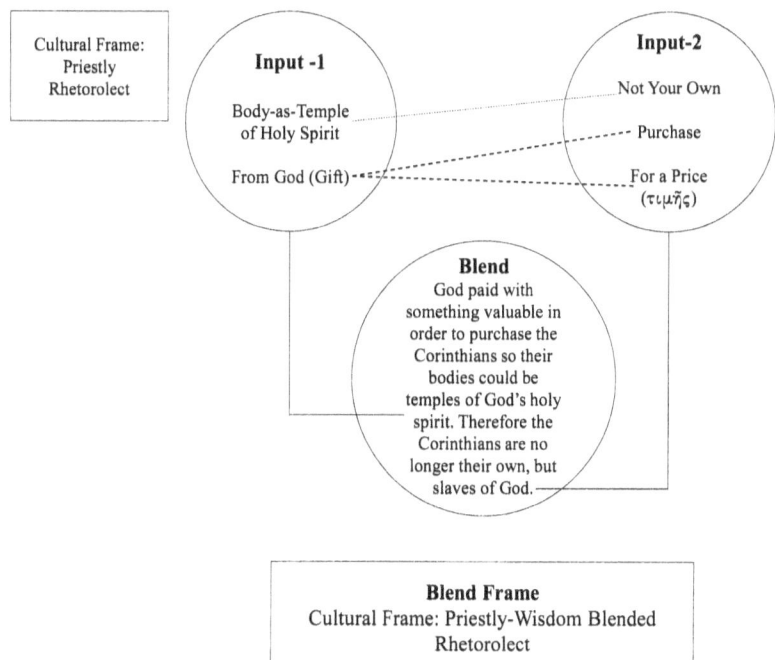

The conceptualization of the Corinthians as both temples and slaves works because of the emergent structure of the blend. The conceptual resources this emergent structure makes available allows Paul to reason that being temples of God's holy spirit means that the Corinthians are no longer masters of their own bodies. This reasoning, I argue, is recruited from wisdom rhetorolect within this overwhelmingly priestly network. Wisdom resources display a concern for correct behavior of members of the household, with slaves ideally deferring to the master. The emergent structure of this mega-blend combines reasoning and resources from priestly and wisdom rhetorolects in such a way that Paul can remind the Corinthians of their proper, sanctified relationship to God (cf. 1 Cor 3:23).

The emergent structure that arises from the mega-blend in 6:19-20a is astonishing in two respects. First, it re-introduces Paul's paradoxical thinking with which he began the pericope. In 6:12d Paul declared that he would not be mastered by anything. Yet, here in 6:19-20a, he is telling the Corinthians that they are slaves who have been purchased by God. Given Paul's argumentation in 6:13-17, however, this is not surprising. As Knust notes, Paul is "reiterating in this passage the view that saintly bodies must be mastered by 'the Lord' rather than the belly or sexual desire."[197] This type of reasoning is also found in Philo's treatise, *Every Good Person Is Free*.[198] As in 1 Cor 3:21-23 and 7:23, Paul argues that the Corinthians are free from all things human that would constrain them. This freedom from desire and other humans, however, only comes as a result of the fact that the Corinthians are the slaves of God.[199] Because of this relationship to God, the body is not for believers' to do with as they wish (6:19b-20a), but rather must be used in a manner befitting its sanctified state.

Second, the emergent structure of this blend turns the usual ideology of beneficial exchange on its head, thereby infusing a paradoxical Pauline Christian element into the priestly-wisdom rhetorolect that arises from the blend. Typically, beneficial exchange works in such a fashion that humans give up something to God in return for God's blessing and favor, this is evident in the law codes of the LXX and in cross-cultural ideologies of sacrifice. In 6:19-20a, however, the Corinthians have done nothing. Rather it is God who is the actor and who has paid a price in order to create the bodies of the Corinthians as sacred spaces.[200] Such reasoning, which comes from the emergent structure of the blend, enriches priestly rhetorolect even as this rhetorolect helps configure the elements of the blend.

The end result of the mega-blend found in 6:19-20a, and for the arguments in 6:12-20 as a whole, is the command Paul gives in 6:20b: "Glorify God with your body!" Rather than being mastered by their bellies and desires, the Christian body is to be a sacred space that is the locus, not for sexual immorality, but for praising God on account of what God has done for the Corinthians.

Conclusion

The gnomic rhetology with which Paul begins the first half of the pericope (6:12) lays the foundation for the host environment of wisdom rhetorolect that conceptually organizes the graphic rhetography that makes up his teaching on the dangers πορνεία poses to the Christian body (6:13-20). This rhetology creates an environment for the

---

[197] Knust, *Abandoned to Lust*, 78.
[198] John Byron, *Slavery Metaphors in Early Judaism and Pauline Christianity: A Traditio-Historical and Exegetical Examination* (WUNT 2nd series 162; Tübingen: Mohr Siebeck, 2003), 107: "The truly free person is the one who has allowed their soul to be ruled by God rather than passions or vices." Byron cites *Prob.* 18-20, 101-106. Also Galloway, *Freedom in the Gospel*, 123-26.
[199] See Martin, *Slavery as Salvation*, 63.
[200] To be sure, there is precedent for this type of divine action in Jewish Scripture. See esp. the call of Abraham (Gen 12:1-3) and the Exodus tradition (Ex 19:3-6).

necessary reflection so critical to wisdom rhetorolect. Yet the integration resources available in wisdom rhetorolect do not provide the rhetorical power to justify the position that Paul's didactic discourse pushes towards, namely that sexual immorality is the worst of all possible sins one could commit with one's body. To achieve this rhetorical goal Paul's discourse draws on the conceptual resources from apocalyptic and priestly rhetorolects. These rhetorolects are invited into the host environment of wisdom to create a more powerful argument than could be achieved by the resources of any one rhetorolect on its own.

Paul relies on apocalyptic and priestly rhetography in his didactic discourse to show the Corinthians why sexual immorality is incompatible with their Christian bodies. This heavy reliance on embodied rhetography has made the use of conceptual integration theory particularly productive in exegeting this segment of his argument. The insights from conceptual blending not only shed light on how Paul's arguments make rhetorical sense, but they also help explain how the cultural resources his language draws from make meaning. Paul's teaching separates the body from its desiring appetites and to do so draws heavily on Hellenistic-Roman concerns about beneficial action and self-mastery. Such concerns were also appropriated by Hellenistic Jews and used as a lens to read their sacred texts. However, the apocalyptic images and rationales that surface in 1 Cor 6:13-17 demonstrate that for Paul πορνεία is first and foremost a religious problem with grave eschatological consequences. Such rhetography would be out of place in the larger non-Jewish Hellenistic cultural milieu. By compressing the vital relation between the believer and Christ from Analogy to Part-Whole and then to Identity, Paul activates not only apocalyptic resources, but also priestly concerns about sexual purity. Such priestly rhetography could draw upon cross cultural resources to fill in necessary background information.

The rhetographical elaboration of Paul's blends in 6:13-20 demonstrates that, in his efforts to show the Corinthians the religious danger posed by πορνεία, Paul does fashion an argument that seems to render any sexual activity problematic. Such a conclusion does not demonstrate a flaw in my interpretive method, as Brian Rosner would likely contend,[201] but rather that Paul's concerns about sexual behavior are firmly located in the diverse cultures of the first century Mediterranean world that worry about desire, the passions, and sex. As Paul moves into the next section of his wisdom teaching on proper sexual comportment, he shifts from showing the Corinthians *why* πορνεία is to be avoided to explaining *how* they can successfully do so. With this shift,

---

[201] See the introduction to this chapter and Rosner, *Paul, Scripture and Ethics*, 124.

Paul's teaching confirms Coulson and Oakley's assertion that "conceptual blends are intimately intertwined with human doings."[202]

---

[202] Coulson and Oakley, "Purple Persuasion," § 4; see Robbins, *Invention*, 1:186

7

How Porneia Should Be Avoided: The Rhetology of 1 Corinthians 7:1-7

Introduction

Having shown the Corinthians why they ought to avoid πορνεία in 6:12-20, in 7:1-7 Paul moves to provide the means by which the Corinthians can enact their flight from sexual immorality. In this section of his teaching, Paul moves away from the reliance on rhetography that so marked 6:12-20 and relies more on rhetology as he explains the modes of sexual behavior that he believes will best protect the Corinthians from the ever present danger of πορνεία. The progression of Paul's argument in 7:1-7 has four discernible sections:

1. An introduction to the section in which Paul offers two main options – abstinence or monogamous heterosexual coupling – to enact the commands he gave in 6:18 and 20 (7:1-2).
2. A rhetological wisdom argument in which Paul commands a married couple to have regular sex (7:3-4).
3. A rhetological concession, a third option, Paul makes for a married couple to cease sexual activity for brief periods (7:5-6).
4. A conclusion in which Paul uses himself as a παράδειγμα, but for the ability to judge wisely, not for his specific ability to be sexually continent (7:7).

In this section of text, which I also read "without quotation marks," Paul offers three options for avoiding the sin of πορνεία.[1] The first option, building off of his wisdom-priestly blended rhetorolect of 6:18-20, is simply not to touch women. By never touching, or having sex, with *any* woman, no (male) person runs the risk of sinning against the holiness of the Christian body via πορνεία.[2] However, since the main

---

[1] Dodd, "Paul's Paradigmatic 'I'," 54. See my section, "The Question of Slogans in 1 Corinthians 6:12-7:7," in Chapter 5.

[2] See Loader, *Sexuality and the Jesus Tradition*, 149-56. Based on what follows, Paul seems to focus on male subjects in 7:1b and not on female same-sex activity. See Bernadette J. Brooten, *Love Between Women: Early Christian Responses to Female Homoeroticism*

goal of Paul's argument in 6:12–7:7 is to ensure that *all* Corinthians protect themselves against πορνεία, he allows the community a second best option, which involves a command for married couples to engage in sexual activity for the sake of satisfying sexual urges rather than (only) for procreation. In a third option Paul blends the behavior from the first two. While this blend grants married couples brief respites from sexual activity, Paul worries that the machinations of Satan will exploit these periods of abstinence and he argues that they should be kept as short as possible. Recognizing that not everyone in Corinth has his gift of sexual continence, Paul would have the community work out its sexual urges in a "safe" way, in marital sexual activity, rather than run the risk of contaminating the community through πορνεία. Such a concern for the varied circumstances and situations in which different members of the Corinthian community find themselves is a hallmark of wisdom discourse.[3]

The Basic Pauline Sexual Options (7:1-2): Wisdom-Priestly Blended Rhetorolect

When Paul turns from showing the Corinthians why πορνεία is so dangerous to teaching the means to avoid it, he touches on a topic about which the Corinthians have apparently written him (7:1a).[4] Paul begins this section by building off of his rhetography of the Christian body-as-sacred-space (6:19-20) and offers them a short maxim that exemplifies his view of the best way to avoid sexual immorality: "And concerning the things which [περὶ δὲ ὧν] you wrote, it is good for a person [καλὸν ἀνθρώπῳ] not to touch a woman" (7:1).[5] I have already argued that 7:1b is best regarded as a gnomic saying Paul uses to persuade his audience, rather than a Corinthian slogan against which he must argue, since it flows seamlessly from the priestly concerns of 6:18-20 and accords with Paul's teaching in the rest of the chapter.[6] Formally,

---

(Chicago: University of Chicago Press, 1996), for a discussion of the latter. Such androcentrism in the use of the term ἄνθρωπος is not unique to Paul; see Sly, *Philo's Perception of Women*, 67-70; Conzelmann, *1 Corinthians*, 115.

[3] Robbins, *Invention*, 1:129; Wilson, *The Mysteries of Righteousness*, 181.

[4] Mitchell has demonstrated that the only requirement necessary for the use of the περὶ δέ formula is that the topic be known to the writer and the audience ("Concerning ΠΕΡΙ ΔΕ").

[5] I translate the δέ as "and" here, as I do in 6:13-14, understanding that "δέ serves to mark that something is different from what precedes it, but only to offset it, not to exclude or contradict it." Smythe, *Greek Grammar*, § 2834.

[6] Tiedemann, *Paulus und das Begehren*, 45-46; idem, *Erfahrung des Fleisches*, 136-42; Weiß, *Der erste Korintherbrief*, 170. See Yarbrough, *Not Like the Gentiles*, 101: "Four times in vv. 8-40 Paul addresses the question of believers' marrying and in each instance he

Paul's exhortation in 7:1b is similar to what he teaches in 7:8b, except that v. 1b is a general maxim – καλὸν ἀνθρώπῳ – that could be spoken to anyone anywhere, whereas v. 8b is directed to a specific group – καλὸν αὐτοῖς, referring to the "unmarried" whom Paul addresses in v. 8a [λέγω δὲ τοῖς ἀγάμοις].[7] Paul, however, recognizes that the Corinthians apparently cannot live out his teaching regarding sexual abstinence (v. 1b), given the cases of sexual immorality [τὰς πορνείας] among them, and so he offers a second best solution: heterosexual coupling in marriage (7:2).[8] Such pragmatic teaching is not unique to Paul. For example, Gaca notes that "In the *Republic* and *Laws* Plato does not present one fixed plan to rein in sexual desire, but he aims to control it by managing the reproductive urge in a variety of ways."[9]

Many have suggested that 7:1b must be a Corinthian slogan because of its supposed "non-Jewish" character.[10] This, however, not only imputes a monolithic character to Judaism in late antiquity, but it also assumes a direct mapping of biblical texts onto Jewish communities. In other words, it assumes a lack of creativity in Jewish appropriation of Scripture in community life. Daniel Boyarin has shown this position to be untenable, especially when dealing with the intersection of Scripture, ethics, and sexual behavior in the multifaceted world of Jewish expression in late antiquity.[11] The position that 7:1b does not fit into a Jewish world view ignores much evidence about what is known about

---

argues against it." But see Roy E. Ciampa, "Revisiting the Euphemism in 1 Corinthians 7.1," *JSNT* 31 (2009): 325-38.

[7] Weiß, *Der erste Korintherbrief*, 176. But see Deming, *Paul on Marriage and Celibacy* (2004), 109 where he seems to equate any maxim with a Corinthian slogan (see also p. 129 n. 91 regarding the phrase "it is better to marry than to burn" in 7:9).

[8] See Gaca, *Fornication*, 47-48 where she compares Plato's ideal sexual reform in the *Republic* to his more pragmatic (and second-best) strictures in the *Laws*.

[9] Gaca, *Fornication*, 57; see Robbins, *Invention*, 1:129.

[10] E.g., R. Collins, *First Corinthians*, 253; Fee, *First Epistle to the Corinthians*, 275 (citing Gen 2:18). See Steven D. Fraade who notes that one argument marshaled against the idea of ascetic tendencies in "Judaism" is based on an understanding of asceticism as pathological: "This tendency is evidenced among scholars who argue that Judaism in general and Judaism of the rabbis in particular is antithetical to asceticism... The argument that Judaism is defined by the centrality of legal observance and therefore contains no asceticism is used, interestingly, by those who make of this a virtue and by those who make of it a weakness." Steven D. Fraade, "Ascetical Aspects of Ancient Judaism," *Jewish Spirituality* (World Spirituality: An Encyclopedic History of the Religious Quest 13; New York: Crossroad, 1987), 278 n. 5. In arguing that asceticism is not inherently antithetical to Judaism, Tiedemann, *Erfahrung des Fleisches*, 115, quotes Fraade.

[11] Boyarin, *Carnal Israel*, ch. 1, "'Behold Israel According to the Flesh': On Anthropology and Sexuality in Late-Antique Judaisms" (pp. 31-60). See also Jacob Neusner, "Varieties of Judaism in the Formative Age," in *Jewish Spirituality* (World Spirituality: An Encyclopedic History of the Religious Quest 13; New York: Crossroad, 1987), 171-97; Rosner, *Paul, Scripture, and Ethics*, 150.

Hellenistic Judaism. First, such a view disregards both the negative views of women found in the biblical texts themselves, which could serve as resources for 1 Cor 7:1b, as well as the variety of figurative interpretations of Scripture practiced in the Hellenistic period that read such "pro-marriage" texts as Gen 1:28 and 2:18 as allegories.[12] Second, while marriage certainly was the norm in various expressions of Judaism during the Second Temple period, as it also was in non-Jewish culture, Hellenistic Jewish writers such as Philo praise groups who do not engage in traditional sexual behavior – the Therapeutae and the Essenes.[13] Finally, there is the famous example of Ben-Azzai that shows how even rabbinical Jews, and not simply their more acculturated Hellenized brethren, were also able to depart from the typical ethos of marriage. Ben-Azzai interprets God's statement about blood vengeance in Gen 9:6, in part, with an argument that God has commanded humanity to be fruitful (Gen 1:27-28). Thus, in his interpretation, he argues that Jews should marry and have children. However, Ben-Azzai himself has neglected both of these duties.[14] When called to explain why his behavior does not accord with his own biblical interpretation Ben-Azzai replies, "What shall I do? My soul desires Torah. Let the world continue by the efforts of others!" (*t. Yebam.* 8:7; cf. *b. Yebam.* 63b).[15]

Boyarin notes that figures such as Ben-Azzai, who refused the duties of marriage and procreation, "were hyperbolically stigmatized as murderers and blasphemers." Such hyperbole, according to Boyarin,

---

[12] Philo, *Contempl.* 12, 68, 78. See my discussion of this in ch. 3; also Loader, *Septuagint, Sexuality, and the New Testament*, 59-69.

[13] Philo, *Cont.* (Therapeutae); *Prob.* 75-91; *Hypoth.* 11.1-18 (Essenes). Kathy Gaca, *Fornication*, 193, 199-200 has shown how a Jewish thinker like Philo can re-interpret his scriptural traditions in light of the cultural concerns of Greek speaking Hellenism so that behavior that might, at first blush, appear "non-biblical" is presented in a positive light. See Tiedemann's discussion of Philo in *Erfahrung des Fleisches*, 117-21. See also Deming, *Paul on Marriage and Celibacy* (2004), 88-94; Weiß, *Der erste Korintherbrief*, 170-72; F. Gerald Downing, *Cynics, Paul and the Pauline Churches* (Cynics and Christian Origins 2; London: Routledge, 1998), 107.

[14] See Fraade, "Ascetical Aspects," 275: "Thus, although rules of sexual purity were liberalized for men – presumably so as not to discourage marital relations – others continued to impose upon themselves a stricter rule. The tension between sexuality and a sage's preoccupation with Torah study is still unresolved."

[15] As quoted from Boyarin, *Carnal Israel*, 134; also cited or quoted in Fraade, "Ascetical Aspects," 274; Tiedemann, *Paulus und das Begehren*, 46; Yarbrough, *Not Like the Gentiles*, 22-23. Ben-Azzai's reason for eschewing marital responsibility is analogous to rationales certain Greek philosophers gave for avoiding marriage; see esp. Deming's discussion of the *Cynic Epistle of Diogenes* in *Paul on Marriage and Celibacy* (2004), 69-70 as well as his discussion of the thought of the Roman thinker Seneca in idem, 73-74. But see Gaca's reservations about using any material from rabbinic Judaism to shed light on Paul (*Fornication*, 14-15).

demonstrates the powerful allure of celibacy even in proto- and early rabbinic culture. Boyarin argues that the insistence on the goodness of marriage and procreation in early rabbinic Judaism "represents ... a point of resistance to the dominant discursive practices of both Jewish and non-Jewish cultures of late antiquity."[16] In light of this, it is not *prima facie* impossible for the phrase "it is good for a person not to touch a woman" to arise out of a Jewish environment and thus be native to Paul's Jewish worldview.[17] Indeed, if Boyarin's observations about Judaisms in late antiquity are correct, Paul's preference for complete avoidance of sexual activity, far from being "non-Jewish," is actually quite representative of the sexual ideals current in various sectors of Hellenistic Judaism.[18]

Careful attention to Paul's use of the resources available in various rhetorolects also provides exegetical coherence to the sentiments expressed in 7:1b and 7:2 within a Jewish thought world. Each of these verses activates resources from different rhetorolects in order to establish the appropriate background information necessary for 7:1b-2 to make cultural sense. The gnomic saying in 7:1b, building directly from his argument in 6:18-20, is configured by priestly rhetorolect and its concomitant concerns about purity. In Exod 19:15, in preparation for the Sinai theophany, Moses tells the people, "do not approach a woman" [μὴ προσέλθητε γυναικί].[19] This, coupled with the various regulations regarding sexual purity necessary for the proper function of the cult in the Pentateuch, represent integration resources available in priestly rhetorolect that allow readers/hearers to make meaning of 1 Cor 7:1b.[20] Such a priestly concern for purity regarding women can be found among non-Jewish Greeks as well. As Anne Carson aptly notes about the status of women in ancient Greek sexual ideology, "Women are pollutable, polluted, and polluting in several ways at once."[21] The priestly concern for purity found in 7:1b continues Paul's line of argumentation from 6:18-20 where he equates the Christian body with a temple filled with God's holy spirit.

---

[16] Boyarin, *Carnal Israel*, 35; see idem, 45-57 where he discusses the multiplicity of rabbinic voices on the topic of sex. See Weiß, *Der erste Korintherbrief*, 171, 174-75.

[17] See esp. my treatment of Philo's views of women in Chapter 3, where I note Richard Baer's discussion of Philo's "pejorative references to the female," *Philo's Use of the Categories Male and Female*, 40. See also Sly, *Philo's Perception of Women*; Wilson, "Sin as Sex and Sex with Sin," 147-68; Wegner, "Philo's Portrayal of Women," 41-66.

[18] See Fraade, "Ascetical Aspects," 266, 268 on the Essenes and celibacy.

[19] See Hippocrates, *Epid.* 6.3.14 for this Greek phrase.

[20] See my discussion of these purity regulations in Chapter 3.

[21] Carson, "Putting Her in Her Place," 158; idem, "Phenomenology of Female Pollution," 87.

The biblical concern about sexual purity involves *any* sexual behavior – thus Paul's use of the saying in 7:1b – but Paul's main concern in this section of text is with a special kind of sexual impurity: the impurity that comes from πορνεία. Because of cases of this sexual sin in the community (7:2; cf. 1 Cor 5), Paul's argument shifts from the integration resources available in priestly rhetorolect, with its concern about purity, to those found in wisdom rhetorolect, where the concern for teaching proper sexual behavior in the context of a marriage is activated. Paul's argument in 7:1-2 thus demonstrates the principles of selective projection. In 7:1b, Paul draws upon and projects those elements in priestly cultural traditions that support the incompatibility between cultic activity and sex. In 7:2 Paul's rhetoric ceases to project elements from this priestly frame and rather draws upon wisdom resources that focus on the benefit of sexual activity within marriage: "but because of the cases of sexual immorality [τὰς πορνείας] let each [man] have his own wife and let each [woman] have her own husband."[22] With the shift to concerns about πορνεία, the usefulness of marriage is activated and the cultic purity concerns of v. 1b drop out of view for the moment.

In making the shift from a priestly to a wisdom frame, Paul is simply pragmatic enough to recognize that which Philo did – that "self-mastery [ἡ σωφροσύνη] ... is powerless to encircle desire and pleasure [τὴν ἐπιθυμίαν καὶ ἡδονήν]; for they are hard to wrestle with and hard to overthrow" (*Leg.* 1.86 [Colson & Whitaker, LCL]).[23] While Hellenistic Jewish thinkers recognized the ethical and religious dangers posed by sexual desire, Jewish wisdom texts also warn that an absence of marriage can sometimes exacerbate the problems caused by sexual appetite.[24] Sirach 36:25-27, for example, teaches about the dangers of an unattached man: "where there is no fence, a piece of property is plundered" (36:25). Sirach 25:16–26:27 exemplifies the dual concerns Jewish wisdom traditions have about sex when it both teaches about the dangers lurking in a bad woman, but also extols the happiness that a man finds in a good wife.

A closer examination of the conceptual network that Paul's teaching creates in 7:1-2 will help fill out the blending of priestly and wisdom rhetorolects in these verses. Such a blend allows Paul to argue for two appropriate responses to the threat of πορνεία – an ideal response that

---

[22] I discuss my translation choices for 7:1-2 below.

[23] See Stowers, *Rereading Romans*, 48: "With the major exception of the early Stoics, writers from the Greco-Roman world did not believe that one could eliminate these unruly appetites and passions that were the source of immoral behavior." See Gaca, *Fornication*, 60–61; 4 Macc 3:2.

[24] R. Collins, *First Corinthians*, 254 notes that this theme is evident in *The Testament of the Twelve Patriarchs* (see esp. T.Levi 9:9-10).

conforms fully to the logic of Christian-body-as-sacred-space, and a second-best option necessary because of the lived reality in the Corinthian community. Johannes Weiß argues that 7:1-2 represents the first instance of a spiritual hierarchy in Christianity wherein Paul offers two acceptable ways for the Corinthians to deal with their sexual bodies.[25] This same spiritual hierarchy recurs in 7:38. In both instances Paul argues that refraining from sexual activity is the best mode of action (ideally), but practicing monogamous sexual activity within marriage also is acceptable (practically) as a way to stave off the dangers of πορνεία.[26]

The complex conceptual network Paul nurtures in 7:1-2 creates the two basic options available to the Corinthians for avoiding πορνεία, although Paul does go on to discuss a blend of these in 7:5. The first option in 7:1b, as noted, activates purity concerns present in a priestly rhetorolect. It is worth nothing that the verb Paul employs in this verse – ἅπτω – can have both cultic and sexual connotations, much like the verb κολλάω which Paul used in 6:16-17.[27] In Num 16:26 and Isa 52:11 the verb is used to warn against touching impure things. In Gen 20:6 and Prov 6:29 the verb is used, interestingly enough, in relation to prohibited sexual activity, although in both of these cases the sexual sin in view is engaging in sex with another man's wife. Like κολλάω, the verb ἅπτω provides a lexical bridge between the cultic and the sexual – as one is not to touch impure or unclean objects, so one is not to "touch" a woman. The purity dangers women present to cultic settings are being activated by this lexical item in this maxim.[28]

In 7:2 the focus shifts from the projected purity dangers of sex in general to Paul's main concern: the danger of πορνεία. Because such cases exist in the Corinthian community – διὰ δὲ τὰς πορνείας (cf. 1

---

[25] Weiß, *Der erste Korintherbrief*, 170-72; also MacDonald, "Virgins, Widows, and Wives," 166. See Yarbrough, *Not Like the Gentiles*, 101 and my discussion on 1 Cor 7:7 below on whether marriage is a "gift" in Paul's teaching. See Thiselton, *First Epistle to the Corinthians*, 503 for the contrary view.

[26] See Fraade, "Ascetical Aspects," 265 on the relation of the ideal and the pragmatic in Philo (citing *Fug.* 36) and idem, 268-69 for this relationship among the Essenes where he notes "...the possibility that the ascetic ideals of the Qumran group had to be adjusted to the *community's* ability to fulfill them..." (p. 268, emphasis in the original). Also Knust, *Abandoned to Lust*, 80.

[27] See BDAG s.v. ἅπτω 3 for a cultic meaning (citing Num 16:26 and Isa 52:11) and 4 for a sexual meaning (citing Gen 20:6 and Prov 6:29); Fee, *First Epistle to the Corinthians*, 275; F.W. Grosheide, *Commentary on the First Epistle to the Corinthians: The English Text with Introduction, Exposition, and Notes* (NICNT; Grand Rapids: Eerdmans, 1953), 155.

[28] See my discussion of this in ch. 3 and in Carson, "Putting Her in Her Place"; idem, "Phenomenology of Female Pollution."

Cor 5:1, 11) – Paul, drawing from wisdom resources, recognizes that for many of the Corinthian Christians the ideal option of not touching a woman will not work.[29] In order to make room in the community for the proper sexual use of the Christian body, Paul activates a wisdom rhetorolect and argues for marriage as a "safe" way to channel the sexual appetite.

The shift in lexical items between v. 1b and v. 2 may help signal this transition. As is well known, the Greek words for man and woman can equally be used to denote husband and wife.[30] Nothing in the lexical items themselves allows the interpreter to distinguish between these two meanings; only context allows for this. I argue that Paul's use of the term ἄνθρωπος in 7:1b and ἀνήρ in 7:2 (as well as in vv. 3-4) can help exegetes explain how Paul's argument progresses in these first two verses. In 7:1b Paul is focusing on sexual relationships in general.[31] He is not invoking marriage, but simply the act of sex itself, in order to highlight its incompatibility with the Christian body-as-sacred-space. His argument here functions within priestly rhetorolect that configures the cultural understating of purity available from this frame. Thus the word γυναικός in 7:1b is best translated as "woman."[32] In 7:2, however, Paul shifts to a wisdom rhetorolect in teaching that heterosexual monogamous coupling – marriage – is an appropriate way to deal with the dangers of πορνεία. Paul narrows the focus to a socially recognized relationship as the proper locus of sexual activity. Here, the reciprocal teaching to men and women suggests a relationship and thus I argue that the words γυναῖκα and ἄνδρα are best translated as "wife" and "husband" respectively in 7:2. Sex in general, between a (male) person and a woman, is ideally avoided. Since the Corinthians have proven unable to control their sexual appetite (7:2a, 5), however, married sex between a husband and wife is a practical way to stave off the dangers of πορνεία.[33]

The shift in translation values I am suggesting is supported by a conceptual analysis of the network created by 7:1-2. By examining how Paul activates different resources within priestly and wisdom rhetorolects, meaning can be made of Paul's arguments in these verses.

---

[29] See Gillian Beattie, *Women and Marriage in Paul and his Early Interpreters* (JSNTSup 296; London: T. & T. Clark, 2005), 21-22 where she notes, contra Dale Martin, that "5.1 makes it clear that πορνεία is already ἐν ὑμῖν, within the boundaries of the church; it is not only a pervasive characteristic of the world (5.10), but it is also found within the community itself (5.11)." See also MacDonald, "Virgins Widows, and Wives," 155.

[30] See Davidson, *Courtesans and Fishcakes*, 74.

[31] Cf. Sir 23:17-18.

[32] For a discussion of this translation issue, see Thiselton, *First Epistle to the Corinthians*, 500.

[33] See Thiselton, *First Epistle to the Corinthians*, 500.

7. How *Porneia* Should be Avoided: 1 Cor 7:1-7

Figure 13: Conceptual Network for 7:1-2

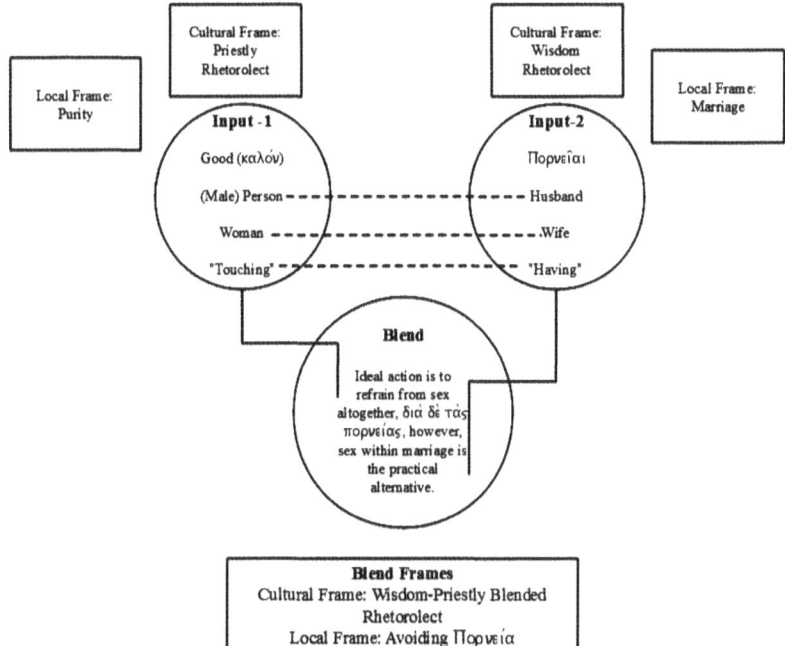

Once again the δέ in Paul's rhetoric does not denote an adversative antithesis, but rather a different side of the same coin (cf. 6:13-14).[34] The rhetorical goal here is to teach the Corinthians how to avoid πορνεία. This can be done *either* by avoiding sex altogether *or* by taking on the roles of husband and wife.

The cross-space mapping between the two inputs spaces is instructive. Input-1, governed by a cultural frame of priestly rhetorolect and a local frame of purity, consists of the ideal situation (καλόν), a male person, a woman (with no apparent relation between the two), and the act of "touching," a lexical item, as noted above, that bridges the cultic and the sexual. In this input space what is ideal is for males and females to avoid having sexual contact. The emphasis on purity found in priestly rhetorolect provides the logic behind this idea. Most of the elements in input-2 are related via cross-space mapping to the elements of input-1, but the organizing frames are different. Input-2 is configured by wisdom rhetorolect, with an emphasis on marriage.[35] In this

---

[34] Again, *pace* Fee, *First Epistle to the Corinthians*, 277.
[35] In exegeting Paul's teaching in 1 Cor 7 it is crucial not to import conceptually anachronous ideas of a Christian "institution" of marriage. See Suzanne Dixon, *Roman Family* (Baltimore: Johns Hopkins University Press, 1992), 72; Huber, *Like a Bride*

input space the ideal [καλόν] does not exist, rather πορνεῖαι do. Because of [διά] this, Paul teaches that it is best for men and women to take on the roles of husbands and wives and, far from not "touching," should "have" each other (cf. 5:1).[36] In this double-scope network the cultural frames do not clash, but blend together in such a way that the local frames each input elicits (purity and marriage, respectively) *both* still remain in the blend. This way of blending frames cognitively harnesses them all to work towards the same goal: avoiding πορνεία. Paul's creative blending in these two verses overpowers none of the frames or elements in either input space. Rather he blends the two in such a way that they work together so that the ideal of sexual purity is maintained even while teaching the benefits of sex *in so far as* men and women take on the roles of husbands and wives.

Commanding Sex (7:3-4): Wisdom Rhetorolect

Having established the marital relationship as the only legitimate space in which the sacred Christian bodies of the Corinthian believers can legitimately engage in sexual activity, Paul continues to focus on marriage by marshalling the resources of wisdom rhetorolect. In 7:3-4 Paul teaches: "Let the husband give the obligation [ὀφειλήν][37] to [his] wife and likewise also the wife to the husband. The wife does not have authority [ἐξουσιάζει] over her own body but the husband [does], and likewise also the husband does not have authority [ἐξουσιάζει] over his own body, but the wife [does]." Here Paul, addressing the ordinary, mundane aspects of marriage to ensure they stave off sexual immorality,[38] commands the married couple to have sex, using the euphemism of "obligation."[39] Paul's teaching on proper behavior between spouses fits

Adorned, ch. 4 (pp. 113-33); and Cynthia B. Patterson, *The Family in Greek History* (Cambridge, Mass.: Harvard University Press, 1998), 109: "Marriage ... should be understood as a social process rather than as a legal moment."

[36] See Thiselton, *First Epistle to the Corinthians*, 501-2 for his discussion of Paul's use of ἔχω in 7:2: "The use of the wide-ranging verb ἔχω ... receives its particular nuance from its close syntagmatic proximity with τὴν ἑαυτοῦ γυναῖκα and τὸν ἴδιον ἄνδρα." Also Fee, *First Epistle to the Corinthians*, 278 who argues that "...this idiom is common in biblical Greek and usually means either to 'have sexually' (Exod. 2:1; Deut. 28:30; Isa. 13:16) or simply to *be* married or to be in continuing sexual relations with a woman..."

[37] See Fee, *First Epistle to the Corinthians*, 272 n. 15 for a discussion of the variant, found in the Syriac traditions and the Majority text, ὀφειλεμένην εὔνοιαν. Idem, 279 n. 56, notes that τὴν ὀφειλὴν ἀποδιδότω is "frequently used in the papyri for payment of debts."

[38] See Goff, "Wisdom, Apocalypticism, and the Pedagogical Ethos of 4QInstruction," 59, 62, 67 for a discussion of Jewish wisdom's traditional focus on mundane aspects of ordinary life.

[39] See Fee, *First Epistle to the Corinthians*, 279. Daniel Boyarin notes how the Mishna argues in a similar fashion regarding the sexual obligation between spouses; "Paul and the

well with the household concerns typical in traditional Jewish wisdom.[40] Moreover, Paul follows his command of mutual sexual obligation with a rationale supporting it, a form typical of wisdom reasoning.[41] Thus, both form and content firmly anchor these verses within wisdom rhetorolect. Paul's instruction in these two verses remains in the domain of the household and consists of teaching regarding proper sexual relations within marriage without recourse to non-wisdom rationales. Paul's discourse here, as in 6:12, does not blend wisdom rhetorolect with any other organizing cultural frames.

Jewish wisdom traditions provide Paul with ample supportive conceptual categories once he begins to teach what sex within a marital union should look like.[42] Speaking to both members of the marital couple, Paul argues that each owes the other a sexual obligation due to the fact that the bodies of each belong to his/her spouse.[43] Once Paul's rhetoric moves down the path of marriage, it is important to note that, in contrast to some of his fellow Hellenistic Jews, Paul does not argue that couples should moderate their sexual activity at all. Sir 9:1, for example, teaches a man not to be overly passionate with his wife (cf. Plutarch, *Conj. praec.* 47). Recall also that Philo worries that "natural pleasure" [ἡ κατὰ φύσιν ἡδονή] will lead "lovers of women" [φιλογύναιοι (cf. 3 Kgdms 11:1)] to "behave unchastely, not with the wives of others, but with their own" (*Spec.* 3.9 [Colson, LCL]).[44] Likewise Pseudo-Phocylides teaches, "Be not inclined to utterly unrestrained lust for a woman. For *Erōs* is no god, but a passion destructive to all [οὐ γὰρ ἔρως θεός ἐστι, πάθος δ' ἀίδηλον ἁπάντων]" (193-94).[45]

Genealogy of Gender," in *A Feminist Companion to Paul* (ed. Amy-Jill Levine; Cleveland: Pilgrim, 2004), 30; repr. from *Representations* 41 (1993).

[40] See my discussion in Chapter 3; Robbins, *Invention*, 1:127.

[41] Robbins, "Argumentative Texture," 32.

[42] For example, once a "woman" becomes a good "wife," teaching such as that found in Prov 18:22 likens her to grace and happiness received from God (cf. Sir 7:19, 26; 26:1, 3).

[43] Unlike the voluntary suspension of one's ἐξουσία Paul argues for in 1 Cor 9 and 10:23-33, here Paul seems to teach that the state of marriage itself transfers authority over the body to one's spouse – there seems to be nothing voluntary about it, beyond (perhaps) entering into the married state to begin with.

[44] Cf. Seneca, *De matrimonio* 85-85 as cited by Suzanne Dixon, "Sex and the Married Woman in Ancient Rome," in *Early Christian Families in Context: An Interdisciplinary Dialogue* (ed. David L. Balch and Carolyn Osiek; Religion, Marriage, and Family; Grand Rapids: Eerdmans, 2003), 123-24.

[45] Text and translation from Wilson, *Sentences of Pseudo-Phocylides*, 187, 221. For this idea expressed in ancient Athenian tragedy, see Simon Goldhill, *Love, Sex and Tragedy: How the Ancient World Shapes Our Lives* (London: John Murray, 2004), 49: "That *Eros* destroys is a general truth which tragedy displays to the citizens of the city."

The concern for moderation in married sexual expression is not as much of a concern (indeed, if it is a concern at all) in the older stratum of Jewish wisdom teaching.[46] However, Hellenistic Jewish moral teaching did not develop in a vacuum, but rather was in conversation with the moral traditions of the wider Hellenistic world. Thus Gaca notes that *erōs* was widely believed to be a force sent by the gods Aphrodite or Eros that compelled people to act against their rationale judgment. She cites Hesiod's teaching that "Limb-loosening Eros subdues the mind and thoughtful will in the breasts of all gods and persons" (*Theog.* 120-2). Moreover, if humans tried to resist this compulsion, "the gods of eros become tyrannical and destructive."[47] Pseudo-Phocylides takes this commonplace idea of the destructive nature of erotic desire and adds a Jewish spin to it – such destructive power, according to this Hellenistic Jewish thinker, demonstrates that Eros is not divine.

Although popular Greek thought held that resistance to *erōs* was futile, the philosophical tradition generally teaches that sexual urges could and should be controlled, even if eradication was considered neither possible nor desirable.[48] Plato argues that "Human sexual desires are the source of countless woes for people individually and for entire cities" (*Laws* 836b2).[49] Yet Plato, according to Gaca, also considers sexual desire a "necessary appetite" that is both "unavoidable and beneficial to a degree." For Plato the goal was moderation in sexual activity.[50] This moderation demonstrated control over one's sexual desire, and thus over one's body, which, in turn, proved one fit to exercise control in other areas as well.[51]

---

[46] See also Loader, *Enoch, Levi, and Jubilees on Sexuality*, 104 who argues that, in the Aramaic Levi Document, "Once the appropriate marriage partner from within the family of Abraham is found, marital and sexual relations are assumed to be normal and unproblematic." See idem, 111.

[47] Gaca, *Fornication*, 65-66. See also Martha C. Nussbaum, "*Erōs* and Ethical Norms: Philosophers Respond to a Cultural Dilemma," in *The Sleep of Reason: Erotic Experience and Sexual Ethics in Ancient Greece and Rome* (ed. Martha C. Nussbaum and Juha Sihvola; Chicago: University of Chicago Press, 2002), 60; Froma I. Zeitlin, "Reflections on Erotic Desire in Archaic and Classical Greece," in *Constructions of the Classical Body* (ed. James I. Porter; The Body, in Theories: Histories of Cultural Materialism; Ann Arbor: University of Michigan Press, 1999), 50.

[48] Gaca, *Fornication*, 40, 66-67. Cf. Philo, *Leg.* 1.86; 4 Macc 3:2.

[49] As translated and quoted by Gaca, *Fornication*, 41.

[50] Gaca, *Fornication*, 40, see also idem, 30-32. See van der Horst, *Sentences of Pseudo-Phocylides*, 240 where he notes: "Self-restraint in marriage is a common theme in antiquity." See also Nussbaum, "*Erōs* and Ethical Norms," 65: "...Athenian culture of the fourth and fifth centuries tries very hard to work out a concept of 'legitimate *erōs*' that will recognize the potentially lethal power of the passion but show how that power can be harnessed toward friendship and education."

[51] Wilson, *Sentences of Pseudo-Phocylides*, 198; see also Davidson, *Courtesans and Fishcakes*, 143-44, 159-67; Knust, *Abandoned to Lust*, 85-86; Gaca, *Fornication*, 41-42:

While Gaca notes that the radical sexual ideologies of early Plato (in the *Republic*) and the early Stoics – Zeno and Chrysippus – do away with marriage as a means for regulating sexual behavior,[52] the later thought of Plato (in the *Laws*) and the writings of the later Stoics Antipater, Hierocles, Musonius, and Epictetus re-inscribe the usefulness of marriage as the proper arena for sexual expression.[53] One notes, however, that sexual passion and the marriage bed did not, in the theories of the moral philosophers, go hand in hand. Martha Nussbaum writes that while it was "possible to conceive the passion of *erōs* for one's own spouse," this was "regarded as an atypical and somewhat ominous phenomenon."[54] Sexual moderation extends to the marital union as well. As Plutarch teaches, "the husband of a modest [σώφρονος] and austere wife must reflect, 'I cannot have her both as a wife and as a *hetaira*'" (*Conj. praec.* 29).[55] Such teachings of the moral philosophers must be taken with a grain of salt, however. As Susanne Dixon argues, "the very fact that these warnings are seen as necessary is an indication that married couples did show the symptoms of sexual infatuation celebrated by the lyrical poets."[56] The same could be said for the wisdom instruction found in Sirach, Philo, and Pseudo-Phocylides on this topic. These Jewish Hellenistic authors were mirroring a concern prevalent in non-Jewish Hellenistic moral philosophy.

Paul's apparent lack of concern about sexual moderation in 7:3-4 demonstrates where he parts ways with some other Hellenistic Jewish thinkers and exhibits creative thinking that works to achieve his local rhetorical purposes. Paul seems to evince some concern about controlling inordinate sexual passion in 1 Thess 4:4-5 where he counsels the

---

Plato "strove to reverse the conventional Greek measures of virility and happiness: Sexual restraint is the mark of the real man and genuine happiness, while sexual pleasure is for sissies." See my discussion of 1 Cor 6:13-14 in ch. 6 above.

[52] Gaca, *Fornication*, 44-45, 60-64; Deming, *Paul on Marriage and Celibacy* (2004), 64-65. But see Gretchen Reydams-Schils, *The Roman Stoics: Self, Responsibility, and Affection* (Chicago: University of Chicago Press, 2005), 145: "The Early Stoics' contributions to the lively debate pro and contra marriage are not consistent."

[53] Gaca, *Fornication*, 47-48, 52, 61; Deming, *Paul on Marriage and Celibacy* (2004), 66, 78-84; Reydams-Schils, *Roman Stoics*, 147-59.

[54] Nussbaum, "*Erōs* and Ethical Norms," 60-61.

[55] Translated by Donald Russell, "Advice to the Bride and Groom," in *Plutarch's Advice to the Bride and Groom and A Consolation to His Wife: English Translations, Commentary, Interpretive Essays, and Bibliography* (ed. Sarah B. Pomeroy; New York: Oxford University Press, 1999), 9.

[56] Dixon, *Roman Family*, 87. Dixon confirms this statement in her essay "Sex and the Married Woman in Ancient Rome," where she concludes "that it was unremarkable – if regrettable – for Roman husbands to display passionate love for their wives." See esp. idem, 111 n. 1 for Dixon's review of recent works of sexuality studies of ancient Rome. See McClure, *Courtesans at Table*, 33.

Thessalonians that they should marry "with holiness and honor" [ἐν ἁγιασμῷ καὶ τιμῇ] unlike the gentiles who do so "with [the] passion of desire" [ἐν πάθει ἐπιθυμίας].[57] However, in 1 Cor 7:3-4 Paul has more pressing concerns, namely that "cases of sexual immorality" have occurred within the community (7:2; cf. 1 Cor 5) and his apparent belief that many among the Corinthians lack self control (7:5). In light of the local rhetorical context, the fact that Paul does not project a Hellenistic concern with sexual moderation into his teaching on proper behavior in marriage is entirely understandable. His rhetorical aims here, the avoidance of impermissible sexual unions, mirror those from earlier Jewish wisdom texts that do not concern themselves much with sexual moderation in marriage.

In addition to displaying a Hellenistic concern about the proper way to control sexual desire within marriage, the Jewish thinker Philo also displays dependence on Greek thought for his teaching that the sole purpose of sex is the production of children, hopefully male heirs (*Ios.* 43), rather than the satisfaction of one's sexual appetite.[58] Pseudo-Phocylides also assumes that the main purpose of marriage is the production of children (175-76). In the case of Philo, Kathy Gaca argues that his understanding of sex only as a means for the production of children stems from the sexual ideology of the Pythagoreans.[59] Such an intellectual tradition is probably at work in Pseudo-Phocylides as well.

Gaca argues that the Pythagoreans, and *not* the later Stoics, were the intellectual progenitors of the notion that sex within marriage was *solely* for the production of children. Gaca calls this sexual ideal "procreationism" and notes that:

> [i]t dictates that men and women who engage in sexual intercourse should do so only in marriage and for the express purpose of reproduction, and that excitement during intercourse should be kept as sedate as possible. In a more extreme version, procreationism forbids all other sexual activity as reckless and morally reprehensible...[60]

---

[57] See Yarbrough, *Not Like the Gentiles*, ch. 3 (pp. 65-87); Knust, *Abandoned to Lust*, 51-52.

[58] See Stowers, *Rereading Romans*, 51: "Sex with a wife who cannot have children is like copulating with a goat or a pig."

[59] Gaca, *Fornication*, 205: "Philo's reputation as 'the Pythagorean Philo' among the early church fathers is borne out by the austerity of his sexual ethic, which is Pythagorean in origin." Gaca also contends that this Pythagorean view of sex influences the later Stoic teaching of Seneca and Musonius, but is actually antithetical to standard Stoic sexual ethics (idem, 114-15).

[60] Gaca, *Fornication*, 96; see her discussion of the "*Preambles to the Laws*, a Hellenistic Pythagorean treatise under the pseudonym 'Charondas,' [which] advocates procreationism in an unambiguously strict sense... He stipulates in no uncertain terms that the man must climax with his penis located nowhere else besides his wife's vagina and for the

This sexual ideology, Gaca maintains, persists in the thought of Philo, the later Stoics Musonius and Seneca, as well as the early Church Fathers.[61] Although Philo picks up this Greek ideology, since it fits well with his distrust of the passions, his fellow Hellenistic Jew, Paul, does not, at least not in 1 Cor 7:3-4. Children never enter the picture in Paul's teaching in 1 Cor 6:12–7:7. A procreationist stance would make no sense for the local rhetorical goals Paul has for teaching about marital sexual relationships. Paul is concerned here with staving off πορνεία and any sexual ideology that would restrict the one safe sexual outlet Paul gives to the Corinthians (see 1 Cor 7:2) would work against his rhetorical goals.[62] Thus a Hellenistic procreationist stance, like the Hellenistic moral concern for moderation, does not get projected into Paul's conceptual network in 7:3-4.

In contrast with the procreationist ideology, the sexual ethic of early and late Stoicism holds that sexual expression is *not* simply for the production of children, but rather as an expression of friendship.[63] As Nussbaum notes, in Stoic teaching "intercourse will be available in ... erotic relationships, when the virtuous judgment of the wise man chooses it. On the other hand, this is not the goal of the relationship."[64] Although in some Stoic thought a man choosing a male object of desire was considered "a higher type of *erōs*,"[65] Gaca argues that the later Stoics uphold the earlier Stoic ideal of friendship as the ultimate goal of sexual activity while relegating this function solely to the heter-

---

purpose of reproduction alone" (idem, 107-108). For his discussion on the significance of reproduction in the Greco-Roman moral tradition, see Yarbrough, *Not Like the Gentiles*, 60-62. On the importance of reproduction for the ancient city, see Brown, *Body and Society*, ch. 1.

[61] See esp. Gaca, *Fornication*, 111-16: "Procreationism in its aphoristic Neopythagorean form gains wider currency by the time of the early Roman empire" (p. 116); see also Phipps, "Is Paul's Attitude Toward Sexual Relations Contained in 1 Cor 7.1?" 129. Deming, *Paul on Marriage and Celibacy* (2004), 68 performs the more standard interpretation of regarding "procreationsim" as an indigenous Stoic ideology. On Musoinius, see Reydams-Schils, *Roman Stoics*, 147-59 who argues that while Musonius viewed procreation as the only legitimate goal of sexual activity, he taught that marriage itself was more than just a means to produce children; see Martha C. Nussbaum, "The Incomplete Feminism of Musonius Rufus, Platonist, Stoic, and Roman," in *The Sleep of Reason: Erotic Experience and Sexual Ethics in Ancient Greece and Rome* (ed. Martha C. Nussbaum and Juha Sihvola; Chicago: University of Chicago Press, 2002), ch. 11 (pp. 283-326).

[62] See Gaca, *Fornication*, 207-208 n. 37; Yarbrough, *Not Like the Gentiles*, 109.

[63] Nussbaum, "*Erōs* and Ethics," 65; Gaca, *Fornication*, 60-64; McClure, *Courtesans at Table*, 33; Reydams-Schils, *Roman Stoics*, 150.

[64] Nussbaum, "*Erōs* and Ethics," 79.

[65] Nussbaum, "*Erōs* and Ethics," 64. But see Davidson, *Courtesans and Fishcakes*, xxiii where he critiques Foucault's focus (and that of subsequent scholarship) on Greek male desire for boys while thinking very little about male desire for women.

osexual married couple.⁶⁶ Regarding the teaching of Musonius Rufus, Gretchen Reydams-Schils argues that "If women can be the equals of men, then Stoics can allow for the possibility of a soul-union between spouses."⁶⁷ Such an ideology fits well into the social ideal in Roman family life of *concordia* between husband and wife, which suggests a high value placed on harmony based on mutual respect between spouses.⁶⁸

Although he does not speak specifically about friendship, Paul alludes to the importance of this ideal, as well as that of *concordia*, when he teaches married couples the importance of sexual reciprocation.⁶⁹ To be sure, Paul's ultimate goal, as in all his teachings in 1 Cor 6:12–7:7, is the avoidance of πορνεία, but it seems that some Hellenistic concerns about the importance of mutuality within the marital unit are projected into the conceptual network Paul creates in 7:3-4. Paul's reasoning in these two verses resembles what Musonius teaches in his tract "What is the Goal of Marriage." According to Musonius, everything should be held in common between the married couple and *nothing* should be regarded as the private possession of one spouse or the other, "not even the body itself." He goes on to teach that "in marriage there must be in every respect a merger of life and a mutual caring between husband and wife... Where this mutual care is complete, and both partners provide it to one another completely, competing with one another for victory in this achievement, the marriage is appropriate and one to be emulated."⁷⁰ Concerns about sexual moderation and emphasis on procreation that are found in Musonius and other Hellenistic-Roman teachers are not adopted by Paul nor projected into 1 Cor 7:3-4. However, Paul freely employs culturally current ideas about the common, mutual ownership of bodies and selectively pro-

---

⁶⁶ Gaca, *Fornication*, 61; see also McClure, *Courtesans at Table*, 33; Reydams-Schils, *Roman Stoics*, 146-47.

⁶⁷Reydams-Schils, *Roman Stoics*, 163. See Martha C. Nussbaum, "The Incomplete Feminism of Musonius Rufus, Platonist, Stoic, and Roman," in *The Sleep of Reason: Erotic Experience and Sexual Ethics in Ancient Greece and Rome* (ed. Martha C. Nussbaum and Juha Sihvola; Chicago: University of Chicago Press, 2002), 283-326 for a more nuanced analysis of the teaching of Musonius vis-à-vis women than found in Reydams-Schils.

⁶⁸ Dixon, *Roman Family*, 83-90; idem, "Sex and the Married Woman in Ancient Rome." Huber, *Like a Bride Adorned*, 125-27; Plutarch, *Conj. praec.* 39, 44, 47.

⁶⁹ See Cynthia Patterson, "Plutarch's *Advice to the Bride and Groom*: Traditional Wisdom through a Philosophic Lens," in *Plutarch's* Advice to the Bride and Groom *and* A Consolation to His Wife: *English Translations, Commentary, Interpretive Essays, and Bibliography* (ed. Sarah B. Pomeroy; Oxford: Oxford University Press, 1999), 136 where she notes "the essential continuity and consistency in conjugal ideals within the ancient world."

⁷⁰ Translated by Nussbaum in an appendix to her "The Incomplete Feminism of Musonius Rufus," 319. See Deming, *Paul on Marriage and Celibacy* (2004), 75-76; Reydams-Schils, *Roman Stoics*, 165.

7. *How* Porneia *Should be Avoided: 1 Cor 7:1-7*   279

jects this concern into his teaching about how couples can avoid falling prey to sexual sin.

Figure 14: Conceptual Network for 7:3-4

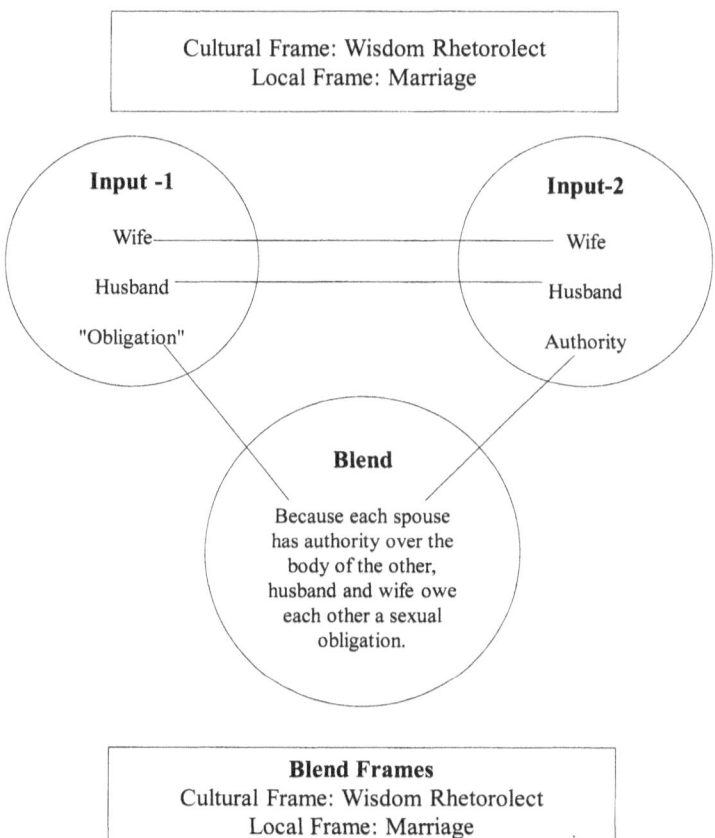

Mapping the conceptual network created by 1 Cor 7:3-4 is a relatively straightforward process, based on the Jewish and non-Jewish cultural information outlined above.

This is a simple mirror network in that each input space contains the same frames.[71] The organizing cultural frame each input space shares carries into the blend, which forms the recognizable command-rationale rhetology common to wisdom rhetorolect. The local frame for both input spaces is marriage, which is established based on the Characters of wife [γυνή] and husband [ἀνήρ]. In the network, there is

---
[71] Fauconnier and Turner, *The Way We Think*, 122-26.

cross-space mapping based on Identity between these two characters. The other elements in each input space have no inherent cross-space relationships with one another. In the blend, however, the authority each spouse possesses over the other spouse's body serves as a rationale for why the members of the marital pair owe a sexual debt to one another. In the blend the vital relation between the characters of husband and wife compress to Similarity.[72] This compression is signaled by the repetition of the lexical item ὁμοίως. Paul selectively projects this concern for mutual relations between spouses into his blend. A concern about sexual moderation and procreation, both available through the local frame of marriage, is not projected into the emergent structure of Paul's teaching. Paul's concern for stopping the practice of πορνεία explains why such selective projection takes place in 7:3-4. The emergent structure that arises from this network focuses the cultural configurations available within wisdom rhetorolect so that unlimited sexual activity, grounded in reciprocal ownership of bodies between spouses, becomes the primary way marriage staves off the dangers of πορνεία.

Paul's wisdom argumentation here is related in important ways to his priestly-wisdom teaching in 6:19-20. In 6:19-20, Paul argues that the bodies of the Corinthians believers are owned by God and they are, thus, not their own. In 7:4, Paul argues that married couples experience yet another claim of ownership on their bodies – husbands and wives do not have authority over their own bodies, but rather their spouses do. When 6:19-20 and 7:4 are read together, Paul's teaching in 7:1-2 make even more logical sense. The tension over who the rightful owner of one's body is – God or one's spouse – helps shed more conceptual light on why Paul teaches that abstinence is the best, but marriage is acceptable. Paul reiterates this point in 7:32-35. For those without a spouse the only master they serve is God. Those who are married, on the other hand, are owned by two parties and this creates a tension of loyalties that Paul would prefer to spare his community if conditions were ideal.

A Time to Pray (7:5-6):
Wisdom-Priestly-Apocalyptic Blended Rhetoric

When Paul teaches married couples that they each have a sexual obligation to the other based on the fact that neither partner in a marriage has authority over his or her body, his rhetoric does not need to roam outside of wisdom rhetorolect since this single rhetorolect provides him with the integration resources necessary to make his argument meaningful. In 7:5-6 Paul moves to nuance the instruction he has giv-

---

[72] Contra Plutarch, *Conj. praec.* 33.

en regarding the two ways to deal with sex and the sanctified Christian body thus far. In these verses Paul allows that a "third way" is possible – a blend of sexual abstinence (7:1b) and regular sexual activity within marriage (7:2-4). This blend allows married couples to refrain from sexual activity for a time, but places restrictions and limits on how this can take place. Paul's rationale and warning in these verses invite priestly and apocalyptic concerns back into his teaching. As he writes the Corinthians, "Do not deprive one another, unless perhaps out of agreement for a time, in order that you might devote yourselves [σχολάσητε] to prayer and [that] you might be together [ἐπὶ τὸ αὐτό] again, lest Satan tempt you on account of your lack of self-control [ἀκρασίαν]. And this I say by way of concession and not as a command."

The first command Paul gives in v. 5 against "robbing" one's spouse of sex flows from his wisdom teaching in vv. 3-4.[73] However, this command admits an exception. If *both* spouses agree to a cessation of sexual activity then *neither* is deprived. Paul allows that married couples can suspend sexual relations, but only for "a time" and only for one reason – so that they might pray. The fact that prayer is *the only* reason Paul allows married couples to stop normal sexual activity evokes reasoning and resources available in priestly rhetorolect, which is at work in 6:17-7:1. Recall that the use of priestly rhetorolect in Paul's teaching in those verses leads to the conclusion, based on the sanctified nature of the Christian body, that ideally it is better to refrain from sex.

Paul worries, however, that even periods of voluntary abstinence might lead to sinful outcomes. As noted above, wisdom texts such as Sirach warn against the dangers that the unmarried, especially unmarried men, pose to the community (Sir 36:25-27). Wisdom resources such as this combined with Paul's experience of the Corinthian community (1 Cor 5, 7:2) make him wary of married couples who are not regularly engaging in sex. Paul thus argues that the couple should always return to regular sexual activity, but he adds a rationale that does not seem completely at home in resources available from either wisdom or priestly rhetorolects. The rationale Paul offers highlights an apparent lack of control that he believes characterizes the Corinthians (a wisdom concern), but it also introduces an apocalyptic character: Satan.[74] It is not *just* that the Corinthians have no control, but Paul also fears that the Adversary will take advantage of this weakness and tempt the sanctified Corinthians into sin. Paul ends this section by reminding the Corinthians that he is not commanding them to give up sex in

---

[73] BDAG s.v. ἀποστερέω.
[74] Robbins, *Invention*, 1:336, 341, 364; see Williams, *Spirit World*, 87-103, 288-90.

order to pray, but rather that he understands that there are those who might feel called to do this.[75] Paul provides these "in between" couples with the proper guidelines for how to do this in a wise fashion. These two verses thus blend resources from wisdom, priestly, and apocalyptic rhetorolects as Paul carefully constructs a small loophole in his sexual teaching of 7:1-4.

John C. Poirier and Joseph Frankovic also note the purity concerns in Paul's teaching in 7:5-6.[76] Their reading provides a helpful corrective to the tendency to explain away the link between sexual abstinence and prayer by situating Paul's teaching within the diverse world of first-century Judaism. Their interpretation falters, however, when they read Paul's concern with purity through the lens of "prophetic celibacy."[77] Following the lead of Vermes, they look to Hellenistic Jewish interpretations of Moses for the interpretive key to unlock 1 Cor 7:5-7.[78] To be sure, Philo states that Moses ceased to have intercourse with his wife when he began to receive prophetic messages from God (*Mos.* 2.68-69). However, their argument that Hellenistic Jewish concerns about prophetic celibacy figures into Paul's sexual instruction to the Corinthians seems to go beyond the evidence.

While Poirier and Frankovic's specific explanation of the background to 1 Cor 7:5-6 is wanting, their contention that Paul is concerned with purity in these verses is correct. Even Will Deming, who argues strenuously for a Cynic-Stoic, rather than Jewish, background to 1 Cor 7, recognizes that Paul's teaching in 7:5-6 about the apparent tension between prayer and sex cannot be explained by Cynic or Stoic material. Like Poirier and Frankovic, Deming cites *T. Naph.* 8:8-9 to illustrate a similar idea: "For there is a time for intercourse with his wife [καιρὸς γὰρ συνουσίας γυναικὸς αὐτοῦ] and a time for continence in his prayer [καιρὸς ἐγκρατείας εἰς προσευχὴν αὐτοῦ]. And there are the two commandments; and if they should not be in order they produce sin."[79] This passage reflects a concern for ritual purity, but it does not make the leap to prophetic concerns that Poirier and Frankovic argue for. Philo links purity with various concerns, including wisdom. He argues that the books of Moses allegorically teach the

---

[75] For a comparative point with rabbinic Judaism, see Fraade, "Ascetical Aspects," 275.

[76] Poirier and Frankovic, "Celibacy and Charism," 1-18.

[77] Poirier and Frankovic, "Celibacy and Charism," 13-15.

[78] Poirier and Frankovic, "Celibacy and Charism," 14.

[79] Translated by Deming, *Paul on Marriage and Celibacy* (2004), 121-22; see Williams, *Spirit World*, 288-89. See also Loader, *Enoch, Levi, and Jubilees on Sexuality*, 115 where he argues that "[p]art of [*Jubilees'*] understanding of appropriate sexual behavior is knowing where and when sexual behaviour and nakedness are appropriate and inappropriate." See also idem, 275-85 for a further discussion of sacred time and space in *Jubilees*.

necessity for the separation of wisdom and bodily things: "For good sense [φρόνησις] and indulgence of bodily necessity [σωματικῆς ἀνάγκης] cannot occupy the same quarters" (*Leg.* 3:151 [LCL, Colson & Whitaker]).[80]

I argue that an explanation to Paul's meaning in 7:5-6 lies in its rhetorical context. Careful attention to the rhetorolects Paul uses to frame his teaching here and in 6:12–7:7 as a whole demonstrates that Paul himself has already provided interpreters with a way to understand these verses. Although Paul continues with wisdom rhetorolect and a local frame of marriage in the first part of v. 5, when he allows a period of sexual separation his rhetology grounds this allowance in a rationale from priestly integration resources. As I noted above, Paul's teaching here attempts to blend the two options he gave the Corinthians in 7:1-4. Just as the priestly concerns for the sanctified body in 6:17-20 ground Paul's teaching in 7:1, so it does in 7:5 as well. The only legitimate reason Paul gives for a couple to refrain from sexual activity is prayer. This recalls Paul's rhetographic construction of the Christian body as sacred space in 6:19 and draws on the commonplace understanding of the proper separation of sexual and cultic practice.

The issue of sexually irregular couplings arises once again, however, in Paul's admonition that the couple refrain from sex only for a short period [πρὸς καιρόν]. The evidence of sexual immorality among them (7:2) leads Paul to conclude that the Corinthians have no self-control [ἀκρασίαν].[81] Self-control, and how to achieve it, are typically matters discussed within a wisdom rhetorolect. However, Paul discusses this wisdom concern within an apocalyptic frame.[82] Recall that Paul uses apocalyptic rhetorolect in 6:13 in order to decompress the belly from its relation to the body and rhetorically fashion it into an entity disanalogous from and opposed to the Lord. Further, Paul draws from apocalyptic rhetorolect in his discussion of the πόρνη in 6:15-17 as an entity opposed to Christ. In 7:5 Paul concretizes his apocalyptic concern about powers opposed to God in the Character of Satan – the ultimate opponent of God.[83] Once again Paul's rhetology for why married couples must resume regular sexual activity rests on an apocalyptic foundation and thus would not be at home in Hellenistic-Roman cultures at large. This apocalyptic frame helps explain Paul's lack of con-

---

[80] See also Philo, *Deus* 8.
[81] See Davidson, *Courtesans and Fishcakes*, 163-64 where he cites Aristotle, *Rhet.* 2.6,4.
[82] See Deming, *Paul on Marriage and Celibacy*, 123.
[83] See Gaca, *Fornication*, 171: "The corporate whore in 1 Cor 6:15 is thus the semantic equivalent of Satan in 1 Cor 7:5; for sexually disobedient Christians are succumbing to the same wicked entity in both cases."

cern with sexual moderation in 7:3-4. Not only is attempting moderation a bad remedy when the true illness is πορνεία, but the lack of self-control Paul assigns to the Corinthians apparently *cannot* be overcome by the Corinthians due to the machinations of Satan, the enemy of God.

Figure 15: Conceptual Network for 7:5

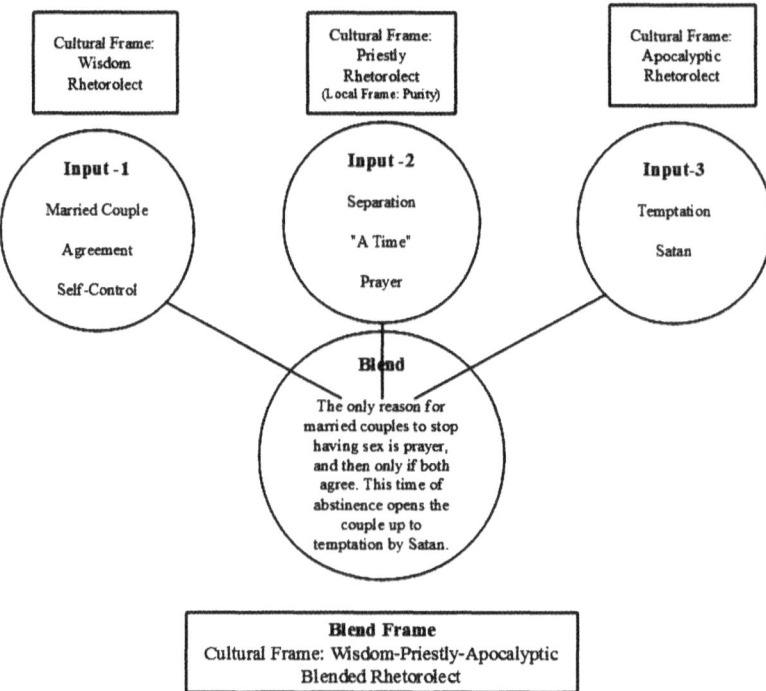

That Paul tries to blend his either/or teaching of 7:1-2 should not strike interpreters as unusual. Striving after greater spiritual gifts is apparently something that some in the Corinthian community did even when it was not beneficial (cf. 1 Cor 12:27-31; 14:18-19). In 7:5 Paul provides a third sexual path for some Corinthians in which they can enact a blend of priestly concern for bodily purity with regular sexual activity that staves off πορνεία. Such an interpretation helps unravel the notorious interpretive crux: to what does the τοῦτο of 7:6 refer? Given that the referent one assigns this demonstrative pronoun affects the way this passage is understood, it is no wonder that much ink has been spilled over its proper interpretation.

In trying to determine the referent for τοῦτο in 7:6, much depends on how interpreters relate 7:1b to Paul's thought. Those interpreters who consider the gnomic saying "it is good for a person not to touch a woman" to be an ideological position of the Corinthians against which Paul must argue typically conclude that the referent for τοῦτο is sexual abstinence (7:5). In this view Paul concedes a little to the Corinthian position while trying to mitigate it: couples may refrain from sex for a short period. In this reading, Paul is pro-marriage and pro-sex and he only allows partial abstinence in order to win over a certain faction of the Corinthian community.[84] Those who maintain that 7:1b represents Paul's, and not the Corinthians', sexual ideology typically take the τοῦτο as referring to sexual activity within marriage (7:2-4). In this reading, Paul prefers celibacy and he concedes sex within marriage only as a means to stop πορνεία, but he would rather everyone be as sexually continent as he is.[85]

I argue for a blend of the two positions outlined above. 1 Cor 7:1b does represent Paul's ideal sexual ideology. However, due to cases of sexual immorality (7:2) and the overall lack of self-control Paul imputes to the Corinthians (7:5), he fears that attempting to avoid sex will only make matters worse in Corinth. Paul thus counsels men and women to form recognized heterosexual monogamous unions in which to practice regular sex as the means to avoid sexual immorality (7:3-4).[86] Paul's concession in 7:6, I argue, refers to his allowance of a period of agreed upon sexual abstinence for the purposes of prayer. However, I do *not* believe this demonstrates Paul to be particularly pro-marriage.[87] Rather, Paul seems to be working through the priestly and wisdom concerns he raises in 7:1-2. His concession in 7:5 represents a blending of these two concerns in order to create more options for the Corinthians. While the *safest* solutions to the problem of πορνεία in Corinth remain *either* complete abstinence *or* regular sex within

---

[84] R. Collins, *First Corinthians*, 260; Fee, *First Epistle to the Corinthians*, 283-84; Schrage, *Der Erste Brief an die Korinther*, 2.70-72; Thiselton, *First Epistle to the Corinthians*, 511; see idem 510-11 for Thiselton's discussion of the five main views on this matter.

[85] Martin, *Corinthian Body*, 210; Nejsum, "Apologetic Tendency." Note that Bruce Winter, "I Corinthians 7:6-7: A Caveat and Framework for 'The Sayings' in 7:8-40," *TynBul* 48 (1997): 57-65, has suggested that the τοῦτο of 7:6 looks forward; see Fee, *First Epistle to the Corinthians*, 283 for a critique of this position held by scholars who wrote before Winter.

[86] Thus, unlike in Greek comedy and in "popular" Greek sexual ideology, for Paul it is marriage and not brothels that becomes the place to properly express one's sexual desire (Athenaeus, *Deipn.* 13.569e). See Davidson, *Courtesans and Fishcakes*, 83-84. This reflects a difference in where the primary sexual sin is considered to lie. In the Greek, Hellenistic, and Roman resources the gravest sexual transgression seems to be the specific act of adultery – see Patterson, *Family in Greek History*, 107-37; Dixon, *Roman Family*, 94-95; McClure, *Courtesans at Table*, 113 – whereas for Paul, it is the broader category of πορνεία, which includes adultery as well (see my treatment of 1 Cor 6:13 in ch. 6).

[87] See Knust, *Abandoned to Lust*, 80.

a marital union, Paul concedes that there is a third way. This way allows couples to practice the higher form of sexual ideology espoused by Paul, drawing upon the cognitive resources available in priestly rhetorolect, while still providing a "safe" sexual outlet for married partners, tapping conceptual structures from wisdom rhetorolect. It is in this third way that Paul comes closest to the sexual ideologies found in the law codes of Leviticus and Deuteronomy.[88] Purity issues are allowed to come into play in Paul's rhetoric, but only as a concession to couples who mutually agree to abstain for cultic reasons. In contrast to the law codes of the Pentateuch, however, Paul does not *command* the Corinthians to integrate purity concerns into their married sexual behavior. Rather Paul, apparently somewhat reluctantly, concedes this option to those who want to understand and order their lives through the frames of both priestly and wisdom rhetorolects.

Paul's Wish and Corinthian Reality (7:7): Wisdom-Priestly Rhetorolect

Paul closes his general teaching regarding how to avoid the sin of πορ-νεία by recapitulating his arguments in 7:1-6.[89] "And I wish all people to be even as I myself am; but each person has his own gift from God [χάρισμα ἐκ θεοῦ], the one thus and the other thus" [ὁ μὲν οὕτως, ὁ δὲ οὕτως]. Paul declares his wish that all people could be sexually continent like he is (7:1, 8; cf. 9:5, 15). This is a counterfactual statement, signaled by the lexical item θέλω.[90] The strong adversative ἀλλά (cf. 6:12; 7:4) signals to Paul's hearers/readers that his wish does not represent reality as lived in Corinth. As he will explicate later in the letter (12:4-11, 27-31; 14), the members of the Corinthian community do not all have the same gifts. Apparently, this extends also to the realm of self-control in matters of sexual expression. If all had the same gifts as Paul, the best way to avoid πορνεία would be to avoid sex altogether. However, the facts on the ground in Corinth demonstrate that not everybody is as gifted as Paul in this regard.[91] Thus Paul commands married couples to engage in regular sex. He allows some to blend together abstinence within a sexual relationship, but under strict controls. Paul seems to fear that members of the community will try to push abstinence beyond their gifts and that this will give Satan an op-

---

[88] See Deborah L. Ellens, *Women in the Sex Texts of Leviticus and Deuteronomy: A Comparative Conceptual Analysis* (New York: T & T Clark, 2008).

[89] On closing texture, see Robbins, *Exploring*, 19-21; idem, *Tapestry*, 50-53.

[90] See Fauconnier and Turner, *The Way We Think*, 31-32.

[91] See Gaca, *Fornication*, 89 for her discussion of the Cynic-Stoic wise "Superman" who can avoid sex, but whose behavior cannot function as an example for the masses. Also MacDonald, "Virgins, Widows, and Wives," 163.

portunity to enter the community.

The language of a "gift from God" that Paul uses in this verse, while certainly not foreign to wisdom rhetorolect, seems to draw more from the integration resources available from priestly rhetorolect. Just as the Corinthians' bodies are temples of the holy spirit only because of what God has done (6:19), so too in 7:7 do the gifts given by God suggest a blend of priestly concerns into Paul's wisdom instruction on the necessity of discernment in sexual matters.

The elements in input-1 (*Fig. 16*) are organized, in this context, by wisdom rhetorolect. Like the father in Proverbs, Paul teaches his Corinthian children with the wish that they imitate him.[92] Moreover, difference that calls for discernment is another element that fits naturally into the integration resources available in wisdom rhetorolect.[93] The elements of input-2 are organized by priestly rhetorolect. Although these elements could, in theory, be organized by a wide array of frames, the local rhetorical context suggests that this input space draws on the resources of priestly rhetorolect, but a peculiarly enriched priestly rhetorolect in which God's gifts are grounded in beneficial exchange in which God, through Christ, is the primary actor (cf. 6:19).

The emergent structure of this network relies on the organization of wisdom and priestly rhetorolects. With this emergent structure Paul ends his general discourse on how to avoid πορνεία by reminding the Corinthians of the proper lens through which to view this problem.

Paul calls for imitation, but an imitation of judgment rather than a specific course of action. The rationale Paul gives for this moves beyond wisdom and into priestly rhetorolect: deciding on what sexual path is best for them requires that the Corinthians examine what gifts they have been given by God. Paul grounds his teaching about different strategies for avoiding πορνεία in the blessings God bestows on God's sanctified people and their holy bodies (6:13-20).[94] Yet discerning these gifts, and acting in accordance with them, requires the eschatological discernment Paul tries to teach the Corinthians throughout the letter. The rich new emergent structure of this wisdom-priestly blend forces the Corinthians beyond a simplistic imitation of Paul's actions toward an imitation of his ability to make wise judgments.

---

[92] See Newsom, "Woman and the Discourse of Patriarchal Wisdom."
[93] Robbins, *Invention*, 1:129.
[94] See Camp, "Wise, Strange, and Holy," 87 for how this moves beyond wisdom.

Figure 16: Conceptual Network for 7:7

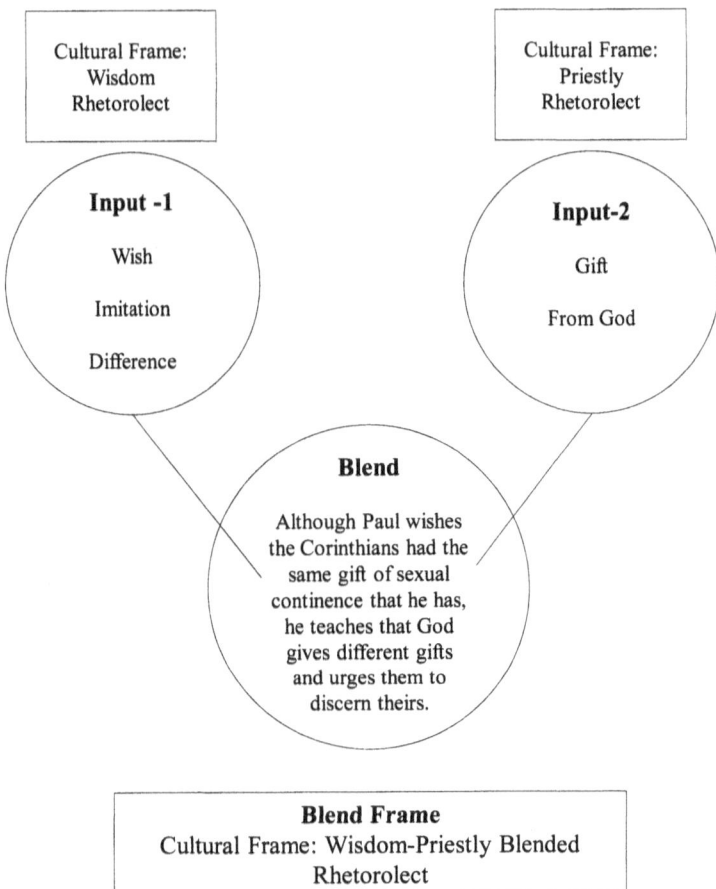

While it seems clear that Paul regards his ability to be sexually continent as a gift from God, the question that has tugged at Christian interpreters over the centuries is whether marriage is to be considered a gift as well.[95] Those, usually Protestant, interpreters who read Paul as being naturally pro-marriage and pro-sex argue that in 7:7 Paul teaches that *both* abstinence *and* marriage are gifts from God – the μὲν ... δέ clauses reflecting the Corinthian position of 7:1b and Paul's retort in 7:2 respectively.[96] Contrary to what the Corinthians believe, these in-

---

[95] R. Collins, *First Corinthians*, 256; Fee, *First Corinthians*, 285; Schrage, *Der Erste Brief an die Korinther*, 2.73-74; Thiselton, *First Epistle to the Corinthians*, 513-14.

[96] Thiselton, *First Epistle to the Corinthians*, cites Luther's *Works* (American ed., St Louis: Concordia, 1973), 28.16: "Marriage is just as much a gift of God, St. Paul says here, as chastity is."

terpreters argue, Paul teaches that marriage is also a gift from God. However, the presence of a blend of these positions in 7:5 complicates this interpretation. Moreover, the reason Paul gives for entertaining the idea of marital sex at all is "on account of cases of sexual immorality" [διὰ τὰς πορνείας] (7:2) and he openly worries about even agreed upon abstinence on the part of married couples because of what he considers to be the Corinthians' innate lack of self-control [ἀκρασίαν]. This hardly seems to be the positive language one might expect Paul to use describing a God given gift.[97] Paul's discussion of marriage in 1 Cor 7 is, to a large extent, accidental. In much the same way that Deming argues marriage "unwittingly" became "the central issue" in the Cynic-Stoic debate about civic responsibility and an individual's allegiance to a higher cause,[98] I argue Paul's discussion of marriage only arises because of his concern over πορνεία. When Paul discusses marriage in this pericope, his main focus is always trained upon the danger of sexual immorality.

Based on the accidental and prophylactic nature marriage plays in Paul's argument, I find it difficult to agree with interpreters who maintain that Paul considers the married state a gift from God. To be sure, Paul does not consider marriage, and the sex that comes with it, to be sinful (7:36). He even teaches that one who marries, instead of sinning, "does well" [καλῶς ποιεῖ], but it is the one who abstains from marriage (and sex) who "will do better" [κρεῖσσον ποιήσει] (7:38). Paul does not censure marriage, but it seems to be a good only in relation to irregular sexual sin. Paul is not shy about his preference, in ideal circumstances, for abstinence. This is perhaps the most important point. Whether Paul considers marriage a "gift" can be endlessly debated. My main concern here is to show that when Paul teaches the Corinthians *how* to avoid πορνεία he would prefer it if all could refrain from sex as he himself does. A second best option is for the Corinthians to get married and engage in regular sexual activity. A much more complicated and perilous third way is a blend of the priestly and wisdom frames that govern the first two options in which couples engage in sex, but refrain only by agreement and only for specific cultic reasons. Paul, the wise teacher of the Corinthians, holds himself up as a παράδειγμα to be emulated. However, Paul is wise enough to know that not all the Corinthians have his gifts, and therefore he gives them more realistic teachings that take into account their differing gifts by offering various

---

[97] See Kurt Niederwimmer, *Askese und Mysterium: Über Ehe* (Göttingen: Vandenhoeck & Ruprecht, 1975), 6 (cited by Thiselton, *First Epistle to the Corinthians*, 513 n. 157).

[98] Deming, *Paul on Marriage and Celibacy*, 58.

permutations of married sexual congress (7:8-40).[99]

Conclusion

The rhetology of Paul's teaching in 7:1-7 builds with the rhetography of 6:12-20 and provides the actionable content to his admonition to flee πορνεία in 6:18. In explaining to the Corinthians how best to avoid sexual immorality, Paul offers two basic sexual options: abstinence (7:1b) or regular sexual activity within a recognized heterosexual union (7:2) organized by priestly and wisdom rhetorolects respectively. To these two basic modes of sexual expression Paul adds a third that blends priestly and wisdom cultural frames in such a way that he allows couples to refrain from sexual activity for a specific religious purpose: prayer (7:5). This third option is fraught with danger and Paul, relying on apocalyptic rhetorolect for his rationale, urges couples to resume regular sexual activity as soon as possible. Paul's teaching in 7:1-7 represents a complex didactic discourse in which Paul endeavors to find the best ways for members of the Corinthian community to avoid πορνεία based on the different gifts each has received from God (7:7). Paul ends the pericope as he began it, with a focus on himself as the παράδειγμα of a wise teacher able to make wise choices – a wisdom he teaches them to emulate.

A Holistic Argument

As I hope to have demonstrated in these chapters, analyzing 1 Cor 6:12–7:7 using conceptual integration theory within a socio-rhetorical framework bears much exegetical fruit. The results of this analysis suggest that this mode of interpreting texts, relatively new to biblical studies, holds promise for understanding other areas of the Pauline corpus as well as other examples of early Christian literature more generally. Conceptual integration theory and socio-rhetorical interpretation work in such a complementary fashion due to the fact that each is concerned with "how language prompts for meaning."[100] Such a concern prods the exegete analyzing Paul's language to examine the larger background resources that frame his discourse as well as examine how the discourse itself is rhetorically effective in the production of a Christian culture.[101] This exegetical investigation has determined that Paul's teaching in 6:12–7:7 is an example of early Christian wisdom discourse that invites apocalyptic and priestly concerns into its argumentation as a

---

[99] See Winter, "1 Corinthians 7:6-7"; Gaca, *Fornication*, 89.
[100] Fauconnier and Turner, *The Way We Think*, 139; see also 277.
[101] This describes oral-scribal intertexture, cultural intertexture, inner texture, and cultural texture respectively.

means to make it more rhetorically effective. Paul offers the Corinthians multiple ways to think about their sanctified bodies as incompatible with πορνεία and, true to form for wisdom, offers a variety of ways the Corinthians can avoid this sin based on their proper discernment of the gifts they have received from God. Paul's *paideia* in this pericope works to create a Christian culture that is wary of sexual activity due to the holiness of the Christian body, but pragmatic enough to offer individual modes of sexual behavior that allow for "safe" sexual expression within this community of sanctified believers.[102]

The gnomic rhetology of 6:12 creates the necessary rhetorical space for reflection that organizes the conceptual networks of 6:12–7:7. After establishing wisdom rhetorolect as the host environment for his didactic discourse, Paul first moves to *show* the Corinthians why πορνεία is incompatible with their sanctified bodies. In order to achieve this, Paul's discourse employs graphic conceptual blends that function on human scale. The host environment of wisdom rhetorolect, however, does not provide Paul with the necessary cognitive resources to argue that πορνεία is the worst bodily sin one could commit. For this, Paul uses resources from apocalyptic and priestly rhetorolects to power his rhetography in 6:13-20. This rhetography first moves to separate the body from its passionate desires and then begins to compress the relationship between the body and Christ from Analogy to Identity. This Identity with the risen Lord is elaborated through the cultic rhetography of the body as a temple, which blends with the image of the Corinthians as slaves purchased by God. Paul's teaching in 6:12-20, then, provides warrants for why πορνεία is to be avoided.

In 7:1-7 Paul's discourse returns to a reliance on rhetology, which is how he began the pericope in 6:12, to *explain* to the Corinthians how they can best enact his command to flee πορνεία. The space for reflection and discernment created by wisdom rhetorolect fully blossoms in this section of the pericope. Here Paul teaches the Corinthians three ways to live a proper sexual life in their sanctified bodies. The two main ways Paul offers for avoiding sexual immorality are either complete abstinence of sexual activity (7:1b) or regular sex within a marital bond (7:2-4). These two options are grounded in the logic and resources of different rhetorolects. If one operates within the realm of priestly rhetorolect, and its concern for purity, the first sexual option makes sense. Shifting to wisdom rhetorolect, however, provides the logic and resources to organize the second option. Given the cases of sexual immorality in Corinth (7:2a), Paul urges the Corinthians to take the latter course given their lack of self-control (7:5). Yet Paul's teach-

---

[102] On the creation of a new Christian *paideia*, see Robbins, *Invention*, 1:15.

ing moves to create a third sexual path. He seems to think, however, that this path is fraught with danger. In 7:5 Paul's teaching blends the two main sexual options he delineated in 7:1-4: Corinthian couples, *if both spouses agree*, may refrain from sex for religious reasons. However, Paul openly worries about their inability to withstand temptation from Satan, and so he urges a quick resumption of sexual activity. Paul wishes that all the Corinthians could follow his sexual praxis, but he recognizes that God does not give the same gifts to everyone. Thus Paul, in true wisdom style, ends his discourse by teaching the Corinthians to discern what gifts they have received from God and to choose the proper sexual path based on these gifts.

Conceptual integration theory and the latest tools of socio-rhetorical interpretation allow my exegesis to make a contribution to the ongoing project of understanding Paul's rhetoric in 1 Cor 6:12–7:7. By reading Paul's teaching in this difficult passage through the lens of wisdom rhetorolect, I believe that many intractable issues have been resolved without recourse to any slogan hypotheses that have so dominated the discussion of these verses in the twentieth century. Paul's use of gnomic sayings (6:12-14; 7:1) not only situates this pericope firmly within the host environment of wisdom, but it also explains the multiplicity of his suggestions for avoiding πορνεία. As Crenshaw notes, in wisdom a "good act constitutes the appropriate one for a given situation."[103] While Paul has a strong preference for abstinence (7:1, 7), his teaching recognizes the heterogeneous nature of the Corinthian community, and his response to the threat of πορνεία takes the different situations of the individual members of the community into consideration. In 6:12–7:7 Paul does not write the familiar περὶ γαμοῦ treatise of Hellenistic moral tradition. Rather he writes περὶ πορνείας, and marriage simply serves as one way, albeit a major way, to solve the religious problem caused by irregular sexual unions.

---

[103] Crenshaw, *Wisdom*, 11.

Conclusion

I have argued that Paul's teaching in 1 Cor 6:12–7:7 is most profitably viewed as an example of early Christian didactic wisdom. In Paul's two pronged attack on the problem of πορνεία he relies on rhetography to show the Corinthians *why* it is the worst of all possible bodily sins and he then employs rhetology when he offers them three modes for *how* to avoid it. As I hope to have demonstrated, however, Paul's didactic wisdom teaching in this pericope is always already energized by an apocalyptic worldview. Moreover, Paul's wisdom in 1 Cor 6:12–7:7 also employs priestly concerns about purity, holiness, and sacred space. The fact that Paul invites the resources and reasoning from other rhetorolects into his didactic argument highlights the fact that Paul is standing within a living stream of Jewish wisdom and moral reflection. The notorious difficulty scholars have in defining wisdom, and neatly demarcating it off from other modes of discourse, is due to the powerful and opportunistic nature of Jewish wisdom discourse, especially Jewish wisdom in the Hellenistic period. Jewish didactic wisdom is concerned to teach people how to live a life of generative righteousness and is willing to use whatever resources are necessary to achieve its goals. Paul, it seems, is most like a Hellenistic Jewish teacher of wisdom when he opens up the boundaries of his didactic discourse by blending wisdom rhetorolect with apocalyptic and priestly integration resources.

The Jewish Resources

The generative aspects of wisdom are related to the role of wisdom in the creation of the world. As God created the world through wisdom, so wisdom continues to generate righteousness in those who properly "fear the Lord." In the Jewish resources I examine, the specific working out of wisdom's admonition to fear the Lord is found in the law. As we have seen, already in Proverbs wisdom is linked to living out the law of God.¹ The identification of wisdom and the law is most firmly cemented in Sirach, for whom the books of Moses contain true wisdom. It is the law that provides, in Ben Sira's understanding, the concrete resources for living a life governed by wisdom.

For Philo, wisdom's role in creation and its expression in the law of Moses go hand in hand. Not only does wisdom, along with the divine λόγος, have a central role in creating the universe, but the law, the expression of God's wisdom, mirrors this created order. For Philo, following Jewish law allows one to achieve the ultimate goal of wisdom, long sought by Greek philosophy, of living life in accord with the structure of nature/creation.

Wisdom's generative nature explains why she is widely sought. Yet, for all the respect accorded to its sages and for all its admonitions to obtain wisdom, most writings within Jewish wisdom tradition are ever vigilant for false expressions or premature declarations of wisdom. This wariness may stem from the problematic nature of human knowledge and wisdom found in Gen 2–3.² Although the examples of Jewish wisdom encountered in the preceding chapters argue for a life-long pursuit of wisdom, they are almost unanimous in their warnings against those who would claim the mantle of wisdom for themselves. I have argued that Jewish wisdom texts reflect an indigenous tradition of self-critique and appear ever ready to put the one wise in his (or her?) own eyes into the position occupied by the fool. Wisdom is a journey and the Jewish resources examined in Chapter 2 evince a deep mistrust of those who claim to have arrived at the destination.

In line with its critique of those who improperly claim wisdom, the resources examined in Chapter 3 demonstrate an understanding of freedom that is always already tied to obeying the Lord and enacting the law. This way of configuring freedom, as noted in Chapter 6, is found in the larger Hellenistic world as well. Only the fool, these resources teach, thinks freedom consists of doing whatever one wishes. Such self-centered action, far from being an expression of freedom, is often described as behavior that ensnares rather than liberates. Philo reconfigures his Jewish wisdom traditions through Greek thought, especially Stoicism. Such a reconfiguration allows him to sum up succinctly the pervasive attitude of freedom in Jewish wisdom via a Greek idiom: the good person is permitted to do whatever he (or she?) wants, since the good person only wants to do that which is beneficial and in line with the law. Therefore, only the good person is truly free.

---

¹ Schnabel, *Law and Wisdom*, 1-7.
² Although recall Sirach's reconfiguration of God's role in the human acquisition of knowledge in Sir 17:1-14. See Robbins, *Invention*, 1:147.

When we turn to examine how the resources of Chapter 3 deal with women, we see a deep ambivalence. The Hellenistic Jewish texts also show a similar ambivalence to sexual activity, even when this activity takes place inside a marital union. In these texts women in general are viewed as figures filled with potential danger. The paradigmatic story of King Solomon going after other gods because of his (sexual) love for his foreign wives demonstrates, in the Jewish wisdom storyline, how even the wisest of kings can fall prey to the dangers of foreign/strange/"other" [ἀλλοτρία] women. Although the Jewish resources personify wisdom as a woman, her nefarious *Doppelgänger* is always tempting young and foolish men with her sexual charms. The fear of woman's evil side rises to such a pitch in the aggressively androcentric writings of Ben Sira and Philo that she becomes the origin of sin and death. In these resources there is a continual "slippage" between woman as symbol and actual women. As Richard Baer notes, regarding Philo, these two elements are never separable – each complements and feeds the other.[3]

To balance this picture, we also saw that if woman (symbolic and actual) performs the role of the good wife, the Jewish wisdom resources, even the misogynist text of Sirach, regard her as a blessing to her husband.[4] Once firmly established with the household and as a partner to a man, real women lose some of their metaphorical danger. They even function, according to Sirach, as a means to tame men. Men without wives, according to this text, are a danger to the stability of the community and must be domesticated.

Yet even in the role of wife, woman is still regarded with suspicion in the Hellenistic era, once again especially in the thought of Ben Sira and Philo. Although each regards marriage and sexual activity within the marital relationship as normal, each warns men against becoming overly passionate with one's own spouse. Such a concern is not found in the older wisdom text of Proverbs, even in its Septuagintal avatar. For certain segments of Hellenistic Judaism, like certain segments of the broader Hellenistic society, marriage – while useful and to some extent necessary – does not completely solve the problem posed by women and sex. When concerns about sexual activity, even in marriage, are blended with resources that stress purity and holiness the negative valance to such activity only increases.

---

[3] Baer, *Philo's Use of the Categories Male and Female*, 35.
[4] Recall how LXX Prov 31 inserts the husband in the encomium to the woman of valor.

Paul's Wisdom

Paul stands within this living and variegated Jewish wisdom tradition. The Jewish resource zones examined in Chapter 3 provide a thick description of how Jewish moral teachings deal with right conduct in sexual matters. Paul's teaching in 6:12–7:7, I argue, is best viewed as early Christian didactic wisdom that grew out of Paul's Hellenistic Jewish background. The wide array of resources available within this rich cultural background, however, is reconfigured through Paul's understanding of the Christ event. The cross of Christ, according to Paul, is the epitome of God's paradoxical wisdom at work in the universe. This wisdom, moreover, has operated since the beginning, before all time. Christ crucified reveals the structure of the cosmos and Paul demands that the Corinthians conform their lives to this reality.

Yet, unlike the Jewish resources, Paul does not believe that law is a necessary or sufficient means to enable the Corinthians to conform to God's paradoxical wisdom. Rather, in the first four chapters of the letter, Paul teaches the Corinthians to develop an eschatological discernment. By modeling themselves after Paul, the Corinthians will be able, through a proper understanding of God's true wisdom, to make wise decisions in a whole host of arenas that are affecting the community (1 Cor 4:16–11:1).

The paradoxical wisdom Paul teaches the Corinthians is rooted in an apocalyptic worldview. This powerful blend of wisdom and apocalyptic integration resources sets the stage for the specific issues Paul tackles in the following chapters. In 1 Cor 6:12–7:7 Paul's wisdom teaching, blending with the integration resources available in apocalyptic and priestly rhetorolects, argues that the Christian (man) must avoid πορνεία. In order to get the Corinthians to *see* why πορνεία is incompatible with the Christian body Paul relies heavily on rhetography in 6:12-20. Through a series of conceptual blends Paul decompresses the Christian body from its passionate desires and progressively compresses the relationship between the believer and Christ from Analogy to Identity. Moreover, Paul elaborates this compression with another blend that constructs the Christian body as sacred temple space. Drawing heavily on the purity and holiness rationales of priestly rhetorolect, Paul creates a Christian body for which any sexual activity is problematic.

Despite the conceptual blends he has created by the end of 1 Cor 6, the facts on the ground in Corinth demonstrate to Paul that the ideal means for avoiding πορνεία, one that conforms fully to the logic of the blend created in 6:18-20, is not possible. Because of this, Paul attempts to enable the Corinthians to employ their eschatological discernment in order to make the right sexual decision in light of the gifts each of them has received from God. Paul, relying now on rhetological demonstrations in 7:1-7, offers the Corinthians three modes of sexual expression that take into consideration their differing gifts and that will provide them with the tools necessary to avoid πορνεία. Although Paul desires that all people be able to conform fully to the ideals of the blends he has created in 6:12-20 (7:1b, 7), he displays his own wisdom by recognizing that this is simply not possible in Corinth.

Promises and Dangers

I hope that the investigation I have undertaken in these pages has demonstrated the exegetical promise that conceptual integration theory holds for those of us studying how early Christian discourse goes about making meaning in various ways. Biblical scholarship has profited immensely from examining these ancient writings through the lens of conceptual metaphor theory. Conceptual blending, I argue, provides exegetes with a similar set of tools for examining a broader spectrum of language.[5] The exegetical fruits generated by using conceptual metaphor theory provide an analogue for the promise conceptual integration theory holds for biblical studies.[6] I have used blending theory within a socio-rhetorical framework because I believe that it addresses similar concerns raised by socio-rhetorical scholars, but other exegetes need not follow my lead in this. Conceptual integration is a powerful theory of human meaning making that, conceivably, can be used in a variety of ways.[7] Conceptual integration theory certainly cannot answer

---

[5] Joseph Grady, Todd Oakley, and Seana Coulson, "Blending and Metaphor," in *Metaphor in Cognitive Linguistics: Selected Papers from the Fifth International Cognitive Linguistics Conference, Amsterdam, July 1997* (ed. Raymond W. Gibbs, Jr. and Gerard J. Steen; Amsterdam: John Benjamins, 1999), 101-24.

[6] Grady, Oakley and Coulson, "Blending and Metaphor," discuss how blending can be used to complement conceptual metaphor theory: "In this article we explore the relationship between BT [blending theory] and CMT [conceptual metaphor theory] and the phenomena they address, arguing that the two approaches are complementary" (p. 101). Such complementarity is possible, they argue, due to the fact that "[s]ince blending is an opportunistic process of on-line space-building, any conceptualization that starts out as a primary metaphor, or other simple conceptual association, is susceptible to being elaborated" (p. 112). See also Oakley, "Conceptual Blending, Narrative Discourse, and Rhetoric."

[7] See Chapter 1, esp. my discussion of the essays in Luomanen, Pyysiäinen, and Uro, eds, *Explaining Christian Origins and Early Judaism*; and Howe, *Because You Bear this Name*. See also Hugo Lundhaug, " 'These are the Symbols and Likenesses of the Resurrection': Conceptualization of Death and Transformation in the *Treatise on the Resurrection* (NHC I,4)," and Ivan Czachesz, "Metamorphosis and Mind: Cognitive Explorations of the Grotesque in Early Christian Literature," pp. 187-205 and 207-30, respectively, in Turid Karlsen Seim and Jorunn Økland, eds., *Metamorphoses: Resurrection, Body and Trans-*

every question that biblical texts prompt, but I hope to have shown the promise it holds for those studies concerned with the meaning potential of biblical discourse.

Enacting exegetical practice using conceptual integration theory has the added benefit of enabling biblical scholars to participate in the larger cognitive science of religion enterprise. Not only does this allow biblical scholars to have productive conversations with other scholars of religion, but also with other colleagues in the academy – in both the humanities and the sciences.[8] The sometimes rancorous relations between scholars who see their primary home in either the Society of Biblical Literature or the American Academy of Religion might, I hope, begin to improve if some of us can engage our respective specialties through a similar cognitive lens. Again, cognitive investigations will not answer every question and they will not be appropriate for many projects. However, the common use of conceptual integration theory allows me, a biblical scholar who specializes in Paul, to learn from Edward Slingerland, a scholar who specializes in (among other things) ancient Chinese thought.[9] And I hope that studies produced by biblical scholars using various tools from the cognitive science of religion will be useful to colleagues in other academic arenas as well. Cognitive approaches provide a solid foundation for comparative and other cross-disciplinary work.

Of course, I specifically use conceptual integration theory within a larger socio-rhetorical framework, and I hope that this exegetical investigation has made a contribution to the ongoing process of developing appropriate and rigorous modes of socio-rhetorical interpretation.[10] For most socio-rhetorical interpreters the promise of conceptual integration theory is recognized as is the exegetical usefulness of rhetorolects as interpretive categories. In this project I undertake a relatively new avenue of investigation that uses conceptual blending with rhetorolects as a means of analyzing the rhetoric of Paul's teaching in 1 Cor 6:12–7:7.[11] Even if they disagree with my specific conclusions, I hope to have used blending theory in such a way that prompts further

---

formative Practices in Early Christianity (Ekstasis 1; Berlin: de Gruyter, 2009). Czachesz's work interacts less with conceptual integration theory than with other aspects of the cognitive science of religion.

[8] Note, as I do in Chapter 1, the recent development of the Cognitive Science of Religion consultation and the Cognitive Linguistics in Biblical Interpretation section in the AAR and SBL, respectively. See also Slingerland's call for cross-disciplinary conversations in *What Science Offers the Humanities*.

[9] See http://faculty.arts.ubc.ca/eslingerland/index.html [cited 26 April 2010].

[10] See Bloomquist, "Paul's Inclusive Language," 165.

[11] See the programmatic program for this type of analysis in Robbins, *Invention*.

refinement from my fellow socio-rhetorical interpreters in future studies.

I understand my work to exist in an ongoing dialogue with other Pauline scholars who use diverse modes of interpretation to solve puzzles Paul's letters generate. Within this community I stand with those such as Renate Kirchhoff and Brian Dodd who are moving away from using slogan hypotheses, as traditionally deployed, in their exegetical work on 1 Corinthians. While Anthony Thiselton does not believe that such a move has created any lasting impact on Pauline scholarship, I hope that studies such as ours may offer future scholars new and creative ways to examine rhetorical invention within the Pauline corpus. I also locate my work among those scholars who attempt to explain the cultural relevance of Paul's argumentation, rather than attempting to derive a precise historical reconstruction of the Corinthian situation. This is not to deny that Paul's rhetoric is employed for a specific local purpose. Rather, it is to acknowledge the limits of our ability to achieve such a precise reconstruction and to focus, rather, on the power of Paul's language. Far from being ahistorical, attending to the cultural power of Paul's rhetoric helps us to understand why early Christian communities outside of Corinth began to read and use Paul's teachings, despite their pronounced difficulties (2 Pet 3:16).

Finally, I must acknowledge what I consider to be the ethically problematic nature of the results of this project.[12] Peter Nejsum eloquently describes the problem facing modern scholars when trying to make sense of the sexual teachings found in Paul's writings:

> Anyone who has ever concerned him or herself with those Biblical texts which contradict the modern moral and theological picture of the world will have noticed that there is a peculiar *apologetic* tendency in Biblical exegesis. An apologetic reading attempts to explain away or at least smooth over the oppositional relationship between the understanding of the world which is behind the texts, and the reader's own modern one; it attempts to "defend" the texts against more or less explicit accusations of sexual asceticism, authoritarianism, oppression of women, and so forth.[13]

Nejsum goes on to note that this apologetic tendency is especially pronounced when trying to reconcile "a currently common view that the satisfaction of sexual desire is part of the 'good life,'" a position he and I share, with what Paul teaches his fledgling communities about

---

[12] Socio-rhetorical interpretation makes a space for, and encourages, such an exploration of the ideological texture of the texts studied and the interpreter who studies them. See Robbins, *Tapestry*, 192-236; idem, *Exploring*, 95-119.

[13] Nejsum, "Apologetic Tendency," 48.

the dangers of sexual immorality.[14] In order to render Paul's arguments in 1 Cor 6:12–7:7 meaningful, there is a tendency among some exegetes to attempt to make these arguments *useful* as well.

In this study, I have used the tools of conceptual integration theory within a socio-rhetorical framework to explore the meaning potential present in Paul's teaching against πορνεία in 1 Cor 6:12–7:7. In order to do this, I have tried to locate Paul's argument within a broader Hellenistic moral landscape, and I have suggested possible discursive resources that help explain how Paul framed his teachings and, thus, how they made meaning. The exegetical conclusions I have come to create a Pauline Christianity, to quote Peter Brown once again, "whose back is firmly turned toward us."[15] Although I have approached my exegetical project with the same amount of preconceptions and ideological baggage as any scholar, my goal has been to understand Paul's rhetoric within its own cultural environment, however strange that environment may appear to those of us living in the twenty-first century. As a result, I find myself standing with Dale Martin who writes, at the end of *The Corinthian Body*:

> As should be clear, I have not attempted an apologia for Paul. Not only do I doubt that he won all his arguments, but in some cases I hope he did not. It would be nice to believe, for instance, that some women refused to accept his and their society's characterizations of them as inferior. But all such hopes remain in the netherworld of historical speculation; we have simply no way of knowing.[16]

Paul wrote in an androcentric universe. Those of us whose intellectual development was nurtured by feminist modes of reading may regard the presence of and activity by women who are clearly powerful within Paul's communities with great hope. Nevertheless, the fact remains that in Paul's letters we have an "incomplete feminism" at best and misogynist conceptual structures at worst.[17] As I have repeated throughout this book, conceptual integration theory proposes that new conceptual blends can only function by reusing and reconfiguring available cultural resources and frames in innovative ways. Paul's argument against πορνεία does just that. The conceptual resources and frames available to Paul conceived of sexual desire and sexual activity, men and women, asceticism and marriage in ways wildly different from the conceptual resources available to those of us living today. We

---

[14] Nejsum, "Apologetic Tendency," 48.

[15] Brown, *Body and Society*, xvii; see my "Introduction," p. 1.

[16] Martin, *Corinthian Body*, 251. But see Antoinette Clark Wire, *The Corinthian Women Prophets: A Reconstruction through Paul's Rhetoric* (Minneapolis: Fortress, 1990).

[17] I have borrowed the phrase "incomplete feminism" from Nussbaum's essay, "The Incomplete Feminism of Musonius Rufus."

should not fault Paul for thinking in the categories of the multiple ancient cultures in which he lived, but neither should we feel compelled either to redeem him or make his thoughts normative.

One of the crucial rhetographical hinges that brings Paul's argument in 1 Cor 6:12–7:7 down to human scale is the image of the πόρνη. In order for Paul's argument to work, the hearers/readers of Paul's instruction need to accept as common sense that some women are so sexually "filthy" that they can be used as the personification of the deviant Other.[18] Paul's argument depends on the negative emotion this character prompts.[19] Again, I would argue that in Paul's language we have "slippage" between woman as symbol and actual women. Yet, as noted above, these two categories are never entirely separate. They justify and reinforce one another. As an ethical reader, I must object to Paul's use and abuse of the "whore" in this pericope. While I have argued that Paul's wisdom teaching against πορνεία is conceptually coherent, this should not be misunderstood to mean that I find it ethically or morally sound.

---

[18] See Nussbaum, *Hiding from Humanity*, 113, 137.
[19] See Damasio, *Descartes' Error*, 173, 179, 197-98.

Bibliography

Reference Resources

Brown, Francis, S.R. Driver, and Charles A. Briggs. *The Brown-Driver-Briggs Hebrew and English Lexicon: With an Appendix Containing Biblical Aramaic.* Boston: Houghton Mifflin, 1906. Repr., Peabody, Mass.: Hendrickson, 1997. [= BDB]

Danker, Frederick William, ed. *A Greek-English Lexicon of the New Testament and Other Early Christian Literature.* 3rd ed. Chicago: University of Chicago Press, 2000. [= BDAG]

Freedman, David Noel, ed. *The Anchor Bible Dictionary.* 6 vols. New York: Doubleday, 1992. [= ABD]

Liddell, Henry George, Robert Scott, and Henry Stuart Jones. *A Greek-English Lexicon.* 9th ed. Oxford: Clarendon, 1989. [= LSJ]

Lust, J., E. Eynikel, and K. Hauspie. *A Greek-English Lexicon of the Septuagint.* 2 vols. Stuttgart: Deutsche Bibelgesellschaft, 1992-1996.

Muraoka, T. *A Greek-English Lexicon of the Septuagint: Chiefly of the Pentateuch and the Twelve Prophets.* Louvain: Peeters, 2002.

Smyth, Herbert Weir. *Greek Grammar.* Cambridge, Mass.: Harvard University Press, 1984.

Primary Resources

1 (Ethiopic Apocalypse of) Enoch. Translated by E. Isaac. Pages 1:5-89 in *The Old Testament Pseudepigrapha.* Edited by James H. Charlesworth. 2 vols. Anchor Bible Reference Library. New York: Doubleday, 1983-1985.

The Apostolic Fathers. Translated by Bart D. Ehrman. 2 vols. Loeb Classical Library. Cambridge, Mass.: Harvard University Press, 2003.

Athenaeus. *The Deipnosophists.* Translated by Charles Burton Gulick. 7 vols. Loeb Classical Library. Cambridge, Mass.: Harvard University Press, 1927-1941.

Biblia Hebraica Stuttgartensia. 5th ed. Stuttgart: Deutsche Bibelgesellschaft, 1997. [= BHS]

Charlesworth, James H., ed. *The Old Testament Pseudepigrapha.* 2 vols. Anchor Bible Reference Library. New York: Doubleday, 1983-1985. [= *OTP*]

Demosthenes. Translated by J.H. Vince et al. 7 vols. Loeb Classical Library. Cambridge, Mass.: Harvard University Press, 1930-1949.

Dio Chrysostom. Translated by J.W. Cohoon and H. Lamar Crosby. 5 vols. Loeb Classical Library. Harvard University Press, 1932-1951.

The Fourth Book of Ezra. Translated by B.M. Metzger. Pages 1:516-59 in *The Old Testament Pseudepigrapha.* Edited by James H. Charlesworth. 2 vols. Anchor Bible Reference Library. New York: Doubleday, 1983-1985.

García Martínez, Florentino. *The Dead Sea Scrolls Translated: The Qumran Texts in English.* Translated by Wilfred G.E. Watson. 2nd ed. Leiden/GrandRapids: Brill/Eerdmans, 1996.

Josephus. Translated by H.St.J. Thackeray, Ralph Marcus, Allen Wikgren, and Louis H. Feldman. 9 vols. Loeb Classical Library. Cambridge, Mass.: Harvard University Press, 1926-1965.

Nestle-Aland. *Novum Testamentum Graece.* 27th ed. Stuttgart: Deutsche Bibelgesellschaft, 1993. [= NA^{27}]

Philo. Translated by F.H. Colson and G.H. Whitaker. 10 vols. Loeb Classical Library. Cambridge, Mass.: Harvard University Press, 1929-1962.

Pietersma, Albert and Benjamin G. Wright, eds. *A New English Translation of the Septuagint and the Other Greek Translations Traditionally Included under That Title.* New York: Oxford University Press, 2007. [= NETS]

Plutarch. *Advice to the Bride and Groom (Coniugalia Praecepta).* Translated by Donald Russell. Pages 5-31 in *Plutarch's* Advice to the Birde and Groom *and* A Consolation to His Wife: *English Translations, Commentary, Interpretive Essays, and Bibliography.* Edited by Sarah B. Pomeroy. New York: Oxford University Press, 1999.

Pseudo-Phocylides. *Sentences.* Translated by Walter T. Wilson. *The Sentences of Pseudo-Phocylides.* Commentaries on Early Jewish Literature. Berlin: de Gruyter, 2005.

Pseudo-Phocylides. *Sentences.* Translated by P. W. van der Horst. *The Sentences of Pseudo-Phocylides: With Introduction and Commentary.* Studia in Veteris Testamenti pseudepigraphica 4. Leiden: Brill, 1978.

Rahlfs, Alfred, ed. *Septuaginta: Id est Vetus Testamentum graece iuxta LXX interpretes.* Stuttgart: Deutsche Bibelgesellschaft, 1979.

The Septuagint Version of the Old Testament and Apocrypha with an English Translation; and with Various Readings and Critical Notes. Translated by Lancelot C.L. Brenton. London: Samuel Bagster & Sons, 1851. Repr., Grand Rapids: Zondervan, 1972.

The Speeches of Aeschines. Translated by Charles Darwin Adams. Loeb Classical Library. New York: G.P. Putnam's Sons, 1919.

Testaments of the Twelve Patriarchs. Translated by H. C. Kee. Pages 1:773-828 in *The Old Testament Pseudepigrapha.* Edited by James H. Charlesworth. 2 vols. Anchor Bible Reference Library. New York: Doubleday, 1983-1985.

The Testaments of the Twelve Patriarchs: A Critical Edition of the Greek Text. Edited by M. de Jonge. Pseudepigrapha Veteris Testamenti Graece 1/2. Leiden: Brill, 1978.

Secondary Resources

Asgeirsson, J.M., A.D. DeConick, and R. Uro, eds. *Thomasine Traditions in Antiquity*. Edited by Leiden: Brill, 2006.
Aune, David Charles. "Passions and Desires in the Pauline Letters: An Exploration of Paul's Moral Psychology." Ph.D. diss., Brown University, 1995.
Baer, Richard A., Jr. *Philo's Use of the Categories Male and Female*. Arbeiten zur Literatur und Geschichte des hellenistischen Judentums 3. Leiden: Brill, 1970.
Bain, David. "Six Greek Verbs of Sexual Congress (βινῶ, κινῶ, πυγίζω, ληκῶ, οἴφω, λαικάζω)." *Classical Quarterly* 41 (1991): 51-77.
Baird, William. *History of New Testament Research, Volume One: From Deism to Tübingen*. Minneapolis: Fortress, 1992.
Balch, David L. and Carolyn Osiek, eds. *Early Christian Families in Context: An Interdisciplinary Dialogue*. Religion, Marriage, and Family. Grand Rapids: Eerdmans, 2003.
Baltenweiler, Heinrich. *Die Ehe im Neuen Testament: Exegetische Untersuchungen über Ehe, Ehelosigkeit und Ehescheidung*. Abhandlung zur Theologie des Alten und Neuen Testaments. Zürich: Zwingli, 1967.
Barrett, C.K. *A Commentary on the First Epistle to the Corinthians*. Harper's New Testament Commentaries. New York: Harper & Row, 1968.
Barton, Stephen C., ed. *Where Shall Wisdom be Found? Wisdom in the Bible, the Church and the Contemporary World*. Edinburgh: T. & T. Clark, 1999.
Bauckham, Richard. *James: Wisdom of James, Disciple of Jesus*. New Testament Readings. New York: Routledge, 1999.
Baur, Ferdinand Christian. "Die Christuspartei in der korinthischen Gemeinde, der Gegensatz des petrinischen und paulinischen Christentums in der alten Kirche, der Apostel Petrus in Rom." Pages 1:1-146 in *Ausgewählte Werke in Einzelgaben*. Edited by Klaus Scholder. 4 vols. Stuttgart-Bad Cannstatt: Friedrich Frommann (Günther Holzboog), 1963-1970. Repr. from *Tübinger Zeitschrift für Theologie* 4 (1831): 61-206.
_____. *Paul, The Apostle of Jesus Christ, His Life and Works, His Epistles and His Doctrine: A Contribution to a Critical History of Primitive Christianity*. Translated by Eduard Zeller. 2 vols. 2nd ed. London: Williams & Northgate, 1873-1875. Repr. Peabody, Mass.: Hendrickson, 2003.
_____. *Paulus, der Apostel Jesu Christi. Sein Leben und Wirken, Seine Briefe und Seine Lehre: Ein Beitrag zu einer Kritischen Geschichte des Urchristentums*. 2 vols. 2nd ed. Leipzig: Fues's Verlag, 1866-1867.
Beal, Timothy K. and David M. Gunn, eds. *Reading Bibles, Writing Bodies: Identity and the Book*. Biblical Limits. London: Routledge, 1997.
Beattie, Gillian. *Women and Marriage in Paul and his Early Interpreters*. Journal for the Study of the New Testament Supplements 296. London: T. & T. Clark, 2005.
Beentjes, Pancratius C., ed. *The Book of Ben Sira in Modern Research: Proceedings of the First International Ben Sira Conference 28-31 July 1996 Soesterberg,*

Netherlands. Beihefte zur Zeitschrift für die alttestamentliche Wissenschaft 255. Berlin: de Gruyter, 1997.
Biddle, Mark E. "Baruch." Pages 176-83 AP in *The New Oxford Annotated Bible.* Edited by Michael D. Coogan. 3rd ed. Oxford: Oxford University Press, 2001.
Bieringer R., ed. *The Corinthian Correspondence.* Bibliotheca ephemeridum theologicarum lovaniensium 125. Leuven: University Press, 1996.
Bird, Phyllis A. *Missing Persons and Mistaken Identities: Women and Gender in Ancient Israel.* Overtures to Biblical Theology. Minneapolis: Fortress, 1997.
Bloomquist, L. Gregory. "Paul's Inclusive Language: The Ideological Texture of Romans 1." Pages 165-93 in *Fabrics of Discourse: Essays in Honor of Vernon K. Robbins.* Edited by David B. Gowler, L. Gregory Bloomquist, and Duane F. Watson. Harrisburg, Pa.: TPI, 2003.
———. "A Possible Direction for Providing Programmatic Correlation of Textures in Socio-Rhetorical Analysis." Pages 61-96 in *Rhetorical Criticism and the Bible: Essays from the 1998 Florence Conference.* Edited by Stanley E. Porter and Dennis L. Stamps. Journal for the Study of the New Testament: Supplement series 195. London: Sheffield Academic Press/Continuum, 2002.
Boyarin, Daniel. *Carnal Israel: Reading Sex in Talmudic Culture.* The New Historicism: Studies in Cultural Poetics 25. Berkeley: University of California Press, 1993.
———. "Paul and the Genealogy of Gender." Pages 13-41 in *A Feminist Companion to Paul.* Edited by Amy-Jill Levine. Cleveland: Pilgrim, 2004. Repr. from *Representations* 41 (1993): 1-33.
Boyer, Pascal. *Religion Explained: The Evolutionary Origins of Religious Thought.* New York: Basic Books, 2001.
Braun, Willi. "Rhetoric, Rhetoricality, and Discourse Performances." Pages 1-26 in *Rhetoric and Reality in Early Christianities.* Edited by Willi Braun. Studies in Christianity and Judaism/Études sur le christianisme et le judaïsme 16. Waterloo, Ontario: Wilfrid Laurier University Press, 2005.
Braun, Willi, ed. *Rhetoric and Reality in Early Christianities.* Studies in Christianity and Judaism/Études sur le christianisme et le judaïsme 16. Waterloo, Ontario: Wilfrid Laurier University Press, 2005.
Brenner, Athalya. *The Intercourse of Knowledge: On Gendering Desire and "Sexuality" in the Hebrew Bible.* Biblical Interpretation series 26. Leiden: Brill, 1997.
Brenner, Athalya, ed. *A Feminist Companion to Wisdom Literature.* Feminist Companion to the Bible 9. Sheffield: Sheffield Academic Press, 1995.
Brenner, Athalya and Fokkelein van Dijk-Hemmes. *On Gendering Texts: Female and Male Voices in the Hebrew Bible.* Biblical Interpretation series 1. Leiden: Brill, 1993.
Brooten, Bernadette J. *Love Between Women: Early Christian Responses to Female Homoeroticism.* Chicago: University of Chicago Press, 1996.
Brown, Peter. *The Body and Society: Men, Women, and Sexual Renunciation in Early Christianity.* New York, Columbia University Press, 1988.

Brown, William P. "The Didactic Power of Metaphor in the Aphoristic Sayings of Proverbs." *Journal for the Study of the Old Testament* 29 (2004): 133-54.

Bruehler, Bart B. *A Public and Political Christ: The Social-Spatial Characteristics of Luke 18:35–19:43 and the Gospel as a Whole in Its Ancient Context.* Princeton Theological Mongraphs 157. Eugene, Or.: Pickwick, 2011.

Buccellati, Giorgio. "Wisdom and Not: The Case of Mesopotamia." *Journal of the American Oriental Society* 101 (1981): 35-47.

Budin, Stephanie Lynn. *The Myth of Sacred Prostitution in* Antiquity. Cambridge: Cambridge University Press, 2008.

Bultmann, Rudolf. *Theology of the New Testament.* Translated by Kendrick Grobel. 2 vols. New York: Charles Scribners' Sons, 1951-55. [= *TNT*]

Burke, Trevor J. "Paul's Role as 'Father' to His Corinthian 'Children' in Sociohistorical Context (1 Corinthians 4:14-21)." Pages 95-113 in *Paul and the Corinthians: Studies on a Community in Conflict. Essays in Honour of Margaret Thrall.* Edited by Trevor J. Burke and J. Keith Elliot. Novum Testamentum Supplements 109. Leiden: Brill, 2003.

Burke, Trevor J. and J. Keith Elliot, eds. *Paul and the Corinthians: Studies on a Community in Conflict. Essays in Honour of Margaret Thrall.* Novum Testamentum Supplements 109. Leiden: Brill, 2003.

Burton-Christie, Douglas. *The Word in the Desert: Scripture and the Quest for Holiness in Early Christian Monasticism.* New York: Oxford University Press, 1993.

Byron, John. *Slavery Metaphors in Early Judaism and Pauline Christianity: A Traditio-Historical and Exegetical Examination.* Wissenschaftliche Untersuchungen zum Neun Testament 2nd series 162. Tübingen: Mohr Siebeck, 2003.

Calvin, John. *Commentary on the Epistles of Paul the Apostle to the Corinthians.* Translated by John Pringle. 2 vols. Grand Rapids: Eerdmans, 1948.

Camp, Claudia V. "Honor and Shame in Ben Sira: Anthropological and Theological Reflections." Pages 171-87 in *The Book of Ben Sira in Modern Research: Proceedings of the First International Ben Sira Conference 28-31 July 1996 Soesterberg, Netherlands.* Edited by Pancratius C. Beentjes. Beihefte zur Zeitschrift für die alttestamentliche Wissenschaft 255. Berlin: de Gruyter, 1997.

_____. "Storied Space, or, Ben Sira 'Tells' a Temple." Pages 64-80 in *"Imagining" Biblical Worlds: Studies in Spatial, Social and Historical Constructs in Honor of James W. Flanagan.* Edited by David M. Gunn and Paula M. NcNutt. Journal for the Study of the Old Testament Supplement series 359. London: Sheffield Academic Press, 2002.

_____. "Understanding Patriarchy: Women in Second Century Jerusalem Through the Eyes of Ben Sira." Pages 1-39 in *"Women Like This": New Perspectives on Jewish Women in the Greco-Roman World.* Edited by Amy-Jill Levine. Society of Biblical Literature Early Judaism and Its Literature 1. Atlanta: Scholars Press, 1991.

_____. "Woman Wisdom and the Strange Woman: Where is Power to be Found?" Pages 85-112 in *Reading Bibles, Writing Bodies: Identities and The Book.* Edited by Timothy K. Beal and David M. Gunn. Biblical Limits. London: Routledge, 1997.

———. *Wisdom and the Feminine in the Book of Proverbs*. Bible and Literature series 11. Decatur, Ga.: Almond: 1985.
———. *Wise, Strange and Holy: The Strange Woman and the Making of the Bible*. Journal for the Study of the Old Testament: Supplement series 320. Gender, Culture, Theory 9. Sheffield: Sheffield Academic Press, 2000.
Carr, David M. *The Erotic Word: Sexuality, Spirituality, and the Bible*. Oxford: Oxford University Press, 2003.
Carroll, John T., Charles H. Cosgrove, and E. Elizabeth Johnson, eds. *Faith and History: Essays in Honor of Paul W. Meyer*. Atlanta: Scholars Press, 1990.
Carson, Anne. "Dirt and Desire: The Phenomenology of Female Pollution in Antiquity." Pages 77-100 in *Constructions of the Classical Body*. Edited by James I. Porter. The Body, in Theories: Histories of Cultural Materialism. Ann Arbor: University of Michigan Press, 1999.
———. "Putting Her in Her Place: Woman, Dirt, and Desire." Pages 135-69 in *Before Sexuality: The Construction of Erotic Experience in the Ancient Greek World*. Edited by David M. Halperin, John J. Winkler, and Froma I. Zeitlin. Princeton: Princeton University Press, 1990.
Castelli, Elizabeth A. *Imitating Paul: A Discourse of Power*. Louisville, Ky.: Westminster John Knox, 1991.
Ciampa, Roy E. "Revisiting the Euphemism in 1 Corinthians 7.1." *Journal for the Study of the New Testament* 31 (2009): 325-38.
Clark, Gillian. "Women and Asceticism in Late Antiquity: The Refusal of Status and Gender." Pages 33-48 in *Asceticism*. Edited by Vincent L. Wimbush and Richard Valantasis. Oxford: Oxford University Press, 1998.
Clark, Elizabeth A. *Reading Renunciation: Asceticism and Scripture in Early Christianity*. Princeton: Princeton University Press, 1999.
Collins, John J. *Between Athens and Jerusalem: Jewish Identity in the Hellenistic Diaspora*. 2nd ed. Biblical Resource series. Grand Rapids: Eerdmans, 2000.
———. "Cosmos and Salvation: Jewish Wisdom and Apocalypticism in the Hellenistic Age." Pages 317-38 in *Seers, Sybils and Sages in Hellenistic-Roman Judaism*, by John J. Collins. Supplements to the Journal for the Study of Judaism 54. Leiden: Brill, 1997. Repr. from *History of Religions* 17 (1977): 121-42.
———. *Jewish Wisdom in the Hellenistic Age*. Old Testament Library. Louisville, Ky.: Westminster John Knox, 1997.
———. "The Sage in the Apocalyptic and Pseudepigraphical Literature." Pages 339-50 in *Seers, Sybils and Sages in Hellenistic-Roman Judaism*, by John J. Collins. Supplements to the Journal for the Study of Judaism 54. Leiden: Brill, 1997. Repr. from pages 343-54 in *The Sage in Israel and the Ancient Near East*. Edited by John G. Gammie and Leo Purdue. Winona Lake, Ind.: Eisenbrauns, 1990.
———. *Seers, Sybils and Sages in Hellenistic-Roman Judaism*. Supplements to the Journal for the Study of Judaism 54. Leiden: Brill, 1997.
Collins, Raymond F. *First Corinthians*. Sacra Pagina series 7. Collegeville, Minn.: The Liturgical Press, 1999.

Conzelmann, Hans. *A Commentary on the First Epistle to the Corinthians.* Hermeneia. Translated by James W. Leitch. Philadelphia: Fortress Press, 1975.
Cook, Johann. *The Septuagint of Proverbs – Jewish and/or Hellenistic Proverbs? Concerning the Hellenistic Colouring of LXX Proverbs.* Vetus Testamentum Supplements 69. New York: Brill, 1997.
Corrington, Gail Paterson. "Paul and the Two Wisdoms: 1 Corinthians 1:18-31 and the Hellenistic Mission." Pages 72-84 in *Proceedings: Eastern Great Lakes and Midwest Biblical Societies.* Edited by Paul Redditt. Eastern Great Lakes Biblical Society and the Midwest Region of the Society of Biblical Literature. Westerville, Ohio: 1986.
Corrington Streete, Gail. *The Strange Woman: Power and Sex in the Bible.* Louisville, Ky.: Westminster John Knox, 1997.
Coulson, Seana. *Semantic Leaps: Frame-Shifting and Conceptual Blending in Meaning Construction.* New York: Cambridge University Press, 2001.
Coulson, Seana and Todd Oakley. "Blending Basics." *Cognitive Linguistics* 11 (2000): 175-96.
———. "Blending and Coded Meaning: Literal and Figurative Meaning in Cognitive Semantics." *Journal of Pragmatics* 37 (2005): 1510-36.
———. "Metonymy and Conceptual Blending." Pages 51-79 in *Metonymy and Pragmatic Inferencing.* Edited by Klaus-Uwe Panther and Linda L. Thornburg. Pragmatics & Beyond New series 113. Amsterdam: John Benjamins, 2003.
———. "Purple Persuasion: Deliberative Rhetoric and Conceptual Blending." Pages 47-65 in *Cognitive Linguistics: Investigations Across Languages, Fields, and Philosophical Boundaries.* Edited by J. Luchenbroers. Human Cognitive Processing 15. Amsterdam: H. Benjamins, 2006. Cited 13 May 2006. Online: http://cogsci.ucsd.edu/~coulson/purple.html.
Crenshaw, James L. *Old Testament Wisdom: An Introduction.* Rev. and enl. ed. Louisville, Ky.: Westminster John Knox, 1998.
Crenshaw, James L., ed. *Studies in Ancient Israelite Wisdom.* The Library of Biblical Studies. New York: Ktav, 1976.
Damasio, Antonio. *Descartes' Error: Emotion, Reason, and the Human Brian.* New York: Grosset/Putnam, 1994.
———. *The Feeling of What Happens: Body and Emotion in the Making of Consciousness* (New York: Harcourt Brace, 1999.
Davidson, James. *Courtesans and Fishcakes: The Consuming Passions of Classical Athens.* London: HarperCollins, 1997.
Davies, Philip R. *Memories of Ancient Israel: An Introduction to Biblical History – Ancient and Modern.* Louisville, Ky.: Westminster John Knox, 2008.
Davis, James A. *Wisdom and Spirit: An Investigation of 1 Corinthians 1:18–3:20 Against the Background of Jewish Sapiential Traditions in the Greco-Roman Period.* Lanham, Md.: University Press of America, 1984.
Dell, Katherine. *"Get Wisdom, Get Insight": An Introduction to Israel's Wisdom Literature.* Macon, Ga.: Smyth & Helwys, 2000.
Delling, Gerhard. *Paulus' Steullung zu Frau und Ehe.* Stuttgart: Kohlhammer, 1931.

Deming, Will. *Paul on Marriage and Celibacy: The Hellenistic Background of 1 Corinthians 7*. Society for New Testament Studies Monograph series 83. New York: Cambridge University Press, 1995.
_____. *Paul on Marriage and Celibacy: The Hellenistic Background of 1 Corinthians 7*. 2nd ed. Grand Rapids: Eerdmans: 2004.
Derrett, J. Duncan M. "Right and Wrong Sticking (1 Cor 6,18)?" *Etudes Bibliques* 55 (1997): 89-106.
De Troyer, Kristin, Judith A. Herbert, Judith Ann Johnson, and Anne-Marie Korte. *Wholly Woman, Holy Blood: A Feminist Critique of Purity and Impurity*. Studies in Antiquity and Christianity. Harrisburg, Penn.: Trinity Press International, 2003.
Di Lella, Alexander A. "Fear of the Lord as Wisdom: Ben Sira 1,11-30." Pages 113-33 in *The Book of Ben Sira in Modern Research: Proceedings of the First International Ben Sira Conference 28-31 July 1996 Soesterberg, Netherlands*. Edited by Pancratius C. Beentjes. Beihefte zur Zeitschrift für die alttestamentliche Wissenschaft 255. Berlin: de Gruyter, 1997.
Dixon, Suzanne. *The Roman Family*. Baltimore: Johns Hopkins University Press, 1992.
_____."Sex and the Married Woman in Ancient Rome." Pages 111-29 in *Early Christian Families in Context: An Interdisciplinary Dialogue*. Edited by David L. Balch and Carolyn Osiek. Religion, Marriage, and Family. Grand Rapids: Eerdmans, 2003.
Dodd, Brian J. "Paul's Paradigmatic 'I' and 1 Corinthians 6.12." *Journal for the Study of the New Testament* 59 (1995): 39-58.
_____. *Paul's Paradigmatic 'I': Personal Example as Literary Strategy*. Journal for the Study of the New Testament: Supplement series 177. Sheffield: Sheffield Academic Press, 1999.
Doll, Peter. *Menschenschöpfung und Weltschöpfung in der alttestamentlichen Weisheit*. Stuttgarter Bibelstudien 177. Stuttgart: Katholisches Bibelwerk, 1985.
Dover, K.J. "Classical Greek Attitudes to Sexual Behavior." Pages 19-36 in *Sexuality and Gender in the Classical World: Readings and Sources*. Edited by Laura K. McClure. Oxford: Blackwell, 2002.
Dowden, Ken. *Death and the Maiden: Girls' Initiation Rites in Greek Mythology*. New York: Routledge, 1989.
Downing, Gerald. *Cynics, Paul and the Pauline Churches*. Cynics and Christian Origins 2. London: Routledge, 1998.
Ellens, Deborah. "Menstrual Impurity and Innovation in Leviticus 15." Pages 29-43 in *Wholly Woman, Holy Blood: A Feminist Critique of Purity and Impurity*. Edited by Kristin De Troyer, Judith A. Herbert, Judith Ann Johnson, and Anne-Marie Korte. Studies in Antiquity and Christianity. Harrisburg, Penn.: Trinity Press International, 2003.
_____. *Women in the Sex Texts of Leviticus and Deuteronomy: A Comparative Conceptual Analysis*. Library of Hebrew Bible/Old Testament Studies 458. New York: T. & T. Clark, 2008.
Engberg-Pedersen, Troels, ed. *Paul Beyond the Judaism/Hellenism Divide*. Louisville: Westminster John Knox, 2001.

Erksine, Andrew. *The Hellenistic Stoa: Political Thought and Action.* London: Duckworth, 1990.

Eriksson, Anders. "Enthymemes in Pauline Argumentation: Reading Between the Lines in 1 Corinthians." Pages 243-59 in *Rhetorical Argumentation in Biblical Texts: Essays from the Lund 2000 Conference.* Anders Eriksson, Thomas H. Olbricht, and Walter Übelacker. Emory Studies in Early Christianity 8; Harrisburg, Pa.: Trinity Press International, 2002.

Eriksson, Anders, Thomas H. Olbricht, and Walter Übelacker, eds. *Rhetorical Argumentation in Biblical Texts: Essays from the Lund 2000 Conference.* Emory Studies in Early Christianity 8. Harrisburg, Penn.: Trinity Press International, 2002.

Eubanks, Philip. "Globalization, '*Corporate Rule*,' and Blended Worlds: A Conceptual-Rhetorical Analysis of Metaphor, Metonymy, and Conceptual Blending." *Metaphor and Symbol* 20 (2005): 173-97.

Fantham, Elaine, Helene Peet Foley, Natalie Boymel Kampen, Sarah B. Pomeroy, and H. A. Shapiro, eds. *Women in the Classical World: Image and Text.* New York: Oxford University Press, 1994.

Fauconnier, Gilles. "Compression and Emergent Structure." *Language and Linguistics* 6 (2005): 523-38.

_____. *Mappings in Thought and Language.* New York: Cambridge University Press, 1997.

_____. *Mental Spaces: Aspects of Meaning Construction in Natural Language.* Cambridge, UK: Cambridge University Press, 1994.

Fauconnier, Gilles and Mark Turner. "Compression and Global Insight." *Cognitive Linguistics* 11 (2000): 283-304.

_____. "Conceptual Integration Networks." *Cognitive Science* 22 (1998): 133-87.

_____. *The Way We Think: Conceptual Blending and the Mind's Hidden Complexities.* New York: Basic Books, 2002.

Fee, Gordon D. *The First Epistle to the Corinthians.* New International Commentary on the New Testament. Grand Rapids: Eerdmans, 1987.

Feldman, Jerome A. *From Molecule to Metaphor: A Neural Theory of Language.* Cambridge, Mass.: MIT Press, 2006 (Paperback edition, 2008).

Fenske, Wolfgang. *Die Argumentation des Paulus in ethischen Herausfoderung.* Göttingen: V & R Unipress, 2004.

Ferguson, Everett, ed. *Christian Teaching: Studies in Honor of Lemoine G. Lewis.* Abilene, Tex.: Abilene Christian University Press, 1981.

Fernandez, James W. *Beyond Metaphor: The Theory of Tropes in Anthropology.* Stanford: Stanford University Press, 1991.

_____. *Persuasions and Performances: The Play of Tropes in Culture.* Bloomington, Ind.: Indiana University Press, 1986.

Fishbane, Michael. *Biblical Interpretation in Ancient Israel.* Rev. ed. New York: Oxford University Press, 1988.

Fisk, Bruce N. "ΠΟΡΝΕΥΕΙΝ as Body Violation: The Unique Nature of Sexual Sin in 1 Corinthians 6.18." *New Testament Studies* 42 (1996): 540-58.

Flood, Gavin. *The Ascetic Self: Subjectivity, Memory and Tradition.* Cambridge: Cambridge University Press, 2004.

Fontaine, Carole R. "The Social Roles of Women in the World of Wisdom." Pages 24-47 in *A Feminist Companion to Wisdom Literature*. Edited by Athalya Brenner. Feminist Companion to the Bible 9. Sheffield: Sheffield Academic Press, 1995.
Fox, Michael V. "The Strange Woman in Septuagint Proverbs." *Journal of Northwest Semitic Languages* 22 (1996): 31-44.
_____. *Proverbs 1-9: A New Translation with Introduction and Commentary*. Anchor Bible 18A. New York: Doubleday, 2000.
Fraade, Steven D. "Ascetical Aspects of Ancient Judaism." Pages 253-88 in *Jewish Spirituality: From the Bible through the Middle Ages*. Edited by Arthur Green. World Spirituality: An Encyclopedic History of the Religious Quest 13. New York: Crossroad, 1987.
Frymer-Kensky, Tikva. *Reading the Women of the Bible: A New Interpretation of Their Stories*. New York: Schocken Books, 2002.
Furnish, Victor Paul. *The Theology of the First Letter to the Corinthians*. New Testament Theology. New York: Cambridge University Press, 1999.
Gaca, Kathy L. *The Making of Fornication: Eros, Ethics, and Political Reform in Greek Philosophy and Early Christianity*. Hellenistic Culture and Society 39. Berkeley: University of California Press, 2003.
_____. "Paul's Uncommon Declaration in Romans 1:18-32 and Its Problematic Legacy for Pagan and Christian Relations." *Harvard Theological Review* 92 (1999): 165-98.
_____. "The Sexual and Social Dangers of *Pornai* in the Septuagint Greek Stratum of Patristic Christian Greek Thought." Pages 35-40 in *Desire and Denial in Byzantium: Papers from the Thirty-first Spring Symposium of Byzantine Studies, University of Sussex, Brighton, March 1997*. Edited by Liz James. Society for the Promotion of Byzantine Studies Publications 6. Brookfield, Vt.: Ashgate/Variorum, 1999.
Gallagher, Shaun. *How the Body Shapes the Mind*. Oxford: Clarendon Press, 2005.
Galloway, Lincoln E. *Freedom in the Gospel: Paul's Exemplum in 1 Cor 9 in Conversation with the Discourses of Epictetus and Philo*. Contributions to Biblical Exegesis and Theology 38. Leuven: Peeters, 2004.
Gammie, John G. and Leo Purdue, eds. *The Sage in Israel and the Ancient Near East*. Winona Lake, Ind.: Eisenbrauns, 1990.
Gibbs, Raymond W., Jr. *Embodiment and Cognitive Science* (New York: Cambridge University Press, 2005.
_____. "Making Good Psychology out of Blending Theory." *Cognitive Linguistics* 11 (2000): 347-58.
Goff, Matthew J. "Wisdom, Apocalypticism, and the Pedagogical Ethos of 4QInstriction." Pages 57-67 in *Conflicted Boundaries in Wisdom and Apocalypticism*. Edited by Benjamin G. Wright, III and Lawrence M. Wills. Society of Biblical Literature Symposium series 35. Atlanta: Society of Biblical Literature, 2005.
_____. *The Worldly and Heavenly Wisdom of 4QInstruction*. Studies on the Texts of the Desert of Judah 50. Leiden: Brill, 2003.

Goldhill, Simon. *Love, Sex and Tragedy: How the Ancient World Shapes Our Lives.* London: John Murray, 2004.
Goulder, Michael D. "Libertines? (1 Cor 5-6)." *Novum Testamentum* 41 (1999): 334-48.
———. *Paul and the Competing Mission in Corinth.* Library of Pauline Studies. Peabody, Mass.: Hendrickson, 2001.
———. "ΣΟΦΙΑ in 1 Corinthians." *New Testament Studies* 37 (1991): 516-34.
Gowler, David B. "Introduction: The Development of Socio-Rhetorical Criticism." Pages 1-36 in *New Boundaries in Old Territory: Form and Social Rhetoric in Mark*, by Vernon K. Robbins. Edited by David B. Gowler. Emory Studies in Early Christianity 3. New York: Peter Lang, 1994.
Gowler, David B., L. Gregory Bloomquist, and Duane F. Watson, eds. *Fabrics of Discourse: Essays in Honor of Vernon K. Robbins.* Harrisburg, Pa.: TPI, 2003.
Grady, Joseph, Todd Oakley, and Seana Coulson. "Blending and Metaphor." Pages 101-24 in *Metaphor in Cognitive Linguistics: Selected Papers from the Fifth International Cognitive Linguistics Conference, Amsterdam, July 1997.* Edited by Raymond W. Gibbs, Jr. and Gerard J. Steen. Amsterdam: John Benjamins, 1999).
Green, Arthur, ed. *Jewish Spirituality: From the Bible through the Middle Ages.* World Spirituality: An Encyclopedic History of the Religious Quest 13. New York: Crossroad, 1987.
Green, Joel B. *Body, Soul, and Human Life: The Nature of Humanity in the Bible.* Studies in Theological Interpretation. Grand Rapids, Mich.: Baker Books, 2008.
Grindheim, Sigurd. "Wisdom for the Perfect: Paul's Challenge to the Corinthian Church (1 Corinthians 2:6-16)." *Journal of Biblical Literature* 121 (2002): 689-709.
Groscheide, F. W. *Commentary on the First Epistle to the Corinthians: The English Text with Introduction, Exposition, and Notes.* New International Commentary on the New Testament. Grand Rapids: Eerdmans, 1953.
Gundry, Robert. *Sôma in Biblical Theology: With Emphasis on Pauline Anthropology.* New York: Cambridge University Press, 1976.
Gunn, David M. and Paula M. NcNutt, eds. *"Imagining" Biblical Worlds: Studies in Spatial, Social and Historical Constructs in Honor of James W. Flanagan.* Journal for the Study of the Old Testament Supplement series 359. London: Sheffield Academic Press, 2002.
Halperin, David M. "Forgetting Foucault: Acts, Identities, and the History of Sexuality." Pages 21-54 in *The Sleep of Reason: Erotic Experience and Sexual Ethics in Ancient Greece and Rome.* Edited by Martha C. Nussbaum and Juha Sihvola. Chicago: University of Chicago Press, 2002.
Halperin, David M., John J. Winkler, and Froma I. Zeitlin, eds. *Before Sexuality: The Construction of Erotic Experience in the Ancient Greek World.* Princeton: Princeton University Press, 1990.
Hawkins, Faith Kirkham. "1 Corinthians 8:1–11:1: The Making and Meaning of Difference." Ph.D. diss., Emory University, 2001.

Hays, Richard B. "Wisdom According to Paul." Pages 111-23 in *Where Shall Wisdom be Found? Wisdom in the Bible, the Church and the Contemporary World*. Edited by Stephen C. Barton. Edinburgh: T. & T. Clark, 1999.
Hengel, Martin. *The Septuagint as Christian Scripture: Its Prehistory and the Problem of Its Canon*. Translated by Mark E. Biddle. Old Testament Studies. Edinburgh: T. & T. Clark, 2002. Repr., Grand Rapids: Baker Books, 2004.
_____. *The Pre-Christian Paul*. Translated by John Bowden. London: SCM Press, 1991.
Holtz, Traugott. "Zur Frage der inhaltlichen Weisungen bei Paulus." *Theologische Literaturzeitung* 106 (1981): 385-400.
Horsley, Richard A. "Wisdom of Word and Words of Wisdom in Corinth." *Catholic Biblical Quarterly* 39 (1977): 224-39.
Horst, P.W. van der. *The Sentences of Pseudo-Phocylides: With Introduction and Commentary*. Studia in Veteris Testamenti pseudepigraphica 4. Leiden: Brill, 1978.
Howe, Bonnie. *Because You Bear This Name: Conceptual Metaphor and the Moral Meaning of 1 Peter*. Biblical Interpretation series 61. Leiden: Brill, 2006.
Huber, Lynn R. *Like a Bride Adorned: Reading Metaphor in John's Apocalypse*. Emory Studies in Early Christianity. New York: T. & T. Clark, 2007.
Hurd, John Coolidge. *The Origin of First Corinthians*. New York: Seabury Press, 1965. Repr., Macon, GA: Mercer University Press, 1983.
Hylen, Susan E. *Allusion and Meaning in John 6*. Beihefte zur Zeitschrift für die neutestamentliche Wissenschaft und die Kunde der älteren Kirche 137. Berlin: de Gruyter, 2005.
James, Liz. ed. *Desire and Denial in Byzantium: Papers from the Thirty-first Spring Symposium of Byzantine Studies, University of Sussex, Brighton, March 1997*. Society for the Promotion of Byzantine Studies Publications 6. Brookfield, Vt.: Ashgate/Variorum, 1999.
Johnson, E. Elizabeth. "The Wisdom of God as Apocalyptic Power." Pages 137-48 in *Faith and History: Essays in Honor of Paul W. Meyer*. Edited by John T. Carroll, Charles H. Cosgrove, and E. Elizabeth Johnson. Atlanta: Scholars Press, 1990.
Johnson, Luke Timothy. *The Writings of the New Testament: An Interpretation*. Rev. ed. Minneapolis: Fortress, 1999.
Johnson, Mark. *The Meaning of the Body: Aesthetics of Human Understanding*. Chicago: University of Chicago Press, 2007.
Jordan, Mark D. *Blessing Same-Sex Unions: The Perils of Queer Romance and the Confusions of Christian Marriage*. Chicago: University of Chicago Press, 2005.
_____. *The Ethics of Sex*. New Dimensions to Religious Ethics 3. Oxford: Blackwell, 2002.
_____. *The Invention of Sodomy in Christian Theology*. Chicago: University of Chicago Press, 1997.
Jordan, Mark D. and Kent Emery, Jr., eds. *Ad Litteram: Authoritative Texts and their Medieval Readers*. Notre Dame, Ind.: University of Notre Dame Press, 1992.

Käsemann, Ernst. *Perspectives on Paul.* Translated by Margaret Kohl. Philadelphia: SCM Press, 1971. Repr., Mifflintown, Pa.: Sigler Press, 1996.

―――. "Zur Thema der urchristlichen Apokalyptik." *Zeitschrift für Theologie und Kirche* 59 (1962): 257-84.

Keuls, Eva C. *The Reign of the Phallus: Sexual Politics in Ancient Athens.* New York: Harper & Row, 1985.

Kirchhoff, Renate. *Die Sünde gegen den einigen Leib: Studien zu* πόρνη *und* πορνεία *in 1 Kor 6,12-20 und dem socio-kulturellen Kontext der paulinischen Adressaten.* Studien zur Umwelt des Neuen Testaments 18. Göttingen: Vandenhoeck & Ruprecht, 1994.

Knust, Jennifer Wright. *Abandoned to Lust: Sexual Slander and Ancient Christianity.* Gender, Theory, and Religion. New York: Columbia University Press, 2006.

Kövecses, Zoltán. *Metaphor in Culture: Universality and Variation.* New York: Cambridge University Press, 2005

Kugler, Robert A. *The Testament of the Twelve Patriarchs.* Guides to the Apocrypha and Pseudepigrapha. Sheffield: Sheffield Academic Press, 2001.

Kümmel, Werner Georg. *Das Neue Testament: Geschichte der Erforschung seiner Probleme.* Freiburg: Karl Alber, 1958.

―――. *The New Testament: The History of the Investigation of Its Problems.* Translated by S. McLean and Howard C. Kee. New York: Abingdon, 1972.

Kurke, Leslie. *Coins, Bodies, Games, and Gold: The Politics of Meaning in Archaic Greece.* Princeton: Princeton University Press, 1999.

Lambert, W. G. *Babylonian Wisdom Literature.* Oxford: Clarendon, 1960.

Lakoff, George. *Women, Fire, and Dangerous Things: What Categories Reveal about the Mind.* Chicago: University of Chicago Press, 1987.

Lakoff, George and Mark Johnson. *Metaphors We Live By.* Chicago: University of Chicago Press, 2003 (1980).

―――. *More Than Cool Reason: A Field Guide to Poetic Metaphor.* Chicago: University of Chicago Press, 1989.

―――. *Philosophy in the Flesh: The Embodied Mind and Its Challenge to Western Thought.* New York: Basic Books, 1999.

Langacker, Ronald W. *Concept, Image, and Symbol: The Cognitive Basis of Grammar.* 2nd ed. Berlin: de Gruyter, 2002.

Lawson, E. Thomas. "The Wedding of Psychology, Ethnography, and History: Methodological Bigamy or Tripartite Free Love?" Pages 1-5 in *Theorizing Religions Past: Archeology, History, and Cognition.* Cognitive Science of Religion series. Walnut Creek, CA: Alta Mira: 2004.

Lawson, E. Thomas and Robert N. McCauley. *Bringing Ritual to Mind.* Cambridge: Cambridge University Press, 2002.

―――. *Rethinking Religion: Connecting Cognition and Culture.* Cambridge: Cambridge University Press, 1990.

Lefkowitz, Mary R. "Wives and Husbands." Pages 67-82 in *Women in Antiquity.* Edited by Ian McAuslan and Peter Walcott. Greece & Rome Studies. Oxford: Oxford University Press, 1996.

Levine, Amy-Jill, ed. *A Feminist Companion to Paul.* Cleveland: Pilgrim, 2004.

_____. "Women Like This": New Perspectives on Jewish Women in the Greco-Roman World. Society of Biblical Literature Early Judaism and Its Literature 1. Atlanta: Scholars Press, 1991.
Lieu, Judith M. Christian Identity in the Jewish and Greco-Roman World. Oxford: Oxford University Press, 2004.
Lightstone, Jack N. Mishnah and the Social Formation of the Early Rabbinic Guild: A Socio-Rhetorical Approach. Studies in Christianity and Judaism 11. Waterloo, Ontario: Wilfrid Laurier University Press, 2002.
Lips, Hermann von. Weisheitliche Traditionen im Neuen Testament. Wissenschaftliche Monographien zum Alten und Neuen Testament 64. Neukirchen-Vluyn: Neukirchener Verlag, 1990.
Loader, William. Enoch, Levi, and Jubilees on Sexuality: Attitudes towards Sexuality in the Early Enoch Literature, the Aramaic Levi Document, and the Book of Jubilees. Grand Rapids, Mich.: Eerdmans, 2007.
_____. The Septuagint, Sexuality, and the New Testament: Case Studies on the Impact of the LXX in Philo and the New Testament. Grand Rapids: Eerdmans, 2004.
_____. Sexuality and the Jesus Tradition. Grand Rapids: Eerdmans, 2005.
Long, Frederick J. "From Epicheiremes to Exhortation: A Pauline Method for Moral Persuasion in 1 Thessalonians." Pages 179-95 in Rhetoric, Ethic, and Moral Persuasion in Biblical Discourse: Essays from the 2002 Heidelberg Conference. Edited by Thomas H. Olbricht and Anders Ericksson. Emory Studies in Early Christianity 11. New York: T. & T. Clark, 2005.
Hugo Lundhaug, "Conceptual Blending in the Exegesis of the Soul." Pages 141-60 in Explaining Christian Origins and Early Judaism. Edited by Patri Luomanen, Ilkka Pyysiäinen, and Risto Uro. Biblical Interpretation series 89. Leiden: Brill, 2007.
Luomanen, Patri, Ilkka Pyysiäinen, and Risto Uro, eds. Explaining Christian Origins and Early Judaism. Biblical Interpretation series 89. Leiden: Brill, 2007.
_____. "Introduction: Social and Cognitive Perspectives in the Study of Christian Origins and Early Judaism." Pages 1-33 in Explaining Christian Origins and Early Judaism. Edited by Patri Luomanen,, Ilkka Pyysiäinen, and Risto Uro. Biblical Interpretation series 89. Leiden: Brill, 2007.
MacDonald, Margaret Y. "Virgins, Widows, and Wives: The Women of 1 Corinthians 7." Pages 148-68 in A Feminist Companion to Paul. Edited by Amy-Jill Levine. Cleveland: Pilgrim, 2004.
Mack, Burton. Logos und Sophia: Untersuchungen zur Weisheitstheologie in hellenistischen Judentum. Studien zur Umwelt des Neuen Testaments 10. Göttingen: Vandenhoeck & Ruprecht, 1973.
_____. Wisdom and the Hebrew Epic: Ben Sira's Hymn of Praise of the Fathers. Chicago Studies in the History of Judaism. Chicago: University of Chicago Press, 1985.
Malherbe, Abraham. Moral Exhortation: A Greco-Roman Sourcebook. Philadelphia: Westminster, 1986.
Martin, Dale. The Corinthian Body. New Haven: Yale University Press, 1995.

_____. *Slavery as Salvation: The Metaphor of Slavery in Pauline Christianity*. New Haven: Yale University Press, 1990.
Martin, Luther H. "Toward a Scientific History of Religions." Pages 7-14 in *Theorizing Religions Past: Archeology, History, and Cognition*. Edited by Harvey Whitehouse and Luther H. Martin. Cognitive Science of Religion series. Walnut Creek, Calif.: Alta Mira: 2004.
Massingberd Ford, J. "St Paul the Philogamist (I Cor. VII in Early Patristic Exegesis)." *New Testament Studies* 11: (1965): 326-48.
McAuslan, Ian and Peter Walcott, eds. *Women in Antiquity*. Greece & Rome Studies. Oxford: Oxford University Press, 1996.
McClure, Laura K. *Courtesans at Table: Gender and Greek Literary Culture in Athenaeus*. New York: Routledge, 2003.
McClure, Laura K., ed. *Sexuality and Gender in the Classical World: Readings and Sources*. Oxford: Blackwell, 2002.
McGinn, Thomas A.J. *The Economy of Prostitution in the Roman World: A Study of Social History and the Brothel*. Ann Arbor: University of Michigan Press, 2004.
Miguens, M. "Christ's 'Members' and Sex (1 Cor 6,12-20)." *Thomist* 39 (1975): 24-48.
Mitchell, Margaret M. "Concerning the ΠΕΡΙ ΔΕ in 1 Corinthians," *Novum Testamentum* 31 (1989): 229-56.
_____. *Paul and the Rhetoric of Reconciliation: An Exegetical Investigation of the Language and Composition of 1 Corinthians*. Hermeneutische Untersuchungen zur Theologie 28. Tübingen: Mohr Siebeck, 1991.
Möller, Karl. *A Prophet in Debate: The Rhetoric of Persuasion in the Book of Amos*. Journal for the Study of the Old Testament: Supplement series 372. Sheffield: Sheffield Academic Press, 2003.
Murphy, Roland E. *The Tree of Life: An Exploration of Biblical Wisdom Literature*. 3rd ed. Grand Rapids: Eerdmans, 2002.
_____. "Wisdom and Creation." *Journal of Biblical Literature* 104 (1985): 3-11.
Murphy-O'Connor, Jerome. "Corinthian Slogans in 1 Cor 6:12-20." *Catholic Biblical Quarterly* 40 (1978): 391-96.
Nejsum, Peter. "The Apologetic Tendency in the Interpretation of Paul's Sexual Ethics." *Studia Theologica* 48 (1994): 48-62.
Neusner, Jacob. "Varieties of Judaism in the Formative Age." Pages 171-197 in *Jewish Spirituality: From the Bible through the Middle Ages*. Edited by Arthur Green. World Spirituality: An Encyclopedic History of the Religious Quest 13. New York: Crossroad, 1987.
Newsom, Carol A. "Woman and the Discourse of Patriarchal Wisdom." Pages 116-31 in *Reading Bibles, Writing Bodies: Identity and the Book*. Edited by Timothy K. Beal and David M. Gunn. Biblical Limits. London: Routledge, 1997.
Nickelsburg, George W. E. "Wisdom and Apocalypticism in Early Judaism: Some Points for Discussion." Pages 17-37 in *Conflicted Boundaries in Wisdom and Apocalypticism*. Edited by Benjamin G. Wright, III and Lawrence M. Wills. Society of Biblical Literature Symposium series 35. Atlanta: Society of Biblical Literature, 2005.

Niebuhr, Karl-Wilhelm *Heidenapostel aus Israel: Die jüdische Identität des Paulus nach ihrer Darstellung in seinen Briefen.* Wissenschaftliche Untersuchungen zum Neuen Testament 62 Tübingen: Mohr Siebeck, 1992.

Niederwimmer, Kurt. *Askese und Mysterium: Über Ehe.* Göttingen: Vandenhoeck & Ruprecht, 1975.

Nussbaum, Martha C. "Eros and Ethical Norms: Philosophers Respond to a Cultural Dilemma." Pages 55-94 in *The Sleep of Reason: Erotic Experience and Sexual Ethics in Ancient Greece and Rome.* Edited by Martha C. Nussbaum and Juha Sihvola. Chicago: University of Chicago Press, 2002.

———. *Hiding from Humanity: Disgust, Shame, and the Law.* Princeton: Princeton University Press, 2004.

———. "The Incomplete Feminism of Musonius Rufus, Platonist, Stoic, and Roman." Pages 283-326 in *The Sleep of Reason: Erotic Experience and Sexual Ethics in Ancient Greece and Rome.* Edited by Martha C. Nussbaum and Juha Sihvola. Chicago: University of Chicago Press, 2002.

———. *The Therapy of Desire: Theory and Practice in Hellenistic Ethics.* Martin Classical Lectures: New series 2. Princeton, N.J.: Princeton University Press, 1994.

Nussbaum, Martha C. and Juha Sihvola, eds. *The Sleep of Reason: Erotic Experience and Sexual Ethics in Ancient Greece and Rome.* Chicago: University of Chicago Press, 2002.

Oakley, Todd V. "Conceptual Blending, Narrative Discourse, and Rhetoric." *Cognitive Linguistics* 9 (1998): 321-60.

———. "The Human Rhetorical Potential." *Written Communication* 16 (1999): 93-128.

O'Dowd, Ryan. *The Wisdom of Torah: Epistemology in Deuteronomy and Wisdom Literature.* Forschungen zur Religion und Literatur des Alten und Neuen Testaments 225. Göttingen: Vandenhoeck & Ruprecht, 2009.

Olbricht, Thomas H. "The Foundations of Ethos in Paul and in the Classical Rhetoricians." Pages 138-59 in *Rhetoric, Ethic, and Moral Persuasion in Biblical Discourse: Essays from the 2002 Heidelberg Conference.* Edited by Thomas H. Olbricht and Anders Ericksson; Emory Studies in Early Christianity 11; New York: T. & T. Clark, 2005), 138-59.

———. "Introduction." Pages 1-6 in *Rhetorical Argumentation in Biblical Texts: Essays from the Lund 2000 Conference.* Edited by Anders Eriksson, Thomas H. Olbricht, and Walter Überlacker. Emory Studies in Early Christianity 8. Harrisburg, Pa.: Trinity Press International, 2002.

Olbricht, Thomas H. and Anders Ericksson, eds. *Rhetoric, Ethic, and Moral Persuasion in Biblical Discourse: Essays from the 2002 Heidelberg Conference.* Emory Studies in Early Christianity 11. New York: T. & T. Clark, 2005.

Oropeza, B. J. *Paul and Apostasy: Eschatology, Perseverance, and Falling Away in the Corinthian Congregation.* Wissenschaftliche Untersuchungen zum Neuen Testament: 2nd series 115. Tübingen: Mohr Siebeck, 2000.

Osiek, Carolyn. "Female Slaves, *Porneia*, and the Limits of Obedience." Pages 255-74 in *Early Christian Families in Context: An Interdisciplinary Dia-*

logue. Edited by David L. Balch and Carolyn Osiek. Religion, Marriage, and Family. Grand Rapids: Eerdmans, 2003.

Pagels, Elaine H. "Paul and Women: A Response to a Recent Discussion." *Journal of the American Academy of Religion* 42 (1974): 538-49.

Panther, Klaus-Uwe and Linda L. Thornburg, eds. *Metonymy and Pragmatic Inferencing*. Pragmatics & Beyond: New series 113. Amsterdam: John Benjamins, 2003.

Patterson, Cynthia B. *The Family in Greek History*. Cambridge, Mass.: Harvard University Press, 1998.

———. "Plutarch's *Advice to the Bride and Groom*: Traditional Wisdom through a Philosophic Lens." Pages 128-37 in *Plutarch's* Advice to the Bride and Groom *and* A Consolation to His Wife: *English Translations, Commentary, Interpretive Essays, and Bibliography*. Edited by Sarah B. Pomeroy. Oxford: Oxford University Press, 1999.

Perdue, Leo G. "The Social Character of Paraenesis and Paraenetic Literature." *Semeia* 50 (1990): 5-39.

———. *Wisdom and Creation: The Theology of Wisdom Literature*. Nashville: Abingdon, 1994.

———. *Wisdom Literature: A Theological History*. Louisville, Ky.: Westminster John Knox, 2007.

Phipps, William E. "Is Paul's Attitude toward Sexual Relations Contained in 1 Cor 7.1?" *New Testament Studies* 28 (1982): 125-31.

Plunkett, Mark Allen. "Sexual Ethics and the Christian Life: A Study of 1 Corinthians 6:12-7:7." Ph.D. diss., Princeton Theological Seminary, 1988.

Pogoloff, Stephen M. *Logos and Sophia: The Rhetorical Situation of 1 Corinthians*. Society of Biblical Literature Dissertation series 134. Atlanta: Scholars Press, 1992.

Poirier, John C. and Joseph Frankovic. "Celibacy and Charism in 1 Cor 7:5-7." *Harvard Theological Review* 89 (1996): 1-18.

Pomeroy, Sarah B. *Goddesses, Whores, Wives, and Slaves: Women in Classical Antiquity*. New York: Schocken Books, 1975.

Pomeroy, Sarah B., ed. *Plutarch's* Advice to the Bride and Groom *and* A Consolation to His Wife: *English Translations, Commentary, Interpretive Essays, and Bibliography*. New York: Oxford University Press, 1999.

Porter, James I., ed. *Constructions of the Classical Body*. The Body, in Theories: Histories of Cultural Materialism. Ann Arbor: University of Michigan Press, 1999.

Porter, Stanley E. "Ancient Rhetorical Analysis and Discourse Analysis of the Pauline Corpus." Pages 249-74 in *The Rhetorical Analysis of Scripture: Essays form the 1995 London Conference*. Edited by Stanley E. Porter and Thomas H. Olbricht. Journal for the Study of the New Testament: Supplement series 146. Sheffield: Sheffield Academic Press, 1997.

———. "How Should ΚΟΛΛΩΜΕΝΟΣ in 1 Cor 6,16.17 be Translated?" *Ephemerides theologicae lovanienses* 67 (1991): 105-106.

Porter, Stanley E. and Thomas H. Olbricht, eds. *Rhetoric and the New Testament: Essays form the 1992 Heidelberg Conference*. Journal for the Study of the

New Testament: Supplement series 90. Sheffield Academic Press, 1993.

———. *Rhetoric, Scripture and Theology: Essays from the 1994 Pretoria Conference*. Journal for the Study of the New Testament: Supplement series 131. Sheffield: Sheffield University Press, 1996.

———. *The Rhetorical Analysis of Scripture: Essays from the 1995 London Conference*. Journal for the Study of the New Testament: Supplement series 146. Sheffield: Sheffield Academic Press, 1997.

Porter, Stanley E. and Dennis L. Stamps, eds. *Rhetorical Criticism and the Bible: Essays from the 1998 Florence Conference*. Journal for the Study of the New Testament: Supplement series 195. London: Sheffield Academic Press/Continuum, 2002.

Preisker, Herbert. *Christentum und Ehe in den ersten drei Jahrhunderten: Eine Studie zur Kulturgeschichte der alten Welt*. Berlin: Trowitzsch & Sohn, 1927.

Radcliffe, Timothy. "'Glorify God in your Bodies': 1 Corinthians 6,12-20 as Sexual Ethic." *New Blackfriars* 67 (1986): 306-314.

Ramsaran, Rollin A. *Liberating Words: Paul's Use of Rhetorical Maxims in 1 Corinthians 1–10*. Valley Forge, Pa.: Trinity Press International, 1996.

———. "Living and Dying, Living is Dying (Philippians 1:21): Paul's Maxim and Exemplary Argumentation in Philippians." Pages 325-38 in *Rhetorical Argumentation in Biblical Texts: Essays from the Lund 2000 Conference*. Edited by Anders Eriksson, Thomas H. Olbricht, and Walter Übelacker. Emory Studies in Early Christianity 8. Harrisburg, Pa.: TPI, 2002.

Rashkow, Ilona N. *Taboo or not Taboo: Sexuality, Family and the Hebrew Bible*. Minneapolis: Fortress, 2000.

Reydams-Schils, Gretchen. *The Roman Stoics: Self, Responsibility, and Affection*. Chicago: University of Chicago Press, 2005.

Ricoeur, Paul. "Toward a Hermeneutic of the Idea of Revelation." *Harvard Theological Review* 70 (1977): 1-37.

Robbins, Vernon K. "Argumentative Textures in Socio-Rhetorical Interpretation." Pages 27-65 in *Rhetorical Argumentation in Biblical Texts: Essays from the Lund 2000 Conference*. Edited by Anders Eriksson, Thomas H. Olbricht, and Walter Übelacker. Emory Studies in Early Christianity 8. Harrisburg, Penn.: Trinity Press International, 2002.

———. "A Comparison of Mishnah Gittin 1:1–2:2 and James 2:1-13 from a Perspective of Greco-Roman Rhetorical Elaboration." Pages 201-16 in *Mishnah and the Social Formation of the Early Rabbinic Guild: A Socio-Rhetorical Approach*, by Jack N. Lightstone. Studies in Christianity and Judaism 11. Waterloo, Ontario: Wilfrid Laurier University Press, 2002.

———. Conceptual Blending and Early Christian Imagination." Pages 161-95 in *Explaining Christian Origins and Early Judaism*. Edited by Patri Luomanen, Ilkka Pyysiäinen, and Risto Uro. Biblical Interpretation series 89. Leiden: Brill, 2007.

———. "The Dialectical Nature of Early Christian Discourse." *Scriptura* 59 (1996): 353-62.

_____. "Enthymeme and Picture in the *Gospel of Thomas*." Pages 175-207 in *Thomasine Traditions in Antiquity*. Edited by J.M. Asgeirsson, A.D. DeConick, and R. Uro. Leiden: Brill, 2006.

_____. *Exploring the Texture of Texts: A Guide to Socio-Rhetorical Interpretation*. Valley Forge, Pa.: Trinity Press International, 1996.

_____. *The Invention of Christian Discourse: Volume I*. Rhetoric of Religious Antiquity series 1. Blandford Forum: Deo, 2009.

_____. *Jesus the Teacher: A Socio-Rhetorical Interpretation of Mark*. Philadelphia: Fortress, 1984. Repr., Minneapolis: Fortress, 1991.

_____. *New Boundaries in Old Territory: Form and Social Rhetoric in Mark*. Edited by David B. Gowler. Emory Studies in Early Christianity 3. New York: Peter Lang, 1994.

_____. "The Present and Future of Rhetorical Analysis." Pages 24-52 in *The Rhetorical Analysis of Scripture: Essays from the 1995 London Conference*. Edited by Stanley E. Porter and Thomas H. Olbricht. Journal for the Study of the New Testament: Supplement series 146. Sheffield: Sheffield Academic Press, 1997.

_____. "The Rhetorical Full Turn in Biblical Interpretation: Reconfiguring Rhetorical-Political Analysis." Pages 48-60 in *Rhetorical Criticism and the Bible: Essays from the 1998 Florence Conference*. Edited by Stanley E. Porter and Dennis L. Stamps. Journal for the Study of the New Testament: Supplement series 195. London: Sheffield Academic Press /Continuum, 2002.

_____. Rhetography: A New Way of Seeing a Familiar Text." Pages 81-106 in *Words Well Spoken: George Kennedy's Rhetoric of the New Testament*. Edited by C. Clifton Black and Duane F. Watson. Waco: Baylor University Press, 2008.

_____. "Social-Rhetorical Criticism: Mary, Elizabeth and the Magnificat as a Text Case." Pages 164-209 in *The New Literary Criticism and the New Testament*. Edited by Elizabeth Struthers Malbon and Edgar V. McKnight. Sheffield: Sheffield Academic Press, 1994.

_____. "Socio-Rhetorical Interpretation." Pages 192-219 in *Blackwell Companion to the New Testament*. Edited by David E. Aune. Oxford: Wiley-Blackwell, 2010.

_____. *The Tapestry of Early Christian Discourse: Rhetoric, Society and Ideology*. New York: Routledge, 1996.

Robertson, Archibald and Alfred Plummer. *A Critical Exegetical Commentary on the First Epistle of St. Paul to the Corinthians*. 2nd ed. International Critical Commentary. New York: Charles Scribner's Sons, 1916.

Robinson, John A.T. *The Body: A Study in Pauline Anthropology*. Philadelphia: SCM Press, 1952. Repr., Bristol, Ind.: Wyndham Hall, 1988.

Rosner, Brian S. "The Function of Scripture in 1 Cor 5,13b and 6,16." Pages 513-18 in *The Corinthian Correspondence*. Bibliotheca ephemeridum theologicarum lovaniensium 125. Edited by R. Bieringer. Leuven: University Press, 1996.

_____. *Paul, Scripture, and Ethics: A Study of 1 Corinthians 5-7*. Arbeiten zur Geschichte des antiken Judentums und des Urchristentums 22. Leiden: Brill, 1994. Repr., Grand Rapids: Baker Books, 1999.

_____. "Temple Prostitution in 1 Corinthians 6:12-20." *Novum Testamentum* 40 (1998): 336-51.
Rossing, Barbara R. "City Visions, Feminine Figures and Economic Critique: A Sapiential *Topos* in the Apocalypse." Pages 181-96 in *Conflicted Boundaries in Wisdom and Apocalypticism*. Edited by Benjamin G. Wright, III and Lawrence M. Mills. Society of Biblical Literature Symposium series 35. Atlanta, Society of Biblical Literature, 2005.
Sandnes, Karl Olav. *Belly and the Body in Pauline Epistles*. Cambridge; Cambridge University Press, 2002.
Schnabel, Eckhard J. *Law and Wisdom from Ben Sira to Paul: A Tradition Historical Enquiry into the Relation of Law, Wisdom, and Ethics*. Wissenschaftliche Untersuchungen zum Neuen Testament: 2nd series 16. Tübingen: Mohr Siebeck, 1985.
Schnelle, Udo. "1 Kor 6:14 – Eine Nachpualinische Glosse." *Novum Testamentum* 25 (1983): 217-19.
Schrage, Wolfgang. *Der erste Brief an die Korinther*. 4 vols. Evangelisch-Katholischer Kommentar zum Neuen Testament 7. Düsseldorf /Neukirchen-Vluyn: Benzinger Verlag/Neukirchener Verlag, 1991-2001.
Schüssler Fiorenza, Elisabeth. "Challenging the Rhetorical Half-Turn: Feminist and Rhetorical Biblical Criticism." Pages 28-53 in *Rhetoric, Scripture and Theology: Essays from the 1994 Pretoria Conference*. Edited by Stanley E. Porter and Thomas H. Olbricht. Journal for the Study of the New Testament: Supplement series 131. Sheffield: Sheffield University Press, 1996.
Shantz, Coleen. *Paul in Ecstasy: The Neurobiology of the Apostle's Life and Thought*. Cambridge: Cambridge University Press, 2009.
Shaw, Teresa M. *The Burden of the Flesh: Fasting and Sexuality in Early Christianity*. Minneapolis: Fortress, 1998.
Sheppard, Gerald T. *Wisdom as a Hermeneutical Construct: A Study in the Sapientializing of the Old Testament*. Beihefte zur Zeitschrift für die alttestamentliche Wissenschaft 151. Berlin: de Gruyter, 1980.
Siebenmann, Paul Charles. "The Question of Slogans in 1 Corinthians." Ph.D. diss., Baylor University, 1997.
Sissa, Guilia. *Greek Virginity*. Translated by Arthur Goldhammer. Cambridge, Mass.: Harvard University Press, 1990.
_____. "Sexual Bodybuilding: Aeschines against Timarchus." Pages 147-68 in *Constructions of the Classical Body*. Edited by James I. Porter. The Body, in Theories: Histories of Cultural Materialism. Ann Arbor: University of Michigan Press, 1999.
Skehan, Patrick W. and Alexander A. DiLella. *The Wisdom of Ben Sira*. Anchor Bible 39. Garden City, N.Y.: Doubleday, 1987.
Slingerland, Edward. "Conceptions of the Self in the *Zhuangzi*: Conceptual Metaphor Analysis and Comparative Thought." *Philosophy East and West* 54 (2004): 322-42.
_____. "Conceptual Metaphor Theory as Methodology for Comparative Religion." *Journal of the American Academy of Religion* 72 (2004): 1-31.

———. *What Science Offers the Humanities: Integrating Body and Culture*. New York: Cambridge University Press, 2008.

———. "Who's Afraid of Reductionism? The Study of Religion in the Age of Cognitive Science." *Journal of the American Academy of Religion* 76 (2008): 275-411.

Sly, Dorothy. *Philo's Perception of Women*. Brown Judaic Studies 209. Atlanta: Scholars Press, 1990.

Stockwell, Peter. *Cognitive Poetics: An Introduction*. London: Routledge, 2002.

Stowers, Stanley K. "A 'Debate' over Freedom: 1 Corinthians 6.12-20." Pages 59-71 in *Christian Teaching: Studies in Honor of Lemoine G. Lewis*. Edited by Everett Ferguson. Abilene, Tex.: Abilene Christian University Press, 1981.

———. "PERI MEN GAR and the Integrity of 2 Cor. 8 and 9." *Novum Testamentum* 32 (1990): 340-48.

———. *A Rereading of Romans: Justice, Jews, and Gentiles*. New Haven: Yale University Press, 1994.

Struthers Malbon, Elizabeth and Edgar V. McKnight. *The New Literary Criticism and the New Testament*. Sheffield: Sheffield Academic Press, 1994.

Stumpp, Bettina Eva. *Prostitution in der römische Antike*. 2nd ed. Antike in der Moderne. Berlin: Akademie Verlag, 1998.

Theis, Joachim. *Paulus als Weisheitslehrer: Der Gerkreuzigte und die Weisheit Gottes in 1 Kor 1-4*. Biblische Untersuchungen 22. Regensburg: Friedrich Pustet, 1991.

Thielman, Frank. *From Plight to Solution: A Jewish Framework for Understanding Paul's View of the Law in Galatians and Romans*. Novum Testamentum Supplements 61. Leiden: Brill, 1989.

Thiselton, Anthony C. *The First Epistle to the Corinthians: A Commentary on the Greek Text*. New International Greek Testament Commentary. Grand Rapids: Eerdmans, 2000.

Thomas, Johannes. *Der jüdische Phokylides: Formsgeschichtliche Zugänge zu Pseudo-Phokylides und Vergleich mit der neutestamentlichen Paränese*. Novum Testamentum et Orbis Antiquus 23. Freiburg, Switzerland/Göttingen: Universitätsverlag/Vandenhoeck & Ruprecht, 1992.

Thompson, John L. "Apostolic Doctrine and Apostolic Advice in 1 Corinthians 7: A Study in Sixteenth-Century Exegesis and Hermeneutics." *American Society of Church History Papers*. Portland, Ore.: Theological Research Exchange Network, 1993.

Thurén, Lauri. "Is There a Biblical Argumentation?" Pages 77-92 in *Rhetorical Argumentation in Biblical Texts: Essays from the Lund 2000 Conference*. Edited by Anders Eriksson, Thomas H. Olbricht, and Walter Übelacker. Emory Studies in Early Christianity 8. Harrisburg, Pa.: Trinity Press International, 2002.

———. "On Studying Ethical Argumentation and Persuasion in the New Testament." Pages 464-78 in *Rhetoric and the New Testament: Essays form the 1992 Heidelberg Conference*. Edited by Stanley E. Porter and Thomas H. Olbricht. Journal for the Study of the New Testament: Supplement series 90. Sheffield Academic Press, 1993.

Tiedemann, Holger. *Die Erfahrung des Fleisches: Paulus und die Last der Lust.* Stuttgart: Radius, 1998.

———. *Paulus und das Begehren: Liebe, Lust und letzte Ziele. Oder: Das Gesetz in den Gliedern.* Stuttgart: Radius, 2002.

Tilley, Christopher. *The Materiality of Stone: Explorations in Landscape Phenomenology.* New York: Berg, 2004.

Tomson, Peter J. *Paul and the Jewish Law: Halakha in the Letters of the Apostle to the Gentiles.* Assen: Van Gorcum, 1990.

Trenchard, Warren C. *Ben Sira's View of Women: A Literary Analysis.* Brown Judaic Studies 38. Chico, Calif.: Scholars Press, 1982.

Turner, Mark. "The Art of Compression." Pages in 93-113 *The Artful Mind: Cognitive Science and the Riddle of Human Creativity.* Edited by Mark Turner. New York: Oxford University Press, 2006.

———. *The Literary Mind.* New York: Oxford University Press, 1996.

Vaage, Leif E. and Vincent L. Wimbush, eds. *Asceticism and the New Testament.* New York: Routledge, 1999.

Vander Stichele, Caroline and Todd Penner. "Paul and the Rhetoric of Gender." Pages 287-310 in *Her Master's Tools? Feminist and Postcolonial Engagements of Historical-Critical Discourse.* Edited by Caroline Vander Stichele and Todd Penner. SBL Global Perspectives on Biblical Scholarship 9. Atlanta: Society of Biblical Literature, 2005.

Vander Stichele, Caroline and Todd Penner, eds. *Her Master's Tools? Feminist and Postcolonial Engagements of Historical-Critical Discourse.* SBL Global Perspectives on Biblical Scholarship 9. Atlanta: Society of Biblical Literature, 2005.

Veale, Tony and Diarmand O'Donoghue. "Computation and Blending." *Cognitive Linguistics* 11 (2000): 253.

von Dehsen, Christian D. "Sexual Relationships and the Church: An Exegetical Study of 1 Corinthians 5–7." Ph.D. diss., Union Theological Seminary, 1987.

von Rad, Gerhard. "The Joseph Narrative and Ancient Wisdom." Pages 439-47 in *Studies in Ancient Israelite Wisdom.* Edited by James L. Crenshaw. The Library of Biblical Studies. New York: Ktav, 1976.

von Thaden, Robert H., Jr."Glorify God in Your Body: The Redemptive Role of the Body in Early Christian Ascetic Literature." *Cistercian Studies Quarterly* 38 (2003): 191-209.

Vos, Johan S. "Die Argumentation des Paulus in 1 Kor 1,10-3,4."Pages 87-119 in *The Corinthian Correspondence.* Bibliotheca ephemeridum theologicarum lovaniensium 125. Edited by R. Bieringer. Leuven: University Press, 1996.

Walsh, Carey Ellen. *Exquisite Desire: Religion, the Erotic, and the Song of Songs.* Minneapolis: Fortress, 2000.

Wanamaker, Charles A. "A Rhetoric of Power: Ideology and 1 Corinthians 1–4." Pages 115-37 in *Paul and the Corinthians: Studies on a Community in Conflict. Essays in Honour of Margaret Thrall.* Edited by Trevor J. Burke and J. Keith Elliot. Novum Testamentum Suppplements 109. Leiden: Brill, 2003.

Watson, Duane Frederick. *Invention, Arrangement, and Style: Rhetorical Criticism of Jude and 2 Peter*. Society of Biblical Literature Dissertation series 104. Atlanta: Scholars Press, 1988.

———. "Why We Need Socio-Rhetorical Commentary and What It Might Look Like." Pages 129-57 in *Rhetorical Criticism and the Bible: Essays from the 1998 Florence Conference*. Edited by Stanley E. Porter and Dennis L. Stamps. Journal for the Study of the New Testament: Supplement series 195. London: Sheffield Academic Press/Continuum, 2002.

Wegner, Judith Romney. "Philo's Portrayal of Women – Hebraic or Hellenic?" Pages 41-66 in *"Women Like This": New Perspectives on Jewish Women in the Greco-Roman World*. Edited by Amy-Jill Levine. Society of Biblical Literature Early Judaism and Its Literature 1. Atlanta: Scholars Press, 1991.

Weiß, Johannes *Der erste Korintherbrief*. 9th ed. Kritischer-exegetischer Kommentar über das Neue Testament 5. Göttingen: Vandenhoeck & Ruprecht, 1910.

Welborn, L.L. *Paul, the Fool of Christ: A Study of 1 Corinthians 1–4 in the Comic-Philosophic Tradition*. Library of New Testament Studies 293. New York: T. & T. Clark, 2005.

Wevers, John William. *Notes on the Greek Text of Exodus*. Society of Biblical Literature Septuagint and Cognate Studies 30. Atlanta: Scholars Press, 1990.

———. *Notes on the Greek Text of Genesis*. Society of Biblical Literature Septuagint and Cognate Studies 35. Atlanta: Scholars Press, 1993.

Whitehouse, Harvey. *Arguments and Icons: Divergent Modes of Religiosity*. Oxford: Oxford University Press, 2000.

———. *Inside the Cult: Religious Innovation and Transmission in Papua New Guinea*. Oxford: Oxford University Press, 1995.

———. *Modes of Religiosity: A Cognitive Theory of Religious Transmission*. Cognitive Science of Religion series. Walnut Creek, Calif.: Alta Mira: 2004.

———. "Theorizing Religions Past." Pages 215-232 in *Theorizing Religions Past: Archeology, History, and Cognition*. Cognitive Science of Religion series. Walnut Creek, Calif.: Alta Mira: 2004.

Whitehouse, Harvey and Luther H. Martin, eds. *Theorizing Religions Past: Archeology, History, and Cognition*. Cognitive Science of Religion series. Walnut Creek, Calif.: Alta Mira: 2004.

———. *Notes on the Greek Text of Leviticus*. Society of Biblical Literature Septuagint and Cognate Studies 44. Atlanta: Scholars Press, 1997.

Williams, Guy. *The Spirit World in the Letters of Paul the Apostle: A Critical Examination of the Role of Spiritual Beings in the Authentic Pauline Epistles*. Forschungen zur Religion und Literatur des Alten und Neuen Testaments 231. Göttingen: Vandenhoeck & Ruprecht, 2009.

Williams, H.H. Drake, III. *The Wisdom of the Wise: The Presence and Function of Scripture within 1 Cor.1:18-3:2*. Arbeiten zur Geschichte des antiken Judentums und das Urchristentums 49. Leiden: Brill, 2001.

Williams, James G. *Those Who Ponder Proverbs: Aphoristic Thinking and Biblical Literature*. Bible and Literature series 2. Sheffield: Almond, 1981.

Wilson, Lindsay. *Joseph, Wise and Otherwise: The Intersection of Wisdom and Covenant in Gensesis 37-50*. Paternoster Biblical Monographs. Carlisle, U.K.: Paternoster, 2004.
Wilson, Walter T. *Love without Pretense: Romans 12:9-21 and Hellenistic-Jewish Wisdom Literature*. Wissenschaftliche Untersuchungen zum Neuen Testament: 2nd series 46. Tübingen: Mohr Siebeck, 1991.
_____. *The Mysteries of Righteousness: The Literary Composition and Genre of the Sentences of Pseudo-Phocylides*. Texte und Studien zum antiken Judentum 40. Tübingen: Mohr Siebeck, 1994.
_____. "Pious Soldiers, Gender Deviants, and the Ideology of Actium: Courage and Warfare in Philo's *De Fortitudine*." *The Studia Philonica Annual: Studies in Hellenistic Judaism* 2005 (17): 1-32.
_____. *The Sentences of Pseudo-Phocylides*. Commentaries on Early Jewish Literature. Berlin: de Gruyter, 2005.
_____. "Sin as Sex and Sex with Sin: The Anthropology of James 1:12-15." *Harvard Theological Review* 95 (2002): 147-68.
Wimbush, Vincent L. and Richard Valantasis, eds. *Asceticism* Oxford: Oxford University Press, 1998.
Winter, Bruce W. "1 Corinthians 7:6-7: A Caveat and Framework for 'The Sayings' in 7:8-40." *Tyndale Bulletin* 48 (1997): 57-65.
_____. *After Paul Left Corinth: The Influence of Secular Ethics and Social Change*. Grand Rapids, Eerdmans, 2001.
_____. *Philo and Paul Among the Sophists: Alexandrian and Corinthian Responses to a Julio-Claudian Movement*. 2nd ed. Cambridge: Cambridge University Press, 1997. Repr., Grand Rapids: Eerdmans, 2002.
_____. *Roman Wives, Roman Widows: The Appearance of New Women in the Pauline Communities*. Grand Rapids: Eerdmans, 2003.
Wire, Antoinette Clark. *The Corinthian Women Prophets: A Reconstruction through Paul's Rhetoric*. Minneapolis: Fortress, 1990.
Witherington, Ben, III. *The Acts of the Apostles: A Socio-Rhetorical Commentary*. Grand Rapids: Eerdmans, 1998.
_____. *Conflict and Community in Corinth: A Socio-Rhetorical Commentary on 1 and 2 Corinthians*. Grand Rapids: Eerdmans, 1994.
_____. *Jesus the Sage: The Pilgrimage of Wisdom*. Minneapolis: Fortress, 1994.
Wright, Benjamin G., III and Lawrence M. Wills, eds. *Conflicted Boundaries in Wisdom and Apocalypticism*. Society of Biblical Literature Symposium series 35. Atlanta: Society of Biblical Literature, 2005.
Wuellner, Wilhelm H. "Where is Rhetorical Criticism Taking Us?" *Catholic Biblical Quarterly* 49 (1987): 448-63.
Yarbrough, O. Larry. *Not Like the Gentiles: Marriage Rules in the Letters of Paul*. Society of Biblical Literature Dissertation series 80. Atlanta: Scholars Press, 1985.
Yee, Gale A. *Poor Banished Children of Eve: Woman as Evil in the Hebrew Bible*. Minneapolis: Fortress, 2003.
Zeitlin, Froma I. "Reflections on Erotic Desire in Archaic and Classical Greece." Pages 50-76 in *Constructions of the Classical Body*. Edited by

James I. Porter. The Body, in Theories: Histories of Cultural Materialism. Ann Arbor: University of Michigan Press, 1999.

Index of Names

Asgeirsson, J. M. 36
Aune, David E. 38

Baer, Richard A. 118, 127–28, 136, 267, 295
Bain, David 249
Baird, William 7
Balch, David L. 232, 273
Baltenweiler, Heinrich 13
Barrett, C.K. 2–3
Barton, Stephen C. 159
Bauckham, Richard 78–79
Baur, Ferdinand Christian 1, 5–7, 10, 12, 15–16, 26–27, 31–32, 160, 211
Beal, Timothy K. 95, 117
Beattie, Gillian 270
Beentjes, Pancratius C. 89, 125
Biddle, Mark E. 35, 98
Bieringer, R. 30
Bird, Phyllis A. 85
Black, Max 43
Bloomquist, Gregory 53, 62, 298
Bowden, John 22
Boyarin, Daniel 198, 265–67, 272
Boyer, Pascal 39
Braun, Willi 186
Brenner, Athalya 114, 139
Brooten, Bernadette J. 263
Brown, Peter 1, 201, 300
Brown, William P. 88
Bruehler, Bart B. 66
Buccellati, Giorgio 77, 81–82
Budin, Stephanie Lynn 258
Bultmann, Rudolf, 40 202-204

Burke, Trevor J., 170 181–83
Burton-Christie, Douglas 4
Byron, John 260

Calvin, John 30
Camp, Claudia V. 115–17, 122–26, 130, 139, 142–44, 287
Carr, David M. 85–86, 129, 131–32
Carroll, John T. 159
Carson, Anne 223, 226, 257, 267, 269
Castelli, Elizabeth A. 181–83
Charlesworth, James H. 164, 166
Ciampa, Roy E. 265
Clark, Elizabeth A. 4, 25, 35, 43, 130, 159, 201, 253, 286
Collins, John J. 28, 71, 78–80, 82–84, 90–93, 96, 98, 109, 115, 117–18, 155, 166, 169, 171, 181–82, 212, 236
Collins, Raymond F. 2–3, 192–93, 196–97, 206, 216, 218, 229, 265, 268, 285, 288
Conzelmann, Hans 2, 171, 181–82, 192-93, 196, 200, 212, 216, 264
Coogan, Michael D. 98
Cook, Johann 79
Corrington Streete, Gail 30, 80, 127, 130, 139, 169
Cosgrove, Charles H. 159
Coulson, Seana 38, 45–48, 50–54, 56–61, 68–69, 78, 110, 185, 188, 199-200, 204,

207, 211, 213–14, 220, 223, 231, 240, 262, 297
Crenshaw, James L. 78–83, 87, 90–91, 95, 119–20, 130, 139, 171, 181–82, 195, 211, 220, 242, 292
Czachesz, Ivan 297

Damasio, Antonio R. 40–41, 59–60, 66–67, 209, 301
Davidson, James 226, 229, 231, 235, 248–50, 270, 274, 277, 283, 285
Davies, Philip R. 87, 148
Davis, James A. 169, 185
DeConick, A.D. 36
Dell, Katherine 81, 181
Delling, Gerhard 13
Deming, Will 5, 18, 24–25, 31–32, 265–66, 275, 277–78, 282–83, 289
Derrett, Duncan M. 30
De Troyer, Kristin 140
Di Lella, Alexander A. 89, 97, 126
Dixon, Suzanne 271, 273, 275, 278, 285
Dodd, Brian J. 3, 21, 33, 147, 182, 184, 191, 193, 197-98, 202, 210, 263, 299
Doll, Peter 82
Dover, K.J. 248
Dowden, Ken 113
Downing, F. Gerald 266
Dundes, Alan 209

Ehrman, Bart 194-95
Ellens, Deborah L. 130, 140, 286
Elliot, Keith 170, 181
Emery, Kent 4
Eriksson, Anders 16, 21, 63–64, 70, 199
Erksine, Andrew 221
Eubanks, Philip 45–46, 48, 53–54, 231

Fantham, Elaine 250

Fauconnier, Gilles 3, 38, 44–51, 53–62, 74–75, 110, 168, 188–91, 207, 204-205, 213–14, 225, 228–31, 233–34, 236–39, 250, 257, 286, 290
Faw, C.E. 194
Fee, Gordon D. 2–3, 162, 181, 184, 192-93, 196-97, 225, 227–29, 235, 244, 257, 265, 269, 271–72, 285, 288
Feldman, Jerome A. 39
Fenske, Wolfgang 209, 213, 227
Ferguson, Everett 24
Fernandez, James W. 53
Fillmore, Charles J. 50, 68
Fishbane, Michael 164, 167
Fisk, Bruce N. 1, 208, 253–55
Flanagan, James W. 143
Fontaine, Carole R. 114, 117
Foucault, Michel, 29
Fox, Michael V. 79–80, 111, 116, 122
Fraade, Steven D. 265–67, 269, 282
Frankovic, Joseph 146, 282
Frymer-Kensky, Tikva 235, 258
Furnish, Victor Paul 2, 196, 200, 206, 210

Gaca, Kathy L. 1, 5, 22, 28–32, 34–35, 114, 135, 137, 156, 226, 231, 235, 265–66, 268, 274–78, 283, 286
Gallagher, Shaun 39
Galloway, Lincoln E. 156–57, 211–13, 216, 219, 221, 260
Gammie, John G. 72
Gibbs, Raymond W. 37, 39–41, 45, 48, 57, 59, 203, 240, 297
Goff, Matthew J. 70–72, 79, 86, 95, 101, 108, 110, 140, 160, 163, 169, 171–76, 180, 183–84, 227, 231, 272
Goldhammer, Arthur 113
Goldhill, Simon 273

Index of Names

Goulder, Michael D. 2–3, 6, 80, 160, 170, 191, 197, 206, 211, 254
Gowler, David B. 111
Grady, Joseph E. 45, 297
Green, Joel B. 41
Grindheim, Sigurd 159
Grobel, Kendrick 40
Groscheide, F.W. 269
Gundry, Robert 203
Gunn, David M. 95, 117, 144

Halperin, David M. 29, 223
Hays, Richard B. 159, 163, 167, 169, 173
Hawkins, Faith Kirkham 195
Hengel, Martin 22, 35
Herbert, Judith A. 140
Holladay, Carl R. 160
Holtz, Traugott 207
Horsley, Richard A. 170
Howe, Bonnie 38, 43–46, 48, 230, 297
Huber, Lynn R. 43–44, 250, 271, 278
Hurd, John C. 3, 5, 8, 10–14, 16–17, 23, 26–27, 32–33, 193, 196–97, 206
Hylen, Susan E. 148

James, Liz 30
Johnson, Elizabeth 159, 170, 173, 176, 184–85
Johnson, Luke Timothy 10, 52, 110
Johnson, Mark 39, 43–44
Jonas, Hans 201
Jordan, Mark 4, 207, 231, 235

Käsemann, Ernst 203-204
Kee, Howard C. 6
Keuls, Eva C. 250
Kirchhoff, Renate 5, 18–21, 27, 31–34, 77, 82, 114, 191, 196, 202, 204, 208–10, 228, 231–32, 234–36, 240, 247, 251, 299

Knust, Jennifer Wright 198, 200, 218, 220, 225–26, 228, 232, 236, 248–50, 259–60, 269, 274, 276, 285
Kövecses, Zoltán 40, 45–46
Kümmel, Werner 6–7
Kurke, Leslie 236, 249–50

Lakoff, George 39, 41, 43–45, 69, 189
Langacker, Ronald W. 188
Lawson, Thomas E. 37, 42
Lefkowitz, Mary R. 257
Leitch, James W. 2
Levine, Amy-Jill 124, 127, 193, 273
Lieu, Judith M. 223, 255
Lightstone, Jack N. 79
Loader, William 113, 137, 156, 192, 232, 247, 257, 263, 266, 274, 282
Long, Frederick J. 253
Lundhaug, Hugo 38, 297
Luomanen, Petri 39, 42, 297

MacDonald, Margaret Y. 193, 201 269–70, 286
Mack, Burton 80, 82, 133, 143–44
Malherbe, Abraham 211
Martin, Dale 2, 5, 17, 23–24, 26–27, 31, 33, 112, 140, 162, 192-93, 195–96, 199-200, 226, 234–35, 239, 251, 253, 257, 260, 285, 300
Martin, Luther H. 37–38, 52
McAuslan, Ian 257
McCauley, Robert N. 42
McClure, Laura K. 142, 222, 229, 231, 236, 239, 248–50, 257–58, 275, 277–78, 285
McGinn, Thomas A. J. 235
McKnight, Edgar V. 15
McLean, S. 6
Merleau-Ponty, Maurice 40
Meyer, Paul W. 159
Miguens, M. 255
Mills, Lawrence M. 235

Mitchell, Margaret M. 2, 8, 15–19, 22, 27, 32–34, 63, 109, 162, 182, 193-97, 199–200, 206, 212, 216, 250–51, 264
Möller, Karl 63–64
Murphy, Roland E. 70, 78–80, 82–84, 90, 131, 181, 183, 195
Murphy-O'Connor, Jerome 196-97

NcNutt, Paula M. 144
Nejsum, Peter 3, 17–18, 25, 191, 195, 201, 207, 257, 285, 299
Neusner, Jacob 14, 265
Newsom, Carol A. 95, 111, 116, 122–23, 139, 181, 287
Niebuhr, Karl-Wilhelm 22
Niederwimmer, Kurt 289
Nussbaum, Martha C. 29, 60, 236, 274–75, 277–78, 301

Oakley, Todd V. 38, 44–45, 47, 61, 75, 110, 188, 190, 199-200, 204, 225, 297
O'Donoghue, Diarmand 44
O'Dowd, Ryan 150, 212
Olbricht, Thomas H. 63, 70, 79, 199, 253
Oropeza, B. J. 54, 204, 232
Osiek, Carolyn 232, 273

Pagels, Elaine H. 195
Panther, Klaus-Uwe 47
Patterson, Cynthia B. 232, 248, 272, 278, 285
Penner, Todd 198
Perdue, Leo G. 44, 72, 80, 82–83, 89–91, 94–95, 110
Phipps, William E. 3, 25, 197, 201,277
Plunkett, Mark Allen 191, 201-202
Plummer, Alfred 206, 228, 235, 253
Pogoloff, Stephen M. 161
Poirier, John C. 146, 282
Pomeroy, Sarah B. 249, 275, 278

Porter, James I. 218, 223, 274
Porter, Stanley E. 62–63, 79, 245
Preisker, Herbert 13
Pringle, John 30
Pyysiäinen, Ilkka 39, 42, 297

Radcliffe, Timothy, 2
Ramsaran, Rollin A. 21, 77, 200, 209
Rashkow, Ilona N. 139
Redditt, Paul 169
Reydams-Schils, Gretchen 275, 277–78
Robbins, Vernon K. 1–3, 15–16, 28, 36, 38–39, 43, 50, 61, 64–72, 74, 77, 79–84, 88–89, 96, 108, 110–11, 140, 150, 158, 160, 164, 166–70, 175–76, 180, 182–83, 186-87, 189, 191-92, 195, 198-200, 206, 208–10, 213, 220, 228, 237, 247, 253, 262, 264–65, 273, 281, 286, 291, 294, 298–99
Robertson, Archibald 206, 228, 235, 253
Robinson, John A.T. 203
Rosner, Brian S. 1, 5, 22–24, 29–32, 78, 191, 206–208, 216, 230, 245, 261, 265
Rossing, Barbara R. 235
Russell, Donald 275

Sandnes, Karl Olav 196, 225–26, 257
Schnabel, Eckhard J. 79, 82, 94, 96, 98–99, 160, 294
Schnelle, Udo 196
Schrage, Wolfgang 2–3, 161–62, 181, 192-93, 196–97, 200, 204, 216, 229, 247, 251, 285, 288
Schüssler Fiorenza, Elisabeth 63
Shantz, Coleen 40
Shaw, Teresa M. 226
Sheppard, Gerald T. 78, 164, 167
Siebenmann, Paul Charles 2–3, 197, 200

Sissa, Guilia 113, 218, 242, 248, 257
Skehan, Patrick W. 125
Slingerland, Edward 37–48, 54, 56, 59–60, 62, 231, 298
Sly, Dorothy 118, 129, 136, 264, 267
Stamps, Dennis L. 62
Steen, Gerard J. 45, 297
Stockwell, Peter 50
Stowers, Stanley K. 24, 27, 193-94, 198, 212–13, 218–20, 222–23, 225–26, 228, 268, 276
Struthers Malbon, Elizabeth 15
Stumpp, Bettina Eva 235

Theis, Joachim 95, 159, 161–63, 168, 170, 172, 176–77, 185
Thielman, Frank 22
Thiselton, Anthony C. 2–3, 16, 33, 161–62, 170–71, 175, 183–84, 193, 196–97, 201, 255, 257, 269–70, 272, 285, 288–89, 299
Thomas, Johannes 80
Thompson, John L. 4
Thornburg, Linda L. 47
Thurén, Lauri 16, 63–64
Tiedemann, Holger 201-202, 264–66
Tilley, Christopher 37
Tomson, Peter J. 22
Trenchard, Warren C. 115, 124–26
Turner, Mark 3, 38, 41, 43–51, 54–58, 60, 62, 74–75, 110, 168, 188-191, 204-205, 207, 213–14, 225, 228–31, 233–34, 236–39, 250, 257, 286, 290

Übelacker, Walter 70
Uro, Risto 36–39, 42, 297

Vaage, Leif E. 25
Valantasis, Richard 25, 202, 226
Vander Stichele, Caroline 198

van der Horst, P.W. 117, 125, 274
van Dijk-Hemmes, Fokkelein 139
Veale, Tony 44
von Dehsen, Christian D. 18
von Lips, Hermann 161
von Rad, Gerhard 84, 119
von Thaden, Robert H., Jr. 226
Vos, Johan S. 161

Walcott, Peter 257
Wanamaker, Charles A. 170, 174, 177–78, 181–82, 184
Watson, Duane F. 36, 62, 199
Wegner, Judith Romney 127, 267
Weiß, Johannes 2, 5, 7–13, 16, 26–27, 31–33, 161, 171, 184, 196–97, 202-203, 206, 211, 216–17, 227, 234, 250, 264–67, 269
Welborn, L. L. 159
Wevers, John William 85, 112, 139–41
Whitehouse, Harvey 37–38, 42, 52
Williams, Guy 241, 252, 281–82
Williams, H. H. Drake III, 216
Williams, James G. 209, 211
Wills, Lawrence M. 163, 174
Wilson, Lindsay 77
Wilson, Walter T. 77–81, 107, 117–19, 128–29, 135, 157, 159, 167, 195, 209–13, 218–20, 226–27, 232, 264, 267, 273–74
Wimbush, Vincent L. 25, 202, 226
Winkler, John J. 223
Winter, Bruce W. 161–62, 182, 226, 250, 285
Wire, Antoinette Clark 300
Witherington, Ben 2–3, 159, 161–62, 169, 181, 183, 185, 192, 197
Wright, Benjamin G. 163, 174, 235
Wuellner, Wilhelm H. 15–16, 64

Yarbrough, O. Larry 3, 5, 13–15, 18, 24, 32–33, 192, 195, 197, 264, 266, 269, 276–77
Yee, Gale A. 87, 113, 119–22

Zeitlin, Froma I. 223, 274

Index of Ancient References

Biblical Texts

Genesis
1   96, 112, 118, 129, 136, 247
1:2   166, 175
1:22   96
1:26   93
1:26-27   92
1:27   112, 154
1:27-28   266
1:28   91, 96, 112, 266
2   112
2-3   85, 294
2-4   85, 89, 93
2:6   90, 94
2:7   93
2:8-10   90
2:9   82, 85
2:10   92
2:15-16   90
2:16   85
2:16-17   86
2:17   85, 89, 92
2:18   115, 265, 266
2:20   115
2:23-24   113, 130
2:24   24, 136-137, 157, 242, 245-48
3   113, 119, 129, 130
3:1-3   86
3:1-24   92
3:2-3   90
3:5   85
3:7   85
3:8   90
3:11   86
3:12   113
3:16-17   130
3:17   113, 130
3:22   86, 88, 130
3:23   82
3:23-24   90
9:6   266
12:1-3   260
12:10-12   135
12:10-20   146
12:13   146
20:6   269
34   156
37-50   77
38:15-26   231
39   22, 119
39:6-7   119
39:9-10   119
39:11-20   119
41:42   153
49:7   156

Exodus
2:1   272
5-14   148
9:14-19   145
11:22   148, 154
14:3-31   154
14:30-31   148
14:31   89
19   139, 149
19:3-6   260
19:4   215
19:4-6   149
19:5-6   100
19:8   149
19:10-11   139
19:11   139
19:12   139
19:15   139, 267
20-23   149
20:17   137, 156
23   215
24:3   149
25:30   143
26:15-30   143
33:9-10   98
33: 21-22   98
34:15-16   121
37:17-24   143
38:34-37   143

Leviticus
11:44   140
12   141
12:4   141
15   140, 141
15:2   140
15:16   140
15:18   140
15:31   140
15:33   140
18   141, 142
18-20   130
18:2-3   141
18:6-18   141
18:19   135, 140
18:19-23   141
18:21   141

18:24-30 141
19:2 140
19:19 142
19:32 121, 133
20:7 140
20:8 140
20:10-21 141
20:22-26 100
20:24 140
20:26 140
21:7-8 142
21:7-13 142
21:13-15 142
21:14 130
22:12-13 142
26:3-13 149
26:13 149
26:14-39 149
26:33 149
26:34 149

Numbers
8:11-14 143
11:4 137
11:34 137
12:1 145
15:40-41 140
16:26 269
25:6-18 144
25:13 144
31:16 128

Deuteronomy
1:13 87
5:21 137, 156
6:2 89
6:13 245
10:12 89
10:20 245
17:19 89
21:10-14 130
23:11 140
23:17 120
23:19 130, 252
26:18-19 100
27:20-23 141
28:1-14 149
28:15-68 149

28:30 272
28:47 150, 152, 222
28:68 150
30:15 150, 215
31: 12-3 89

Joshua
24:14 89

1 Samuel[1]
12:14 89

2 Kingdoms
7:1-13 87
20:2 245

3 Kingdoms
2:35 87, 120
2:46 87
3:9 87
3:9-12 172
3:16-28 121
5:9 171
5:9-11 87
5:9-14 120
5:14 87, 120
5:15-19 87
7:26-29 143
7:34-36 143
7:35 143
10:1-3 121
10:23-25 87, 120
11:1 121, 136, 246, 273
11:1-4 87
11:2 120-21, 246
11:4 120-21, 123, 150, 246
11:9-13 120
19:10 180
19:14 180

[1] Note: Although I reference LXX books in making my arguments, many of my conversation partners use MT books.

4 Kingdoms
18:6 245

2 Chronicles
3:15-4:10 143
4:7 143
4:19-22 143
4:20 143
36:15-16 180

1 Esdras
4:20 245

1 Maccabees
1:63 226

4 Maccabees
1:1 155
1:3-4 155
1:17 155
1:13 155
1:22 138
1:30 155
1:34 226
2:2 156
2:5 156
2:6 137, 156
2:19-20 156
3:2 156, 268, 274
5-7 155
6:31 155
8-14 155
9:23 95
13:1 155
15:1-17:6 155
16:23 155
18:1-2 155

Psalms
32:10 164
66:11 89
112:1 89
128:1 89

Proverbs
1-9 95, 111, 114, 122, 150, 181
1:1 88, 121

Index of Ancient References

1:7 89, 95, 121
1:8 95, 181
2:1 181
2:1-2 95
2:16-19 255
2:32 121
3:1 95, 181
3:5 104, 167
3:7 104, 105, 167
3:15 116
3:16 88
3:18 88
3:18-20 82
3:19-20 88
3:21 95
3:22 95
3:35 121
4:1 116
4:1-2 95, 181
4:6 116
4:6-7 116
4:10 95, 181
4:10-19 121
4:20 95, 181
4:22 151
5 122
5-9 122
5:1 95, 181
5:2-23 255
5:3 122, 223
5:5 122-23, 223
5:6 123
5:15-19 116
5:19 116
5:20 116, 122, 246
6 122
6:2 150-51, 222
6:5 150, 222
6:20 95, 181
6:23-25 255
6:25 122, 223
6:26 122
6:29 122, 269
7 122
7:1 95, 181
7:1-3 95
7:4 116
7:4-5 117

7:5 122, 246
7:6-27 255
7:10 122, 223
7:11 122
7:13 122-123, 223
7:14 142
7:15 142
7:16-17 123
7:16-18 223
7:18 123
7:19-20 122
7:21 150, 222
7:21-23 150, 222
7:22 22
7:22-23 223
7:23 150, 222
7:22 152
7:22-23 123, 150
7:26-27 123, 223
7:27 122
8:11 116
8:17 116
8:18 121, 180
8:20 123
8:22-31 88, 92
8:36 151
9 122, 124
9:10 89, 95, 123
9:11 123
9:12 94
9:13 122
9:13-17 123, 223
9:16 150
9:18 122-23, 223, 246
10:1 95
10:4 151
10:13 184
10:16 88
10:19 115
10:24 137
11:8 150, 222
11:9 150, 151, 222
11:12 115
11:16 114
11:29 151
11:30 94
12:4 114
12:12 137

12:13 150, 222
12:27 150, 222
13:3 115
13:4 137
13:12 137
13:14 90, 94, 150, 222
13:19 137
13:24 184
14:1 114, 115
14:2 89
14:27 90, 94, 150, 222
15:4 88
15:8 142
15:20 95
15:24 88
15:32 151
15:33 89, 95
16:22 88, 150
17:2 151
17:21 95
17:25 115
18:7 150, 222
18:22 114, 273
19:13 142
20:1 151
20:3 151
20:25 150, 222
21:6 150, 222
21:27 142
22:4 95-96
22:5 150-51, 222
22:11 151
22:15 184
22:24 89
22:24-25 151
22:25 150, 222
23:13-14 184
23:20 142
23:33 229
24:9 151
25:10 151
25:20 254
26:1-12 121
26:3 184
26:12 105, 167
27:20 115
29:3 121, 229
29:6 150, 222

28:7 96
28:9 96
29:3 122
29:5 151
29:20 115
29:21 151
29:23 95
30:20 142
31 115, 117, 295
31:10 114
31:10-31 114, 116
31:11-27 121, 180
31:13-19 114
31:20 114
31:22-21 114
31:23 114
31:24 114
31:25 115
31:27 114
31:28 115
31:28-29 114
31:30 115
31:31 114

Ecclesiastes
1:13 105
2:3-8 180
2:16 100
2:17 105
2:26 96
3:18-22 100
5:5 115
7:27 150, 222
8:16 105
9:7-10 100
9:9 115
9:12 150, 222
10:5-7 151
10:13-14 115

Song of Solomon
1:2 132
1:5 131
1:5-6 132
2:7 132
3:5 132
3:7 131
3:9 131

3:11 131
4:8-12 132, 134
4:9 132
4:10 132
4:11 132
4:12 132
5:1 132, 134
5:1-2 132
5:2 132
5:4 132-133
5:6 132
8:6 132
8:11-12 131

Wisdom of Solomon
1:1–6:21 91
1:2-3 91
1:3 100
1:4-5 100
1:6–2:1 106
1:14 92
1:13 91
1:15 91, 99
1:16 92
1:26 91
2:1 154
2:12 99
2:21 154
2:23 99, 154
2:23-24 92
3:2-4 155
3:4 91
3:6 155
3:8 155
3:10-11 154
3:12 118
3:13 91, 117
4:1 91, 118
4:1-9 95
4:3 118
4:22 95
5:15 91
6:4 99
6:9 99
6:12-14 106
6:17 99
6:17-18 99
6:17-20 98

6:18 99
6:21 100
6:22–10:21 91
6:22 105
6:24 106
7:1 106
7:1-6 106
7:6 106
7:7 106, 172
7:12 116
7:15 91
7:17-21 91
7:21 91
7:22-23 100
7:24 100
7:25 100
7:25-26 91
7:27 100
7-9 106
8:2 100, 132, 134
8:6 91
8:9-15 106
8:13 91
8:16 154
8:17 91, 100
8:21 106, 172
9:1-2 91, 93
9:1-18 219
9:2 91
9:4 91
9:5 106, 153
9:7 153
9:9 91, 99
9:13-17 106, 172
9:15 153
9:17 106, 172
9:18 106
19:3 153
10-11 91
10:15 100, 154
10:17 100
10:18-19 154
10:20 154
11-19 91
12:1 256
12:23 154
13:1 134
14:11 150, 151, 222

14:12 134, 137
14:13 134
14:24 134
14:26 135
15:3 91
16-19 91
17:2 154
18:4 99, 100

Sirach
Prologue 96, 97
1:1-2 89
1:11 153
1:11-30 89
1:12 89
1:14 89
1:20 89
1:26 97
1:30 105, 107
2:1-9 152
2:3 245
3:18 105, 167
3:18-24 162
3:20-24 98
3:21-24 106
3:26-28 152
4:11 105
4:12 89
4:17-19 152, 222
6:9 229
6:24-25 152, 222
6:29-31 153
6:30 153
7:1-2 152
7:3 152
7:19 114, 115, 273
7:24 126
7:24-25 134
7:25 134
7:26 114, 125, 273
8:8-9 90
9 124
9:1 125, 273
9:1-9 255
9:2 125, 226
9:3 124, 150, 222
9:3-9 124
9:4 124

9:5 124
9:6-8 124
9:8-9 124
9:13 150, 222
11:14 152
14:20 97
14:20-27 97
14:22-27 97
15:1 97
15:2 59, 97
15:15 105
15:18 89
16:1-3 118
17:1 89, 92
17:1-14 294
17:6 89
17:6-7 105
17:7 89
17:10 89
17:30 105
18:1 89
18:1-6 89
18:28 105
18:30 228
19:1 242
19:2 242
19:3 242
19:19 155
19:20 89, 97
20:5-8 115
21:11 89
21:13 90
21:19 153
21:19-21 222
21:21 153
22:3 126
22:6 184
23 133
23:2 184
23:3-5 134
23:5-6 133
23:16-23 231
23:16-27 255
23:17 133, 232
23:17-18 270
23:18 133
23:23 133
24 98, 144

24:1-9 89
24:1 98
24:2 98
24:3-7 98
24:4 98
24:8 98
24:9 98
24:10 98
24:10-12 143
24:22 98, 152
24:23 98
24:25-27 98
24:28 105
25:2 255
25:13-26 125
25:12 143
25:24 113
26:1 114, 273
26:3 114, 273
26:3-4 115
26:5-9 125
26:10 125
26:12 126
26:14 115
26:14-16 115
26:17 143
26:18 143
26:22 255
27:7-30 152
27:20 150, 222
27:26 150, 151, 222
27:27 222
27:29 150, 151
28:17 184
30:1 184
33:2 153
33:25 184
33:20 125
36:18 225, 226
36:18-26 226
36:24 115
36:25 134
36:25-27 134, 281
37:11 125
37:30 226
38:23 232
38:24-25 138
40:9 184

40:27 89, 90
41:14 92, 124
41:17 133
41:17-22 255
42:6 125
42:9 126
42:9-14 134
42:10 126
42:11 126
42:12 126
42:13 126
42:15-43:33 89
43:33 89
44-50 133, 143
44:12-15 143
45:14 143
45:16 143
45:21 143
45:23 143
45:23-24 144
46:16 143
47:19 121, 125, 247
47:14 133
47:19 133, 150, 246, 255
47:20 246
50 144
50:1-21 143
50:27 144
51:2 150, 151, 222
51:13-14 98
51:26 152, 222

Isaiah
13:16
29:14 164, 171
40:13 175
52:11 269

Jeremiah
2:24 131
9:23 167
13:11 245

Baruch
3:9–4:4 98

Ezekiel
16 131
23 131

Daniel
1:17 171
1:20-21 171
2:18-19 171
2:21 164, 166
2:22 171
2:23 172
2:28 160
2:28-29 171
2:47 171

Susanna
56 113

Hosea
1-3 131

Matthew
5:12 180
12:2 211
12:4 211
12:12 211
19:3 211
19:5 245
22:17 211
23:37 180

Mark
2:24 211
3:4 211
10:2 211
12:14 211

Luke
6:2 211
6:4 211
6:9 211
11:47-48 180
13:34 180
14:3 211
20:22 211

John
5:10 211

Acts
7:51-52 180
15:20 10
15:29 10
21:18-26 194
21:19 194
21:20-24 194
21:25 10, 194

Romans
3:25
7:7 137
10:6-8 185
11:33-36 185
12:9-21 77, 81
13:9 137

1 Corinthians
1–4 11, 35, 73, 81, 107, 153-54, 159-85, 170, 173, 177, 184, 186, 198, 211, 227
1:1 168
1:1-16 238
1:1–6:11 8
1:5 161
1:8 164
1:9 168
1:10 160
1:10-17 160, 161
1:10-4:13 182
1:10-4:21 182
1:10-5:8 11
1:11 10, 160
1:11-12 162
1:12-13 177
1:12 7, 162
1:17 161, 163
1:17-18 184
1:18 163-166, 172-73, 198
1:18–2:5 159, 163-70, 172, 174
1:18–3:4 161-162, 179-80
1:19 164, 165, 171
1:20 164

Index of Ancient References

1:21 164-65, 171-72, 175, 184
1:23 165
1:23-24 198
1:24 163-72, 175
1:25: 164-65, 184
1:26 151, 162, 165, 198
1:26-29 168
1:27 165
1:28 165, 166, 178
1:29 167
1:30 162, 164-66, 170-72, 175
1:31 167
2-3 173
2:1 165, 171, 179
2:1-5 178
2:2 165, 229
2:3 162, 165
2:4 165
2:4-5 184
2:5 165
2:6 170-75
2:6-13 172-73
2:6-7 174
2:6-13 193
2:6-16 159
2:6–3:4 159, 163-64, 170-76
2:7 160, 163, 171, 175, 179
2:8 170-71, 174
2:9 171
2:10-13 171-72, 174
2:10-16 175, 177
2:13 172
2:14 172
2:15 172, 193
2:16 175
3:1 173
3:1-4 173-75, 180
3:3-4 174
3:4-5 161
3:5 162, 177
3:5-9 177
3:5-17 179
3:5-23 179
3:5–4:13 161, 176-80
3:5–4:21 161
3:6-7 162
3:6-8 178
3:9 162, 175, 178
3:10 162, 177-78
3:10-15 178
3:11 178
3:12-15 179
3:16 234
3:16-17 178, 207, 255
3:17 179
3:18 168, 179
3:18-20 162, 198
3:18-23 107
3:19 164, 184
3:19-20 164
3:21 200
3:21-22 162, 184
3:21-23 260
3:22 162
3:22-23 155
3:23 162, 229, 259
4:1 162, 177
4:1-5 179
4:1-13 179
4:5 179
4:7 169, 179
4:8 179-180, 218
4:8-13 151, 162, 179, 180, 182
4:9 162
4:10 180
4:10-13 181
4:12-21 180-84
4:13 162
4:14 181
4:14-15 181
4:15 72, 181
4:15-21 182-83
4:16 181, 182, 191
4:16–11:1 219, 296
4:17 183
4:18-20 184
4:20 184
4:21 184
5 27, 206, 226, 229, 268, 276, 281
5–6 11, 17, 23
5–7 18, 22-24
5–10 182, 183
5:1 17, 232, 270, 271
5:1–11:1 17, 109, 163, 185
5:3 182
5:6 234
5:9 11, 195
5:9-13 11
5:10 270
5:11 270
5:12 182
5:13 183
5:13–6:11 11
6:2 234
6:3 155, 234
6:7 182
6:9 234
6:9-12 191
6:11 191, 238
6:12 2, 20-21, 27, 34, 73, 77, 109, 133, 138, 147, 156-57, 182, 187, 190-91, 195-97, 199, 200-201, 206-28, 247, 259-60, 273, 286, 291
6:12-14 220, 292
6:12-20 2-3, 8, 11, 14, 18-21, 24, 27, 36, 58, 67, 68, 109, 186-87, 195-96, 202, 204, 206-208, 218, 232, 255, 260, 263, 290-91, 296-98
6:12–7:7 2-6, 9, 28, 34-36, 38, 53-54, 59-60, 62, 67, 70-75, 77, 80-81, 83, 108-110, 112-13, 117, 138, 147-48, 158, 160, 173, 176, 178, 181, 186-87, 191, 196-202, 205-206, 225, 263-64, 277-78, 283, 290-93, 296, 300-301

6:13 27, 132-33, 156, 196-97, 200, 233-234, 283, 285
6:13-14 73, 200, 208, 225-33, 263, 271, 275
6:13-17 207, 254-55, 259, 261
6:13-20 203, 206, 260-61, 287, 291
6:14 196, 202, 205, 251
6:15 21, 182, 195, 234-40, 283
6:15-16 222
6:15-17 208, 226, 233-52, 255, 283
6:15-20 173, 27
6:16 121, 157, 255
6:16-17 240-52, 253, 269
6:17 256
6:17-20 283
6:17-7:1 281
6:18 23, 30, 183, 196, 197, 253-55, 290
6:18-20 138, 141, 207, 208, 252-60, 263-64, 267, 296
6:19 234, 287
6:19-20 247, 255-60, 264, 280
6:20 193
7 14, 17-18, 23-26, 194-95, 272, 282, 289
7–11 17
7:1 2-3, 8, 14, 17-18, 23-25, 27, 33, 77, 95, 133, 187, 192-93, 195, 197, 201, 263, 277, 281, 283-86, 288, 290-92, 297
7:1-2 264-72, 280, 284-85
7:1-4 282-83, 292
7:1-6 286
7:1-7 3, 9, 10, 14, 23, 36, 67-68, 109, 129, 186-87, 192, 194-95, 208, 263, 290-91, 297
7:1–11:16 11
7:2 134, 195, 201, 276-77, 281, 283, 285, 288-291
7:2-4 192, 281, 285, 291
7:2-6 192
7:3-4 187, 263, 270, 272-80, 281, 284-85
7:4 286
7:5 73, 187-88, 192, 270, 276, 283, 289, 290-92
7:5-6 263, 280-86
7:7 182, 192, 195-96, 263, 269, 286-90, 292, 297
7:8 182, 192-93, 265, 286
7:8-9 192, 193
7:8-16 192, 193
7:8-40 192, 264, 290
7:10-11 192
7:12-16 192
7:17-24 192-193
7:25 192-193
7:25-40 192-93
7:32-35 135, 138, 280
7:32-38 194
7:36 289
7:38 269, 289
7:39-40 193
7:40 182, 192
8–10 27
8:1 27, 193, 197
8:1–11:1 195
8:2 172
8:4 27, 197
8:8 197
8:13 182
8:20 101
9 182, 191, 200, 219, 273
9:1-23 8
9:1-17 182
9:5 286
9:15 286
9:16 162
9:23 234
9:24 234
9:24-27 8
10:1-23 8
10:6-13 215
10:7-8 226
10:14 183, 196, 252
10:23 27, 196, 197
10:23-33 273
10:24–11:1 8
10:33 182
11:1 182, 191
11:2-16 198
11:2-34 8
11:17-24 27
11:17-34 11
12 8, 11, 23, 202, 237
12:1 193
12:4-11 286
12:27-31 192, 195, 284, 286
12:28 194
12:1–14:40 11
14 8, 192, 195, 286
14:18-19 284
15 8, 173, 202, 205
15:2 229
15:3-9 229
15:29 238
15:44 173, 251
15:46 173
16:1 193
16:1-7 8
16:1-9 11
16:3 219
16:7-9 8
16:10-14 8
16:12 193
16:15-20 8
16:17 10
16:21-24 8

2 Corinthians
3:17 219
6:14–7:1 12

8-9 193
11 185
12:21 206

Galatians
5:1 219

Philippians
2:5-11 185, 198

1 Thessalonians
4 14
4:4-5 275

James
1:12-15 118

2 Peter
3:16 299

Early Jewish and Christian Texts

1 Enoch
2:1–5:8 166
5:8 164, 166, 168, 172
6-9 120
12:4 120
15:3-7 120
19:1 120
19:1-3 135, 137
37:3-5 172
38:3 171
41:3 171
41:3-9 166
49:1-4 171
49:4 165
51:3 171
52:1 171
52:5 171
60:11 171
60:11-23 166
63:2-3 160, 171
68:1 171
71:4 171
93:11-14 168, 172
96:1-3 155

99:2 176
99:10 164
99:12 166
100:9 178
101:1-9 166
102:1 178
103:2 171
104:10-12 171
108:1 176
108:15 160, 171

4 Ezra
4:2 160, 168, 172
4:2-3 167
4:5 166
4:7 166
4:10 171-72
4:10-11 172
4:21 166, 171
5:9-10 171
5:32 174
5:34-35 167, 172
5:36 166
5:39 168
5:40 172
5:51-55 94
6:1-6 175
7:14 155
7:49 174
7:72 176
7:81 176
8:12 176
8:29 176
8:47-49 168
9:11 176
10:38 171, 174
13:38 176
14:26 166, 171
14:46-47 166, 171

Testament of the Twelve Patriarchs
Testament of Reuben
4:6 255
5:1-7 255
5:5 252

Testament of Levi
9:9-10 268

Testament of Naphtali
8:8-9 282

Dead Sea Scrolls
4Q184 (4QWiles of the Wicked Woman)
9-11 123

4Q416 (4QSap.WorkA^b)
Frag. 2 co. IV

Philo
De Abrahamo (Abr.) –
On the Life of Abraham
3-6 101
13 102
16 157
77 101
78 101
94 146
98 146
100 135
101 135
118 101
132 101
142 101
168 101
202 101
213 101
229 101
255 101
275 101
275-76 101

De agricultura (Agr.) – *On Agriculture*
20 102
43 102

De cherubim (Cher.) – *On the Cherubim*
18 102

47 102
107 156

De confusione linguarum (*Conf.*) – On the Confusion of Tongues
39 107
49 94
110-25 107

De congressu eruditionis gratia (*Congr.*) – On Preliminary Studies
44 102
48 101
114 107

De vita contemplativa (*Contempl.*) – On the Contemplative Life
12 266
31 165, 184
34 157
59 136
68 118, 266
75 165, 184
78 266

De decalogo (*Decal.*) – On the Decalogue
8 134
45 145
58 104
142 137

Quod deterius potiori insidari soleat (*Det.*) – That the Worse Attacks the Better
115-117 93
116 92
125 102
126 102

Quod Deus sit immutabilis (*Deus.*) – That God is Unchangeable
8 283

11 138
115 138
148 102
160 94

De ebrietate (*Ebr.*) – On Drunkenness
48 104
55 128
81 92
84 101
86 147
87 147
88 76
91 76, 80, 103, 107
212 157

De fuga et inventione (*Fug.*) – On Flight and Finding
58 102
109 92

De gigantibus (*Gig.*) – On Giants
24 102
29-30 138
29-31 106
56 102
65 137
108 103

Quis rerum divinarum heres sit (*Her.*) – Who is the Heir?
52-53 129
57 129
269-70 157

Hypothetica (*Hypoth.*) – Hypothetica
11.1-18 266

De Iosepho (*Ios.*) – On the Life of Joseph
40 120
40-53 146
41 120

43 120, 135, 276
54 157
54-55 120
153 120, 223

Legum allegoriae (*Leg.*) – Allegorical Interpretation
1.19 93
1.21 93, 136, 247
1.31-32 93
1.43-45 93
1.45 93
1.47 94
1.52 107
1.64 92
1.64-65 93
1.65 92, 94
1.86 268, 174
1.92 93
1.93 102, 183
1.143 92
2.8 136
2.17 136, 138
2.38 129
2.49 92, 157
2.49-50 129, 137-138, 247
2.70 157
2.72 138
2.79 157
2.89-90 184
3.42 94
3.113 138
3.141 104
3.149 196, 223
3.151 283
3.152 93
3.156 196, 223
3.194 196, 223
3.206 106, 107
3.219 92
3.252 94

De migratione Abrahami (*Migr.*) – On the Migration of Abraham
39 94
40 92, 106-107

Index of Ancient References

41 92
45 102
76 102
89 103
90 103
93 103
102 104
122 101
130 102-103
134 107, 172
134-38 162
135 107
136-38 107
143 103
149 101
129-130 101
171 106

De vita Mosis (Mos.) –
On the Life of Moses
1 128
1.4 102, 104
1.25 157
1.80 102
1.162 102
1.296 128
1.297 128
1.298 128
1.299 157
1.300 128
1.301 128
1.305 128
2:2 101, 104
2.2-3 145
2.14 101
2.25 104
2.48 101
2.49-50 102, 183
2.66-186 104
2.67 104, 146
2.68 104, 146
2.68-69 282
2.69 146
2.185 157
2.204 102
2.211 101
2.212 104
2.292 101, 104

2.562 101

De opificio mundi (Opif.)
– *On the Creation of the World*
1-3 102
3 101
16 93
20 93
24 93
36 93
69 93
76 136
81 136
128 104
129 93
130 93
134-45 93
139 93
141 94
146 93
151 113
151-52 137
152 137
158 93
161 138
164 157
165 128
167 138
168 138

De plantatione (Plant.) –
On Planting
27 102
28 102

De posteritate Caini (Post.) – *On the Posterity of Cain*
28 102
169 102

De praemiis et poenis (Praem.) – *On Rewards and Punishments*
82 103
86 107
137 157

Quod omnis probus liber sit (Prob.) – *That Every Good Person is Free*
6-7 220
17 157, 216
18 157
18-20 260
21 158, 216
45 157, 216
59 158, 216-217
60 158, 216
75-91 266
88 165, 184
96 165, 184
101-106 260
113 155

De providentia (Prov.) –
On Providence
1 101-102

De sacrificiis Abelis et Caini (Sacr.) – *On the Sacrifices of Cain and Abel*
21 157
23 157, 196, 223
32 196, 223
43 102
45 157
48 102
64 107
127 158, 216

De sobrietate (Sobr.) – *On Sobriety*
55 92

De somniis (Somm.) – *On Dreams*
1.207 102

De specialibus legibus (Spec.) – *On the Special Laws*
1.332 134
2.100 102
2.194 102

3.9 136, 247, 273
3.32 135
3.34 136
3.35-36 136
3.51 120, 128
4.69 102
4.78 137
4.79 138
4.84 137
4.157 102
4.175 102

De virtutibus (Virt.) – On the Virtues
1-50 128
34 128
34-39 157
39 128
60 102
61 102
62 92
163 107
175 103
184 103

Sentences of Pseudo-Phocylides
175-76 117, 276
193-94 125, 273
194 132

Josephus
Antiquitates judaicae (A.J.) – Jewish Antiquities (Ant.)
4.206 252
8.190-191 246
8.192 246
8.193 246

Didache
6:1-3 194
6:2 194
6:3 194, 195
9:1-3 194
11:1-2 194

11:3 194, 195
11:3-6 194

Other Ancient Texts

Aeschines
In Timarchum (Tim.) – Against Timarchus
19 258
22 253
31 253
39 253
41 253
87 253
94 253
108 219, 253
116 253
183 258
185 248
188 253, 258

Aristotle
Problemata (Probl.) – Problems
896a 226

Rhetorica (Rhet.) – Rhetoric
2.6,4 283

Athenaeus
Deipnosophistae (Deipn.)
13.569e-f 249, 285

Demosthenes
In Neaeram (Neaer.) [Or. 59] – Against Neara
73 258
86 258
111 258
116 258

Dio Chrysostom
De regno iii (3 Regn.) [Or. 3] – Kingship 3
9-10 219
10 222, 224

De servitude et libertate i (1 Serv. lib.) [Or. 14] – Slavery and Freedom 1
1 216
3 216
4-8 216
13 216
14 217
16 217
17 217, 222

De quod felix sit sapiens (Fel. Sap.) [Or. 23] – The Wise Man is Happy
8 219

De geno (Gen.) [Or. 25] – The Guiding Spirit
1 217

De virtute (Virt.) [Or. 69] – Virtue
2 219
8 217
9 217

De lege [Or. 75] – Law
3 215

De libertate (Lib.) [Or. 80] – Freedom
3 217
9 222
10 222
11 22
12 22

Hesiod
Theogonia (Theog.) – Theogony
120.2 274

Hippocrates
Epidemiae (Epid.) – Epidemics
6.3.14 139, 267

Plato
Leges (Leg.) – Laws
836b2 274

Plutarch
*Conjugalia Praecepta
(Conj. paec.)*
29 275
33 280
39 278
42 249
44 249, 278
47 273 , 278

Demtr. (Demetrius)
26.3 257

Seneca
*Epistulae morales (Ep.) –
Epistles*
1.69 218
1.71 218

www.ingramcontent.com/pod-product-compliance
Lightning Source LLC
Chambersburg PA
CBHW030300010526
44108CB00038B/811